THE GUINNESS WHO'S WHO OF HEAVY METAL

SECOND EDITION

General Editor: Colin Larkin

GUINNESS PUBLISHING

Dedicated to Kurt Cobain

First Edition 1992
Second Edition published in 1995 by
GUINNESS PUBLISHING LTD
33 London Road, Enfield, Middlesex EN2 6DJ, England

All Editorial correspondence to
The Editor
Square One books Ltd
Iron Bridge House, 3 Bridge Approach, Chalk Farm, London NW1 8BD

British Library Cataloguing-in-Publication data
A catalogue record for this book is available from the British Library

ISBN 0-85112-656-1

Conceived, designed, edited and produced by Colin Larkin for
SQUARE ONE BOOKS LTD
Iron Bridge House, 3 Bridge Approach, Chalk Farm, London NW1 8BD

Editor and Designer: Colin Larkin
Assistant Editor: Alex Ogg
Picture Editor: Alex Ogg
Editorial and production assistant: Susan Pipe
Special thanks to David Roberts of Guinness Publishing

Reprint 10 9 8 7 6 5 4 3 2 1 0

Printed and bound in Great Britain by the Bath Press

Editor's Note

The Second Edition of *The Guinness Who's Who Of Heavy Metal* forms a part of the multi-volume series taken from the *Guinness Encyclopedia Of Popular Music*. 15 specialist single volumes have already been published and new editions and titles are being planned for the near future.

Already available:
The Guinness Who's Who Of Indie And New Wave Music.
The Guinness Who's Who Of Reggae.
The Guinness Who's Who Of Film Musicals
The Guinness Who's Who Of Rap, Dance And Techno,
The Guinness Who's Who Of Fifties Music.
The Guinness Who's Who Of Sixties Music.
The Guinness Who's Who Of Seventies Music.
The Guinness Who's Who Of Jazz.
The Guinness Who's Who Of Country Music.
The Guinness Who's Who Of Blues.
The Guinness Who's Who Of Soul.
The Guinness Who's Who Of Folk Music.
The Guinness Who's Who Of Stage Musicals.
The Guinness All Time Top 1000 Albums.

This new edition builds on the first by adding many new bands that have grown in stature since publication in 1992. We have almost doubled the extent and number of words, and we have expanded and re-written almost every entry. I have responded to the many letters received over the past three years adding artists that readers felt should have been included - even though they are often not strictly heavy metal bands. There is a fine line between Heavy Rock (Bad Company, Thunder, etc.), AOR (Journey, Kansas, etc.), Grunge (Nirvana, Stone Temple Pilots, etc.) and guitar-based indie bands such as Sugar and the Smashing Pumpkins. All are included together with the more traditional metal monsters: Metallica, Van Halen and Queensrÿche. I have attempted to include as many current and relevant heavy metal bands as space and deadlines permitted. We have now included record labels in the discography section together with many videos. Suggestions and complaints should be addressed to me at the address shown on page 2. I would like to thank, in addition to the contributors Alex Ogg, who buried himself into this project with great dedication, humour and enthusiasm and Susan Pipe for sharing the same room with Alex and his cheese and coleslaw sandwiches. Alex re-wrote much of the existing text and added many new entries. He would like to thank David McDonald from Scotland who handled the largest bulk of new contributions spanning several sub-genres, and although he kept our fingernails short towards deadline, the quality of his work never failed. N.W.O.B.H.M. expert Adrian T'Vell came in to the team late and handled many entries and updates at short notice, always happy to cope with whatever was thrown at him. He also offered us a valuable factual reading of the book's contents and did the majority of the photo research. Gavin Baddeley, meanwhile, specialized in the dark stuff in this book, again producing many entries quickly and offering invaluable advice and updates on existing profiles. Look out for his forthcoming book on Satanic rock music.

Several record company personnel acted above and beyond the call in the completion of this volume. We would especially like to thank, in no particular order, Mary (Music For Nations), Dan (Earache), Ulrike (Nuclear Blast), Mark (Roadrunner) and Marshall (Rock The Nation). Last minute photo assistance came from Steve of *Dissident* magazine, while his fellow internee

Duff also noted a couple of ommissions during layout. Appreciation to Sue And Dave Williams of Frontier Promotions who supplied properly written biogs and new product without having to beg. Thanks to Phil Knox-Roberts and Andrea Gibbs at WEA for usually responding to my requests. Thanks to my partner and closet metal fan Diana Luke for allowing me to share her CD collection. Thanks also to Dan and Tom Larkin for their 'young person's opinion' of the subject. They have both become mad keen metal aficionados, although Nine Inch Nails and Therapy? before breakfast on a Sunday morning is just a bit too much for us to take.

Colin Larkin, February 1995

A

A Foot In Coldwater

This prolific rock band produced four albums during their five-year career. Canadian in origin, they comprised Alex Machin (vocals), Paul Naumann (guitar), Bob Horne (keyboards), Hugh Leggat (bass) and Danny Taylor (drums). Concentrating on a traditional approach to songwriting, their work was characterized by Machin's expressive vocals and Naumann's melodic guitar lines. Leggat went on to form the Rolling Stones-influenced Private Eye, and later a progressive outfit under his own surname. Machin, meanwhile, would perform vocal duties with Champion.
Albums: *A Foot In Coldwater* (Love 1972), *Second Foot In Coldwater* (Love 1973), *All Around Us* (Elektra 1974), *Breaking Through* (Anthem 1977).

A II Z

This band from Manchester, England, made a small but significant contribution to the New Wave Of British Heavy Metal. (N.W.O.B.H.M.). Formed in 1979, they featured vocalist Dave Owens, guitarist Gary Owens, bassist Cam Campbell and drummer Karl Reti. After signing to Polydor and releasing the much-hyped 'No Fun After Midnight', they landed support slots to Girlschool and Black Sabbath, introducing them to a wider audience. However, after the release of a poorly produced live album, their Iron Maiden and Samson-styled material met with increasing apathy and they disbanded. Gary Owens went on to play with Tytan, after auditioning, unsuccessfully, for Girl. In 1981 the Owens brothers reformed the band with Tony Backhouse (bass) and ex-Tora Tora drummer Simon Wright (b. 19 June 1963). They released one single, 'I'm The One Who Loves You'. Late in 1982 Simon Wright also joined Tytan, subsequently replacing Phil Rudd in AC/DC.
Album: *The Witch Of Berkeley - Live* (Polydor 1980).

A.C.

Formed in Boston, Massachusetts, USA, in 1988, A.C.'s career has proved as unconventional as the white knuckle noise they produce. Their first record was a split 7-inch single in 1988, followed by a number of limited pressing singles and EPs (the best of which was the *Morbid Florist* EP), and compilation appearances. There was also a scarcely credible 7-inch with 5,345 'tracks' on it. They quickly earned themselves a reputation for what even veteran thrash metal observers decried as 'merely noise'. Spokesperson Seth admitted in the 90s that: 'We broke up because our old guitarist didn't know how to play anything else on guitar'. They reformed in short order, however, with a new, more able axeman, and a deal with Earache for their *Everyone Should Be Killed* set (sadly only 58 songs this time around). Which was described by the band itself as sounding: 'like a vacuum cleaner with us screaming over it'.
Album: *Everyone Should Be Killed* (Earache 1994).

Aaron, Lee

Canadian vocalist Lee Aaron (b. Karen Lynn Greening, 21 July 1962, Belleville, Ontario, Canada) first achieved notoriety by naively posing nude for a magazine on the advice of an unscrupulous manager, and consequently faced a struggle to prove that she had more to offer than looks alone. *The Lee Aaron Project*, recorded with backing from Triumph's Rik Emmett, Santers, Frank Soda and Moxy, was a positive step, displaying the powerful, husky Aaron voice, although the sometimes cliched lyrics left something to be desired. However, domestic interest resulted in a deal with Attic, and *Metal Queen* improved on the debut as Aaron worked with guitarists John Albani (ex-Wrabit) and George Bernhardt to produce more suitable material, the former becoming Aaron's long-term song writing partner. *Call Of The Wild* moved in a more sophisticated direction, although Bob Erin's production sounded a little dated, and confident shows supporting Bon Jovi and headlining helped Aaron maintain her high European profile. *Lee Aaron* realised her potential at last, with Peter Coleman's sympathetic production and Aaron and Albani's work with songwriters such as Joe Lynn Turner resulting in a classy and accessible album which finally brought some domestic success. *Bodyrock* achieved Canadian double platinum sales as Aaron continued in what was a more comfortable style, and *Some Girls Do* consolidated her Canadian status, although the lack of worldwide record deals denied her wider fame.
Albums: *The Lee Aaron Project* (Fantasy 1982), *Metal Queen* (Attic 1984), *Call Of The Wild* (Attic 1985), *Lee Aaron* (Attic 1987), *Bodyrock* (Attic 1989), *Some Girls Do* (Attic 1991), *Emotional Rain* (Hipchic 1994). Compilation: *Powerline: The Best Of Lee Aaron* (Attic 1992).

Aaronsrod

Angelo Jensen formed the heavy metal band Aaronsrod in 1984. Hailing from Hawaii, the unit comprised Brian Spalding (guitar), Neil Delaforce

(vocals/guitar), Edward Dysarz (bass/vocals) and Gerard Gonsalves (drums). Jensen, originally from Italy, was brought up in a vaudeville family. He made his debut at six years old and found performing to be such an exhilarating experience that he was determined to embark on a similar career. *Illusions Kill*, released in 1987 was a solid statement, culling influences from Iron Maiden and Def Leppard to a more American sound, typical of Motley Crüe. Despite their promise, however, Aaronsrod have remained subsequently unsuccessful; their only major break to date coming as support act to Ratt.
Album: *Illusions Kill* (Roadrunner 1987).

AB/CD

Calling themselves AB/CD, a pun on the Australian group AC/DC, this Swedish rock group was formed by students Braijan (vocals), Bengus (guitar), Nalcolm (guitar), Clim (bass) and Raijmon Left (drums). They came together in 1986 for a one-off performance at an end of college term party. The resemblance to AC/DC went beyond a similarity in name, extending to an aptitude for heavy, good-time rock. An astute record producer got them into the studio to record an album, which was subsequently released on the Doremi label. Although the set was well-received and the group obviously talented, fears of court action by the Australians scared off prospective overseas offers. Reluctant to go out under any other name, thus ruining the joke, the group disbanded within a year.
Album: *Victim Of Rock* (Doremi 1986).

Abattoir

Inaugurated during 1983 in Los Angeles, California, USA, this heavy rock group was formed by Mel Sanchez (bass), Mark Caro (guitar) and Juan Garcia (guitar). With the later addition of 'Danger' Wayne (drums) and Rawl Preston (lead vocals), they performed their first concert at the Los Angeles Troubadour. By the time of Abattoir's debut studio recordings, Preston had been replaced by an ex-member of Sceptre, John Cyriis. One of the songs from this session, 'Screams From The Grave', found its way on to the compilation, *Metal Massacre IV*. The result of this was a series of tours supporting top-flight metal acts such as W.A.S.P. and Metallica. However, by this time the personnel had undergone some changes with Danny Amaya replacing Wayne on the drumstool, and a certain amount of disenchantment with Abattoir's progression led to the departure of Cyriis and Garcia, who later re-emerged with their own band, Agent Steel. With the replacement guitarist Danny Olivero and singer Steve

Gaines, the group continued with the recording of their debut album, *Vicious Attack*. The group suffered yet more personnel changes when Gaines left to join Bloodlust. In his place, Mike Towers' contributions developed a more subdued sound, which manifested itself on their second album. By 1988, founder member Mel Sanchez had joined Evildead, signalling the demise of Abattoir shortly thereafter
Albums: *Vicious Attack* (Roadrunner 1985), *The Only Safe Place* (Noise 1986).

Absu

Texas black metal act (though they prefer the term 'Mythological Occult Music') led by the pseudonymous Emperor Proscriptor Magikus (percussion/voices), formed in 1989 'under the moon and equinox'. The initial line-up actually comprised two entirely different musicians (Gary and Danny, who recorded the *Temples Of Offal* EP in November 1991), until Magikus joined along with Daviel Athron Mysticia from their former band, Megas. Influenced by progressive rock as well as US and German death metal, they released their debut album in April 1993, its full title reading *Barathrum: Visita Interiora Terrae Rectificando Invenies Occultul Lapidem* (Latin for 'visiting the insides of the earth', or the abyss). Their own name, incidentally, is the word for abyss taken from the ancient Sumerian mythos. Daviel was subsequently replaced by Shaftiel (voices, guitar), though Magikus (otherwise engaged as an accountant for a computer firm, incredibly) remains the central figure.
Album: *Barathrum: V.I.T.R.I.O.L.* (Osmose 1993).

AC/DC

This theatrical Australian hard rock band was formed in 1973 by Malcolm Young (b. 6 January 1953, Glasgow, Scotland; rhythm guitar) after the demise of his previous outfit, the Velvet Underground (no relation to the US group). Young, whose elder brother George had already achieved stardom in Australia as a member of the Easybeats, also enlisted his younger brother Angus Young (b. 31 March 1959, Glasgow, Scotland; guitar). Their sister later suggested that Angus wear his school uniform on stage, a gimmick that rapidly became their trademark. The two brothers made their debut appearance in a bar in Sydney on 31 December 1973, along with Dave Evans (vocals), Larry Van Knedt (bass) and Colin Burgess (drums). In 1974, the Young brothers and Evans moved to Melbourne, where Mark Evans (b. 2 March 1956, Melbourne, Australia; bass) and Phil Rudd (b. 19 May 1954, Melbourne, Australia; drums) joined the band. Another immigrant from the

UK, Bon Scott (b. Ronald Scott, 9 July 1946, Kirriemuir, Scotland, d. 19 February 1980; vocals), graduated from being the band's chauffeur to becoming their vocalist when Dave Evans refused to go on stage one night in September 1974. (Evans would go on to form Rabbit, releasing two albums for CBS in Australia, before joining Hot Cockerel in 1984 and releasing *David Evans And Thunder Down Under* in 1986). Scott had previously recorded with two Australian outfits, pop group the Valentines (1966-68) and rockers Fraternity (1970-74). Indeed, after he emigrated from Scotland in 1951, he had also spent five consecutive years as drum champion (under-17 section) with the Perth Pipe Band. After such a wholesome start a prison conviction for assault and battery earmarked a more volatile side to his nature, and also resulted in him being refused admission to the army. In 1965 he joined the Spectors, before the aforementioned assignations with the Valentines in 1966, and Fraternity between 1970 and 1974. The AC/DC line-up which welcomed him had already recorded a solitary single, 'Can I Sit Next To You?', but it was his voice that graced their first two albums, *High Voltage* and *TNT*. Both sets were produced by George Young and his writing partner, another former Easybeat, Harry Vanda. Neither of them were issued outside Australia, though Atlantic in Britain did offer a selection of material from both records under the title *High Voltage* in 1976. These albums established the group as a major draw in their native territory, and brought them to the attention of Atlantic, who promptly relocated the band to London in January 1976. However, bassist Mark Evans would be replaced by Cliff Williams (b. 14 December 1949, Romford, Essex, England; ex-Home) in June 1977 after tiring of touring. Evans would go on to Finch/Contraband, then a variety of bands including Swanee, Heaven, Best and Party Boys. Once AC/DC began to tour outside Australia, the band quickly amassed a cult following, as much for the unashamed gimmickry of its live show as for its furious, frequently risque brand of hard rock. *Let There Be Rock* broke them as a chart act in the UK, with its contents including the perennial crowd-pleaser, 'Whole Lotta Rosie'. However, it was *Highway To Hell* in 1979 which established them as international stars. This, the band's first album with producer Mutt Lange, also proved to be their last with Bon Scott. On 20 February 1980, after a night of heavy drinking, he was left unconscious in a friend's car, and was later found to be dead, having choked on his own vomit. The coroner recorded a verdict of misadventure.

Scott's death threatened the band's future, but his replacement, former Geordie lead singer Brian Johnson (b. 5 October 1947, Newcastle, England), proved more than equal to the task. His first album with the band, *Back In Black*, reached number 1 in the UK and Australia, and spawned the hit single 'Rock 'n' Roll Ain't Noise Pollution'. 1981 saw the release of *For Those About To Rock*, plus the band's first headlining appearance at the Castle Donington festival and two Top 20 UK singles. After *Flick Of The Switch* in 1983, drummer Phil Rudd left the band to become a helicopter pilot in New Zealand, to be replaced by Simon Wright (b. 19 June 1963; ex-A II Z and Tytan) - who in turn departed to join Dio in 1990. His replacement was Chris Slade (b. 30 October 1946; ex-Manfred Mann's Earthband, Firm and Gary Moore). In keeping with their superstar status, AC/DC maintained an increasingly relaxed schedule through the 80s, touring to support each carefully-spaced album release. There were further 'casualties', however. When Macolm Young proved unfit to tour in 1988 his cousin, Stevie Young (ex-Starfighters), would temporarily deputise. Paul Greg would also step in for Cliff Williams on the US leg of their 1991 tour. A year earlier *The Razor's Edge* had proved to be one of the more successful albums from their later career, producing a Top 20 UK hit, 'Thunderstruck'. In 1992 they issued a live album, while the attendant single, 'Highway To Hell', made the UK top 20. With Brian Johnson long having buried the ghost of Bon Scott, the band shows no signs of varying its winning musical formula.

Albums: *High Voltage* (Albert 1974 - Australia only), *TNT* (Albert 1975 - Australia only), *High Voltage* (Atlantic 1976), *Dirty Deeds Done Dirt Cheap* (Atlantic 1976), *Let There Be Rock* (Atlantic 1977), *Powerage* (Atlantic 1978), *If You Want Blood You've Got It* (Atlantic 1978), *Highway To Hell* (Atlantic 1979), *Back In Black* (Atlantic 1980), *For Those About To Rock We Salute You* (Atlantic 1981), *Flick Of The Switch* (Atlantic 1983), *Fly On The Wall* (Atlantic 1985), *Who Made Who* (Atco 1986), *Blow Up Your Video* (Atlantic 1988), *The Razor's Edge* (Atco 1990), *Live* (Atco 1992). Compilations: *Box Set 1* (EMI 1987), *Box Set 2* (EMI 1987).

Videos: *Let There Be Rock* (1986), *Fly On The Wall* (1986), *High Voltage* (1988), *Promo Collection* (1990), *Who Made Who?* (1991).

Further reading: *AC/DC*, Malcolm Dome (1982), *The AC/DC Story*, Paul Ezra (1982), *Hell Ain't No Bad Place To Be*, Richard Bunton (1982), *Illustrated Biography*, Mark Putterford (1992).

Accept

This German heavy rock quintet comprised Udo Dirkschneider on vocals, guitarists Jan Kommet and

Wolf Hoffman, drummer Frank Friedrich and bassist Peter Baltes. Formed in 1977, their power metal sound was characterized by Dirkschneider's guttural howl and the warp speed drumming of Stefan Kaufmann, who replaced Friedrich after the band's debut album. 1981's *Breaker* also featured guitarist Jorg Fischer, who left following a support tour to Judas Priest (though he did return briefly in the late 80s). *Restless And Wild* from 1983 epitomized their blitzkrieg style. This had an undeniable influence on the thrash movement which developed during the late 80s, though *Metal Heart* adopted a more melodic approach. Unhappy with this style, Dirkschneider quit and formed his own outfit, Udo. A series of replacement vocalists came and went, including Rob Armitage (ex-Baby Tuckoo), David Reese and Jim Stacey (Stacey stepping in to complete tracks on *Eat The Heat* after Reese and Baltes underwent a physical confrontation on tour in the US). Several lacklustre albums were released during these years, which received little critical acclaim or commercial reward. Internal problems persisted, with Kaufmann contracting a muscular disease and being replaced by Ken Mary (House Of Lords). The band eventually disintegrated in 1989, but for *Restless And Wild* and *Balls To The Wall* at least, their reputation as a high echelon metal act remains. Reese would form Bang Galore Choir while old sparring partner Baltes contributed to Don Dokken. The band reunited in the 90s with a revised line-up (namely Dirkschneider, Hoffman, Baltes and Kaufmann).

Albums: *Accept* (Brain 1979), *I'm A Rebel* (Logo 1980), *Breaker* (Brain 1981), *Restless And Wild* (Heavy Metal 1983), *Balls To The Wall* (Portrait 1984), *Metal Heart* (Portrait 1985), *Kalizoku-Ban* (Portrait 1986), *Russian Roulette* (Portrait 1986), *Eat The Heat* (RCA 1989), *Live In Japan* (1992), *Objection Overruled* (RCA 1993). Compilations: *Best Of Accept* (Metronome 1983), *Hungry Years* (Razor 1991), *The Collection* (Castle 1991).

Accuser

Derivative German heavy metal quartet evidently influenced by Slayer and Metallica. The group was formed in 1986 by vocalist/bassist Eberhard Weyel and drummer Volker Borchert after leaving Breaker.

Accept

Following a period of trial and error formations (including utilising Thomas Kircher on bass), they finally recruited guitarists Frank Thomas (ex-Expect No Mercy) and Rene Schutz to record *The Conviction*. This was a powerful, if unoriginal, album, working to a set of rules and guidelines that had been drawn up by others. *Experimental Errors*, a mini-album, followed two years later. *Who Dominates Who?* continued the rigidly formularized approach, and their European tour with Mucky Pup the same year met largely with indifference.

Albums: *The Conviction* (Atom 1987), *Experimental Errors* (Atom 1988, mini-album), *Who Dominates Who?* (Atom 1989).

Ace Lane

This heavy metal group was formed in 1982 by ex-Gaskin bassist Stef Prokopczuk and vocalist Mick Clarke. With drummer Roy Whyke and guitarists Gary Sleet and Paul Brook completing the line-up, they released *See You In Heaven* the following year. This featured identikit hard-rock songs, distinguished by some blistering guitar work from Sleet and Brook. Failing to secure press attention or significant sales, they were condemned to obscurity, and subsequently split-up.

Albums: *See You In Heaven* (Mausoleum 1983).

Acheron

Acheron are Florida-based exponents of the Satanic black metal movement of the early 90s. Creator, guitarist and vocalist Vincent Crowley is also founder of the anti-Christian youth movement the Order of the Evil Eye. Musically, the band have clear death metal roots with their rapid hammering guitars and guttural vocal style. What distinguishes them from the increasing number of Satanic metal acts appearing during the early 90s is the authenticity of their material. Much of this derives from the involvement of the Reverend Peter Gilmore, a priest in the notorious Church of Satan, who contributes not only advice on the infernal content of the lyrics, but also provides the atmospheric keyboard intros that link the songs on Acheron's albums. *Hail Victory* is a release that contains an expanded version of *Satanic Victory*, adding eight songs and nine intros to the original.

Albums: *Rites of the Black Mass* (Turbo 1992), *Satanic Victory* (Turbo 1994), *Lex Talionis* (Turbo 1995).

Acid

This Belgian heavy metal band were formed in 1980 but saw their career receive little acclaim outside their own country, doubtless due to no record company being prepared to release their material abroad. The original line-up comprised Kate (vocals), Demon (guitar), Dizzy Lizzy (guitar), T-Bone (bass) and Anvill (drums). Their stylistic origins owed much to Previous Page, while their material was a derivative thrash-boogie blend reminiscent of Motörhead. They showed considerable enterprise and initiative by releasing their three albums independently, but Kate's leather dominatrix act still failed to garner an audience outside of the low countries.

Albums: *Acid* (Giant 1983), *Maniac* (Megaton 1983), *Engine Beast* (Giant 1985), *Don't Lose Your Temper* (SPV 1989).

Acid Bath

Louisiana-based metal outfit fronted by Dax Riggs (vocals), whose music reflects the atmosphere of the swamplands which form the singer's backyard. The band's material also exhibits a strong affection for the nether world and the art of the serial killer - in this case literally - their debut album, produced by DRI guitarist Spike Cassidy, featured a painting by mass murderer John Wayne Gacy on its cover. The album's title was described by Riggs as depicting 'the state of mind you get to when you're high - the point where you're capable of just floating away from whatever connects you to the world'.

Album: *When The Kite String Pops* (Roadrunner 1995).

Acid Reign

Heavy metal band formed in Harrogate, Yorkshire, England, in 1987. The band's original line-up consisted of H (vocals), Kev (guitar), Gaz Jennings (guitar), Ian Gangwer (bass) and Ramsey Wharton (drums). They wasted no time in recording a demo entitled *Moshkinstein*, which led to them being signed by the Music For Nations subsidiary label, Under One Flag. The band's debut release in 1988, a mini-album also entitled *Moshkinstein*, was well received, offering a blend of Anthrax-style riffing with the band's own basic metal sound. They also became popular on the UK club circuit with their quirky stage antics and down-to-earth attitude. The band's first full length album, *The Fear*, released in 1989, is best described as thrash metal with humour. However, all was not well within the ranks and shortly after its release Gaz and Ian were replaced by Mac (ex-Holoslade bassist) and Adam (ex-Lord Crucifer guitarist). The band toured Britain extensively including support slots with Nuclear Assault and Exodus in Europe. They then re-recorded 'Humanoi', a track from the previous album, as well as putting out a cover version of Blondie's hit

'Hanging On The Telephone' (originally recorded by the Nerves). Their second album, *Obnoxious*, was a major musical departure, announcing their songwriting maturity. Unfortunately, it was not well taken by fans of their previous releases and, feeling disillusioned following the departure of Adam and then Kev (now with Lawnmower Deth), the band announced their split in January 1991. They played a farewell gig at the Marquee, London, on October 28 of that year. As a postscript Under One Flag released a compilation album entitled *The Worst Of Acid Reign*, made up of previously unreleased material, live and demo tracks. Meanwhile Adam would go on to join Gaz in Cathedral, as did Ramsey slightly later in that band's evolution.
Albums: *Moshkinstein* (Under One Flag 1988, mini-album), *The Fear* (Under One Flag 1989), *Obnoxious* (Music For Nations 1990). Compilation: *The Worst Of Acid Reign* (Under One Flag 1991).

Acrophet

This heavy metal band hailed from Brookfield, Wisconsin, USA, and was formed in 1986 by guitarist Dave Pellino. He was joined by Dave Bauman (vocals/bass), Todd Saike (guitar) and Jason Mooney (drums). Technically, they were a competent unit, but originality was not a prominent feature of this thrash metal band. Nevertheless, inspired by Anthrax, Slayer and Megadeth, they managed to release a self-produced demo within a year of formation, and by the autumn of 1988 offered *Corrupt Minds*. This brought them a little attention, and was followed by *Faded Glory* in April 1990. Though the album revealed Acrophet to be a tighter outfit, the same progression was not evident in their songwriting capabilities.
Albums: *Corrupt Minds* (Roadrunner 1988), *Faded Glory* (Roadrunner 1990).

AD (80s)

Kenny Livgren (b. 18 September 1949, Kansas, USA; guitar/vocals) wasted little time after leaving Kansas before embarking on a solo career and putting together AD. Alongside Michael Gleason (vocals/keyboards), Dave Hope (bass) and Dennis Holt (drums), Livgren used the platform to peddle his new found Christian beliefs (which had been a factor in the dissolution of Kansas). Though his solo releases have also continued, Livgren has proved more prolific as the leading light behind this group, who record in a soft rock/AOR vein. Much of the interest in this output, however, which often ventures into Yes/orchestral rock territory, is from recalcitrant former Kansas fans. That constituency would have

been pleased to see the inclusion of 'Portrait' (drawn from *Point Of No Return*, Kansas' 1977 album) revisited on *Reconstructions*. This album also saw the introduction of vocalist Warren Ham. AD should not be confused with the 90s rap/rock group of similar name.
Albums: *Time Line* (CBS 1984), *Art Of State* (CBS 1985), *Reconstructions* (Sparrow 1987), *Prime Mover* (Sparrow 1988).

Adam Bomb

This pop-metal outfit was heavily influenced by Bon Jovi and Europe. Self-styled sex symbol cum vocalist Adam Brenner (ex-TKO) persuaded guitarist Jimmy Crespo (ex-Flame, Aerosmith), drummer Sandy Slavin (ex-Riot) and bassist Phil Feit to join forces and record *Fatal Attraction* in 1985. *Pure S.E.X.* emerged in 1990 to indifferent reviews, much of it being leftover material from the first album.
Albums: *Fatal Attraction* (Geffen 1985), *Pure S.E.X.* (FM Revolver 1990).

Adams, Bryan

b. Bryan Guy Adams, 5 November 1959, Kingston, Ontario, Canada. Bryan Adams has grown to be the most popular mainstream Canadian rocker of the late 80s/early 90s. His solo career commenced in 1978 (having previously worked with Sweeney Todd) when he began writing songs with Jim Vallance, a former member of Prism, who was keen to retire from live work but not from songwriting. Some of these early collaborations were recorded by Loverboy, Bachman Turner Overdrive, Bonnie Tyler and others. In 1980 Adams signed a deal with A&M Records, putting together a band which included Vallance on drums, plus Ken Scott (lead guitar) and Dave Taylor (bass). Their debut single, 'Let Me Take You Dancing', was followed by a self-titled album (which featured a cameo from Jeff 'Skunk' Baxter of Steely Dan), though neither charted. 1982 was largely spent touring with Foreigner (whose Lou Gramm would guest on the forthcoming album), the Kinks and Loverboy. The resultant *You Want It, You Got It*, scraped into the lower regions of the US charts. A third album, *Cuts Like A Knife*, released in 1983, was Adams' breakthrough, reaching number 8 and going platinum in the US (although it did not chart in the UK until three years later). It saw Vallance vacate the drumstool for Mickey Curry, though he would maintain his songwriting partnership with Adams. The first single from the album, 'Straight From The Heart', also made the US Top 10, with the help of MTV airplay and two follow-up singles, 'Cuts Like A Knife' and 'This Time', reached the Top 20 and Top

30 respectively. Adams' fourth album, *Reckless*, was issued near the end of 1984 and returned the singer to the Top 10. It also gave him his first major UK chart placing, reaching number 7. The single, 'Run To You', fared well on both sides of the Atlantic, as did 'Somebody'. He scored a US number 1 in mid-1985 with 'Heaven', the b-side of which was 'Diana', a tribute to the UK princess, which helped create the tabloid headlines: 'Princess Di Flirts With Canadian Rock Star'.

Adams was introduced by actor Jack Nicholson at the July 1985 Live Aid concert in Philadelphia, though UK audiences had to cope with transmission problems. He would also write and help perform the Canadian benefit record for Ethiopia, 'Tears Are Not Enough'. The defiant and celebratory 'Summer Of '69' returned him to the Top 10 in the US and he ended a successful year duetting with Tina Turner on 'It's Only Love' (though there was one further, bizarre release in December, when he coupled the festive 'Christmas Time' with 'Reggae Christmas'). His fifth album, *Into The Fire*, was released in March 1987 and became a Top 10 hit in both the US and the UK, boasting songs of a more political bent, informed by Adams' charity work and tours in support of Amnesty International (Adams is also a staunch vegitarian). It would also see the final effort of the Adams/Vallance songwriting partnership, and the end of a five album tenure with producer Bob Clearmountain. 'Heat Of The Night' provided Adams with his fifth US Top 10 hit, although subsequent single releases fared less well. Indeed, the late 80s proved a comparitively tranquil time for the artist, as he took stock of his career and waited for a window in producer Mutt Lange's diary. He would, however, contribute to records by Dion, Mötley Crüe, Belinda Carlisle, Charlie Sexton and others. In 1988 he guested at the Nelson Mandela birthday party concert at Wembley Stadium in London, and in 1990 appeared with Roger Waters and others at the special Berlin performance of *The Wall*. All was eclipsed, however, by his contribution to the 1991 Kevin Costner film, *Robin Hood, Prince Of Thieves*. '(Everything I Do) I Do It For You' was a phenomenal chart success, topping the UK singles listings for an incredible 16 weeks, the longest run since Frankie Laine's 18-week domination with 'I Believe' back in 1953 (it also sold three million copies and hit the number 1 mark in the US). Its follow-up, 'Can't Stop This Thing We Started', and another strong ballad, 'Thought I'd Died And Gone To Heaven', also charted strongly. All featured on his hugely successful 1992 album, *Waking Up The Neighbours*, which underwent no less than 18 months in production. 1994 saw him return from a major tour of South-East Asia (in the process becoming the first Western artist to visit Vietnam) for six headlining nights at Wembley Arena. His new-found commercial breakthrough may have diminished his stature in the eyes of those fans who once made up the main constituency of his followers, but as a performer and songwriter the greater body of his work remains firmly within the rock tradition.
Albums: *Bryan Adams* (A&M 1980), *You Want It, You Got It* (A&M 1981), *Cuts Like A Knife* (A&M 1983), *Reckless* (A&M 1984), *Into The Fire* (A&M 1987), *Waking Up The Neighbours* (A&M 1992). Compilation: *So Far So Good* (A&M 1994). Video: *Reckless* (1988).

Adams, S.A.

One of metal's unsung underground warriors, Adams first started fusing punk with hard rock in the Fury, whose career stretched over four years and three line-ups. However, some of his previous band mates have also included Rick Rubin (producer), Mike Nach (Wicked Marya) and Mike Portnoy (Dream Theater). Recording credits also add Raven, Manowar, Pro-Pain, Type Of Negative and Coroner to his list of achievements. Turning ssolo, Adams took pains to state to the press how he was determined to enlist musicians interested in carving their own musical niche rather than re-interpreting prevalent trends. To this effect he eventually found 'Big Bad Bill' Janusz (bass) and Rocky D (drums; ex-Fury) to back his guitar and potent vocals. However, this line-up only gelled after the release of his debut album, *Exiled On Green Street*, which saw him accompanied solely by a four-track and a DAT machine. The new group toured the east coast of the US before landing a deal with Rock The Nation Records. In the summer of 1994 they recorded then re-recorded a debut album proper, *Redemption*, to far superior effect, also including in the process a mail-order only CD with studio out-takes and live versions.
Albums: *Exiled On Green Street* (1993), *Redemption* (RTN 1994).

Adrenalin

This sophisticated AOR outfit, influenced by Styx, Foreigner and Journey, was put together by the brothers Romeo and Pastoria in 1984. The seven-piece band comprised Marc Gilbert (vocals), Flash (guitar), Michael Romeo (guitar), Jimmy Romeo (saxophone), Marc Pastoria (keyboards), Bruce Schafer (bass) and Brian Pastoria (drums). Adrenalin were signed by MCA and released two quality melodic rock albums. The title-track of *Road Of The Gypsy* was also included on the *Iron Eagle* film soundtrack. Success eluded the band and they were subsequently dropped by their label in 1987. That year also saw the departure of Gilbert and Flash, with ex-Grand Funk Railroad vocalist/guitarist Mark Farner stepping in as replacement. As Grand Funk songs started to appear in their live set, so the band eventually became known as Mark Farner And Adrenalin. Unable to secure a recording contract and attract media attention, Farner quit the following year, with Joey Hammody taking over soon after as the new vocalist.

Albums: *American Heart* (MCA 1985), *Road Of The Gypsy* (MCA 1986).

Aerosmith

One of the USA's most popular hard-rock acts, Aerosmith was formed in 1970 when vocalist Steven Tyler (b. Steven Victor Tallarico, 26 March 1948, New York, USA; vocals) met Joe Perry (b. Anthony Joseph Perry, 10 September 1950, Boston, Massachusetts, USA; guitar) while the latter was working in a Sunapee, New Hampshire ice cream parlour, the Anchorage. Tyler was in the area visiting the family-owned holiday resort, Trow-Rico. Perry, then playing in the Jam Band, invited Tyler (who had previously released one single with his own band Chain Reaction, 'When I Needed You', and another, 'You Should Have Been Here Yesterday', with William Proud And The Strangeurs) to join him in a Cream-styled rock combo. Together with fellow Jam Band member Tom Hamilton (b. 31 December 1951, Colorado Springs, Colorado, USA; bass) and new recruits Joey Kramer (b. 21 June 1950, New York, USA; drums) and Ray Tabano (guitar), the group's original line-up was now complete. However, Tabanao was quickly replaced by former member of Justin Tyme, Earth Inc., Teapot Dome and Cymbals Of Resistance, Brad Whitford (b. 23 February 1952, Winchester, Massachusetts, USA). After playing their first gig at the Nipmuc Regional High School the band took the name Aerosmith (rejecting other early monikers including 'Hookers'). Their popularity throughout the Boston area grew rapidly, and a triumphant gig at Max's Kansas City witnessed by Clive Davis led to a recording deal with Columbia/CBS Records. In 1973 Aerosmith secured a minor chart placing with their self-titled debut album. Although its attendant single, 'Dream On', initially peaked at number 59, it became a Top 10 hit when reissued in 1976. *Get Your Wings* introduced a fruitful working relationship with producer Jack Douglas. Nationwide tours established the quintet as a major attraction, a position consolidated by the highly successful *Toys In The Attic*, which has now

sold in excess of six million copies. A fourth album, *Rocks*, achieved platinum status within months of its release. Aerosmith maintained their pre-eminent position with *Draw The Line* and the powerful *Live! Bootleg*, but despite popular acclaim, failed to gain the approbation of many critics who dubbed the group 'derivative', particularly of Led Zeppelin. Tyler's physical resemblance to Mick Jagger, and his foil-like relationship with guitarist Perry, also inspired comparisons with the Rolling Stones, with whom they shared several musical reference points.

In 1978 Aerosmith undertook a US tour of smaller, more intimate venues in an attempt to decelerate their rigorous schedule. They appeared in the ill-fated *Sgt. Pepper's Lonely Hearts Club Band* film (as the Future Villain band), and although their rousing version of 'Come Together' reached the US Top 30, tension between Tyler and Perry proved irreconcilable. The guitarist left the group following the release of the disappointing *Night In The Ruts* and subsequently founded the Joe Perry Project. Jimmy Crespo joined Aerosmith in 1980, but the following year Brad Whitford left to pursue a new career with former Ted Nugent band member, Derek St Holmes. Newcomer Rick Dufay debuted on *Rock In A Hard Place*, but this lacklustre set failed to capture the fire of the group's classic recordings. Contact between the group and Perry and Whitford was re-established during a 1984 tour. Antagonisms were set aside, and the following year, the quintet's most enduring line-up was performing together again. *Done With Mirrors* was a tentative first step, after which Tyler and Perry underwent a successful rehabilitation programme to rid themselves of drug and alcohol dependencies, synonymous with the group's hedonistic lifestyle. In 1986 they accompanied rappers Run DMC on 'Walk This Way', an Aerosmith song from *Toys In The Attic* and a former US Top 10 entry in its own right. The collaboration was an international hit, rekindling interest in Aerosmith's career. *Permanent Vacation* became one of their best-selling albums, and the first to enter the UK chart, while the highly-acclaimed *Pump* and *Get A Grip* emphasized their revitalization. Feted by a new generation of acts, including Guns N'Roses, the quintet are now seen as elder statesmen, but recent recordings show them leading by example.

Albums: *Aerosmith* (CBS 1973), *Get Your Wings* (CBS 1974), *Toys In The Attic* (CBS 1975), *Rocks* (CBS 1976), *Draw The Line* (CBS 1977), *Live! Bootleg* (CBS 1978), *Night In The Ruts* (CBS 1979), *Rock In A Hard Place* (CBS 1982), *Done With Mirrors* (Geffen 1985), *Permanent Vacation* (Geffen 1987), *Pump* (Geffen 1989), *Get A Grip* (Geffen 1993). Compilations: *Greatest Hits* (CBS 1980), *Classics Live*

(CBS 1986), *Classics Live II* (Columbia 1987), *Anthology* (Raw Power/Castle 1988), *Big Ones* (Geffen 1994), *Box Of Fire* (Columbia 1994, CD box set of all CBS albums with bonus rarities disc).
Videos: *Video Scrapbook* (1988), *Live Texas Jam '78* (1989), *Things That Go Pump In The Night* (1990), *The Making Of Pump* (1991), *Big Ones* (1994).
Further reading: *The Fall And Rise Of Aerosmith*, Mark Putterford.

Afghan Whigs

From Cincinnati, and originally stalwarts of the Sub Pop empire, in the 90s Afghan Whigs were classified widely as favoured proponents of grunge, though there is much of a more traditional nature in their music. Their *Uptown Avondale* EP, for example, was a collection of classic soul covers, while as early as *Up In It* they were bastardising country rock on tracks like 'Son Of The South'. The band numbers Rick McCollum (guitar), Steve Earle (drums) and John Curley (bass) alongside the distinctive vocals ('I think Camel cigarettes are a big influence on my voice') of mainman Greg Dulli (vocals/guitar). With his origins in Hamilton, a steeltown 30 miles outside of Cincinnati, Dulli quit his film course to attempt to pick up acting parts (apparently making it into the last 50 at the auditions for the *Breakfast Club*'s 'weirdo'). He first met bassit John Curley in jail, where they were being held overnight for urinating in front of a police officer and drug-dealing respectively. When Afghan Whigs went major, Dulli insisted that he produce their records and direct their videos (in fact before signing Dulli had handled band management). Elektra agreed to his conditions, and to financing a movie project. Their major label debut, *Gentlemen*, concerned familiar Afghan Whigs subjects: alienation and the seedier side of life. One of the songs, 'My Curse', was so personal that Dulli couldn't sing it himself - employing Marcy Mays of Scrawl instead. Marketing the album also became the subject of a College Music Journal seminar. In 1994 Dulli was part of the supergroup who recorded a soundtrack for the Stuart Sutcliffe (Beatles) biopic, singing as John Lennon. Other band members were Mike Mills (REM), Don Fleming (Gumball) Dave Grohl (Nirvana) and Thurston Moore (Sonic Youth).
Albums: *Big Top Halloween* (Ultrasuede 1988), *Up In It* (Sub Pop 1990), *Congregation* (Sub Pop 1992), *Gentlemen* (Elektra 1993).

After Hours

This British heavy rock quartet, based in Southampton, was formed from the ashes of XS and Love Attack. Comprising John Francis (vocals), Tim Payne (guitar), Rick Young (keyboards), Martin Walls (bass) and Mark Addison (drums), After Hours specialized in melodic pomp/AOR, although tougher edges were also occasionally apparent. *Take Off*, their debut, was an excellent collection of songs in the Foreigner/Whitesnake tradition. Afterwards the line-up fluctuated to accomodate Andy Nye (keyboards; ex-MSG) and Alan Jackman (drums; ex-the Outfield), until further sightings became increasingly rare.
Albums: *Take Off* (FM Revolver 1988).

Aftermath

This heavy metal band hailed from Tucson, Arizona, USA, and were formed by vocalist Richard Shayka and guitarist Cliff Finney in 1984. Enlisting the services of John E. January (guitar), Joe Nutt (bass) and Rick Von Glahn (drums), they recorded a self-titled eight-track demo that was rejected by many major labels in the USA. However, newly-formed Dutch label Mushroom signed them in 1988. *Don't Cheer Me Up* materialized the same year; a derivative collection of melodic metal, with the odd anthemic number and power-ballad included. A different band, incidentally, to the Chicago doom metal merchants who had two songs issued on the *Metal Forces* album in the UK.
Album: *Don't Cheer Me Up* (Mushroom 1988).

Agent

This Canadian heavy rock quintet was formed in Vancouver in 1981, by the three-man nucleus of Bob Smart (guitar), Craig Zurba (keyboards) and Andre Kunkel (bass). After a series of short-lived line-ups, they stabilized with the addition of vocalist Rick Livingstone and drummer Dave Allen in 1983. They attracted the interest of Virgin Records after winning a 'Battle Of The Bands' style contest and were approached by ex-Doobie Brother, Jeff 'Skunk' Baxter, who produced their debut album. Influenced by Foreigner, Styx, Kansas and Loverboy, their style was commercial though unspectacular melodic rock.
Album: *Agent* (Virgin 1986).

Agent Steel

This heavy metal unit was formed in Los Angeles, California, USA, and had been around in various guises since the early 80s. The most popular line-up consisted of John Cyriis (vocals; ex-Abbatoir), Juan Garcia (guitar), Bernie Versye (guitar), Michael Zaputil (bass) and Chuck Profus (drums). Signing to Combat Records the band released their debut, *Operation Redeye*, in 1985, but it was the same year's *Skeptics Apocalypse* which was well-received by both

music press and the public. However, the group ran into difficulty with both their record label and internal wrangles owing to Cyriis' reputed eccentricity. With label problems resolved, the band released an EP entitled *Mad Locust Rising* and quickly followed this up with their finest recording, the trash-fixated *Unstoppable Force*. However, they experienced further disruption when Cyriis decided he wanted to relocate the band to Florida. The rest of the group were less than delighted with the provisional change in locale and left (or rather stayed). Cyriis carried on with various musicians in the new location but could never quite match previous standards. Disillusioned, he dissolved the group in 1988 and, after a brief tenure alongside Profus in Pontius Prophet, has since quit the music business.
Albums: *Operation Redeye* (Combat 1985), *Skeptic's Apocalypse* (Combat 1985), *Unstoppable Force* (Music For Nations 1987).
Video: *Mad Locust Rising* (1987).

Agnostic Front

Originally comprising Roger Miret (vocals), Alex Kinon (guitar), Vinnie Stigma (guitar), Rob Kabula (bass) and Louie Beatto (drums), Agnostic Front offered the definitive example of the New York hardcore scene of the mid-80s. Growing up on stage at CBGB's, like many of that scene's participants, as their career progressed they adopted more and more elements which identified them instead with the heavy metal scene. Politically not the most circumspect of bands, even by hard rock's standards, their avowed right wing stance and staunch nationalism helped set them apart from other punk and hardcore bands. Whatever the lyrics, Miret discharged them with quite remarkable ferocity (he allegedly spent his spare time breeding pit bull terriers). Following *Cause For Alarm* Jimmy Merrick replaced Beatto on drums, while guitarist Matt Henderson joined for *One Voice*. This featured lyrics written by Miret during an 18 month prison stretch on drugs charges. Temporary vocalist Alan Peters would join Crawlpappy on his release. Although their reputation mounted over the years, little changed in Agnostic Front's musical formula, their principal strength always remaining the live arena. They played their last live show together at CBGB's on December 20 1992. Miret's younger brother, Freddy Cricien, meanwhile, would put together Madball with other former members of Agnostic Front.
Albums: *Victim In Pain* (Rat Cage 1984), *Cause For Alarm* (Combat Core 1986), *Liberty & Justice For...* (Combat 1987), *Live At CBGB* (In-Effect/Relativity 1989), *One Voice* (Relativity 1991).

Air Raid

This short-lived US quartet specialized in sophisticated and melodic symphonic rock. The band originated in 1980 and featured Arthur Offen (vocals/keyboards), Rick Hinkle (guitar), Tommy Walker (bass) and Rick Brown (drums). Their self-titled debut released in 1981 was strongly reminiscent of Styx and Journey. Technically, the band were without fault, but they lacked the necessary spark of originality to make any real impact. Failing to attract media attention, they disbanded shortly after the album was released.
Album: *Air Raid* (20th Century 1981).

Airey, Don

Airey is a talented UK keyboards player, who has contributed to a wide range of bands and projects during the 70s and 80s. Unable to make a long-term commitment (or, perhaps, to find the right musicians to work with), he has made short-lived appearances with Colosseum II, Rainbow, Ozzy Osbourne, Whitesnake, Black Sabbath, MSG, Alaska, Jethro Tull and Gary Moore. In 1986 he decided to set some time aside to work on a solo project. *K2* was an ambitious concept album centred on the mystique of the second highest mountain in the world, and the dangers of climbing it. With the help of Gary Moore, Cozy Powell and Colin Blunstone, the album came to life, but appealed more to new-age music aficionados than to serious rock fans.
Album: *K2, Tales Of Triumph And Agony* (1986).

Airrace

This British heavy rock quintet was formed in 1983 by vocalist Keith Murrell and guitarist Laurie Mansworth. Recruiting Jim Reid (bass), Jason Bonham (drums) and Toby Sadler (keyboards), they signed to Atlantic Records the same year. The band's most striking feature was the highly accomplished vocal style of Murrell. His powerful Lou Gramm-like warblings led to obvious Foreigner comparisons, but in an approving rather than critical sense. Their Beau Hill-produced debut released in 1984 flopped but remains an undiscovered classic of the melodic rock genre. The band split up soon after its release, with Murrell joining Mamas Boys and Jason Bonham forming Virginia Wolf, then Bonham. Mansworth resurrected Airrace in 1986 with a new line-up, but the band soon vanished again.
Album: *Shaft Of Light* (Atlantic 1984).

Alaska

This UK heavy rock unit was the phoenix that rose from the ashes of Bernie Marsden's S.O.S. Marsden, also a veteran of Babe Ruth and Whitesnake, was joined by Robert Hawthorn (vocals), Brian Badham (bass/piano), and John Marter (drums; ex-Mr. Big and Marillion). The band produced symphonic rock with pomp and circumstance, Hawthorn's vocals contrasting subtly with Marsden's famous blues-influenced style. The band's first big break came in 1984, when they supported Manowar at the Headbanger's Ball in Holland. Sadly, after two albums Alaska disintegrated, with Marsden joining the ill-fated MGM, who split up before releasing any material. Alaska's 'Headlines' was used in a UK television commercial in 1988 for the *Sunday Sport* newspaper. The song was reissued as a single, but failed to make the charts.

Albums: *Heart Of The Storm* (Music For Nations 1984), *The Pack* (Music For Nations 1985).

Alcatrazz

This American band were heavy metal exponents in the Deep Purple tradition. Formed by ex-MSG and Rainbow vocalist Graham Bonnet in 1983, the initial line-up featured virtuoso guitarist Yngwie Malmsteen, ex-New England members Jimmy Waldo (keyboards) and Gary Shea (bass), plus former Alice Cooper drummer Jan Uvena. *No Parole From Rock 'n' Roll* was chest thumping hard-rock in the David Coverdale/Ronnie James Dio style, complete with intricately textured and classically influenced guitar breaks. Steve Vai (ex-Frank Zappa) replaced Malmsteen after a disappointing live album to record *Disturbing The Peace*. This was a disjointed affair comprising a mixture of heavy rock and instrumental showcase numbers. Vai joined Dave Lee Roth's band in 1986, with ex-Axis guitarist Danny Johnson taking over six-string duties. *Dangerous Games* followed but was poorly received, lacking both power and direction. The band broke up in 1987 with Johnson forming Private Life and Bonnet teaming up with guitarist Chris Impelliteri.

Albums: *No Parole From Rock 'n' Roll* (Rockshire 1984), *Disturbing The Peace* (Capitol 1985), *Dangerous Games* (Capitol 1986), *Live Sentence* (Grandslam 1989).

Alexa

Discovered by Paul Sabu (Only Child, Sabu), this Switzerland-born, US-based vocalist (b. Alexa Anastasia) combined hard rock overtures with pop hooks. Trading on a strong visual image, Sabu was again on hand to produce her self-titled debut album, which invited further comparisons to Lita Ford, Lee Aaron and other top-flight female larynxes. However, poor sales have ensured that it has been difficult to

trace her movements since its release.

Album: *Alexa* (Savage 1989).

Alias

Hard rock band formed in Sarasota, Florida, in March 1985, the members - Mark Severns (guitar), Phil Arnt (percussion), Carl Hayden (vocals) and Dirk Van Tilborg (bass/keyboards) - meeting whilst playing in local cover bands. Combining diverse influences ranging from Frank Zappa to Weather Report as well as more traditional metal outfits (Scorpions, Dokken), they recorded their first demo in July 1985. Signing to Grudge Records in February 1987, their debut mini-album was released six months later. Relocating to Los Angeles in 1989 the group backed several major artists including Ace Frehley, White Lion and Nightranger. However, it would be a full seven years before the release of a second album in 1994, another attempt to build 'classic metal' songs around clean production and exemplary playing technique. Not to be confused with the Canadian Alias inaugurated by former members of Sherriff.

Albums: *Alias* (Grudge 1987, mini-album), *Metal To Infinity* (RTN 1994).

Alice Cooper

b. Vincent Damon Furnier, 4 February 1948, Detroit, Michigan, USA. Alice Cooper became known as the 'master of shock rock' during the 70s and remained a popular hard-rock artist into the 90s. The Furnier family moved to Phoenix, Arizona, where Vincent began writing songs while in junior high school. Inspired by a dream to become as famous as the Beatles and Rolling Stones, Furnier formed a group in the early 60s called the Earwigs. By 1965 their name had changed to the Spiders and then the Nazz (no relation to Todd Rundgren's band of the same name). Both the Spiders and Nazz played at local dances and recorded singles that were moderately popular regionally. In 1968, the Nazz, which also included Mike Bruce (lead guitar), Dennis Dunaway (bass), Glen Buxton (guitar) and Neal Smith (drums), changed its name to Alice Cooper, reportedly due to Furnier's belief that he was the reincarnation of a 17th century witch by that name. The name Alice Cooper was also attached to Furnier, who invented an androgynous, outrageously attired character to attract attention. The band played deliberately abrasive rock music with the intention of shocking and even alienating those attending its concerts. In 1969 the Alice Cooper band found a kindred spirit in Frank Zappa, who signed them to his new Straight Records label. The group recorded

Alice Cooper

two albums, *Pretties For You* and *Easy Action*, before switching to Warner Brothers Records in 1970. By that time Cooper had taken on more extreme tactics in his live performances, using a guillotine and electric chair as stage props and a live snake as part of his wardrobe. The finishing touch was the thick black eye make-up which dripped down his face, affording him his trademark demonic appearance. As the group and its singer built a reputation as a bizarre live act, their records began to sell in greater quantities. In 1971 'Eighteen' was the first single to reach the US charts, at number 21. Cooper's commercial breakthrough came the following year with the rebellious 'School's Out' single and album, both of which made the US Top 10 as well as topping the UK chart. A streak of best-selling albums followed: the number 1 *Billion Dollar Babies*, then *Muscle Of Love*, *Alice Cooper's Greatest Hits* and *Welcome To My Nightmare*, all of which reached the US Top 10. The last was his first true solo album as the band fractured and Cooper officially adopted the Alice Cooper name as his own.

In contrast to his professional image, the offstage Cooper became a Hollywood celebrity, playing golf and appearing on television talk shows, as well as developing a strong friendship with Groucho Marx, with whom he planned a television series. In tribute to the legendary comedian he purchased one of the 'O's from the famous Hollywood sign and dedicated it to his memory. The late 70s saw him appearing in films such as *Sextette* and *Sgt. Pepper's Lonely Hearts Club Band*. In 1978 Cooper admitted chronic alcoholism and entered a New York hospital for treatment. *From The Inside*, with songs co-written by Bernie Taupin, reflected on the experience. His band continued touring, and between 1979 and 1982 featured ex-Iron Butterfly lead guitarist Mike Pincra. Cooper continued recording into the early 80s with diminishing results. In 1986, after a four-year recording absence, he signed to MCA Records, but none of his albums for that label reached the US charts. A 1989 set, *Trash*, his first for Epic Records, returned him to the Top 40 and yielded a Top 10 single, 'Poison', his first in 12 years. *Hey Stoopid* found him accompanied by Joe Satriani, Steve Vai and Slash and Axl from Guns N'Roses, while his 90s tours saw Cooper drawing a new, younger audience who considered him a heavy metal pioneer. An impression which was immortalized by Cooper's appearance in *Wayne's World*, wherein the haphazard protagonists kneel before their idol and insist they are 'not worthy'.

Albums: *Pretties For You* (Straight 1969), *Easy Action* (Straight 1970), *Love It To Death* (Warners 1971),

Killer (Warners 1971), *School's Out* (Warners 1972), *Billion Dollar Babies* (Warners 1973), *Muscle Of Love* (Warners 1973), *Welcome To My Nightmare* (Anchor 1975), *Alice Cooper Goes To Hell* (Warners 1976), *Lace And Whiskey* (Warners 1977), *The Alice Cooper Show* (Warners 1977), *From The Inside* (Warners 1978), *Flush The Fashion* (Warners 1980), *Special Forces* (Warners 1981), *Zipper Catches Skin* (Warners 1982), *Dada* (Warners 1983), *Live In Toronto* (Breakaway 1984), *Constrictor* (MCA 1986), *Raise Your Fist And Yell* (MCA 1987), *Trash* (Epic 1989), *Hey Stoopid* (Epic 1991), *Live 1968* (Edsel 1992), *Live At The Whiskey A Go Go* (Edsel 1992), *The Last Temptation* (Epic 1994). Compilations: *School Days* (Warners 1973, double album), *Alice Cooper's Greatest Hits* (Warners 1974), *Freak Out Song* (Castle 1986), *Beast Of* (Warners 1989).

Videos: *The Nightmare Returns* (1987), *Welcome To My Nightmare* (1988), *Alice Cooper Trashes The World* (1990), *Box Set* (1990), *Prime Cuts* (1991).

Further reading: *Alice Cooper*, Steve Demorest (1974), *Me: Alice: The Autobiography Of Alice Cooper*, Alice Cooper with Steven Gaines (1976), *Rolling Stone Scrapbook: Alice Cooper*, Rolling Stone (1975).

Alice In Chains

Formed in 1987 in Seattle, USA, by vocalist Layne Staley and guitarist/vocalist Jerry Cantrell with Mike Starr (bass) and Sean Kinney (drums), Alice In Chains developed a sound which mixed Black Sabbath-style riffing with Staley and Cantrell's unconventional vocal arrangements and strong songwriting. Cantrell had drifted from his home in Tacoma to Seattle, homing in on a musician's collective entitled the Music Bank. He brought in the rhythm section of Kinney and Starr, before Staley, brought up a Christian scientist, was rescued from a local funk metal act. After dispensing with early moniker Fuck, the group became Alice In Chains, a name coined by Staley for 'a parody heavy metal band that dressed in drag'. The group won a major recording deal despite some record executives being scared off by Staley's aggressive performance at an early showcase. *Facelift* received excellent reviews, but took off slowly, boosted by US touring with Van Halen, the difficult opening slot on the US Clash Of The Titans tour, featuring Slayer, Anthrax and Megadeth, and European dates with Megadeth and the Almighty. 'Man In The Box' became an MTV favourite, and the album went gold in the autumn of 1991, just as Nirvana's success began to make Seattle headline news. The band released the gentler *Sap*, featuring guests from Heart, Soundgarden and Mudhoney, before recording their second full album.

Dirt was a dark, cathartic work with many personal lyrics, including 'Rooster', telling of Cantrell's father's Vietnam War experience, which became a live centrepiece, but critical attention focused on a sequence of songs referring to Staley's past heroin problems, descending from the happy initiate of 'Junkhead' ('...we are an elite race of our own/The stoners, junkies and freaks') through depths of addiction to the realisation of the need to break away from dependency in 'Angry Chair' ('Little boy made a mistake/Pink cloud has now turned to gray'). Despite the controversy, *Dirt* was deservedly acclaimed, becoming critics' album of the year in many metal magazines, and entered the US charts at number 6. 'Would?' became a hit, boosted by an appearance playing the song in the *Singles* movie, and the band supported Ozzy Osbourne in the USA, with Staley in a wheelchair for the early dates, having broken his foot, before Starr departed. Ex-Ozzy bassist Michael Inez stepped in, and the band embarked on sold-out European and US headline tours. Cancellation of European stadium shows supporting Metallica in mid-1993 due to exhaustion led to speculation about a setback in Staley's recovery, but Alice In Chains returned in fine style, contributing to the *Last Action Hero* soundtrack and playing superbly on the third Lollapalooza tour. In early 1994 *Jar Of Flies* became the first EP to top the US album charts, entering at number 1. Staley would put together side-project Gacy Bunch (after mass murderer John Wayne Gacy) with Pearl Jam's Mike McCready and Barrett from Screaming Trees, amid rumours that Alice In Chains had split. Rumours exacerbated by the return of Staley's misfortunes in August 1994 when gigs, including Woodstock II, were cancelled, due to further 'health problems'.

Albums: *Facelift* (Columbia 1990), *Sap* (Columbia 1992, mini-album), *Dirt* (Columbia 1992), *Jar Of Flies* (Columbia 1994, mini-album).

Alien (Sweden)

This melodic hard-rock quartet was formed in Sweden in 1986. Assimilating influences such as Survivor, Styx, Foreigner, Kansas and Journey, they delivered a highly polished, if rather derivative, debut album in 1988. Earlier they had earned a domestic number 1 with a cover of the old Graham Bonnet hit, 'Only One Woman'. Original vocalist Jim Gilhead was replaced by the ex-Madison frontman Peter Sandberg soon after the album was released. The remainder of the band included Tony Borg (guitar), Ken Sandin (bass), Jimmy Wandroph (keyboards) and Toby Tarrach (drums). With a distinct lack of promotion from Virgin Records, they made little impact outside their native Sweden and split soon after the release of their second album.

Albums: *Alien* (Virgin 1988), *Shitfin' Gear* (Virgin 1990).

Alien (USA)

Metal band from New York, USA, comprising Frank Starr (vocals), Rik Kristi (guitar), Damien 'The Beast' Harlow (bass), Roxann Harlow (drums) and Brian Fair (guitar). Although they remained together just long enough to release a solitary mini-album, this has become a popular cult item among hard rock followers. Kristi would later join with ex-Steeler bass player Rik Fox on the west coast. However, the band's exploits would be overshadowed by the news that Harlow had lived up to his grisly moniker and been charged with a count of first-degree murder during a botched burglary.

Album: *Cosmic Fantasy* (Mongol Horde 1983; mini-album).

Alkatrazz

This group was formed in Maidstone, Kent, England, in 1980 by vocalist Craig Stevens and guitarist Bob Jenner. Recruiting the services of Gary Bevan (bass) and Nick Parsons (drums), they signed to RCA Records as one of the hopefuls of the New Wave Of British Heavy Metal movement. *Young Blood* featured hard-rock reminiscent of UFO. Unable to make a breakthrough with this, they switched to an Americanized AOR approach with *Radio 5*. This drive for commercial success also failed and RCA dropped them soon after the album was released.

Albums: *Young Blood* (RCA 1981), *Radio 5* (RCA 1982).

Alliance

This short-lived, American melodic rock quintet was formed in 1980 by the talented vocalist Mark Bucchare. With guitarist Pat Hand, keyboardist Mark Heckert, bassist Bradley Davidson and drummer David Pridemore completing the line-up, their music was characterized by note-perfect harmonies, razor-sharp arrangements and understated guitar work. Their self-titled debut however, lacked both the image and real direction necessary to elevate them above the plethora of other Styx/Kansas/Journey clones around at the time. Disillusioned by the lack of recognition and label support, they disbanded the following year.

Album: *Alliance* (Handshake 1982).

Allied Forces

Formed in 1983, Allied Forces were a Dutch hard

Alien (Sweden)

rock quintet, from the province of Brabant. Featuring Ronnie Gershwin (vocals), Marc Gershwin (guitar), Harold Cucken (guitar), Steven Highwood (bass) and Pete Van de Sluice (drums), they built up a solid reputation touring the European circuit as support for Anvil and TNT. Following a series of delays, *The Day After* was eventually released in 1987 on the German Flametrader label. Produced by ex-Vandenberg bassist Dick Kemper, they acknowledged a variety of influences which included Golden Earring, Scorpions and Europe, but without ever resorting to plagiarism. Highwood and Cucken quit in 1988 with Ferry Schmuter stepping in to take over four-string duties. The band then pursued a more melodic direction, but have yet to provide evidence of this on vinyl.
Album: *The Day After* (Flametrader 1987).

Allies

This US group were formed from the ashes of the religious pomp-rock outfit, the Sweet Comfort Band, in 1983. Comprising Bob Carlisle (vocals/guitar), Randy Thomas (guitar/keyboards), Kenny Williams (keyboards/saxophone/vocals), Matthew Chapman (bass) and Jim Erickson (drums), their first two albums are fine examples of melodic Christian rock in a Kansas/Stryper vein. 1987's *Shoulder To Shoulder* saw the band diversifying their approach, with blues, funk and soul influences being given more prominence in their compositions. The album was a disappointment, judged by many critics to be overloaded with nondescript power-ballads. *Long Way To Paradise* tried unsuccessfully to recapture the ground lost by this change in style, but was let down by weak material.
Albums: *Allies* (Light 1984), *Virtues* (Light 1985), *Shoulder To Shoulder* (Dayspring 1987), *Long Way To Paradise* (Dayspring 1987).

Allman Brothers Band

Formed in Macon, Georgia, USA, in 1969 by guitarist Duane Allman (b. 20 November 1946, Nashville, Tennessee, USA, d. 29 October 1971), the band included brother Gregg Allman (b. 8 December 1947, Nashville, Tennessee, USA; keyboards/vocals), Richard Betts (b. 12 December 1943, Palm Beach, Florida, USA; guitar), Berry Oakley (b. 4 April 1948, Chicago, Illinois, USA, d. 11 November 1972; bass), Butch Trucks (b. Jacksonville, Florida, USA; drums) and Jai Jai Johanson (b. 8 July 1944, Ocean Springs, Mississippi, USA; drums). The above line-up was the culmination of several southern-based aspirants, of which the Hour Glass was the most prolific. This pop/soul ensemble featured Duane and Gregg Allman, but broke up when demo tapes for a projected third album were rejected by their record company. Duane then found employment at the Fame studio where he participated in several sessions, including those for Aretha Franklin, Wilson Pickett and King Curtis, prior to instigating this new sextet. The Allman Brothers established themselves as a popular live attraction and their first two albums, *The Allman Brothers Band* and *Idlewild South*, were marked by strong blues-based roots and an exciting rhythmic drive. However it was a sensational two-album set, *Live At The Fillmore East* that showcased the group's emotional fire. 'Whipping Post', a 22 minute *tour de force*, remains one of rock music's definitive improvisational performances. The set brought the band to the brink of stardom, while Duane's reputation as an outstanding slide guitarist was further enhanced by his contribution to *Layla*, the seminal Derek And The Dominos' album. However, tragedy struck on 29 October 1971 when this gifted musician was killed in a motor-cycle accident.

The remaining members completed *Eat A Peach*, which consisted of live and studio material, before embarking on a mellower direction with *Brothers And Sisters*, a style best exemplified by the album's hit single, 'Ramblin' Man'. A second pianist, Chuck Leavell, was added to the line-up, but just as the group recovered its momentum, Berry Oakley was killed in an accident chillingly similar to that of his former colleague on 11 November 1972. Not surprisingly, the Allman Brothers now seemed deflated, and subsequent releases failed to match the fire of those first recordings. Their power was further diminished by several off-shoot projects. Gregg Allman (later to marry Cher twice) and Dickie Betts embarked on solo careers while Leavell, Johanson and new bassist Lamar Williams formed Sea Level. The Allmans broke up acrimoniously in 1976 following a notorious drugs trial in which Gregg testified against a former road manager. Although the other members vowed never to work with the vocalist again, a reconstituted 1978 line-up included Allman, Betts and Trucks. *Enlightened Rogues* was a commercial success, but subsequent albums fared less well and in 1982 the Allman Brothers Band split for a second time. A new incarnation appeared in the 90s with a line-up of Greg Allman (vocals/organ), Dicky Betts (vocals/lead guitar), Warren Haynes (vocals/slide and lead guitar), Allen Woody (bass), Jaimoe (drums), Butch Trucks (drums) and Mark Quinones (percussion). Their 1994 album, *Where It All Begins*, was recorded effectively live in the studio, with production once more by Allman Brothers veteran Tom Dowd. The work displayed on their first five

albums remains among the finest recorded during the late 60s and early 70s, in particular for the skilful interplay between two gifted, imaginative guitarists. Albums: *The Allman Brothers Band* (Capricorn 1969), *Idlewild South* (Capricorn 1970), *Live At The Fillmore East* (Capricorn 1971, double album), *Eat A Peach* (Capricorn 1972, double album), *Brothers And Sisters* (Capricorn 1973), *Win Lose Or Draw* (Capricorn 1975), *Wipe The Windows, Check The Oil, Dollar Gas* (Capricorn 1976, double album), *Enlightened Rogues* (Capricorn 1979), *Reach For The Sky* (Arista 1980), *Brothers Of The Road* (Arista 1981), *Ludlow Garage (Live)* (Polygram 1990, double CD), *Seven Turns* (Epic 1990), *Shades Of Two Worlds* (Epic 1991), *An Evening With* (Epic 1992), *Where It All Begins* (Epic 1994). Compilations: *The Road Goes On Forever* (Capricorn 1975, double album), *Dreams* (Polydor 1989; six album/four CD box set), *A Decade Of Hits* (Polygram 1991).
Video: *Live At Great Woods* (1993).
Further reading: *The Allman Brothers: A Biography In Words And Pictures*, Tom Nolan (1976).

Almighty

This Scottish hard rock quartet was formed in 1988 by vocalist/guitarist Ricky Warwick (husband of Vanessa, hostess of *Headbanger's Ball* on MTV), guitarist Tantrum, bassist Floyd London and drummer Stump Munroe. Along with Little Angels, Quireboys and the Dogs D'Amour, the Almighty spearheaded a revival in British heavy rock during the late 80s, drawing their inspiration from bands such as the Cult, Ramones and Motörhead. Signing to Polydor the following year, they released *Blood, Fire And Love* to widespread critical acclaim. The title was changed from *Blood, Fire And Roses* to avoid any possible confusion with Guns N'Roses. This was swiftly followed by a perfunctory live mini-album, which included a stunning cover of Bachman Turner Overdrive's standard, 'You Ain't Seen Nothin' Yet'. *Soul Destruction* emphasized the growth of the group's songwriting abilities. It spawned the UK Top 20 hit, 'Free 'n' Easy', and gained them recognition throughout Europe. However, internal tensions led to the dismissal of Tantrum, with Canadian Peter Friesen, whom the band had met during his time in Alice Cooper's band, filling the gap. The band broke from recording sessions to open the 1992 Donington Monsters of Rock festival with a fiery performance, a recording of which was released with initial copies of *Powertrippin'*. Mark Dodson's production gave the band a heavier sound, drawing Metallica and Soundgarden comparisons, yet retaining the Almighty's characteristic aggressive delivery, while a more mature lyrical approach enhanced the band's already strong songwriting platform. Single success with 'Addiction' was followed by heavy touring as the band supported Iron Maiden across Europe, played stadium dates with Metallica, and took on a gruelling club trek to lay the groundwork in the USA. On their return, the Almighty headlined one of the most acclaimed UK tours of 1993 with the Wildhearts and Kerbdog in tow. However, despite a UK Top 5 placing for *Powertrippin'*, the band were faced with demands for new material from Polydor within four months of its release. This led to a parting of the ways, with the Almighty sacking manager Tommy Tee and signing to Chrysalis in early 1994. Now rehoused in London, the debut album for their new label was produced by Chris Sheldon (responsible for Therapy?'s *Troublegum*).
Albums: *Blood, Fire And Love* (Polydor 1989), *Blood, Fire and Love - Live* (Polydor 1990), *Soul Destruction* (Polydor 1991), *Powerstrippin'* (Polydor 1993), *Crank* (Chrysalis 1994).

Alpha Centauri

This exceptionally talented but little-known Canadian heavy rock quintet was formed in 1976 by Kurt Smith (vocals/guitar) and Jesse Redmon (keyboards/vocals). With Garth Hannum (bass/vocals) and Randy Thompson completing the line-up, they specialized in highly dramatic, often grandiose arrangements, awash with keyboards, but punctuated in places by some fierce guitar work. Their self-titled debut was an undiscovered gem of the pomp-rock genre. Released as a limited edition, it is still much sought-after by collectors.
Album: *Alpha Centauri* (Salt 1977).

Altar Of The King

Formed in April 1991 in San Francisco as Now Hear This, this hard rock quartet first met in audition jams for lead singer Bogdan Jablonski's then band, Warsaw, at Jackson St. Studios. This process saw the group evolve to include Bob Coons (guitar; brother of Laaz Rockit's vocalist), Tony Anthony (bass; once auditioned for Metallica) and Steve Quartarola (drums; ex-Black Ice, Vise, Cry Wolf, Lust). For Jablonski's part he had been singing in Bay Area bands for over ten years, and studied under Barbara Streisand and Frank Sinatra vocal coach Judy Davis. He had also sung background vocals for Testament. The group played their first shows soon after this line-up was settled, recording their material at Fantasy Studios in Berkeley in 1993 for release as a demo (which saw original name *Now Hear This* revived as its title). This was touted round until European label

Rock The Nation heard it and a deal was concluded. 1994 saw these tracks remixed for release at Trax East Studios in New Jersey, while the group supported the likes of Primus, Helix and others on the road.
Album: *Altar Of The King* (RTN 1994).

Amboy Dukes

Originally from Detroit, Michigan, USA, the Amboy Dukes - John Drake (vocals), Ted Nugent (lead guitar), Steve Farmer (rhythm guitar), Rick Lorber (keyboards), Bill White (bass) and Dave Palmer (drums) - achieved notoriety for their rendition of 'Baby Please Don't Go', which took Them's classic version as its inspiration, but added Ted Nugent's snarling guitar. A US Top 20 hit, its brashness set the tone for the group's subsequent albums on which Farmer's rather pretentious lyrics often undermined the music on offer. Frequent changes in personnel (Drake, Lorber and White were replaced, in turn, by Rusty Day, Andy Solomon and Greg Arama), made little difference to the Amboy Dukes' development as the group increasingly became an outlet for Nugent's pyrotechnics. He unveiled a new line-up in 1974 with *Call Of The Wild*, the first of two albums recorded for Frank Zappa's Discreet label. The guitarist then abandoned the band's name altogether and embarked on a solo career.
Albums: *The Amboy Dukes* (Mainstream 1967), *Journey To The Centre Of Your Mind* (Mainstream 1968), *Migrations* (Mainstream 1969), *Marriage On The Rocks* (Polydor 1969), *Survival Of The Fittest* (Polydor 1971). As Ted Nugent And The Amboy Dukes: *Call Of The Wild* (Discreet 1974), *Tooth, Fang And Claw* (Discreet 1975).

Americade

This New York hard rock quartet was put together by the De Marigny brothers in 1981. Vocalist P.J. and guitarist Gerard teamed up with ex-Rachel duo Nick Sadano (bass) and Walt Woodman III (drums). Sadano was replaced by Dave Spitz (brother of Dan, the Anthrax guitarist) before any material was recorded. Meanwhile they gained a reputation for covering Van Halen numbers at high-velocity. They split in 1984, but Gerard De Marigny resurrected the name in 1989 with ex-Malice vocalist Mark Weitz, bassist Greg O'Smith (ex-W.O.W.) and Paul Cammarata on drums.
Album: *American Metal* (Adem 1982).

Amorphis

Formed in Helsinki, Finland, in 1990, Amorphis were originally the idea of guitarist Esa Holopinen and drummer/synthesizer player Jan Rechberger, who recruited vocalist/guitarist Tomi Koivusaari and bass player Olli-Pekka Laine. Their first demo, *Disment Of Soul*, arrived a few months later. It was on the strength of this that they secured a multi-album recording contract with Relapse Records, famed for their catalogue of American grind bands. December 1991 saw the band record six tracks for a shared album with labelmates Incantation (never actually released). Two songs from this session did see the light of day, however, as part of a limited edition 7-inch EP. In May 1992 the quartet travelled to Stockholm, Sweden, to record 11 tracks for their debut album, *The Karelian Isthmus*, with engineer/producer Tomas Skogsberg. A crushing demonstration of state-of-the-art death metal, the dramatic atmosphere of the songs would soon be further enhanced by the addition of keyboard player Kasper Martenson. In the wake of the album's success, Relapse elected to release the abandoned split LP session as part of its Underground series as *Privilege Of Evil*. September 1993 saw Amorphis return to Stockholm to record 10 further tracks for their second full length album, *Tales From The Thousand Lakes*. As the title may have suggested, this saw a sound incorporating elements of 70s progressive rock, with the band taking their theme as a historical tribute to Finland and the national literature that is *The Kalevaia*.
Albums: *The Karelian Isthmus* (Relapse/Nuclear Blast 1992), *Privilege Of Evil* (Relapse 1993, mini-album), *Tales From The Thousand Lakes* (Relapse/Nuclear Blast 1993).

Anathema

Formed in Liverpool, England, in the summer of 1990, doom metal band Anathema owe much to early 70s Black Sabbath, most notably their low, ominous riffs and depressive hippie affectations. Combined with this are more contemporary influences, highlighted by abrasive guitar and vocal performances, taken from the death metal genre of the early 90s. Perhaps the oddest element of Anathema's material lies in the moments of morbid poetic romanticism, most evident in their lyrics and occasional use of the angelic tones of female vocalist, Ruth (Anathema's original line-up comprised vocalist Darren, guitarist Danny, bassist Jamie and drummer John). The results of this odd hybrid hold together surprisingly well and Anathema enjoy a strong cult following among doom metal fans. 'We began like a cross between a thrash and death metal band', they concede, evidence of which was first made available in their four-track demo, *An Illiad Of Woes*, released in November 1990 under their original title, Pagan Angel. A second demo, *All Faith Is Lost*, again cut at the MA Studios where both Vincent and replacement bass player Duncan work, arrived in July 1991. In its wake they were contacted by Switzerland label Witchunt, which led to a limited edition single, 'They Die'/'Crestfallen'. This was the first recording from the band with Duncan, Jamie having elected to return to college. Eventually the band earned a contract with the musically sympathetic Peaceville Records, initially contributing one track, 'Lovelorn Rhapsody', to the *Volume 4* compilation. Their first release 'proper' in 1992, the *Crestfallen* EP, was sufficiently well-received to warrant an album the following year. Slow, pretentious, melancholy and heavy, Anathema exude a gravity often missing from the heavy metal genre. Along with fellow English doom bands My Dying Bride and Paradise Lost, they represent an intriguing, ponderous, semi symphonic movement in 90s heavy metal.

Album: *Serenades* (Peaceville 1993).

Angel

This Los Angeles-based band are perhaps more widely recalled for their outrageous image and stage shows than for their musical prowess. Their self-titled debut, recorded with a line-up of Frank DiMino (vocals), Edwin Lionel 'Punky' Meadows (guitar), Greg Giuffria (keyboards), Mickey Jones (bass), and Barry Brandt (drums), was an excellent slab of heavy pomp rock, with lengthy songs swathed in Giuffria's atmospheric keyboards and featuring the long-time stage favourite, 'Tower'. *Helluva Band* continued in a similar vein, although the longest track, 'The Fortune', was exceptional and tended to obscure the rest of the material, and the band's famous white satin stage clothing made its debut on the album sleeve. *On Earth As It Is In Heaven* saw a distinct change in musical direction, as the band adopted a pop-rock sound, and introduced a clever logo which read identically when upside down, but a poor production let the album down. *White Hot*, with Felix Robinson replacing Jones, was helped by Eddie Leonetti's more sympathetic production, and produced minor US hits in 'I Ain't Gonna Eat Out My Heart Anymore' and 'The Winter Song'. Leonetti subsequently produced *Sinful* and the in-concert set, *Live Without A Net*, which had been recorded on the *White Hot* tour and suffered from the lack of material drawn from *Sinful*. Angel's record sales never quite reflected their popularity as a live act, and the loss of their recording contract led to the band's break-up in 1981, with Giuffria going on to success with Giuffria and House Of Lords, and Robinson appearing in an early White Lion line-up.

Albums: *Angel* (Casablanca 1975), *Helluva Band* (Casablanca 1976), *On Earth As It Is In Heaven* (Casablanca 1977), *White Hot* (Casablanca 1977), *Sinful* (Casablanca 1979), *Live Without A Net* (Casablanca 1980). Compilation: *Anthology* (Casablanca 1992).

Angels

During the late 70s and the early 80s, the Angels, formed in 1975, were Australia's most successful rock band, enjoying massive record sales for both singles and albums, and also the distinction of being the number one live act in the country. The group are based around the brothers John (guitar) and Rick Brewster (guitar) with Doc Neeson (vocals), who had been together in jug and rock 'n' roll revival bands such as the Keystone Angels in Adelaide since 1971. The line-up filled out by Chris Bailey (bass) and Graham Bidstrup (drums, replacing original sticksman Buzz Throckman), the Angels toured incessantly, culminating in an extended tour of the USA where they were known as Angel City. Their no-nonsense go-getting rock was never innovative, but they worked hard to captivate their audiences at every opportunity, writing lyrics that were concise and easy to sing along to. However, the band did not make much headway in America and, as happened with so many others, their audience in Australia tired of them and several albums were ignored. But unlike lesser outfits, the Angels continued working and gradually won over a new audience, supporting Guns N'Roses at LA's Whiskey in 1988, though by this time only Neeson and Rick Brewster remained from the original line-up. Once again becoming hugely popular in their native country, they achieved an Australian number 1 chart position for the first time in 1990, with an album recorded in Memphis, Tennessee, with Led Zeppelin/Z.Z. Top producer Terry Manning.

Albums: *The Angels* (Albert 1977), *No Exit* (Albert 1979), *Face To Face* (Epic 1980), *Dark Room* (Epic 1980), *Night Attack* (Epic 1982), *Two Minute Warning* (MCA 1984), *The Howling* (MCA 1986), *Liveline* (MCA 1988), *Beyond Salvation* (Chrysalis 1990).

Angels With Dirty Faces

Taking their name from an old Sham 69 rallying call, Angels With Dirty Faces formed in the north west of England in early 1991, the line-up consisting of Simon Gibbs (vocals), Jason Woolley (guitar), Jeremy Dykes (bass) and Paul Roscrow (drums). Their debut release was a self-financed mini-album, *A Little Taste*, which was warmly received in *Kerrang!* magazine by guest reviewers Henry Cluney (Stiff Little Fingers) and Neil Schon (Journey). Following a heavy gigging

Angels With Dirty Faces

schedule through 1992 and 1993 they signed to RTN subsidiary Blue Flame and released their full-length debut the following year.

Album: *Sounds Of The World Turning* (Blue Flame 1994).

Angelwitch

Angelwitch were one of the first rock groups to be associated with the New Wave Of British Heavy Metal movement which originated in 1979. The band, a power trio, put together by guitar virtuoso Kevin Heybourne, featured Kevin Riddles (bass) and Dave Dufort (drums). (Dufort's sister, Denise, occupied the same position in Girlschool.) Their self-titled debut album drew heavily on satanic and witchcraft imagery and combined this with doom-laden riffs and virriolic guitar breaks. Their only chart success was with 'Sweet Danger' which reached number 75 in the UK chart for just one week in June 1980. Soon after the release of *Angelwitch* the band split up, but Heybourne retained the name and drafted in Dave Hogg and Pete Gordelier on drums and bass respectively, plus vocalist Dave Tattum. After two uninspiring albums they ground to a halt, but

Heybourne resurrected the band in 1989 with drummer Spencer Holman and bassist Grant Dennis for a one-off album, recorded live in Los Angeles.

Albums: *Angelwitch* (Bronze 1980), *Screaming And Bleeding* (Rock Machine 1985), *Frontal Assault* (Killerwatt 1986), *Screamin' Assault* (Killerwatt 1988), *Live* (Music For Nations 1990). Compilation: *Doctor Phibes* (Raw Power 1986).

Annihilator

Basically a vehicle for the talents of classically trained Canadian guitarist Jeff Waters (b. Ottawa, Canada). Annihilator set the underground scene alight with a demo entitled 'Phantasmagoria', before relocating to Vancouver and releasing their debut, *Alice In Hell*. This was a *tour de force* of intricate thrash with all guitars and bass parts played by Waters, who also produced and wrote the material, with Randy Rampage (vocals; ex-DOA) and Ray Hartmann (drums) - augmented by Anthony Greenham (guitar) and Wayne Darley (bass) after the recording. The sizzling guitar work helped the record become the best-selling debut in Roadrunner's history. The band subsequently suffered from an unstable line-up, with

Annihilator

Greenham being replaced almost immediately by Dave Scott Davis, while Rampage departed when touring was complete, with ex-Omen frontman Coburn Pharr stepping in. *Never, Neverland* was another excellent effort, displaying rather more lyrical maturity than the debut, and a new version of 'Phantasmagoria'. Band stability remained an issue, and Davis' departure on the eve of a European tour as guests of Judas Priest caused problems due to the sheer complexity of the material, but the group managed to produce creditable performances nevertheless. After a lengthy break, Annihilator returned with new guitarist Neil Goldberg and another vocalist, Aaron Randall. *Set The World On Fire*, though less well received by the metal press than previous offerings, revealed some promising progression beyond thrash boundaries into more melodic spaces, and sold well. The remix and unreleased tracks compilation *Bag Of Tricks* would be the band's last for Roadrunner, debuting for new home Music For Nations with *King Of The Kill*. This saw Waters take over lead vocals and Randy Black on drums, adding Dave Davis (guitar) and Cam Dixon (bass) later.

Albums: *Alice In Hell* (Roadrunner 1989), *Never, Neverland* (Roadrunner 1990), *Set The World On Fire* (Roadrunner 1993), *King Of The Kill* (Music For Nations 1994). Compilation: *Bag Of Tricks* (Roadrunner 1994).

Anthem

This Japanese group, formed in 1981, specialized in cloning western rock music. After numerous personnel changes, the 1990 line-up comprised Elizo Sakamoto (vocals), Hiroya Fukada (guitar), Nuoto Ski Bata (bass) and Tahamasa Ohuchi (drums), though none were original members. Influenced by the style and melodies of UFO, Thin Lizzy, Kiss and more recently Megadeth, they have produced a series of solid but unassuming albums. Their second album proper (*Bound To Break*) was produced by Chris Tsangarides (of Thin Lizzy fame) and was a major success in the Far East.

Albums: *Anthem* (Medusa 1985, mini-album), *Tightrope* (Medusa 1986), *Bound To Break* (Medusa 1987), *Gypsy Ways* (Medusa 1988).

Anthrax

This New York-based thrash metal outfit came to the fore in 1982 with a line-up comprising Scott 'Not' Ian (rhythm guitar), Neil Turbin (vocals), Dan Spitz (lead guitar), Dan Lilker (bass) and Charlie Benante (drums). Managed by Johnny Z, head of the independent Megaforce Records, the quintet released

Fistful Of Metal in 1984. Despite its tasteless sleeve, the album garnered fair reviews and was a small but steady seller. For a time Ian, Lilker and Benante were also part of Stormtroopers Of Death (S.O.D., who were revived briefly in 1991), a hardcore band with a satirical outlook, and Lilker subsequently left Anthrax to pursue just such a direction with Nuclear Assault. Turbin also departed, with his initial replacement, Matt Fallon, being quickly succeeded by Joey Belladonna. This line-up released the *Armed And Dangerous* EP in 1985, and their rising popularity led to a contract with Island Records. *Spreading The Disease* was deservedly well-received, and the band's European profile was raised considerably by their support slot on Metallica's Damage Inc tour. *Among The Living*, co-produced by the band with Eddie Kramer, established Anthrax as a major force in the speed metal scene, producing UK hits in 'I Am The Law' and 'Indians', and their riotously entertaining live shows made them many friends among press and public alike. A humorous rap song, 'I'm The Man', became both a hit and a favourite encore. However, *State Of Euphoria* was a disappointing, patchy affair, with the group suffering an undeserved media backlash over their image, until sterling live work restored their reputation, with Anthrax's commitment to expanding their audiences' musical tastes demonstrated by their choice of UK support acts, Living Colour and King's X. *Persistence Of Time* showed a real return to form, a dark and relentless work which produced another hit in the unlikely shape of a high-speed cover of Joe Jackson's 'Got The Time'. Classed by the band as an EP, *Attack Of The Killer B's* was essentially a collection of b-sides for the curious fan, but became one of Anthrax's most popular albums, with the hit collaboration with Public Enemy, 'Bring The Noise', leading to the two bands touring together in a co-headlining package. Shortly after the band signed a new deal with Elektra Records, Belladonna was fired, with ex-Armored Saint frontman John Bush stepping in. *Sound Of White Noise* was hailed as the band's finest hour, a post-thrash *tour de force* of power metal with bursts of hardcore speed. Bush's creative input helped Ian and Benante to write some of their best work, while Dave Jerden's production updated and re-energized the Anthrax sound. 1994 saw Bush start his own R&B offshoot, Ho Cake, which includes former Armored Saint personnel Joey Vera (bass) and Jeff Duncan (guitar), as well as Shawn Duncan (drums), Tony Silbert (keyboards) and Bruce Fernandez (drums; ex-Dread Zeppelin).

Albums: *Fistful Of Metal* (Megaforce 1984), *Spreading The Disease* (Island/Megaforce 1986), *Among The*

Living (Island/Megaforce 1987), *State Of Euphoria* (Island/Megaforce 1988), *Persistence Of Time* (Island/Megaforce 1990), *Attack Of The Killer B's* (Island/Megaforce 1991), *Sound Of White Noise* (Elektra 1993), *Live - The Island Years* (Island 1994). Videos: *Oidivnikufesin N.F.V.* (1988), *Videos P.O.V.* (1990).

Anti-Nowhere League

Leading lights in the early 80s UK punk scene along with contempories GBH and Exploited, this quartet from Tunbridge Wells, Kent, betrayed their talent in biker leather, chains and hardcore obscenity. Led by Animal (b. Nick Karmer; vocals) and Magoo (guitar), their catalogue of sexual outrage veered from the satirical to the genuinely offensive, with a string of four-letter words, rabid misogyny and the glorification of bestiality. Their most memorable moment was a thrashy re-run of Ralph McTell's 'Streets Of London' which replaced the song's folky sentimentality with the barbed, snarling rhetoric of the gutter. Thousands of copies of the single were seized and destroyed by the police as the b-side, 'So What', was deemed obscene. This incident however, did nothing to prevent the group reaching number 1

in the UK Independent single charts, a feat accomplished a further three times in 1982 with 'I Hate People', 'Woman' and 'For You'. As their punkish appeal receded, the group abbreviated their name to the League and turned to a punk/metal hyrbrid in keeping with their biker image. Surprsingly, the results were not as appalling as might have been imagined, with *The Perfect Crime* boasting several fine songs, not least the very nearly subtle '(I Don't Believe) This Is My England'. The group disbanded in 1988 but there have been several revivals, including the one-off 1989 reunion recorded for release as *Live And Loud*.
Albums: *We Are...The League* (WXYZ 1982), *Live In Yugoslavia* (ID 1983), *The Perfect Crime* (GWR 1987), *Live And Loud* (Link 1990). Compilation: *Long Live The League* (Dojo 1986).

Anvil

Formerly known as Lips, Anvil was a Canadian four-piece from Toronto that made a significant impression on the speed-metal rock scene during the early 80s. The group comprised frontman Lips (vocals/guitar), who had given his name to the group's previous incarnation, Dave Allison (guitar), Ian

Anthrax

Dickson (bass) and Robb Reiner (drums). The band were technically excellent, playing at breakneck speed and with an intensity that few of their peers could equal. Their first three albums were exemplary, with *Metal On Metal* containing the strongest material. Following a series of legal disputes with their label, as well as internal conflicts concerning musical differences, there was a four-year gap between successive studio albums. *Backwaxed* was a compilation, released against the band's wishes, which featured songs they had recorded but rejected. *Strength Of Steel*, released in 1987, was a satisfactory come-back; but it was overshadowed by the concurrent work of Slayer, Megadeth and Metallica. Ironic given that Anvil were now being acknowledged as having had a profound influence on these bands in their formative years. *Pound For Pound* was followed by a compilation of live material, before Allison quit in 1989.

Albums: *Hard 'n' Heavy* (Attic 1981), *Metal On Metal* (Attic 1982), *Forged In Fire* (Attic 1983), *Strength Of Steel* (Attic 1987), *Pound For Pound* (Metal Blade 1988), *Past And Present - Live* (Roadrunner 1989). Compilation: *Backwaxed* (Attic 1985).

Apes, Pigs & Spacemen

Metal band who took their name from what they considered to be a gap in Charles Darwin's rationale - the theory of evolution not accounting for a 30 million year gap in fossil records, nor why humans only use 10% of their brain capacity. The answer, to this quartet formed in Derby in 1993, was that 'An advanced lifeform came to earth from space and mated with what we consider a lower life-form, an ape. The offspring became what he now call humanity'. The pig element, meanwhile, arrived because 'we're now growing organs in pigs for the purpose of being transplanted into humans. But we eat pigs...'. Such elemental logic was reflected in the musical dynamic of the band, fronted by lead singer and thinker Paul Miro, backed by friends Sam Carr (drums), Kettle (guitar) and Bart (bass). Within a year of their formation in 1993 they were putting the finishing touches to a debut EP, *Antiseptic*, produced by Simon Efemey, of Wildhearts, Helmet and Pantera fame. 1994 brought rave reviews for their support slots to Freak Of Nature and others.

Apocalypse

Apocalypse were the most important heavy metal outfit to emerge from Switzerland after Celtic Frost. Comprising Carlos R. Sprenger (vocals), Julien Brocher (guitar), Pierre Alain Zurcher (guitar), Jean Claude Schneider (bass) and Andre Domenjoz (drums), their central influence came from speed metal bands such as Slayer. Formed in 1984, a series of short-lived line-ups ensued before stability was reached and they secured a contract with Under One Flag. Their debut album was mixed by Metallica-supremo Flemming Rasmussen and featured high-energy power metal, although the sound was ultimately flawed by insubstantial vocals. Not to be confused with any of the several other pop and rock acts who have used the name Apocalypse.
Album: *Apocalypse* (Under One Flag 1988).

Apocrypha

Hailing from Las Vegas, USA, Apocrypha were the brainchild of techno-wizard rock guitarist Tony Fredianelli. Their music was characterized by his intricate guitar work which combined classical and rock styles to startling effect. Formed in 1988, the original line-up featured Fredianelli, Steve Plocica (vocals), Chip Chrovian (guitar), Al Rumley (bass) and Mike Poe (drums). *Forgotten Scroll* and *Eyes Of Time* were excellent speed-metal albums, but somewhat lacking in variety. Breck Smith and Dave Schiller replaced Rumley and Poe respectively before the band recorded *Area 54*. Released in 1990, it revealed an outfit who had matured considerably as songwriters. Seemingly well equipped to compete with artists such as Megadeth and Metallica, the group nevertheless ground to a halt soon after.
Albums: *Forgotten Scroll* (Roadrunner 1988), *Eyes Of Time* (Roadrunner 1989), *Area 54* (Roadrunner 1990).

April Wine

Formed in 1969 in Montreal, Quebec, this hard rock group became an immediate success, going on to make inroads in the American market after establishing itself as a platinum act in Canada. Through fluctuating line-ups they arrived at steady membership by the late 70s, including original lead singer Myles Goodwyn (b. 23 June 1948, Halifax, Nova Scotia, Canada), Brian Greenway (b. 1 October 1951; guitar), Gary Moffet (b. 22 June 1949; guitar), Steve Lang (b. 24 March 1949; bass) and Jerry Mercer (b. 27 April 1939; drums). Among their first admirers were former Rascals members Dino Dinelli and Gene Cornish, who produced early material for the group. The line-up for their first album had featured Goodwyn on guitar and vocals, David Henman on guitar, Jim Clench on bass and Richie Henman on drums. *Electric Jewels* saw the line-up switch with Gary Moffet coming in on guitar, and Jerry Mercer on drums to replace the Henman brothers. Clench was replaced on *The Whole World's Going' Crazy* by

Steve Lang, with Greenaway added as third guitarist in time for *First Glance*. Despite uneven album performances, April Wine placed three Top 40 singles and five albums in the US charts, their greatest commercial successes coming with the gold album *Harder...Faster* and the platinum *The Nature Of The Beast*. The group split in the mid-80s but reformed at the turn of the new decade.

Albums: *April Wine* (Aquarius 1972), *On Record* (Aquarius 1973), *Electric Jewels* (Aquarius 1974), *Live* (Aquarius 1975), *Stand Back* (Aquarius 1975), *The Whole World's Goin' Crazy* (London 1976), *Live At The El Macambo* (London 1977), *First Glance* (Capitol 1978), *Harder...Faster* (Capitol 1979), *The Nature Of The Beast* (Capitol 1981), *Power Play* (Capitol 1982), *Animal Grace* (Capitol 1984), *Walking Through Fire* (Capitol 1985).

Video: *Live In London* (1989).

Arcade

As Ratt began to disintegrate, vocalist Stephen Pearcy was quick to jump ship for a new project with old friend Fred Coury (drums, ex-Cinderella). From beginnings as a Pearcy solo project, a band soon evolved under the name Taboo, later changing to Arcade, with the recruitment of bassist Michael Andrews, ex-Sea Hags guitarist Frankie Wilsey (subsequently known, curiously, as Wilsex), and ex-Michael Monroe guitarist Johnny Angel, who was later replaced by Donnie Syracuse. *Arcade* (titled *Calm Before The Storm* in Europe) was a big, brash hard rock affair, peering into areas where Pearcy felt his old act had failed to go, with the vocalist making a conscious effort to change his vocal style. Both *Arcade* and a lengthy US club tour did well despite difficult times for hard rock in the face of grunge, with the band's greatest difficulty being hecklers demanding old Ratt material. *A/2* showed a harder approach from a band toughened by months of road work, with some experimental moves adding alternative flavours to heavy arena metal dominated by Wilsex and Syracuse's guitar onslaught, although Pearcy's vocals now retreated towards his former style.

Albums: *Arcade* (Epic 1993), *A/2* (Epic 1994).

Armageddon

This short-lived, mid-70s supergroup specialized in psychedelia-tinged melodic rock. The band comprised ex-Yardbirds and Renaissance vocalist Keith Relf, guitarist Martin Pugh formerly of Steamhammer, bassist Louis Cennamo (also ex-Renaissance) and ex-Johnny Winter drummer Bobby Caldwell. Their self-titled debut, released in 1975, graced the US album charts. It featured long esoteric compositions that fused rock, jazz, blues and symphonic influences. This album is now much sought-after by collectors. Relf would go on to form Illusion in 1975, but was fatally electrocuted a year later, ending a still promising career. Jeff Fenholt was recruited as the new vocalist, but things did not work out as planned; the band split up after recording tracks for a second album. These have yet to be released.

Album: *Armageddon* (A&M 1975).

Armored Saint

This Los Angeles heavy metal quintet was formed in 1981. The band originally comprised John Bush (vocals), Dave Prichard (guitar), Phil E. Sandoval (guitar), Joey Vera (bass) and Gonzo (drums). Gigging incessantly around the Los Angeles bar and club circuit led to them being asked to contribute a track to the *Metal Massacre II* compilation album. This, in turn, attracted the attention of Chrysalis Records, who signed them in 1984. *March Of The Saint* appeared the same year to widespread apathy. Poor production resulted in the band's dynamic energy being totally dissipated in a muddy wall of noise. They moved away from the one-dimensional thrash approach on their next two albums, with John Bush's powerful vocal style giving them a strong identity. Sandoval left to form Megattack during the recording of the second album. The band continued as a four-piece for some time, before Jeff Duncan (ex-Odin) was drafted in as replacement. With no commercial success after three albums, their contract with Chrysalis ended. The band returned with an excellent live album on Metal Blade Records, followed almost three years later by *Symbol Of Salvation*, their most accomplished work to date. Duncan was superseded by Alan Barlam (ex-Hellion) in 1989 while Dave Prichard died of leukaemia on the 27th of February 1990. In 1992 Bush left to replace Joey Belladonna in Anthrax and the rest of the band also dispersed (though Vera and Ducan reunited with Bush in his side-project, Ho Cake). Vera also released a solo album for Metal Blade in 1994, which featured a guest spot from Bush.

Albums: *March Of The Saint* (Chrysalis 1984), *Delirious Nomad* (Chrysalis 1985), *Raising Fear* (Chrysalis 1987), *Saints Will Conquer - Live* (Metal Blade/Enigma 1988), *Symbol Of Salvation* (Metal Blade/Enigma 1991). Joey Vera solo: *A Thousand Faces* (Metal Blade 1994).

Artch

This Norwegian heavy metal quintet was formed in Sarpsborg, Norway, during 1982, by bassist Bernt A.

Jansen and guitarist Cato Olsen. It took a three-year search to find the right musicians to complete the line-up, with drummer Jorn Jamissen, guitarist Geir Nilssen and vocalist Espen Hoss finally meeting the original duo's requirements. Tragically, Hoss was killed in a motorcycle crash, and a replacement was eventually found in Icelandic-born Eirikur Hauksson. Influenced by Black Sabbath, Candlemass, Celtic Frost and Deep Purple, their debut album assimilated all these elements within a dense, melodic framework. Brutal riffs, anthemic choruses and grandiose arrangements were the medium. The album received a favourable response, but the band were reluctant to promote it with a full scale tour. Little has been heard of them since.

Album: *Another Return* (1988).

Artillery

This Danish heavy metal band was formed in 1982 by the guitarist brothers Michael and Morten Stutzer. After several trial and error line-ups, vocalist Flemming Rodsdorf, bassist Peter Torsland and drummer Carter Nielsen were recruited. Influenced by Slayer and Anvil, the band specialized in somewhat formulaic thrash-metal, recording three workman-like albums to date.

Albums: *Fear Of Tomorrow* (Roadrunner 1985), *Terror Squad* (Roadrunner 1986), *By Inheritance* (Roadrunner 1990).

ASAP

The acronym stands for Adrian Smith And Project. This heavy metal unit started off as a sideline interest for the Iron Maiden guitarist, under the unlikely moniker The Entire Population Of Hackney, after a jam session at the Marquee Club in 1986. He intended to use it as an outlet for more conventional songs that did not fit into the Maiden concept. Recruiting guitarists Andy Barnett (who had formerly worked alongside Smith in Urchin) and Dave Colwell, bassist Robin Clayton, keyboardist Richard Young and drummer Zak Starkey (son of Ringo Starr), they recorded *Silver And Gold* in 1989. Smith decided to leave Iron Maiden at this point to concentrate fully on his solo career. His output, however, proved uninspiring. *Silver And Gold* sold poorly and was followed by silence.

Album: *Silver And Gold* (Enigma 1989).

Ashphalt Ballet

This USA heavy metal/'biker-rock' outfit are heavily influenced by the Cult, Lynyrd Skynyrd and Aerosmith (their name is derived from the description of a motorcyclist crashing and skidding along the road at high speed). Fronted by gravel-throated vocalist Gary Jefferies, they soon built up a small but loyal following through incessant gigging on the Los Angeles bar and club circuit. Formed in San Diego in 1988, the line-up is completed by Danny Clarke (guitar), Julius J. Ulrich (guitar), Terry Phillips (bass) and Mikki Kiner (drums). Jeffries was ex-Broken Rule, while the other members of the band had worked together as Mistreated. They signed to Virgin in 1991 and their first album was released early the following year. This epitomized their no-nonsense, raunchy rock 'n' roll style, but offered little that had not been heard before.

Album: *Ashphalt Ballet* (Virgin 1992).

Asia

A supergroup comprised of well-known musicians from British art-rock bands, Asia formed in early 1981 and included John Wetton (b. 12 July 1949, Derby, England; vocals), keyboardist Geoff Downes, Steve Howe (b. 8 April 1947, London, England; guitar) and Carl Palmer (b. 20 March 1947, Birmingham, England; drums/percussion). At the time, Wetton had recently left the English progressive band UK, Howe and Downes had just vacated Yes and Palmer had left Emerson, Lake And Palmer. The group's self-titled debut album was released a year later and, although dismissed by critics as unadventurous and overly commercial, it topped the US album charts for nine weeks, becoming one of the year's bestsellers. A single, 'Heat Of The Moment', also reached the US Top 5. Neither fared as well in the group's homeland. A follow-up single, 'Only Time Will Tell', was a moderate US success. The group released its second album, *Alpha*, in 1983 and although it was a Top 10 hit in the US, as was the single 'Don't Cry', its sales failed to match those of the debut. Wetton then left the group, to be replaced by Greg Lake (b. 10 November 1948, Bournemouth, England), another Emerson, Lake and Palmer alumnus. As testament to the residual affection for the band a live television concert from Japan drew over 20 million US viewers in late 1983. In late 1985 Wetton rejoined the band and a third album, *Astra*, was released. However, its comparatively low chart position precipitated the band's dissolution. By early 1990 Howe had left to join a regenerated Yes, with Pat Thrall, an ex-Pat Travers Band member, moving in to take his place. *Then And Now*, released the same year, was a mixture of six earlier recordings and four new songs. The group would then move from European label Musidisc to a new home on Music For Nations' subsidiary Bullet Proof.

Albums: *Asia* (Geffen 1982), *Alpha* (Geffen 1983),

Astra (Geffen 1985), *Then And Now* (WEA 1990), *Aqua* (Musidisc 1992), *Aria* (Bullet Proof 1994).

Athiest

Formerly known as Ravage, this US heavy metal band changed their name to Athiest in 1987 when the line-up of Randy Burke (guitar), Roger Patterson (bass), Kelly Shaeffer (vocals/guitar) and Steve Flynn (drums) came together. From amateurish origins, the band developed into a powerful and accomplished 'death-metal' outfit. Playing at breakneck speed, their sound was characterized by Shaeffer's gurgling vocal style. They released a debut album in 1990 to favourable reviews and built up a loyal following in their native state of Florida, USA.

Albums: *Piece Of Time* (Active 1990), *Unquestionable Presence* (Music For Nations 1991).

Atilla

This speed-metal trio from New York, not to be confused with the Dutch Atilla, was assembled by guitarist John De Leon in 1983. Enlisting the services of vocalist/bassist Vincent Paul and drummer A.T. Soldier, they made their vinyl debut with a track on Mausoleum's sampler album, *Metal Over America*, in 1985. *Rolling Thunder*, produced by Rods' drummer Carl Canedy, was released the following year, but made little impact. It featured an uninspired fusion of hard-rock and thrash, including a version of the Alice Cooper classic, 'School's Out'. The band disintegrated shortly after the album's release.

Album: *Rolling Thunder* (Mausoleum 1986).

Atlantic

Firmly in the classic AOR tradition, Atlantic musicians Phil Bates (lead vocals/guitar/keyboards), Simon Harrison (guitar/keyboards), Glen Williams (keyboards), Chris Taylor (keyboards), Paul Hoare (bass) and Andy Van Evans (guitar) represent an unfashionably large musical nucleus, complicated by the fact that drummer Andy Duncan does not play live, being replaced on such occasions by Phil Ridden. The group was formed in the summer of 1991 when Harrison was working on a television pilot theme song. He discovered his kindred spirit Bates in his quest for a suitable backing singer. The latter had already performed session tracks for Billy Ocean, Long John Baldry and producer Tony Visconti, while his own bands, Trickster and Quill, had supported ELO and Boston. His many session commissions included an appearance on the *Gladiators* television theme tune. His recent history up until the formation of Atlantic saw him singing with ELO Part 2. Together with an assembly line of local musicians,

plus producer Colin Thurston (Duran Duran etc.) and session drummer Duncan (Trevor Horn, Simple Minds) the duo concocted a set of AOR rock and power ballads, released by the Music For Nations imprint. A touring band was assembled, while a single, 'Every Beat Of My Heart', was utilised to promote the album.

Album: *Power* (Music For Nations 1994).

Atom Seed

This London-based quartet formed in 1989 with a line-up of Paul Cunningham (vocals), Simon James (guitar), Chris Dale (bass - original bass player Chris Huxter would soon depart to form New England) and Amir (drums), and quickly established a reputation as one of Britain's hardest-working and most exciting live bands. Signing to FM Revolver in 1990, Atom Seed released the *I Don't Want To Talk About It* EP, before making their full debut with *Get In Line*. Faith No More and Red Hot Chili Peppers were obvious reference points for *Get In Line's* remarkably mature material, and the lively delivery retained all the youthful energy of their live shows. With a subsequent major deal with London, the Atom Seed's future seemed bright, despite Amir's departure, with Jerry Hawkins replacing him. However, the band spent considerable time writing and demoing new material for London, who seemed disappointed with the performance of the reissued debut and single 'Rebel', and both their live profile and enthusiasm dwindled as a result. *The Dead Happy* EP was to be Atom Seed's sole London release before they were dropped, and the disillusioned band broke up. A second album, *Hard Sell Paranoia*, remains unreleased.

Album: *Get In Line* (FM Revolver 1990).

Atomic Rooster

Formed in 1969 at the height of the UK progressive rock boom, the original Rooster line-up comprised Vincent Crane (b. 1945, d. February 1989; organ), Nick Graham (bass) and Carl Palmer (b. 20 March 1951, Birmingham, England; drums). Crane and Palmer had just departed from the chart-topping Crazy World Of Arthur Brown and it was assumed that their new group would achieve sustained success. After only one album, however, the unit fragmented with Graham joining Skin Alley and Palmer founding Emerson, Lake And Palmer. Crane soldiered on with new members John Cann (guitar/vocals) and Paul Hammond (drums), drafted in from Andromeda, who were featured on the album *Death Walks Behind You*. Their excursions into hard rock produced two riff-laden yet catchy UK hit singles in 1971:

Atom Seed

'Tomorrow Night' and 'The Devil's Answer', as Crane adopted the Ray Manzarek (Doors) style of using keyboards to record bass parts. With assistance from Pete French of Cactus the trio recorded their third album *In Hearing Of*, but just when they seemed settled, they split. Cann and Hammond would join Bullet, then Hardstuff. French formed Leafhound. The irrepressible Crane refused to concede defeat and recruited new members, guitarist Steve Bolton, bassist Bill Smith and drummer Rick Parnell (son of the orchestra leader, Jack Parnell). The new line-up was completed by the famed singer Chris Farlowe. A dramatic musical shift towards blue-eyed soul won few new fans, however, and Crane finally dissolved the band in 1974. Thereafter, he collaborated with former colleague Arthur Brown, but could not resist reviving the fossilised Rooster in 1979 (the same year he teamed up with Crane once more for the 'Don't Be A Dummy' Lee Cooper jeans advertisement, backed by members of Gillan and Status Quo). After two anti-climactic albums with new drummer Preston Hayman then a returning Hammond, Crane finally killed off his creation. The final Atomic Rooster studio album had included guest stints from Dave Gilmour (Pink Floyd), Bernie Tormé (Gillan) and John Mazarolli on guitars in place of Cann. In 1983 he accepted an invitation to record and tour with Dexys Midnight Runners and appeared on their album *Don't Stand Me Down*. For some time he had been suffering from depression and he took his own life in 1989.

Albums: *Atomic Rooster* (B&C 1970), *Death Walks Behind You* (B&C 1970), *In Hearing Of* (Pegasus 1971), *Made In England* (Dawn 1972), *Nice 'N' Greasy* (Dawn 1973), *Atomic Rooster* (EMI 1980), *Headline News* (Towerbell 1983). Compilations: *Assortment* (B&C 1974), *Home To Roost* (Mooncrest 1977, double album), *The Devil Hits Back* (Demi Monde 1989), *BBC In Concert* (Windsong 1994).

Atomkraft

After a series of false starts and four years of frustration, UK heavy metal band Atomkraft finally secured a recording deal with Neat Records in 1985. They were among the first British thrash-metal bands, and built a solid reputation supporting labelmates Venom. The band comprised Tony Dolan (guitar), Rob Matthews (guitar), D.C. Rage (bass), Ged Wolf (drums), and vocalist Ian Swift. By the time *Future Warriors* emerged in 1985, their one dimensional thrashing sounded rather dated in comparison to the new American outfits that had recently appeared. After a further two average releases, Atomkraft split, with Dolan going on to join the revamped Venom in 1989.

Albums: *Future Warriors* (Neat 1985), *Queen Of Death* (Neat 1986), *Conductors Of Noise* (Neat 1987).

Atrophy

This speed metal outfit hailed from Tucson, Arizona, USA. The band was formed in 1987 by vocalist Brian Zimmerman and guitarist Chris Lykins. Recruiting Rick Skowron (guitar), James Gulotta (bass) and Tim Kelly (drums), they recorded a demo album, *Chemical Dependency*, the same year. This attracted the attention of thrash specialists, Roadrunner Records, who immediately recognized them as a band with great potential. *Socialized Hate* was an impressive debut, featuring heavy duty riffing, screaming guitars and thoughtful lyrics. Their second album saw some musical progression, with the material showing a greater awareness of melody and a slightly less extreme approach.

Albums: *Socialized Hate* (Roadrunner 1988), *Violent By Nature* (Roadrunner 1990).

August Redmoon

This Californian heavy rock quartet was formed in 1980 by drummer Dave Young. With the addition of vocalist Michael Henry, Greg Winslow (bass) and Ray Winslow (guitar) they adopted a traditional approach to hard rock. Incorporating Kiss, Van Halen and Aerosmith influences plus an added 'speed-metal' element, they recorded *Fools Are Never Alone* in 1982. Following a long line of management and label disputes, the band changed their name to Terracuda in 1984, but split up before entering a recording studio. Henry, Young and Gary Winslow went on to form Eden.

Album: *Fools Are Never Alone* (1982).

Autograph

Hailing from Los Angeles, USA, rock band Autograph was formed in 1983 by vocalist Steve Plunkett and bassist Randy Rand. With the addition of Steve Lynch (guitar), Steven Isham (keyboards) and Keni Richards (drums), the band signed to RCA the following year. Comprising five exceptionally talented musicians, they delivered a stunning combination of sophisticated and melodic AOR that had enormous pop-metal crossover potential. 'Turn Up The Radio' from their debut *Sign In Please*, became a belated US Top 50 hit in 1985, with the album following suit, eventually peaking at number 29 in the *Billboard* chart. Two further excellent albums were released with 1987's *Loud And Clear* representing the pinnacle of the band's creativity. Isham quit in 1988 to start a new project with ex-Dio guitarist Craig Goldie.

Autograph continued as a four-piece, but failed to attract media attention or repeat their initial success. They subsequently became disillusioned and disbanded in 1989, having failed to realize their potential.

Albums: *Sign In Please* (RCA 1984), *That's The Stuff* (RCA 1985), *Loud And Clear* (RCA 1987).

Autopsy

Drummer/vocalist Chris Reifert formed this death metal act with guitarist Danny Coralles and Eric Cutler after his involvement with Death on *Scream Bloody Gore*. Sadus bassist Steve DiGiorgio guested on *Severed Survival* before Ken Sovari was recruited for a European tour with Bolt Thrower and Pestilence, but he was then replaced by Cutler's brother, Steve. The *Retribution For The Dead* EP and *Mental Funeral* saw Autopsy continue in their sludgy death vein with gore-laden lyrics, but *Fiend For Blood* again featured DiGiorgio before Josh Barohn (ex-Suffocation) was recruited as bassist. *Acts Of The Unspeakable* continued the grisly lyrical approach, but ran into problems over gruesome cover artwork, with album covers being destroyed by Australian authorities and similar t-shirts confiscated by German customs.

Albums: *Severed Survival* (Peaceville 1989), *Mental Funeral* (Peaceville 1991), *Fiend For Blood* (Peaceville 1992, mini-album), *Acts Of The Unspeakable* (Peaceville 1992).

Avalon

This Dutch heavy metal quintet was formed in 1984 by guitarist Jack Pisters and vocalist Richard Muermans. Recruiting Maarten Huiskamp (keyboards), Erik Fox (bass) and Jacques Kraal (drums) they specialized in combining the hard-driving rock style of Iron Maiden with very intricate and off-beat guitar work that at times verged on the *avant garde*. They released an excellent mini-album in 1986 on the independent Dynamo label. This focused attention on the band's imaginative lyrics and futuristic guitar sound. Unfortunately, as soon as the album appeared the band underwent several personnel changes, which resulted in its eventual demise. They are not be confused with either the Capitol recording artists from the US, the London recording artists from Canada, or, for that matter, the folk artists, all of whom share the same name.

Album: *The Third Move* (Dynamo 1986, mini-album).

Avatar

Formerly known as Metropolis, the heavy metal group Avatar were formed in Florida, USA, in 1978 by the Oliva brothers. Comprising Jon Oliva (vocals/guitar/keyboards), Chris Oliva (guitar), Steve Wacholz (drums) and Keith Collins (bass), they specialized in hard-edged power-metal, with melodic undercurrents. The most distinctive elements of which were Jon Oliva's soaring vocals and Chris Oliva's razor-sharp guitar runs. They made their vinyl debut with *City Beneath The Surface*, a three-track EP of brutal and uncompromising metal at its very best. They subsequently changed their name to Savatage and went on to achieve international recognition and success. The EP is now highly valued by collectors of American heavy metal.

Avenger (Germany)

This hi-tech thrash metal quartet originated in Herne, West Germany. Formed in 1984, the band comprised Peter Wagner (vocals/bass), Thomas Gruning (guitar), Jochen Schroeder (guitar) and Jorg Michael (drums). Its debut album combined a speed-metal style with intricate Rush-like bridges and interludes. The songs were complex and technically proficient but were let down somewhat by the vocals, which lacked both power and range. After the release of the mini-album *Depraved To Black*, they became known as Rage and went on to receive critical acclaim throughout the European music media.

Albums: *Prayer Of Steel* (Wishbone 1985), *Depraved To Black* (Wishbone 1985, mini-album).

Avenger (UK)

This Newcastle-based, speed-metal outfit was formed by ex-Blitzkrieg duo Brian Ross (vocals) and Mick Moore (bass). With the addition of Gary Young (drums) and Lee Cheetam (guitar) they recorded the single, 'Too Wild To Tame', before Ross switched places with Satan's vocalist Ian Swift. *Bloodsports* followed, a prime example of the New Wave Of British Heavy Metal and notable for some inspired guitar work from Cheetam. A series of guitarists arrived and departed in rapid succession, with American Greg Reiter eventually being recruited on a permanent basis. *Killer Elite* was followed by a disastrous American tour. Returning to England, Swift left to join Atomkraft and the band fell apart.

Albums: *Blood Sports* (Neat 1984), *Killer Elite* (Neat 1985).

Aviary

This short-lived, esoteric art-rock outfit was formed in 1978 by Brad Love (vocals/keyboards) and Toby Bowen (guitar). With the recruitment of Paul Madden (keyboards), Ken Steimonts (bass/vocals) and Richard Bryans (drums) the line-up was

complete. Assimilating influences as diverse as Yes, Queen, ELP, the Beatles and classical music, they recorded a pretentious and overblown debut characterized by high-pitched vocals and harmonies. Unable to attract favourable media attention, the band split up soon after the album was released. Brad Love went on to record a solo album in 1982.
Album: *Aviary* (Epic 1979).

Aviator

This New York hard rock quartet was formed in 1984 by guitarist Richie Cerniglia and drummer Michael Ricciardelli. With the addition of vocalist Ernie White and bassist Steve Vitale, they signed to RCA in 1986. Influenced by Bon Jovi, Europe and Thin Lizzy their highly commercial debut album was produced by Neil Kernon. The songs were identikit pop-metal, and the band struggled to find their own image. The album sold poorly and Aviator were subsequently dropped by RCA. A series of line-up changes ensued, but the band has been unable to secure another recording contract to date.
Album: *Aviator* (RCA 1987).

Axe

Rock band Babyface, comprising Edgar Riley (vocals), Bobby Barth (guitar), Mike Turpin (bass) and Teddy Mueller (drums), recruited Mike Osbourne as a second guitarist in 1979 and changed their name to Axe. Purveying highly-sophisticated pomp-rock, they built up a loyal following in the USA and released a trio of superbly crafted albums. Disaster struck in 1984 when vocalist Riley was killed in a car crash. The band dissolved itself, with Barth joining Blackfoot for a short period in 1985, before re-forming Axe in 1989 with ex-UFO drummer Andy Parker.
Albums: *Axe* (MCA 1979), *Living On The Edge* (MCA 1980), *Offering* (Atco 1981).

Axewitch

This Swedish heavy metal quartet originated in Stockholm in 1981. The initial line-up comprised Anders Wallentoft (vocals), Magnus Jarls (guitar), Mikael Johansson (guitar), Tommy Brage (bass) and Mats Johansson (drums). They started life as a doomy thrash-metal outfit, but, unable to attract press coverage, they decided on a radical change in direction. *Hooked On High Heels* saw the band sporting fashionable clothes, expensive hair-styles and a much more commercial approach similar to Mötley Crüe. However, the record-buying public was not impressed and the album sold poorly. The band split up shortly afterwards.

Albums: *The Lord Of Flies* (Neon 1983), *Visions Of The Past* (Neon 1984), *Hooked On High Heels* (Neon 1985).

Axis

This USA power-trio was formed by ex-Derringer duo Danny Johnson (guitar/vocals) and Vinnie Appice (drums). With the addition of bassist Jay Davis, they recorded *It's A Circus World* in 1978. This was a derivative hard-rock album that drew from the early 70s as a source of inspiration. The band disintegrated soon after the album's release, with Appice joining Black Sabbath and later Dio. Johnson replaced Steve Vai in Alcatrazz, then teamed up with Jay Davis again in Private Life.
Album: *It's A Circus World* (RCA 1978).

Axxis

This highly competent German hard rock quartet comprised Walter Pietsch (guitar/vocals), Bernhard Weiss (guitar/vocals), Werner Kleinhans (bass) and Richard Michalski (drums/vocals). Their diverse style recalled Boston and Black Sabbath and back again via Europe and the Scorpions. Axxis released *Kingdom Of The Night* in 1986 to favourable reviews and landed the support slot on Black Sabbath's European tour the same year. They could not transform this into album sales however, as the band lacked both consistency and real direction.
Album: *Kingdom Of The Night* (Parlophone 1986).

B

B'zz

Formed from the ashes of heavy metal 'biker-band' Boyzz, this group featured Michael Tafoya (guitar), David Angel (bass) and Anatole Halinkovitch (keyboards). With the recruitment of Tom Holland (vocals) and Steve Riley (drums), they rejected their previous Hells Angels image and concentrated instead on pop-metal crossover material. Their debut album, released in 1982, fused elements of Kiss, Cheap Trick and Foreigner, but met with little success. The band disintegrated when Holland left to form a new outfit under his own name. Riley subsequently went on to play with W.A.S.P.
Album: *Get Up* (Epic 1982).

b.l.o.w.

Something of a mid-90s supergroup, heavy metal outfit b.l.o.w. were formed in 1994 by Dave Godding (vocals; ex-No Sweat), brothers Bruce (guitar) and Jimmy Dickinson (keyboards; both ex-Little Angels), drummer Mark Richardson and final recruit, bass player Nick Boyes. Their first demo exceeded expectations, even given their pedigree, and included a more pyschedelic/pop influenced approach than might have been anticipated. A cover of Peter Tosh's 'Legalise It' typified their eclectic and much-admired live set throughout 1994.
Album: *Man And Goat Alike* (Cottage Industry 1995, mini-album).

Babes In Toyland

This hardcore trio spearheaded a new wave of US female bands at the turn of the 90s. Their origins can be traced back to 1987, when Kat Bjelland (b. Woodburn, Oregon, USA - adopted, though she did not know it until she was much older; vocals/guitar) moved to Minneapolis. Previously she had played in a band, Sugar Baby Doll, with Courtney Love (Hole) and Jennifer Finch (L7) when she was stationed in San Francisco. The trio was completed by Michelle Leon (bass) and Lori Barbero (drums/vocals). They first came to prominence via the legendary singles club at Sub Pop Records, then made a deep impression on a European support tour with Sonic Youth. A debut album, prooduced by Jack Endino, was recorded live with the vocals overdubbed. Soon after, WEA A&R representative Tim Carr saw the band live in Minneapolis and was impressed. After signing to the label, they recorded the 1992 mini-album, *To Mother*. Bjelland, meanwhile, was busy defending the band from the suspicious minds of a media that wanted to latch on to the 'girl group' phenomena as an amorphous movement: 'Men and women play their instruments to a completely different beat. Women are a lot more rhythmic - naturally - than men. It doesn't even have anything to do with music, it all has to do with timing'. In 1992 Leon left the group and was replaced by Maureen Herman (b. Chicago, Illinois, USA). *Fontanelle* received excellent reviews throughout the rock and indie press, and a support tour with Faith No More brought them further plaudits, as they signed with their first manager, Debbie Gordon. However, when the group took a breather in 1993, press speculation suggested their imminent demise. Lori Barbero would form her own label, Spanish Fly, home of Milk, while Kat worked with husband Stuart Grey, singer with Australian noise outfit Lubricated Goat, on two projects, Crunt and KatSu. Babes In Toyland reconvened in time for the the Lollapalooza tour and looked set to continue their ascendency, aided principally by Bjelland's distinctive guitar style and anachronistic appearance, until in 1993 it was rumoured she had relocated to Seattle to form yet another band with Grey.
Albums: *Spanking Machine* (Twin Tone 1990), *To Mother* (WEA 1991, mini-album), *Fontanelle* (WEA 1992), *Painkillers* (WEA 1994).

Baby Animals

This Australian indie-metal quartet were formed in 1990 by vocalist Suzi Demarchi and guitarist Dave Leslie. Recruiting bassist Eddie Parise and drummer Frank Delenza, they signed to the Imago label and debuted with a self-titled album in February 1992. Influenced by Heart, the Pretenders, AC/DC, INXS and Siouxsie And The Banshees, their sound is characterized by Demarchi's provocative growl and the understated guitar work of Leslie. They made a considerable impact in the UK as support act to Bryan Adams on his 1991 tour, but otherwise have remained a cult taste.
Albums: *Baby Animals* (Imago 1992), *Shaved And Dangerous* (Imago 1993).

Baby Chaos

Scottish-based rock crew, formed in Stewarton in 1992, whose entertaining debut album went some way towards holding up their press assertions of incendiary intent. They were signed by East West after appearing on BBC2's *The Late Show* in the

Babes In Toyland

Spring of 1993. Fronted by gifted if wayward vocalist/guitarist Chris Gordon, the rest of the band includes Bobby Dunn (bass), Davey Greenwod (drums) and Grant McFarlane (guitars). Comparisons to stablemates the Wildhearts were inevitable, with tracks like 'Sperm' and 'Breathe' revealing an emotional span beyond component expectations. A steady rise in profile was achieved via a relentless touring schedule, including nearly 100 gigs (with the likes of Terrovision, Wildhearts and Shed 7) between September 1994 and May 1994.

Album: *Safe Sex, Designer Drugs & The Death Of Rock 'n' Roll* (East West 1994).

Baby Tuckoo

Baby Tuckoo were formed in 1983 by ex-Geddes Axe guitarist/keyboard player Andy Barott, alongside Rob Armitage (vocals), Neil Saxton (guitar), Paul Smith (bass) and Tony Sugden (drums). They soon built up a following in their home town of Bradford and then set their sights on bigger things, becoming part of the second generation N.W.O.B.H.M. movement along with Chrome Molly and Chariot. Signed in 1984 to independent label Ultra Noise they released an impressive debut album, *First Born*, which blended together British and American influences and drew comparisons to Whitesnake. Despite this, they were dropped by their record company soon after. A second album followed in similar musical vein and live they proved a popular attraction. Nevertheless the participants decided to split in 1986. Rob Armitage joined Accept for a brief spell and Barrott became part of Chrome Molly.

Albums: *First Born* (Ultra Noise 1984), *Force Majeure* (Music For Nations 1985).

Babys

Considerable attention attended the launch of this much-touted British rock group. John Waite (b. 4 July 1955, London, England; vocals/bass), Mike Corby (b. 3 July 1955, London, England; guitar/keyboards), Walter 'Wally' Stocker (b. 27 March 1954, London, England; guitar) and former Spontaneous Combustion and Strider member Tony Brock (b. 31 March 1954, Bournemouth, Dorset, England; drums) were promoted as the most promising newcomers of 1976, but while *The Babys* offered a competent blend of pop and rock, similar to that of the Raspberries, it lacked an identifiable sound and image. Obscured by the punk explosion, the quartet looked to the USA for commercial succour over the ensuing years. Jonathan Cain replaced Corby following the release of *Head First*, but although the Babys did achieve considerable US success, including

two Top 20 singles with 'Isn't It Time' and 'Every Time I Think Of You', they remained in the shadow of AOR stalwarts Fleetwood Mac, Foreigner and Journey. Waite subsequently embarked on a high-profile solo career.

Albums: *The Babys* (Chrysalis 1976), *Broken Heart* (Chrysalis 1977), *Head First* (Chrysalis 1978), *Union Jacks* (Chrysalis 1980), *On The Edge* (Chrysalis 1980). Compilations: *Anthology* (Chrysalis 1981), *Unofficial Babys* (NEMS 1982).

Bad Boy

The origins of this Milwaukee, USA, rock band date back to the mid-70s, when Steve Grimm (guitar/vocals) teamed up with John Marcelli (bass). The first incarnation of Bad Boy had included Lars Hanson (drums) and Joe Lavie (guitar). The band chemistry was wrong however, and their debut album was a disappointing, half-hearted affair. Things improved with their second release, as the band moved in a heavier direction and made greater use of an up-front guitar sound. Following a period of inactivity between 1978-82, the band hit back with a revamped line-up that saw Xeno (keyboards) and Billy Johnson (drums) alongside Grimm and Marcelli. Unfortunately, they switched back to a melodic pop-rock style once more. Both albums sold poorly and the band split up as a result.

Albums: *The Band That Made Milwaukee Famous* (United Artists 1977), *Back To Back* (United Artists 1978), *Private Party* (Indie 1982), *Electric Eyes* (Indie 1984).

Bad Brains

This black US hardcore punk and dub reggae outfit originated in 1978. The band were all playing together earlier in a fusion outfit 'doing Chick Corea and Stanley Clarke type stuff'. They moved from Washington, D.C. to New York where they established a reputation as prime exponents, alongside the Dead Kennedys and Black Flag, of the new 'hardcore' hybrid of punk, based on a barely credible speed of musicianship. The line-up consisted of H.R. (b. Paul Hudson; vocals) and brother Earl Hudson (drums), Dr. Know (guitar) and Darryl Jennifer (bass). They would break up their sets with dub and reggae outings and attracted a mixed audience, which was certainly one of their objectives: 'We're a gospel group, preaching the word of unity'. It is frustrating that so little studio material remains to document this early period, though the singles 'Pay To Cum' and 'Big Takeover' are regarded as *bona fide* genre classics. They were due to support the Damned in the UK in October 1979. selling most of their equipment to buy aeroplane tickets. On arrival, however, they were denied work permits. They continued through the 80s, although H.R. went on to a solo career. In May 1988 he was temporarily replaced by ex-Faith No More vocalist Chuck Moseley, while Mackie (ex-Cro-Mags) took over on drums. The move, which allowed the remaining founding members to gig, was singularly unsuccessful. Famed for their exhilarating live shows, especially H.R.'s athletics, noted US rock critic Jack Rabid rated them, on form, the best he had ever seen. More recently bands like Living Colour have sung their praises as one of the forerunners of articulate black rock music, while in 1994 even Madonna took notice, offering them a place on her Maverick imprint, with H.R. returning to the fold.

Albums: *Bad Brains* (ROIR 1982, cassettle only), *Rock For Light* (PVC 1983), *I Against I* (SST 1986), *Live* (SST 1988), *Attitude: The ROIR Session* (ROIR-Important 1989), *Quickness* (Caroline 1989), *The Youth Are Getting Restless* (Caroline 1990), *Rise* (1993).

Bad Company

This solid, highly acclaimed UK heavy rock group formed in 1973 with a line-up comprising Paul Rodgers (b. 17 December 1949, Middlesbrough, England; vocals), Simon Kirke (b. 27 August 1949, Wales; vocals/drums), Mick Ralphs (b. 31 May 1944, Hertfordshire, England; vocals/guitar) and Boz Burrell (b. Raymond Burrell, 1946, Lincolnshire, England; bass guitar). With Ralphs (ex-Mott The Hoople) and Rodgers and Kirke (both ex-Free), Bad Company were akin to a blues-based supergroup, with much of their style derived from the traditions established by Free, not least because of Paul Rodgers' distinct vocals. Their best-selling, self-titled debut album established the premise - strong vocals placed beside tough melody lines and hard riffing. A string of albums through the mid/late 70s brought them chart success on both sides of the Atlantic while a series of arduous stadium tours maintained their reputation as an exemplary live act. They achieved singles success with a number of powerful songs (notably 'Can't Get Enough Of Your Love' and 'Feel Like Makin' Love'), well produced and faultlessly played, although lyrically they were often pedestrian. A three year hiatus ended with the release of *Rough Diamonds*, which provided another UK Top 20 album success (US number 26). After nearly a decade of extensive gigging and regularly released albums, they finally dissolved in 1983. A new version of the group with former Ted Nugent vocalist Brian Howe replacing Rodgers came together in 1986 for the reunion album, *Fame And Fortune*. The band's subsequent releases have been mediocre, a pale shadow of their first two albums. The late 80s/early 90s Bad Company model revolved around sole surviving original member Mick Ralphs. However, 1994 saw the re-mastering and re-release of their legacy, masterminded by George Marino in New York.

Albums: *Bad Company* (Island 1974), *Straight Shooter* (Island 1975), *Run With The Pack* (Island 1976), *Burnin' Sky* (Island 1977), *Desolation Angels* (Island 1979), *Rough Diamonds* (Swan Song 1984), *Fame And Fortune* (Atlantic 1986), *Dangerous Age* (Atlantic 1988), *Holy Water* (Atlantic 1990), *Here Comes Trouble* (Atlantic 1992). Compilation: *10 From 6* (Atlantic 1986).

Bad English

Towards the end of the 80s a new generation of 'supergroups' emerged from the USA, including Mr Big, Badlands, Damn Yankees, Alias, and arguably the most successful of them all, Bad English. The group was formed in 1988 by ex-Babys' vocalist and successful solo artist John Waite, ex-Santana and Journey guitarist Neal Schon, ex-Babys and Journey keyboard player Jonathan Cain, ex-Babys' bassist Ricky Phillips, and ex-Wild Dogs' drummer Dene Castronovo. Their 1989 self-titled debut album was an instant success in the USA combining hard-edged, melodic rock with big ballads. It reached the US Top 10 helped on its way by the Dianne Warren-penned 'When I See You Smile', which was a US number 1 hit in 1990 (UK number 61). Success in the UK was not forthcoming and the album barely dented the Top 40, while a similar fate befell the single. 1991's follow up, *Backlash,* was backed up by the single 'Straight To Your Heart'. Internal disagreements struck the band causing them to split soon after its release, with Waite resuming his solo career; Phillips and Castronovo joining the Jimmy Page and David Coverdale project; while Schon and Cain were rumoured to be reforming Journey. Despite their short history, Bad English left behind a legacy of quality melodic rock which achieved a high degree of commercial success.

Albums: *Bad English* (Epic 1989), *Backlash* (Epic 1991).

Bad News

Originally written by Adrian Edmondson as apart of UK television's *The Comic Strip Presents* series in 1982, the *Bad News Tour* told the story of an ambitious (but inept) London heavy metal band played by Edmondson as vocalist/guitarist Vim Fuego, Rik Mayall as bassist Colin Grigson, Nigel

Planer as the dim rhythm guitarist Den Dennis and finally Comic Strip co-writer/founder member Peter Richardson as drummer Spider Webb - on tour and en-route to Grantham with a television documentary crew. The music and lyrics for the show were put together by Edmondson and composer Simon Brint as a clever parody on the cliches of the UK heavy metal scene. After the success of the *American National Lampoon*-based *Spinal Tap* movie and the resulting move into legend, Edmondson decided to bring Bad News back for another Comic Strip episode, writing a basic storyline that would mean they would really have to play live. In 1986, armed with a recording contract with EMI Records, a producer in Queen's Brian May, clever management and photo sessions by Gered Mankowitz, they set about recording an album of songs and sketches. The full promotional machinery of interviews, television appearances and a slot at the Donnington festival in August, all required for the film, were set in motion. Four months later they had a short tour set up which included a couple of charity concerts with Iron Maiden. 1987 saw *More Bad News* shown in the cinemas as support to another comic strip film, *Eat The Rich*, which incidentally starred Lemmy from Motörhead. This was backed up with a cover version of Queen's 'Bohemian Rhapsody' on single, and a self-titled debut album. The music was badly received but in retrospect was actually both well constructed and executed. Following the album they set out on a two month tour and released a second single, 'Cashing In On Xmas'. However, by this time the joke had worn too thin for both press and public and the actors returned to their day jobs. The name briefly appeared the next year when EMI released the bootleg album which contained the Edmondson-produced outtakes of music and comedy and a Brian May remix of the 'Christmas' single.

Albums: *Bad News* (EMI 1987), *Bootleg* (EMI 1988).
Compilation: *Collection* (Castle 1994).
Videos: *Bad News Tour And A Fistful Of Traveller's Cheques* (1986), *More Bad News* (1987).

Bad Steve

This UK speed metal outfit was put together in 1983 by former Accept members Rubi Rubach (bass), Jan Komet (guitar) and Fritz Friedrich (drums). Recruiting vocalist Phil Magoo (ex-Sin City) and guitarist Akku Becher (ex-Kanaan), they finally landed a deal with Mausoleum Records after being turned down by many major labels in Germany. *Killing The Night* emerged in 1984 and they supported Accept throughout Europe to promote it. The album lacked energy, drive and quality songs and compared unfavourably to Accept's material, the yardstick by which the band were naturally judged. It failed to sell and the band disintegrated, with Rubach going on to play with UDO for a short time.
Album: *Killing The Night* (Mausoleum 1984).

Badlands

This blues-based, UK hard-rock band was put together in 1988 by vocalist Ray Gillen (ex-Black Sabbath and Blue Murder) and former Ozzy Osbourne guitarist Jake E. Lee. With the addition of bassist Greg Chaisson and drummer Eric Singer (d. 1994), they signed to Atlantic and released a self-titled debut album the following year. Using the early 70s as a source for inspiration, their music invited comparison with Led Zeppelin, Bad Company, Humble Pie and Free. Singer joined Alice Cooper's band and was replaced by Jeff Martin before the recording of their second album in 1991. *Voodoo Highway* received widespread critical acclaim, with Gillen's classic soulful vocal style contrasting beautifully with Lee's explosive guitar pyrotechnics. The album oozed class, emotion and energy from every note, and included an inspired cover of James Taylor's 'Fire And Rain'.
Albums: *Badlands* (Atlantic 1989), *Voodoo Highway* (Atlantic 1991).

Baird, Dan

Guitarist/vocalist Dan Baird (b. Daniel John Baird, 12 December 1953, San Diego, California, USA) sacked himself from the Georgia Satellites in the early 90s feeling unable to keep the band going after a difficult time in his private life, leading to the Satellites' break-up. However, the now Kentucky-based singer was rejuvenated by a break from the music business, and soon put a new band together, enlisting old bandmate Mauro Magellan (drums), bassist Keith Christopher and ex-Replacements keyboard player Slim Dunlap on guitar, and signed a deal with Def American. *Love Songs For The Hearing Impaired* (a joke aimed towards his label's name) was a fresh, upbeat blend of R&B with country influences and the self-deprecating sense of humour which had characterised his Satellites work, with studio guests including Tom Petty And The Heartbreakers' Benmont Tench on keyboards and fiddler Byron Berline. Success returned in tandem with Baird's enthusiasm as he scored a US hit with 'I Love You Period'.
Album: *Love Songs For The Hearing Impaired* (Def American 1992).

Balaam And The Angel

This UK rock band included both post-punk gothic and 60s elements in their output. They were originally made up of the three Morris brothers, Jim (b. 25 November 1960, Motherwell, Scotland; guitar/recorder/keyboards), Mark (b. 15 January 1963, Motherwell, Scotland; lead vocals/bass) and Des (b. 27 June 1964, Motherwell, Scotland; drums). They began their career playing working mens clubs as a childrens' cabaret act in their native Motherwell, encouraged by their father who had insisted they all watch television's *Top Of The Pops* as children. They eventually moved down to Cannock in Staffordshire, where they are still based. An early gig at the ICA in London, 1985, saw a completely different approach to that with which Balaam would become identified. Playing in bare feet and pyjamas, they procured numerous covers of 60s love paeans, and a recorder solo. Somewhat falsely categorized as a gothic group after supporting the Cult on three successive tours, they were, in fact, self-consciously colourful in both appearance and approach. Early in their career they founded Chapter 22 Records, along with manager Craig Jennings. Their debut on the label came when 'World Of Light' appeared in 1984, although 'Day And Night' was their most impressive release from this period. Their debut set, *The Greatest Story Ever Told*, was named after the headline under which their first interview in *Melody Maker* appeared, and saw them rehoused on Virgin Records. Apparently intended to be reminiscent of the Doors, while there were stylistic similarities, it fell some way short of the visionary qualities associated with the west coast phenomenon. In September 1988 the band's second album was released after they had returned from support slots with Kiss and Iggy Pop in the USA. A new guitarist, Ian McKean, entered because of the need for two guitar parts on *Live Free Or Die*. They were dropped by Virgin however, and their first tour for over four years took place in 1990. Press speculation that Mark would join the Cult as replacement bass player for Jamie Stewart collapsed as Ian Astbury decided that he was too much of a 'front man'. In 1991, they truncated their name to Balaam, marking the switch with the release of a mini-album, *No More Innocence*.

Albums: *The Greatest Story Ever Told* (Virgin 1986), *Live Free Or Die* (Virgin 1988), *No More Innocence* (Intense 1991), *Prime Time* (Bleeding Hearts 1993).

Balance

This US melodic AOR group were put together in 1979 by vocalist Peppy Castro (ex-Wiggy Bits) and session men Doug Katsaros (keyboards) and Bob

Bang Tango

Kulick (guitarist and older brother of Kiss' Bruce Kulick). Augmented by other hired hands, they debuted in 1981 with a self-titled album that came over as a three-way amalgam of Toto, Kansas and Journey. As interest built, the trio signed on bassist Dennis Feldman and former Brand X drummer Chuck Burgi to stabilize their line-up. *In For The Count*, which followed, assumed a harder direction and incorporated Foreigner influences. Attracting an encouraging media response, the album surprisingly failed to take off. Disillusioned, the band went their separate ways in 1982. Bob Kulick subsequently joined Meat Loaf's band prior to forming Skull. In 1987 Kulick, Feldman and Burgi were stated to be working together again with former Blue Öyster Cult vocalist Eric Bloom, but no recordings were forthcoming.
Albums: *Balance* (Portrait 1981), *In For The Count* (Portrait 1982).

Bang Tango

This Los Angeles, California, USA quintet was assembled in 1987 from the remnants of several local club circuit rock bands. Comprising Joe LeSte (vocals), Mark Knight (guitar), Kyle Stevens (guitar), Kyle Kyle (bass) and Tigg Ketler (drums), they secured a deal with MCA Records. This followed the release of a highly regarded live mini-album which the band partly financed themselves. Initially they concentrated on a sleazy, low-life image and incorporated influences such as Aerosmith and the Cult. This manifested itself on *Psycho Cafe*, a refreshingly honest, but slightly offbeat hard rock album which was characterized by LeSte's laconic vocal style. *Dancin' On Coals* released in 1991, indicated that the band had matured remarkably in two years, both in a creative and performing sense. This album featured a greater degree of musical sophistication, with soulful and more blues-based material included. Looking poised for international success and recognition, the group would leave MCA for the Music For Nations independent, revitalizing their career with the self-proclaiming *New Generation*. *Love After Death*, its 1994 follow-up, featured Nicky Hopkins on one of his last session appearances, adding piano to '1000 Goodbyes'.
Albums: *Live Injection* (Bang Tango 1987, mini-album), *Psycho Cafe* (Mechanic/MCA 1989), *Dancin' On Coals* (Mechanic/MCA 1991), *New Generation* (Music For Nations 1994), *Love After Death* (Music For Nations 1995).

Bangalore Choir

Heavy metal team Bangalore Choir, named after a torpedo-like explosive device, are an ambitious group. They were formed in 1991 by former Accept vocalist David Reece, and also feature ex-Razor Maid guitarists Curt Mitchell and John Kirk, plus Ian Mayo (bass) and Jackie Ramos (drums), who were previously with Hurricane Alice. Their collective pedigree has undoubted potential, but *On Target* failed to reach it. Reece is a strong frontman, but his phrasing and delivery is so closely modelled on David Coverdale and Jon Bon Jovi that the comparison becomes distracting.
Album: *On Target* (1992).

Banished

Buffalo-based death metal crew who rose from the ashes of Baphomet, who released one album in 1991. The name change was caused by a German group who claimed prior use of the title, and Banished was selected to avert possible legal consequences. Their debut material under the new name was not entirely problem-free either. Several commentators were struck by the sleeve artwork of their 1993 album, inked by Tim Vigil from Faust Comic Books, which guitarist Tom Frost justified thus: '...it's not like a sexist thing in the sense that it's real. The picture has all women in it, even the demon in the middle is a woman, with a huge strap on horn...'.
Albums: As Baphomet: *The Dead Shall Inherit* (Deaf 1991). As Banished: *Deliver Me Unto Pain* (Death 1993).

Barnes, Jimmy

With the disintegration of the Australian band Cold Chisel in 1982, lead singer Jimmy Barnes embarked on a solo career. He teamed up with ex-Baby Jonathan Cain and produced *Body Swerve* and a self-titled album in quick succession. These were characterized by Barnes's rough and raunchy vocal delivery, and included erudite selections of blues, soul and R&B numbers. *Freight Train Heart* had a much bigger budget, as Geffen Records were hoping to break Barnes in the USA. With contributions from Journey's Neil Schon, Desmond Child, Mick Fleetwood and Jim Vallence, the result was a classic American rock album. Surprisingly, the album did not take off and Geffen dropped Barnes in 1988. A credible double live album, appropriately titled *Barnestorming*, was recorded in Melbourne on his 1987-88 tour of Australia. This surfaced on import on the Mushroom label, and eventually led to a new contract with Atlantic Records. *Two Fires* emerged in 1990; yet another quality album of gritty rockers and gut-wrenching ballads. Once again, it made little impact outside Australia.

Barren Cross

44

Albums: *Body Swerve* (Mushroom 1984), *Jimmy Barnes* (Mushroom 1985), *Freight Train Heart* (Geffen 1987), *Barnestorming* (Mushroom 1988, double album), *Two Fires* (Atlantic 1990), *Heat* (Atlantic 1993).

Baron Rojo

This Spanish heavy metal outfit was formed in Madrid in 1980 by the brothers Armando (vocals/guitar) and Carlos (guitar/vocals) de Castro. With the addition of former session musicians Jose Luis Campuzano (bass) and Hermes Calabria (drums), they specialized in an early 70s approach, redolent of an amalgam of UFO, Uriah Heep and Black Sabbath. Their appeal has been limited in Europe and the USA by the Spanish vocals, but they have made some inroads in South America. In an attempt to widen their audience, they recorded an English vocal version of *Volumen Brutal*, but the result was disappointing due to poor phrasing and an awkward lyrical translation (despite the presence of Mel Collins on saxophone and Colin Towns from Gillan on keyboards). They make no attempt to follow fashions and are now regarded as an anachronistic, but well-respected curiosity on the international rock scene.
Albums: *Larga Vida Al Rock And Roll* (Chapa Discos 1981), *Volumen Brutal* (Chapa Discos 1982), *Metal Morphosis* (Chapa Discos 1983), *Baron Rojo Vivo* (Chapa Discos 1984), *Tierra De Nadie* (Zafiro 1987), *No Va Mas!* (Zafiro 1988).

Barren Cross

This Christian rock outfit from California was formed by guitarist Ray Parris and drummer Steve Whitaker in 1981. Enlisting the services of Jim Laverde (bass) and Mike Lee (vocals), they were initially reminiscent of Iron Maiden or Van Halen. *Rock For The King* featured turbo-charged metallic anthems with fluid guitar work, delivered with steely conviction. Lyrically, the band explored themes such as abortion, drug abuse and terrorism, but explained rather than simply condemned these issues. Later releases saw the band afford greater use of melody, but without compromising their ideals or striving for commercial recognition. *Hotter Than Hell* is a magnificent live album, which fully showcases the band's talents. It provided a much needed shot in the arm for the credibility of Christian metal, which had suffered adverse press coverage for several years.
Albums: *Rock For The King* (Starsong 1986), *Atomic Arena* (Enigma 1987), *State Of Control* (Virgin 1989), *Hotter Than Hell - Live* (Medusa 1990).

Barth, Bobby

After the disintegration of UK heavy metal band Axe in 1984, lead singer Bobby Barth embarked on a solo career, following a short, but unfruitful association with Blackfoot. Dispensing with the hard-rock style he grew up with, Barth recorded an album of sentimental ballads and middle-of-the-road AOR. The songs featured expansive arrangements, which included swathes of keyboards and a brass section. The album made little impact and Barth reformed Axe in 1989.
Album: *Two Hearts-One Beat* (Atco 1986).

Bastard

This German quartet was formed in Hanover in 1977 by Karl Rothert (bass/vocals) and Keith Kossoff (guitar). With the help of guitarist Uli Meisner and drummer Toto Petticoato, they took the Scorpions, AC/DC and Bad Company as their blueprint for heavy duty rock 'n' roll. Their first two albums sadly failed to embellish on these influences. The live album was an improvement, with the band adding sparkle and character to songs that sounded dull on record.
Albums: *Back To Nature* (Lava 1978), *Tearing Nights* (Lava 1978), *Live And Alive* (Lava 1980).

Bathory

This Swedish satanic-metal project was masterminded by the enigmatic, multi-instrumentalist Quothorn. The band originally comprised Quothorn (vocals/guitar), Kothaar (bass) and Vvorthn (drums), but the latter two left after recording just a single track for a heavy metal compilation album. Aided by session musicians, Quothorn decided to go it alone and recorded a series of black metal albums during the latter half of the 80s. He attracted a cult following, many of whom were satanists, but refrained from taking his music out on the road. *Hammerheart*, released in 1990, was an ambitious concept album based on Viking legend and his most (relatively) accessible work to date.
Albums: *Bathory* (Under One Flag 1984), *Raise The Dead* (Under One Flag 1984), *The Return* (Under One Flag 1985), *Under The Sign Of The Black Mark* (Under One Flag 1986), *Blood, Fire, Death* (Under One Flag 1988), *Hammerheart* (Noise 1990), *Twilight Of The Gods* (Black Mark 1992).

Baton Rouge

Originally know as Meridian, the band were formed in New Orleans, USA, in 1986 by Kelly Keeling (lead vocals/guitar) and Lance Bulen (lead guitar/vocals), the line-up being completed by Corky McClellan

(drums/vocals), Scott Bender (bass/vocals) and David Cremin (keyboards/guitars/vocals). Within a year the band moved away from the covers-orientated Louisiana club circuit to Los Angeles, where two years of songwriting and rehearsal paid off with a major record deal after only six live shows. *Shake Your Soul*, produced by Jack Ponti, who also wrote with the band, was an album of blues-influenced melodic hard rock with powerful harmonies, reminiscent of Def Leppard, augmenting Keeling's striking vocals. Extensive USA touring, including dates supporting Alannah Myles, coupled with heavy radio airplay for their debut single, 'Walks Like A Woman', allowed the quintet to build up a healthy live following, to the extent that they played a headline show to a 10,000 crowd in Milwaukee. A slightly heavier approach was adopted for *Lights Out In The Playground*, again produced by (and co-written with) Ponti. This marked the debut of former Keel guitarist Tony Palmucci, who replaced the departed Cremin, but the characteristic Baton Rouge sound remained.
Albums: *Shake Your Soul* (Atlantic 1990), *Lights Out In The Playground* (Atlantic 1991).

Battleaxe

Formed in 1983 and hailing from Sunderland, Battleaxe made a minor dent on the north-east England heavy metal scene after appearing with two tracks on the Guardian compilation album, *Roxcalibur*. They quickly followed up with a single, 'Burn This Town', in 1981. They maintained a solid line-up with Dave King (vocals), Steve Hardy (guitar), Brian Smith (bass) and Ian McCormack (drums), and eventually signed up with Music For Nations who released both of their albums to little public interest. With other acts from their area like Venom and Raven getting all the attention they split up in 1985.
Albums: *Burn This Town* (Music For Nations 1983), *Power From The Universe* (Music For Nations 1984).

Battlecry

This Christian rock band was formed in California in 1984 by Dave Chumchal (vocals/guitar/keyboards) and Doug Morris (guitar). With the recruitment of Robert Kirk Giverink (guitar), Mariko Martinez (keyboards/vocals), Ronald P. Simmons (bass/vocals) and Bret Kik Keys (drums), their sound was heavily laden with keyboards and characterized by high-pitched, note-perfect harmonies. Their sole release was an impressive collection of melodic AOR that paid respect to Yes and Journey's blueprint.
Album: *Red, White And Blue* (1985).

Beau Geste

Beau Geste is the pseudonym of the exceptionally talented US multi-instrumentalist Bryan Hughes. With the aid of session musicians he recorded *Another Night In The City* in 1986. It served as a tribute to Hughes's technical and artistic capabilities, seeing him take on responsibility for writing the material and contributing vocals, bass, keyboards and guitar parts. However, the end result was less impressive, a melodic AOR album lacking character and real energy.
Album: *Another Night In The City* (1986).

Beck, Bogert And Appice

The plan for guitar virtuoso Jeff Beck (b. 24 June 1944, Surrey, England) to form a power trio with the ex-Vanilla Fudge rhythm section was first mooted in 1969. Both drummer, Carmine Appice (b. 15 December 1946, New York, USA), and bassist, Tim Bogert (b. 27 August 1944, Richfield, New Jersey, USA), were dissatisfied with their present band. The plans were spoiled when Beck was involved in a serious car crash that put him out of action. Meanwhile, Bogert and Appice formed the heavy rock band Cactus, until in 1972 their paths again crossed with Beck and they put together the heavy rock unit Beck, Bogert And Appice. The self-titled commercially successful debut was instrumentally superb, but suffered from a lack of songwriting ability and strained vocals. Twenty years later the album sounds ponderous and is justifiably disowned by its members.
Albums: *Beck, Bogert And Appice* (Epic 1973), *Live In Japan* (Epic/Sony 1975).

Beck, Jeff

b. 24 June 1944, Wallington, Surrey, England. As a former choir boy the young Beck was interested in music from an early age, becoming a competent pianist and guitarist by the age of 11. His first main band was the Tridents, who made a name for themselves locally. After leaving them Beck took on the seemingly awesome task of stepping into the shoes of Eric Clapton, who had recently departed from the 60s R&B pioneers, the Yardbirds. Clapton had a fiercely loyal following, but Beck soon had them gasping with his amazing guitar pyrotechnics, utilizing feedback and distortion. Beck stayed with the Yardbirds adding colour and excitement to all their hits until October 1966. The tension between Beck and joint lead guitarist Jimmy Page was finally resolved during a US tour. Beck walked out and never returned. His solo career was launched in March 1967 with an unexpected pop single, 'Hi-Ho Silver Lining', wherein Jeff's unremarkable voice was heard on a sing-along number which was saved by his trademark guitar solo. The record was a sizeable hit and has demonstrated its perennial appeal to party-goers by re-entering the charts overal occasions since. The follow-up, 'Tallyman', was also a minor hit, but by now Jeff's ambitions lay in other directions. From being a singing, guitar-playing, pop star he relaunched a career that led him to become one of the world's leading rock guitarists. The Jeff Beck Group, formed in 1968, consisted of Beck, Rod Stewart (vocals), Ron Wood (bass), Nicky Hopkins (piano) and Mickey Waller (drums). This powerhouse quartet released *Truth*, which became a major success in the USA, resulting in the band undertaking a number of arduous tours. The second album, *Cosa Nostra Beck-Ola*, had similar success, although Stewart and Wood had now departed for the Faces. Beck also contributed some sparkling guitar and received equal billing with Donovan on the hit 'Goo Goo Barabajagal (Love Is Hot)'. In 1968 Jeff's serious accident with one of his hot-rod cars put him out of action for almost 18 months. A recovered Beck formed another group with Cozy Powell, Max Middleton and Bob Tench, and recorded two further albums, *Rough And Ready* and *Jeff Beck Group*. The latter became a sizeable hit. Beck was now venerated as a serious musician and master of his instrument, and figured highly in various guitarist polls. In 1973 the erratic Beck musical style changed once again and he formed the trio Beck, Bogert And Appice with the two former members of Vanilla Fudge. Soon after Beck introduced yet another musical dimension, this time forming an instrumental band. The result was the excellent *Blow By Blow*, thought by many to be his best work. His guitar playing revealed extraordinary technique, combining rock, jazz and blues styles. *Blow By Blow* was a million seller and its follow-up, *Wired*, enjoyed similar success. Having allied himself with some of the jazz/rock fraternity Beck teamed up with Jan Hammer for a frantic live album, after which he effectively retired for three years. He returned in 1980 with *There And Back* and, now rejuvenated, he found himself riding the album charts once more. During the 80s Beck's appearances were sporadic, though he did guest on Tina Turner's *Private Dancer* and work with Robert Plant and Jimmy Page on the Honeydrippers' album. The occasional charity function aside, he has spent much of his leisure time with automobiles (in one interview Beck stated that he could just as easily have been a car restorer). In the mid-80s he toured with Rod Stewart and was present on his version of 'People Get Ready', though when *Flash* arrived in 1985, it proved his least successful album to date. The release of a box-set in 1992,

chronicling his career, was a fitting tribute to this accomplished guitarist and his numerous guises (the latest of which had been guitarist on Spinal Tap's second album). Following an award in 1993 for his theme music (with Jed Stoller) for the Anglia TV production *Frankie's House* he released *Crazy Legs*, a tribute to the music of Gene Vincent. For this Beck abandoned virtuosity, blistering solos and jazz stylings for a clean, low-volume rock 'n' roll sound, demonstrating once more his absolute mastery of technique. As if not already amply endowed with strings to his bow he also made his acting debut, playing Brad the serial killer in *The Comic Strip Presents...Gregory: Diary Of A Nutcase*

Albums: *Truth* (EMI 1968), *Cosa Nostra Beck-Ola* (EMI 1969), *Rough And Ready* (Epic 1971), *Jeff Beck Group* (Epic 1972), *Blow By Blow* (Epic 1975), *Wired* (Epic 1976), *Jeff Beck With The Jan Hammer Group Live* (Epic 1977), *There And Back* (Epic 1980), *Flash* (Epic 1985), with Terry Bozzio, Tony Hymas *Jeff Beck's Guitar Shop* (Epic 1989), *Crazy Legs* (Epic 1993). Compilation: *Beckology* (Epic 1992, CD box set).

Becker, Jason

This classically-trained US guitarist first came to prominence in the late 80s with fellow guitar wizard Marty Friedman in the band Cacophony. Combining blues, rock and classical styles he built up a reputation for playing at breakneck speed with a melodic intensity and feel that was reminiscent of Alvin Lee. He took time out between Cacophony albums in 1988 to record *Perpetual Burn*, a solo instrumental showcase for his remarkable six-string acrobatics. After the recording of Cacophony's second album, Becker accepted Dave Lee Roth's offer to be permanent replacement for Steve Vai. Becker appeared on Roth's *A Little Ain't Enough* album in 1991, contributing some stunning guitar work, and silenced the critics' premature claims that he would not be able to match his flamboyant predecessor.

Album: *Perpetual Burn* (Roadrunner 1988).

Becker, Margaret

This US Christian rock singer first achieved recognition with Steve Camp in 1986, singing on a duet with Camp on his *One On One* album. With her solo career taking off as a result, she concentrated on a melodic and easily accessible pop-rock style, dominated by brooding and atmospheric ballads. Becker has released four quality albums to date, with the vast majority of the songs being self-written. However, she has yet to make a significant impression outside the Christian music scene, despite excellent albums like *The Reckoning*.

Albums: *Never For Nothing* (Sparrow 1987), *The Reckoning* (Sparrow 1988), *Immigrant's Daughter* (Sparrow 1990), *Simple House* (Sparrow 1991).

Bedlam

Formed in 1972 and originally known as Beast, Bedlam comprised former Truth singer Frank Aiello (vocals), Dave Ball (guitar), Dennis Ball (bass) and Cozy Powell (drums). Each of the group, barring Aiello, were previously members of the Ace Kefford Stand and Big Bertha, but this new act was convened following Powell's tenure with Jeff Beck and Dave Ball's spell in Procol Harum. Despite early optimism, *Bedlam* failed to establish the UK quartet as a commercial proposition and they split in 1974. Powell and Aiello then formed Cozy Powell's Hammer, while their ex-colleagues left music altogether.

Album: *Bedlam* (Chrysalis 1973).

Benatar, Pat

b. Pat Andrzejewski, 10 January 1953, Brooklyn, New York, USA. Pat Benatar, after training as an opera singer, became a major hitmaker in the early 80s, adept at both mainstream rock and powerful ballads, often focusing on personal relationships and sexual politics. She married Dennis Benatar after graduating from high school and relocated to Virginia. By the 70s she had returned to New York, where she was discovered by Rick Newman in 1979 at the latter's Catch A Rising Star club. With Newman as manager, she signed to Chrysalis Records that year and released her debut album *In The Heat Of The Night*, produced by Mike Chapman, which became a substantial hit and spawned three US chart singles. Benatar (who retained the name after divorcing), released her second album, *Crimes Of Passion*, in 1980. This collection, which later won a Grammy for Best Female Rock Vocal Performance, rose to number 2 in the US charts, while the hard-rocking 'Hit Me With Your Best Shot', became her first *Billboard* Top 10 single. *Precious Time* was released in 1981 and this time reached number 1 in the US. Although no Top 10 singles resulted, Benatar won another Grammy for 'Fire And Ice'. In 1982 Benatar married producer Neil Geraldo, who played guitar in her band and wrote most of her material, and released *Get Nervous*, which reached US number 4. The following year, a live album, also including two new studio tracks, was released. One of those tracks, 'Love Is A Battlefield', reached number 5 in the US, the same position attained in 1984 by 'We Belong', from the next album, *Tropico*. The former

single eventually became a UK Top 20 hit in 1985 after initially stalling a year earlier at 49 and was re-issued in the wake of the British success of 'We Belong'. That same year, 'Invincible', from the film *Legend Of Billie Jean*, was Benatar's last US Top 10 single of the decade. An album, *Seven The Hard Way*, followed later that year but indicated a decline in Benatar's popularity. Inactivity marked the next couple of years as Benatar devoted her attentions to motherhood. A compilation album, *Best Shots*, was released in 1987. Although moderately successful in her homeland, it became a major hit in Europe, putting her into the UK Top 10 album charts for the first time. Since 1988 Benatar has also, reportedly, pursued an acting career.

Albums: *In The Heat Of The Night* (Chrysalis 1979), *Crimes Of Passion* (Chrysalis 1980), *Precious Time* (Chrysalis 1981), *Get Nervous* (Chrysalis 1982), *Live From Earth* (Chrysalis 1983), *Tropico* (Chrysalis 1984), *Seven The Hard Way* (Chrysalis 1985), *Wide Awake In Dreamland* (Chrysalis 1988), *True Love* (Chrysalis 1991), *Gravity's Rainbow* (Chrysalis 1993).

Compilation: *Best Shots* (Chrysalis 1987).

Videos: *Benatar* (1985), *Best Shots* (1986).

Further reading: *Benatar*, Doug Magee.

Benediction

Birmingham death metal band formed in the late 80s, featuring singer Dave Ingram, with guitarists Darren Brooke and Peter Rew, and bass player Frank Healy. Original vocalist 'Barny' (Mark Greenway) joined Napalm Death, while drummer Ian Treacy quit in late 1993 (for session work, eventually becoming part of Celestial), to be replaced by Paul Brooks, a veteran of several thrash, punk, indie and even reggae bands. Signed to Germany's Nuclear Blast stable, in the 90s European touring with Atheist established the band throughout the continent, with the possible exception of their native country, a fact frequently bemoaned by the group. A half-live affair, *The Grotesque - Ashen Epitaph*, also comprised two new studio tracks, along with material recorded on their well-received European tour.

Albums: *Subconscious Terror* (Nuclear Blast 1990), *Grand Leveller* (Revolver 1991), *Dark Is The Sea* (Nuclear Blast 1992), *Transcend The Rubicon* (Nuclear Blast 1993), *The Grotesque - Ashen Epitaph* (Nuclear Blast 1994; mini-album).

Bengal Tigers

This short-lived Australian heavy metal band was formed in Melbourne in 1983 by vocalist Gordon Heald and guitarist Barney Fakhouri. Enlisting the services of Steve Tyler (bass) and Mick Egan

(drums/vocals), they signed to the Mushroom label and released a mini-album the following year. Influenced by AC/DC, Iron Maiden and Scorpions, they purveyed cliched heavy metal, that, sadly, lacked both identity and energy.
Album: *Metal Fetish* (Mushroom 1984, mini-album).

Betsy

In 1988 Bitch, the Los Angeles-based sado-masochistic band who were obsessed with leather, whips and chains, decided to clean up their act. They changed their name to Betsy and adopted a less extreme angle. The band still comprised Betsy Weiss (vocals), David Carruth (guitar), Ron Cordy (bass) and Robby Settles (drums), but the sexual side of the band's image was played down. Signing to Roadrunner Records, their sole release was not noticeably different from the old Bitch musical style; heavy metal with lacklustre vocals, albeit with less tawdry lyrics. The album sank without trace and they reverted back to leather underwear and the Bitch tag within a year.
Album: *Betsy* (Roadrunner 1988).

Beyond

Formed in Derby, England, in 1988 the band consists of John Whitby (vocals), Andy Gatford (guitar), Jim Kersey (bass) and Neil Cooper (drums). Quickly gaining popularity on the live club circuit and obtaining a publishing contract with Island Music, they attracted the attention of EMI Records thanks to some early demos. The band initially signed a year-long development arrangement with the label during which time they released two singles on the small independent Big Cat Records label. These were the EP, *Manic Sound Picnic*, and the single, 'No Excuse', both released in 1990. The following year the band released their first single for the EMI label proper, 'One Step Too Far'. This was quickly followed by 'Empire' on the relaunched EMI subsidiary Harvest Records. A cross between Jane's Addiction, Voivod and Faith No More, the band's debut album was well received by both the music press and the public. In support of the album they toured the UK and Europe with Living Colour and an EP, *Raging*, was also added to the band's discography.
Album: *Crawl* (Harvest 1991), *Chasm* (Harvest 1993).

Big F

This Los Angeles, USA, trio comprised Mark Christian (guitar), John Shreve (bass/vocals) and Rob Donin (drums). Their stock in trade was a 'mind-blowing wall of noise', dominated by crashing drums and screeching feedback, while vocalist Shreve screamed incessantly above the maelstrom. Psychedelia, Jimi Hendrix, the Stooges, the Cult and *avant garde* influences appeared as reference points, while rumours persisted that Shreve was in fact the alter-ego of Berlin's John Crawford. Whatever, the sub-Led Zeppelin riffs and affected stylings of Big F were unlikely to find any success on the scale of 'Take My Breath Away'.
Album: *The Big F* (Elektra 1989).

Big House

This Canadian quartet specialize in melodic and hard-edged AOR. They were formed in 1987 by drummer Sjor Throndson and vocalist Jan Ek who both wanted to prove that Canada had other things to offer besides Rush and Bryan Adams. Recruiting guitarist K.B.Broc and bassist Jay Scott King, the current line-up was finalized in 1989. After incessant gigging in their native Canada, the band were signed by RCA Records. They debuted in 1992 with a self-titled album that incorporated elements of Bon Jovi, Ratt and Aerosmith, and with time and record company backing, they could develop into a major force.
Album: *Big House* (Boom Town 1992).

Billion Dollar Babies

This short-lived group revolved around Michael Bruce (b. 21 November 1948, California, USA; guitar/vocals), Dennis Dunaway (b. 15 March 1946, California, USA; bass) and Neal Smith (b. 10 January 1946, Washington, USA; drums). Founder members of Alice Cooper, the trio were summarily fired in 1974 by lead singer Vince Furnier, known henceforth as 'Alice Cooper'. Protracted legal entanglements delayed this riposte, which took its name from one of their former group's best-selling albums. Sessionmen Bob Dolin (keyboards) and Mike Marconi (guitar) completed the line-up, but the resultant album, *Battle Axe*, was a major disappointment. Its uncomfortable mix of technology and heavy metal did not prove popular and the quintet was then dissolved. Bruce embarked on a solo career and thereafter teamed up with ex-Angel drummer Barry Brandt to pursue a jazz-orientated path. Dunaway and Smith formed the Flying Tigers while Dolin and Marconi reverted to studio work.
Album: *Battle Axe* (Polydor 1977).

Billy Satellite

This Californian quartet was formed in 1983 by Monty Byrom (guitar/vocals/keyboards) and Danny Chauncey (guitar/keyboards). With bassist Ira Walker and drummer Tom Falletti completing the line-up, they bridged the musical divide between the commercial radio-rock of Boston, and the bluesy southern-style of Lynyrd Skynyrd. Signing to EMI in 1984, they released a single album before disbanding. Byrom and Chauncey went on to join New Frontier and .38 Special respectively. Eddie Money later covered the band's 'I Wanna Go Back', scoring a minor hit in the USA in the process.

Album: *Billy Satellite* (Capitol 1984).

Billy The Kid

This brash pop-metal quartet was formed in Los Angeles during 1984 by vocalist Stephen Frederick and guitarist Bill L'Kid. With the addition of Jeffrey Velvet (bass) and Randy Delay (drums), they signed a contract with MCA the following year. Fusing the energy and flamboyance of Van Halen with the commercial sensibility of REO Speedwagon, they cut the impressive and appropriately titled *Sworn To Fun* in 1985. Failing to attract media interest, they disbanded soon after the album's release.

Album: *Sworn To Fun* (MCA 1985).

Biohazard

The mean streets of Brooklyn, New York, saw the formation of Biohazard in 1988 by Evan Seinfeld (bass, vocals), Billy Graziedi (guitar, vocals), Bobby Hambel (guitar) and Danny Schuler (drums), and the harsh realities of urban life provide constant lyrical inspiration for this socially and politically aware hardcore band. Modest beginnings supporting the likes of the Cro-Mags and Carnivore at the famous L'Amour club led to an independent debut, *Biohazard*. Constant touring built such a cult following that the band were able to sign to Roadrunner for one album and a subsequent major deal with Warner Brothers at the same time in 1992. *Urban Discipline* was recorded in under two weeks on a tiny budget, but proved to be the band's breakthrough album. Blisteringly heavy with lyrics to match - 'Black And White And Red All Over' was an anti-racism tirade to dispel a mistakenly-applied fascist label stemming from the debut's 'Howard Beach', which concerned a racially-motivated Brooklyn murder - the album drew massive praise, as did wild live shows during heavy touring with Kreator in Europe and Sick Of It All in the US. The band also recorded a well-received track with rappers Onyx for the *Judgement Night* soundtrack. The Warners debut, *State Of The World Address*, was recorded in seven weeks, and demonstrated that major label status did not mean any compromise on Biohazard's part, with a furiously heavy Ed Stasium production and an aggressive performance which gathered a succession of rave reviews. The band embarked on a successful US tour with Pantera and Sepultura as album sales took off, but a second appearance at Donington came to a controversially premature end due to the stage management's safety worries over Biohazard's penchant for encouraging their audience to join them on stage *en masse*. However, further European touring, including several festival dates, was problem-free, with the band constantly enhancing a deserved reputation for their ferocious live shows, before returning to the US for dates with House Of Pain and Danzig.

Albums: *Biohazard* (Maze 1990), *Urban Discipline* (Roadrunner 1992), *State Of The World Address* (Warners 1994).

Birtha

Birtha were one of the first USA all-female bands to try and penetrate the exclusively male bastion of heavy rock. Comprising Rosemary Butler (bass/vocals), Sherry Hagler (keyboards), Liver Favela (drums) and Shele Pinizzotto (guitar/vocals), they released two excellent hard-rock albums during the early 70s. They specialized in tight harmonies and a style not dissimilar to that of early Uriah Heep. They were regarded as a novelty at the time, which on reflection is a little unjust. Their tasteless publicity handout during their early 70s UK tour with the Kinks stating 'Birtha has balls' doubtless failed to help. Along with Fanny they undoubtedly helped pave the way for future female rockers such as the Runaways.

Albums: *Birtha* (Probe 1972), *Can't Stop The Madness* (Probe 1973).

Bitch (Switzerland)

Bitch were formed in Zurich, Switzerland, in 1979 by the Schmid brothers Eric (vocals), Jimmy (drums) and Geoffrey (guitar). Adding Marc Portman (guitar) and Roddy Landolt (bass), they combined 70s symphonic-rock with a New Wave Of British Heavy Metal approach. Elements of Deep Purple, Krokus, Emerson, Lake And Palmer and Angelwitch were evident in the two albums they released during the early 80s. However, the band's name was always more provocative than their music, and unable to find an appreciative audience, they disappeared from the scene in 1982.

Albums: *First Bite* (Bellaphon 1980), *Some Like It Hard* (Bellaphon 1982).

Bitch (USA)

This Los Angeles-based quartet made an impact in

1982 with their debut EP, more as a result of their shock value, rather than any originality. Led by female vocalist Betsy Weiss, a former ska singer, they released *Be My Slave*, with David Carruth (guitar), Mark Anthony Wells (bass) and Robbie Settles (drums) completing the line-up. With Ron Cordy replacing Wells, it took a further four years before the appropriately titled *The Bitch Is Back* emerged. Regarded with little affection by the mainstream audience, they relaunched themselves as Betsy in 1988, with a cleaner AOR-like image. This was met with indifference and the band became Bitch again within a year, reverting to their original Motörhead/Girlschool metal boogie format.

Albums: *Damnation Alley* (Metal Blade 1982, minialbum), *Be My Slave* (Metal Blade 1983), *The Bitch Is Back* (Metal Blade 1987).

Bitches Sin

Formed in Cumbria, England in 1980, during the growth of the New Wave Of British Heavy Metal movement, Bitches Sin comprised Ian Toomey (guitar), Alan Cockburn (vocals), Perry Hodder (bass), Peter Toomey (guitar) and Bill Knowles (drums). Cockburn was later replaced by Frank Quegan, while Mike Frazier took over on bass. Purveying high-energy metallic rock, they combined UFO and Deep Purple influences with modern technology and were reminiscent of Diamond Head in places. Their first single, 'Sign Of The Times', achieved success in Holland after it was championed by radio disc jockey Hanneke Kappen. They subsequently contributed a track to a *Heavy Metal Heroes* compilation album, which helped to further their reputation. A plethora of personnel changes hindered their progress, however. They would release two studio albums, neither of which fulfilled their initial promise, and had actually disbanded before *Invaders* materialized. The Toomey brothers reappeared in 1988 as Flash Point, self-financing the release of a debut album.

Albums: *Predator* (Heavy Metal 1982), *Invaders* (King Klassic 1986).

Black 'N' Blue

Formerly known as Boogie Star, Black 'N' Blue were formed in Portland, Oregon, USA, in 1981. After a series of line-up shuffles, the band stabilized with Jaime St. James (vocals), Tommy Thayer (guitar), Jeff Warner (guitar), Patrick Young (bass) and Peter Holmes (drums). Relocating to Los Angeles in 1982, they forged a contract with Geffen Records and delivered their self-titled debut album in 1984. Produced by Dieter Dierks, the album was classic hard rock and surprisingly un-American; shunning the party-metal approach of Ratt and Quiet Riot and having more in common with the Scorpions and Def Leppard. Failing to attract media attention, the band dropped this approach and tried to emulate the style of Kiss and Mötley Crüe from then on. With Gene Simmons (Kiss's bassist) producing their third and fourth albums, the accusations of imitation grew even stronger. Unable to generate commercial success, the band disintegrated in 1989. Patrick Young went on to Dokken, vocalist James joined Madhouse, Thayer teamed up with Harlow and the remaining pair formed Wet Engine. Black 'N' Blue were an excellent band, who grew to regret the decision to compromise an original talent.

Albums: *Black 'N' Blue* (Geffen 1984), *Without Love* (Geffen 1985), *Nasty, Nasty* (Geffen 1986), *In Heat* (Geffen 1988).

Black Crowes

Exposed to a wide variety of music from an early age by their musician father, brothers Chris (b. Christopher Mark Robinson, 20 December 1966, Atlanta, Georgia, USA; vocals) and Rich Robinson (b. Richard S. Robinson, 24 May 1969, Atlanta, Georgia, USA; guitar) formed the band under the name Mr. Crowe's Garden in 1984. A procession of six bassists and three drummers passed through before the band stabilized with Johnny Colt (bass) and ex-Mary My Hope drummer Steve Gorman. His predecessor, Jeff Sullivan, went on to join Drivin' N' Cryin'. Jeff Cease joined the group as a second guitarist in 1988 from Nashville band, Rumble Circus, to augment and toughen both the songs and the live sound. As the Black Crowes, they were signed to the Def American label by George Drakoulias. Given the very heavy nature of the other members of the label's roster such as Slayer and Danzig, the purist rock 'n' roll style of the Crowes was a stark contrast. Drakoulias produced the debut, *Shake Your Money Maker*, a remarkably mature album from such a young band, blending soul and uncomplicated R&B reminiscent of vintage Rolling Stones and Humble Pie. Another influence was made obvious by the stirring cover of Otis Redding's 'Hard to Handle'. The record's highlight was 'She Talks To Angels', an emotive acoustic ballad about the frailties of a drug addict, featuring a superb vocal and highly accomplished lyric from Chris Robinson. The album was released to critical acclaim, and the band went on the road, supporting first Steve Stevens' Atomic Playboys and then Junkyard in the USA, plus a handful of UK dates, some opening for the Dogs D'Amour and the rest as headliners. Their live

Black Crowes

performances drew further Stones comparisons, the band's image being very much rooted in the 70s, with Chris Robinson's thin frame dominating the stage like a young Mick Jagger. With heavy radio and *MTV* airplay exposing the Crowes to a wide audience, the first single 'Jealous Again' was a deserved US hit, and the band were invited to fill the prestigious support slot for the final leg of Aerosmith's 'Pump' tour on their return to the US. Canadian keyboard player Ed Hawrysch, recommended by former Green On Red member Chuck Leavell, who had played on the album, joined the band in early 1991 as the live shows became more progressive, incorporating jam sessions on new material, and the band were invited on to another high-profile tour as guests of Z.Z. Top. However, their uncompromising attitude led to Z.Z. Top's management asking the Crowes to leave the tour following a home town show in Atlanta, due to Chris Robinson's persistent, if oblique, criticism of the corporate sponsorship of the tour. Somewhat ironically, the band fired the support act for their subsequent headline shows after discovering that they had made advertisements for a similar major company.

By this stage the band had achieved a sufficient level of chart success to enable them to continue as a headline act, and their popularity led to an invitation to join the European Monsters of Rock tour, opening at the prestigious Donington festival in England and culminating in a massive free show in Moscow. Prior to these dates, the band were forced to take a five week break (which was to be their longest in 22 months of touring) when Chris Robinson collapsed suffering from exhaustion following an acoustic showcase at Ronnie Scott's club in London. The singer recovered to undertake the tour, plus a UK trek to complete the band's world tour. This ended with further controversy, with Colt and vocalist Robinson becoming embroiled in a fight with a member of the crowd in the Edinburgh Playhouse. Almost immediately after the tour was complete, the band parted company with Jeff Cease, who had drifted apart from the other members on the road, replacing him with former Burning Tree guitarist/vocalist Marc Ford, a friend of Chris Robinson's. Rather than rest on their laurels, the band went straight into pre-production for their second album. Although the recording sessions were interrupted while the Robinsons went to their mother's bedside as she recovered from a heart attack, basic tracks were completed in a total of eight days. Using a truncated version of a title found by the elder Robinson in an old hymn book, *The Southern Harmony And Musical Companion* was released in the spring of 1992, again

to positive reviews. The musical progression of the band, and of the brothers as songwriters, was obvious; the greater expanse of sound provided by the permanent addition of Hawrysch coupled with the use of female backing singers allowed the band to develop from the simpler arrangements of *Shake Your Money Maker*. New recruit Ford, given responsibility for the majority of guitar solos, turned in a superb performance, with one particularly notable lead on 'Sometimes Salvation'. Robinson had advanced lyrically, finding new depths, and making full use of the backing singers for less straightforward vocal arrangements. Overall, the album has a feel which echoes the great Southern rock bands of the 70s, such as Lynyrd Skynyrd, and, while each track works individually, the album seems to build from driving opener 'Sting Me' towards the musical and emotional peak of 'My Morning Song', with a gentle coda in an acoustic rendition of Bob Marley's 'Time Will Tell'. With both the album and opening single 'Remedy' a success, the Black Crowes immediately returned to the road for the High As The Moon tour, their massive popularity ensured healthy attendances in recessionary times - a free show in Toronto's G Rose Lord Park drew a 75,000 crowd, with people entering the park at a rate of 1,000 per minute at one point. Both the live performances and the customized lighting rig garnered great critical praise. 1994 finally saw the release of *Amorica*. This arrived complete with artwork featuring a women's Stars 'n' Stripes-bedecked briefs, which barely cover her embarassment, taken from a 1976 copy of *Hustler*. A previously completed album (*Tall*) had been scrapped, with only five songs retained, with producer Jack Puig brought in to help rectify matters. Live shows saw the debut of percussionist Chris Trujillo, adding further atmosphere as the now seven-piece band produced some brilliantly tight-but-loose performances.

Albums: *Shake Your Money Maker* (Def American 1990), *The Southern Harmony And Musical Companion* (Def American 1992), *Amorica* (American 1994).

Further reading: *The Black Crowes*, Martin Black.

Black Flag

Formed in 1977 in Los Angeles, California, Black Flag rose to become one of America's leading hardcore groups. The initial line-up - Keith Morris (vocals), Greg Ginn (guitar), Chuck Dukowski (bass) and Brian Migdol (drums) - completed the *Nervous Breakdown* EP in 1978, but the following year Morris left to form the Circle Jerks. Several members would join and leave before Henry Rollins (vocals), Dez

Cadenza (guitar) and Robo (drums) joined Ginn and Dukowski for *Damaged*, the group's first full-length album. Originally scheduled for release by MCA, the company withdrew support, citing outrageous content, and the set appeared on the quintet's own label, SST. This prolific outlet has not only issued every subsequent Black Flag recording, but boasts a catalogue which includes Hüsker Dü, Sonic Youth, the Minutemen, the Meat Puppets and Dinosaur Jr. Administered by Ginn and Dukowski, the latter of whom left the group to concentrate his efforts more fully, the company has become one of America's leading, and most influential, independents. The former musician continued to lead Black Flag in tandem with Rollins, and although its rhythm section was still subject to change, the music's power remained undiminished. Pivotal albums included *My War* and *In My Head* while their diversity was showcased on *Family Man*, which contrasted a side of Rollins' poetry with four excellent instrumentals. However, the group split up in 1986 following the release of a compulsive live set, *Who's Got The 10 1/2?*, following which Ginn switched his attentions to labelmates Gone. Rollins went on to a succesful solo career. The glory days of Black Flag are warmly recalled in one of Rollins' numerous books for his 2.13.61. publishing empire, *Get In The Van*.

Albums: *Damaged* (SST 1981), *My War* (SST 1984), *Family Man* (SST 1984), *Slip It In* (SST 1984), *Live '84* (SST 1985, cassette only), *Loose Nut* (SST 1985), *The Process Of Weeding Out* (SST 1985, instrumental mini-album), *In My Head* (SST 1985), *Who's Got The 10 1/2?* (SST 1986). Compilations: *Everything Went Black* (SST 1983, double album), *The First Four Years* (SST 1983), *Wasted...Again* (SST 1988).

Further reading: *Get In The Van*, Henry Rollins (1994).

Black Oak Arkansas

A sextet formed in the late 60s, Black Oak Arkansas took its name from the USA town and state where singer Jim 'Dandy' Mangrum (b. 30 March 1948) was born. The other members of the group hailed from nearby towns: Ricky Reynolds (b. 28 October 1948, Manilan, Arkansas, USA; guitar), Stanley Knight (b. 12 February 1949, Little Rock, Arkansas, USA; guitar), Harvey Jett (b. Marion, Arkansas, USA; guitar), Pat Daugherty (b. 11 November 1947, Jonesboro, Arkansas, USA; bass) and drummer Wayne Evans, replaced on the third album by Thomas Aldrich (b. 15 August, 1950, Jackson, Mississippi, USA). Before forming the band, the future members were part of a gang that shared a house. At first calling themselves the Knowbody Else,

the group recorded an unsuccessful album for Stax Records in 1969. Two years later they changed their name and signed with Atco Records, for whom they recorded a self-titled album that introduced them to the US charts. Touring steadily, this hard rock/southern boogie band built a core following, yet its records never matched its concert appeal. Of their 10 US-charting albums between 1971 and 1976, *High On The Hog* proved the most commercially successful, peaking at number 52. It featured the best-selling 1974 Top 30 single, 'Jim Dandy' (sung by female vocalist Ruby Starr, who reappeared on the 1976 *Live! Mutha* album). In 1975, guitarist Jett was replaced by James Henderson (b. 20 May 1954, Jackson, Mississippi, USA) and the following year, after switching to MCA Records, Black Oak Arkansas had only one further minor chart single, 'Strong Enough To Be Gentle'. By 1977 only Mangrum remained from the original band and although they signed to Capricorn Records, there was no further record success. Mangrum did, however, keep variations of the group on the road during the 80s as well as recording a solo album in 1984.

Albums: As the Knowbody Else: *The Knowbody Else* (Stax 1969). As Black Oak Arkansas: *Black Oak Arkansas* (Atco 1971), *Keep The Faith* (Atco 1972), *If An Angel Came To See You, Would You Make Her Feel At Home?* (Atco 1972), *Raunch 'N' Roll/Live* (Atlantic 1973), *High On The Hog* (Atco 1973), *Street Party* (Atco 1974), *Ain't Life Grand* (Atco 1975), *X-Rated* (MCA 1975), *Live! Mutha* (Atco 1976), *Balls of Fire* (MCA 1976), *10 Year Overnight Success* (MCA 1976), *Race With The Devil* (Capricorn 1977), *I'd Rather Be Sailing* (Capricorn 1978), *Black Attack Is Back* (Capricorn 1986). Compilations: *The Best Of Black Oak Arkansas* (1977), *Early Times* (1993), *Hot & Nasty: The Best Of* (1993). Jim Dandy solo: *Randy As Hell* (1984).

Black Rose (UK)

Black Rose were formed in Newcastle, England, in 1983 by vocalist Steve Bardsley and guitarist Chris Watson. With the addition of Mick Thompson (bass) and Malla Smith (drums), they followed a musical direction similar to other north east bands such as Raven, Venom and Blitzkrieg. After contributing tracks to a number of heavy metal compilation albums, they signed to Bullet Records and released *Boys Will Be Boys* in 1984. Following a Dutch tour to promote the album, Graham Hunter replaced Chris Watson. A second album recorded in 1986 showed that the band had made little musical progress. Pat O'Neill replaced Watson on guitar, but with poorly attended live-shows and an ever-diminishing fanbase, the band folded in 1987.

Albums: *Boys Will Be Boys* (Bullet 1984), *Walk It, How You Talk It* (Neat 1986).

Black Rose (USA)

The US version of Black Rose was formed by singer/actress Cher and guitarist Les Dudek in 1979. Employing the services of Warren Ham (vocals/guitar), Ron Ritchotte (guitar), Michael Finnigan (keyboards), Trey Thompson (bass) and Gary Ferguson (drums), they specialized in rock/pop crossover material, with a slight country influence. Their debut and only album was highly polished, with slick arrangements and an expensive production. When Cher and Dudek's tempestuous romance ended, Black Rose split. Ritchotte went on to play with Stan Bush And Barrage then Steppenwolf.

Album: *Black Rose* (Casablanca 1980).

Black Sabbath

Group members Terry 'Geezer' Butler (b. 17 July 1949, Birmingham, England; bass), Tony Iommi (b. 19 February 1948, Birmingham, England; guitar), Bill Ward (b. 5 May 1948, Birmingham, England; drums) and 'Ozzy' Osbourne (b. 3 December 1948, Birmingham, England; vocals) were originally known as Earth, a name they changed to Black Sabbath in 1969. The members of this band grew up together in the musically fertile English Midlands, and their name hints at the heavy, doom-laden and yet ingenious music they produced. The name had first been invoked as a song title used by Polka Tulk, a pre-Earth blues outfit featuring Iommi, Ward, Butler and Osbourne. It does not come from a book by the occult writer Denis Wheatley, as is often stated, but from the cult horror film of that title. However, many of Sabbath's songs deal with alternative beliefs and ways of life in keeping with Wheatley's teachings. The title-track of *Paranoid* also confronts mental instability, and other songs are concerned with the affects of narcotic substances such as cocaine and marijuana. The line-up remained unchanged until 1973 when Rick Wakeman, keyboard player for Yes, was drafted in to play on *Sabbath Bloody Sabbath*. By 1977 personnel difficulties within the band were beginning to take their toll, and the music was losing some of its earlier orchestral, bombastic sheen, prompting Ozzy Osbourne to pursue a solo career the following year. He was replaced by ex-Savoy Brown member Dave Walker until Ronnie James Dio accepted the job. Dio had been a central figure in the early 70s band Elf, and spent three years with Ritchie Blackmore's Rainbow. However, Dio's tenure with the band was to be short-lived, and he left in 1982. The replacement vocalist was Ian Gillan. It is this Sabbath incarnation which is commonly regarded as the most disastrous for band and fans alike, *Born Again* failing to capture any of the original vitality of the group. In 1986 the entire line-up was rethought. Iommi was the only original member of the band, which now consisted of Geoff Nichols (b. Birmingham, England; keyboards; Nichols had been the group's keyboard player since 1980 when still a member of Quartz, but now joined full-tme), Glenn Hughes (b. England; vocals), Dave Spitz (b. New York City, New York, USA; bass), and Eric Singer (b. Cleveland, Ohio, USA; drums). This was an accomplished combination, Singer having been a member of the Lita Ford band, and Glenn Hughes having worked with such legendary outfits as Trapeze and Deep Purple. In 1986 the surprisingly blues-sounding *Seventh Star* was released, the lyrics and music for which had been written by Iommi. In the first of a succession of personnel changes, Hughes left the band to be replaced by Ray Gillen, an American singer who failed to record anything with them. Tony Martin was the vocalist on 1987's powerful *The Eternal Idol* and 1988's *Headless Cross,* the album which skilled and renowned drummer Cozy Powell produced and appeared on. Martin has remained with them since in an on/off relationship which saw him replaced at various times by Rob Halford (Judas Priest), Ozzy and Dio, as a sort of permanent understudy. By late 1991 Sabbath was suffering from flagging record sales and declining credibility so Iommi recruited their original bassist, Butler, and attempted to persuade drummer Bill Ward to rejoin too. Ward, however, was not interested, Cozy Powell was still recuperating after being crushed by his horse, and so Vinnie Appice became Sabbath's new incumbent (Bev Bevan of ELO had been part of the band for *Born Again*, and returned at various times. Other temporary drummers have included Terry Chimes of the Clash). After much speculation, a return to the band by Ronnie Dio completed the 1982/3 line-up. Ozzy's attempts, meanwhile, to reform the original group for a 1992 tour faltered when the others demanded an absolutely equal share in the spoils. 1994 saw the release of a tribute album, *Nativity In Black*, which featured appearances from all four original members in various guises, plus Megadeth, White Zombie, Sepultura, Biohazard, Ugly Kid Joe, Bruce Dickinson, Therapy?, Corrosion Of Conformity and Type O Negative - those being just a handful of the names indebted to Sabbath's legacy.

Albums: *Black Sabbath* (Vertigo 1970), *Paranoid* (Vertigo 1970), *Master Of Reality* (Vertigo 1971), *Black Sabbath Vol. 4* (Vertigo 1972), *Sabbath Bloody*

Sabbath (World Wide Artists 1974), *Sabotage* (NEMS 1975), *Technical Ecstasy* (Vertigo 1976), *Never Say Die* (Vertigo 1978), *Heaven And Hell* (Vertigo 1980), *Live At Last* (NEMS 1980), *Mob Rules* (Vertigo 1981), *Live Evil* (Vertigo 1982), *Born Again* (Vertigo 1983), *Seventh Star* (Vertigo 1986), *The Eternal Idol* (Vertigo 1987), *Headless Cross* (IRS 1989), *Tyr* (IRS 1990), *Dehumanizer* (IRS 1992), *Cross Purposes* (EMI 1994). Compilations: *We Sold Our Soul For Rock 'n' Roll* (NEMS 1976, double album), *Greatest Hits* (NEMS 1980), *Collection: Black Sabbath* (Castle 1985, double album), *Blackest Sabbath* (Vertigo 1989), *Backtrackin'* (Backtrackin' 1990, double album), *The Ozzy Osbourne Years* (Essential 1991, 3-CD box set). Videos: *Never Say Die* (1986), *The Black Sabbath Story Vol. 1 (1970-1978)* (1992).
Further reading: *Black Sabbath*, Chris Welch.

Black Sheep

This group was formed in New York in 1974 by vocalist Louis Grammatico and guitarist Donald Mancuso. Recruiting Larry Crozier (keyboards), Bruce Turgon (bass) and Ron Rocco (drums), they signed with Capitol Records the following year. Influenced by Bad Company, Free and Led Zeppelin, they recorded two excellent hard rock albums, characterized by Grammatico's powerful, yet soulful vocal style. Unable to make an impact, the band split up, with Grammatico changing his name to Lou Gramm and finding considerable success with Foreigner. Turgon, after a spell with Warrior, later helped co-write Gramm's first solo album.
Albums: *Black Sheep* (Capitol 1975), *Encouraging Words* (Capitol 1976).

Black Train Jack

New York hardcore troupe brought up in the CBGB's era, owing obvious stylistic debts to Agnostic Front, Murphy's Law *et al*, but with more of an ear for melody. Indeed the band centres around local legend Ernie, who had previously formed hardcore semi-legends Token Entry, remaining their drummer for several years. Switching to guitar, he was joined in Black Train Jack by former Token Entry roadies Brian (bass) and four octave, classically-trained vocalist, Rob. The line-up was completed by Nick (drums), recruited from the group's neighbourhood of Astoria, Queens. They took their name, meanwhile, from a touring incident when all four of them headed off-road in Brian's jeep and ended up in a sewage plant. Henry Rollins' *Hard Volume* was playing from the tape-deck, and as the group emerged, covered head to foot in silage, they adapted a line from 'Wreckage' which stated, appropriately, 'You've got a ticket on the blacktrain, Jack'. Their crunching guitar music was unveiled properly on a debut album co-produced with manager Anthony Countey, which crossed a street-perspective with the pop sentiments of Bow Wow Wow, or, closer to home, Descendents/All.
Album: *No Reward* (Roadrunner 1994).

Black Widow

A progressive rock band from Leicester, England, the group was formed as soul band Pesky Gee in 1966 by Jim Gannon (vocals/guitar/vibraphone) with Kay Garrett (vocals), Kip Trevor (vocals/guitar/harmonica), Zoot Taylor (keyboards), Clive Jones (woodwind), Bob Bond (bass) and Clive Box (drums). Pesky Gee made one album for Pye, before re-forming without Garrett as Black Widow. The band's first album and its elaborate stage act (choreographed by members of Leicester's Phoenix Theatre company) were based by Gannon on research into black magic rituals. Black Widow's 'Come To The Sabbat' appeared on the CBS sampler, *The Rock Machine Turns You On*, which was a Top 20 hit in 1969. The group toured throughout Europe and appeared at the Isle of Wight Festivals of 1969 and 1970. A debut album reached the Top 40 in the UK and after its release Romeo Challenger and Geoff Griffiths replaced Box and Bond. Later albums abandoned the witchcraft theme and were unmemorable. On *Three*, John Culley from Cressida replaced Gannon who later worked with Trevor on an abortive project to turn the *Black Widow* stage show into a Broadway musical. Gannon went on to play with songwriter Kenny Young in Fox and Yellow Dog before joining Sherbet and moving to Australia where he leads a club band called Bop Till You Drop. Trevor worked as a session singer and music publisher while Challenger plays drums for Showaddywaddy.
Albums: *Sacrifice* (CBS 1970), *Black Widow* (CBS 1971), *Three* (CBS 1971). Pesky Gee solo: *Exclamation Mark!* (Pye/Dawn 1969).

Blackeyed Susan

This US hard rock quintet were formed in 1991 by ex-Britny Fox vocalist Dean Davidson. With Erik Levy (bass), Rick Criniti (guitar), Tony Santoro (guitar) and Chris Branco (drums) completing the line-up, the band soon negotiated a deal with Mercury Records. They debuted with *Electric Rattlebone*, a blues-based set of hard rock songs that paid respect to Aerosmith, Humble Pie, Cinderella and the Rolling Stones in more or less equal portions. Although far from original, the material was delivered with conviction. Widely compared to fellow retro-rockers the Black Crowes, they have yet to emulate

that level of commercial or artistic stature.
Album: *Electric Rattlebone* (Mercury 1991).

Blackfoot

Southern USA rock practitioners Blackfoot initially comprised Rick Medlocke (guitar/vocals), Charlie Hargrett (guitar), Greg Walker (bass) and Jakson Spires (drums/vocals). The quartet shared common origins with Lynyrd Skynyrd (Medlocke co-writing four songs and singing lead on two tracks on the latter's platinum *First And Last*) and in turn offered a similar blues/rock-based sound, centred on their leader's confident playing. Medlocke himself was the grandson of Shorty Medlocke, a popular Jacksonville, Florida, bluegrass musician of the 50s, whose 'Train, Train' would be successfully covered by both Blackfoot and, in the 90s, Warrant. Rick took the name Blackfoot from his own native Indian tradition. Session pianist Jimmy Johnson produced Blackfoot's early work at the revered Muscle Shoals studio, but despite this impressive pedigree, the group was unable to translate an in-concert popularity, especially in the UK, into record sales. *Strikes*, the unit's first release for Atlantic/Atco, offered a heavier perspective, while the cream of their early work was captured live on *Highway Song*. After which the group bowed to record company pressure and pursued a more commercial approach which did not always convince. Ken Hensley, formerly of Uriah Heep, joined the line-up for *Siogo* and *Vertical Smiles*, and was eventually replaced by Bobby Barth of Axe, but Blackfoot was disbanded following the latter's release. The name was revived at the end of the decade with a revised line-up, with Medlocke now backed by Neal Casal (guitar), Rikki Mayer (bass; ex-Lizzy Borden) and Gunner Ross (drums). However, none of these survived for Blackfoot's 1994 album with new label Bullet Proof/Music For Nations, with Mark Woerpel (guitar/vocals; ex-Wardrive), Benny Rappa (drums/vocals) and Tim Stunson (bass) stepping in to support the venerable Medlocke. Rappa was replaced by ex-W.A.S.P. drummer Stet Howland for touring.

Albums: *No Reservations* (Island 1976), *Flyin' High* (Epic 1977), *Blackfoot Strikes* (Atco 1978), *Tomcattin'* (Atco 1980), *Maurauder* (Atco 1981), *Highway Song* (Atco 1982), *Siogo* (Atco 1983), *Vertical Smiles* (Atco 1984), *Medicine Man* (Loop 1990), *After The Reign* (Bullet Proof 1994).

Blackfoot Sue

Previously known as Gift and led by twin brothers Tom (bass/keyboards/vocals) and Dave Farmer (both

Blackfoot

b. 2 March 1952, Birmingham, England; drums), this group was completed by Eddie Galga (b. 4 September 1951, Birmingham, England; lead guitar/keyboards) and Alan Jones (b. 5 January 1950, Birmingham, England; guitar/vocals). The quartet scored a UK Top 5 hit in 1972 with 'Standing In The Road', but although its rhythmic performance appealed successfully to pop and rock audiences, Blackfoot Sue proved unable to retain such a deft balance. They scored a minor hit the same year with 'Sing Don't Speak', but heavier elements displayed on subsequent albums were derided by commentators viewing the group as a purely 'teeny-bop' attraction. Blackfoot Sue broke up following the release of *Strangers* which appeared in the midst of the punk boom, with several members going on to soft-rock outfit Liner.

Albums: *Nothing To Hide* (Jam 1973), *Gun Running* (Passport 1975), *Strangers* (Passport 1977).

Blackmore, Ritchie

b. 14 April 1945, Weston-Super-Mare, Avon, England. Guitarist Blackmore spent his early career in Mike Dee And The Jaywalkers before joining Screaming Lord Sutch And His Savages in May 1962. Within months he had switched to the Outlaws, a popular, principally instrumental, group which also served as the studio houseband for producer Joe Meek. Blackmore's exciting style was already apparent on the group's releases, notably 'Keep A Knockin'/'Shake With Me', and on sessions for Heinz and Mike Berry. The guitarist briefly joined the former singer's group, the Wild Boys, in 1964, and completed a suitably idiosyncratic solo single, 'Little Brown Jug'/'Getaway', before forging an erratic path as a member of Neil Christian's Crusaders, the Savages (again) and the Roman Empire. When a short-lived act, Mandrake Root, broke up in October 1967, Ritchie opted to live in Hamburg, but the following year was invited back to London to join organist Jon Lord in the embryonic Deep Purple. Although initially envisaged as an 'English Vanilla Fudge' the group quickly became a leading heavy metal act, with Blackmore's powerful, urgent runs an integral part of their attraction. He left the group in 1975, unhappy with their increasingly funk-based sound, and joined forces with the USA-based Elf to form Ritchie Blackmore's Rainbow. This powerful band became a highly popular hard rock attraction, but was blighted by its leader's autocratic demands. Multiple firings ensued as the guitarist searched for the ideal combination, but such behaviour simply enhanced a temperamental reputation. He was nonetheless involved in the Deep Purple reunion, undertaken in 1984, although animosity between the guitarist and vocalist Ian Gillan resulted in the latter's departure. Blackmore's prowess as a guitar 'hero' is undisputed, while his outstanding technique has influenced everyone from the N.W.O.B.H.M. bands to conventional modern rock outfits.

Compilations: *Ritchie Blackmore Volume 1: Early Sessions To Rainbow* (1990), *Ritchie Blackmore Volume 2* (1991), *Session Man* (RPM 1993).

Blackout

The origins of this Dutch quintet date back to 1983, when Godzilla were assembled from the remnants of the bands Van East and Zenith. Godzilla specialized in mainstream pop-rock material, but switched to 'speed-metal' and changed their name to Blackout in 1984. The band comprised Bas Van Sloten (vocals), Mannes Van Oosten (guitar), Jean Hoffman (guitar), Alfred Dreuge (bass) and Jan Boxem (drums). After securing a deal with Roadrunner Records, they released *Evil Game* the same year. This proved a workman-like collection of songs, constructed around heavy-duty, quick-fire riffs and dual lead soloing. Failing to make any significant impact, they disappeared from the scene within a year of the album's release.

Album: *Evil Game* (Roadrunner 1984).

Blackthorne

This band was assembled by former Balance/Alice Cooper/Meat Loaf guitarist Bob Kulick, with a line-up of former Quiet Riot members Chuck Wright (bass, ex-House Of Lords), Frankie Banali (drums, ex-W.A.S.P.) and Jimmy Waldo (keyboards, ex-Alcatrazz), along with former Rainbow/MSG/Alcatrazz singer Graham Bonnet. Such an experienced team inevitably attracted the supergroup tag, but they were keen to play down their collective past to allow the band to be judged on its own merits; and not merely as a short-term project. The Kulick-produced *Afterlife* saw the band ignore trends and play in a classic hard rock style, with Kulick's powerful guitar lines adding considerable weight to heavy, yet accessible material, which included a reworking of the Rainbow hit, 'All Night Long' (as Bonnet felt that the original version was 'not as heavy as it should have been').

Album: *Afterlife* (Music For Nations 1993).

Blackwych

This Irish metal band was put together by the three James brothers in 1985. Comprising vocalist Ciaran, guitarist Declan and bassist Niall, they recruited Bobby Tierney as a second guitarist, plus drummer Chris Andralinus to complete their line-up.

Influenced by Thin Lizzy, Mama's Boys and the New Wave Of British Heavy Metal, they made their debut on the Irish sampler, *The Green Metal Album*. Under-rehearsed when they entered the studio to record *Out Of Control*, the album proved a rudimentary affair, with flat, tuneless vocals. Reeling from poor reviews, the group split shortly afterwards.

Album: *Out Of Control* (Metal Masters 1986).

Blessed Death

This American doom/thrash/hardcore outfit was formed in New Jersey in 1984 by vocalist Larry Portelli and guitarist Jeff Anderson. Enlisting the services of Nick Florentino (guitar), Kevin Powelson (bass) and Chris Powleson (drums), they were initially influenced by Black Sabbath, Slayer and Anthrax. *Kill Or Be Killed* highlighted the remarkable vocal talent of Portelli whose range extended from a low guttural growl, to a high pitched banshee-like screech. Bass-laden riffs, thunderous drums and vitriolic guitar blasts bridged the ground between the doom and thrash metal factions. *Destined For Extinction* incorporated hardcore nuances reminiscent of Bad Brains and Jello Biafra. Produced by Alex Perialas and Raven drummer Rob Hunter, it was heralded as a great achievement, combining excellent sound quality with uncompromising and thought-provoking lyrics. Unfortunately, the positive reviews did not translate into commercial success, and nothing has been heard of the band since.

Albums: *Kill Or Be Killed* (1986), *Destined For Extinction* (1987).

Blind Date

This mysterious US pop-metal quartet first came together in San Francisco in 1975, with its members employing strange pseudonyms (their original choice of name was Ratz). Featuring Dane Bramage (vocals/bass/keyboards), Brad Billion (guitar/vocals), Arnie Baddie (guitar/vocals) and Pinky Chablis (drums), their music payed homage to Cheap Trick, Kansas and REO Speedwagon. Produced by Jeff Glixman, *Blind Date*, released in 1979, actually comprised songs written four years previously. The instrumental, 'Twin Engines', gained a certain degree of fame after being used as a theme tune to a European rock radio programme. The band faded back into obscurity after the album's release, despite signing with the Regency Records label.

Album: *Blind Date* (Windsong 1979).

Blind Fury

Formerly known as Satan, these UK purveyors of stereotypical black-metal changed their name, personnel and direction in 1984. Still based in Newcastle, Blind Fury comprised Lou Taylor (vocals), Steve Ramsey (guitar), Russ Tippins (guitar), Graeme English (bass) and Sean Taylor (drums). Eighteen months of writing and rehearsing led to *Out Of Reach*, a commercial hard rock album that played down their previous associations with witchcraft and the occult. Success proved elusive however, and they disbanded in 1986. Taylor had periods of activity with Persian Risk and Tour De Force, while the remainder of the band reformed Satan.

Album: *Out Of Reach* (Roadrunner 1985).

Blind Illusion

This group was formed in Richmond, California, USA, during 1978, by guitarist/vocalist Mike Biederman and bassist Les Claypool. An extensive series of personnel changes ensued over the next 10 years before the band released any product. With the addition of Larry Lalonde (guitar) and Mike Miner (drums), plus the return of Biederman and Claypool from stints with Blue Öyster Cult and Primus respectively, they finally entered a studio in 1988 to record *The Sane Asylum*. This was a techno-thrash affair, comparable in places to Megadeth and Metallica, but without the bite or ferocity.

Album: *The Sane Asylum* (Under One Flag 1988).

Bloodgood

This Christian heavy metal band was formed in Washington DC, USA, in 1985 by guitarist David Zaffiro and bassist Mike Bloodgood. With Les Carlsen (vocals) and Mark Welling (drums) completing the line-up, they were initially strongly influenced by Iron Maiden and Saxon. However, as time progressed, the band matured and diversified their sound considerably, with their latter albums courting Def Leppard, Whitesnake and Van Halen comparisons. Without doubt, the band have been the most credible white metal outfit on the circuit for many years. Kevin Whistler took over the drumstool from Welling in 1989, and guitarist David Zaffiro recorded a solo, *The Other Side*, the same year.

Albums: *Bloodgood* (Frontline 1985), *Detonation* (Frontline 1987), *Rock In A Hard Place* (Frontline 1988), *Out Of Darkness* (Intense 1989), *Hotter Than Hell* (Roadracer 1990).

Blue Cheer

Renowned as one of the world's loudest groups, Dickie Petersen (vocals/bass), Bruce Leigh Stephens (guitar) and Paul Whaley (drums) harboured dreams of a more conventional direction until seeing Jimi Hendrix perform at the celebrated Monterey Pop

Festival. Taking their name from a potent brand of the hallucinogenic drug, LSD. San Francisco's Blue Cheer made an immediate impact with their uncompromising debut album, which featured cacophonous interpretations of 'Summertime Blues' (US number 14) and 'Parchman Farm'. A second set, *Outsideinside*, was completed in the open air when the trio's high volume destroyed the studio monitors. Stephens left the group during the sessions for *New! Improved*, and his place was taken by former Other Half guitarist Randy Holden. *Blue Cheer* then unveiled a reconstituted line-up of Petersen, Burns Kellogg (keyboards), Bruce Stephens (bass) and Norman Mayall (drums/guitar). Stephens was then replaced by former Kak guitarist, Gary Yoder, for the quartet's fifth album, *The Original Human Being*. This impressive set featured the atmospheric, raga-influenced 'Babaji (Twilight Raga)', and is widely acclaimed as the group's most cohesive work. The band was dissolved during the early 70s, but reformed the following decade following an emotional reunion between Petersen and Whaley. Blue Cheer continued to pursue the former's bombastic vision and a 1990 release, *Highlights And Lowlives*, coupled the group with Anthrax producer Jack Endino. In the early 90s the band was reappraised, with many of the Seattle grunge rock bands admitting a strong affection for Blue Cheer's ground-breaking (not to mention earth-shaking) work.

Albums: *Vincebus Eruptum* (Philips 1968), *Outsideinside* (Philips 1968), *New! Improved! Blue Cheer* (Philips 1969), *Blue Cheer* (Philips 1970), *The Original Human Being* Philips (1970), *Oh! Pleasant Hope* (Philips 1971), *The Beast Is Back* (Important 1985), *Blitzkrieg Over Nuremburg* (Thunderbolt 1990). Compilations: *The Best Of Blue Cheer* (Phillips 1982), *Louder Than God* (1987), *Highlights And Lowlives* (Nibelung 1990).

Blue Murder

This project was masterminded by ex-Thin Lizzy and Tygers Of Pan Tang guitarist John Sykes, after he left Whitesnake. Enlisting the services of Tony Franklin on bass and Cozy Powell on drums (the latter quickly replaced by Carmine Appice) Sykes decided to record as a three-piece outfit. This followed a long and fruitless search for a suitable vocalist to front the band. The material included on their self-titled debut drew heavily on Sykes's Whitesnake legacy, but featured more extended compositions, with sophisticated arrangements and lengthy instrumental breaks. It was criticized upon its release, perhaps prematurely and unfairly, as it does contain a number of classy songs. Franklin would leave in 1991 following the recording of tracks for the band's second album.

Album: *Blue Murder* (Geffen 1989), *Nothin' But Trouble* (Geffen 1993).

Blue Öyster Cult

The genesis of Blue Öyster Cult lay in the musical ambitions of rock writers Sandy Pearlman and Richard Meltzer. Based in Long Island, New York, the pair put together a group - known variously as the Soft White Underbelly and Oaxaca - to perform their original songs. By 1969 the unit, now dubbed the Stalk-Forrest Group, had established around Eric Bloom (b. 11 December 1944; guitar/vocals), Donald 'Buck Dharma' Roeser (b. 12 November 1947; guitar/vocals), Allen Lanier (b. 25 June 1986; keyboards/guitar), Joe Bouchard (b. 9 November 1948; bass/vocals) and Albert Bouchard (drums). The quintet completed a single, 'What Is Quicksand', before assuming their Blue Öyster Cult appellation. Early releases combined Black Sabbath-styled riffs with obtuse lyricism which engendered an 'intelligent heavy metal' tag. Cryptic titles, including 'A Kiss Before The Redap' and 'OD'd On Life Itself' compounded an image - part biker, part occult - assiduously sculpted by Pearlman, whose clean production technique also removed any emotional inflections. 'Career Of Evil' from *Secret Treaties* - co-written by Patti Smith - showed an increasing grasp of commercial hooklines, which flourished on the international Byrds-sounding hit, '(Don't Fear) The Reaper'. Smith continued her association with the band on *Agents Of Fortune*, contributing to 'Debbie Denise' and 'The Revenge Of Vera Gemini'. A romantic companion to Allen Lanier, she later added 'Shooting Shark' to the band's repertoire for *Revolution By Night* and single release. Fantasy writer Michael Moorcock, meanwhile, would contribute to *Mirrors* and *Cultosaurus Erectus*. However, the release of the live *Some Enchanted Evening* had already brought the group's most innovative era to an end, despite an unlikely hit single, 'Joan Crawford Has Risen From The Grave', drawn from *Fire Of Unknown Origin* (which included another composition co-written with Moorcock). Sustained by continued in-concert popularity; notably on the *Black And Blue* tour with Black Sabbath, elsewhere predictability had crept into their studio work. Former road crew boss Rick Downey replaced Al Bouchard in 1981, while the following year Roeser completed a solo album, *Flat Out*, as the Cult's own recordings grew noticeably less prolific. *Imaginos* in 1988 was the band's re-interpretation of a Bouchard solo album which had never been released. Though of dubious origins, critics welcomed it as the band's best work for several years. Afterwards Joe Bouchard would leave the group to form Deadringer with Neal Smith (ex-Alice Cooper), Dennis Dunaway, Charlie Huhn and Jay Johnson. 1992 saw the group write and perform the majority of the soundtrack album to the *Bad Channels* horror film.

Albums: *Blue Öyster Cult* (Columbia 1971), *Tyranny And Mutation* (Columbia 1973), *Secret Treaties* (Columbia 1974), *On Your Feet Or On Your Knees* (Columbia 1975, live double album), *Agents Of Fortune* (Columbia 1976), *Spectres* (Columbia 1977), *Some Enchanted Evening* (Columbia 1978), *Mirrors* (Columbia 1979), *Cultosaurus Erectus* (Columbia 1980), *Fire Of Unknown Origin* (Columbia 1981), *Extraterrestial Live* (Columbia 1982), *The Revolution By Night* (Columbia 1983), *Club Ninja* (Columbia 1985), *Imaginos* (Columbia 1988). Compilations: *E.T.I.* (Columbia 1982, double album), *Career Of Evil - The Metal Years* (Columbia 1990). Donald Roeser solo: *Flat Out* (Portrait 1982). Video: *Live 1976* (1991).

Body Count

Ice-T's spin-off metal/hardcore band who rose to alarming fame via the inclusion of the track 'Cop Killer' on their debut Warner Brothers album. Other songs included titles like 'KKK Bitch' and 'Bowels Of Hell', but it was 'Cop Killer' which effectively ended Ice-T's tenure with his record company, and brought him the status of public enemy number one within the American establishment. Body Count made their debut during the inaugural Lollapalooza US festival tour in 1991, preceding the release of the album. The line-up was completed by Ernie-C (guitar), D-Roc (guitar), Mooseman (bass) and Beatmaster V (drums), whom Ice-T knew from Crenshaw High School in South Central. Although occasionally suffering from the misogynistic street language common to much US west coast rap, their material contained forceful anti-drug and anti-racism themes, particularly 'Momma's Gotta Die Tonight', which addressed the issue of institutionalised bigotry being passed down through successive generations. The band continued touring, and were fortunate enough to be given the opening slot on the Guns N'Roses/Metallica North American trek, exposing them to a more mainstream audience. In the meantime the Los Angeles Police Department were taking extreme exception to 'Cop Killer', a song which they viewed as dangerous and inflammatory ('I got my twelve guage sawed off, I got my headlights turned off, I'm 'bout to bust some shots off, I'm 'bout to dust some cops off'). The fury aimed at Ice-T, now officially number 2 in the FBI National Threat list, came thick and fast; Charlton Heston read out the lyrics to 'KKK Bitch' to astonished shareholders at Time Warner's AGM. 'Cop Killer' also appeared in the Warner's block-buster *Batman Returns*, which consequently faced calls for boycotts. Among the other opponents were Oliver North, president George Bush, and the Texas police force, who called for a nationwide boycott of Time Warner, including their Disneyland complex. The possibility of millions being wiped off Warners' share value had seen a U-turn. The pivotal moment came when death threats were received by record company employees, and the track was eventually replaced with a spoken word message from former Dead Kennedys' frontman and noted anti-censorship lobbyist, Jello Biafra. Undettered, Ice-T has resolved to continue in authority-tackling mode, and Body Count persist as an ongoing musical concern. Indeed, a second album, this time for new label Virgin, offered arguably far greater musical depth.

Albums: *Body Count* (Sire 1992), *Born Dead* (Virgin 1994).

Bolin, Tommy

b. 1 August 1951, Sioux City, Iowa, USA, d. 4 December 1976, Miami, Florida, USA. Tommy Bolin was a highly versatile progressive rock guitarist who successfully branched into fusion with considerable success and respect. Bolin became interested in music after seeing Elvis Presley in concert in 1956. He quickly learned to play Elvis songs on guitar and won local amateur contests. His first groups, Denny and the Triumphs and American Standard, found little or no success, and Bolin took work backing blues guitarist Lonnie Mack. In 1968 he formed Ethereal Zephyr, later shortened to Zephyr. Signed to Probe Records, their debut release was a US Top 50 album in 1969. Following the failure of their follow-up Bolin departed and formed the jazz/fusion group Energy with flautist Jeremy Steig, based in Colorado. Bolin also worked on an unreleased Steig album that also featured Jan Hammer and Billy Cobham. The latter then asked Bolin to play guitar on his *Spectrum* album in 1973 (which reputedly inspired Jeff Beck to try his hand at fusion). Having become a 'name' guitarist he was asked to replace Domenic Troiano (who himself had replaced Joe Walsh) in the James Gang. Bolin performed on their 1973 *Bang* album and the following year's *Miami*. After contributing to sessions for jazz drummer Alphonse Mouzon's *Mind Transplant* album, he was hired in 1975 by Deep Purple, to replace the departed Ritchie Blackmore.

He subsequently wrote and co-wrote many songs for the English hard-rock group's *Come Taste The Band*. During the early stages of that band's dissolution in late 1975 Bolin went solo, recording the critically-acclaimed *Teaser* for Nemperor Records and, the following year, *Private Eyes* for Columbia. In each case he toured with the Tommy Bolin Band to promote the albums. In December 1976, Bolin was found dead in a Miami hotel room, the victim of a drug overdose.

Albums: With Zephyr: *Zephyr* (Probe 1969), *Going Back To Colorado* (Warners 1971). With Billy Cobham: *Spectrum* (Atlantic 1973). With James Gang: *Bang* (Atco 1973), *Miami* (Atco 1974). With Alphonse Mouzon: *Mind Transplant* (1975). With Deep Purple: *Come Taste The Band* (Purple 1975). Solo: *Teaser* (Nemperor 1975), *Private Eyes* (Columbia 1976). Compilation: *The Ultimate... Tommy Bolin* (Geffen 1989).

Bolt Thrower

Deriving their name from a character in a popular war game story, Bolt Thrower are an extreme 'grindcore' rock band based in Birmingham, England. Comprising Al West (vocals), Gavin Ward (guitar), Barry Thomson (guitar), Jo Bench (bass) and Andy Whale (drums), they released two attention-grabbing demos, 'In Battle There Is No Law' and 'Concessions Of Pain'. They finally managed to gain a recording contract on the strength of their session for BBC DJ John Peel, broadcast on Radio 1 in January 1988. The same year their debut album emerged, featuring an aggressive fusion of hardcore and thrash with indecipherable vocals, this time from replacement vocalist Karl Willets. Titled after their first demo, the contents were housed on the Vinyl Solution imprint, after which the group would permanently move to Earache. *Realms Of Chaos* was the first result of this union, arriving in striking cover art from the Games Workshop empire, which stressed the band's fondness for both fantasy and militaria. Tours with the musically like-minded Napalm Death, Morbid Angel and Carcass brought these songs of conflict to a progressively wider audience. Their bludgeoning, wall of noise ethos was continued in *Warmaster*, by which time the press had developed the tag 'war metal' for Bolt Thrower. More intricate and less obvious was *The IVth Crusade*, with a more melodic style prevalent between aural assaults, and the Games Workshop art dropped in favour of a 19th Century painting by Delacroix. The production skills of Colin Richardson also brought new lustre and clarity to the band's sound. However, Bolt Thrower remained unable to affect their press stereotyping: 'In the beginning we were called a hardcore band, a thrash metal band. Then, this whole grindcore and death metal thing... we've always thought that none of those labels defined us, that we were always separate in a way'. Unhappy with this situation, their fourth album for Earache saw Willets and Whale provide their swansong performances. The remainder of Bolt Thrower elected to continue without them and in late 1994 recruited Martin Van Drunen (ex-Asphyx, Pestilence; vocals) and Martin Kearns (drums).

Albums: *In Battle There Is No Law* (Vinyl Solution 1988), *The Peel Sessions* (Strange Fruit 1988), *Realm Of Chaos* (Earache 1989), *Warmaster* (Earache 1991), *The IVth Crusade* (Earache 1992), *...For Victory* (Earache 1994).

Bombers

This Australian-based, hard-rock/boogie group were formed in 1989 by ex-Status Quo bassist Alan Lancaster. Recruiting John Brewster (guitar/harmonica), Steve Crofts (slide guitar), Tyrone Coates (vocals/saxophone) and Peter Heckenberg (drums), they signed to Polydor for whom their *Aim High* arrived in 1990. Musically, they meander through territory familiar to fans of Lancaster's former employers, with Coates's pumping saxophone and Crofts' slide guitar adding some individuality to the material. Largely ignored outside Australia, with the exception of diehard Quo fans, they are nevertheless a quality act.

Album: *Aim High* (Polydor 1990).

Bon Jovi

This commercial hard rock band was formed in New Jersey and fronted by Jon Bon Jovi (b. John Francis Bongiovi Jnr, 2 March 1962, Perth Sayreville, New Jersey, USA; vocals). His four co-conspirators were: Ritchie Sambora (b. 11 July 1959; guitar), David Bryan (b. David Rashbaum, 7 February 1962, Edison, New Jersey, USA; keyboards), Tico Torres (b. 7 October 1953; drums) and Alec John Such (b. 14 November 1956; bass). Bongiovi, of Italian descent, met Rashbaum at Sayreville High School, sharing a mutual interest in rock music. They soon joined eight other musicians in the R&B cover band Atlantic City Expressway. When Rashbaum moved to New York to study at the Juilliard School of Music, Bongiovi followed. Bluffing his way into the Power Station recording studios, he performed menial tasks for two years before Billy Squier agreed to produce his demo tape. One track, 'Runaway', was played on local radio and appeared on a local artist compilation album (his work would also grace oddities like the novelty track, 'R2D2 I Wish You A Merry Christmas'). Reunited with Rashbaum, he acquired the services of Sambora, an established session musician, Such (ex-Phantom's Opera) and Torres (ex-Knockouts). By July 1983, they had a recording contract with Polygram and support slots with Eddie Money and Z.Z. Top, the latter at Madison Square Gardens. Jon Bon Jovi's looks attracted immediate attention for the band, and he turned down the lucrative lead role in the dance film *Footloose* in order to concentrate on his music. Their debut album preceded a headline tour and supports with the Scorpions, Whitesnake and Kiss. *7800 Degrees Fahrenheit* was greeted with cynicism by the media, which was already reticent at the prospect of the band's manicured image and formularized heavy rock. A mediocre album only fuelled their scorn. The band responded with style. *Slippery When Wet* was the biggest selling rock album of 1987, although it originally appeared at the end of 1986. Two of its tracks; 'You Give Love A Bad Name' and 'Livin' On A Prayer', were US hits. Headlining the Monsters Of Rock shows in Europe, they were joined on stage by Gene Simmons and Paul Stanley (Kiss), Dee Snider (Twisted Sister) and Bruce Dickinson (Iron Maiden) for an encore of 'We're An American Band'. It merely served to emphasize the velocity with which Bon Jovi had reached the top of the rock league. The tour finally closed after 18 months in Australia, while the album sold millions of copies. When *New Jersey* followed, it contained 'Living In Sin', a Jon Bon Jovi composition which pointed to his solo future, although the song owed a great debt to his hero Bruce Springsteen. The rest of 1989 was spent on more exhaustive touring, before the band temporarily retired. As Jon Bon Jovi commented, it was time to 'Ride my bike into the hills, learn how to garden, *anything* except do another Bon Jovi record'. He subsequently concentrated on his solo career, married karate champion Dorothea Hurley and appeared in his first movie, *Young Guns II*. However, the commercial incentive to return to Bon Jovi would be hard to resist. *Keep The Faith*, though it saw locks shorn and the sound stripped down, was an impressive album, satisfying critics and anxious fans alike who had patiently waited almost four years for new material. If any had considered the group a spent commercial force then the success of the slick ballad, 'Always', a chart fixture in 1994, revealed no such decline. On the back of its success Bon Jovi would occupy the UK number 1 spot with the compilation set, *Crossroads*, amid rumours that bass player Alec John Such was about to be replaced by Huey McDonald. Bryan, meanwhile, released his first solo album, through Phonogram in Japan.

Albums: *Bon Jovi* (Vertigo 1984), *7,800 Degrees Fahrenheit* (Vertigo 1985), *Slippery When Wet* (Vertigo 1986), *New Jersey* (Vertigo 1988), *Keep The Faith* (Phonogram 1992). Compilation: *Crossroads - The Best Of* (Phonogram 1994). Jon Bon Jovi solo: *Blaze Of Glory* (Vertigo 1990). Richie Sambora solo: *Stranger In This Town* (Mercury 1991). David Bryan solo: *On A Full Moon* (Phonogram 1994).

Videos: *Breakout* (1986), *Slippery When Wet* (1988), *Dead Or Alive* (1989), *New Jersey* (1989), *Access All Areas - A Rock 'n' Roll Odyssey* (1990), *Crossroads - The Best Of* (1994).

Bonfire

This heavy metal band was formed in Ingolstadt, Germany. They came together in 1985 from the ashes of Cacumen, which had featured Claus Lessmann (vocals) and Hans Ziller (guitar) in their ranks. Other early members of Bonfire included Horst Makr Thorn (guitar) and a nameless drummer, who was sacked and replaced temporarily by Ken Mary from House Of Lords. Edgar Patrik (ex-Sinner, Tyran Pace and Paul Samson) joined in time for their third album, while Thorn was replaced by Angel Schaeffer (ex-Pretty Maids and Sinner) in 1988. An early introduction to UK audiences was convened at 1988's Reading festival. Afterwards they completed recording for their third album, *Point Blank*, produced by Michael Wagner, which gave them critical and commercial success in the UK and Europe. Despite this, Ziller departed leaving the 90s line-up comprising Lessmann, Schaeffer, Patrik, Michael Voss (guitar) and Jorg Deisinger (bass). Despite working in a similar vein to the Scorpions they failed to achieve the same sort of crossover appeal. Lessman split the band in 1993, teaming up with Ziller once more to form a folk rock group in the aftermath.

Albums: *Don't Touch That Light* (RCA 1986), *Fireworks* (RCA 1987), *Point Blank* (RCA 1989), *Knockout* (RCA 1991).

Bonham

This heavy rock band was founded by Jason Bonham (b. 1967, England), who was given his first drum kit at the age of four by his father, Led Zeppelin's John Bonham. After playing in local groups, Jason Bonham toured and recorded in 1987 with Jimmy Page and, after his father's death, performed with the surviving members of Led Zeppelin in New York in 1988. After stints with Airrace and Virginia Wolf he formed his own band with ex-Robert Plant's Honeydrippers guitarist Ian Hatton (b. 1962, Kidderminster, Worcestershire, England), John Smithson (b. 1963, Sussex, England; keyboards/bass)

Bon Jovi

and Daniel McMaster (b. 1968, Barrie, Ontario, Canada; vocals). The group's first single would be 'Wait For You', recorded with Alice Cooper's producer Bob Ezrin, augmented by an impressive debut album which took many cynical critics, unconvinced by the drummer's familial connections, by surprise.

Album: *The Disregard Of Time Keeping* (WTG/Epic 1989).

Bonnet, Graham

b. 12 December 1947, Skegness, Lincolnshire, England. Bonnet first garnered attention in 1968 as half of the Marbles, who enjoyed a UK Top 5 hit with the emotional 'Only One Woman'. Subsequent singles, both with the group and as a solo act, proved unsuccessful and he later turned to acting, starring in the film *Three For All*. Bonnet resumed recording in 1977 on Ringo Starr's Ring O Records, but although *Graham Bonnet* was not a major seller in Britain, the album achieved gold status in Australia. In 1979 Bonnet replaced Ronnie James Dio in Ritchie Blackmore's Rainbow. With his almost James Dean-like image, the choice of Bonnet as Dio's replacement was the subject of some consternation amongst the group's more traditional heavy metal fans. The singer was featured on *Down To Earth*, one of the group's most popular albums, and also graced the hit singles 'Since You've Been Gone' and 'All Night Long'. But Rainbow's legendary instability led to Bonnet's departure the following year. He resumed his solo career with *Line Up* in 1981 and earned himself a UK Top 10 single with 'Night Games'. Later he returned to collectivism by joining MSG for one album, *Assault Attack*, before relocating to the west coast of the US to become vocalist for Alcatrazz. 1993 saw him put together metal 'supergroup' Blackthorne, whose repertoire included an update of 'All Night Long'.

Album: *Graham Bonnet* (Ring O 1977), *Line Up* (Vertigo 1981).

Bootsauce

This Canadian funk/rap/metal crossover quintet were formed in Montreal in 1989. Comprising Drew Ling (vocals), Pere Fume (guitar), Sonny (guitar), Baculis (bass) and Rob Kazenel (drums), the sound they produced was not unlike a three-way hybrid of Earth Wind And Fire, Red Hot Chili Peppers and Weather Report. At times verging on *avant garde* and jazz-rock, they nevertheless possessed an irreverent sense of humour that set them aside from the mainstream. A riotous cover of Hot Chocolate's 'Everyone's A Winner', together with 'Sex Machine', were released on the single format to boost sales of the group's debut album.

Album: *The Brown Album* (Next Plateau 1991).

Borich, Kevin

b. New Zealand. Regarded as one of his continent's leading guitarists, Borich came to Australia with the New Zealand band La De Das in 1976. After a tour of the UK in 1980 other members left, leaving Borich as lead guitarist in a trio which he eventually renamed the Kevin Borich Express. The Express earned a reputation as one of the hardest working groups in the country, touring and playing incessantly. His style was influenced by Jimi Hendrix and Robin Trower, though his excellent guitar work often overshadowed his ordinary vocals and songwriting. On album his talent has not been adequately explored, although his guitar playing on the La De Das' version of 'All Along the Watchtower' was exemplary. An involvement with the hugely popular Party Boys cover band led to the gradual dissolution of his own band from 1983 onwards.

Albums: *Celebration* (Image 1976), *The Lonely One* (Image 1977), *Live* (Avenue 1979), *No Turning Back* (Mercury 1979), *Angels Hand* (Mercury 1980), *Kevin Borich Express* (Mercury 1980). With Renee Geyer: *Blues Licence* (1979). With Dutch Tilders: *The Blues Had A Baby And They Called It Rock And Roll* (1981). Compilation: *The Best Of Kevin Borich* (Image 1977).

Boston

As a result of home-made demos recorded by the enterprising Tom Scholz (b. 10 March 1947, Toledo, Ohio, USA) one of the finest AOR albums of all time was unwittingly created. The tapes impressed Epic Records and Scholz joined with friends, Fran Sheehan (b. 26 March 1949, Boston, Massachusetts, USA; bass), Brad Delp (b. 12 June 1951, Boston, Massachusetts, USA; guitar/vocals), Barry Goudreau (b. 29 November 1951, Boston, Massachusetts, USA; guitar) and Sib Hashian (b. 17 August 1949, Boston, Massachusetts, USA; drums). The name Boston was adopted and their first release was a US Top 3 album success which eventually sold 10 million copies worldwide and spent two years in the US charts. The memorable single, 'More Than A Feeling', was an instant classic, containing all the ingredients of adult-orientated rock; upfront guitar, powerful lead vocal with immaculate harmonies and heavy bass and drums. Two years later they repeated the formula virtually note for note with *Don't Look Back* (featuring the same futuristic space-craft masquerading as guitars on the cover) which also topped the US charts. During this time Scholz, formerly a product designer for the Polaroid Company, invented a mini-amplifier marketed as the Rockman. Goudreau would grow tired of the band's lengthy sabbaticals and release a solo album before quitting to form Orion. Never a prolific band, Boston in the guise of Scholz and Delp returned seven years later with *The Third Stage* which spawned two further US hit singles, 'Amanda' (which reached number 1) and 'We're Ready'. Those fans wanting to replace worn copies of the previous albums merely had to purchase this one. It too went straight to the top spot giving Boston a unique record in rock history, combining the biggest selling debut album with three number 1 albums and total sales of over 20 million copies.

Albums: *Boston* (Epic 1976), *Don't Look Back* (Epic 1978), *Third Stage* (MCA 1986), *Walk On* (MCA 1994). Solo album: Barry Goudreau: *Barry Goudreau* (Portrait 1980).

Boulevard

This Canadian band was formed in 1984 by saxophonist and ex-session musician Mark Holden. With the addition of David Forbes (vocals), Randy Gould (guitar), Andrew Johns (keyboards), Randy Burgess (bass) and Jerry Adolphe (drums), the six-man line-up was complete. Initially, they pursued a highly melodic AOR direction, similar to Toto and REO Speedwagon. *Into The Street* marked a move towards a more hard rock approach, with Foreigner, Bad Company and Bon Jovi influences. They have established a solid fan base in their native Canada, but this success has yet to be translated elsewhere, despite the efforts of Bryan Adams' manager Bruce Allen on their behalf.

Albums: *Boulevard* (MCA 1987), *Into The Street* (MCA 1990).

Bow Wow

The name translates literally into 'Barking Dog'; a fitting title for Japan's finest exponents of melodic heavy metal. Formed in 1976, the band comprised Kyoji Yamamoto (vocals/guitar), Mitsuhiro Saito (vocals/guitar), Kenji Sano (bass) and Toshiri Niimi (drums). Intriguingly, they incorporated classical Japanese musical structures within a framework of westernized hard rock. Influenced by Kiss, Led Zeppelin and Aerosmith, they released a sequence of impressive albums during the late 70s. Characterized by explosive guitar work and breathtaking arrangements, the only disappointment to western ears was the Japanese vocals, which doubtless restricted their international appeal. On *Asian Volcano*, their eleventh album released in 1982, the vocals were sung in English for the first time, but the band sounded uncomfortable with the transition. They played the Reading Festival the same year and were afforded an encouraging reception. Two subsequent shows at London's Marquee Club were recorded for the live album, *Holy Expedition*, which followed in 1983. At the end of that year the band changed their name to Vow Wow, adding an extra vocalist and keyboard player to pursue a more melodic direction. Lead guitarist Yamamoto has released two solo albums, representing an instrumental fusion of classical, rock and jazz styles; *Horizons* and *Electric Cinema* in 1980 and 1982 respectively. Outside the Far East success has continued to elude this first-class rock outfit, despite Whitesnake man Neil Murray joining for a short time in 1987.

Albums: *Bow Wow* (Invitation 1976), *Signal Fire* (Invitation 1977), *Charge* (Invitation 1977), *Super Live* (Invitation 1978), *Guarantee* (Invitation 1978), *The Bow Wow* (Invitation 1979), *Glorious Road* (SMS 1979), *Telephone* (SMS 1980), *X Bomber* (SMS 1980), *Hard Dog* (SMS 1981), *Asian Volcano* (VAP 1982), *Warning From Stardust* (VAP 1982), *Holy Expedition* (Heavy Metal 1983). As Vow Wow: *Beat Of Metal Motion* (VAP 1984), *Cyclone* (Eastworld 1985), *III* (Eastworld 1986), *Live* (Passport 1987), *V* (Arista 1987), *VIB* (EMI 1989), *Helter Skelter* (Arista 1989).

Boyzz

Influenced by Steppenwolf, Black Oak Arkansas and Lynyrd Skynyrd, the US-based Boyzz combined hard-driving rock 'n' roll, with southern-style boogie. With a strong leather-clad, biker image, their sole album, *Too Wild To Tame*, featured Dirty Dan Buck (vocals), Anatole Halinkovitch (keyboards), Gil Pini (guitar), Mike Tafoya (guitar), David Angel (bass) and Kent Cooper (drums). Unable to transform media interest into record sales, the band disintegrated soon after the album's release. Halinkovitch, Tafoya and Angel later went on to form B'zz.

Album: *Too Wild To Tame* (Epic 1978).

Brad

The involvement of Pearl Jam guitarist Stone Gossard in this one-off project inevitably and unfairly saw Brad tagged as Gossard's solo outing, when in reality it was a collaboration with two old friends, Pigeonhead/Satchel vocalist and keyboard player Shawn Smith and Satchel drummer Regan Hagar, plus bassist Jeremy Toback. The band was originally called Shame, but Los Angeles musician Brad Wilson held a copyright on the name which he was not prepared to give up, and the band subsequently

named themselves Brad in tongue-in-cheek retaliation. They entered the studio with only album opener 'Buttercup' written, and wrote, recorded and mixed *Shame* in just 17 days. The result was an enthralling and atmospheric work, blending funk, rock, jazz and soul with a melancholy lyrical air, and the fact that much of the material stemmed from studio jams lent the album a loose, laid-back feel. Gossard produced a largely understated performance which complemented Smith's piano and organ lines, backed by a solid economical groove from the rhythm section, while Smith's smoky, soulful vocals added another dimension to the band, and drew comparisons to Prince and Stevie Wonder amid a heap of deserved critical praise.
Album: *Shame* (Epic 1993).

Brats

This Danish quartet was formed in Copenhagen in 1979 by guitarists Michael Denner and Hank Sherman. Recruiting Yens (bass/vocals) and Monroe (drums), they signed to CBS and recorded a debut album the following year. Appropriately titled *1980*, it featured a dozen hard rock tracks, punctuated by some dazzling guitar work from Denner. The band fell apart shortly after the album's release, with guitarists Denner and Sherman joining forces with King Diamond (vocals), Timmy Grabber (bass) and Kim Ruzz to become Mercyful Fate. This corresponded with a change in direction towards satanic heavy metal.
Album: *1980* (CBS 1980).

Breathless

This six-piece melodic AOR band was formed in the USA's mid-west in 1978. Breathless was assembled by ex-Michael Stanley Band vocalist Jonah Koslen who, after a successful search, completed the line-up with Alan Greene (guitar), Mark Avsec (keyboards), Bob Benjamin (bass) and drummers Rodney Psycka and Kevin Valentine. They signed to EMI in 1979 and released two albums in the space of 18 months. Their lightweight, Kansas meets Toto-style melodic compositions failed to win an appreciative audience. The band split in 1981, with Koslen releasing a solo album, *Aces*, two years later.
Albums: *Breathless* (EMI 1979), *Nobody Leaves This Song Alive* (EMI 1980).

Breslau

This German hard rock quartet was formed in 1981 by vocalist Jutta Weinholt and guitarist Alex Parche. Adding Zweibel Truhol (bass) and Cay Wolf (drums), they recorded their first and only album the following

year. Influenced by Iron Maiden, Scorpions and Kiss, *Volksmusik* was notable for Weinholt's powerful and unusual vocal style. The music was derivative, however. Unable to generate any interest, the band disintegrated a few months later. Weinholt reappeared in 1988 as lead vocalist with Zed Yago.
Album: *Volksmusik* (1982).

Briar

This pop-rock quartet was formed in Birmingham, England, during 1983 by Kevin Griffiths (vocals/bass) and Daren Underwood (guitar). With Dave Fletcher (guitar) and Dean Cook (drums), they released a self-financed single that was given considerable airplay by BBC Radio 1 disc jockey, Peter Powell. A Radio 1 live session was followed by a recording contract with Heavy Metal Records. *Too Young* emerged in 1985, an over-produced affair that was full of lightweight guitar, high-pitched harmonies and inoffensive lyrics. The album flopped and the band were forced to return to the club circuit. *Take On The World*, a self-financed cassette was released in 1986, which eventually led to a new contract with CBS. Half the album comprised a selection of cover versions which included Richie Valens's 'La Bamba' and Sister Sledge's 'Frankie', which may have suggested a note of desperation sinking in.
Albums: *Too Young* (Heavy Metal 1985), *Take On The World* (CBS 1986), *Crown Of Thorns* (CBS 1988).

Bricklin

This American, six-piece rock band was founded by the Bricklin brothers in 1986. Featuring Brian Bricklin (guitar/keyboards), Scott Bricklin (vocals/keyboards), Ian Cross (guitar/keyboard/vocals), James Goetz (bass/vocals) and Eddie Bader (drums), the band secured a contract with A&M Records in 1987. Adopting a commercial approach, their music was comparable in style to Toto, Loverboy, It Bites and Kansas. Although technically excellent and superbly produced, their two albums lacked individuality and distinction.
Albums: *Bricklin* (A&M 1987), *Bricklin II* (A&M 1989).

Brighton Rock

This highly popular Canadian band who followed in the footsteps of Don Dokken and Loverboy, came together in 1984 in Toronto where they stabilized their line up with Gredd Fraser (guitar), Gerry McGhee (vocals), John Rogers (keyboards), Steve Skreeb (bass) and Mark Cavarzan (drums). Recording a self-financed EP to attract attention, the policy proved a success as Warner Brothers re-issued the debut. In 1987 they released their first full album which won critical acclaim - however, it was its successor which put them into the arenas, at least in their native territory. The group eventually dispersed in 1992 when they failed to convert domestic popularity into worldwide standing.

Albums: *Young, Wild And Free* (Warners 1987), *Take A Deep Breath* (Warners 1988), *Love Machine* (Warners 1991).

Britny Fox

This American 'glam-metal' quartet was formed in Philadelphia in 1987 by vocalist 'Dizzy' Dean Davidson (ex-World War III drummer) and former Cinderella guitarist Michael Kelly Smith. With the addition of bassist Billy Childs and ex-Waysted drummer Johnny Dee, they signed to CBS and released their debut album the following year. This was an amalgam of AC/DC, Mötley Crüe and Quiet Riot influences, characterized by Davidson's raucous snarl, and included an inspired cover of Slade's 'Gudbuy To Jane', plus nine originals. *Boys In Heat* saw the band mellow a little; the make-up was discarded and replaced with a rough, street-wise rock 'n' roller image. Davidson's vocals were further refined and the material edged, significantly, towards Cinderella's style. Britny Fox toured with Bon Jovi and Alice Cooper, but were unable to convert successful concert performances into album sales. Davidson quit in 1990 and went on to form Blackeyed Susan, with Tommy Paris being drafted in as his replacement almost a year later. *Bite Down Hard* emerged in 1991, with the songs following a much heavier direction. Against expectations, the band had made a triumphant return, and looked poised for greater success in the second phase of their career. However, it was not to be, and Britny Fox were finally laid to rest in early 1993.

Albums: *Britny Fox* (Columbia 1988), *Boys In Heat* (Columbia 1989), *Bite Down Hard* (East West 1991).

Brocas Helm

Influenced by the New Wave Of British Heavy Metal, Brocas Helm were formed in 1983 and comprised vocalist/guitarist Robbie Wright, bassist Jim Schumacher and drummer Jack Hays. Drawing inspiration from Iron Maiden, Venom and Angelwitch, they specialized in identikit heavy metal adapted from these sources. The emphasis was on uptempo numbers, which were let down by weak vocals and an average rhythm section. They disbanded during 1986.

Albums: *Into Battle* (First Strike 1984), *Undefeated* (First Strike 1985).

Broken Bones

This British hardcore band was formed in Stoke-on-Trent, England, during 1983 by ex-Discharge guitarist Tony 'Bones' Roberts. Recruiting brother Terry on bass, vocalist Nobby and drummer Cliff, they closely followed the metal/punk crossover approach of Bones's former group. With controversial lyrics and a rigidly formularized approach, they have progressed little since their inception. After a period of inactivity, they returned in 1989 with Quiv and D.L. Harris as new faces on lead vocals and bass respectively. *Losing Control* appeared shortly afterwards, a vitriolic blast of angst-ridden hardcore, but again, little different from previous servings.

Albums: *Dem Bones* (Fall Out 1984), *Live 100 Club* (Fall Out 1985), *F.O.A.D.* (Fall Out 1987), *Bone-Crushers* (Fall Out 1987), *Losing Control* (Heavy Metal 1989), *Trader In Death* (Heavy Metal 1990), *Stitched Up* (Music For Nations 1991).

Video: *Live At Leeds* (1984).

Broken Hope

Thoroughly brutal musicians based in Illinois, USA, comprising Joe Ptacek (vocals), Jeremy Wagner (guitar), Ed Hughes (bass) and Ryan Stanek (drums). The group was formed in 1989 when Stanek first approached Wagner at a party, with the simple goal of becoming the heaviest of death metal acts on the local scene. Nursing a four song demo tape, which was traded throughout the fertile underground metal network, the founding members realised an addition to their sound was required and pulled in Brian Griffin as second guitarist, who abandoned his budding career as a studio engineer at Wave Digital. It was here that the group entered the studio in the summer of 1990 to record a second demo, which cemented previous impressions and led to several offers from independent labels. They eventually signed with new local imprint Grind Core International, for whom they made their long-playing debut in February 1992 with *Swamped Inn Gore*. However, representatives of the more financially viable Metal Blade Records witnessed the band at the Milwaukee Metalfest VI, and when Broken Hope lost faith in their first home and looked for new offers, Metal Blade stepped in. The resulting *Bowels Of Repugnance* reinstated the band's belief in matching ferocious musicianship with clinical production standards.

Albums: *Swamped Inn Gore* (Grind Core International 1992), *Bowels Of Repugnance* (Metal Blade 1994).

Bronz

This band were the first to be launched on the US market by Bronze Records. The five musicians that co-operated in this marketing ploy were from Bath, England, and comprised ex-Nightwing vocalist Max Bacon, guitarists Chris Gouldstone and Shaun Kirkpatrick, bassist Paul Webb and drummer Carl Matthews. In spite of using four producers and an embarrassingly large budget, their debut album was a ramshackle affair that was inferior to the well-established outfits of the genre. After one album, the band split, with Bacon going on to achieve success later with GTR.

Album: *Taken By Storm* (Bronze 1984).

Brujeria

In reality, the mysterious Brujeria is an extreme death metal side project for Fear Factory guitarist Dino Cazares and his friends and colleagues. The band name comes from the black magic which some Mexican drug dealers use to inspire fear in religious locals. The publicity surrounding the release of *Matandos Gueros* painted a similar picture, alleging that the band were in fact seven psychotic Mexican drug barons, Satanists to a man, led by vocalist Juan Brujo, and featuring three bassists (Guero Sin Fe, Fantasma, Hongo) for a particularly heavy bottom end. The line-up was completed by Asesino on guitar, Grenudo on drums and the mysterious Jr Hozicon/Director Diabolico. The original album cover featured a photograph of a severed head, allegedly that of another Mexican drug dealer, but it was relegated to the inner sleeve and replaced by a black sleeve which warned of the graphic nature of this and other photographs contained therein. The album itself was a fierce collection of short, sharp songs which echoed early Napalm Death and Carcass in style, with lyrics growled exclusively in Spanish, and seemed to offer a similar purpose to that served by Stormtroopers Of Death on the New York hardcore scene by adding a touch of humour and parody to the death/grind network with its deliberately grandiose approach. Meanwhile, suspected contributors such as Cazares, Fear Factory vocalist Burton C. Bell, and Faith No More bassist Bill Gould continued to fearfully deny any involvement.

Album: *Matandos Gueros* (Roadrunner 1993).

Brutal Truth

During a break in activities with Nuclear Assault, bassist Dan Lilker began working with guitarist Brent McCarty and drummer Scott Lewis to indulge his passion for hardcore. Joined by vocalist Kevin Sharp, the band created their own brand of high-speed hardcore with industrial and death metal elements. Finding this music more to his liking, Lilker left his old outfit to concentrate fully on Brutal Truth (the trio's past work had also included stints with S.O.D., Anthrax, Winter and J.C.T.). Signing with 'grindcore' specialists Earache, the band released *Extreme Conditions Demand Extreme Responses*, a collection of exceptionally fast and fierce material with political themes, to a positive reception, and received further good press for their live shows, playing US dates with labelmates Napalm Death, Carcass and Cathedral. A European tour with Fear Factory followed, leaving a trail of damaged PA systems behind them as well as Lewis, who was replaced by Rich Hoak. The group then teamed up with Coventry based techno act Larcency for the 'Perpetual Conversion' single, which also featured a cover version of Black Sabbath's 'Lord Of This World'. The equally venomous *Need To Control* came in an unusual format - a boxed set containing 5, 6, 7, 8 and 9-inch vinyl, with two additional covers of Celtic Frost's 'Dethroned Emporer' and Pink Floyd's 'Wish You Were Here'. Lilker also worked part-time in another side-project, Exit-13, as the parent band embarked on a tour of America, Australia and Japan.

Albums: *Extreme Conditions Demand Extreme Responses* (Earache 1992), *Need To Control* (Earache 1994).

Brutality

One of the most popular acts to emerge out of Florida, USA's burgeoning death metal scene, Brutality had actually developed over several years following formation in 1988. As is typical of the genre, they subsisted in these early days via the demo network, though there were also two singles ('Hell On Earth', 'Sadistic') for European label Nuclear Blast. These introduced Brutality's trademark sound, aggressive, purging rhythms topped by Scott Reigel's distinctive vocals. The violence of the sound, more fully visited on debut album *Screams Of Anguish* and the subsequent *When The Sky Turns Black*, was all-encompassing.

Albums: *Screams Of Anguish* (Nuclear Blast 1993), *When The Sky Turns Black* (Nuclear Blast 1994).

Bruzer

Bruzer were a short-lived collaboration between established US musicians playing a mixture of hard rock and techno-pop in the style of Cheap Trick. The line-up comprised Paul Frank (vocals), Jeff Steele (bass), Vinnie Appice (drums, ex-Derringer, later Black Sabbath), Mitchell Froom (keyboards, later of

Gamma) and Rick Ramirez (guitar, ex-Striker). *Round One*, released in 1982, was well received, but the band splintered, before the interest shown could be consolidated into commercial success.

Album: *Round One* (Handshake 1982).

Budgie

This hard rock group was formed in Cardiff, Wales, by John Burke Shelley (b. 10 April 1947, Cardiff, South Glamorgan, Wales; bass/acoustic guitar/lead vocals) and Ray Phillips (drums) in 1968. Joined by Tony Bourge (b. 23 November 1948, Cardiff, South Glamorgan, Wales; lead guitar/vocals) the trio established a substantial following in the south Wales college and club circuit and were subsequently signed to MCA Records. Plying their trade in a basic, heavy riffing style, the standard was set with the first single, charmingly entitled 'Crash Course To Brain Surgery'. The vagaries of early 70s British album artwork were typified by the treatment given to Budgie's releases and promotional material, depicting a ludicrous image of a budgerigar variously posed dressed as a fighter pilot (staring nobly out into the far horizon), a Nazi Gestapo officer, or as a squadron of fighter budgies flying in formation, tearing into combat. Founder member Phillips quit in 1974 before the recording of their fourth album and was replaced by Pete Boot (b. 30 September 1950, West Bromwich, Staffordshire, England), who in turn departed that year before Steve Williams took over. The exiled drummer would form Ray Phillips' Woman back in Wales, then Tredegar in 1982. With the success of *In For The Kill*, Budgie won over a wider audience, although they were held in higher esteem in Europe during this period. Their sixth album, *If I Was Brittania I'd Waive The Rules*, their first on A&M Records, was the last to feature Bourge, who left in 1978, joining Phillips in Tredegar. He was replaced by former George Hatcher Band guitarist John Thomas. The group's popularity grew in the USA resulting in Budgie concentrating on touring there for two years. Returning to Britain, and now signed to RCA, Budgie found themselves fitting in well with the new heavy rock scene, and despite being labelless for much of the mid-80s, their reputation and influence on a younger generation of musicians brought them consistent work until Shelley wound up the group in 1987. He subsequently worked with a new trio, Superclarkes. Phillips would use Budgie's original *nom de plume*, Six Ton Budgie, for a new line-up featuring his son, Justin, on guitar, who still play out regularly with versions of his former group's standards.

Albums: *Budgie* (MCA 1971), *Squawk* (MCA 1972), *Never Turn Your Back On A Friend* (MCA 1973), *In For The Kill* (MCA 1974), *Bandolier* (MCA 1975), *If I Was Brittania I'd Waive The Rules* (A&M 1976), *Impeckable* (A&M 1978), *Power Supply* (Active 1980), *Nightflight* (RCA 1981), *Deliver Us From Evil* (RCA 1982). Compilation: *Best Of* (MCA 1982).

Buffalo

Buffalo emerged in Sydney, Australia, in 1970 and soon picked up a healthy following of heavy rock fans. Signed by the prestigious Vertigo label, the band's albums sold slowly but steadily enough to retain the interest of the label. The group received adverse press owing to the overtly sexist nature of the covers of their first three albums and also for some of the song lyrics (eg 'Skirt Lifter'), which limited their appeal. Buffalo were an anomaly among bands in Australia during the 70s in that they were as popular in Europe, particularly France, as they were in their homeland. The outfit were musically akin to the likes of Black Sabbath and Deep Purple while retaining their own rock sound, enhanced by Norm Roue's slide guitar playing and the powerful performances of vocalist Dave Tice. Eventually the dearth of original members led the band to split, after recording five albums. The first of which went gold three years after release. Bassist Pete Wells, played slide guitar in Rose Tattoo with Angry Anderson, while Tice joined original drummer, Paul Balbi, in the Count Bishops in the UK.

Albums: *Dead Forever* (Vertigo 1972), *Volcanic Rock* (Vertigo 1973), *Only Want You For Your Body* (Vertigo 1974), *Mother's Choice* (Vertigo 1976), *Average Rock And Roller* (Vertigo 1977). Compilation: *Best Of* (Vertigo 1980).

Bulldozer

This death metal trio was formed in Milan, Italy, during 1984 by classically trained guitarist Andy Panigada and bassist/vocalist A.C. Wild. With the recruitment of drummer Don Andras, they recorded *The Day Of Wrath* in 1985. This slice of frantic thrash was hamstrung by out-of-phase vocals and a muddy production. They built up a small but loyal cult following, gaining notoriety for their extreme style and profane bad taste. Two more albums followed a similar pattern, before 1988's *Neurodeli* played down the satanic emphasis in the lyrics. Presumably no more will be heard from Bulldozer with Wild's appointment as Metal Master's label representative.

Albums: *The Day Of Wrath* (Roadrunner 1985), *The Final Separation* (Roadrunner 1986), *IX* (Roadrunner 1987), *Neurodeli* (Roadrunner 1988).

Bulletboys

This American hard rock quartet was formed in 1987 by Mike Sweda (guitar, ex-King Kobra) and Marq Torien (vocals, ex-Ratt). They were joined by Lonnie Vincent (bass) and Jimmy D'Anda (drums) and took their musical brief from AC/DC, Van Halen and Montrose. Championed by producer Ted Templeman, they signed to Warner Brothers and recorded their self-titled debut album the following year. Torien's flamboyant persona courted comparisons with Dave Lee Roth, while Sweda's guitar histrionics were based on a style first made famous by Eddie Van Halen. *Freakshow* saw the band broaden their musical horizons and incorporate blues and funk influences into the basic hard rock structures.

Albums: *Bulletboys* (Warners 1988), *Freakshow* (Warners 1991), *Za-Za* (Warners 1993).

Burning Tree

Hailing from Los Angeles, USA, this three-piece unit specialized in early 70s blues-based power rock. Marc Ford (guitar/vocals), Mark Dutton (bass/vocals) and Doni Gray (drums) re-invented, re-hashed and re-interpreted the riffs, licks and solos first unleashed by artists including Eric Clapton, John Mayall and Jimi Hendrix. In essence they were revivalists using Cream as a musical template to work from. They celebrated rather than simply duplicated, breathing new life into well-worn arrangements by a combination of sheer conviction and the application of technology. It was not enough to bring them the longevity associated with the great blues artists however, with Gray joining ex-Quireboys' singer Spike in a new project, God's Hotel.

Album: *Burning Tree* (Epic 1990).

Burtnick, Glen

After working with Helmet Boy, Jan Hammer and Neil Schon, Glen Burtnick (b. USA; vocals/guitar/keyboards) declined the offer to join Bon Jovi in favour of working on a solo career. Securing a deal with A&M Records, he employed session musicians to help record his debut, *Talking In Code*. A sophisticated and highly-polished selection of pop-rock anthems, the album was infused with elements of funk and soul. On *Heroes And Zeroes*, Bruce Hornsby, Anton Fig and Neil Schon made guest appearances, but the songs covered mainly the same ground as before. In 1990 he joined Styx in place of Tommy Shaw, to record their comeback album, *Edge Of The Century*.

Albums: *Talking In Code* (A&M 1986), *Heroes And Zeroes* (A&M 1987).

Burzum

Founded in 1991 by Norwegian Satanist Count Grishnakh (real name Varg Vikernes), Burzum became one of the leading lights in Scandinavia's black metal revival of the early 90s. Largely a solo project, Grishnakh composes, sings and plays almost all of Burzum's material himself. The project first surfaced under the name of Uruk Hai in 1987. Significantly, the name Uruk Hai is taken from JRR Tolkien's fantasy classic, *The Lord Of The Rings*. In it, the Uruk Hai are a particularly brutal tribe of orcs (the orcs are the subhuman villains of the book). Burzum is the orcish language, while Grishnakh is a treacherous orc that plays a small, but pivotal role in proceedings. Count Grishnakh, who takes his name from this fictional character, used Tolkien's epic struggle between good and evil as a model for his own brand of Satanism, casting himself among the hordes of darkness. Grishnakh would go on to collaborate with Euronymous, godfather of the Scandinavian black metal revival. The Count played for Euronymous' band Mayhem, released material on his Deathlike Silence label, and played a leading hand in the curious hate cult known as the Black Metal Circle. Meanwhile Burzum recordings were receiving increasing acclaim on the heavy metal underground, with their tortured mix of overheated guitars, screamed vocals and strange, ambient, keyboards. In the Spring of 1993 Grishnakh, along with a number of other prominent members of the Black Metal Circle, was arrested for a series of church burnings. Then, in late Summer, Grishnakh was arrested for the brutal murder of Euronymous. He was subsequently convicted in 1994, but showed no remorse, instead relishing the notoriety the crime attracted. Sentenced to 21 years (the maximum possible under Norwegian law) Grishnakh continues to record increasingly strange and twisted material in gaol. Satanism and the works of Tolkien now take a back seat to the right wing occultism and Viking paganism which are currently his chief obsessions, with many of his lyrics now sung in Old Norse.

Albums: *Burzum* (Deathlike Silence 1992), *Aske* (Deathlike Silence 1993), *Hvis Lyset Tar Oss* (Misanthropy 1994), *Det Som Engang Var* (Misanthropy 1994).

Bush, Stan

This US singer first came to prominence with country/rock band Boulder. Bush went solo in 1983, recording a self-titled album that invited comparisons to the sophisticated pop-rock style of Billy Squier and John Parr. He linked up with the occasional band Barrage in 1987 to pursue a more hard rock direction.

Albums: *Stan Bush* (Columbia 1983), *Stan Bush & Barrage* (Scotti Bros/Polydor 1987), *Every Beat Of My Heart* (1993).

Buzzov.en

Revelling in their own musical and aesthetic ugliness, Buzzov.en formed from the ashes of Sewer Puppet in the early 90s. Based in North Carolina, and featuring Kirk Fisher (vocals/guitar), Brian Hill (bass) and Ashley Williamson (drums), they played anywhere dumb enough to entertain them, until by 1991 they had raised the money for a studio recording of their first demo tape, *Buttrash*. One of the songs from that demo, 'Wound', would be released as a single by a friend setting up his own, local label. However, the cassette also ended up in the hands of John Yates, founder of San Francisco imprint Allied Recordings. Sending the group back to the studio, he had them record the *Wound* EP (though this time it did not include the song of similar title). On the back of this, and east coast gigs where the music was largely distinguished by its savagery and, particularly, volume, Buzzov.en embarked on building a cult audience. They completed their debut album in San Francisco with Billy Anderson (who had previously lent his production expertise to projects by Steel Pole Bath Tub, Melvins and others). After experimenting with a second guitarist the group made Buddy Apostolis a permanent fixture, and hit the road for some 200 gigs inside a year. A show at 1993's CMJ Music Convention led to them signing to Roadrunner through Monte Conner, and the following year saw them back in the studio with Billy Anderson, recording their second 'studio' album in just nine days (the first, however, had only taken three). Content to play anytime, anywhere, Buzzov.en, with their astonishing, GG Allin-inspired stage displays, have yet to capture that capability on record, but are getting closer all the time.

Albums: *To A Frown* (Allied Recordings 1992), *Sore* (Roadrunner 1994). Compilations: *Music For The Proletariat* (Very Small 1993), *Vinyl Retentive* (Very Small 1993, double album).

Byron, David

b. David Garrick, 29 January 1947, Essex, England, d. 28 February 1985. Byron began his music career as vocalist with the Stalkers, an Essex-based act which, by 1969, had evolved into Uriah Heep. Although subjected to critical denigration, the group became one of the 70s leading hard rock/heavy metal attractions, thanks in part to the singer's powerful delivery. In 1975, Byron completed a solo album, *Take No Prisoners*, as excessive alcohol consumption put his position within the line-up under increasing pressure. He was fired the following year, but hopes of an artistic rebirth with Rough Diamond proved ill-founded and this highly-touted attraction featuring Dave Clempson broke apart within a year. Bereft of a regular group, he completed *Baby Faced Killer*, but the set appeared during the height of the punk boom, and was not a commercial success. A similar fate befell the ensuing Byron Band whose ill-focused *On The Rocks* did little to further their leader's progress. They folded soon after its release, after which the disconsolate vocalist attempted to sustain his career, with increasingly faltering results. He died in 1985 as a result of a heart attack.

Albums: *Take No Prisoners* (1975), *Baby Faced Killer* (1977), *This Day And Age* (1980). As the Byron Band: *On The Rocks* (Creole 1981), *Bad Widow* (Rockport 1984).

Bystander

This American melodic rock quartet was formed in 1981. Influenced by Loverboy and Kansas, the band comprised Andy Kiely (vocals/bass), Bucky Naughton (guitar/vocals), John E. Allison (guitar/vocals) and Jimmy Callaghan (drums). Allison and Callaghan arrived after the release of their album, replacing Mike Weaver and Stanley Steele. The self-financed *Not So Innocent* was an admirable debut and surpassed the efforts of many of the more well-established acts in the genre.

Album: *Not So Innocent* (1987).

C

Cacophony

This speed metal band was formed in the USA in 1986, built around the nucleus of up-and-coming guitar wizards Marty Friedman and Jason Becker. Recruiting drummer Atma Anur and ex-Le Mans vocalist Peter Marrino, they debuted with *Speed Metal Symphony*, a predominantly instrumental album, that fused classical, blues and hard rock styles. Friedman and Becker then went on to record individual solo albums in a similar vein, before commencing work on another band project. *Go Off*, released in 1989, saw the arrival of Jimmy O'Shea and Kenny Stavropoulos on bass and drums, respectively. This album

reinforced the band's hi-tech instrumental approach, and featured complex passages where the guitars of Friedman and Becker duelled for supremacy. The album was a commercial failure and Cacophony subsequently dissolved in 1990, with Stavropoulos joining Starship, Becker teaming up with Dave Lee Roth and Friedman being recruited by Megadeth.
Albums: *Speed Metal Symphony* (Roadrunner 1987), *Go Off* (Roadrunner 1989).

Cadillac Tramps

From Orange County, California, USA, the Cadillac Tramps did not take too kindly to their press tag of 'bar-drunk brawly blues band', claiming they offered a much more sophisticated sound - yet that description was close enough to reality to warrant repetition. Comprising Gabby (lead vocals), Brian Coakley (guitar/vocals), Johnny Wickersham (guitar/vocals), Warren Renfrow (bass) and Dieter (drums), they riffed their way to prominence via an acclaimed, sweaty live show that earned a solid reputation for the band on the Southern Californian club circuit, with their admirers including Eddie Vedder of Pearl Jam (who personally filmed one show). Their third album and first for Music For Nations' subsidiary Bullet Proof was headed by a title-track which concerned Coakley's HIV positive friend.
Album: *It's All Right* (Bullet Proof 1994).

Cancer

This band emerged from Telford, Shropshire, and quickly established themselves as the UK's leading death metal exponents. *To The Gory End* saw the trio of John Walker (vocals/guitar), Ian Buchanan (bass) and Carl Stokes (drums) adopt a traditional death metal sound with suitably gory and offensive imagery, but the addition of American guitarist James Murphy (ex-Death/Obituary) expanded both Cancer's live sound and their approach to songwriting. The Scott Burns-produced *Death Shall Rise* showed considerable progression, but Murphy's continued residence in the USA proved impractical and he departed to form Disincarnate. Barry Savage (b. Barry White) proved to be an able replacement, adding an individual and less Americanized edge to the Cancer sound. The new maturity in evidence on *The Sins Of Mankind* brought not only overdue respect but also a major deal with East West. This made them the first death metal band to sign to a major deal (discounting single territory or distribution contracts afforded Morbid Angel and Carcass). Their first album for East West, *Black Faith*, was the second to be recorded with Simon Efemy.
Albums: *To The Gory End* (Vinyl Solution, 1990),

Death Shall Rise (Vinyl Solution 1991), *The Sins Of Mankind* (Vinyl Solution 1993), Black Faith (East West 1995)..

Candlemass

This Swedish doom metal quintet formed in 1985. Comprising Messiah Marcolin (vocals), Lars Johansson (guitar), Mats Bjorkman (guitar), Leif Edling (bass) and Jan Lindh (drums), their style combined elements of Black Sabbath, Black Widow and Mercyful Fate. Marcolin's eccentric appearance gave the band a visual focus; dressed in a monk's habit, his deep, bellowing tones added a touch of mystique to their live performances. *Nightfall,* their most accomplished work, fused crushing rhythms with delicate, neo-classical interludes to startling effect. *Tales Of Creation* saw the band afforded a larger recording budget with new label Music For Nations. However, their approach had become rather formularized by this stage, and although the album was technically superior to earlier efforts, the songs left a distinct feeling of *déjà-vu*. A live album followed in an attempt to recapture lost ground. It soon became apparent that the band were trapped in a creative *cul de sac*, with their initial followers continuing to move on to other things. A situation doubtless grasped by Marcolin when he left in 1991, to be replaced by Thomas Wilkstrom (ex-Talk Of The Town). Edling for his part would go on to form Abstrakt Algebra.
Albums: *Epicus, Doomicus, Metallicus* (Black Dragon 1986), *Nightfall* (Axis 1987), *Ancient Dreams* (Axis 1988), *Tales Of Creation* (Music For Nations 1989), *Live* (Music For Nations 1990), *Chapter Six* (Music For Nations 1992).

Cannata

Jeff Cannata first came to prominence under the name Arc Angel in 1983. Following five years of producing, arranging and guesting on a variety of projects, he finally took enough time out in 1988 to record *Images Of Forever*. Being responsible for the vocals, guitar, keyboards, bass and drums, the album served as testimony to the man's remarkable musical ability. The material invited comparisons with the best works of Boston, Starcastle and Angel, as did a subsequent set finally released five years later.
Album: *Images Of Forever* (CBS 1988), *Watching The World* (1993).

Cannibal Corpse

This controversial death metal act was formed in Buffalo, New York, by Chris Barnes (vocals), guitarists Bob Rusay and Jack Owen, Alex Webster

(bass) and Paul Mazurkiewicz (drums). The band adopted an almost cartoon-like approach to their material, which stood out even from the extreme grotesqueries of the death scene, and Cannibal Corpse have thrived on the controversy created by offensive song titles such as 'Meat Hook Sodomy', 'Necropedophile' and the infamous 'Entrails Ripped From A Virgin's Cunt', and their equally offensive lyricism. The band's cover art has not been immune to criticism either, with some retailers refusing to carry both *Butchered At Birth* and *Tomb Of The Mutilated* until gruesome Vincent Locke cover paintings were replaced. Musically, the band have made steady progress from their *Eaten Back To Life* debut, refining a death metal assault to match the song titles, although Rob Barrett replaced Rusay on *The Bleeding*. The band were also exposed to a major audience via a cameo appearance in the *Ace Ventura: Pet Detective* movie, playing 'Hammer Smashed Face'.
Albums: *Eaten Back To Life* (Metal Blade 1990), *Butchered At Birth* (Metal Blade 1991), *Tomb Of The Mutilated* (Metal Blade 1992), *Hammer Smashed Face* (Metal Blade 1993, mini-album), *The Bleeding* (Metal Blade 1994).

Captain Beyond

Based in Los Angeles, this Anglo-American 'supergroup' was formed in 1972 around Rod Evans (b. 19 January 1947, Slough, Berkshire, England; vocals, ex-Deep Purple), Bobby Caldwell (drums, ex-Johnny Winter) and two former members of Iron Butterfly, Larry 'Rhino' Rhinehardt (b. 7 July 1948, Florida, USA; guitar) and Lee Dorman (b. 15 September 1945, St. Louis, Missouri, USA; bass). Although *Captain Beyond* established the unit's hard-rock style, this initial line-up proved incompatible and Caldwell was replaced by Marty Rodriguez for *Sufficiently Breathless*. The departure of Evans precipitated a lengthy period of inactivity but in 1976 the remaining trio was joined by Willy Daffern (vocals), Reese Wynans (keyboards; ex-Stevie Ray Vaughan) and Guille Garcia (percussion). This final version broke up following the release of *Dawn Explosion*.
Albums: *Captain Beyond* (Capricorn 1972), *Sufficiently Breathless* (Capricorn 1973), *Dawn Explosion* (Capricorn 1977).

Carcass

This Liverpool, England, hardcore/death metal group

Cannibal Corpse

was formed in 1987. The band, all vegetarians, comprised Jeff Walker (vocals/bass; ex-Electro Hippies), Bill Steer (vocals/guitar; ex-Napalm Death) and Ken Owen (drums). The line-up was later enlarged with the addition of a second guitarist, Michael Amott (ex-Carnage). Their approach is characterized by morbid death-grunts over a barrage of chaotic, bass-dominated music. Carcass's lyrical content primarily concerns itself with mutilation, vomiting, putrefaction, intestinal rupturing and steaming entrails - all dealt with in strict medical and anatomical terminology - 'Intenacious, intersecting/Reaving fats from corporal griskin...Skeletal groats triturated, desinently exsiccated'. Carcass signed to Columbia Records following *Heartwork*, which dramatically reduced previous 'gore' content, incorporating a more modern image complete with H. R. Giger artwork. They also introduced ex-Devoid guitarist Carlo Regedas (the third such addition since 1990), and toured the UK with Body Count, then the US with Pitch Shifter. For a band whose appeal initially seemed destined to remain of cult interest, Carcass now appear to be on the threshold of commercial possibility.

Albums: *Reek Of Putrefaction* (Earache 1988), *Symphonies Of Sickness* (Earache 1989), *Necrotism-Descanting The Insalubrious* (Earache 1991), *Heartwork* (Earache 1993).

Carnivore

This American heavy metal band was formed by ex-Fallout duo Louie Batteaux (alias Lord Petrus T; drums) and Peter Steele (vocals/bass) in New York in 1983. With the addition of guitarist Keith Alexander, they attracted media interest by basing their image on a *Mad Max II*/post apocalyptic scenario. Dressed in animal skins, they achieved a degree of notoriety with their racially naïve lyrics. Their musical compositions, revealed on a self-titled debut, relied on basic thrash metal with little originality. Marc Piovanetti replaced Alexander on 1987's *Retaliation*, which resulted in a marked improvement in the band's guitar sound. However, this was not sufficient to enable them to compete realistically with first division acts such as Slayer, Testament or Anthrax. Piovanetti left in 1988, to join Crumbsuckers.

Albums: *Carnivore* (Roadrunner 1986), *Retaliation* (Roadrunner 1987).

Cathedral

This excellent UK doom/grind band was formed by vocalist Lee Dorrian after his departure from Napalm Death, with bassist friend Mark Griffiths, former Acid Reign guitarists Garry Jennings and Adam

Lehan and drummer Ben Mockrie. This line-up was in place for the release of a four-track demo, *In Memorium*. Interestingly, this included a cover of Pentagram's 'All Your Sins' - a band which Cathedral would later draw members from. Dorrian's vocals changed remarkably from his Napalm days to suit a style which drew heavily from early Black Sabbath and late 60s/early 70s underground rock. *Forest Of Equilibrium* was an impressive debut, with ex-Penance/Dream Death drummer Mike Smail standing in for the departed Mockrie. A permanent replacement was then found in Mark Ramsey Wharton in time for the *Soul Sacrifice* EP, as Cathedral's live ability was amply demonstrated on the 'Gods Of Grind' UK tour with Carcass, Entombed and Confessor, and dates with Trouble and the Obsessed. A US tour with Brutal Truth, Napalm Death and Carcass followed, and although Griffiths departed, Cathedral signed a US deal with Columbia. *The Ethereal Mirror*, produced by Trouble, Danzig and Mick Jagger collaborator Dave Bianco, deservedly received a wealth of critical acclaim, and the band toured the UK with Sleep and Penance in tow before recording the *Statik Majik* EP with Cronos guitarist Mike Hickey guesting on bass. This included the 23 minute epic 'The Voyage Of The Homeless Sapien'. However, Lehan and Wharton left after a US tour with Mercyful Fate, and a new line-up with former Pentagram members Victor Griffin (drums) and Joe Hasselvander (guitar) was assembled for a Black Sabbath support tour. However, personality clashes led to Hasselvander's premature departure. Cathedral re-emerged as a quartet in late 1994 with Dorrian and Jennings joined by Scott Carlson (ex-Repulsion; bass) and Dave Hornyak (drums).

Albums: *Forest Of Equilibrium* (Earache 1991), *The Ethereal Mirror* (Earache 1993).

Cats In Boots

This short-lived Japanese-American group came together when guitarist Takashi 'Jam' Ohashi and bassist Yasuhiro 'Butch' Hatae, of the successful Tokyo-based band Seiki Matsu, recruited vocalist Joel Ellis, a native of Cleveland, Ohio, and drummer Randy Meers, originally from Houston, Texas, from the remains of Los Angeles-based Merry Hoax. The American members relocated to Tokyo to record demos, and these tapes were released as a mini-album which shot rapidly to number 1 on the Japanese indie chart. The resultant interest saw the quartet sign to EMI. The Mark Opitz-produced *Kicked And Klawed* was a raucous and thoroughly enjoyable debut, with the band's raw, trashy hard rock drawing comparisons to Mötley Crüe, Aerosmith and Vain, and was a huge

Carcass

success in Japan, reaching number 3. However, despite great reviews and considerable *MTV* airplay, album sales were only moderate elsewhere, and with the almost simultaneous departure of both Ellis and their recording deal, Cats In Boots disintegrated.

Albums: *Demonstration - East Meets West* (Bronze 1988, mini-album), *Kicked And Klawed* (EMI 1989).

Celtic Frost

Formed in Switzerland in 1984 from the ashes of the thrash metal-inspired Hellhammer, Celtic Frost's focal point has always been Thomas Gabriel Warrior (guitar/vocals). Together with Martin Eric Ain (bass) and Stephen Priestly (drums), the group's 1984 debut was a thrash metal landmark, with guttural vocals splintering the grim musical tapestry. Ain was replaced by bassist Dominic Steiner for *To Mega Therion*, while Reed St. Mark became drummer for *Emperors Return*. It is their third album, *Into The Pandemonium,* which has become Celtic Frost's legacy to the metal world, a mjaor work which has loosely been described as '*avant garde* thrash'. It saw the return of Ain as well as the introduction of second guitarist Ron Marks. *Cold Lake* was much more mainstream and featured the return of Priestly (drums), alongside Curt Victor Bryant (bass) and Oliver Amberg (guitar). Following a glam rock bent, it proved too much of a departure from their natural sound to be a success, as fans deserted them in droves. The band's popularity slid dramatically, with a slight resurgence after the much improved *Vanity/Nemesis*. The 90s saw St. Mark rejoin after a spell with Mind Funk, with the band promising new material in the tradition of their early efforts.

Albums: *Morbid Tales* (Noise 1984), *To Mega Therion* (Noise 1985), *Emperor's Return* (Noise 1986), *Into The Pandemonium* (Noise 1987), *Cold Lake* (Noise 1988), *Vanity/Nemesis* (Noise 1990). Compilations: *The Celtic Frost Story* (EMI 1990), *Parched With Thirst Am I, And Dying (1984-1992)* (Noise 1992, double album).

Video: *Live At The Hammersmith Odeon* (1989).

Cement

Cement were formed by ex-Faith No More vocalist Chuck Moseley after one too many physical and verbal confrontations with his former employers (apparently taking the stage in pyjamas for their

Celtic Frost

Town & Country club date on their second UK tour in May 1988 was the last straw). Afterwards he served time as replacement for HR in Bad Brains, but this was another ill-starred assignation. He then worked as frontman for Haircuts That Kill before emerging with Cement in 1993. This more permanent outfit were formed in Los Angeles with Sean Maytum (ex-Beer Nuts; guitar), Senon Williams (bass) and Doug Duffy (ex-Pygmy Love Circus; drums). They gigged heavily on the west coast before producing a 13 track self-titled album for Dutch East India Records in 1993 (on World Service, through Rough Trade, in the UK). Critics suggested 'Old Days' from the set may have concerned Faith No More, but this aside did not detract from a solid hard rock effort.

Albums: *Cement* (Dutch East India 1993), *The Man With The Action Hair* (Rough Trade Germany 1994).

Cemetary

Formed in Sweden in 1989, after two well-received demos (*Incarnation of Morbidity* and *Articulus Mortis*) Cemetary secured a record deal in 1992. The resultant album, *An Evil Shade of Grey*, was a competent, but unremarkable, exercise in death metal. *Godless Beauty* saw Cemetary develop beyond the stylistic restraints of the genre, and incorporate new, fresher elements into their sound. Dominant amongst these were gothic rock influences and sampled dialogue from horror films. The resultant effect was a powerful and melodramatic musical exploration of depression and suicide. *Black Vanity* is a continuation of this death metal/gothic rock crossbreed, and features the line-up of Mathias Lodmalm (vocals/guitar), Anders Iwers (guitar), Thomas Jofesson (bass) and Markus Nordberg (drums).

Albums: *An Evil Shade of Grey* (Black Mark 1992), *Godless Beauty* (Black Mark 1993), *Black Vanity* (Black Mark 1994).

Centaurus

This US, blues-based rock quartet was formed in 1977 by guitar virtuoso Nick Paine. Enlisting the services of Nick Costello (bass), Louis Merlino (vocals) and Joey Belfiore (drums), they took their musical lead primarily from Led Zeppelin and Aerosmit. Paine's guitar work, certainly, was structured on the style made famous by Jimmy Page. Their sole release is noticeably derivative, but the excellent production and rawness of the band's delivery makes it more than worthwhile. They split soon after the album hit the racks, with Costello going on to join Toronto.

Album: *Centaurus* (Azra 1978).

Chain Reaction

Not the minor US act from whom Aerosmith would draw membership, this Canadian hard rock/techno-pop quartet was formed in 1981 by Warren Barvour (guitar) and Phil Naro (vocals). Recruiting Ray Lessard (bass) and John Livingston (drums), they secured a contract with Attic Records the following year. Influenced by Van Halen, REO Speedwagon and Foreigner, they recorded *X Rated Dream*; a collection of pop-rock anthems, lifted only by some explosive guitar bursts from Barvour. Naro left to work with Talas in 1983 and the band subsequently disintegrated.

Album: *X Rated Dream* (Attic 1982).

Champion

When David Byron quit Rough Diamond in 1977, the remaining band members recruited US vocalist Garry Bell as replacement and subsequently changed their name to Champion. With former Humble Pie guitarist Dave Clempson, ex-Wings drummer Geoff Britton plus Damon Butcher (keyboards) and Willy Bath (bass) completing their line-up, Champion's music never lived up to the promise suggested by their impressive pedigree. Picked up by Epic Records, they released a self-titled album in 1978 of blues-based rock. Failing to attract media attention, they disbanded shortly after the disc was released.

Album: *Champion* (Epic 1978).

Chastain, David T.

This highly productive, new-age guitar virtuoso emerged from Cincinnati, USA. As well as releasing solo albums under his own name, he recorded with CJSS and Chastain, to provide outlets for the vast amount of material that he composes. After leaving Spike in 1984 with bassist Mike Skimmerhorn, the duo formed the two semi-permanent outfits CJSS and Chastain, with the latter being a vehicle for the faster, louder and heavier material. With the help of ex-Rude Girl vocalist Leather Leone and drummer Fred Coury, *Mystery Of Illusion* was recorded under the Chastain moniker in 1985. The predominantly uptempo approach, with raunchy vocals and fluid guitar work, was well received by the critics, and consequently Chastain became David's major concern. A series of albums followed in quick succession, each one an identikit version of the debut. Eight high-speed rockers and two ballads were the typical formula. Ken Mary (ex-Alice Cooper) took over the drumstool in 1986 as Chastain's work rate reached overload. *Instrumental Variations* and *Within The Heat* indicated a move towards a jazz-rock style. *For Those Who Dare* saw Chastain, the band, back in the studio again. It comprised the same formularized approach as before. There is no doubt that David Chastain has sacrificed much of his original credibility in repeatedly releasing average material, though at least his 90s works, *Elegant Seduction* and *Next Planet Please*, have offered some technical respite and variation. The latter, again recorded with regular bass collaborator David Harbour, also saw him utilize a Roland GR-1 guitar synthesizer for the first time.

Albums: As David T. Chastain: *The 7th Of Never* (Roadrunner 1987), *Instrumental Variations* (Roadrunner 1987). As Chastain: *Mystery Of Illusion* (Shrapnel 1985), *Ruler Of The Wasteland* (Roadrunner 1986), *The Voice Of The Cult* (Roadrunner 1988), *Within The Heat* (Roadrunner 1989), *For Those Who Dare* (Roadrunner 1990), *Elegant Seduction* (Music For Nations 1991), *Next Planet Please* (Music For Nations 1994).

Cheap 'N' Nasty

This melodic UK rock 'n' roll quartet were formed in 1990 by former Hanoi Rocks guitarist Nasty Suicide (b. Jan Stenfors). Recruiting Alvin Gibbs (bass; ex-UK Subs), Timo Caltio (guitar) and Les Riggs (drums), they signed to China Records the following year. Debuting with *Beautiful Disaster*, the band lacked image and direction, and Suicide seemed uncomfortable in his dual role of guitarist and vocalist. Specializing in mid-paced rockers, which relied heavily on vocal harmonies to carry the melody lines, the most distinctive cut was undoubtedly the album's title-track. Suicide would soon return to a neo-Hanoi Rocks berth in a new band formed with Sam Yaffa and Michael Monroe, Demolition 23.

Album: *Beautiful Disaster* (China 1991).

Cheap Trick

One of rock's most entertaining (if least consistent) attractions, Cheap Trick formed in Chicago, Illinois, USA, in 1973. Rick Neilsen (b. 22 December 1946, Rockford, Illinois, USA; guitar/vocals) and Tom Petersson (b. Peterson, 9 May 1950, Rockford, Illinois, USA; bass/vocals) began their careers in various high-school bands, before securing a recording deal as members of Fuse. This short-lived outfit folded on completing a debut album, and the duo subsequently formed a new group with Thom Mooney and Robert 'Stewkey' Antoni from the recently disbanded Nazz. Mooney was subsequently replaced by drummer Brad Carlson (aka Bun E. Carlos, b. 12 June 1951, Rockford, Illinois, USA), and with the departure of 'Stewkey', the initial Cheap Trick line-up was completed by vocalist Randy 'Xeno' Hogan. He in turn was replaced by Robin Zander (b.

23 January 1952, Loves Park, Illinois, USA; guitar/vocals), a former colleague of Carlson in the short-lived Toons. Relocated to America's mid-west, the quartet followed the gruelling bar-band circuit before a series of demonstration tapes secured a recording deal. Although *Cheap Trick* is generally regarded as a disappointment, it introduced the group's inventive flair and striking visual image. The heart-throb good-looks of Zander and Petersson clashed with Carlos' seedy garb, while Neilsen's odd-ball costume - baseball cap, bow-tie and monogrammed sweater - compounded this unlikely contrast. Having spent a frenetic period supporting Queen, Journey and Kiss, Cheap Trick completed a second collection within months of their debut. *In Color* offered a smoother sound in which a grasp of melody was allowed to flourish and established the group's ability to satisfy visceral and cerebral demands. It contained several engaging performances, including 'I Want You To Want Me', 'Hello There' and 'Clock Strikes Ten', each of which became in-concert favourites. *Heaven Tonight* consolidated the group's unique approach while 'Surrender' contained the consummate Cheap Trick performance, blending the British pop of the Move with the urgent riffing of the best of America's hard rock. *At Budokan* followed a highly-successful tour of Japan, and this explosive live set became the quartet's first platinum disc, confirming them as a headline act in their own right. However, *Dream Police* added little to the sound extolled on the previous two studio releases, and indeed the title song was originally recorded for the group's debut album. Producer George Martin did little to deflect this sterility on *All Shook Up*, while *Found All The Parts*, a mini-album culled from out-takes, suggested internal problems. A disaffected Petersson left the group in 1982, but although Pete Comita initially took his place, the latter quickly made way for Jon Brandt. Neither *One On One*, nor the Todd Rundgren-produced *Next Position Please* halted Cheap Trick's commercial slide, but *Standing On The Edge* offered hopes of a renaissance. A 1986 recording, 'Mighty Wings', was used on the soundtrack of the successful *Top Gun* film, while the return of Petersson the same year re-established the group's most successful line-up. *Lap Of Luxury* achieved multi-platinum status when an attendant single, 'The Flame', topped the US chart in 1988 while *Busted* scaled similar heights, confirming Cheap Trick's dramatic resurrection as a major US act.

Albums: *Cheap Trick* (Epic 1977), *In Color* (Epic 1977), *Heaven Tonight* (Epic 1978), *Cheap Trick At Budokan* (Epic 1979), *Dream Police* (Epic 1979), *Found All The Parts* (Epic 1980, mini-album), *All*

Cheetah

Shook Up (Epic 1980), *One On One* (Epic 1982), *Next Position Please* (Epic 1983), *Standing On The Edge* (Epic 1985), *The Doctor* (Epic 1986), *Lap Of Luxury* (Epic 1988), *Busted* (Epic 1990), *Woke Up With A Monster* (Warners 1994), *Budokan 2* (Epic/Sony 1994, rec 1978). Compilations: *The Collection* (Castle 1991), *Greatest Hits* (Epic 1992). Video: *Every Trick In The Book* (1990).

Cheetah

Having played in numerous bands since the late 70s London born sisters Lyndsay and Chrissie Hammond went to work as music researchers before signing up with the Albert Productions Company in their adopted homeland of Australia. Under the wing of Vanda & Young they began to work on original material with session musicians who had previously backed Maggie Bell in Midnight Flyer. The resulting 1982 album, *Rock N' Roll Women*, was largely ignored for its music content as press attention focused on the fact that they were, indeed, 'Rock N' Roll Women'. Their fate as serious musicians sealed, not least by their own choice of title, and unable to shake off the public perception of them which resulted, the band splintered. Lyndsay later formed Rockhouse but their album remained 'in the can'.
Album: *Rock N' Roll Women* (Epic 1982).

Child, Desmond, And Rouge

This commercially minded and chart-oriented US soft rock outfit was formed in 1975 by keyboardist Desmond Child, backed by an array of musicians. With college friends Maria Vidal, Myriam Naomi Vaille and Diana Graselli completing the line-up as vocalists, they attracted the interest of Kiss guitarist Paul Stanley. Signing to Capitol Records, their debut album released in 1978 was a *pot-pourri* of styles, including elements of pop, rock, funk, blues and soul. The follow-up, *Runners In The Night*, adopted a more hard rock stance, but was also met with indifference. The band became redundant as Child decided to concentrate on writing and production, rather than actually playing. He has composed for Cher, Michael Bolton, Bon Jovi, Alice Cooper, Kiss and Jimmy Barnes among others. 'You Give Love A Bad Name' and 'Livin' On A Prayer', co-written with Bon Jovi, and the Kiss million-seller, 'I Was Made For Loving You', have been his greatest successes to date. Child made a return to recording in 1991 for Elektra Records, which despite the competent performance again failed to set the charts alight.
Albums: *Desmond Child And Rouge* (Capitol 1979), *Runners In The Night* (Capitol 1980). As Desmond Child: *Discipline* (Elektra 1991).

China

This melodic rock band was formed in Switzerland during 1987 by guitarists Freddy Laurence and Claudio Matteo. Recruiting Math Shiverow (lead vocals), Marc Lynn (bass) and John Dommen (drums), they signed with Phonogram the following year. Influenced by Thin Lizzy, Europe and Scorpions, their self-titled debut appeared in 1988 to a positive media response. It was characterized by Shiverow's high-pitched but note perfect vocals and the dual guitar attack of Matteo and Laurence. *Sign In The Sky*, recorded two years later, saw ex-Krokus guitarist Patrick Mason take over on vocals, and Brian Kofmehl replace Lynn on bass. It was a more mature album in several respects with the songwriting displaying greater depth and a full, crisp production, courtesy of Stephan Galfas. A live mini-album followed but, as yet, China have failed to receive the recognition that their talents deserve.
Albums: *China* (Vertigo 1988), *Sign In The Sky* (Vertigo 1990), *Live* (Vertigo 1990, mini-album).

China Sky

This group was formed in Florida, USA, in 1987 by ex-Danny Joe Brown and Molly Hatchet guitarist John Ingram. With the addition of vocalist Ron Perry and bassist Richard Smith, they specialized in rough-edged AOR, with a distinctly southern influence. They recorded a self-titled debut in 1988, which attracted attention due to the fact that 'The Last Romantic Warrior' was reminiscent of Derek And The Dominos' 'Layla'. The band split up soon after the album's release.
Album: *China Sky* (Parc 1988).

Chinatown

This UK band started life as a glam-rock outfit known as Chinastreet and comprised vocalist Steve Prangell, guitarists Pat Shayler and Danny Gwylym, John Barr (bass) and Steve Hopgood (drums). In 1981 they changed their name to Chinatown and switched to a hard rock style similar to Thin Lizzy and UFO. Their sound was characterized by Prangell's stratospheric vocals and the dual guitar interplay of Shayler and Gwylym. After one album, recorded live, the band split up with only drummer Steve Hopgood resurfacing later. He went on to play with Persian Risk and Paul Di'Anno's Battlezone.
Album: *Play It To The Death* (Airship 1981).

Chrome Molly

This hard rock/thrash quartet was formed in Leicester, England, during 1984, by vocalist Steve Hawkins and guitarist John Antcliffe. With the addition of Nick Wastell (bass) and Chris Green (drums), they recorded their debut, *You Can't Have It All*, the following year. This was a competent collection of mid-paced rockers. Mark Godfrey replaced Green on drums and Tim Read took over from Antcliffe on lead for the recording of their third album, *Angst*. This collection was afforded a bigger budget, as the band had now been picked up by the I.R.S. label. It included an excellent cover of Squeeze's 'Take Me I'm Yours', but the remainder was much as before. Joined by second guitarist Andy Barrott (ex-Baby Tuckoo), they landed the support slot on Alice Cooper's 1988 UK tour, including a date at Wembley Arena. Their live reputation was indeed a formidable one, embossed by Hawkins' fetish for placing a cordless microphone down his cycling shorts. But this did little to stimulate album sales, and Chrome Molly were hastily dropped by their label. Far from disheartened, they began writing new material and eventually secured a contract with Music For Nations. *Slaphead* appeared in 1990, to yet another flat response from the music media despite an evident increase in quality.

Albums: *You Can't Have It All* (Powerstation 1985), *Stick It Out* (Powerstation 1987), *Angst* (IRS 1988), *Slaphead* (Music For Nations 1990).

Cianide

Death metal band with origins in Chicago, Illinois, USA. Represented by Mike Perun (bass/vocals), Scott Carroll (guitar) and Jeff Kabella (drums), Cianide are a power trio who, like so many others from their genre, made their initial impression via the thriving demo cassette network. *Funeral* in 1990 and *Second Life* in 1991 brought the group's crushing musicianship and steadfast exhortations on the nature of decomposition to the world, until the group went overground in 1992 with *The Dying Truth*. Building on their influences (Hellhammer, Celtic Frost, Venom, Death), *A Descent Into Hell* delivered a further caustic epistle, including a cover of Canadian death metal crew Slaughter's 'Death Dealer'.

Albums: *The Dying Truth* (1992), *A Descent Into Hell* (Bullet Proof 1994).

Cinderella

This Philadelphia-based band were formed in 1983 by guitarist/vocalist Tom Keifer and bassist Eric Brittingham with Michael Kelly Smith (guitar) and Tony Destra (drums), although the latter pair departed in 1985 to form Britny Fox, and were replaced by Jeff LaBar (ex-White Foxx) and Jody Cortez respectively. Polygram signed Cinderella on Jon Bon Jovi's recommendation after he witnessed a particularly wild Philadelphia club gig. Fred Coury replaced Cortez after the recording of *Night Songs*, which, while hardly original, ably demonstrated Keifer's songwriting abilities. The band's AC/DC-Aerosmith style proved popular, with raucous live shows helping produce hits in 'Shake Me' and 'Nobody's Fool' as the debut shot up the US charts. *Long Cold Winter* established a more individual sound as Cinderella adopted a classy blues-rock style which ideally suited Keifer's throaty tones, and 'Gypsy Road', 'Don't Know What You Got (Till It's Gone)', and 'Coming Home' continued their ascent. *Heartbreak Station*, however, was less successful as the band added further R&B elements for a Rolling Stones feel, though 'Shelter Me' was another hit. Coury's departure (ex-Shadow King drummer Kevin Valentine briefly replaced him) and throat problems for Keifer meant a lengthy break before *Still Climbing*, a strong comeback which followed the more powerful approach of *Long Cold Winter*, with John Mellencamp drummer Kenny Aaronoff filling in as Cinderella auditioned new drummers over the Internet. The replacement would be Kevin Conway.

Albums: *Night Songs* (Polygram 1986), *Long Cold Winter* (Polygram 1988), *Heartbreak Station* (Polygram 1990), *Still Climbing* (Polygram 1994).
Video: *Night Songs* (1987).

Circus Of Power

Emerging from the gutter of New York's late 80s lower East Side, this heavily tattooed quartet deliver a unique and uncompromising brand of blues-based heavy metal. Alex Mitchell's paint-stripping vocals coupled with Ricky Beck-Mahler's grungy guitar riffs are the band's trademarks, whilst Gary Sunshine (bass) and Ryan Maher (drums) provide the necessary ammunition in the rhythm section. Distilling influences such as the Dictators, AC/DC, Motörhead and white blues guitarists like Johnny Winter and Rick Derringer, they purvey solid, raunchy rock 'n' roll, underpinned by a keen sense of melody and dynamics. The lyrical subject matter concerns itself with 'wrong side of the street' narratives, reflecting their origins in the drug-infested Alphabet City community they call home. With three albums for RCA behind them and a successful support slot on Black Sabbath's 1990 tour, they remained relatively unknown outside their native New York. RCA consequently dropped the group, which may have been a rash decision, particularly in the light of Columbia's decision to step in with a contract.

Albums: *Circus Of Power* (RCA 1988), *Still Alive* (RCA 1989), *Vices* (RCA 1990), *Magic And Madness* (Columbia 1993).

Cirith Ungol

Taking their name from one of the towers in *Lord Of The Rings*, this gothic heavy metal outfit materialized in 1980. Hailing from Ventura, California, USA, the band comprised ex-Titanic duo Jerry Fogle (guitar) and Robert Garven (drums), ex-roadie Tim Baker (vocals) and Greg Lindstrom (bass), the latter eventually replaced by Michael Flint. Characterized by high-pitched vocals and complex, at times cumbersome arrangements, their style was highly introspective, or less kindly, morbid. Their *Frost And Fire* debut has been referred to by some commentators as 'The Worst Heavy Metal Album Of All Time' They did progress somewhat, improving song constructions and introducing up-tempo numbers to break the monotony. Nevertheless, success continued to elude them as they struggled to find an audience for their hopelessly out-dated brand of fantasy metal.
Albums: *Frost And Fire* (Liquid Flames 1981), *King Of The Dead* (Roadrunner 1984), *One Foot In Hell* (Roadrunner 1986).

City

This Californian quintet specialized in sophisticated rock, with a distinctly commercial pop-edge. Formed in 1986, the band comprised Bill Trudel (vocals), Stuart Mathis (guitar), Peter McLan (keyboards), Wade Biery (bass) and Jerry Speiser (drums). Strongly influenced by Toto, Kansas and Mr. Mister, they debuted in 1987 with *Foundation*, but split up immediately after the album's release. Trudel went on to work with ex-Jeff Paris musician Michael Thompson, while McLan handled production duties for Men At Work.
Album: *Foundation* (Chrysalis 1987).

CJSS

This US group was a part-time side project for virtuoso guitarist David T. Chastain. Ably assisted by Mike Skimmerhorn (bass), Les Sharp (drums) and Russell Jenkins (lead vocals), CJSS offered an outlet for Chastain's melodic and more accessible compositions. They recorded two albums during the mid-80s, characterized by impeccable musicianship and inventive guitar work. In theory, the material still retained enough rough edges to appeal to rock fans but, at the same time, was sophisticated enough to cross over to a mainstream audience. In practice, this did not work out and CJSS have been inactive since 1987.
Albums: *World Gone Mad* (Roadrunner 1986), *Praise The Loud* (Roadrunner 1986).

Clarke, 'Fast' Eddie

Highly underrated guitarist Eddie Clarke (b. 5 October 1950, Isleworth, Middlesex, England) will always be remembered for his six years with Motörhead. Clarke had been playing in various bands since 1965 but his big break came in 1973 when he joined Zeus, the group put together by Curtis Knight (the blues/soul man who played with Jimi Hendrix) where he remained for 18 months. Following Zeus he formed Blue Goose along with Nicky Hogarth and Chris Perry. After his departure Blue Goose recorded recorded an album for Anchor Records which included 'Over The Top', a track written by Clarke. His next band, Continuous Performance, formed with Charlie Tumalhi, produced only a handful of demos, a disappointment which led to him quitting music in 1975. It was finally through his friend, drummer Phil Taylor, that he joined Motörhead in 1976. Here he enjoyed worldwide fame as a foil to Lemmy's brutal bass that no other guitarist has matched, even taking lead vocal on the blues song 'Step Down' from the *Bomber* album. Clarke played on all Motörhead albums between 1977 and 1982. During 1978 (a quiet period for the band) Clarke and Taylor joined vocalist 'Speedy' Keen and Johnny Thunders bassist Billy Wrath in the Muggers, playing a number of gigs under that banner. In 1982 he produced Tank's debut album, *Filth Hounds Of Hades*, guested on Twisted Sisters *Under The Blade* and quit Motörhead through musical differences. He soon struck up a partnership with Pete Way (bassist for UFO) and formed Fastway, but Way subsequently accepted an offer to join Ozzy Osbourne, which turned out to be short-lived, leaving him to form Waysted. Clarke then recruited drummer Jerry Shirley from Humble Pie, vocalist Dave King and bassist Charlie McCracken. This line-up lasted for two years and was the only stable line-up Fastway enjoyed. Further line-ups included ex Damned/UFO bassist Paul Grey. Eventually Clarke gave the band up in favour of solo work and overseeing archive Motörhead releases for Receiver Records.
Albums: With Curtis Knight And Zeus: *Zeus* (Phillips 1973), *Second Coming* (Dawn 1974): With Fastway: *Fastway* (CBS 1983), *All Fired Up* (CBS 1984), *Waiting For The Roar* (CBS 1986), *Trick Or Treat OST* (CBS 1987), *On Target* (GWR 1988), *Bad Bad Girls* (Legacy 1990). With Phil Taylor: *Naughty Old Santas Xmas Classics* (Receiver 1989). With The Muggers: *Muggers Tapes* (Castle 1993). Solo: *It Aint Over Till It's Over* (Chequered Flag 1993).

Clawfinger

This Swedish rap-metal outfit formed in 1990 when

the main protagonists, Zak Tell (vocals), Norwegian guitarists Erland Ottem and Bard Torstensen, and Jocke Skog (programmer/keyboards/vocals), met in Stockholm's Rosegrove Hospital, where they all worked as orderlies. The still-nameless band cut an early version of 'Nigger' - an anti-racist track questioning the use of the term by black people themselves, which conversely drew accusations of racism to Clawfinger - which was picked up by a local radio station, catching the attention of East West Records. *Deaf, Dumb, Blind* was described by *Metal Hammer* magazine as 'the finest rock/rap album ever', and although Rage Against The Machine comparisons were obvious, due to the musical style, socio-political lyrical content and the profusion of profanity contained therein, Clawfinger's heavier approach, with electronic bass and drums and guitars plugged directly into the mixing desk for extra punch, had more in common with Faith No More and Public Enemy. Early live shows with live bass and drums included UK dates with Alice In Chains and Anthrax, where the band's inexperience on stage was obvious, but heavy touring quickly turned Clawfinger into a potent and popular live act. A second album, *Use Your Brain*, was slated for release in early 1995.

Album: *Deaf, Dumb, Blind* (East West 1993).

Cloven Hoof

Formed in 1979, this UK band were strongly influenced by early Kiss. The personnel took on the pseudonyms of Air, Fire, Earth and Water and dressed in appropriately ridiculous stage costumes. Specializing in kitsch glam-metal, with an underlying satanic element, they recorded two amateurish, but naively charming albums before the original line-up and band concept fell apart. The only remaining member, bassist Lee Payne, reformed the band in 1987 with Russell North (lead vocals), Andy Wood (guitar) and Jon Brown (drums). Ditching the old image in favour of a hard rock/thrash approach, they signed to FM Revolver Records. *Dominator*, produced by Guy Bidmead (of Motörhead fame) materialized in 1988, but was highly derivative. *A Sultan's Ransom*, which moved towards a thrashier style, fared little better and was universally slated in the music press. The band continued, undaunted by such setbacks, until finally giving up the ghost in the 90s.

Albums: *Cloven Hoof* (Neat 1984), *Live...Fighting Back* (Moondance 1987), *Dominator* (FM Revolver 1988), *A Sultan's Ransom* (FM Revolver 1989).

Clutch

This Washington DC noise-metal quartet was formed in 1991 by childhood friends Neil Fallon (vocals), Tim Sult (guitar), Dan Maines (bass) and Jean-Paul Gaster (drums), and drew from hardcore, metal, punk and industrial traditions for their abrasive, intense sound. The band signed to Earache Records, releasing the *Passive Restraints* EP and establishing their style, and although the EP was not a major commercial success, it brought Clutch to East West Records' attention. *Transnational Speedway League: Anthems, Anecdotes And Undeniable Truths* showed no signs of compromises being made due to major label status as Clutch maintained their angry hardcore groove, with a charismatic performance from Fallon. The Clutch live repertoire had grown in stature and confidence since their early European tour with Biohazard, as the band toured heavily with the likes of Fear Factory and Prong.

Album: *Transnational Speedway League: Anthems, Anecdotes And Undeniable Truths* (East West 1993).

Cobra

This US hard rock quintet was formed in 1982 by ex-Krokus guitarist Mandy Meyer and former Target vocalist Jimi Jamison. With the recruitment of Jack Holder (guitar), Tommy Keiser (bass) and Jeff Klaven (drums) they were soon signed by CBS Records. Their music, a fusion of the blues-rock approach of Whitesnake and Bad Company and the heavier, power-metal style of Van Halen and Iron Maiden, was immediately impressive. Legal and contractual problems were instrumental in the band's demise after just one album release. Meyer joined Asia, Jamison teamed up with Survivor and Keiser later appeared in Krokus.

Album: *First Strike* (Epic 1983).

Cockney Rejects

Discovered by Jimmy Pursey of Sham 69, this east London based skinhead group came to the fore in 1980 with an irreverent brand of proletariat punk/rock. The group comprised Jefferson Turner (vocals), Vince Riordan (bass/vocals), Micky Geggus (guitar/vocals) and Keith Warrington (drums). Daring and anti-everything, they were virtually a parody of the 'kick over the traces' punk attitude, while also betraying a stubborn parochialism in keeping with their group title. The 'anarchic' contents of their albums were reflected in their garishly tasteless record sleeves. Yet they had a certain subversive humour, titling their first two albums *Greatest Hits* when the sum of their UK Top 40 achievements rested with 'The Greatest Cockney Ripoff' at number 21 and the West Ham United football anthem, 'I'm Forever Blowing Bubbles', at number 35. On their second album they included the 'Oi! Oi! Oi!' song/chant, thereby giving birth to a musical sub-genre which came to define the brash inarticulacy of skinhead politics. Their gigs during this time also became an interface for working class culture and the extreme right, though just like Sham the Rejects were judged guilty by default. By the time of 1982's *The Wild Ones* the group were veering away from their original punk influences towards heavy metal. Significantly, their new producer was UFO bassist Pete Way. Equally significantly, their career was well on the decline by that point.

Albums: *Greatest Hits Volume 1* (Zonophone 1980), *Greatest Hits Volume 2* (Zonophone 1980), *The Power And The Glory* (Zonophone 1981), *The Wild Ones* (AKA 1982), *Rock The Wild Side* (Heavy Metal 1984), *Greatest Hits Volume 3 (Live And Loud)* (Link 1987), *Lethal* (Neat 1990). Compilations: *We Are The Firm* (Dojo 1986), *Unheard Rejects* (Wonderful World 1985, early/unreleased recordings).

Cold Sweat

Following his departure from Keel, guitarist Marc Ferrari put together his own band, but not without a series of problems. The initial choice of name, Ferrari, encountered objections from the famous car manufacturers, despite the fact that it was genuinely the guitarist's surname, and second choice, Cryin' Shame, clashed with that of a veteran jazz band. Hence Cold Sweat, from a Thin Lizzy song, was finally adopted. To add to the difficulties, original vocalist Oni Logan was stolen away by ex-Dokken guitarist George Lynch for his Lynch Mob band. Rory Cathey was recruited to join Ferrari, ex-Waysted guitarist Erik Gamans, bassist Chris McLernon, and drummer Anthony White on *Break Out*. While Kevin Beamish's production was a little too clean, the melodic hard rock material and performances on display were impressive, with some superb guitar interplay between Ferrari and Gamans. Cathey proved his worth as a frontman on stage to complete a talented live act. However, despite some US touring with Dio and their own club dates, the album received little additional promotion, and disappeared. Ferrari later showed up in actor Tia Carrere's backing band in the *Wayne's World* film.

Album: *Break Out* (MCA 1990).

Company Of Wolves

This US hard rock group, formed in the late 80s, comprised Kyf Brewer (vocals), Steve Conte (guitar), John Conte (bass) and Frankie Larocka (drums; ex-Bryan Adams and John Waite touring bands). Revealing a wide range of influences encompassing Kiss, Aerosmith, Bad Company, Led Zeppelin and David Bowie, these were re-processed with such frantic energy and attitude that they almost convinced. However, a near-thing proved of no value to their record company and they were dropped after the release of a solitary album, their own split following in 1991.

Album: *Company Of Wolves* (Mercury 1990).

Concrete Blonde

After spending several years in the embryonic form of Dream 6 (under which name they released an EP for Happy Hermit in France), Hollywood, California, USA rock band Concrete Blonde formed in 1986. The founders of the group, former Sparks personnel Earle (production) and Jim Mankey (guitars) plus Johnette Napolitano (bass/vocals), were joined by Harry Rushakoff (drums) for their debut on IRS Records. Its alluring mix of energy, sensitivity and streetwise wit secured Concrete Blonde a positive response from both the music press and maturer rock audiences. For *Free* Napolitano handed over bass duties to new member Alan Bloch, allowing her to concentrate on singing. Irrespective of which she remained the focus of the band - her remarkable voice, which sounds both assertive and vulnerable, gives Concrete Blonde much of its poignancy and power. *Bloodletting* is perhaps the band's strongest album in terms of emotional intensity, with its painful dissection of an ailing relationship (all songwriting handled by Napolitano). It saw the introduction of new percussionist Paul Thompson (ex-Roxy Music), with the group now effectively a trio of Napolitano, Jim Mankey and Thompson. Their most recent release, *Mexican Moon*, includes Hispanic influences, and continues the vein of sincere, sassy and seductive rock which has made Concrete Blonde such a welcome presence over the last decade.

Albums: *Concrete Blonde* (IRS 1986), *Free* (IRS 1989), *Bloodletting* (IRS 1990), *Walking In London* (IRS 1992), *Mexican Moon* (IRS 1993).

Coney Hatch

This Canadian quartet was formed in 1981 by vocalist Carl Dixon and guitarist Steve Shelski. Taking their name from a (corruption of) a north London lunatic asylum, the line-up was stabilized with the addition of Andy Curran (bass) and Dave Ketchum (drums). They debuted in 1982 with a self-titled album, produced by Max Webster supremo Kim Mitchell. It still remains their essential work, featuring a variety of styles from blues-rock to *avant garde* jazz via heavy metal. Dixon's vocals are outstanding, with Shelski's eclectic guitar bursts providing the perfect foil. Barry Connors took over the drumstool after *Outta Hand*, a disappointing and lacklustre follow-up, which was not helped by a lifeless production. *Friction* marked a slight return to form, but the band disintegrated before they could capitalize on its success. Occasional reunion gigs still take place in their native territory.

Albums: *Coney Hatch* (Mercury 1982), *Outta Hand* (Vertigo 1983), *Friction* (Vertigo 1985).

Coroner

Coroner were founded in Switzerland in 1985 by Ron Royle (vocals), Tommy T. Baron (guitar) and Marquis Marky (drums). They were signed by Noise Records in the following year after recording a demo entitled *Death Cult*. Guesting on vocals for the demo was Thomas G. Warrior, leader of cult *avant garde* thrash band Celtic Frost. Coroner were to maintain a close relationship with their countrymen - and now labelmates - over the years to come (even roadying for them on Celtic Frost's 1986 US tour). While Coroner have always had a less experimental approach to thrash metal than Celtic Frost, it is possible to detect a number of intricate and unusual guitar riffs in their caustic, rapid fire approach. For a time it looked like the band might even establish themselves among the leaders of the speed metal genre, but as its popularity expired, Coroner were increasingly side-lined by younger death metal bands. Their future as a unit now looks doubtful and their *Best Of* compilation (featuring remixes, instrumentals and four new tracks) may prove to be their swan song.

Albums: *RIP* (Noise 1987), *Punishment For Decadence* (Noise 1988), *No More Colour* (Noise 1989), *Mental Vortex* (Noise 1991), *Grin* (Noise 1993). Compilation: *Best Of* (Noise 1995).

Corrosion Of Conformity

This seminal hardcore crossover band, originally known as No Labels, was formed in Raleigh, North Carolina, by Reed Mullin (drums), Woody Weatherman (guitar) and Mike Dean (bass/vocals) in 1982, and rose to become one of the biggest draws in the US underground with their stunning live shows. *Eye For An Eye*, with vocals supplied by Eric Eyke, separated them from the pack by mixing hardcore speed with Black Sabbath and Deep Purple-influenced power riffing. A more metallic crossover style became evident with *Animosity*, although the group lost neither their aggression nor their hardcore ideals. The blistering *Technocracy*, with Simon Bob (ex-Ugly Americans) on vocals, saw the band's audience expand with the rise of thrash, but record

company problems and the loss of Simon Bob and Dean led to Corrosion Of Conformity's collapse. However, just as it seemed that *Six Songs With Mike Singing* was to be their epitaph, Corrosion Of Conformity returned, with Mullin and Weatherman joined by Karl Agell (vocals, ex-School Of Violence), Pepper Keenan (guitar/vocals) and Phil Swisher (bass). Impressive tours with DRI and Danzig helped gain a new deal, and the acclaimed *Blind* saw the band adopt a slower, more melodic, but still fiercely heavy style. It also continued the hardcore lyrical stance of an increasingly politically active band, challenging social, political and ecological issues. Success with 'Vote With A Bullet' and electrifying live shows, including a UK tour supporting Soundgarden, re-established Corrosion Of Conformity as a force, but the departure of Agell and Swisher slowed the momentum once more. *Deliverance*, with Keenan taking lead vocals and Dean back in place, saw the band incorporate even more diverse influences into their weighty sound, adding southern rock grooves and, perhaps most surprisingly, Thin Lizzy-style guitar harmonies for a varied album which was a considerable departure from their hardcore musical roots.

Albums: *Eye For An Eye* (No Core 1984), *Animosity* (Death/Metal Blade 1985), *Technocracy* (Metal Blade 1987, mini-album), *Six Songs With Mike Singing* (Caroline 1988, rec. 1985, mini-album), *Blind* (Relativity 1991), *Deliverance* (Columbia 1994).

Coverdale Page

Following Whitesnake's headline appearance at the 1990 Donington Festival, and the comparatively poor sales of *Slip Of The Tongue*, vocalist David Coverdale put his band on ice, and had all but retired. Former Led Zeppelin guitarist Jimmy Page was, however, searching for a singer to work with at the time, and Coverdale was suggested by his booking agent during a conversation with Page's manager. The pair met in New York in March 1991, and gelled on personal and professional levels very quickly. Their first attempt at writing together produced an album track, 'Absolution Blues', and the duo began writing and recording their debut, enlisting the services of Heart drummer Denny Carmassie and bassists Jorge Casas and Ricky Phillips in the studio. The partnership was viewed rather cynically by sections of the music press as a corporate rock supergroup, and was subject to much speculation on all fronts - Legends was rumoured as a possible band name for some time - before the appearance of the simply-titled *Coverdale Page*. The album saw the duo rediscovering their blues-rock roots, and was widely regarded as the finest work produced by either for quite some time. Majestic ballads like 'Take Me For A Little While' and the mellow 'Take A Look At Yourself' sat easily amid the thunderous hard rock of 'Shake My Tree', 'Waiting On You', and 'Pride And Joy', while the atmospheric delivery of 'Over Now' evoked the epic air of the Zeppelin classic, 'Kashmir'. The album hit the Top 5 on both sides of the Atlantic, and Carmassi's Bonhamesque performance ensured that his services were retained for the live band, along with bassist Guy Pratt and ex-Dave Lee Roth keyboard player Brett Tuggle. However, the band were unable to arrange a financially viable world tour, with recession-hit promoters sceptical of their drawing power in a poor market for traditional heavy rock, and without that support, album sales dwindled. The group played six shows in Japan in December 1993, successfully mixing Whitesnake and Zeppelin material with Coverdale Page originals, but these performances were to be the band's swan song. It looks unlikely that the main protagonists will work together in the future, especially given Page's reunification with Robert Plant for the *Unledded* project.

Album: *Coverdale Page* (EMI 1993).

Craaft

This German melodic rock quartet was formed in 1984 by guitarist Marcus Schleicher and ex-Krokus bassist Tommy Keiser. Adding Tom Schneider (drums), Franz Keil (keyboards) and Klaus Luley (vocals; ex-Tokyo), they provided a breath of fresh air in the mid-80s teutonic rock scene, which was otherwise dominated by identikit speed metal bands. Surprisingly, the band sounded more American than German, combining Nightranger, Whitesnake and Toto influences to great effect. Luley is a highly talented vocalist, using his considerable range and power to carry the melody lines, while the use of keyboards to fill out the sound is achieved in a subtle and understated fashion. They have released two excellent albums to date, the first produced by Peter Hauke of White Lion, but have received little recognition outside Germany.

Albums: *Craaft* (Epic 1986), *Second Honeymoon* (RCA 1988).

Cradle Of Filth

English band who have joined the Satanic black metal revival of the early 90s. Visually, Cradle of Filth are influenced by the Scandinavian bands who led the

Corrosion Of Conformity

movement, such as Mayhem and Emperor. This influence includes adopting a penchant for the black and white make-up known as 'corpse-paint', funereal garb, fire-breathing and drenching themselves in blood. While the Scandinavian black metal bands have become increasingly interested in the occult, right-wing philosophies of Viking mythology, Cradle of Filth have a more gothic, quasi-poetic musical outlook. This is evidenced in their darkly poignant lyrics, use of a cello player and haunting singing of Andrea Mayer (a German Satanist who has since married a member of Emperor). The core of Cradle of Filth's sound however, remains a blizzard of apocalyptic guitars and tortured vocals.
Albums: *The Principle of Evil Made Flesh* (Cacophonous Records 1994).

Crash 'N' Burn

This Anglo-German hard rock quartet were previously known as Riff. Formed by vocalist William Lennox in 1991, with fellow members Becking (guitar), Thomas (bass) and Brendel (drums), the group signed by RCA, and debuted with *Fever* in 1991. A blues-based heavy rock album, it utilized state-of-the-art recording technology to transpose the group's keen melodies. Replete with promotional single, 'Hot Like Fire', it announced a band of considerable flair and energy, and seemed likely to win over the most hardened critics.
Album: *Fever* (RCA 1991).

Crawler

This UK heavy rock group was an offshoot of Back Street Crawler, the band that had featured the late and legendary Paul Kossoff. Crawler comprised Terry Wilson Slesser (vocals), Geoff Whitehorn (guitar), John 'Rabbit' Bundrick (keyboards; ex-Free), Terry Wilson (bass) and Tony Braunagel (drums). They released two blues-rock albums during the late 70s, which were ignored amid the punk rock explosion of the day (though their debut's 'Stone Cold Sober' was a particularly resonant piece). The group disbanded in 1978, with Whitehorn going back to session work and Slesser reappearing later in Charlie.
Albums: *Crawler* (CBS 1977), *Snake, Rattle And Roll* (CBS 1978).

Creaming Jesus

This satirical UK hardcore/metal quintet were formed in 1987 by vocalist Andy and guitarists Richard and Mario. With the addition of drummer Roy and bassist Tally, they signed to the independent Jungle label. Their amusingly titled debut saw chainsaw guitars collide with machine-gun drumming, whilst the lyrics dealt with contemporary issues such as television evangelists, sexual perverts, childhood anxieties and warmongerers. Never big on subtlety, Creaming Jesus, whose name in itself is enough to send the weak-hearted into apoplexy, have sustained a rudimentary talent over a succession of albums.
Albums: *Too Fat To Run, Too Stupid To Hide* (Jungle 1990), *Guilt By Association* (Jungle 1992), *Chaos For The Converted* (Jungle 1994).

Creed

This US blues-based boogie outfit was formed in 1977 by vocalist Steve Ingle and guitarist Luther Maben. Enlisting the services of Hal Butler (keyboards), James Flynn (bass) and Chip Thomas (drums) they were soon signed by Asylum Records. Their self-titled debut appeared in 1978 and was notable for 'Time And Time Again', an epic southern-style guitar work-out, comparable in stature to Lynyrd Skynyrd's 'Freebird'. Unable to attract enough media attention, the band split up soon after the album's release.
Album: *Creed* (Asylum 1978).

Creek

Hailing from North Carolina, USA, this hard rock band shortened their name from Sugarcreek in 1986 to avoid any association with the country music scene. Comprising Jerry West (guitar/vocals), Rick Lee (keyboards/vocals), Mike Barber (bass), Tim Clark (vocals/percussion) and Lynn Samples (drums), they specialized in highly melodic pomp-rock, making extensive use of four-part vocal harmonies. Influenced by Styx, Kansas and Journey, they have released two exceptional albums on shoestring budgets. John Harwell and Robbie Hegler replaced Samples and Barber on drums and bass respectively in 1987.
Albums: *The Creek* (Music For Nations 1986), *Storm The Gate* (Beaver 1989).

Crimson Glory

Formerly known as Pierced Arrow and Beowolf, this Florida-based heavy metal quintet settled on the name Crimson Glory in 1982. Comprising Midnight (vocals), Jon Drenning (guitar), Ben Jackson (guitar), Jeff Lords (bass) and Dana Burnell (drums), they spent a full three years writing material and developing a sound. They emerged in 1986 with a self-titled debut on Roadrunner Records, which fused the techno-rock of Queensrÿche with the uncompromising power-metal of Iron Maiden. Their was also a nod to religious themes, not least in the choice of their name, though the group denied any connection to the 'white metal' movement. The band also sported silver masks to add an element of artistic mystique to their identity. *Transcendence* was an ambitious concept album, which explored the themes of destiny, theocracy and philosophy. It received widespread critical acclaim and put the band on the launching pad to international recognition. Internal disputes then led to a line-up reshuffle with Jackson and Burnell ousted. Ravi Jakhorta was recruited on drums and the band continued as a four-piece. They eventually discarded the masks on *Strange And Beautiful*, their third and most complete work to date. Here they incorporated a wider range of influences, added organ and acoustic bridges and showed an increased awareness of dynamics. Seemingly only a matter of time before the Midnight/Drenning songwriting partnership achieved more significant success, the band's absence for much of the early 90s served to diffuse their impact.

Albums: *Crimson Glory* (PAR 1986), *Transcendence* (Roadrunner 1988), *Strange And Beautiful* (Roadrunner 1991).

Cro-Mags

This US thrashcore band was formed in 1984 by bassist (and sometime singer) Harley Flanegan, a follower of the Hare Krishna doctrine, who nevertheless represents an intimidating, multi-tattooed presence on stage. After a series of false starts, vocalist John 'Bloodclot' Joseph, drummer Mackie and guitarists Doug Holland (ex-Kraut; who joined in time for *Best Wishes*) and Parris Mitchell Mayhew were recruited to cement the band's line-up. When Joseph left Flanegan would take over vocal duties. They specialized in a fusion of thrash, hardcore and heavy metal and the influences of Motörhead, the Dead Kennedys and Metallica were quite apparent on their debut, *The Age Of Quarrel*. They built up a small but loyal cult of supporters, and regularly headlined major hardcore events at New York's CBGB's during the mid to late 80s. Primarily remarkable for their sheer sonic intensity, the group were at the forefront of a musical genre which became increasingly adopted by the metal fraternity as time wore on. Unlike most, however, Cro-Mags offered lyrical diversity and invention to back up their 'mosh' epics, notably on tracks like 'The Only One', which delivered a sermon on their leader's religious position. Line-up changes were numerous, the most pertinent of which was Mackie's decision to join Bad Brains.

Albums: *The Age Of Quarrel* (GWR 1987), *Best Wishes* (Profile 1990), *Alpha Omega* (Century Media 1992).

Cross

After two solo albums, Roger Taylor (b. 26 July 1949, Norfolk, England; vocals/guitar) needed a new challenge outside the confines of Queen. He formed the Cross in summer 1987 with Clayton Moss (guitar), Spike Edney (keyboards), Peter Noone (bass; *not* the Peter Noone of Herman's Hermits fame) and Josh Macrae (drums) concentrating on a low-key pop-rock approach. The group made its debut in September 1987 with 'Cowboys And Indians', a mix of dance and rock music not a million miles away from mid-period Queen. 1988's *Shove It*, its title-track preceding it as a single, was a nondescript collection of half-hearted rockers which lacked distinction, partly due to Taylor's limited vocal ability. Ironically the best track, 'Heaven For Everyone', was delivered by Freddie Mercury, though when this was issued as a single it was in a new version with Taylor at the microphone. *Mad, Bad And Dangerous To Know*, a title inspired by the poetry of Byron, was something of a misnomer, though it did feature a more raucous version of the Cross sound than that previously unveiled. Much of the album had been written by other band members while Taylor was working with Queen, though he did contribute some strong guitar work and two overtly political songs in 'Old Men (Lay Down)' and 'Final Destination'. Mike Moran assisted on keyboards in place of Edney, unavailable due to touring commitments with Elton John. However, Parlophone were losing interest in the group and their third album, *Blue Rock*, was issued in Germany and Japan only. Following the death of Freddie Mercury, extra-curricular work for Taylor included another solo album with further songs of a serious political nature. This activity ruled out any iniment return to the Cross name, and the band played what many considered to be a farewell gig at London's Marquee club in December 1992.

Albums: *Shove It* (Virgin 1988), *Mad, Bad And Dangerous To Know* (Parlophone 1990), Blue Rock (Electrola 1991).

Crowbar

This quartet emerged as one of the leading lights of the New Orleans extreme metal scene with a sound which blended Black Sabbath/St Vitus-styled heaviness with hardcore aggression. Kirk Windstine (vocals/guitar), Kevin Noonan (guitar), Todd Strange (bass) and Craig Nunenmacher (drums) made their debut with the dark and doom-laden *Obedience Through Suffering*, after which Noonan was replaced by Matt Thomas, a former band-mate of Pantera frontman Phil Anselmo in Razor White. Anselmo, an old friend who collaborated with Windstein on side-projects such as *Down* and *Both Legs Broken*, helped refine and improve the band's sound with his sympathetic production on *Crowbar*, which included a brutally heavy interpretation of Led Zeppelin's 'No Quarter', adapted stylishly to the Crowbar sound to produce a valid cover version. The band added to their good press on the road with Paradise Lost in the UK and Pantera in the US, releasing the *Live +1* EP (which was packaged with *Crowbar* in the UK) to coincide, before returning to the studio with the stated intention of making *Crowbar* sound 'like Jethro Tull'.

Albums: *Obedience Through Suffering* (Grindcore 1992), *Crowbar* (Pavement 1993).

Crown Of Thorns

Heavy metal band (nothing to do with similarly-titled IRS recording artists) formed in 1991 ostensibly because: 'we just kept bumping into each other on the tour circuit'. A promise to work together at a future date was eventually honoured when Micki Free (guitar; ex-Shalamar) and Jean Beauvoir (vocals, guitar; ex-Plasmatics, Little Steven, Voodoo X) put Crown Of Thorns together with Michael Page (bass) and Tony Thompson (drums; ex-Power Station). The first song they wrote together, 'Hike It Up', would be the standout track on their debut, self-titled mini-album. With the production assistance of Kiss' Paul Stanley on five tracks, and songwriting imput from Beau Hill and Jim Vallance (Bryan Adams, Scorpions, Aerosmith) the set was unfortunately not given a release outside of the UK due to label problems, the band contenting itself with widespread touring instead.

Album: *Crown Of Thorns* (Now And Then 1993, mini-album).

Crumbsuckers

This New York 'thrashcore' quintet was formed in Long Island in 1983 by vocalist Chris Notaro and guitarist Chuck Lenihan. With the addition of Gary Meskill (bass), Dave Wynn (guitar) and Dan Richardson (drums), they signed to Combat Records and cut *Life Of Dreams* in 1986. This was an uncompromising blast of hardcore angst with metallic undercurrents, which helped establish a large cult following for the band. *Beast On My Back* saw Wynn replaced by Ronnie Koebler, as the band moved away from their hardcore roots and entered the thrash metal domain. Marc Piovanetti and Joe Hegarty replaced Lenihan and Notaro respectively in 1989, with the band subsequently changing their name to Heavy Rain. The Crumbsuckers' transition to Metallica and Slayer-like metal was now complete.

The band's rhythm section would later re-emerge in **Pro-Pain**.

Albums: *Life Of Dreams* (Combat Core/Rough Justice 1986), *Beast On My Back* (Combat/Music For Nations 1988).

Cry Of Love

These North Carolina retro-rockers began life in 1989 on the local covers' circuit around Raleigh, as a trio of Audley Freed (guitar), Robert Kearns (bass) and Jason Patterson (drums), but only really took off with the arrival of vocalist/guitarist Kelly Holland. Cry Of Love (a name taken from a Jimi Hendrix album) quickly signed major recording and management deals in the wake of his entrance. *Brother* was a classic slice of soulful hard rock, with a sound akin to Free and Bad Company enhanced by atmospheric live takes, Holland producing a performance worthy of Paul Rodgers in his heyday, while the inevitable Hendrix comparisons were heightened by Freed's tasteful lead work. With the success of the Black Crowes opening ears to classic rock styles, Cry Of Love's popularity leapt, with the superb 'Peace Pipe' hitting number 1 on the US *Billboard* Album Rock Track chart, while the band produced a series of dazzling live performances on the road with Robert Plant, Lynyrd Skynyrd, Bad Company and Z.Z. Top. This was in addition to their own heavy club touring schedule where they freely jammed on extended versions of album material, and preceded their second UK tour with a well-received second stage spot at Donington 1994. It therefore came as something of a surprise when Holland departed later that year.

Album: *Brother* (Columbia 1993).

Crybabys

This bluesy rock 'n' roll quartet from the UK were formed in 1991 by former Boys' guitarist 'Honest' John Plain. Recruiting Darrell Barth (guitar/vocals), Mark Duncan (bass) and Robbie Rushton (drums) they signed with Receiver Records the same year. Drawing inspiration from Mott The Hoople, Hanoi Rocks and the Georgia Satellites, the Crybabys successfully bridged the gap between punk and rock 'n' roll. Shambolic, chaotic and full of stamina, they debuted with *Where Have All The Good Girls Gone?* This compared favourably with the best that either the similarly-inclined Dogs D'Amour (whom Barth would later join) or Quireboys produced in the period.

Album: *Where Have All The Good Girls Gone?* (Receiver 1991).

Cryptic Slaughter

This US speed metal quartet was formed in 1985 by vocalist Bill Cook and guitarist Les Evans. Enlisting the services of Rob Nicholson (bass) and Scott Peterson (drums), they specialized in short, abrupt songs that were carried along by warp-speed drumming and hell-for-leather riffing. They recorded four albums in total for the Metal Blade and Roadrunner labels between 1986-88, roughly in the mould of all-out thrashers like D.R.I., Suicidal Tendencies or Gang Green. The band split up in 1990 however, and their passing was scarcely mourned even within that select fraternity.

Albums: *Convicted* (Metal Blade 1986), *Money Talks* (Metal Blade 1987), *Stream Of Consciousness* (Roadrunner 1988), *Speak Your Peace* (Metal Blade 1990).

Cubanate

Confrontational English metal duo, aesthetically likened to the Henry Rollins band, who managed to earn death threats early in their careers after calling a Belfast audience 'cocksuckers'. The other half of Cubanate's ability to infuriate and upset resides in their musical approach, which utilizes samplers and DAT alongside guitar riffs and hardcore techno percussion (though in their early touring forays with Carcass they were unable to present a further live percussionist and guitarist due to financial restrictions). Marc Heal (vocals/programming) and Phil Barry (guitar) nevertheless managed to sustain quite an impression on their own, with a musical hybrid similar but more extreme than that engendered by central Europeans Front 242 and KMFDM. This first came to public attention via the striking 'Bodyburn' single. They offered fuller exposition of this creed on their debut album, recorded in just six days and on a budget of £4,000.

Album: *Cyberia* (Dynamica 1995).

Culprit

US hard rock quintet based in Seattle which was formed in 1980 from the ashes of Orpheus and Amethyst. Comprising John DeVol (guitar), Scott Earl (bass), Bud Burrill (drums), Jeff L'Heureux (vocals) and Kjartan Kristoffersen (guitar), they combined the power-metal style of Iron Maiden with the intricate melodic arrangements of Rush. Signing to Mike Varney's Shrapnel label, they debuted with *Guilty As Charged* in 1983. This was favourably received by the music media, and they built a large following throughout Washington state. However, such success was short-lived as the band was beset by drug problems and internal musical disagreements.

They finally disintegrated in 1985, and a planned reunion in 1987 failed to reach fruition.

Album: *Guilty As Charged* (Shrapnel 1983).

Cult

Originally known as first Southern Death Cult then Death Cult, the band were formed by lead singer Ian Astbury (b. 14 May 1962, Heswell, Merseyside, England) in 1981. After a youth spent in Scotland and Canada (where he gained early exposure to the culture of native Indians on the Six Nations Reservation, informing the early stages of the band's career), Astbury moved into a Bradford, Yorkshire, house and discovered a group in rehearsal in the basement. The group's personnel included Haq Qureshi (drums), David 'Buzz' Burrows (guitar) and Barry Jepson (bass). As their vocalist, Astbury oversaw a rapid rise in fortunes, their fifth gig and London debut at the Heaven club attracting a near 2,000-strong audience. Southern Death Cult made their recording debut in December 1982 with the double a-side, 'Moya'/'Fatman', and supported Bauhaus on tour in early 1983. However, by March the group had folded, Astbury reeling from his perceived image of 'positive punk' spokesman, and the fact that his native Indian concept was being diluted by the group's format. His new band, operating under the truncated name Death Cult, would, he vowed, not become a victim of hype in the same way again (Qureshi, Jepson and Burrows would go on to join Getting The Fear, subsequently becoming Into A Circle before Qureshi re-emerged as the centrepiece of Fun-Da-Mental's 'world dance' ethos under the name Propa-Ghandi). A combination of the single, demo and live tracks was posthumously issued as the sole SDC album. Death Cult comprised the rhythm section of recently deceased gothic band Ritual, namely Ray 'The Reverend' Mondo (drums) and Jamie Stewart (bass), plus ex-Ed Banger And The Nosebleeds and Theatre Of Hate guitarist Billy Duffy (b. 12 May 1959, Manchester, England). They made their debut in July 1983 with an eponymous four-track 12-inch, at which time Astbury also changed his own name (he had previously been using Ian Lindsay, which, it later transpired, was his mother's maiden name). After an appearance at the Futurama festival Mondo swapped drumming positions with Sex Gang Children's Nigel Preston (d. 7 May 1992), a former colleague of Duffy's in Theatre Of Hate. However, 1984 brought about a second and final name change - with the band feeling that the Death prefix typecast them as a 'Gothic' act, they became simply the Cult. They recorded their first album together, *Dreamtime*, for release in September 1984, its sales boosted by a

number 1 single in the indepedent charts with the typcially anthemic 'Spiritwalker'. Another strong effort followed early the next year, 'She Sells Sanctuary', but this was to prove Preston's swansong. Mark Brzezicki of Big Country helped out on sessions for the forthcoming album until the permanent arrival of Les Warner (b. 13 February 1961), who had previously worked with Johnny Thunders, Julian Lennon and Randy California. The band's major commercial break came with *Love* in 1985, which comprised fully-fledged hard rock song structures and pushed Duffy's guitar lines to the fore. It spawned two UK Top 20 hit singles in the aforementioned 'She Sells Sanctuary' and 'Rain'. *Electric* saw the band's transition to heavy rock completed. There was no disguising the group's source of inspiration, with Led Zeppelin being mentioned in nearly every review. Part-produced by Rick Rubin, *Electric* was a bold and brash statement of intent, if not quite the finished item. It became a success on both sides of the Atlantic, peaking at number 4 and 38 in the UK and US charts respectively. The gigs to promote it saw the band add bass player Kid 'Haggis' Chaos (b. Mark Manning; ex-Zodiac Mindwarp And The Love Reaction), with Stewart switching to rhythm guitar. Both he and Warner were dispensed with in March 1988, the former joining 4 Horsemen. Reduced to a three-piece of Astbury, Stewart and Duffy, the sessions for *Sonic Temple* saw them temporarily recruit the services of drummer Mickey Curry. It was an album which combined the atmospheric passion of *Love* with the unbridled energy of *Electric*. A 1989 world tour saw the band augmented by Matt Sorum (drums) and Mark Taylor (keyboards; ex-Alarm, Armoury Show). Stewart quit in 1990, while Sorum would go on to a tenure with Guns N'Roses. *Ceremony* was released in 1991, with the help of Charley Drayton (bass) and the returning Mickey Curry. This was a retrogressive collection of songs, that had more in common with *Love* than their previous two albums. Nevertheless, having already established an enormous fan-base, success was virtually guaranteed. 1994's *The Cult* saw them reunited with producer Bob Rock once more, on a set which included a Kurt Cobain tribute, 'Sacred Life'.
Albums: As Southern Death Cult: *Southern Death Cult* (Beggars Banquet 1986). Compilation: *Complete Recordings* (Situation Two 1991). As the Cult: *Dreamtime* (Beggars Banquet 1984), *Love* (Beggars Banquet 1985), *Electric* (Beggars Banquet 1987), *Sonic Temple* (Beggars Banquet 1989), *Ceremony* (Beggars Banquet 1991), *The Cult* (Beggars Banquet 1994). Compilation: *Pure Cult* (Beggars Banquet 1993).

Videos: *Dreamtime Live At The Lyceum* (1984), *Electric Love* (1987), *Sonic Ceremony* (1992), *Pure Cult* (1993).

Currie, Cherie

Lead vocalist with the Runaways, Currie opted for a solo career after the release of *Queens Of Noise* in 1977. Under the wing of Kim Fowley and guitarist Steven T, she recorded *Beauty's Only Skin Deep* which also featured her sister, Marie, on backing vocals. Released to coincide with the Runaways' *Live In Japan*, it failed to make the charts and received poor press. Her elusive second album, *Messin' With The Boys*, credited to Cherie And Marie, was a much heavier affair and utilized the talents of session men/Toto members Steve Lukather and Mike Porcaro. The title-track was released as a single but ultimately failed to capture the solo success that fellow Runaways Joan Jett and Lita Ford would gain. Currie quit music in 1980 to become an actress and after a starring role alongside Jodie Foster and Randy Quaid in the film *Foxes*, she vanished from the public eye.
Albums: *Beauty's Only Skin Deep* (Mercury 1978), *Messin' With The Boys* (Mercury 1979).

Cyclone

Formerly known as Centurion, Cyclone were formed in Vilvoorde, Belgium, by vocalist Guido Gevels and guitarist Pascal van Lint in 1981. With the addition of Johnny Kerbush (guitar), Stefan Daamen (bass) and Nicholas Lairin (drums), they initially took their cue from the New Wave Of British Heavy Metal. They later switched to a more thrash-orientated approach, styling themselves on Anthrax. They subsequently negotiated a one-album deal with Roadrunner Records and debuted with *Brutal Destruction* in 1986. The label neglected to renew the group's contract and Cyclone disbanded the following year.
Album: *Brutal Destruction* (Roadrunner 1986).

Cynic

This death metal act were formed in Florida, USA, in 1987 by guitarist/vocalist Paul Masvidal, guitarist Jason Gobel, bassist Tony Choy, and drummer Sean Reinert, and recorded a number of acclaimed demos where brutal death metal was mixed with highly complex jazz/fusion-style riffs and rhythms. However, until the release of *Focus*, it seemed that the band were destined to be better known for providing session musicians for other bands, as Masvidal and Reinert played on Death's *Human* album and tour, while Choy worked first with Pestilence and then with

Atheist, whom he subsequently joined on a permanent basis. *Focus*, with Shawn Malone replacing Choy, was a complex, multi-textured album, displaying some remarkable musicianship without quite lapsing into self-indulgence, and one reviewer's description of 'King Crimson meets Death' seemed apt. The band were finally able to tour extensively in their own right, although, ironically, a temporary bassist was recruited for some dates due to Malone's music degree study commitments.

Album: *Focus* (Roadrunner 1993).

D

D'Molls

This Chicago-based heavy metal band featured Desi Rexx (vocals/guitar), Billy Dior (drums), S.S. Priest (guitar), Nigel Itson (vocals) and Lizzy Valentine (bass). Their self-titled 1988 debut album caused quite a stir at the time of its release, with its self-assured Aerosmith-meets-Poison approach. However, the songwriting on the follow-up, *Warped*, was weak, being rigidly formularized and lacked the cutting edge of its predecessor. They relocated to Los Angeles, but with poor reviews and sales to match, they disbanded in 1991. Rexx would work with former Derringer guitarist Danny Johnson, while Itson joined Millionaire Boys Club.

Albums: *D'Molls* (Atlantic 1988), *Warped* (Atlantic 1990).

D.A.D.

Originally known as Disneyland After Dark, D.A.D. came together in Copenhagen, Denmark, in 1985. Comprising Jesper Binzer (vocals/guitar), Jacob A. Binzer (guitar), Stig Pedersen (bass) and Peter L. Jensen (drums), they combined high-energy metallic rock 'n' roll with an irreverent sense of humour, reminiscent of Cheap Trick and Z.Z. Top at their playful best. After two entertaining and musically competent albums on the independent Mega label, they were signed by Warner Brothers in 1989 (reputedly for over $1,000,000) and marketed as their 'next big thing'. Their energetic and eccentric live performances were highly impressive, with scenarios including exploding helmets and instruments, but they could not generate the same intensity in the

studio. Consequently, *No Fuel Left For The Pilgrims* did not live up to the label's advance promotion. *Riskin' It All* emerged in 1991 and showed that the band had not been disillusioned by the press backlash. It was, instead, a splendid hard rock album, sparkling with offbeat energy and their own peculiar, tongue-in-cheek style.

Albums: *Call Of The Wild* (Mega 1986), *Disneyland After Dark Draws A Circle* (Mega 1987), *No Fuel Left For The Pilgrims* (Warners 1989), *Riskin' It All* (Warners 1991).

Dakota

This US melodic rock outfit was formed in Chicago in 1979 by vocalists/guitarists Jerry Hludzik and Billy Kelly. Recruiting Lou Crossa and Jeff Mitchell on keyboards, Bill McMale (bass) and John Robinson (drums), they based their style on the music of Styx, Toto and Kansas. Heavily dominated by keyboards and watertight vocal harmonies, the band released two quality studio albums of pomp rock, before disbanding in 1984.

Albums: *Dakota* (Columbia 1980), *Runaway* (Columbia 1984).

Damien Thorne

This American heavy metal quintet was formed in Chicago in 1985 by vocalist Justin Fate and guitarist Ken Starr. The group took their name from the 'Anti-Christ' in the book/film *The Omen*. After enlisting the services of Michael Monroe (guitar), Sanders Pate (bass) and Pete Pagonis (drums), they concentrated on a dual guitar approach similar to Judas Priest. They signed to Roadrunner Records and debuted with *Sign Of The Jackal* the following year. Produced by Virgin Steel vocalist David Defeis, this incorporated Iron Maiden, Def Leppard and Metallica influences, but these were not sufficiently modified or re-interpreted to an extent where they gave the band an identity of their own.

Album: *Sign Of The Jackal* (Roadrunner 1986).

Damn The Machine

Refusing an offer to rejoin Megadeth after playing on the demo sessions for *Rust In Peace*, guitarist Chris Poland subsequently recorded a fine solo effort, *Return To Metalopolis*. Afterwards he would form Damn The Machine in Los Angeles in 1991 with his drummer brother Mark, bassist Dave Randi, and guitarist/vocalist Dave Clemmons. The band were signed by A&M Records on the strength of a live-in-the-studio demo. *Damn The Machine* eschewed Megadeth-style thrash, opting for a progressive blend of traditional power metal and the jazz stylings which

Poland had explored in his solo work to produce a complex yet listenable album. However, despite considerable interest and near-universal press support, the band surprisingly broke up shortly after their debut European dates opening for Dream Theater.

Album: *Damn The Machine* (A&M 1993).

Damn Yankees

Formed in 1989, the Damn Yankees were one of several supergroups, which included Bad English, to emerge in the USA towards the end of the decade. Ex-Styx guitarist/vocalist Tommy Shaw had already been writing with the larger-than-life guitarist and solo artist Ted Nugent and they were soon joined by Jack Blades on bass/vocals (from the recently demised Nightranger) and Michael Cartellone, a previously unknown drummer. Warner Brothers beat Geffen Records in the race to sign the band, and their self-titled debut album was released in 1990. The music was hard-edged melodic rock much heavier than the style Styx and Nightranger were noted for, with Shaw and Blades handling the bulk of the vocal duties, while Nugent contributed lead vocals to the outrageous 'Piledriver'. The album went Top 10 in the US, with the help of a Top 5 single - the power ballad 'High Enough'. Damn Yankees, however, were not simply a record company creation. They proved they could produce sparkling live performances too, gaining a glowing reputation for their shows. These included tantalizing snippets from the respective back catalogues of Styx, Nightranger and Ted Nugent's solo work. The melodic influence of Shaw and Blades combined with the melodramatic antics of Nugent created a highly successful unit in terms of both critical acclaim and commercial success.

Albums: *Damn Yankees* (Warners 1990), *Don't Tread* (Warners 1992).

Danger, Danger

This melodic and atmospheric hard rock band were formed in 1988 by former Michael Bolton bassist Bruno Ravel. Enlisting the services of Ted Poley (ex-Prophet vocalist), Kasey Smith (keyboards), Steve West (drums) and Tony Rey (guitar), their style lies somewhere between White Lion and Bon Jovi. They were picked up by Imagine Records and debuted with a self-titled album in 1989. Produced by Lance Quinn and Mike Stone, this featured an impressive collection of infectious rockers and dynamic power-ballads. Rey quit to concentrate on his other project, Saraya, in 1989, and was replaced by Andy Timmins. Signing to Epic, they released *Screw It* in 1992, which built on the solid foundations of their debut, but included a greater element of arrogant street attitude. It revealed considerable crossover potential which, with careful nurturing, could produce a major songwriting force.

Albums: *Danger, Danger* (Imagine 1989), *Screw It* (Epic 1992).

Dangerous Toys

This group was formed by ex-Onyx members Scott Dalhover (guitar), Mike Watson (bass) and Mark Geary (drums) in Texas in 1987. With the recruitment of ex-Watchtower vocalist Jason McMaster, the band signed to CBS and debuted with a self-titled album in 1989. This revealed strong Guns N'Roses and Aerosmith influences, alongside their previous techno-thrash style. Danny Aaron was added as second guitarist shortly after the album was released to add greater flexibility on the road. They scored minor successes in the US singles market with 'Teas'n, Pleas'n' and 'Scared', the latter a tribute to their idol, Alice Cooper. Both also reached number 1 on the MTV video chart. Collaborating with Desmond Child, they recorded 'Demon Bell' for inclusion on the soundtrack to the horror film, *Shocker*, following which they supported the Cult and Bonham on a lengthy US west coast tour. *Hellacious Acres* would see further minor success with 'Gimme No Lip' and 'Line 'Em Up'. Aaron departed in 1992 to be replaced by Paul Lidel (ex-Dirty Looks) in time for the sessions which produced *Pissed*. This album, their first for Music For Nations' subsidiary Bullet Proof, was recorded in exactly one month in Los Angeles.

Album: *Dangerous Toys* (CBS 1989), *Hellacious Acres* (CBS 1991), *Pissed* (Bullet Proof 1994).

Daniel Band

Canadian heavy metal band formed in 1981 by vocalist/bassist Dan McGabe and guitarist/keyboardist Bill Findlay. The line-up, which remained remarkably stable over the course of the band's career, was completed by Tony Rossi (vocals/guitar) and Matt Delduca (drums). Taking their cue from April Wine, Triumph and Y&T, they specialized in melodic hard rock, with extended guitar and keyboard passages. Unlike many Christian rockers, the religious message was subservient to some excellent music.

Albums: *On Rock* (Streetlight 1982), *Straight Ahead* (Refuge 1983), *Run From The Darkness* (Refuge 1984), *Rise Up* (Refuge 1986), *Running Out Of Time* (Refuge 1987).

Danzig

Danzig are largely a vehicle for the lyrical and musical talents of enigmatic frontman, Glenn Danzig. Using musicians from his previous bands, the Misfits and Samhain (guitarist John Christ and bass player Eerie Von), plus stylish hardcore veteran Chuck Biscuits on drums (ex-D.O.A., Black Flag, Circle Jerks) he put together Danzig in 1987 and sold the concept to Rick Rubin's Def American label the following year. The resultant album realised all of the promise shown in Glenn's former projects, producing something with a soulful profundity that he had previously only hinted at. While Satanicaly inclined, Danzig have managed to avoid most of the pitfalls that have plagued other bands who court a devilish image. Younger, more overtly aggressive acts like Deicide or Slayer have presented an image of the Prince of Darkness dominated by rage and pain. Danzig introduced a series of other dimensions to his portrayal of the Satanic in artfully composed songs, from the seductive to the quietly sinister. Yet this subtlety tempered their appeal within the heavy metal fraternity, many of whom demanded a more direct or traditional approach, and Danzig remained a connoisseur's metal band. Their second release, *Lucifuge*, did little to change this. None of the elements used are in themselves original - vocals in the style of 50s crooners, rich black blues guitars, evocative heavy metal riffs - but it is the cunningly seamless way in which they are combined which generates Danzig's dark magic. A third long-playing release, *How the Gods Kill*, was, arguably, the archetypal Danzig album, forming a bridge between the high melodrama of heavy metal and the alluring menace of gothic mood. *Black Aria* was a solo project for Glenn Danzig, which is something of a departure stylistically from his previous, guitar-based, material. It consists of quasi-classical instrumentals, with one side dedicated to portraying the story of Satan's fall from grace. In late 1993 the mainstream rock crowd discovered Danzig via the runaway success of the video for 'Mother' on MTV. 'Mother' was in fact a track from their debut, but it took five years for this twisted classic to gain widespread recognition. *Danzig 4* followed and was met with critical accusations that it was a deliberately commercial outing for the band, designed to please their new audience. It is true that it contained little of the rousing anthemic rock which had peppered previous albums, but this fourth instalment was still distinctively Danzig (indeed, it echoed Samhain days to a degree). Glenn Danzig had long since demonstrated that he could yell up a storm with the Misfits, but this collection also proved that he was at his most menacing and creative when he was at his quietest. During touring to support *Danzig 4* Joey Castillo replaced Biscuits.

Albums: *Danzig* (Def American/Geffen 1988), *Danzig II - Lucifuge* (Def American/Geffen 1990), *How The Gods Kill* (Def American/Geffen 1992), *Black Aria* (Plan 9 1993), *Danzig 4* (American Recordings 1994).

Dare

This UK melodic rock quintet was formed in 1987 by ex-Thin Lizzy keyboard player, Darren Wharton. The band's name was derived from Wharton's christian name, the suggestion taken from Lemmy of Motörhead. Relocating to Manchester after Lizzy's demise, it took Wharton six months to find musicians on his own wavelength. He eventually teamed up with Vinny Burns (guitar), Shelley (bass), James Ross (drums) and Brian Cox (keyboards), taking on vocals and additional keyboards himself. They debuted with *Out Of The Silence* in 1988, a grandiose, keyboard-dominated album, reminiscent of Giuffria, Journey and House Of Lords. The follow-up, *Blood From Stone*, released three years later, adopted an approach rooted in hard rock structures and featured up-front guitar along with improved vocals from Wharton. Tipped to make a significant impact on the international rock scene, harsh reality intervened as the band became another fixutre on 'might have been' lists.

Albums: *Out Of The Silence* (A&M 1988), *Blood From Stone* (A&M 1991).

Dark Angel

Formed in Los Angeles, California, USA, in 1983, Dark Angel specialize in 'ultra-heavy thrash metal'. The original line-up consisted of Don Doty (vocals), Jim Durkin (guitar), Eric Meyer (guitar), Rob Yahn (bass) and Jack Schwarz (drums). Early demos saw the band sign to Axe Killer Records resulting in the release of *We Have Arrrived* in 1984. Unfortunately this was a clumsy effort which at times made them sound unrehearsed. Soon after its release, Rob Yahn and Jack Schwarz left to be replaced by Mike Gonzalez (bass) and Gene Hoglan (drums), who would become the band's chief lyricist. Signing a new deal with Combat Records, they released *Darkness Descends*. This brutally heavy and uncompromising album showed the band to have made the transition into a tight, cohesive unit. There was a lull in their recording career until they reappeared in 1989 with *Leave Scars*. If anything, this release was even heavier. Featuring new vocalist Ron Rinehart, it also contained a cover version of Led Zeppelin's 'Immigrant Song'. The band then embarked on a

European tour recording a live mini-album, *Live Scars,* which was released in 1990 as a stop-gap until the next studio project. Before commencing work on that the band underwent another line-up shuffle replacing Jim Durkin with ex-Viking guitarist Brett Eriksen. Together they recorded *Time Does Not Heal,* a turbulent vortex of twisted riffs and savage drums. Definitely not a band for the faint-hearted, Dark Angel continued to combine unsavoury lyrics with ferocious musicianship, though by this point the impact had waned. Hoglan would go on to cause further sonic mayhem in Death.

Albums: *We Have Arrived* (Axe Killer 1984), *Darkness Descends* (Under One Flag 1986), *Leave Scars* (Under One Flag 1989), *Live Scars* (Under One Flag 1990, mini-album), *Time Does Not Heal* (Under One Flag 1991). Compilation: *Decade Of Chaos* (Under One Flag 1992).

Dark Lord

This guitar-oriented, hard-rock outfit was formed in Venice, Italy, in 1984 by six-string virtuoso Alex Masi and drummer Sandro Bertoldini. With the addition of vocalist Gable Nalesso and bassist Al Guariento, they released a self-titled mini-album that showcased the talents of Masi, a classically trained guitarist in the style of Yngwie Malmsteen and Steve Vai. *State Of Rock,* another mini-album, followed, and saw the arrival of new bass player Randzo Zulian and vocalist Emanual Jandee. Masi quit and relocated to Los Angeles soon after the album's release, joining Sound Barrier, who later became Masi. After two years of inactivity, Jandee and Bertoldni re-formed *Dark Lord* with Paolo Mufato (guitar) and Alex Favaretto (bass). *It's Nigh' Time* was the result, but it lacked the sophistication and experimentation of Masi's era, and consequently made little impact outside Italy.

Albums: *Dark Lord* (1984, mini-album), *State Of Rock* (1985, mini-album), *It's Nigh' Time* (1988).

Dark Star

Formerly known as Berlin, the band were formed in the British Midlands in 1980, during the heyday of the New Wave Of British Heavy Metal. Dark Star comprised Rick Staines (vocals/synthesizer), David Harrison (guitar), Robert Key (guitar), Mark Oseland (bass) and Steve Atkins (drums). They debuted with 'Lady Of Mars', a track on EMI's compilation, *Metal For Muthas Volume II.* Stylistically, they alternated between pure heavy metal and US pomp-rock and consequently found it difficult to win supporters from either camp. The band ground to a halt shortly after the release of their self-titled debut in 1981. Six years later, Staines, Harrison and Key re-formed the band. With the help of session musicians they recorded *Real To Reel,* but unable to attract media attention, they disbanded shortly thereafter.

Albums: *Dark Star* (Avatar 1981), *Real To Reel* (FM Revolver 1987).

Deaf Dealer

This heavy metal band was formed in Jonquiere, Canada, in 1980. The original line-up consisted of Andy La Roche (vocals), Ian Penn (guitar), Marc Hayward (guitar), J.P. Forsyth (bass) and Dan McGregor (drums). Through early demos the band quickly gained popularity on the underground tape-trading scene and also had a track included on the *Metal Massacre IV* compilation album, released on the Metal Blade label in 1983. They then disappeared from the scene until resurfacing in 1985 as Deaf Dealer with a new vocalist, Michael Flynn. After several false starts on the recording of their debut album, *Keeper Of The Flame* was finally released on Roadrunner Records in 1986. A worthy power metal release, it nevertheless sank without trace amid strong competition from several musically similar outfits. The band tried to persevere but in the face of such adversity folded in 1987.

Album: *Keeper Of The Flame* (Roadrunner 1986).

Death

Primarily the brainchild of vocalist/guitarist Chuck Schuldiner, the godfather of the 'death metal' movement, who formed his first, embryonic outfit in Florida, USA, in 1983. Through early demos recorded with various local musicians (notably guitarist Rick Rozz and drummer Kam Lee) as Mantas, he gained a recording contract with Combat Records in America, with the provision that the product would also be released in Europe on the Music For Nations' subsidiary label, Under One Flag. Playing some of the fastest, most aggressive white noise ever to be recorded, Schuldiner moved the band from Florida to San Francisco, and Death came into existence. It is here the story becomes complicated due to the sheer number of different musicians who have passed through the Death ranks. For their 1987 debut, *Scream Bloody Gore,* the line-up consisted of Schuldiner (vocals/guitar/bass) and Chris Reifert (drums). The album, as its title implied, was a torrid listening experience, putting the band firmly on the map as purveyors of musical extremities and the originators of the death metal style, as Schuldiner ground out cinematic riffs to his evocation of night-time terror. For *Leprosy* the band's line-up grew to include Schuldiner (vocals/guitar), Rick Rozz (guitar), Terry Butler (bass) and Bill Andrews (drums), with the themes of the debut expanded into less fantastical concerns. By the time of *Spiritual Healing,* Rozz had left the band to be replaced by James Murphy. This third chapter in the group's evolution saw Schuldiner advance a political perspective which blended true crime stories with news reportage, peppered with digs at both the establishment and the evangelist preachers who were beginning to target the group. The band toured Europe as support to Kreator, but on the eve of their departure, mainman Schuldiner left. Against all odds (and common sense) they decided to carry on and undertake this, their most important tour. His replacements for the duration of the exercise were ex-Devastation drummer Louie Carrisalez (handling vocal duties) and ex-Rotting Corpse guitarist Walter Thrashler, both of whom had previously been members of Death's roadcrew. The tour was not a great success, with European fans refusing to accept the group without its figurehead. On their return to America they soon went their separate ways, with both drummer Bill Andrews and bassist Terry Butler going on to re-form their original band, Massacre. It was at this point that Schuldiner decided to resurrect Death to record what is considered by many to be their best work. Joining him in this new incarnation

of the band were Cynic guitarist Paul Masvidal, Sadus bassist Steve DiGiorgio and Cynic drummer Sean Reinert. The album, entitled *Human,* was released in 1991 and unveiled material of a much more varied composition than had previously been the case - even going as far as to include a melodic instrumental track, entitled 'Cosmic Sea'. After its release Schuldiner promised to put together a full-time unit from the musicians who had played on the album, with the intention of a European tour in 1992. However, by the following year Gene Hoglan (ex-Dark Angel; drums) and Skott Karino (guitar) had been recruited. For the sessions which produced *Individual Thought Patterns,* however, the supporting cast was Andy Larocque (guitar; ex-King Diamond) plus DiGiorgio (bass) and Hoglan (drums). The album's better moments included two cuts which attacked the music industry ('Overactive Imagination', 'Trapped In A Corner'), while production was helmed by Scott Burns.

Albums: *Scream Bloody Gore* (Under One Flag 1987), *Leprosy* (Under One Flag 1988), *Spiritual Healing* (Under One Flag 1990), *Human* (Roadrunner 1992), *Individual Thought Patterns* (Roadrunner 1993), *Symbolic* (Roadrunner 1995). Compilation: *Fate: The Best Of Death* (Under One Flag 1992).

Death

Death Angel

This group was formed in San Francisco, California, USA, the home of the Bay Area 'thrash' phenomenon in 1982. The band consisted of five cousins, namely Mark Osegueda (vocals), Rob Cavestany (guitar), Gus Pepa (guitar), Dennis Pepa (bass) and Andy Galeon (drums). Their debut, *The Ultra-Violence,* was a brutal blend of high speed thrash riffs and thunderous drums. The band quickly followed it up with *Frolic In The Park* in 1988. This showed the band had progressed both musically and lyrically, though many perferred the outright carnage of their opening salvo. Death Angel then experienced internal problems but managed to pull through, signing to Geffen Records after touring with Motörhead, and releasing the highly-acclaimed *Act III* in 1990. However, while touring to promote the latter album their bus drove off the road and crashed in the early hours of the morning in the middle of the desert between Phoenix and Las Vegas. Drummer and youngest member Andy Galeon was critically hurt, with injuries that would take over a year to heal. Unfortunately, their problems escalated with the departure of vocalist Mark Osegueda, who was not prepared to be inactive during Galeon's recuperation. The remaining members, with their recovered cousin and drummer, became the Organization.
Albums: *The Ultra-Violence* (Under One Flag 1987), *Frolic In The Park* (Enigma 1988), *Act III* (Geffen 1990).

Death Mask

Formed in New York, America in 1985 this heavy metal band consisted of Steven Michaels (vocals), Benny Ransom (guitar), Chris Eichhorn (bass) and Lee Nelson (drums). All the band had been members of various New York street gangs, and taking it off the streets they channelled their aggression into the music. They attracted the attention of Jon-Mikl Thor, the muscle-bound vocalist of the band Thor, who produced their debut album. The band signed to the Killerwatt Records label and released their debut entitled *Split The Atom* in 1986. Production duties were handled by Thor, and guitarist Steve Price. Unfortunately the music on offer did not reflect the band's tough street image, being a mixture of mediocre thrash metal and hard rock. Even though Thor included one of the album tracks, entitled 'I'm Dangerous', on the soundtrack to his film *Zombie Nightmare* the band failed to make any impact and soon sank without trace.
Album: *Split The Atom* (Killerwatt 1986).

Dedringer

Originally titled Deadringer, they formed in late 1977 in Leeds, England, as a competent but average rock group comprising John Hoyle (vocals), Neil Hudson (guitar), Al Scott (rhythm guitar), Lee Flaxington (bass) and Kenny Jones (drums). They built up a small but loyal following throughout 1978 and came to the attention of Virgin Records through their A&R man, who decided to manage them when Virgin failed to sign them. In 1980 they signed to pop/new romantic label DinDisc who issued a handful of singles and an album, before setting off touring in support of Triumph and Gillan. In 1981, following the release of their best single, 'Maxine', they decided to split up. A year later Scott reformed the group with Neil Garfitt (vocals) and Chris Graham (bass). Armed with a new recording deal with Neat Records they adopted a more aggressive style typical of bands like Fist and Tygers Of Pan Tang, but after a second uninspired long playing collection they fell apart.
Albums: *Direct Line* (DinDisc 1980), *Second Arising* (Neat 1983).

Deep Purple

Deep Purple evolved in 1968 following sessions to form a group around former Searchers' drummer Chris Curtis (b. 26 August 1942, Liverpool, England). Jon Lord (b. 9 June 1941, Leicester, England; keyboards) and Nick Simper (bass), veterans, respectively, of the Artwoods and Johnny Kidd And The Pirates, joined guitarist Ritchie Blackmore (b. 14 April 1945, Weston-super-Mare, England) in rehearsals for this new act, initially dubbed Roundabout. Curtis dropped out within days, and when Dave Curtis (bass) and Bobby Woodman (drums) also proved incompatible, two members of Maze, Rod Evans (vocals) and Ian Paice (drums), replaced them. Having adopted the Deep Purple name following a brief Scandinavian tour, the quintet began recording their debut album, which they patterned on USA group Vanilla Fudge. *Shades Of Deep Purple* thus included dramatic rearrangements of well-known songs, including 'Hey Joe' and 'Hush', the latter becoming a Top 5 US hit when issued as a single. Lengthy tours ensued as the group, all but ignored at home, steadfastly courted the burgeoning American concert circuit. *The Book Of Taliesyn* and *Deep Purple* also featured several excellent reworkings, notably 'Kentucky Woman' (Neil Diamond) and 'River Deep Mountain High' (Ike And Tina Turner), but the unit also drew acclaim for its original material and the dramatic interplay between Lord and Blackmore. In July 1969 both

Evans and Simper were axed from the line-up, which was then buoyed by the arrival of Ian Gillan (b. 19 August 1945, Hounslow, Middlesex, England; vocals) and Roger Glover (b. 30 November 1945, Brecon, Wales; bass) from the pop group Episode Six. Acknowledged by aficionados as the 'classic' Deep Purple line-up, the reshaped quintet made its album debut on the grandiose *Concerto For Group And Orchestra*, scored by Lord and recorded with the London Philharmonic Orchestra. Its orthodox successor, *Deep Purple In Rock*, established the group as a leading heavy metal attraction and introduced such enduring favourites as 'Speed King' and 'Child In Time'. Gillan's powerful intonation brought a third dimension to their sound and this new-found popularity in the UK was enhanced when an attendant single, 'Black Night', reached number 2. 'Strange Kind Of Woman' followed it into the Top 10, while *Fireball* and *Machine Head* topped the album chart. The latter included the riff-laden 'Smoke On The Water', now lauded as a seminal example of the hard rock oeuvre, and was the first release on the group's own Purple label. Although the platinum-selling *Made In Japan* captured their live prowess in full flight, relations within the band grew increasingly strained, and *Who Do We Think We Are?* marked the end of this highly-successful line-up. The departures of Gillan and Glover robbed Deep Purple of an expressive frontman and imaginative arranger, although Dave Coverdale (b. 22 September 1949, Saltburn, Lancashire, England; vocals) and Glenn Hughes (ex-Trapeze, bass) brought a new impetus to the act. *Burn* and *Stormbringer* both reached the Top 10, but Blackmore grew increasingly dissatisfied with the group's direction and in May 1975 left to form Rainbow. US guitarist Tommy Bolin, formerly of the James Gang, joined Deep Purple for *Come Taste The Band*, but his jazz/soul style was incompatible with the group's heavy metal sound, and a now-tiring act folded in 1976 following a farewell UK tour. Coverdale then formed Whitesnake, Paice and Lord joined Tony Ashton in Paice Ashton And Lord, while Bolin tragically died of a heroin overdose within months of Purple's demise. Judicious archive and 'best of' releases kept the group in the public eye, as did the high profile enjoyed by its several ex-members. Pressure for a reunion bore fruit in 1984 when Gillan, Lord, Blackmore, Glover and Paice completed *Perfect Strangers*. A second set, *House Of Blue Lights*, ensued, but recurring animosity between Gillan and Blackmore resulted in the singer's departure following the in-concert *Nobody's Perfect*. Former Rainbow vocalist, Joe Lynn Turner, was brought into the line-up for *Slaves And Masters* as Purple steadfastly

maintained their revitalized career. Gillan re-joined in 1993 only to quit, yet again, shortly after, while his old sparring partner, Blackmore, would also bail out the following year, to be replaced by Joe Satriani.
Albums: *Shades Of Deep Purple* (Parlophone 1968), *The Book Of Taliesyn* (Harvest 1969), *Deep Purple* (Harvest 1969), *Concerto For Group And Orchestra* (Harvest 1970), *Deep Purple In Rock* (Harvest 1970), *Fireball* (Harvest 1971), *Machine Head* (Purple 1972), *Made In Japan* (Purple 1973), *Who Do We Think We Are?* (Purple 1973), *Burn* (Purple 1974), *Stormbringer* (Purple 1975), *Come Taste The Band* (Purple 1975), *Perfect Strangers* (Polydor 1984), *House Of Blue Light* (Polydor 1987), *Nobody's Perfect* (Polydor 1988, double live album), *Slaves And Masters* (RCA 1990), *The Battle Rages On* (RCA 1993), *The Final Battle* (RCA 1994), *Come Hell Or High Water* (RCA 1994). Compilations: *24 Carat Purple* (Purple 1975), *Made In Europe* (Purple 1976), *Last Concert In Japan* (EMI 1977), *Shades Of Deep Purple* (Harvest 1977), *Powerhouse* (Purple 1977), *Singles: As & Bs* (Harvest 1978), *Deepest Purple* (Harvest 1980), *Live In London: Deep Purple* (Harvest 1982), *Anthology: Deep Purple* (Harvest 1985), *Scandinavian Nights* (Connoisseur 1988, double album), *Knebworth '85* (Connoisseur 1991), *Anthology 2* (EMI 1991).
Videos: *California Jam* (1984), *Video Singles* (1987), *Bad Attitude* (1988), *Concert For Group And Orchestra* (1988), *Deep Purple* (1988), *Doing Their Thing* (1990), *Scandinavian Nights* (1990).
Further reading: *Illustrated Biography*, Chris Charlesworth.

Deep Switch

Formed in Norwich, England, late in 1985, Deep Switch - Jinx (vocals), Gander (bass), Reverend Nice (guitars) and Simon DeMontford (drums) played few gigs and received almost no press at all. It was thanks to the underground fanzine the *Organ* that the band achieved cult status with a blistering review of their only self-financed album. Musically they blended elements of Alice Cooper and Wrathchild (UK) with a sense of humour which stretched the boundaries of taste. One track, 'Pigfeeder', must be singled out for its clever political theme based on George Orwell's book, *Animal Farm*. By the time word of the band filtered out of the underground to the likes of heavy metal magazine *Kerrang* and DJ Tommy Vance at Radio 1 (who played 'Pigfeeder' once) they had split up, with DeMontford joining the Bombshells.
Album: *Nine Inches Of God* (Switch 1986).

Def Leppard

This supremely popular hard rock band was formed

in Sheffield by Pete Willis (b. 16 February 1960, Sheffield, England; guitar), Rick Savage (b. 2 December 1960, Sheffield, England; bass) and Tony Kenning (drums), as Atomic Mass. They assumed their current name when Joe Elliott (b. 1 August 1959, Sheffield, England; vocals) joined the band. The quartet initially hired a tiny room in a spoon factory, which served as a rehearsal area, for £5 per week. Early in 1978, Willis met another young guitarist, Steve Clark (b. 23 April 1960, Sheffield, England, d. 8 January 1991, London, England), and invited him to join. Clark agreed only on condition that they would play some 'proper' shows, and in July that year Def Leppard debuted at Westfield School before an audience of 150 children. After several gigs, the band voted to dismiss their drummer, replacing him with Frank Noon, who was working with another Sheffield group, the Next Band. In 1979 they recorded a debut EP for Bludgeon Riffola Records, which included 'Ride Into The Sun', 'Getcha Rocks Off' and 'The Overture'. Shortly after its release, Noon returned to the Next Band, and Rick Allen (b. 1 November 1963, Sheffield, England) became Def Leppard's permanent drummer. Later that year the band supported Sammy Hagar and AC/DC on short UK tours. This generated considerable interest and they were then offered a deal by Vertigo Records. Their Tom Allom-produced debut, *On Through The Night*, was issued in 1980. The band subsequently staged their first headlining tour of Britain and also visited America for the first time - something which prompted fans to accuse them of 'selling out', making their displeasure known by throwing cans at the band during their appearance at the Reading Festival that summer. *Pyromania* in 1983 saw the first change in the band's line-up since 1979. After missing many pre-production meetings and turning up drunk for a recording session, Pete Willis was sacked and replaced by ex-Girl guitarist Phil Collen (b. 8 December 1957, Hackney, London, England). The album was Def Leppard's most successful to date, but they were unable to build on that momentum. On New Year's Eve 1984, tragedy struck when drummer Rick Allen was involved in a car crash in which he lost his left arm. The band maintained faith with their percussionist, and did not resume work until Allen had perfected a specially designed kit which made it possible for him to play most of the drums with his feet. His recovery severely delayed the recording of *Hysteria*, which was finally released in 1987 and eventually sold a staggering 15 million copies worldwide. It topped both the British and American charts, and produced two Top 5 US singles, 'Armageddon It' and the anthemic 'Pour Some Sugar

On Me'. To promote the album, the band embarked on a 14-month world tour, which ended at the Memorial Arena, Seattle, in October 1988. This was destined to be Steve Clark's last show with the band. As they began work on their belated follow-up to *Hysteria*, Clark was found dead in his London flat after consuming a mixture of drugs and alcohol. The rest of the band subsequently revealed that they had spent years trying to dissuade Clark from his self-abusive lifestyle. Faced once again by tragedy, Def Leppard soldiered manfully through the recording sessions for their fifth album, *Adrenalize*, which was released in March 1992 and immediately scaled the charts, topping the US list almost on release. Greeted with the usual mixture of critical disdain and public delight (the group's fans had chosen the title), Def Leppard celebrated by performing at the Freddy Mercury tribute concert at Wembley Stadium. This event also sought to introduce replacement guitarist Vivian Campbell (b. 25 August 1962, Belfast, Northern Ireland; ex-Dio, Trinity, Whitesnake and Shadow King), who had made his debut at a low-key Dublin gig.

Albums: *On Through The Night* (Mercury 1980), *High 'N' Dry* (Mercury 1981), *Pyromania* (Mercury 1983), *Hysteria* (Mercury 1987), *Adrenalize* (Mercury 1992). Compilations: *CD Box Set* (Mercury 1989), *Retro Active* (Mercury 1993).
Videos: *Historia* (1988), *In The Round, In Your Face* (1989), *Visualize* (1993).
Further reading: *Animal Instinct*, David Fricke.

Deicide

This controversial Satanic metal outfit were formed in 1987 in Florida as Amon, with the line-up of Glen Benton (bass/vocals), guitarists Eric and Brian Hoffman, and Steve Asheim (drums). The band became notorious owing to their conflict with the Christian establishment in America, and with animal rights groups due to Benton's exaggerated statements concerning mutilation of small animals. Repeated bomb threats from the Animal Militia during European tours culminated in an actual explosion at a Stockholm venue in 1992 during support band Gorefest's set. In addition, an alleged suicide pact between the band members when they reach 33 years of age and the fact that the outspoken Benton branded his own forehead with an inverted cross created an air of evil charisma which *Deicide*'s workmanlike death metal could barely match. Coupled with the publicity, it at least served to establish them as a major death metal act. *Legion* saw considerable progression, with a more focused approach channelling Deicide's aggression into better musicianship and songs. The band subsequently released two raw Amon demos, 'Feasting The Beast' and 'Sacrificial', as *Amon: Feasting The Beast*, and *Once Upon The Cross* .

Albums: *Deicide* (RC 1990), *Legion* (RC 1992). As Amon: *Amon: Feasting The Beast* (RC 1993), *Once Upon The Cross* (RC 1995).

Demolition 23

New York-based rock band whose rise to prominence was initially sponsored by three of the group's former occupation - as part of legendary sleaze rockers Hanoi Rocks. That band sundered with the death of drummer Razzle in 1984, since when Michael Monroe, Nasty Suicide and Sam Yaffa had involved themselves in a variety of solo and group projects. However, none of these proved truly satisfactory, and in the summer of 1993 Demolition 23 was born. Guitarist Jay Henning joined them for a 10 week residency at downtown Manhattan club, the Grand. An unusal tenure for a new band, their popularity was confirmed by a set which mixed Hanoi Rocks' standards with US punk rock anthems drawn from the Dead Boys, New York Dolls, Heartbreakers, MC5 and the Stooges. Guest performers included Joey Ramone (Ramones), Ian Hunter, Kory Clarke (Warrior Soul) and Sebastian Bach (Skid Row). With the band now established as Monroe (vocals/harmonica), Suicide (guitar), Yaffa (bass) and Jimmy Clark (drums), they recorded their debut album in five days at the Power Station in New York. An important collaborator was Steven Van Zandt, who produced and also co-wrote much of the material. Released in Japan in June 1994, where the Hanoi legacy still burns strong, it was eventually welcomed as a mutual return to form when released in mainland Europe and the US.

Album: *Demolition 23* (Music For Nations 1994).

Demon

This Midlands-based quintet were formed in the early 80s by vocalist Dave Hill and guitarist Mal Spooner in the halcyon days of the New Wave Of British Heavy Metal movement. Backed by Les Hunt (guitar), Chris Ellis (bass) and John Wright (drums), after two albums they had outgrown the formularised approach of this genre and diversified into more melodic and mature rock music, fired with passion and a keen sense of dynamics. *The Plague* was designed as a musical equivalent to Orwell's *1984*, a powerful statement of intent on both a musical and lyrical level. *British Standard Approved* and *Heart Of*

Deicide

Our Time followed, which consolidated the band's position as the UK's leading exponents of underground melodic rock. Following the tragic death of Mal Spooner in 1985, keyboardist Steve Watts teamed up with Dave Hill as the band's new writing force. Subsequently augmented by Scot Crawford on drums and guitarists Steven Brookes and John Waterhouse, the group went on to release a string of highly polished, atmospheric studio albums and a double live set recorded in Germany. Still struggling to achieve widespread recognition and exposure well into their second decade, it is Demon's commitment to maintaining standards as much as their longevity which distinguishes them.

Albums: *Night Of The Demon* (Carerre 1981), *The Unexpected Guest* (Carerre 1982), *The Plague* (Carerre 1983), *British Standard Approved* (Clay 1985), *Heart Of Our Time* (Clay 1985), *Breakout* (Clay 1987), *Taking The World By Storm* (Clay 1989), *One Helluva Night - Live* (Sonic 1990, double album), *Hold On To The Dream* (Sonic 1991), *Blow-Out* (Sonic 1992). Compilation: *Anthology* (Clay 1991).

Derringer, Rick

b. Richard Zehringer, 5 August 1947, Fort Recovery, Ohio, USA. Originally a member of the chart-topping McCoys ('Hang On Sloopy' etc.), Derringer went on to produce two of their later albums, paving the way for his new career. Along with his brother Randy, Rick formed the nucleus of Johnny Winter's backing group. After producing four of Winter's albums, he joined the Edgar Winter Group and produced their best-selling 1973 album, *They Only Come Out At Night*. Meanwhile, Derringer finally recorded his first solo album, the heavy metal-tinged *All American Boy*, which would introduce vocalist Vinny Appice (later of Black Sabbath), in 1974. Appice, plus band colleagues Danny Johnson (guitar) and Kenny Aaronson (bass) would depart to form Axis after the release of *Live* in 1977. For his part, after several albums with the group Derringer, Rick reverted to solo billing and appeared as guest guitarist on albums by Steely Dan (he was the Ricky mentioned in 'Ricky Don't Lose That Number'), Bette Midler, Todd Rundgren, Donald Fagen, Kiss, Cyndi Lauper, Meat Loaf, Barbra Streisand and 'Weird Al' Yankovic. Afterwards he would turn his attention to production and soundtrack work. However, the 90s saw him return to solo recording, having turned down several previous attempts to lure him: 'They all saw me as some kind of screaming, sweating rock 'n' roller, but I've grown out of that now'. It was Mike Varney at Shrapnel Records who finally won the day, teaming him with bassist and co-producer Kevin Russell for *Back To The Blues* and *Electra Blues*.

Albums: *All American Boy* (Blue Sky 1974), *Spring Fever* (Blue Sky 1975), *Derringer* (Blue Sky 1976), *Sweet Evil* (Blue Sky 1977), *Live* (Blue Sky 1977), *If You Weren't So Romantic* (CBS 1978), *Guitars And Women* (CBS 1979), *Face To Face* (CBS 1980), *Good Dirty Fun* (Passport 1983), *Back To The Blues* (Shrapnel 1993), *Electra Blues* (Shrapnel 1994).

Des Barres, Michael

Des Barres was formerly lead vocalist with 70s glam-rockers Silverhead. Before going solo, he was also a short-lived member of Detective and Chequered Past, and made a guest appearance on Gene Simmons' solo album in 1978. Five years on from his debut effort, he replaced Robert Palmer as the vocalist in Power Station in 1985. Both of his solo albums, meanwhile, have been erratic, featuring an *ad hoc* collection of styles and ideas that, whilst rock-based, are not easily pigeon-holed into any particular genre.

Albums: *I'm Only Human* (Dreamland 1980), *Somebody Up There Likes Me* (MCA 1986).

Destiny

This Swedish melodic rock quintet was formed in 1980 by bassist Stefan Bjornshog. Following a plethora of short-lived line-up changes, the band finally stabilized in 1984 with Bjornshog plus Magnus Osterman (guitar), John Proden (guitar), Peter Lundgren (drums) and Hakan Ring (vocals). They debuted the following year with *Beyond All Sense*, which comprised an uninspiring collection of identikit Eurorock numbers. Attracting little media interest, Osterman, Proden and Ring quit the band and were replaced by Jorgen Pettersson, Floyd Konstatin (ex-King Diamond) and Zenny Hanson respectively. This line-up recorded *Atomic Winter*, which was more aggressive and leaned towards the thrash genre. Nevertheless it fared little better than its predecessor. Konstantin and Pettersson quit shortly after the album was recorded, and the band reverted to a four-piece with the addition of Gunnar Kindberg. *Destiny*, released in 1990, was their finest work to date, but the band remain virtually unknown outside their native Sweden.

Albums: *Beyond All Sense* (1985), *Atomic Winter* (1988), *Destiny* (1990), *Nothing Left To Fear* (Music For Nations 1991).

Destruction

Along with Kreator, this speed metal band were at the forefront of the 80s German thrash scene, although they never quite achieved the former's level of success.

Rick Derringer

Schmier (bass/vocals), Mike (guitar) and Tommy (drums) made a rather raw debut with *Sentence Of Death*, but quickly refined their sound into potent, powerful thrash for the excellent *Infernal Overkill*. Second guitarist Harry joined following the recording of the equally ferocious *Eternal Devastation* to bolster the live sound, although Tommy also departed to be replaced by Olly, and the pair made their debut on the *Mad Butcher* E.P. *Release From Agony* saw the band make full use of the extra dimension the second guitar added, although their increasing musical dexterity and more intricate song structures did nothing to temper Destruction's aggression and heaviness, and the band began to extend themselves abroad, playing with Motörhead across Europe and on a few dates of Slayer's US tour. *Live Without Sense* was an adequate display of the band's on-stage power, but Destruction's fortunes took a downturn after they supported Celtic Frost on their Cold Lake UK tour. Internal dissent led to Schmier's departure, with the rest of the band electing to pursue a more melodic direction. *Cracked Brain* was recorded with new bassist Chris and stand-in vocalist Andre but was disappointing, and further credibility was lost with a pointless cover of the Knack's 'My Sharona', and Destruction soon folded.
Albums: *Sentence Of Death* (SPV 1985, mini-album), *Infernal Overkill* (SPV 1987), *Eternal Devastation* (SPV 1986), *Release From Agony* (SPV 1987), *Live Without Sense* (Noise 1989), *Cracked Brain* (Noise 1990). Compilation: *Best Of Destruction* (SPV 1992).

Detective

Superb Anglo-American Led Zeppelin-inspired supergroup fronted by actor and ex-Silverhead vocalist Michael Des Barres and ex-Yes keyboard player Tony Kaye. With the addition of Michael Monarch on guitar, Bobby Picket on bass and the powerful drummer Jon Hyde they soon began to make waves in the clubs of Los Angeles. When Jimmy Page spotted them he signed them to his Swan Song label and put them straight in the studio. Hyde's drumming proved so John Bonham-like that Page himself undertook most of the production work (under the pseudonym Jimmy Robinson) to do the band's sound justice (which he did). Detective soon built up a reputation among their professional peers but fame seemed to elude them. A second album lacked the direction and production of the first and did little to elevate them into the first division. It did, however, lead them into a starring role for an episode of the American situation comedy series, *WKRP In Cincinnati*. Barres split the band soon after and made a guest appearance on Gene Simmons' solo album

before launching his own band in 1980. Monarch joined Meat Loaf's backing band and Kaye later returned to Yes while Hyde, sadly, gave up the music business.
Albums: *Detective* (Swan Song 1977), *It Takes One To Know One* (Swan Song 1978).

Detente

This heavy metal band with a punk attitude were formed in Los Angeles in 1984, by vocalist Dawn Crosby and drummer Dennis Butler. Recruiting guitarists Caleb Quinn and Ross Robinson, along with bassist Steve Hochheiser through small-ad columns, the line-up was complete. They signed to Roadrunner Records and debuted in 1986 with *Recognize No Authority*. Produced by Dana Strum (now of Slaughter), it was characterized by Crosby's vitriolic vocal tirade and the heavy-duty riffing of Quinn and Robinson. The album sank without trace and subsequently Hochheiser and Robinson left to form Catalepsy. Detente continued with Greg Cekalovich (guitar) and George Robb (bass) and later ex-Abattoir guitarist Mike Carlino. They lost their contract with Roadrunner in 1988 and the band have been inactive since.
Album: *Recognize No Authority* (Roadrunner 1986).

Di'Anno's, Paul, Battlezone

When Paul Di'Anno (b. 17 May 1959, Chingford, London, England) was unceremoniously 'asked to leave' Iron Maiden he set about forming his own band. After playing in the American-influenced Lonewolf and Dianno, he put together the first incarnation of the band known as Paul Di'Anno's Battlezone in London, England, in 1985. Joining Di'Anno in this venture were ex-Deep Machine and Tokyo Blade guitarist John Wiggins, John Hurley (guitar), Pete West (bass) and Bob Falck (drums). The band signed to the Raw Power label and released their debut album, *Fighting Back*, in 1986. It was a welcome return to the style of music Di'Anno plays best - hard and fast power metal in the classic British tradition. Tours took the band through Europe (where they appeared at the Dynamo Open Air Festival) and America. At the end of which Falck left the band to join Overkill. Around the same time Hurley also departed. Their replacements were drummer Steve Hopgood and guitarist Graham Bath, both ex-Persian Risk. A label switch preceded album number two, and *Children Of Madness* was released by Powerstation in 1987. Slightly Americanized, and harking back to Di'Anno's Lonewolf days, the material was not as strong as the band's previous release. Battlezone soon fell apart leaving their leader alone to regroup. The band's last line-up consisted of Di'Anno (vocals), Graham Bath (guitar), Randy Scott (guitar), Mel Gibbons (bass) and Wayne Hewitt (drums). They gigged but never managed to secure a recording contract and subsequently folded. Di'anno later turned up as guest vocalist with the re-formed Praying Mantis on a Japanese tour, before forming Killers with former members of Passion, Jagged Edge and Tank.

Albums: *Fighting Back* (Raw Power 1986), *Children Of Madness* (Powerstation 1987).

Diamond Head

Formed in Stourbridge, England, in 1979, the original line-up of Diamond Head comprised Sean Harris (vocals), Brian Tatler (guitar), Colin Kimberley (bass) and Duncan Scott (drums). The band were one of the pioneers of the New Wave Of British Heavy Metal and their debut single, 'Sweet And Innocent', was a catchy melodic rocker showcasing the band's blues influences and Harris's impressive vocal talents. After gigging extensively, the band recorded a session for the Friday night rock show on BBC's Radio 1. 'Play It Loud' and 'Shoot Out The Lights' were both released in 1981 to minor critical acclaim. The press even went as far as to hail the band as the new Led Zeppelin. With interest growing they decided to self-finance their debut, which they sold through the pages of *Sounds* magazine under the title *Lightning To The Nation*. This was quickly snapped up by the German-based Woolfe Records in the same year, and released on import. The album was full of catchy melodic rock, soaring vocals and tasteful guitar work, and attracted the attention of several major record companies. As a stop-gap, the band released a 12-inch EP, *Diamond Lights*, again on DHM Records in 1981, before signing to MCA. Their first release for the label was an EP, *Four Cuts*, which was quickly followed up by their most popular album to date, *Borrowed Time*. Again the material was Led Zeppelin-style hard rock, and the band also included a couple of re-recorded tracks that had originally appeared on their first album. During sessions for the follow-up, *Canterbury*, both Kimberley and Scott exited. They were quickly replaced by former Streetfighter bassist Merv Goldsworthy (later a member of F.M.) and drummer Robbie France. The album was a brave change of direction for the band, still melodic but much more inventive and unconventional. Unfortunately, this change in style was not well received and despite a very successful appearance at the Monsters Of Rock Festival it flopped, and the group split up in 1985. Tatler then re-mixed their debut album, dropped two

of the original tracks and added four previously released single tracks. This was then released under the new title of *Behold The Beginning* (1986). Tatler went on to form Radio Moscow while Sean Harris teamed up with guitarist Robin George in the ill-fated Notorious album project. Even though Diamond Head were no longer in existence, they retained a healthy press profile owing to the acclaim heaped on them by Metallica drummer Lars Ulrich, who made no secret of the fact that the band were one of his main influences and inspired him to begin his musical career. Metallica subsequently recorded a cover version of Diamond Head's old stage favourite, 'Am I Evil'. Early in 1991 Harris and Tatler reformed Diamond Head with newcomers Eddie Nooham (bass) and Karl Wilcox (drums). The band undertook a short, low-key UK club tour using the name Dead Reckoning, then declared officially that they had reformed. The first release from this new incarnation was a limited edition 12-inch single, 'Wild On The Streets'. Housed on the newly relaunched Bronze label in 1991 it showed the band had returned in fine form and rediscovered the spirit lost in 1985. By the time they had pieced together a new collection (after shelving a projected mini album the year before) many of the rock world's biggest names were only to pleased to help out (including Tony Iommi of Black Sabbath, Dave Mustaine of Megadeth, and still-fervent supporter Lars Ulrich).

Albums: *The White Label Album* (Happy Face 1980), *Lightning To The Nations* (Woolfe 1981), *Borrowed Time* (MCA 1982), *Canterbury* (MCA 1983), *Behold The Beginning* (Heavy Metal 1986), *Am I Evil* (FM/Revolver 1987), *Death & Progress* (Bronze 1993).

Video: *Diamond Head* (1981).

Dianno

This British band was formed in 1982 by ex-Iron Maiden vocalist Paul Di'Anno (vocals), John Wiggins (guitar), Peter J. Ward (guitar/vocals), Mark Venables (keyboards/vocals), Kevin Browne (bass/vocals), and Mark Stewart (drums). Originally known as Lonewolf, they spent their first year touring Europe playing American style melodic AOR rock. In 1983 John Wiggins was replaced on guitar by Lee Slater and Lonewolf signed to FM Revolver. Soon after the contract was in place Lonewolf were forced to change their name following complaints from a group of the same title. On their debut album *Dianno*, the unit came across as an English band trying to sound American, though their version of Cliff Richard's 'Heart User' was a surprise inclusion. The album did not sell well and at the end of the year Dianno fell

apart with Paul Di'Anno going on to form Paul Di'Anno's Battlezone, then Killers.
Album: *Dianno* (FM Revolver 1984).

Dickinson, Bruce

b. Paul Bruce Dickinson, 7 August 1958, Worksop, Nottinghamshire, England. Former public school-boy Dickinson left the heavy metal group Samson to join pioneering contemporaries, Iron Maiden, replacing Paul Di'Anno in 1981. By the following year Dickinson had fully established himself within the line-up through his performances on the road and on the UK number 1 album, *Number Of The Beast*. 1990 was a busy year for Dickinson's solo pursuits. His aspirations to become a novelist were realized in his comic-novel, *The Adventures Of Lord Iffy Boatrace*, a sub-standard attempt at the style of Tom Sharpe. However, legions of Iron Maiden fans propelled the book into the best-seller ratings. Also that year, Dickinson's solo album, *Tattooed Millionaire*, reached number 14, while the title-track climbed into the UK Top 20. A version of Mott The Hoople's 'All The Young Dudes' also reached the UK Top 30. A keen fencer, Dickinson had at one time been ranked seventh in the men's foils for Great Britain, serving only to embellish his reputation as metal's renaissance man. He finally quit Maiden in 1993, a year after releasing a second book, *The Missionary Position*. A second solo album for EMI also followed, a year later.
Albums: *Tattooed Millionaire* (EMI 1990), *Balls To Picasso* (EMI 1994).
Further reading: *Lord Iffy Boatrace*, Bruce Dickinson (1990), *The Missionary Position*, Bruce Dickinson (1992).

Dictators

Formed in 1974 in New York City, the Dictators pre-dated the punk rock of bands such as the Ramones and Sex Pistols by two years, yet they exhibited many of that genre's hallmarks from their inception. Purveying loud, three-chord rock without long solos and drawing their lyrical inspiration and visual image from such disparate facets of popular culture as fast food, professional wrestling, cult movies and late-night television, the Dictators built a devoted fan-base in their hometown and selected hip pockets in the USA and Europe, but were unable to succeed commercially and are rarely acknowledged for their pioneering efforts in helping to establish the new rock 'n' roll of the 70s and 80s. The group originally consisted of guitarists Scott 'Top Ten' Kempner and Ross 'The Boss' Funicello, bassist Adny Shernoff and drummer Stu Boy King. Vocalist 'Handsome Dick Manitoba' (b. Richard Blum) guested on the group's debut album and subsequently joined. King left after the release of that album and was replaced by Richie Teeter, and bassist Mark 'The Animal' Mendoza also joined at that time (1975), allowing Shernoff to switch to keyboards. That first album, *The Dictators Go Girl Crazy*, featured original songs by Shernoff with titles such as 'Teengenerate', '(I Live For) Cars And Girls' and a cover of Sonny And Cher's 'I Got You Babe'. It was released on Epic Records, which then dropped the group when the album failed to catch on. After the personnel shuffle of 1975, the Dictators signed to Asylum/Elektra Records in late 1976 and released *Manifest Destiny*, their only album to chart. Before they recorded their third and last album, *Bloodbrothers*, in 1978, Mendoza left to join heavy metal outfit Twisted Sister. When the third album failed, they were dropped by Elektra and disbanded. The Dictators have reunited several times for single concert dates, one of which was recorded and released as a cassette-only album in 1981, *Fuck 'Em If They Can't Take A Joke*. During the 80s Kempner went on to form the Del-Lords, another straight-ahead rock group popular in New York, which recorded a few albums. Manitoba and Shernoff formed the quasi-metal band Manitoba's Wild Kingdom. Ross The Boss Funicello joined the short-lived Shakin' Street. The Dictators reunited once more in December 1993 to play at the 20th Anniversary celebrations for CBGB's.
Albums: *The Dictators Go Girl Crazy* (Epic 1975), *Manifest Destiny* (Asylum 1977), *Bloodbrothers* (Asylum 1978), *Fuck 'Em If They Can't Take A Joke* (ROIR 1981).

Die Cheerleader

British four-piece consisting of Rita Blazyca (guitar), Sam Ireland (vocals), Debbie Quargnolo (bass) and lone male member Andy Semple (drums). Die Cheerleader play chunky, punk-edged, hard rock, featuring feisty, semi-surreal songs about relationships and life's many downturns. In the process they have managed to straddle both the heavy metal and indie genres, capturing the attention of rock journalists from both camps and securing a publishing deal with poet and punk legend Henry Rollins. Tours with well-regarded punk and rock bands Terrorvision, Bad Religion and Iggy Pop helped to establish their reputation as a hard working, talented live act. *Filth By Association* collected their well-received first three EPs (*D.C.E.P.*, *Saturation* and *69 Hayloft Action*) in a remixed form, along with two new tracks to complete the package.
Album: *Filth By Association* (Abstract 1993).

Bruce Dickinson

Die Kreuzen

This punk/thrash band was formed in Milwaukee, USA, in 1981, their name derived from the German for 'the crosses'. The band, featuring Dan Kubinski (vocals), Brian Egeness (guitar), Keith Brammer (bass) and Eric Tunison (drums), started life with a highly regarded album of embryonic thrash (incorporating all six tunes from their 1982 debut EP, *Cows And Beer*). Since that debut their material has revealed a much stronger inclination towards traditional rock structures, though they were widely congratulated for bringing intelligence and lyrical diversity to the heavy metal sphere. *Century Days*, for example, includes both piano and horns on several tracks, whilst maintaining an allegiance to the band's traditionally hard sound. Brammer would transfer to Wreck in 1989. Signed to Chicago independent Touch And Go, their 1991 album was produced by Butch Vig (Killdozer, Tad, Nirvana).
Albums: *Die Kreuzen* (Touch & Go 1984), *October File* (Touch & Go 1986), *Century Days* (Touch & Go 1988), *Gone Away* (Touch & Go 1989, mini-album), *Cement* (Touch & Go 1991).

Die Krupps

Tracing their origins to the turn of the 80s, German outfit Die Krupps have been a pioneering force in experimental music ever since. The band was formed in 1981 by Jurgen Engler (vocals, keyboards, guitars and group spokesman; ex-famed German punk band Male) and Ralf Dorper (previously part of Propaganda). Together with Front 242 they helped to formulate the Body Music sub-genre of Euro rock, a sound lush in electronics but harsh in execution. Several albums of synthesized material emerged, and were duly snapped up by Die Krupps' loyal fan base. However, Engler spent the mid-80s, which were largely quiet for the band, ingesting the new sounds pioneered by Metallica and others who were pushing back the frontiers of metal. When Die Krupps eventually returned in 1992 they took all by surprise by adding layers of metal guitar, consequently picking up a new audience which spanned several genres. The most famous of two excellent sets in that year was a tribute album to the band who had revolutionized Engler's thinking: 'Metallica were coming to Germany for some dates and I wanted to present something to them because I really admired what they did. So we put together this tape, and that's all it was intended for, but our label heard of it and wanted to put it out...'. Lars Ulrich was reportedly highly impressed with the results, though he proved unable to meet an engagement to help out on the recording of *The Final Option*. This set saw the recruitment of Lee Altus (guitar; ex-Heathen) and Darren Minter (drums), and a continuation of Die Krupps' bleak lyrical thematic (notably on 'Crossfire', a reaction to the Yugoslavian conflict). A remix album, with contributions from Gunshot, Jim Martin (ex-Faith No More), Andrew Eldritch (Sisters of Mercy) and Julian Beeston (Nitzer Ebb, who in 1989 had remodelled the group's classic 'Wahre Arbeit, Wahrer Lohn') was also unveiled.
Albums: *Stahlwerksinfonie* (Zick Zack 1981), *Volle Kraft Voraus* (WEA 1982), *Entering The Arena* (Statik 1984), *Metalle Maschinen Musik 91-81 Past Forward* (Rough Trade 1991, double album), *One* (Rough Trade 1992), *Metal For The Masses Part II - A Tribute To Metallica* (Rough Trade 1992), *The Final Option* (Rough Trade 1993), *The Final Mixes* (Rough Trade 1994). Compilation: *Die Krupps Box* (Rough Trade 1993, 3-CD box set).

Die Monster Die

Formed in Athens, Georgia, the original impetus for Die Monster Die (self-described as 'the highest and lowest intellect combined into one mass') came from guitarist/bassist Evan Player's discovery of the Dead Kennedys' *Fresh Fruit For Rotting Vegetables*. The band he consequently put together, the first incarnation of Die Monster Die, dispersed in the late 80s, with Player departing for a new life in New York. At about which time drummer and New Orleans native Kenny Sanders also settled in the city, obliging his divine calling to 'become a rock star'. The two met through industrial metal outfit Stalwart. When both left that group in 1991 Die Monster Die was reborn. Sanders invited Alice Cohen, of Philadelphian extract, to sing with the group, having formerly appeared in Shag Motor Pony and the Vels. She agreed, also sharing bass duties with Player. With Shawn Tracy expanding the sound with second guitar the group released its first single, 'Planet'/'Backwater Trailer Park Blues'. A series of chaotic live performances ensued, highlighted by outlandish costumes and garish stage behaviour.

Dio, Ronnie James

b. Ronald Padavona, 10 July 1940, New Hampshire, USA. Dio was raised in New York, USA, and served his musical apprenticeship in the late 50s with school-based bands like the Vegas Kings, Ronnie And The Rumblers and Ronnie And the Redcaps (one single, 'Lover'/'Conquest', in 1958). From 1961-67 he led Ronnie Dio And the Prophets, not solely as a vocalist, but also playing the piano, bass guitar, and even trumpet. A multi-talented musician, he also acted as a record producer. In that time the Prophets released at least seven singles, including a gimmick version of 'Love Potion No. 9' which had the same song on both sides, plus an album. In 1967, with his cousin, David Feinstein, he formed the Electric Elves, a band which, in the early 70s, changed its name to Elf. In the middle of 1970, the entire band was involved in a car-crash, in which guitarist Nick Pantas died. Dio took on lead vocals in Elf and played the bass. Elf were discovered by Roger Glover and Ian Paice of Deep Purple in 1972, and the group would go on to support Deep Purple on two American tours as well as signing to their Purple imprint in the UK. In 1975 Glover gave Dio the opportunity to appear on his *The Butterfly Ball,* and the widespread recognition which ensued helped persuade Ritchie Blackmore, who had already recorded one track, 'Black Sheep Of The Family', with Elf, and recently left Deep Purple himself, to hook up. The remnants of Elf, with the exception of the ousted Steve Edwards, became Rainbow. This saw Dio develop from the honky-tonk influence of his former band to the harder rock of Blackmore and Rainbow. Dio's tendency to write about supernatural events, thoughts and fantasies also began to emerge at this stage, combining with the succession of often excellent musicians in Rainbow (the former members of Elf had been rapidly discarded) to produce four albums of high quality and enduring appeal. In 1979 Dio left Rainbow, taking his gift for singing and songwriting to Black Sabbath, where he built on the previously phenomenal, but now waning success of the band, doing much to rejuvenate the flagging supergroup. *Heaven And Hell* arrived alongside the New Wave Of British Heavy Metal, outclassing most of its rivals with its tight, solid, bass-dominated sound and science fiction lyrics. After an acrimonious world tour in 1983, Dio left to form his own band, Dio, which comprised Vinny Appice (drums), Jimmy Bain, former bassist with Rainbow, Vivian Campbell (guitar) and Claude Schnell (keyboards). Together, they recorded four albums, with Dio taking on all the lyrics and songwriting himself, allowing his creative muse a completely free rein. While the subject matter remained other worlds, times and beings, the style ranged from anthemic to epic. A lack of direction led to stagnation, and by 1987, when Craig Goldie replaced Campbell, the band was failing. In 1991 Dio renewed his acquaintance with Black Sabbath, joining them for a UK tour and recording *Dehumanizer* with them the following year. However, November saw Judas Priest's Rob Halford stand in for Dio when he refused to appear with the band in California after hearing of Ozzy Osbourne's intention to reform the original Sabbath line-up as part of his solo farewell tour. Dio, whom some commentators had taken to describing as the Cliff Richard of heavy metal, simply returned to the studio with yet another incarantion of his eponymous band.

Albums: With Ronnie Dio And The Prophets: *Dio At Dominos* (Lawn 1963). With Elf: *Elf* (Epic 1972), *LA59* (Purple 1974), *Trying To Burn The Sun* (MGM 1984), *Live* (MGM 1976). With Rainbow: *Ritchie Blackmore's Rainbow* (Oyster 1975), *Rainbow Rising* (Polydor 1976), *Live On Stage* (Polydor 1977), *Long Live Rock And Roll* (Polydor 1978), *Live In Germany* (Connoisseur 1990, double album). With Black Sabbath: *Heaven And Hell* (Vertigo 1980), *Mob Rules* (Vertigo 1981), *Live Evil* (Vertigo 1983), *Dehumanizer* (IRS 1992). With Dio: *Holy Diver* (Vertigo 1983), *The Last In Line* (Vertigo 1984), *Sacred Heart* (Vertigo 1985), *Intermission* (Vertigo 1986), *Dream Evil* (Vertigo 1987), *Hey Angel* (Vertigo 1990), *Lock Up The Wolves* (Vertigo 1990). Compilation: *Diamonds* (Vertigo 1992). Solo: *Carolina County Ball* (Purple 1974).
Videos: Dio: *Live In Concert* (1986), *Special From The Spectrum* (1986).

Dirty Looks

Founded in the early 80s by Dutch-born Hendrik Ostergaard, Dirty Looks released three albums on three different independent labels before achieving a major deal with Atlantic Records in 1987. Ostergaard handled both vocals and guitar, ably supported by Paul Lidel (guitar), Jack Pyers (bass) and Gene Barnett (drums). Their debut, *Cool From The Wire*, showed the band to be purveyors of straight-ahead, no nonsense power metal very much in the AC/DC mould. Both the crushing style of guitar riffing and the vocal delivery of Ostergaard made comparisons with the Australian supremos inevitable. However, such was the energy and commitment the band brought to recording and live performances that their indebtedness quickly became forgivable. The follow-up, *Turn Of The Screw*, was not as successful, despite critical acclaim. *Bootlegs* saw the band presenting the same style of relentless power boogie, albeit now with a return to a smaller label.

Albums: *Dirty Looks* (Axekiller 1985), *I Want More* (Storm 1986), *In Your Face* (Mirror 1987), *Cool From The Wire* (Atlantic 1987), *Turn Of The Screw* (Atlantic 1988), *Bootlegs* (Shrapnel 1991), *One Bad Leg* (Rockworld/Music For Nations 1995).

Dirty Tricks

This blues-based UK heavy rock outfit were formed in 1974 by vocalist Kenny Stewart and guitarist John Fraser Binnie. With bassist Terry Horbury and drummer John Lee completing the line-up, they drew inspiration from Bad Company, the Faces, Black Sabbath and Deep Purple. They never graduated from support status, because their attempt to bridge the divide between hard-rock and heavy metal was sabotaged by weak material. They released three albums on Polydor during the mid-70s, which failed to reflect the energy they generated in a live setting. In 1976 Andy Beirne took over the drumstool, but the band were soon overwhelmed by the growing punk movement. Beirne later joined Grand Prix, Terry Horbury teamed up with speed metal outfit Vardis and guitarist John Fraser Binnie was recruited by Rogue Male in 1984.

Albums: *Dirty Tricks* (Polydor 1975), *Night Man* (Polydor 1976), *Hit And Run* (Polydor 1977).

Dirty White Boy

This 'supergroup' was put together by Earl Slick (ex-guitarist with David Bowie, John Waite and John Lennon bands) and Glenn Eisley, former vocalist of Giuffria. Adding ex-Autograph drummer Keni Richards and bassist F. Kirk Alley to the line-up, their style and approach was the antithesis of what one might expect from their collective pedigrees. Throwing caution to the wind, they went for a no-holds-barred, down-and-dirty rock 'n' roll attack on their debut album. Produced by Beau Hill (of Ratt), *Bad Reputation* found these seasoned musicians re-discovering their roots and enjoying themselves in the process. 'Let's Spend Momma's Money', released as a single, also attracted approving glances.

Albums: *Bad Reputation* (Polygram 1990).

Dismember

Swedish band Dismember are a product of the increasingly active Scandinavian death metal scene. Like most of their peers Dismember are rather short on subtlety and originality. In terms of musical vitriol and intensity, however, they are a force to be reckoned with. They have also developed a talent for attracting controversy and outrage, which is a valuable asset in the shock-hungry death metal genre. Most notably, upon the release of *Like `an Ever Flowing Stream*, several hundred copies were seized at UK customs. The justification for this was the track 'Skin Her Alive', which HM Customs contended was obscene. The song dealt with a murder which had taken place in the flat beneath that of vocalist Matti Karki, and the lyrics tried to explore the thoughts of the killer. Despite widespread mainstream consensus that death metal did not deserve freedom of speech, the album was acquitted of obscenity in court. Dismember continued flouting good taste, dressing their

drummer, Fred Estby, as Jesus Christ in a demonic parody of the crucifixion on video shoots and album artwork. *Indecent And Obscene* refers to the attempted prosecution of their debut and comes complete with a track designed to provoke similar outrage, entitled 'Eviscerated (Bitch)'.

Albums: *Like An Ever Flowing Stream* (Nuclear Blast 1991), *Indecent And Obscene* (Nuclear Blast 1993).

Diving For Pearls

This cult AOR quintet formed in New York in 1988, when ex-Urgent guitarist Yul Vazquez joined Danny Malone (vocals), Jack Moran (keyboards), David Weeks (bass) and ex-Jean Beauvoir drummer Peter Clemente, taking their unusual name from an Elvis Costello lyric ('Shipbuilding'). The band signed within nine months to Epic Records on a development deal, and were subsequently able to record their full debut. *Diving For Pearls*, produced by David Prater, was received with a wave of acclaim in AOR circles, with comparisons to a diverse array of acts for their classy blend of keyboard-flavoured commercial hard rock with superb vocals and melancholy lyrics from Malone. However, given minimal promotion, the album simply failed to sell, and Diving For Pearls broke up when they lost their deal. Malone later reappeared in Band Of Angels.

Album: *Diving For Pearls* (Epic 1989).

DNA

This US band was a short-lived collaboration between guitarist Rick Derringer and drummer Carmine Appice. With the assistance of Duane Hitchings (keyboards) and Jimmy Johnson (bass), they released *Party Tested* in 1983. This featured a wide range of styles that included jazz, rock, funk, blues and pop. The playing was beyond criticism, but the songs were devoid of soul, and the album as a whole lacked unity and cohesion. Failing to win support in the media, DNA disintegrated when Carmine Appice accepted the offer to join Ozzy Osbourne's band. He subsequently formed King Kobra.

Album: *Party Tested* (Polydor 1983).

DOA

Explosive hardcore band based in Vancouver, Canada, who formed in 1978. The line-up featured Joey 'Shithead' Keithley (lead vocals/guitar), Randy Rampage (bass/vocals), Chuck Biscuits (drums), and also Brad Kent (guitar; ex-Avengers). Early releases included the *Disco Sucks* EP on their own Sudden Death Records, an impossibly rare artefact. Apart from their long playing debut, 1980 also saw Dave Gregg added as second guitarist to fill out the band's sound (Kent was only a temporary member). In the early 80s they toured incessantly, and not only defined their own sound but much of the subsequent 'hardcore' genre. The *Positively DOA* EP and *Hardcore 81* are hugely important to the development of north American punk. The latter actually gave the movement an identity, not only in name, but a political agenda too. The band's most successful line-up collapsed in 1982. Biscuits left to join the Circle Jerks (and subsequently Black Flag, Danzig), while Randy Rampage went on to a solo career. In came Gregg 'Dimwit' James (drums; ex-Subhumans, Pointed Sticks, actually Chuck Biscuits' elder brother) and Brian 'Wimpy Boy' Goble (bass/vocals; ex-Subhumans). DOA's product in this incarnation is almost as invigorating. However, the third album 'proper' would realise fully the potential of the two which preceded it. *Let's Wreck The Party* was a definitive, hard-rocking, intelligent punk record. After its release, James departed and was replaced on drums by Jon Card (ex-Personality Crisis and SNFU). Chris Prohourn aka 'Humper The Dumper' (guitar/vocals; ex-Red Tide) joined as well, when Dave Gregg started his own band, Groovaholics. Keithley, meanwhile, appeared alongside old friend Jello Biafra in the film *Terminal City Ricochet*, as a biker cop. One of the most influential and popular of Canada's punk bands.

Albums: *Something Better Change* (Friend's 1980), *Hardcore '81* (Friend's 1981), *Let's Wreck The Party* (Alternative Tentacles 1985), *True (North) Strong And Free* (Rock Hotel/Profile 1987), *Murder* (Restless 1990), *Talk Minus Action Equals Zero* (Roadrunner 1991), *13 Flavours Of Doom* (1992). Compilation: *Bloodied But Unbowed* (CD Presents 1984). With Jello Biafra: *Last Scream Of The Missing Neighbours* (Alternative Tentacles 1990, mini-album). Video: *Assassination Club* (1984).

Doc Holliday

Not to be confused with Frank Carillo's band from the early 70s, although both groups were American and played Southern boogie/rock. This version of Doc Holliday formed in 1980 with Bruce Bookshire (guitar/vocals), Rick Skelton (guitar), Eddie Stone (keyboards) and Robert Liggio (drums), and followed the 'heavier' style of Blackfoot, mixed with more obvious influences such as the Outlaws and the Allman Brothers. Having released two excellent albums without gaining mass acceptance they made what existing fans saw as a mistake in changing musical tack with an album in 1983 more suited to the listening tastes Journey or Styx fans. When this too failed they broke up. In 1986 they returned with a harder edge added to their original style and finally gained overdue attention with *Danger Zone*. *Song For The Outlaw Live* also earned strong reviews, though afterwards they fell silent.

Albums: *Doc Holliday* (A&M 1981), *Doc Holliday Rides Again* (A&M 1982), *Modern Medicine* (A&M 1983), *Danger Zone* (Metal Masters 1986), *Song For The Outlaw Live* (Loop 1989).

Dog Eat Dog

Impassioned New York metal crossover crew comprising John Connor (vocals), Dan Nastasi (guitar/vocals), Sean Kilkenny (guitar), Dave Neabore (bass) and David Maltby (drums). However, the stylistic diversity of their debut releases, the 1993 EP *Warrant*, and 1994 album, *All Boro Kings*, also saw them traverse hip hop, hardcore and dancehall reggae as well as more traditional rock riffing. Significantly, it featured contributions from Darryl Jenifer of Bad Brains, with production overseen by Jason Corsaro (Soundgarden, Danzig, Madonna etc.). Accused of jumping the Rage Against The Machine bandwagon in some quarters, the group nevertheless provided an intoxicating blend of forceful musics, while 'No Fronts' offered a caustic reply to their detractors in the press: 'No front, no tricks, no soap box politics, no guns, just blunts, we kick this just for fun'. If that sounded like a chip off Cypress Hill's block, then comparisons were accentuated by the introduction of the Solid Ground hip hop crew, and even a brass section. Playing live with both hip hop (Goats, Onyx) and metal/alternative acts (Biohazard, Bad Brains) further extended their audience.

Album: *All Boro Kings* (Roadrunner 1994).

Dogs D'Amour

This rock outfit was originally formed in Birmingham, England, during 1983, with a line-up comprising Tyla (guitar), Ned Christie (vocals), Nick Halls (guitar), Carl (bass) and Bam Bam (drums). After making their London debut in April 1983 and recording a track for the Flicknife compilation, *Trash On Delivery*, they underwent a rapid series of personnel changes. Halls, Bam Bam and Christie departed prompting Tyla to assume lead vocal responsibilities. He and Carl recruited replacements, Dave Kusworth (guitar) and Paul Hornby (drums). They relocated to Finland where their hard rock style won them an underground following. After returning to the UK in 1985, further changes in the line-up were underway, with Bam Bam replacing Hornby, while Kusworth departed in favour of the elegantly named Jo-Dog. Later that year, the procession of changes continued with the departure of Carl in favour of Doll By Doll bassist Mark Duncan, who lasted until 1987 when Steve James arrived. The group finally broke through with the minor hit, 'How Come It Never Rains', and the mini-album, *A Graveyard Of Empty Bottles*. The follow-up, 'Satellite Kid', also reached the UK Top 30, as did their album, *Errol Flynn*. The latter met some resistance in the USA where it was forcibly retitled *The King Of The Thieves*. Having at last stabilized their line-up, Dogs D'Amour failed to establish themselves in the top league of hard rock acts but continued to tour extensively. During a lull in the early 90s James formed the Last Bandits while Bam Bam joined the Wildhearts. The group reformed in 1993 with Darrell Barth (ex-Crybabys) replacing Jo Dog. However, by 1994 the group had ground to a halt, with Tyla considering a solo career while Steve James and Bam Bam formed Mary Jane.

Albums: *The State We're In* (Kumibeat 1984), *The (Un)Authorized Bootleg* (China 1988), *In The Dynamite Jet Saloon* (China 1988), *A Graveyard of Empty Bottles* (China 1989), *Errol Flynn* (China 1990), *More Uncharted Heights Of Disgrace* (China 1993).

Dokken

This Los Angeles band was put together by vocalist Don Dokken. His first break came when producer Dieter Dierks recruited him to supply (eventually un-used) back-up vocals on the Scorpions' *Blackout* in 1982. Dierks then allowed Dokken the left-over studio time to produce demos. These rough recordings impressed Carrere Records enough to secure a contract, and he enlisted the services of guitarist George Lynch, drummer Mick Brown and bassist Juan Croucier (who later left to form Ratt and was replaced by Jeff Pilson) to form Dokken, the band. Essentially Dokken's music is an intimate fusion of hard rock, melody and atmospherics. It was these qualities that Elektra Records saw in the band when they signed them in 1982. They re-mixed and re-released their Carrere debut, *Breaking The Chains*, which made the lower end of the US *Billboard* album charts. From this point on, Elektra allowed the band a substantial recording budget, with producers Michael Wagener, Geoff Workman, Tom Werman and Roy Thomas Baker being used at different times. The band recorded three excellent studio albums for Elektra before internal disputes between Lynch and Don Dokken led the band to split in 1988. A farewell

Dogs D'Amour

live album, *Beast From The East* followed, and is a fitting epitaph to a fine band. Lynch went on to form Lynch Mob, while Don Dokken negotiated a solo deal with Geffen Records and released *Up From The Ashes* in 1990.

Albums: *Breaking The Chains* (Carrere 1982), *Tooth And Nail* (Elektra 1984), *Under Lock And Key* (Elektra 1985), *Back For The Attack* (Elektra 1987), *Beast From The East* (1988, double album), *Back In The Streets* (Repertoire 1989). Don Dokken solo: *Up From The Ashes* (Geffen 1990).

Dollface

Indie/metal band formed in autumn 1992, comprising Adrian Portas (b. Sheffield, England; vocals/guitar), John Alexander (b. Surrey, England; bass), Rob Todd (b. Wales; guitar) and Dave Mage (b. Buckinghamshire, England; drums). Signing to Kill City Records in 1993, they made their debut with the *Methedrine* EP, then another four-track effort, *Rock Stars*. This, with endearing songs like 'Dead Boyfriend' and the ironic title-track, brought them to the attention of several in the media who admired their straightforward approach to dynamic rock. Their consequent position on many 'most likely to' critical lists as 1994 closed confirmed that arrival.

Dominique, Lisa

Dominique is a former beautician and sister of guitarist Marino. She started her career in the UK singing in Marino's band, but came to prominence through the pages of *Kerrang* magazine, appearing regularly as a pin-up. With interest already generated, she decided on a career in the music business and was signed by FM Revolver/Heavy Metal Records. With the help of Marino (guitar), Pete Jupp (drums) and other session musicians, she debuted with *Rock 'N' Roll Lady* in 1989. The album was universally slated by the music media, and Lisa was subsequently dropped. Undaunted by such a setback, she signed to Castle Communications and delivered *Lisa Dominique* in 1991. Again, this was not well-received in the heavy metal fraternity, or anywhere else for that matter.

Albums: With Marino: *Wanna Keep You Satisfied* (LRM 1985). Solo: *Rock 'N' Roll Lady* (FM Revolver 1989), *Lisa Dominique* (Essential 1991).

Done Lying Down

Led by Boston-born Jeremy Parker (vocals/guitar), Done Lying Down are nevertheless a UK-based outfit who were widely venerated by a number of sources throughout 1994. The line-up filled out by English personnel Ali Mac (bass), Glen Young (guitar) and James Sherry (drums), their list of achievements in that year included a series of EPs (*Heart Of Dirt, Family Values, Negative One Friends* and *Just A Misdemeanour*) which brought gradually increasing indie chart returns, radio sessions for John Peel, and video appearances on UK television's *Chart Show*, alongside feverish touring with Girls Against Boys, Compulsion, Ned's Atomic Dustbin and many others. The first of their EPs, released in 1993, was produced by Membranes/Sensurround leader and journalist John Robb. The three tracks were headed by 'Dissent', a forceful cut accentuated by a stop-start construction reminiscent of Nirvana (a comparison which stuck to the band throughout the course of their early career). An album, *John Austin Rutledge*, was named after a friend of Parker who co-wrote some of the songs therein: 'All he wanted was a credit, but we decided to name it after him and put his photo on the cover!', advised a slightly contrary Parker.

Album: *John Austin Rutledge* (Black And White Indians/Abstract 1994).

Doro

Dorothee Pesch (b. 3 June 1964, Dusseldorf, Germany), the leading light and vocalist of the German heavy metal band Warlock, dissolved the unit after the release of 1987's *Triumph And Agony*. Retaining only bassist Tommy Henriksen, she embarked on a solo career under the Doro moniker. To complete the new line-up she recruited guitarist John Devin and drummer Bobby Rondinelli. Using Joey Balin as a writing partner, *Force Majeure* offered a departure from her previous heavy teutonic style, moving towards a more mainstream AOR approach in a bid for commercial success. It featured an embarrassing cover of Procol Harum's 'A Whiter Shade Of Pale' as the opening track and fared poorly. Ditching the entire band in favour of hired hands, she recorded *Doro* with Gene Simmons (of Kiss) as producer. Musically, this was even further away from her roots, an attempt to achieve chart success which verged on desperation. *Rare Diamonds* was a compilation of older material, giving Doro time for a radical re-think about her next career move. When she did re-merge in 1993 with *Angels Never Die* the interest was minimal.

Albums: *Force Majeure* (Vertigo 1989), *Doro* (Vertigo 1990), *Angels Never Die* (Vertigo 1993). Compilation: *Rare Diamonds* (Vertigo 1991).

Dr. Mastermind

Formed in the USA during 1986, Dr. Mastermind were part of a new wave of guitar-orientated rock bands. Comprising Kurt James (ex-Steeler and Driver

Done Lying Down

guitarist), Deen Castronovo (drums) and the enigmatic Dr. Mastermind on bass and vocals, they were a power trio in every sense of the word. Frenetically paced songs, which never quite degenerated into tuneless thrash, were punctuated by high-octane and complex guitar breaks. After the release of their debut album, Castronovo joined Cacophony, and James left for Turbin. Rick Hosert and Pete Lachman were drafted in as replacements on drums and guitar respectively, but this new line-up failed to produce.

Album: *Dr. Mastermind* (Roadrunner 1986).

Dread Zeppelin

Novelty hard rock combo featuring an overweight Elvis Presley look-alike from California who leads his band through a succession of Led Zeppelin covers played in reggae and calypso style. The band's line-up is as bizarre as its theme, and features the aforementioned TortElvis (vocals), Jah Paul Jo (guitar), Carl Jah (guitar), Put-Mon (bass), Ed Zeppelin (bongos) and Fresh Cheese (b. Bruce Fernandez; drums). Formed in January 1989, they supposedly met when Tortelvis rammed his milkfloat in to the back of the band's car. They scored natural media curiosity and a minor hit single with 'Your Time Is Gonna Come' from their first album, and then with 'Stairway To Heaven' from the second. Robert Plant was reportedly highly amused at their appearance, though not so the Graceland estate of Elvis Presley. Tortelvis quit the band in 1992. Fernandez would go on to join Anthrax singer John Bush's side project, Ho Cake, while the rest of the band went 'straight'.

Albums: *Un-Led-Ed* (IRS 1990), *5,000,000* (IRS 1991).

Dream Theater

Dream Theater arrived on the US techno-rock scene in 1988. Initially comprising Berklee College Of Music students John Petrucci (guitar), John Myung (bass) and Mike Portnoy (drums), they subsequently drafted in old schoolfriend Kevin Moore (keyboards) and began to record demos. Along with a contract to MCA, they also picked up the services of vocalist Charlie Dominici, adopting their new name in favour of original choice, Majesty. A debut album showcased strong material, incorporating elements of Rush, Queensrÿche, and Yngwie Malmsteen, in addition to the English progressive tradition embodied by King Crimson and Genesis. Dynamic, multi-faceted hard rock songs, characterized by countless slick time changes and impeccable musicianship, were the band's trademark. The album received a favourable response from the music media, but was strangely ignored by the record-buying public. Dismayed at the poor album sales, MCA terminated their contract and Dominici quit shortly afterwards. It took the group a year to extricate themselves from the deal, and a rigorous auditioning process began to find a new singer. The winning candidate would be Canadian James LaBrie, formerly of Winter Rose, and also Carl Dixon's replacement in Coney Hatch. After their earlier label and personnel tribulations, the release of two albums in the 90s saw them regain their initial momentum, with both mainstream and metal critics acknowledging their fluency in meshing a variety of styles around a hard rock core.

Albums: *When Dream And Day Unite* (MCA 1989), *Images And Words* (Atco 1993), *Awake* (East West 1994).

Video: *Images And Words* (1994).

DRI

This thrash metal band were formed in Houston, Texas, USA, in 1982. The band's original line-up consisted of Kurt Brecht (vocals), Spike Cassidy (guitar), Dennis Johnson (bass) and Kurt's brother, Eric Brecht (drums). Originally calling themselves Dirty Rotten Imbeciles, they shortened it to DRI and signed to Roadrunner Records in the UK. In the US they would first use their own indpendent label, subsequently signing with Metal Blade/Enigma. Their debut album, *Dirty Rotten LP*, was released in 1984, and preceded the band's relocation to San Francisco. It quickly established DRI at the forefront of their genre with its vicious mixture of punk, hardcore and thrash metal (Slayer's Dave Lombardo would cite them as a major influence). Before the next album, *Dealing With It*, founder member Eric Brecht left the band to be replaced by Felix Griffin, though this was only one of numerous personnel changes over the band"s lifetime. DRI continued to bridge punk and metal audiences, even going as far as to call their third album *Crossover*. They would eventually move into a more traditional speed metal style for the release of *Four Of A Kind* in 1988. Perhaps to remind their fans of their 'roots', the band re-mixed and re-released the *Dirty Rotten LP* in the same year, also including four extra tracks which had originally been released as an EP, *Violent Pacification*, back in 1984. Soon after this the band hit problems on a short tour of Mexico as new bass player John Menor was viciously attacked and robbed. However, this did not deter the band from producing their most accomplished album to date, *Thrash Zone*, though it would prove to be their swansong.

Albums: *Dirty Rotten LP* (Rotten 1984), *Dealing*

Doro

With It (Metal Blade/Enigma 1985), *Crossover* (Metal Blade/Enigma 1987), *Four Of A Kind* (Metal Blade/Enigma 1988), *Dirty Rotten LP* (Rotten/Roadrunner 1988, remixed version of debut with 4 extra tracks), *Thrash Zone* (Metal Blade/Enigma 1989).
Video: *Live At The Ritz* (1989).

Drive, She Said

Formed in 1986 by the former American Tears, Touch, and Michael Bolton keyboard player Mark Mangold, and previously unknown vocalist/guitarist Al Fritsch. Mangold was also a successful songwriter, co-writing Cher's hit, 'I've Found Someone', along with Bolton. After signing to CBS in 1988 their self-titled debut album was released a year later in the USA and contained guest appearances by artists such as multi-instrumentalist Aldo Nova, Fiona Flanigan, and Bob Kulick of Balance, Kiss, and Meat Loaf fame. The collection of light-edged melodic rock songs, which included a reworking of the Touch classic 'Don't You Know What Love Is?', was aimed directly at the American market, but failed to make any significant impact. It sold well on import in the UK, however, prompting the independent Music For Nations label to sign the band for the European market (Mangold reportedly being unhappy at CBS' marketing attempts). The album was subsequently released in the UK in 1990 and was quickly followed by a club tour. *Drivin' Wheel*, a slightly harder-edged album, was released in 1991, preceded by the single, 'Think About Love', both of which failed to achieve any significant success. Undeterred by the lack of chart success, they toured the UK with FM in 1992 before embarking on sessions for a third album.
Albums: *Drive, She Said* (CBS 1989), *Drivin' Wheel* (Music For Nations 1991).

Driver

This short-lived, Canadian power-trio were formed in 1976 by vocalist/guitarist Peter Glinderman. With the addition of bassist Dennis Coats and drummer Stephen Rexford, they signed to A&M the following year. *No Accidents*, their only album release, remains one of the undiscovered classics of the hard rock genre. It features an inspired collection of high energy blues-based rockers, saturated with infectious hooks, bridges and choruses. Ideas were explored and exhausted in just three minutes. 'Lookin' For A New Way To Say I Love You' became a modest US hit. A band who disappeared into oblivion, when it was was obvious they deserved so much more.
Album: *No Accidents* (A&M 1977).

Drivin' N' Cryin'

Guitarist/vocalist Kevn Kinney, having relocated to Atlanta after splitting from his old punk band the Prosecutors, met bassist Tim Nielsen in a local club, and the two formed Driving' N' Cryin'. *Scarred But Smarter* was recorded in a week and a half with a real garage rock trio sound, and the band recruited drummer Jeff Sullivan from Mr Crowe's Garden, who later became the Black Crowes, and began to broaden their musical style, incorporating country and R&B influences, while expanding their audience with gruelling club touring. *Whisper Tames The Lion*, by way of contrast to the debut, was rather overproduced, but *Mystery Road*, with a second guitarist in ex-REM roadie Buren Fowler, was more representative of the band's true sound. However, Driving' N' Cryin' had become musically somewhat schizophrenic at this stage, mixing heavy rockers with country songs, although the latter made little impression within insular US C&W radio circles. *Fly Me Courageous* thus saw a conscious effort to focus on the rock direction of their live shows, and while it met a mixed reception from reviewers, respectable US sales finally established the band as a force. *Smoke* refined the harder approach with a tough sound and Ramones-like simplicity, while Kinney kept the more acoustic-based material for his solo albums.
Albums: *Scarred But Smarter* (Island 1986), *Whisper Tames The Lion* (Island 1988), *Mystery Road* (Island 1989), *Fly Me Courageous* (Island 1990), *Smoke* (Island 1993).

Dub War

A collision of ragga and punk, shot through with steely metallic guitar, Dub War emerged in 1994 as a high octane, highly political extension of hard rock's new found ability to merge new styles with old. Formed in Newport, Wales, in 1993, the four-piece, who comprise Jeff Rose (guitar), Richie Glover (bass), Martin Ford (drums) and Benji (vocals), all came from diverse musical backgrounds. Glover had played in several minor punk bands, while Benji's apprenticeship came in reggae dancehalls, and he had previously worked with Mad Professor. The group made its debut at the end of 1993 with a self-titled 12-inch EP, which simultaneously managed to appear in three different *New Musical Express* charts - the 'Vibes', 'Turn Ons' and 'Hardcore' listings. Following a debut mini-album in 1994, they switched to Earache Records for the *Mental* EP, joining Pop Will Eat Itself and Manic Street Preachers on touring engagements. *Mental* featured remixes from Senser, Brand New Heavies and Jamiroquai, and was followed by a further EP, *Gorrit*. Their first full album came in February 1995 with *Pain*, by which time the band had established a strong live following to augment their press profile.

Albums: *Dub Warning* (1994, mini-album), *Pain* (Earache 1995).

Dumpy's Rusty Nuts

Dumpy (b. Graham Dunnell, July 1949, London, England) had been playing with various bands since the mid-60s. His first big break came in 1977 with new wave outfit the Rivvets. Four years later he returned to his love of blues and formed Dumpy's Rusty Nuts. Taking on guitar and vocals, he was joined by Malcolm McKenzie (bass) and Chris Hussey (drums). Together they recorded the 'Biker Anthem' and 'Just For Kicks' before running into trouble with BBC Radio 1 who objected to the band's name - for a while 'nuts' became 'bolts'. Dumpy, a natural entertainer, followed the rock traditions started by Jackie Lynton and blended joke telling with the music, which helped to gain them a cult following in the pubs and clubs. Prior to a major tour with the Blues Band, McKenzie left to join Nuthin' Fancy and was replaced by Jeff Brown. Over the next few years records sold few copies, a situation exacerbated by ever-fluctuating line-ups, transient personnel including Mark Brabbs (drums; ex-Tank), Alan Fish and Mick Kirton (bass and drums; both ex-Groundhogs), Alan Davey and Danny Thompson (bass and drums; on loan from Hawkwind) and guitarist Mick Grafton from Cloven Hoof. It was Dumpy's connections with Lemmy and Hawkwind that kept him in the public eye with 1987's *Get Out On The Road* being his most successful release, largely thanks to Davey, Thompson and Dave Brock from Hawkwind guesting. The band took one last shot at the big time in October 1990 when they entered the studio to record a cover of the Jo Jo Gunn classic, 'Run Run Run', with Kim Wilde producer Steve Glenn. The single was to be released to coincide with a major support slot on the Status Quo tour. However, all did not go according to plan - the single only appeared in promo fashion and, under orders, they had to cut much of the humour from their live set. This robbed them of their ability to impress and rendered them just another blues rock band. Since then there have been no new records and they have returned to the pub circuit. McKenzie later went on to manage Thunder while Alan Fish formed Egypt.

Albums: *Somewhere In England* (Landslide 1984), *Hot Lover* (Gas 1985), *Get Out On The Road* (Metal Masters 1987), *Firkin Well Live* (Razor 1988).

Videos: *Live At The Marquee 1986* (1988), *Vintage Video* (1990), *Live At The Hippodrome 1989* (1990).

E

Earthshaker

This Japanese heavy metal band was modelled on the styles of Y&T, Deep Purple and Van Halen. Formed by guitarist Shinichiro Ishihara in 1981, even its name was taken from Y&T's third album. After a series of false starts the band was completed with the addition of Masafumi Nishida (vocals), Takayuki Kai (bass) and Yoshihiro Kudo (drums). Relocating to San Francisco in 1983, they utilized the talents of ex-Gamma keyboardist Mitchell Froom on the following year's *Fugitive* opus. As a consequence the band's sound became less aggressive, which only served to highlight their obvious limitations. They have continued to release albums as a four-piece, but have made little impact outside their native Japan.

Albums: *Earthshaker* (Music For Nations 1983), *Fugitive* (Music For Nations 1984), *Midnight Flight* (Music For Nations 1984), *Live* (Nexus 1985), *Over The Run* (Eastworld 1986), *Treachery* (Eastworld 1989), *Live Best* (Eastworld 1990).

Electric Boys

This Swedish funk-metal band was formed by vocalist/guitarist Conny Bloom (b. Blomquist) and bassist Andy Christell in 1988. As a duo, the pair recorded 'All Lips 'N' Hips', and finding themselves with a domestic hit, completed the band by recruiting guitarist Franco Santunione and drummer Niclas Sigevall. The self-produced *Funk-O-Metal Carpet Ride* was a strong debut, with memorable songs delivered in a heavy punk style with a distinct psychedelic edge, and led to world-wide deals with Atco in the USA and Phonogram elsewhere. The band replaced five songs on the original version of the debut with new, Bob Rock-produced efforts, and the revised *Funk-O-Metal Carpet Ride* made quite an impact, emerging as the rock world was opening its collective mind to the likes of Living Colour and Dan Reed Network. The band's colourful image and live shows only served to enhance their growing reputation. However, the funk-metal bubble had burst by the time that the more heavily psychedelic *Groovus Maximus* appeared, and despite the potential of the Beatles-influenced 'Mary In The Mystery World' (the album was actually recorded at Abbey Road), the Electric Boys struggled, and after a US tour with Mr Big, Santunione and Sigevall departed.

Martin Thomander (guitar) and Thomas Broman (drums; ex-Great King Rat) replaced them on *Freewheelin'* which abandoned funk in favour of a more 70s-inspired Aerosmith/Led Zeppelin groove, but this impressive comeback could not restore the band's waning fortunes, and they broke up shortly after release.

Albums: *Funk-O-Metal Carpet Ride* (Mercury 1989), *Groovus Maximus* (Mercury 1992), *Freewheelin'* (Music For Nations 1994).

Electric Hellfire Club

Their name is derived from the English 18th Century group of Satanic society swingers known as the Hellfire Club. The band was formed in an attempt to emulate the playful, pleasure-loving devilment of their 18th Century inspiration in a musical (thus 'Electric') form. At the band's heart is the vocalist, synthesiser programmer and Satanist Thomas Thorn. Thorn had previously been in the seminal industrial dance act the Thrill Kill Kult under the name Buck Ryder. In 1991 he had become alienated by their increasingly commercial direction and contemptuous attitude to darker topics. He left and formed the Electric Hellfire Club with a diverse group of musicians, including the Reverend Doctor Luv (keyboards), Ronny Valeo (guitars) and Janna Flail (drums) who was later replaced on percussion by Richard Frost. All of them brought different influences into the band's sound, from heavy metal and ethnic music, to punk and techno. Thorn's own fascination with 60s psychedelia adds to this cocktail to create a style which is distinctive and colourful. Frivolous and sinister in equal parts, the Electric Hellfire Club roam far from the clichéd stamping grounds of Satanic rock.

Albums: *Burn, Baby, Burn!* (Cleopatra 1994).

Electric Love Hogs

This Los Angeles quintet originated when vocalist John Feldmann and guitarist Donny Campion linked with drummer Bobby Fernandez in a San Diego covers band. The addition of second guitarist Dae Kushner and funk-oriented bassist Kelly LeMieux, who was recruited following a wrong number phone call, saw the band move towards original material, incorporating LeMieux's slap bass into a trad/speed metal framework for an energetic hybrid style. The band adopted the Electric Love Hogs name as a reaction against the crop of Los Angeles glam bands on the late 80s club scene whom they felt were taking the music business too seriously. London Records were willing to sign the band without making them change their name, and *Electric Love Hogs* was a bright

debut, offering a strong, punchy sound curtesy of Mark Dodson (although more interest centred on two tracks produced by Mötley Crüe's Tommy Lee), but didn't quite have the individuality to separate the band from the funk-metal pack. The band's live work was nonetheless impressive as they toured the USA with L.A. Guns and the UK with Ugly Kid Joe before returning to the studio.

Album: *Electric Love Hogs* (London 1992).

Electric Sun

This German group was formed by Uli Jon Roth (guitar/vocals) after he left the Scorpions. At first he was assisted by Ule Ritgens on bass and Clive Edwards on drums. He was quickly signed by the Brain label and released *Earthquake* in 1979. This was a highly spiritual record with guitar work that aspired to imitate Jimi Hendrix and the west coast acid rock movement. This fusion of jazz and rock music with occasionally unusual guitar parts was let down by Roth's vocals. On *Firewind*, released in 1981, Clive Edwards was replaced by Sidhatta Gautama. The music improved and now contained pieces influenced by the oriental tradition, even though the vocals remained the same. The next release, *Beyond The Astral Skies*, took four years to complete, but when finally released it revealed a great leap forward by Roth. In addition to the jazz rock pieces, there were also neo-classical movements which allowed Roth free reign to indulge his religious beliefs and demonstrate his musical ability and technique. The record's opening verse ran: 'The astral skies shall open wide, The night the master comes, And all the mountains will step aside'. The biggest improvement was in the vocals, with Roth still singing lead but having the support of seven other vocalists.

Albums: *Earthquake* (Brain 1979), *Firewind* (Brain 1981), *Beyond The Astral Skies* (EMI 1985).

Electro Hippies

This eccentric grindcore outfit formed in Liverpool, England, in 1988. Specializing in low-technology studio techniques, they went on to issue a sequence of albums for Peaceville, and, later, Necrosis. In each case, a distorted, bass-laden barrage was over-ridden by stomach-churning vocals that lacked both finesse and cohesion (though that was hardly the intention anyway). The group's initial line-up included the surname-less Simon (drums), Dom (bass/vocals) and Andy (guitar/vocals). Chaotic and extreme, Electro Hippies used their platform to chastise the whole recording industry. Their mantle was upheld in the first case by Radio 1 DJ John Peel, for whom the group recorded a July 1987 session consisting of some

Electric Boys

nine tracks. Titles likes 'Starve The City (To Feed The Poor)' and 'Mega-Armageddon Death Part 3' summed up both their appeal and limitations.

Albums: *Peel Sessions* (Strange Fruit 1987), *The Only Good Punk Is A Dead One* (Peaceville 1988), *Electro Hippies Live* (Peaceville 1989), *The Peaceville Recordings* (Peaceville 1989), *Play Loud Or Die* (Necrosis 1989).

Elf

This US heavy rock unit was formed in 1967 by vocalist Ronnie James Dio (b. Ronald Padavona, 10 July 1940, New Hampshire, USA) with cousin Dave Feinstein on guitar, plus Gary Driscoll (drums), Doug Thaler (keyboards) and Nick Pantas (guitar). They actually worked under the title Electric Elves until 1970 when the entire band was involved in a car-crash, in which guitarist Nick Pantas died and Thaler was hospitalized. Mickey Lee Soule (keyboards/guitar) was added to a reshuffled line-up, who were spotted by Roger Glover and Ian Paice of Deep Purple in 1972. A production and recording deal was arranged, with Elf supporting Deep Purple on two American tours. However, the group's bar-room blues and boogie always came across better live than in the studio (witness posthumous live album for MGM). In 1973 Elf recruited bassist Craig Gruber, allowing Dio to concentrate on vocals. Their guitarist, Feinstein, gave up touring and was replaced first by Doug Thaler, previously keyboard player for the Elves, and then Steve Edwards. From 1974 Mark Nauseef (later Ian Gillan and Thin Lizzy) played percussion for the band. In 1975 Glover gave Dio the opportunity to appear on his project, *The Butterfly Ball*, and this gave Dio the widespread recognition he desired. Ritchie Blackmore stepped in to co-opt Elf into his Rainbow project, though after five months only Dio remained as former Elf musicians Gruber, Lee Soule and Driscoll were summarily dispensed with.

Albums: *Elf* (Epic 1972), *LA59* (Purple 1974), *Trying To Burn The Sun* (MGM 1975), *Live* (MGM 1976).

Elixir

This UK heavy metal quintet was formed in the mid-80s and featured Paul Taylor (vocals), Kevin Dobbs (bass), Phil Denton (b. c.1962, Luton, Bedfordshire, England; guitar), Norman Gordon (guitar) and Nigel Dobbs (drums). Their debut album, released in 1988, was preceded by a session for the Radio 1 Friday Rock show. A second album saw them joined by ex-Iron Maiden drummer Clive Burr, plus Mark White on bass, replacing the Dobbs brothers. Their stylistic origins date back to the N.W.O.B.H.M., utilizing twin lead guitars to alternate between circular power-riffs and intricate solos. Early Iron Maiden and Def Leppard were strong influences, with their lyrical content split roughly in half between mythology/epic struggles ('Son Of Odin', etc.) and the equally cliched themes of sex, violence and drugs. After the band's dissolution Denton returned to playing the clubs with covers band Rough Diamond (not the 70s supergroup).

Albums: *Elixir* (Goasco 1988), *Lethal Potion* (Sonic 1990).

Eloy

This German progressive-space rock band is essentially a vehicle for the creative talents of lead vocalist/lead guitarist/songwriter Frank Bornemann, with a somewhat unstable backing line-up. The band released their debut, *Inside*, in 1973, and achieved enormous success in Germany with a succession of albums in the vein of Pink Floyd and Yes but with a heavier, guitar-based approach. These usually featured instrumentally complex epics based on Bornemann's science fiction-flavoured concepts, but despite a domestic major label deal, and a consistent English language approach, it wasn't until *Planets* that Eloy were able to release their material outside their homeland. Bornemann, at this stage joined by Hannes Filberth (keyboards), Hannes Arkona (keyboards/guitar), Klaus-Peter Matziol (bass) and Fritz Randow (drums), was by now updating the Eloy sound, culminating in the excellent *Metromania*, where modern keyboard textures added colour to more compact, less indulgent songs, but this line-up crumbled as the rhythm section departed. Bornemann was subsequently less prolific as his duties as owner and manager of Hanover's Horus Sound Studios took more of his time, but Eloy made a comeback with *Destination* and then *The Tide Returns Forever*, with Michael Gerlach's keyboards helping Bornemann produce an altogether more technical sound along the lines of latter-day Rush while retaining all of Eloy's individual character.

Albums: *Inside* (Electrola 1973), *Floating* (Electrola 1974), *Power And The Passion* (Electrola 1975), *Dawn* (Electrola 1976), *Oceans* (Electrola 1977), *Silent Cries, Mighty Echoes* (Electrola 1978), *Live* (Electrola 1978), *Colours* (Electrola 1983), *Metromania* (Electrola 1984), *Ra* (Electrola 1989), *Destination* (SPV 1993), *The Tide Returns Forever* (SPV 1995).

Emperor

Members of the bizarre Norwegian Satanic club led by Euronymous of Mayhem known as the Black Metal Circle, Emperor form part of the black metal

revival of the 90s. Musically, they whip up a cacophonous storm of blistering guitars and bellowed vocals, with aggressive, devilish themes and a few strange, quasi-classical flourishes. In 1993 they released a split CD with Scandinavian pagan heavy metal band Enslaved. In the same year the Black Metal Circle were connected with a series of church burnings in Norway and Samoth, Emperor's sinisterly flamboyant frontman, was arrested in connection with the crimes. He was later released, but Emperor drummer Faust was not and, in addition to arson, was convicted of the 1992 murder of a homosexual. Despite this, and the murder of fellow black metal Satanist Euronymous, Emperor continue to fly the Scandinavian black metal banner.
Albums: *Emperor* (Candlelight 1993), *In the Nightside Eclipse* (Candlelight 1994).

Entombed

This Swedish death metal band were formed in Stockholm in 1987 as Nihilist, releasing four acclaimed demos; *Drowned, Premature Autopsy, But Life Goes On* and *Only Shreds Remain*. After breaking up Nihilist the band reunited a few days later as Entombed, with a line-up of Lars Goren-Petrov (vocals), Ulf Cederlund (guitar), Alex Hellid (guitar), Lars Rosenburg (bass) and Nicke Andersson (drums). *Left Hand Path* adequately demonstrated the band's potential with an atmospheric and individual sound, and live shows were equally impressive. Petrov departed shortly after the debut, but Orvar Safstrom only lasted for one single ('Crawl') before ex-Carnage bassist Johnny Dordevic took over on the well-reviewed *Clandestine*. After an extensive US tour with Morbid Angel, he too was ousted in favour of the returning Petrov for the Gods Of Grind UK jaunt with Carcass, Cathedral and Confessor. *Hollowman* was swiftly followed by the hugely impressive *Wolverine Blues* as Entombed continued to ignore death metal convention, establishing themselves as one of the genre's leading acts, and creating more accessible material by incorporating traditional rock song structures and the rhythmic groove which they first explored on *Clandestine* into their fierce death metal framework. Entombed's popularity continued to rise as they toured Europe on a frighteningly intense bill with label mates Napalm Death, while an EP, *Out Of Hand*, saw high class covers of material by Kiss ('God Of Thunder') and Repulsion ('Blackbreath').
Albums: *Left Hand Path* (Earache 1990), *Clandestine* (Earache 1991), *Hollowman* (Earache 1993, mini-album), *Wolverine Blues* (Earache 1993).

Enuff Z'Nuff

This Chicago, USA, pop-metal crossover quartet comprised Donnie Vie (vocals), Derek Frigo (guitar; ex-Le Mans), Chip Z'Nuff (bass) and Vikki Fox (drums). Influences such as Cheap Trick and the Beatles were apparent through the band's extensive use of three-part harmonies, which carried the melody line in many of the songs. On a visual level, they initially appeared as multi-coloured fashion casualties from the early 70s, sporting an ambitious and often dazzling array of sunglasses, waistcoats, boots and accessories (regalia most notably paraded on MTV via the video to their minor hit, 'New Thing'). This image has since been played down with the release of *Strength*, an impressive and mature musical offering that combined infectious hooks, abrasive guitar work and a sparkling production to dramatic effect. Following Atco's internal problems with mothership Atlantic, the trio moved to Arista, though their third album saw them lose Fox to the Vince Neil band. His replacement would be Ricky Parent (ex-War And Peace), allegedly a distant relative of Arnold Schwarzenegger.
Albums: *Enuff Z'Nuff* (Atco 1989), *Strength* (Atco 1991), *Animals With Human Intelligence* (Arista 1993).

Epitaph

Epitaph's career comprises two distinct phases, linked together by founder member and guitarist/vocalist Cliff Jackson. The first two albums had little to do with their later hard-rock style and featured a jazz-tinged AOR flavour. The band disintegrated in 1975, but Jackson resurrected Epitaph in 1979 with Heinz Glass (guitar), Harvey Janssen (bass), Michael Karch (keyboards) and Fritz Randow (drums). *Return From Reality* adopted an aggressive approach, characterized by the heavy-duty guitar work of Glass. Karch was fired after the album was released, and surprisingly, *See You In Alaska* which followed, was rather lightweight compared to its predecessor. *Live* redressed the balance and saw the band in good shape once more. However, internal disputes resulted in the departure of Glass, Randow and Janssen soon after the album's release. Klaus Walz, Norbert Lehmann and Bernie Kolbe were drafted in as replacements on guitar, drums and vocals respectively, to record *Danger Man* in 1982. Unable to generate renewed interest, the band folded in 1983. Kolbe and Jackson went on to Kingdom, while Randow joined Victory.
Albums: *Outside The Law* (Billingsgate 1974), *Stop, Look And Listen* (Polydor 1975), *Return From Reality* (Brain 1979), *See You In Alaska* (Brain 1980), *Live* (Metronome 1981), *Danger Man* (Metronome 1982).

Entombed

Ethel The Frog

Featuring P. Sheppard (vocals), Tognola (guitar), Hopkinson (bass) and Paul Conyers (drums), Ethel The Frog, taking their name from a *Monty Python* sketch, first came to the public's attention via a track on EMI's *Metal For Muthas Vol. I* compilation in 1980. This album was intended to introduce unsigned British heavy metal bands and is most notable for boasting two early Iron Maiden tracks. The concept was very much to advance the New Wave Of British Heavy Metal of which Ethel The Frog was a part. However, their track, 'Fight Back', was disappointingly basic heavy metal. Soon after they recorded and released their own debut, *Ethel The Frog*. Sadly this did not capture the public's interest and met with critical disdain. Disillusioned, they split in 1980, with Conyers and Tognola moving on to Salem and 'Eleanor Rigby' covers.
Album: *Ethel The Frog* (EMI 1980).

Europe

A Swedish heavy rock band, Europe found international success in the late 80s. In 1982, Joey Tempest (19 August 1963, Stockholm, Sweden; vocals), John Norum (guitar) and John Leven (bass) founded Force in the Stockholm suburb of Upplands-Vasby. After winning a national talent contest, the group recorded two Rush-influenced albums for the Swedish market before signing to Epic in 1986. By now Norum had left and the renamed Europe included guitarist Kee Marcello (ex-Easy Action), Michael Michaeli (keyboards) and drummer Ian Haughland. With English-language lyrics, the first Epic album was produced by Kevin Elson and included hits with 'Carrie', 'The Final Countdown' (a UK number 1), 'Rock The Night' and 'Cherokee'. *The Final Countdown* would go on to triple platinum status, but also set the group a standard they have failed to maintain. However, Europe's continued success in Japan and the US was assisted by the group's lengthy world tours. Later hits included 'Superstitious' from the Ron Nevison-produced second album, but *Prisoners Of Paradise*, with Beau Hill as producer, sold poorly. Joey Tempest would go on to sign a solo deal with Polygram in 1994.
Albums: *Europe* (Hot 1983), *Wings Of Tomorrow* (Hot 1984), *The Final Countdown* (Epic 1986), *Out Of This World* (Epic 1988), *Prisoners In Paradise* (Epic 1992). Compilation: *Europe 1982 - 1992* (Epic 1993).

Every Mother's Nightmare

This US 'sleaze-rock' band, surprisingly originating from the home of country music, Nashville, were formed in 1989 by vocalist Rick Ruhl and guitarist Steve Malone. With the addition of bassist Mark McMurty and drummer Jim Phipps, they signed a deal with Arista in 1990. Their self-titled debut, released the same year, combined Kiss, Aerosmith, Tesla and Bon Jovi influences to powerful effect. Their dynamism and musical palate gave the songs a cutting edge that elevated the resultant collection above mere plagiarism.
Album: *Every Mother's Nightmare* (Arista 1990).

Evil Dead

After his split with the eccentric Agent Steel in 1988, guitarist Juan Garcia (also ex-Abattoir) went on to form Evil Dead featuring a line-up of Albert Gonzalez (guitar), Phil Fiores (vocals), and Rob Ailinz (drums; ex-Necrophilia). A strong and professional thrash metal act, Evil Dead nevertheless lacked identity or the kind of individuality Agent Steel frontman John Cyriss was able to give his volatile five-piece. In the increasingly crowded thrash and death metal genres, Garcia's act are struggling to hold the attention of the young, and somewhat fickle, extreme metal audiences.
Albums: *Rise Above* (Steamhammer 1988), *Annihilation Of Civilisation* (Steamhammer 1990).

Excalibur

This group was formed in Yorkshire, England, in 1981 by Paul McBride (vocals), Paul Solynskyj (b. 27 October 1966, England; guitar), Martin Hawthorn (bass), and Mick Dobson (drums). The band got together while they were still schoolboys and legend has it that they would fall asleep in class after a heavy night's gigging. On leaving school, Excalibur continued to tour heavily, while its members also attempted to hold down day jobs. Conquest Records signed the band in 1985 after an employee heard Excalibur one night by accident. *The Bitter End* mini-album was released in 1985, containing slightly predictable but melodic heavy metal. In 1986 Excalibur expanded to a five-piece with the addition of Steve Blades (b. 20 May 1968, Scotland; guitar/keyboards). This was followed by a session for BBC Radio I's *Friday Rock Show* which was broadcast in July 1986 and again in September. The four tracks that the band recorded were later released by Clay Records as the *Hot For Love* EP in 1988. That year saw Excalibur appear on a BBC television programme, *On A Personal Note*, where they performed 'Hot For Love' and 'Running Scared' alongside slots from Def Leppard and Little Angels. Before the year's end Dobson was replaced by Dave Sykes on drums, as the group supported Uriah Heep for most of their UK tour. In 1989 the band signed to Active Records and immediately began recording a debut album proper. The first taster was a track entitled 'Carole Ann', an acoustic number which drew comparisons to Bon Jovi. After *One Strange Night* was released to critical acclaim, Excalibur headed out on their first full headlining tour of the UK in February 1990. They supported Saxon on UK and European dates, though there were further personnel changes to endure. Livermore had replaced Martin Hawthorn in 1989, and he now left to make way for Dean Wilson (b. 5 March 1966, England; bass). In 1991 Excalibur were in the studio recording their follow-up album, when Paul McBride announced that he was leaving the band, placing their career on hold.

Albums: *The Bitter End* (Conquest 1985, mini-album), *One Strange Night* (Active 1990).

Exciter

Formed in Ottawa, Canada, in 1979 as a three-piece outfit, the band's original line-up consisted of Dan Beehler (drums/vocals), John Ricci (guitar) and Allan Johnson (bass), their name taken from an old Judas Priest track. An impressive demo attracted the attention of Shrapnel Records which as well as featuring the band on an early *U.S. Metal* compilation also released the demo as an album entitled *Heavy Metal Maniac* in 1983. This was belligerent, Motörhead-influenced power metal and quickly gained the band a strong following in Europe. They then changed labels and released *Violence & Force* for Roadrunner Records in 1984. Produced by ex-Rods drummer Carl Canedy, it was a much more stylish release benefiting from better production and higher quality material. By the next release, the band had changed European labels once again. Their third album, *Long Live The Loud*, appeared on the Music For Nations label in 1985. Recorded and produced in London with producer Guy Bidmead, this album did not seem as immediate as previous releases and saw them lose some of their early raw power. However, this did not deter the band from undertaking an extensive European tour in support of the release. Afterwards Ricci left to be replaced by Brian McPhee, an old friend of the band, who added a new dimension to their fourth album, *Unveiling The Wicked*. Unfortunately, even McPhee's excellent guitar work could not alleviate the sense of tiredness in the music, and after a short tour of Brazil the band decided to add a vocalist/frontman to give them a stronger identity. This resulted in the recruitment of Rob Malnati. Once again they changed labels, signing to the small, Canadian independent Maze Records.

Their last album, *Exciter*, failed to sell and shortly after its release the band sank into obscurity playing on the local club scene.

Albums: *Heavy Metal Maniac* (Shrapnel 1983), *Violence & Force* (Music For Nations 1984), *Long Live The Loud* (Music For Nations 1985), *Unveiling The Wicked* (Music For Nations 1986), *Exciter* (Maze/Music For Nations 1988), *Better Live Than Dead* (1993).

Exit-13

Environmentally-themed 'grind rock' group from Pennsylvania, USA, Exit-13 are a side-project for Brutal Truth bass player Dan Lilker (also ex-S.O.D. and others). Joined by Relapse Records co-owner Bill Yurkiewicz (vocals/samples), guitarist Steve O'Donnell and former Brutal Truth drummer Scott Lewis, the band's debut fused traditional doom metal components with blues and jazz textures. An unlikely combination, it saw the record described as mixing 'Stevie Ray Vaughan and early Napalm Death' in one quarter. Yurkiewicz's lyrics continued to explore desperate themes on *Ethos Musick* - the opening track, subtly titled 'Societally Provoked Genocidal Contemplation', opened with the line 'This whole world is fucking sick', before concluding its first verse with 'Insanity frees my mind to wonder, I gleefully ponder humanity's murder'. Elsewhere the group ruminated further on their race's capacity for self-degradation and cruelty, and the lasting effect of industrial activities on the planet. It certainly provided an intriguing contrast to hear such 60s idealism braced against some of the present decade's most fearsome noise.

Albums: *Ethos Musick* (Nuclear Blast/Relapse 1994).

Exodus

Formed in San Francisco, USA, in 1982, Exodus were one of the earliest thrash metal bands. Their very first line-up included Metallica guitarist Kirk Hammett, though he would not record with the band. Their first album was an important landmark in the thrash arena, with its highly aggressive musical and lyrical approach, dealing with all manner of extremes and brutalities. It was recorded by the line-up of Paul Baloff (vocals), Gary Holt (guitar), Rick Hunolt (guitar), Rob McKillop (bass) and Tom Hunting (drums). Vocalist Steve Sousa replaced Baloff (who formed the ill-advised Pirahna) for *Pleasures Of The Flesh*, which was marginally mellower, but a daunting proposition nonetheless. Even after the subsequent departure of Hunting, who was replaced by John Tempesta, Exodus continued to record worthy material, but failed to match the commercial success of contemporaries such as Metallica and Anthrax. They steadfastly refused to compromise or waver from their straightforward thrash style, and managed to maintain a level of popularity sufficient to gain a major label record deal. However, their own exodus was confirmed in 1992 after *Force Of Habit* saw them, as the title suggested, banging their heads against brick walls.

Albums: *Bonded By Blood* (Music For Nations 1985), *Pleasures Of The Flesh* (Music For Nations 1987), *Fabulous Disaster* (Music For Nations 1989), *Impact Is Imminent* (Capitol 1990), *Good Friendly Violent Fun* (Roadrunner 1991), *Force Of Habit* (Roadrunner 1992). Compilation: *The Best Of Exodus - Lessons In Violence* (Music For Nations 1992).

Export

This British rock band was formed in 1980 by former Hardstuff vocalist Harry Shaw and guitarist Steve Morris. Enlisting the services of bassist Chris Alderman and drummer Lou Rosenthal, they specialized in Americanized AOR. Their material is characterized by note-perfect harmonies, sterling guitar work and infectious hooklines similar to Kansas, Starz and REO Speedwagon. After a well-received self-titled debut in 1981, they were picked up by Epic, who recognized the enormous potential they possessed. Two albums were delivered, with Lance Quinn (of Bon Jovi) at the production helm for 1986's *Living In Fear Of A Private Eye*. Surprisingly, the band failed to take off in the USA and Epic dropped them due to poor sales figures. Steve Morris produced Torino's debut album in 1987 while Export continued to search for a (not forthcoming) new contract.

Albums: *Export* (His Masters Vice 1981), *Contraband* (CBS 1984), *Living In Fear Of A Private Eye* (Epic 1986).

Extreme

This Boston quartet comprise Gary Cherone (b. 26 July 1961, Malden, Massachussets, USA; vocals) Nuno Bettencourt (b. 20 September 1966, Azores, Portugal; guitar) Pat Badger (b. 22 July 1967, Boston, Massachussets, USA; bass) and Paul Geary (b. 24 July 1961, Medford, Massachussets, USA; drums). The origins of the band can be traced to local act the Dream, whose sole six-track EP in 1983 featured Cherone and Geary. As Extreme the original line-up found themselves on television in 1985 via a video clip for 'Mutha (Don't Wanna Go To School Today') as part of an MTV competition, but it was the arrival

Extreme Noise Terror

of Bettencourt in 1986 and Badger the following year that gave them lift-off. A recording contract with A&M Records was soon secured and the group made their vinyl debut with 'Play With Me' for the soundtrack to *Bill And Ted's Excellent Adventure*. The inevitable self-titled debut album followed. Encompassing elements of pop, metal, funk and blues, their songwriting powers were still in their infancy at this stage and although competent, the album met with widespread critical indifference. *Pornograffitti* was a stunning second release, being an ambitious concept affair, sub-titled 'A Funked Up Fairy Tale' based on the life and times of the album's central character. The big breakthrough came when the simple acoustic ballad, 'More Than Words', reached number 1 and number 2 in the US and UK singles charts respectively. The band's music was now characterized by Bettencourt's innovative guitar work, intelligent lyrics and a diverse style that transcended a variety of musical genres. Their appearance at the Freddie Mercury concert, which interrupted sessions for *III Sides To Every Story*, gave them considerable exposure beyond the heavy metal fraternity. Prior to the band's appearance at Castle Donington in the summer of 1994, Mike Mangini (ex-Annihilator) replaced Paul Geary on drums. The following year Bettencourt announced plans to release a solo album through Colorblind, the label he runs through A&M. Albums: *Extreme* (A&M 1989), *Pornograffitti* (A&M 1990), *III Sides To Every Story* (A&M 1992, double album), *Waiting For The Punchline* (A&M 1995).

Extreme Noise Terror

A band whose name truly encapsulates their sound, Extreme Noise Terror formed in January 1985 and were signed by Manic Ears Records after their first ever gig. Their debut release was a split album with Chaos UK, and although there were musical similarities, ENT, along with Napalm Death, were already in the process of twisting traditional punk influences into altogether different shapes. Along with the latter, they became the subject of DJ John Peel's interest in 1987, recording a session (one of three) which would eventually see release on the Strange Fruit imprint. Afterwards drummer Mick Harris, who had left Napalm Death to replace the group's original drummer, in turn departed, joining Scorn. His replacement was Stick (Tony Dickens), who joined existing members Dean Jones (vocals), Phil Vane (vocals) and Pete Hurley (guitar). Mark Bailey had by now replaced Mark Gardiner, who himself had replaced Jerry Clay, on bass. Touring in Japan preceded the release of *Phonophobia*, while continued Peel sessions brought the group to the attention of the KLF's Bill Drummond. He asked them to record a version of the KLF's '3am Eternal', with the intention of the band appearing on *Top Of The Pops* live at Christmas to perform the tune (The BBC decided this was not in the best interests of their audience). Eventually released as a limited edition single, the two band's paths crossed again in 1992 when the KLF were invited to perform live at the 1992 Brit Awards. This crazed event, which included the firing of blanks into the audience, has already passed into music industry legend. Back on their own, 1993 saw Extreme Noise Terror touring widely, and the group signed to premier noise stable Earache the following year. By this time the line-up had swelled to include Lee Barrett (bass; also Disgust) replacing Bailey, and Ali Firouzbakht (lead guitar), with a returning Pig Killer on drums. Together they released *Retro-bution*, ostensibly a compilation, but nevertheless featuring the new line-up on re-recorded versions of familiar material.
Albums: *Radioactive* (split with Chaos UK, Manic Ears 1985), *A Holocaust In Your Head* (Hurt 1987), *The Peel Sessions* (Strange Fruit 1990), *Phonophobia* (Vinyl Japan 1992), *Retro-bution* (Earache 1995). Video: *From One Extreme To The Other* (1989).

F

F.M.

Formed in 1985 from the remnants of three prominent N.W.O.B.H.M. bands, this British quintet quickly established themselves as a superior AOR outfit with a relentless touring schedule, supporting Magnum, Status Quo and Meat Loaf. Comprising ex-Wildlife brothers Steve Overland (guitar/vocals) and Chris Overland (guitar), drummer Pete Jupp provided the Samson connection, while Didge Digital (keyboards) and Merv Goldsworthy (bass; ex-Diamond Head) completed the line-up. Specializing in lightweight harmonic rock characterized by Chris Overland's high-pitched, and at times melodramatic vocals. *Indiscreet* was well received by the critics, being a well-produced, glossy and easily accessible debut, which surprisingly sold poorly. After a three-year gap, a serious re-think, and the use of outside writers, *Tough It Out* emerged. The album built on their previous strengths, but adopted a slightly harder style. Epic Records declined to give the album the necessary promotional back-up to push the band towards major status. Disillusioned and frustrated, they disbanded in 1990, but re-formed the following year (with Andy Barnett in place of Chris Overland). Signing to the independent Music For Nations label, they released *Taking It To The Streets*, which represented a back to basics approach. Afterwards Ditial's tenure with the band would also end. F.M. have established themselves as steady-sellers in an over-subscribed AOR metal market, despite recent albums veering towards blues workouts.

Albums: *Indiscreet* (Portrait 1986), *Tough It Out* (Epic 1989), *Taking It To The Streets* (Music For Nations 1991), *Aphrodisiac* (Music For Nations 1992), *Indiscreet* (Music For Nations 1993), *Live Acoustical Intercourse* (Alfa 1993, Japan only), *No Electricity Required (Live)* (Music For Nations 1994). Compilation: *Only The Strong* (Conniseur Collection 1994). Video: *Live Acoustic Intercourse* (1994).

Faith No More

Formed in San Francisco in 1980, Faith No More, titled after a greyhound the members had bet on, were among the first outfits to experiment with the fusion of funk, thrash and hardcore styles which effectively became a new musical sub-genre. The band initially comprised Jim Martin (b. 21 July 1961, Oakland, California, USA; guitar; ex-Vicious Hatred), Roddy Bottum (b. 1 July 1963, Los Angeles, California, USA; keyboards), Bill Gould (b. 24 April 1963, Los Angeles, California, USA; bass), Mike Bordin (b. 27 November 1962, San Francisco, California, USA; drums) and Chuck Moseley (vocals). Bottum had attended the same school as Bould, while Bordin was recruited from his course at Berkeley University in tribal rhythm. Gould had met Moseley on the Los Angeles club circuit in 1980, while Martin had been recommended by Metallica's Cliff Burton. This line-up recorded a low-budget, self-titled debut on the independent Mordam label, followed by the ground breaking *Introduce Yourself* on Slash, a subsidiary of Warner Brothers. It encompassed a variety of styles but exuded a rare warmth and energy, mainly through Moseley's melodramatic vocals, and was well received by the critics (not least for signature tune, 'We Care A Lot'). However, internal disputes led to the firing of Moseley on the eve of widespread press coverage and favourable live reviews, though it had been reported that the band underwent a period when every single member walked out at some point. Moseley would go on to gig, temporarily, with Bad Brains, before

putting his own band together, Cement. Against the odds his replacement, Mike Patton (b. 27 January 1968, Eureka, California, USA), was even more flamboyant and actually more accomplished as a singer (it was also rumoured that Courtney Love of Hole auditioned/rehearsed with the group). *The Real Thing*, the album which followed Patton's recruitment, was a runaway success, with the single, 'Epic', denting the UK Top 20 singles chart. Their style was now both offbeat and unpredictable, yet retained enough melody to remain a commercial proposition. Despite the universal adulation, however, it transpired that the band still pretty much hated each other off stage. *Live At The Brixton Academy* was released as a stop-gap affair, while the band toured on for nearly three years on the back of the worldwide success of their last studio album. After Patton temporarily defected back to his original, pre-Faith No More outfit, Mr Bungle, the group finally returned with *Angel Dust*. A tougher, less acessible record in keeping with the group's origins (despite a cover of the Commodores' 'I'm Easy'), it made the US Top 10 as their commercial ascent continued. However, in 1994 following a good deal of press speculation, the ever volatile line-up of Faith No More switched again as Jim Martin was ousted in favour of Trey Spruance, who had formerly worked in Patton's earlier and sometimes concurrent band, Mr Bungle.

Albums: *Faith No More* (Mordam 1984), *Introduce Yourself* (London 1987), *The Real Thing* (London 1989), *Live At The Brixton Academy* (London 1991), *Angel Dust* (London 1992), *King For A Day...Fool For A Lifetime* (London 1994). Video: *Live At Brixton* (1990).

Faithful Breath

This progressive heavy metal band from Germany have a long and chequered history, dating back to 1974. The initial nucleus of the band comprised Heinz Mikus (guitar/vocals), Horst Stabenow (bass) and Uwe Otto (drums). Influenced by King Crimson and Deep Purple, their debut album was *Fading Beauty* in 1974. This featured intricate arrangements and keyboards, but lacked both melody and memorable hooks. After a lengthy gap and the ditching of keyboards, the band concentrated on guitar-oriented hard rock. Three competent albums followed, but each suffered from inexperienced self-production. Successful appearances at two Dutch rock festivals in 1983 attracted the attention of Mausoleum Records. Jurgen Dusterloh took over the drumstool and Andy Bibi Honig was added as a second guitarist for the recording of *Gold 'N' Glory*.

Faith No More

Produced by Michael Wagener, it remains the band's finest recorded work. Further line-up changes ensued as the band moved towards the thrash end of the hard rock spectrum. In 1987, they changed their name to Risk, with only Mikus surviving from the original line-up.

Albums: *Fading Beauty* (Sky 1974), *Back On My Hill* (Sky 1980), *Rock Lions* (Sky 1981), *Hard Breath* (Sky 1983), *Gold 'N' Glory* (Mausoleum 1984), *SKOL* (Ambush 1985), *Live* (Noise 1986).

False Prophets

'Our aim is to disarm the mechanics of oppression through persistent 'making and doing' of words and music in an invocation of the ancient magic which empowers humankind through the massing of voices in sacred speech/song.' With this impressive philosophy in mind, False Prophets comprising Stephan Ielpi (vocals), Debra De Salvo (guitar/vocals), Steven Taylor (guitar/vocals), Nick Marden (bass/vocals) and Billy Atwell III (drums/vocals) - burst into life in the early 80s as part of the famed US hardcore scene which also spawned Black Flag and Hüsker Dü. Their hypothesis was intelligence, intellect and knowledge as opposed to the horror show shock tactics used by so many US punk acts. This approach led to a contract with Jello Biafra's Alternative Tentacles label in 1986, from which sprang *False Prophets* and *Implosion*. These albums showed a willingness to experiment and break away from pure punk thrash-outs. *Invisible People*, on Konkurrel, saw them start the new decade in style. An innovative fusion of hardcore punk, Latin rhythms, hard rock and polemic sculpted into a uniquely compelling record. They continue their quest for equality and freedom through the 90s with this theory as their cornerstone: 'All music, particularly rock, is ecstatic activity, and ecstasy itself is revolutionary.'

Albums: *False Prophets* (Alternative Tentacles 1986), *Implosion* (Alternative Tentacles 1987), *Invisible People* (Konkurrel 1990).

Fandango

American melodic hard rock outfit formed in 1976 by vocalist Joe Lynn Turner and guitarist Rick Blakemore. Enlisting the services of Larry Dawson (keyboards), Bob Danyls (bass) and Abe Speller (drums), they signed to RCA the following year. They produced four albums in four years, with each successive release featuring more accomplished and memorable compositions. Influenced by Kiss, Deep Purple, Journey and Styx, their style was rigidly formularized and totally geared to US FM radio playlists. The band disintegrated in 1981, with Turner embarking on a solo career. His first release was *Fandango*, which comprised tracks re-recorded from the band's four albums. Turner subsequently went on to play with Rainbow, Yngwie Malmsteen's Rising Force and Deep Purple.

Albums: *Fandango* (RCA 1977), *One Night Stand* (RCA 1978), *Last Kiss* (RCA 1979), *Cadillac* (RCA 1980).

Fast Forward

This one-off side project from former Stories vocalist Ian Lloyd came to fruition in 1984. With the help of producer Bruce Fairbairn (of Loverboy and Bon Jovi fame) and a series of highly regarded session musicians, the end result was *Living In Fiction*, a highly polished melodic rock album, featuring razor-sharp harmonies, swathes of keyboards and an infectious pop sensibility. Guest appearances included Mick Jones and Lou Gramm from Foreigner and Beau Hill (Ratt producer) on keyboards. Songwriting contributions from Bryan Adams and Jim Vallance added further interest to the project, yet, surprisingly, it was a commercial flop. Consequently, plans to record a second album were abandoned.

Album: *Living In Fiction* (Island 1984).

Faster Pussycat

The mid-80s Los Angeles glam/sleaze scene which produced Guns N'Roses also saw the formation of Faster Pussycat in 1986 around vocalist Taime Downe and guitarist Mick Cripps - although Cripps later departed for L.A. Guns along with original bassist, Kelly Nickels. Downe, formerly co-owner of LA club The Cathouse, recruited guitarists Brent Muscat and Greg Steele, bassist Eric Stacy and drummer Mark Michals, and, with a name taken from Russ Meyer's *Faster, Pussycat! Kill! Kill!* film, the band signed to Elektra in December 1986. *Faster Pussycat* was recorded with Poison producer Ric Browde on a low budget, and was an infectious collection of Aerosmith/Rolling Stones-influenced numbers, with the band's sense of humour shining through in 'Bathroom Wall', 'Don't Change That Song' and 'Babylon'. A UK tour with Guns N'Roses and US dates with Alice Cooper, Dave Lee Roth and Motörhead helped build respectable album sales and the band had matured considerably by the time they recorded *Wake Me When It's Over* with John Jansen. This buried the glam image under a heavier sound and greater lyrical depth, with 'Pulling Weeds' addressing the abortion issue, while the emotive 'House Of Pain' examined the effects of divorce through a child's eyes. The humour still permeated through, however, on 'Slip Of The Tongue' and 'Where There's A Whip There's A Way'. Michals left in disgrace, jailed on drugs charges, on the eve of a European tour with the Almighty and Dangerous Toys, and Frankie Banali filled in before Brett Bradshaw took the drumstool for further US touring with Kiss and Mötley Crüe. *Whipped* showed further progression and a diverse approach, but emerged into a much different musical climate. Despite the quality of the album, Faster Pussycat fell victim to a combination of the recession and the success of the Seattle bands - ironically, Downe was a Seattle native - with Elektra dropping them while they toured America with Kiss. The band split shortly thereafter. Taime Downe was later spotted helping out Pigface.

Albums: *Faster Pussycat* (Elektra 1987), *Wake Me When It's Over* (Elektra 1989), *Whipped* (Elektra 1991).

Fastway

After quitting Motörhead in May 1982 guitarist 'Fast' Eddie Clarke went into partnership with bassist Pete Way from UFO, drummer Jerry Shirley from Humble Pie and previously unknown vocalist Dave King. Way left soon after to form Waysted and was replaced by Charlie McCracken. Within a year they had formulated a style far removed from Motörhead and soon drew comparisons to Deep Purple and Led Zeppelin, yet they won few fans despite a strong debut album and a minor hit single with 'Easy Living'. Finding a degree of fame in America boosted their confidence and they recorded a second album with producer Eddie Kramer. Again this was a good collection, but it remained largely ignored in Europe and unfortunately a similar fate befell it in America, prompting Shirley and McCracken to quit. After a new line-up and a third album a little success came with the recording of the soundtrack to the rock/horror film *Trick Or Treat,* which kept them in the American charts for 11 months. Yet they failed to capitalise on it. Clarke returned to the UK in 1988 and rebuilt the band with Paul Gray (bass; ex-Eddie And The Hot Rods, Damned, UFO), Steve Clarke (drums) and former Joan Jett lyricist Lea Hart on vocals and guitar. *On Target* failed to capture public interest and Clarke and Hart formed a new line-up with American bassist K.B. Bren and a drummer known as 'Riff Raff'. With the addition of members of Girlschool this line-up recorded *Bad Bad Girls*, which turned out to their last line-up and album. Once more the curse of Clarke being ex-Motörhead overshadowed his involvement in Fastway. The failure

Fastway

of the press to view the band as a separate entity was always the rock on which Fastway ran aground, and finally floundered. Clarke would subsequently launch a solo career under his own name.

Albums: *Fastway* (CBS 1983), *All Fired Up* (CBS 1984), *Waiting For The Roar* (CBS 1986), *Trick Or Treat* (CBS 1987), *On Target* (GWR 1988), *Bad Bad Girls* (Legacy 1990).

Fates Warning

Formed in Cincinatti, Ohio, USA, in 1982, initially as Misfit, the original line-up of Fates Warning consisted of John Arch (vocals), Jim Matheos (guitar), Victor Arduini (guitar), Joe DiBiase (bass) and Steve Zimmerman (drums). After a couple of early demos the band were invited to contribute a track to the *Metal Massacre V* compilation released on Metal Blade Records in 1984. The label signed the band immediately to a long-term recording agreement and released the band's debut album, entitled *Night On Broken*, in the same year. The album was very reminiscent of early Iron Maiden due to the song compositions and John Arch's vocal style. Shortly after its release guitarist Victor Arduini left the band to be replaced by Frank Aresti. The next two albums, *The Spectre Within* and *Awaken The Guardian*, released in 1985 and 1986 respectively, showed the band's music to be more progressive and complex than first impressions had suggested. However, vocalist John Arch was unhappy with the musical direction that Fates Warning had begun to pursue and left, but was soon replaced by Ray Alder, whose voice was better suited to the material. This was most noticeable on *No Exit*. Released in 1988, it was widely recognized as the band's finest work to date, partially thanks to producer Max Norman, who strove for a clean, Queensrÿche-like sound. Soon after its release drummer Steve Zimmerman left the band to be replaced by Mark Zonder. *Perfect Symmetry* was released in 1989 after the band had completed a couple of rather uneasy European tours. The result was an album that in some places sounded orchestral in its arrangements, and featured Dream Theater keyboard player Kevin Moore as a guest musician. Come the next album, *Parallels*, released in 1991, the band returned to their earlier techno-pomp metal influences. It was well received by the press, who were beginning to acknowledge a band who had a lot to offer and deserved more recognition than had previously been awarded them.

Albums: *Night On Broken* (Metal Blade 1984), *The Spectre Within* (Metal Blade 1985), *Awaken The Guardian* (Metal Blade 1986), *No Exit* (Metal Blade 1988), *Perfect Symmetry* (Metal Blade 1989), *Parallels* (Metal Blade 1991).

Fear Factory

This Los Angeles-based band are one of the few truly innovative acts in death metal, mixing industrial-style electronic rhythms and samples with grinding guitars and harsh vocals to create their own brutal soundscape. Formed in late 1991 with the line-up of Burton C. Bell (vocals), Dino Cazares (guitar, who has an additional side project, Brujeria), Andrew Shives (bass) and Raymond Herrera (drums), the band rapidly made an impact with two tracks on the *LA Death Metal* compilation, produced by Faith No More bassist Bill Gould, and subsequently signed to Roadrunner. The Colin Richardson-produced *Soul Of A New Machine* established Fear Factory as a genuine death metal force, with a good collection of songs delivered with originality and ferocity, while the band set about developing their live show on their debut tour with Brutal Truth in Europe, followed by US dates with Sick Of It All and Biohazard. *Fear Is The Mind Killer*, a mini-album of remixes by Canadian industrialists Front Line Assembly, demonstrated further dimensions and possibilities available to the Factory sound by adding an industrial dance edge, bringing the band further acclaim.

Albums: *Soul Of A New Machine* (Roadrunner 1992), *Fear Is The Mind Killer* (Roadrunner 1993, mini-album).

Femme Fatale

This American quintet formed in Alberquerque, New Mexico, in 1987. However, it did not take long before they relocated to the bright lights of Los Angeles in the quest for wider exposure and A&R attention from record companies. Fronted by Lorraine Lewis, they were quickly snapped up by MCA Records who assigned Jim Faraci (of L.A. Guns fame) as producer. Musically, they strived to corner the same market as Bon Jovi, relying on a pop-metal/hard rock crossover approach. In interviews Lewis repeatedly stated her objective was to be the biggest 'pin up girl' in rock. The band, completed by Mazzi Rawd (guitar), Bill D'Angelo (guitar), Rick Rael (bass) and Bobby Murray (drums), recorded a self-titled debut album which played heavily on their vocalist's sexuality. This approach often overshadowed Lewis's genuine ability, and although it was received favourably by the critics, it was quickly consigned to the bargain bins while the band disappeared without trace. Lewis would go on to work with Roxy Petrucci (ex-Vixen) and Gina Stile (ex-Poison Dollys) in a new all-female outfit.

Album: *Femme Fatale* (MCA 1988).

Fields Of The Nephilim

This British rock group were formed in Stevenage, Hertfordshire, in 1983. The line-up comprised Carl McCoy (vocals), Tony Pettitt (bass), Peter Yates (guitar) and the Wright brothers, Nod (b. Alexander; drums) and Paul (guitar). Their image, that of neo-western desperados, was borrowed from films such as *Once Upon A Time In America* and *The Long Ryders*. They also had the bizarre habit of smothering their predominantly black clothes in flour and/or talcum powder. Their version of Goth-rock, tempered with transatlantic overtones, found favour with those already immersed in the sounds of the Sisters Of Mercy and the Mission. Signed to the Situation Two label, Fields Of The Nephilim scored two major UK Independent hit singles with 'Preacher Man' and 'Blue Water', while their first album, *Dawn Razor*, made a modest showing on the UK album chart. The second set, *The Nephilim*, reached number 14, announcing the group's arrival as one of the principal rock acts of the day. Their devoted following also ensured a showing on the national singles chart, giving them minor hits with 'Moonchild' (1988 - also an independent chart number 1), 'Psychonaut' (1989) and 'Summerland (Dreamed)' (1990). In October 1991 McCoy left the group taking the 'Fields Of The Nephilim' name with him. The remaining members have since vowed to carry on. With the recruitment a new vocalist, Alan Delaney, they began gigging under the name Rubicon in the summer of 1992, leaving McCoy yet to unveil his version of the Nephilim.

Albums: *Dawn Razor* (Situation 2 1987), *The Nephilim* (Situation 2 1988), *Elyzium* (Beggars Banquet 1990), *Earth Inferno* (Beggars Banquet 1991), *BBC Radio 1 In Concert* (Windsong 1992), *Revelations* (Beggars Banquet 1993).

Videos: *Forever Remain* (1988), *Morphic Fields* (1989), *Earth Inferno* (1991).

Fifth Angel

Formed in Seattle in 1985, Fifth Angel comprised Ted Pilot (vocals), Kendall Bechtel (guitar), Ed Archer (guitar), John Macko (bass) and Ken Mary (drums). On the back of promising club dates they came to the attention of Mike Varney, who signed them to his Shrapnel label. A self-titled debut album backed up with touring commitments won them many fans and now brought them to the attention of Epic Records, who had the album remixed and reissued in 1988. *Time Will Tell* sold well but the band were unable to live up to expectations and they broke up later that year with only drummer Mary going on to a degree of success with the Alice Cooper

Band and House Of Lords.

Albums: *Fifth Angel* (Shrapnel 1986), *Fifth Angel* (Epic 1988, remix of debut), *Time Will Tell* (Epic 1989).

Fight

Inspired by the aggressive new metal sounds of the likes of Pantera, Skid Row and Metallica, Judas Priest vocalist Rob Halford formed Fight as a solo project to explore material which he felt was inappropriate for Priest, but it eventually led to a bitter and acrimonious split from his old band as they celebrated 20 years together. Taking Priest drummer Scott Travis with him, Halford recruited guitarists Russ Parish (ex-War And Peace) and Brian Tilse plus bassist Jay Jay (both from local Phoenix, Arizona, band Cyanide) for *War Of Words*. While Pantera comparisons were obvious, Fight proved themselves not to be the clone band some had feared with the intense material given individual character by Halford's distinctive vocal delivery, and the band delivered with powerful live shows. However, the intense tour schedule proved too much for Parish, who was replaced by Robbie Lockner for the Anthrax US tour and then permanently by Mark Chausse as Fight performed with Metallica across the USA and released the *Mutations* mini-album, a collection of live tracks and covers, including 'Freewheel Burnings', before going to work on their second album proper.

Albums: *War Of Words* (Epic 1993), *Mutations* (Epic 1994, mini-album).

Fiona

b. Fiona Flanagan, New Jersey, USA. Fiona had always harboured ambitions to be a star since her teenage years singing in clubs with various rock bands in New York. Eventually she took the first steps towards achieving that dream by signing a deal with Atlantic Records in 1985, who put her in the studio with guitarist Bobby Messano from the Starz, along with session men Donnie Kisselbach (bass), Joe Franco (drums) and Benjy King (keyboards). After a false start with production problems former Good Rats vocalist Peppi Marchello took over. The resulting self-titled album received good press and predictable comparisons to Heart and Pat Benatar ensued. The second album displayed a more mature sound thanks to producer Beau Hill (at that time her boyfriend) and guest appearances from Nile Rogers and Kip Winger and Reb Beach from the Alice Cooper band (at the time forming their own unit, Winger). The album contained a poignant cover of 'Thunder And Lightning' by German singer Chi Coltrane, which if released as a single just might have provided a much needed hit. She did, however, come to the attention of film producer Richard Marquand who cast her in his rock musical, *Hearts Of Fire*, in which she sang alongside Bob Dylan and actor Rupert Everett. Her last album for Atlantic was greeted with a measure of indifference and her career has remained on hold ever since, despite winning a new contract from Geffen Records.

Albums: *Fiona* (Atlantic 1985), *Beyond The Page* (Atlantic 1986).

Fire Merchants

This hi-tech power trio of well-seasoned session musicians was put together by ex-Andy Summers bassist Doug Lunn. Enlisting John Goodsall (ex-Brand X and Peter Gabriel) on guitar and keyboards, the line-up was eventually completed following a long search for the right drummer. Ex-Frank Zappa and Genesis' sticksman Chester Thompson was drafted in as the perfect candidate, allowing the band to stabilize in October 1987. Released two years later, their self-titled debut album was an all-instrumental affair, offering an eclectic fusion of jazz, rock and blues.

Album: *Fire Merchants* (Roadrunner 1989).

Firm

It seemed to be a marriage made in heaven when ex-Led Zeppelin guitarist Jimmy Page and former Free/Bad Company vocalist Paul Rodgers began working together as the Firm in 1984. Enlisting ex-Uriah Heep/Manfred Mann drummer Chris Slade (the Damned's Rat Scabies also auditioned) and virtual unknown Tony Franklin on bass, an acquaintance of Page's from work with Roy Harper, the partnership never quite gelled in a manner to match either protagonist's earlier achievements. However, the band was not without musical merit, with Slade's precise backbeat providing a solid base for Page and the stylish Franklin to create a distinctive sound on *The Firm*, with Rodgers in fine voice on varied material from the lengthy and Zeppelinesque 'Midnight Moonlight' to the more commercial strains of 'Radioactive', which was a minor hit, plus a cover of 'You've Lost That Loving Feeling'. Live dates proved successful, with Page producing his customary show-stopping solo spot replete with laser effects, although neither Page nor Rodgers were willing to reprise their previous work. *Mean Business* continued in the warm, understated and bluesy style of the debut, but failed to raise the band to new heights, and the Firm split after the subsequent world tour. Page and Rodgers returned to their respective solo careers, while Slade joined AC/DC and Franklin teamed up with John Sykes in Blue Murder.

Albums: *The Firm* (Atlantic 1985), *Mean Business* (Atlantic 1986).

Fish

b. Derek William Dick, 25 April 1958, Dalkeith, Edinburgh, Scotland. Fish acquired his nickname from a landlord who objected to his lengthy periods in the bath. He sang for Nottingham band the Stone Dome before auditioning for progressive rockers Marillion by writing lyrics for their instrumental, 'The Web'. The group established a strong following by constant touring before releasing their debut single 'Market Square Heroes'. Fish's bombastic vocals, markedly similar to Peter Gabriel, strengthened critics' arguments that Marillion were mere Genesis copyists. Despite this, Marillion went from strength to strength, with Fish structuring a series of elaborately linked concept albums, which were still capable of yielding hit singles including 'Garden Party' and the melodic ballad, 'Kayleigh'. His lyrics were strongly influenced in style and content by the work of Peter Hammill, former leader of progressive 70s group Van Der Graaf Generator, a debt he acknowledged by inviting Hammill as special guest on Marillion's 1983 tour of Britain. After the huge success of *Clutching At Straws*, he began to disagree with the band about their musical direction and left in 1988 to embark on a solo career, and was replaced by Steve Hogarth. Fish's debut solo album utilized stylistically diverse elements such as folk tunes and brass arrangements, as shown on the hit 'Big Wedge', but he also retained a mixture of hard rockers and ballads. In 1989 he worked with Peter Hammill on his opera, *The Fall Of The House Of Usher*, but their voices clashed and Fish was replaced on the project by Andy Bell of i. A more successful collaboration was the single 'Shortcut To Somewhere', recorded with Genesis keyboard player Tony Banks in 1986. His 1993 release was a desultory album of cover versions, including the Kinks' 'Apeman' and the Moody Blues' 'Question'.

Albums: *Vigil In A Wilderness Of Mirrors* (EMI 1990), *Internal Exile* (EMI 1991), *Songs From The Mirror* (EMI 1993), *Sushi* (Dick Bros 1994), *Suits* (Dick Bros 1994).

Fishbone

Funk metal hybrid from Los Angeles, USA, who have now been active for over a decade. Five of the seven band members met through the Los Angeles School Bussing Program; a scheme designed to encourage black and white kids to visit each other's schools. Although their recorded output is sparse given their longevity, their hard political edge and high octane

Fish

rythmic onslaught is every bit as deserving of mass attention as the Red Hot Chili Peppers or Living Colour. Their line-up boasts Chris 'Maverick Meat' Dowd (b. Christopher Gordon Dowd, 20 September 1965, Las Vegas, Nevada, USA; trombone, keyboards), 'Dirty' Walter Kibby (b. Walter Adam Kibby II, 13 November 1964, Columbus, Ohio, USA; trumpet, horn, vocals), 'Big' John Bigham (b. 3 March 1969, Lidsville, USA), Kendall Jones (b. Kendall Rey Jones, USA; guitar), Philip 'Fish' Fisher (b. 16 July 1967, El Camino, Los Angeles, California, USA; drums - has guested for Little Richard, Bob Dylan and others), John Fisher (b. John Norwood Fisher, 9 December 1965, El Camino, Los Angeles, California, USA; bass) and Angelo Moore (b. Angelo Christopher Moore, 5 November 1965, USA; lead vocals). Norwood was stabbed on stage early in their career when Fishbone played alongside hardcore bands like the Dead Kennedys (the influence of Bad Brains is obvious in their output). After a debut mini-album the production expertise of David Kahne saw them touch on a more conventional metal direction, before exposing their true talents for the first time on *Truth And Soul*. This was helped in no small part by the airplay success of a cover of Curtis Mayfield's 'Freddie's Dead'. Subsequent recordings saw Fishbone branching out and working with rap artists like the Jungle Brothers, though *The Reality Of My Own Surroundings* had more in common with the hard-spined funk of Sly Stone. 'Fight The Youth' and 'Sunless Saturday' demonstrated a serious angle with socio-political, anti-racist and anti-drug lyrics in contrast to their lighter side on the humorous 'Naz-tee May'en'. Fishbone live shows continued to sell out without a hit to be seen, and Moore caused a minor sensation by ending a London show naked but for his saxophone. However, just as transatlantic commercial breakthrough offered itself with the *Monkey* set, bizarre press stories began to circulate concerning the activities of Jones, who, at the instigation of his father, had left the flock to join a religious cult. The group, whom he had renounced, were accused of attempted kidnap in their attempts to retrieve him.
Albums: *Fishbone* (Columbia 1985, mini-album), *In Your Face* (Columbia 1986), *Truth And Soul* (Columbia 1988), *The Reality Of My Surroundings* (Columbia 1991), *Give A Monkey A Brain & He'll Swear He's The Centre Of The Universe* (Columbia 1993).

Fist (Canada)

This Canadian heavy rock quartet were formed in 1978 by vocalist/guitarist Ron Chenier. After several false starts and numerous line-up changes the band stabilized with Chenier, plus Laurie Curry (keyboards), Bob Moffat (bass) and Bob Patterson (drums). Influenced by Triumph, Rush and Led Zeppelin, they released six albums of generally average hard rock between 1979 and 1985, with *In The Red* from 1983 being undoubtedly the strongest. This featured the highly talented Dave McDonald on lead vocals instead of Chenier, who lacked both range and power. In order to prevent confusion with the British band Fist, their albums were released under the name Myofist in Europe.
Albums: *Round One* (TCD 1979), *Hot Spikes* (A&M 1980), *Thunder In Rock* (A&M 1982), *In The Red* (A&M 1983), *Danger Zone* (A&M 1985).

Fist (UK)

Formed as Axe in Newcastle-upon-Tyne, England, in 1978, changing their name at the beginning of the following year, the band's original line-up consisted of Keith Satchfield (vocals/guitar), Dave Irwin (guitar), John Wylie (bass) and Harry Hill (drums). They released a couple of mediocre singles via Neat Records in 1979. However, seeing potential, MCA signed the band and released their debut album, *Turn The Hell On*, in 1980. This was a lacklustre affair of standard hard rock and was largely overlooked by both press and the public. Fist were subsequently dropped by MCA, and Satchfield left in 1981. Determined to carry on, the rest of the group replaced the departed vocalist/guitarist with Glenn Coates (vocals) and John Roach (guitar), then re-signed to Neat Records and released their second album, *Back With A Vengeance*, in 1982. Even though this was an improvement on their previous release, it still failed to attract any real interest, and Fist's end was in sight.
Albums: *Turn The Hell On* (MCA 1980), *Back With A Vengeance* (Neat 1982).

5X

Japanese hard rock band founded in 1981 by ex-Midnight Cruiser guitarist George Azuma and former Oz vocalist Carmen Maki. With Kinta Moriyama (bass) and Jun Harada (drums) completing the line-up, they adopted a style that incorporated elements of Motörhead, Van Halen and AC/DC, also veering towards thrash metal at times. By their third album, which saw them adopt a slightly altered name offering their singer more prominent billing, they had moved into mainstream rock territory, and it appeared that vocalist Carmen Maki was striving to become the Japanese equivalent of Heart's Ann Wilson.
Albums: *Human Targets* (EMI 1982), *Live X* (EMI 1982), *Carmen Maki's 5X* (Eastworld 1983).

Flotsam And Jetsam

This 'thrash metal' band was formed in Phoenix, Arizona, USA, in 1984 by drummer David Kelly Smith and bassist Jason Newsted. Adding vocalist Eric A.K. and guitarists Mike Gilbert and Ed Carlson, they debuted with tracks on the *Speed Metal Hell II* and *Metal Massacre IV* compilations. This led to a contract with Roadrunner Records and the release of *Doomsday For The Deceiver* in 1986. Hard, fast and punchy riffs were the band's trademarks, but their progress was hampered by the departure of Newsted to Metallica, shortly after the album's release. Eventually, Troy Gregory was recruited as a permanent replacement and *No Place For Disgrace* emerged in 1988. This sadly revealed that the band had progressed little in two years, and the new material lacked imagination. In an attempt to break into the singles market, they recorded a cover of Elton John's 'Saturday Night's Alright For Fighting', which failed commercially. Dropped by Roadrunner, they were eventually signed up by MCA in 1990 and released *When The Storm Comes Down*. Produced by Alex Periallis (of Testament and Anthrax fame), it was aggressive and power-paced, but suffered from an overall monotony of pace and tone.

Albums: *Doomsday For The Deceiver* (Roadrunner 1986), *No Place For Disgrace* (Roadrunner 1988), *When The Storm Comes Down* (MCA 1990), *Cuatro* (MCA 1993).

For Love Not Lisa

This guitar-based alternative rock band were formed in Oklahoma, USA in 1990 by guitarist Miles, vocalist/guitarist Mike Lewis, bassist Doug Carrion and drummer Aaron Preston. They relocated to Los Angeles in mid-1991, although they soon moved away from the culture shock of the Hollywood scene, and signed a major recording deal while steering well clear of the notorious pay-to-play clubs. *Merge* was an effective debut, mixing punk and rock influences into a varied style with good songwriting, and the band backed it up with live shows where they revealed an experiment side which included Lewis' unusual penchant for ad-libbing most of his lyrics bar the choruses. However, whether For Love Not Lisa can rise above the glut of major label grunge-flavoured bands signed in Nirvana and Pearl Jam's wake was the question left on critics' lips.

Album: *Merge* (East West 1993).

Forbidden

Originally travelling under the moniker Forbidden Evil, this band was formed in San Francisco, California, in 1985. It's original line-up consisted of Russ Anderson (vocals), Glen Alvelais (guitar), Craig Locicero (guitar), Matt Camacho (bass) and Paul Bostaph (drums). They quickly gained a strong following playing numerous support slots with more established Bay Area bands such as Testament and Exodus. Through their early demos the band signed to Combat Records (product would be released in Europe on the Music For Nations subsidiary label, Under One Flag). Their name was truncated to Forbidden while the full title was saved for their debut long player, *Forbidden Evil*. This arrived in 1988 to critical acclaim within the Bay Area thrash community and some of the mainstream metal magazines. They toured Europe in support of the release during 1989, appearing at the Dynamo Open Air Festival in Holland. This was recorded and the subsequent live album, *Raw Evil At The Dynamo*, was released the same year. During preparation for their next studio album Glen Alvelais left the band, but was replaced by ex-Militia guitarist Tim Calvert in time for the recordings. *Twisted Into Form*, released in 1990, was again received well by the media, with its blend of hard-hitting thrash metal, cleverly structured songs and excellent guitar interplay. The band's long-term impact was then dealt a potentially lethal blow by a split between Megaforce Records and Atlantic, which left them without an outlet for much of the early 90s. For *Distortion*, however, they signed to German label Gun Records, adding new drummer Steve Jacobs to the Locicero/Calvert/Anderson axis.

Albums: *Forbidden Evil* (Metal Blade 1988), *Raw Evil At The Dynamo* (Metal Blade 1989, mini-album), *Twisted Into Form* (Metal Blade 1990), *Distortion* (Gun 1994). Compilation: *Point Of No Return: The Best Of* (Metal Blade 1993).

Ford, Lita

b. 23 September 1959, London, England. Ford was one of the original members of the Kim Fowley-conceived Runaways, first joining the band at age 15. A disagreement within the ranks in 1979 over musical direction led to the Runaways break-up, leaving Ford to explore a solo career on the US glam/metal circuit (initially subsidised by her day job as a beautician). Her debut album was recorded for Mercury with the assistance of Neil Merryweather on bass, though it was Ford's guitar playing which took centre stage. *Dancin' On The Edge* made a minor impact on the US album charts reaching number 66, though this was a less seamless collection. Almost four years later in 1988 came *Lita*. Housed on RCA (a third album for MCA, *The Bride Wore Black*, had been abandoned) it reached the Top 30 and spawned the US number 12 hit, 'Kiss Me Deadly', plus a Top 10 hit on the duet with Ozzy Osbourne, 'Close My Eyes Forever'. Later that year she married W.A.S.P. guitarist Chris Holmes, though this would be an ill-starred union. *Stiletto* continued to display Ford's commitment to the formula rock format prevalent in the USA, but she would leave RCA following disappointing sales for 1991's *Dangerous Curves*.

Albums: *Out For Blood* (Mercury 1983), *Dancin' On The Edge* (Mercury 1984), *Lita* (RCA 1988), *Stiletto* (RCA 1990), *Dangerous Curves* (RCA 1991). Compilation: *Best Of* (BMG 1992).

Video: *Lita Live* (1988), *A Midnight Snack* (1990).

Foreigner

A band which took its name from the fact that original members were drawn from both sides of the Atlantic, and this mixture of influences is much in evidence in its music. Mick Jones (b. 27 December 1944, London, England; guitar/vocals) formed the band in 1976, having spent time in Nero & The Gladiators (one hit, 'Entry Of The Gladiators', in 1961). The rest of the 60s were taken up with sessions, while the early 70s saw him working with musicians such as Johnny Halliday as well as his second major band, Wonderwheel. Later he recorded one album with Spooky Tooth, then worked with Leslie West and Ian Lloyd, before taking a job as an A&R man who never signed anyone. Prepared to give the music scene one last try, Jones auditioned musicians, eventually forging a line-up which consisted of Ian McDonald (b. 25 June 1946, London, England; guitar/keyboards/vocals), formerly of King Crimson, Lou Gramm (b. Lou Grammatico, 2 May 1950, Rochester, New York, USA; vocals), who had played with Black Sheep in the early 70s, Dennis Elliott (b. 18 August 1950, London, England; drums), Al Greenwood (b. New York, USA; keyboards) and Edward Gagliardi (b. 13 February 1952, New York, USA; bass). In 1977 the band released *Foreigner*, and in a poll conducted by *Rolling Stone* magazine, came out as top new artists. Jones and Gramm wrote most of the band's material, including classic tracks such as 'Feels Like The First Time' and 'Cold As Ice'. Despite playing at the Reading Rock Festival in England twice in the 70s, Foreigner had more consistent success in the USA. In 1979 Rick Wills (b. England; bass) replaced Gagliardi, having served a musical apprenticeship with King Crimson and Peter Frampton. Gagliardi reportedly 'fell on the floor and passed out' on being told the news. *Head Games*, meanwhile, proved most notable for its 'exploitative' sleeve design, which contrasted with the subtle brand of rock it housed. 1980 saw the departure of McDonald and Greenwood which led to the guest appearances of Thomas Dolby and Junior Walker on *4*, produced by Mutt Lange. 'Waiting For A Girl Like You' was the hit single lifted from the album. Though it demonstrated the band's highly musical approach, taking the form of a wistful yet melodious ballad, it pigeonholed the group as purveyors of the epic AOR song. A reputation which was hardly infringed by the release of 'I Want To Know What Love Is', which proved to be Foreigner's greatest commercial success. It topped the charts on both sides of the Atlantic and featured the New Jersey Mass Choir backing Gramm's plaintive vocal. In the mid-80s the members of Foreigner were engaged in solo projects, and the success of Gramm's *Ready Or Not* in 1987 led to widespread speculation that Foreigner were about to disband. This was not the case, as *Inside Information* proved, though in other respects it was a poor record and a portent of things to come. In 1989 Gramm enjoyed success with another solo project, *Long Hard Look*, before leaving the band officially in 1990 to form Shadow King. Jones refused to face the inevitable, and, amid much press back-biting, recruited Johnny Edwards to provide vocals for *Unusual Heat*. By 1994 both Jones and Gramm grasped the nettle and got back in touch, launching a reunited Foreigner, though both Wills and Elliott (the latter going on to a career as a master ornamental wood lather) were deemed surplus to requirements. The 1994 model then, boasted a line-up of Bruce Turgon (bass; a former colleague of Gramm in Black Sheep), Jeff Jacobs (keyboards; ex-Billy Joel circa *Storm Front*) and Mark Schulman (drums; ex-Billy Idol, Simple Minds), in adition to Jones and Gramm. Whether or not their legacy grows further, Foreigner will continue to epitomize the classic sound of 'adult orientated rock' better than anybody.

Albums: *Foreigner* (Atlantic 1977), *Double Vision* (Atlantic 1978), *Head Games* (Atlantic 1979), *4* (Atlantic 1981), *Agent Provocateur* (Atlantic 1985), *Inside Information* (Atlantic 1987), *Unusual Heat* (Atlantic 1991), *Mr Moonlight* (BMG 1994). Compilations: *Records* (Atlantic 1982), *The Very Best Of And Beyond* (Atlantic 1992). Mick Jones solo: *Everything That Comes Around* (Atlantic 1989).

44 Magnum

Japanese heavy metal outfit formed in 1977 by vocalist Tatsuya Umehara and guitarist Satoshi Hirorse. With the addition of Hironori Yoshikawa on bass and Satoshi Miyawaki on drums, they persevered for many years in the shadow of higher profile Japanese bands such as Loudness, Earthshaker and Vow Wow. They eventually secured a record contract in 1982 and debuted with *Danger* the following year. Although the musicianship was competent, their ideas and style were too obviously influenced by British and American acts such as Van Halen, Deep Purple and Led Zeppelin.

Albums: *Danger* (Moon 1983), *Street Rock 'n' Roller* (Roadrunner 1984).

Four Horsemen

This heavy metal/rock 'n' roll outfit was formed in 1991 by former Cult bassist, Haggis, who in a previous life had been Kid Chaos of Zodiac Mindwarp And The Love Reaction, while his parents have always known him as Mark Manning. Recruiting Frank C. Starr (vocals), Ken 'Dimwit' Montgomery (drums), Dave Lizmi (guitar) and Ben Pape (bass), they negotiated a deal with Rick Rubin's Def American label (with whom the band's leader had worked during his stint with the Cult). With Haggis on rhythm guitar, their music drew heavily from AC/DC, the Black Crowes and the Georgia Satellites, though most critics could not see past their Cult affiliations Their debut album, *Nobody Said It Was Easy*, was a powerful collection of heavy duty rockers based on loud riffs and infectious chorus lines. Just like Haggis' former employers they exaggerated every cliche in the book, yet this approach did not groan under the same weight of lofty ideals and was consequently more fun. Manning was last sighted promoting his book of illustrations, *A Bible Of Dreams*, in conjunction with Bill Drummond of the KLF.

Album: *Nobody Said It Was Easy* (Def American 1991).

Freak Of Nature

Following the break-up of White Lion, frontman Mike Tramp assembled Freak Of Nature with guitarist Kenny Korade, former Lion bassist Jerry Best, drummer Johnny Haro and ex-VVSI/House Of Lords guitarist Dennis Chick, a replacement for original member, Oliver Steffenson. Away from record company pressures, the band developed a strong collection of melodic rock songs with a distinctly harder edge than White Lion, with Tramp concentrating on introspective, personal lyrics, again in contrast to the simpler themes of his previous group. '92' dealt with a traumatic year in Tramp's personal and professional life, while 'Rescue Me' tackled the difficult subject of his brother's addiction problems. While acquiring recording contracts for Europe and Japan, Freak Of Nature had trouble finding a deal for the USA owing to their unwillingness to compromise, but were prepared to

be patient and let their music and growing live reputation break the band. A lengthy touring schedule, taking in the USA, Japan and Europe from May 1993 made the band many friends, and served to reinforce the idea of Freak Of Nature as a band rather than a Tramp solo project. Late 1994 saw the introduction of new guitarist Marcus Mand in place of Kenny Korade.

Albums: *Freak Of Nature* (Music For Nations 1993), *Gathering Of Freaks* (Music For Nations 1994).

Free

Formed in the midst of 1968's British blues boom, Free originally comprised Paul Rodgers (b. 17 December 1949, Middlesbrough, Cleveland, England; vocals), Paul Kossoff (b. 14 September 1950, London, England, d. 19 March 1976; guitar), Andy Fraser (b. 7 August 1952, London, England; bass) and Simon Kirke (b. 28 July 1949, Shrewsbury, Shropshire, England; drums). Despite their comparative youth, the individual musicians were seasoned performers, particularly Fraser, a former member of John Mayall's Bluesbreakers. Free gained early encouragement from Alexis Korner, but having completed an excellent, earthy debut album, *Tons Of Sobs*, the group began honing a more individual style with their second set. The injection of powerful original songs, including 'I'll Be Creeping', showed a maturing talent, while Rodgers' expressive voice and Kossoff's stinging guitar enhanced a growing reputation. The quartet's stylish blues/rock reached its commercial peak on *Fire And Water*. This confident collection featured moving ballads; 'Heavy Load', 'Oh I Wept' and compulsive, uptempo material, the standard-bearer of which is 'All Right Now'. An edited version of this soulful composition reached number 2 in the UK and number 4 in the US in 1970, since when the song has become one of pop's most enduring performances, making periodic re-appearances in the singles chart. A fourth set, *Highway*, revealed a mellower perspective highlighted by an increased use of piano at the expense of Kossoff's guitar. This was due, in part, to friction within the group, a factor exacerbated when the attendant single, 'The Stealer', failed to emulate its predecessor's success. Free split up in May 1971, paradoxically in the wake of another hit single, 'My Brother Jake', but regrouped in January the following year when spin-off projects faltered, although Kossoff and Kirke's amalgamation (Kossoff, Kirke, Tetsu And Rabbit) proved fruitful. A sixth album, *Free At Last*, offered some of the unit's erstwhile fire and included another UK Top 20 entrant, 'Little Bit Of Love'. However, Kossoff's increasing ill-health and Fraser's

Freak Of Nature

departure for the Sharks undermined any new-found confidence. A hastily convened line-up consisting of Rodgers, Kirke, John 'Rabbit' Bundrick (keyboards) and Tetsu Yamauchi (b. 1946, Fukuoka, Japan; bass) undertook a Japanese tour, but although the guitarist rejoined the quartet for several British dates, his contribution to Free's final album, *Heartbreaker*, was muted. Kossoff embarked on a solo career in October 1972; Wendel Richardson from Osibisa replaced him on a temporary basis, but by July the following year Free had ceased to function. Rodgers and Kirke subsequently formed Bad Company.

Albums: *Tons Of Sobs* (Island 1968), *Free* (Island 1969), *Fire And Water* (Island 1970), *Highway* (Island 1970), *Free Live* (Island 1971), *Free At Last* (Island 1972), *Heartbreaker* (Island 1973). Compilations: *The Free Story* (Island 1974, double album), *Completely Free* (Island 1982), *All Right Now* (Island 1991).

Video: *Free* (1989).

Frehley's Comet

Following drug and alcohol-related problems, US guitarist Ace Frehley (b. Paul Frehley, 22 April 1951, Bronx, New York, USA) left Kiss in 1981. After a four-year period of rehabilitation, he began writing and playing again, signing to the Megaforce label in 1987. Recruiting Tod Howarth (vocals/guitar), John Regan (bass) and Anton Fig (drums), Frehley's Comet was born. With an emphasis on Americanized hard rock, with a commercial edge, their self-titled debut was given a favourable reception from critics and Kiss fans alike. In time, Tod Howarth's creative input began to change the band's sound, pushing them in a more lightweight, AOR direction. This was clearly illustrated on *Second Sighting*. Ace, concerned that this new direction might alienate his loyal fan base, relieved Tod Howarth of vocal duties on *Trouble Walkin'* (issued as an Ace Frehley solo album), drafting in guitarist Richie Scarlet as replacement. This album was a backward step musically in an attempt to appeal to the same market as Kiss; employing that band's drummer Peter Criss as guest vocalist and covering Paul Stanley's (Kiss guitarist) 'Hide Your Heart'. The rest of the band became frustrated by Frehley's controlling interest and quit halfway through the tour to support the album. Ace hit rock bottom and has not surfaced since.

Albums: *Frehley's Comet* (Atlantic 1987), *Live + 1* (Atlantic 1988), *Second Sighting* (Atlantic 1988), *Trouble Walking* (WEA 1989).

Video: *Live 4* (1990).

Frehley, Ace

b. Paul Frehley, 22 April 1951, Bronx, New York, USA. Ace Frehley rose to fame as the lead guitarist for premier USA hard rock band Kiss during its prime years. Often nicknamed 'Space Ace' by fans, Frehley released his first, self-titled solo album in September 1978, with albums by the other three members of Kiss also cut simultaneously. Released on Casablanca Records, the album, which found the guitarist attempting more diverse musical styles than he was allowed to follow within the context of Kiss, reached the Top 30 and spawned a number 13 single, the Russ Ballard-penned 'New York Groove'. Frehley left Kiss in 1983, following a near-fatal car accident, and attempted to free himself of a drug habit over the next four years. He formed his own band, Frehley's Comet, in 1987, with whom he recorded three studio albums.
Albums: *Ace Frehley* (Casablanca 1978).

Friedman, Marty

This technically brilliant guitarist has a long and impressive pedigree. Stints with Vixen, Hawaii and Cacophony helped formulate and define his characteristic quick-fire style, before embarking on a solo career. *Dragon's Kiss* was an impressive instrumental debut, combining heavy-duty riffs and intricate solos with Far Eastern influences and undertones. Friedman later went on to produce speed-metallers Apocrypha, before commencing work on a second solo project. This was put on hold after he accepted an invitation to join Megadeth in February 1990, though it did finally emerge three years later. By *Introduction* the guitarist had moved on to a spacious, new-age technique, on a set more expansive in tone that anything he had previously recorded in the rock field.
Album: *Dragon's Kiss* (Roadrunner 1988), *Scenes* (Roadrunner 1993), *Introduction* (Roadrunner 1994).

Fudge Tunnel

UK noise operatives Fudge Tunnel were formed in 1989 by 18 year old vocalist, guitarist and songwriter Alex Newport when he moved to Nottingham. He quickly sought out like-minds in the shape of Dave Ryley (bass) and Adrian Parkin (drums). Their first ever release, 1990's *Sex Mammoth* EP, was immediately made Single Of The Week in the *New Musical Express*. Six months later came *The Sweet Sound Of Excess* EP, then touring commitments with Silverfish and Godflesh. 1991 saw them gain a permanent home at Earache Records, which culminated in the release of their debut album, which arrived with the self-explanatory title of *Hate Songs In E Minor*. This immensely caustic epistle was released

in May 1991 after initial copies, featuring a drawing of a decapitation taken from the John Minnery book, *How To Kill*, were confiscated by Nottingham vice police. The acclaim the Colin Richardson-produced disc eventually accrued in metal and indie magazines was huge however, with barely a word of dissent and plenty more which earmarked Fudge Tunnel as the ultimate in brutal music. A commercially successful EP, *Teeth* (UK indie chart number 4 - a major landmark for such extreme music) preceded the release of a second album, *Creep Diets*. Despite continued progress, the band were unhappily bracketed with the emerging Seattle 'grunge' sound (which they had actually anticipated) and some of the momentum waned. As well as touring 1993 saw Newport working with Max Cavalera (Sepultura) on the Nailbomb project. Fudge Tunnel then reconvened at Sawmill Studios in Cornwall for their third album, *The Complicated Futility Of Ignorance* saw the grunge comparisons dropped as the group processed a further increase in their already massively violent sound.
Albums: *Hate Songs In E Minor* (Earache 1991), *Fudge Cake* (Pigboy/Vinyl Solution 1992; comprises *Sex Mammoth* and *Sweet Sound Of Excess* EPs), *Creep Diets* (Earache 1993), *The Complicated Futility Of Ignorance* (Earache 1994).

G

G-Force

G-Force were the brainchild of ex-Skid Row, Colosseum II, and Thin Lizzy guitarist Gary Moore. After leaving Lizzy shortly after playing on the band's *Black Rose* in 1979, Moore headed for Los Angeles with the intention of forming a new group there. He teamed up with some reputable local musicians and, not wishing at that time to be known as the Gary Moore Band, they chose to travel under the moniker of G-Force. Joining Moore in this project were Tony Newton (vocals), Willie Dee (bass) and Mark Nauseef (drums). The band played some low-key gigs in and around the Los Angeles area and signed to Jet Records, for whom they released their debut album in 1980. A strong slice of melodic hard rock with definite commercial prospects, it nevertheless flopped. The band folded soon after its release.
Album: *G-Force* (Jet 1980).

G.B.H.

Formerly known as Charged G.B.H. (truncating the name by the release of 1986's *Oh No It's G.B.H. Again!* EP), the band originated as the initial impetus of the punk movement was petering out in 1980, counting the Exploited and Discharge among their peer group. Comprising Cal (b. Colin Abrahall; vocals), Jock Blyth (guitar), Ross (bass) and Wilf (drums), they brokered a violent and aggressive image (G.B.H., of course, standing for grievous bodily harm), sporting multi-coloured mohican haircuts and *de rigeur* studded and chained leathers. Musically, they combined influences such as the Ramones and Venom into a hardcore metallic barrage of testosterone-led frustration. With 'smash-the-system' sloganeering in place of lyrics, they were an uncompromising and extreme musical outfit during the early 80s, and exerted some influence on the thrash and hardcore movements which followed. While musically they could always be exciting, any enjoyment was downgraded by the poverty of intellect behind the lyrics (notable examples being the anti-feminist tract, 'Womb With A View', from *City Baby's Revenge*, or 'Limpwristed', from *Midnight Madness*). Their success was also always going to be limited by an inability to progress musically. Kai replaced Wilf on drums in 1989, as the band veered away from regimented hardcore towards speed metal. This trend has continued with the arrival of new bassist Anthony Morgan. Even the mohicans had disappeared on their 1993 tour to promote *From Here To Reality*, which the *New Musical Express* kindly reviewed as having 'no redeeming features whatsoever'.

Albums: *Leather, Bristles, Studs And Acne* (Clay 1981, mini-album), *City Baby Attacked By Rats* (Clay 1982), *Live At City Garden* (Clay 1982), *City Babies Revenge* (Clay 1983), *Midnight Madness And Beyond* (Rough Justice 1986), *A Fridge Too Far* (Rough Justice 1989), *No Need To Panic* (Rough Justice 1989), *Diplomatic Immunity* (Clay 1990), *From Here To Reality* (Music For Nations (1990), *Chruch Of The Truly Warped* (Rough Justice 1993). Compilations: *Leather, Bristles, No Survivors And Sick Boys* (Clay 1982), *The Clay Years 81-84* (Clay 1986).

Videos: *Live At Brixton* (1983), *A Video Too Far* (1989).

G.G.F.H.

G.G.F.H. (an acronym for Global Genocide Forget Heaven) consists of two Californians, Brian J Walls and Ghost. Highly media-literate and pessimistic, G.G.F.H.'s music paints a picture of pain, ignorance and perversity with a palette of harsh electronic music, robotic vocals and sampled dialogue. Their main obsession, however, is the way a paranoid establishment creates sensationalist panics to feed to the TV-addicted populace. *Eclipse*, their first full album, concentrated on the media panic around Satanism with auditory samples from talk shows and cheap films as its backdrop. The second album, *Disease*, dropped the Satanic theme in favour of the more generic territory of serial murder, sexual violence and urban alienation. The grinding hum of *Eclipse* was replaced by a lighter, more electronic, though no less disturbing, tone for *Disease*. The grim *Halloween* EP, released in a limited edition in 1991, was re-released in an extended form as their third full album, consisting of demo material recorded between 1986 and 1989.

Albums: *Eclipse* (Dreamtime 1991), *Disease* (Dreamtime 1993), *Halloween* (Dreamtime 1994).

Galactic Cowboys

This US metallic art-rock quartet was formed in 1990 by vocalist Ben Huggins and guitarist Dane Sonnier. With the addition of bassist Monty Colvin and drummer Alan Doss, they specialized in complex and densely melodic song structures that typically exceeded the six-minute mark. Combining elements of Kings X, Metallica and Neil Young with state-of-the-art technology, they produced one of 1991's most impressive debut albums. Defying simple categorization, they surprised the listener with what initially seemed the *ad hoc* juxtaposition of incompatible styles. Somehow, the strange fusion worked; manic thrashing giving way to harmonica solos, which in turn are followed by four-part vocal harmonies. The Galactic Cowboys' flair for innovation was further confirmed by 1993's *Space In Your Face*, a second chapter in what promises to be an intriguing career.

Albums: *Galactic Cowboys* (MCA 1991), *Space In Your Face* (MCA 1993).

Gamma

After the failure of his solo album guitarist Ronnie Montrose reunited with former Montrose members Jim Alcivar (keyboards) and Alan Fitzgerald (bass) and, with the addition of Davey Patison on vocals and Skip Gallette on drums, formed Gamma in 1979. Following the release of a debut album the line-up changed with another ex-Montrose member, Denny Carmassi, taking over drumming duties, and newcomer Glen Letsch on bass. This new line-up recorded *Gamma 2* - a much stronger album which spawned a hit single in 'Voyager' and a successful tour of America and Europe. Alcivar left soon after to be

replaced by Michell Froom. Despite being a fine synthesizer player in his own right, his input led to keyboard saturation on the third album, relegating Montrose's perennially excellent guitar playing to second string status. Gamma then toured with Foreigner in 1983 but failed to record again as Montrose attempted to reform the band of his name with original vocalist Sammy Hagar. Davey Pattison later surfaced with Robin Trower and Montrose, never fulfilling his wish, returned to a solo career.
Albums: *Gamma* (Elektra 1979), *Gamma 2* (Elektra 1980), *Gamma 3* (Elektra 1982).

Gamma Ray

After leaving Helloween in 1989, the band he founded, guitarist Kai Hansen teamed up with ex-Tyran Pace vocalist Ralf Scheepers. The intention was to record an album of already composed material which had been deemed unsuitable for Hansen's previous band. Joining them for this proposed project were Uwe Wessel (bass), Mathias Burchardt (drums) and a host of guest musicians. Signing to Noise Records they entered the Horus Sound Studios in Germany with producer Tommy Newton. The resulting recordings were released under the Gamma Ray moniker as *Heading For Tomorrow* in 1990. The album was an excellent blend of powerful melodic heavy metal with song structures reminiscent of Queen. Having proved a favourite with press and public alike, Hanson began to realize the group's potential and decided to form a working unit out of the musicians who had played on the project to tour in support of the album. The now fully assembled Gamma Ray consisted of Ralf Scheepers (vocals), Hansen (guitar/vocals), Dirk Schlacter (guiter), Wessel (bass) and Uli Kusch (drums). They toured extensively throughout Europe and Japan where they gained a substantial following, and, as a stop-gap between albums, released an EP of new material, *Heaven Can Wait*. Come the next album, *Sigh No More*, the band were in fine form; extensive touring had disciplined them into a tight, cohesive unit. Though heavier than its predecessor the album boasted quality heavy metal with melody and power, serving as a more than worthy encore to their impressive debut.
Albums: *Heading For Tomorrow* (Noise 1990), *Sigh No More* (Noise 1991).

Gang Green

This quartet from Boston, Massachusetts, USA, specializing in a fusion of hardcore and thrash, was put together by guitarist/vocalist Chris Doherty. Although formed originally in 1982, it was the 1985 re-incarnation that inked a deal with Taang! Records (Doherty had spent some of the intervening period with Jerry's Kids). After numerous line-up changes, a degree of stability was achieved for *You Got It* with Doherty, plus Brian Bertzger (drums), Fritz Erickson (guitar; replacing Chuck Stilphen), and Joe Gittleman (bass), the latter eventually replaced by ex-DRI member Josh Papp. Extolling the virtues of alcohol and skateboarding, and ridiculing the PMRC at every opportunity, their music was fast, aggressive and occasionally abusive. One career highlight was the mini-album, *I81B4U*, where the group's irreverent sense of fun puts 'two fingers up' at Van Halen's *OU812*. They also released one record as a skateboard-shaped picture disc. Unable to progress on the songwriting front, their sound nevertheless grew louder and more impressive as time wore on, particularly on *Older, Budweiser*, which also took their obsession with the eponymous beer to new excesses.
Albums: *Another Wasted Night* (Taang! 1986), *You Got It* (Roadracer 1987), *I81B4U* (Roadracer 1988, mini-album), *Older, Budweiser* (Emergo 1989), *Can't Live Without It* (Emergo 1990), *King Of Bands* (Roadrunner 1991).

Gaye Bykers On Acid

This UK rock group employed an image which combined traditional biker attire with elements of psychedelia and hippie camp. They were led by the colourful figure of Mary Millington, aka Mary Mary (b. Ian Garfield Hoxley; vocals), alongside Kevin Hyde (drums), Robber (b. Ian Michael Reynolds; bass) and Tony (b. Richard Anthony Horsfall; guitar). They were later complemented by disc jockey William Samuel Ronald Monroe ('Rocket Ronnie'). Mary Mary, who had once come second in Leicester's Alternative Miss Universe competition, was often to be seen in platform shoes and dresses, which fuelled the critics' confusion with regard to the band's name and gender orientation. Their debut album, *Drill Your Own Hole*, required purchasers to do just that, as the record was initially issued without a hole in its centre. After leaving Virgin they set up their own label, Naked Brain, quite conceivably because nobody else would have them. Subsequent to the band's demise, which may or may not prove permanent, Kevin instigated a new band, G.R.O.W.T.H., with Jeff (ex-Janitors). Tony teamed up with Brad Bradbury in Camp Collision, while Mary Mary joined ex-members of Killing Joke, Ministry and PiL in the multi-member outfit Pigface. The 90s would bring a more permanent home for his talents in the shape of Hyperhead, formed with Karl Leiker (ex-Luxuria, Bugblot).

Albums: *Drill Your Own Hole* (Virgin 1987), *Stewed To The Gills* (Virgin 1989), *GrooveDiveSoapDish* (Bleed 1989), *Cancer Planet Mission* (Naked Brain 1990), *From The Tomb Of The Near Legendary* (1993).
Video: *Drill Your Own Brain* (1987).

Geddes Axe

Far from having anything to do with a tribute to Rush's bass player, guitarists Martin Wilson and Andrew Barrot took their name from a school book titled *Geddex Axe 1921-1922*. Coming together in 1980 with Andy Millard (vocals), Dave Clayton (drums) and Mick Peace (bass), the band decided to follow in the footsteps of fellow Sheffield citizens Def Leppard and record a self-financed E.P. Entitled *Return Of The Gods* it failed to generate the public interest that Def Leppard had aroused. After one further single, 'Sharpen Your Wits', the band underwent a major personnel change with Barrot joining Baby Tuckoo (and later Chrome Molly), Millard and Clayton quitting and being replaced with Nick Brown, Tony Rose and John Burke respectively. A revamped live set included the progressive 'Valley Of The Kings' (sadly unrecorded) and cover versions of Kiss songs. Indie label Bullet picked them up and released a much-improved 12-inch single, 'Escape From New York', yet it failed to gain any ground for them and by 1983 they had split up for good.

Genitorturers

During the early 90s sexual fetish trappings - such as rubber and leather garb and increasingly extravagant bodily piercings - became fashionable. So it was no surprise that a band surfaced who used elaborate sado-masochistic imagery as the basis for their act. The band in question was the Genitorturers, who were discovered by IRS Records when they were looking for acts for a film featuring rock bands with spectacular stage shows. The film project was abandoned, but the Genitorturers got a deal and recorded their Sadean debut, *120 Days of Genitorture*. The founder, vocalist and core of the band, Gen, is a statuesque dominatrix who is not only a professional body piercer but also works as an organ reclamation technician in a local hospital. She is a persuasive spokesperson for the new piercing ethos which sees sado-masochism as not only a sexual, but spiritual and tribal practice. This translates into an unforgettable stage show, featuring everything from whips and chains, to live nipple and genital piercing. Inevitably, the Genitorturers' striking visual aspects rather eclipse their music, which is a somewhat pedestrian blend of power metal and hardcore punk, combined with a few modern touches such as sampled dialogue. Gen's vocals are gruff and assertive, and the whole package is reminiscent of the Plasmatics, the punk posse of another blonde rock sex queen, Wendy O'Williams.
Album: *120 Days of Genitorture* (Under One Flag 1993).

Geordie

Hailing from the north east of England, Tynesiders Brian Johnson (b. 5 October 1947, Newcastle, England; vocals), Victor Malcolm (guitar), Tom Hill (bass) and Brian Gibson (drums) started life as a poor man's Slade. Their unconsciously professional style was based on the pop end of the hard rock spectrum, with a stage act that included an audience participation opus, the dialectal 'Geordie's Lost His Liggy', which involved Johnson hoisting Malcolm onto his shoulders. After one single for Regal Zonophone, 'Don't Do That', tickled the hit parade, they were signed by EMI, whose faith was justified when 'All Because Of You' from 1973's *Hope You Like It* made the UK Top 20. Two lesser entries - 'Can You Do It' and 'Electric Lady' - followed, and the group's albums sold steadily if unremarkably. Geordie's power as a concert attraction outlasted this chart run, and when the going got rough in the watershed year of 1976-77, the quartet signed off with *Save The World* - a consolidation rather than development of their derivative music. They were remembered not for their hits but as the *alma mater* of Johnson who, after a lean period in which he was heard in a vacuum cleaner commercial, replaced the late Bon Scott in AC/DC.
Albums: *Hope You Like It* (EMI 1973), *Masters Of Rock* (EMI 1974), *Don't Be Fooled By The Name* (EMI 1974), *Save The World* (EMI 1976). Compilation: *Featuring Brian Johnson* (Red Bus 1981).

George, Robin

The style of British born guitarist/producer Robin George, despite his geographical origins, is pure US AOR. George began his career playing guitar in the Byron Band, fronted by one time Uriah Heep vocalist David Byron. His fine guitar work can be heard to good effect on their debut album, *On The Rocks* (Creole Records), in 1981, though after a year with them he left to pursue a solo career. He first signed to Arista Records in 1983, cementing the relationship with the release of a single, 'Go Down Fighting', the melodic guitar work of which quickly brought attention and a reputation as the UK's answer to Billy Squier. Despite this Arista dropped him and instead he went on to work in a production capacity with Heavy Metal Records, helping various acts including

Wrathchild (UK). In 1984 Bronze Records picked him up and the release of 'Heartline' preceded his first full album, *Dangerous Music*, both of which were noted for their pristine production and the bass work of Pino Pallidino (Paul Young Band). Despite the good auspices 'Heartline' remained his only real success and was later reissued in 1985, again selling well. He remained in production until 1990 when he formed a partnership with ex-Diamond Head vocalist Sean Harris in Notorious. This was an ill-fated project that advanced neither career and they soon parted. George has since returned to the mixing desk.
Albums: *Dangerous Music* (Bronze 1984). With Notorious: *Notorious* (Warners 1990).
Video: *Dangerous Music* (1985).

Giant

Hailing from Nashville, USA, Giant developed in the mid-80s when seasoned session guitarist Dann Huff met on various projects with keyboard player Alan Pasqua, notably Whitesnake's *1987* album. However, it was not until 1988 that Giant evolved into a fully-fledged unit with Huff's younger brother, David, joining as drummer and Mike Brignardello on bass (the Huff brothers had formerly been in partnership as part of Christian rockers, White Heart). By this time Dann Huff had taken on llead vocal duties after an unsuccessful search for a suitable singer. Candidates for this job had included the highly successful songwriter and backing vocalist, Tom Kelly. Giant signed to A&M Records in 1988 and released their debut album, *Last Of The Runaways*, a potent brew of hard rock, strong on melody and presentation, in the USA in 1989. This included the Top 10 hit single, 'I'll See You In My Dreams'. The success of the album and single in the USA and impressive sales on import in the UK prompted A&M to give *Last Of The Runaways* a European release in 1990 to a moderate degree of success. This was followed by a series of highly acclaimed club dates around the UK. In 1991, Huff, Pasque and Brignardello played together on Amy Grant's *Heart In Motion*, and prepared material for a new album. However, *Time To Burn* would not feature Pasqua, and though it was again critically lauded, soon after release Epic, to whom Giant had now transferred, dropped the band.
Album: *Last Of The Runaways* (A&M 1989), *Time To Burn* (Epic 1992).

Gillan, Ian

b. 19 August 1945, Hounslow, Middlesex, England. Heavily influenced by Elvis Presley, vocalist Gillan formed his first band at the age of 16. In 1962 he was invited to join local semi-professional R&B band the Javelins, who eventually split up in March 1964. Gillan next formed the Hickies, but abandoned the project to join established soul band, Wainwright's Gentlemen. Soon he was unhappy with this group and he readily accepted an invitation to join the fully professional outfit, Episode Six, in May 1965. A succession of tours and singles failed to produce any domestic chart placings, however, and by early 1969 the band was beginning to disintegrate. In May of the same year Gillan, and Roger Glover (b. 30 November 1945, Brecon, South Wales; bass) were recruited to join Deep Purple, forming the legendary 'Mk II' line-up with Ritchie Blackmore, Jon Lord and Ian Paice. Deep Purple gradually established themselves as a major rock band, helped by their dynamic live show and an aggressive sound characterized by a mix of long instrumentals and Gillan's powerful vocals. The latter part of 1972 saw Deep Purple, acknowledged as the biggest-selling rock band in the world, enter the *Guinness Book Of Records* as the loudest pop group of the day. Their status was consolidated with the release of the live album, *Made In Japan*. In August 1972 Gillan decided to leave the band, but was persuaded to remain with them until June 1973. By the time of his last show with Deep Purple on 28 June, he had already purchased the De Lane Lea studio in London, and it was on this venture that he concentrated on leaving the band, forming Kingsway Studios. He recorded a solo album in 1974 for the Purple label, to whom he was still signed, but it was rejected as too radical a musical departure, and has never been released. After a brief attempt to launch Ian Gillan's Shand Grenade, which included Glover, in late 1975, it was the Ian Gillan Band which began recording *Child In Time* in the first days of 1976. The line-up was Gillan, Ray Fenwick (guitar), Mike Moran (keyboards), Mark Nauseef (drums) and John Gustafson (bass). This first album was much lighter in tone than Deep Purple, but included some excellent songs. The next two albums, now with Colin Towns on keyboards, demonstrated a notable jazz-rock influence, particularly on *Clear Air Turbulence*, which was also distinguished by its striking Chris Foss-designed cover. None of these albums was particularly successful commercially, and after a disappointing tour in spring 1978, Gillan disbanded the group.
Within just a few months of dissolving the Ian Gillan Band, he was back in the studio with a new outfit, inspired by a Towns' song, 'Fighting Man'. New members Leon Genocky (drums), Steve Byrd (guitar) and John McCoy (bass) joined Ian Gillan and Towns to record *Gillan* in summer 1978. The lack of a

record deal meant that this excellent album was never released in the UK, although several of the tracks did appear on the next album, *Mr. Universe*, recorded early in 1979 with Pete Barnacle on drums. The title-track was based on a song of the same name which Ian Gillan had recorded with Episode Six. The album as a whole marked the return of the imposing frontman to solid rock music. In so doing, this collection was instrumental in developing the New Wave Of British Heavy Metal, a label even more applicable to Gillan's next album, *Glory Road*. Now with Bernie Tormé on guitar and former Episode Six drummer Mick Underwood, Gillan produced one of his finest albums, the first copies of which contained a second, free album, *For Gillan Fans Only*. After the slightly disappointing *Future Shock*, Tormé left to be replaced by guitarist Janick Gers of White Spirit, who featured on *Double Trouble*, a double album comprising one studio and one live album, recorded mainly at the 1981 Reading rock festival, at which the band were appearing for the third consecutive year, a testimony to their popularity. Summer 1982 saw the release of *Magic*, another album of quality though sadly also the group's last. After many years of speculation and rumour, a Deep Purple reformation seemed imminent and Gillan wound up his band amid a certain amount of acrimony and uncertainty, early in 1983. Finding that he had ended Gillan somewhat prematurely, he joined Black Sabbath, a move he claims was motivated by financial necessity. Artistically, the time he spent with this band is deplored by both Gillan and Sabbath fans. After one album and a tour with Sabbath, the much talked about Deep Purple reunion took off and Gillan had his opportunity to escape. After eleven years apart, and all with successful, if turbulent careers during that time, the essential question remained whether or not the various members of the band would be able to get on with each other. A successful tour and a sell-out British concert at the 1985 Knebworth Festival seemed to suggest the reunion had worked, but by the time of the second album, *House Of The Blue Light*, it was clear that the latent tensions within the band were beginning to reappear. Between Deep Purple tours, and adding to the speculation about a break-up, Gillan and Glover recorded an album together; a curious but thoroughly enjoyable collection of material, it seemed to fulfil a need in both musicians to escape from the confines of the parent band. The 1988/1989 Deep Purple tour revealed the true extent of the rift between the members, and Gillan's departure was formally announced in May 1989. It was effectively over from January, when he was informed that he need not attend rehearsals for the next album. Gillan's response was to perform a short tour as his alter ego, Garth Rockett, in spring 1989, before recording vocals for the Rock Aid Armenia version of 'Smoke On The Water', in July. By the end of 1989 Gillan had assembled a band to record a solo album, which he would finance himself to escape record company pressures, and record under his own name to avoid the politics of group decisions. The line-up featrued Steve Morris (guitar), from the Garth Rockett tour; Chris Glen (bass) and Ted McKenna (drums), both formerly of the Michael Schenker Group; Tommy Eyre (keyboards); Mick O'Donoghue (rhythm guitar) and Dave Lloyd (backing vocals/percussion). The album, *Naked Thunder*, released in July 1990, was labelled middle-of-the-road by some critics, while Gillan himself described it as 'hard rock with a funky blues feel.' After touring in support of it, Gillan returned to the studio to prepare a second solo album. Now formulating a highly productive partnership with Steve Morris, he recruited Brett Bloomfield on bass and Leonard Haze on drums and produced an excellent album as a four-piece rock band, blending straightforward music with Gillan's often bizarre sense of humour and off-beat lyrics. *Toolbox* was released in October 1991 to critical acclaim. Gillan rejoined Deep Purple in 1992, undertook new recording sessions with the band and toured, before yet again quitting. However, the career decision taken in 1994 was indeed a strange one, seeing him reunited with his very first band, the Javelins, for a moribund collection of 60s covers. However, Gillan's durability alone makes him a central player in the British rock tradition, despite such occasional lapses.

Albums: With Episode Six: Compilation: *Put Yourself In My Place* (PRT 1987). With Deep Purple: *Concerto For Group And Orchestra* (Harvest 1970), *In Rock* (Harvest 1970), *Fireball* (Harvest 1971), *Machine Head* (Harvest 1972), *Made In Japan* (Purple 1972), *Who Do We Think We Are?* (Purple 1973), *Powerhouse* (Purple 1977), *In Concert 1970/72* (Harvest 1980), *Perfect Strangers* (Polydor 1984), *House Of The Blue Light* (Polydor 1987), *Nobody's Perfect* (Polydor 1988), *The Battle Rages On* (RCA 1993), *The Final Battle* (RCA 1994). With the Ian Gillan Band: *Child In Time* (Oyster 1976), *Clear Air Turbulence* (Island 1977), *Scarabus* (Scarabus 1977), *I.G.B. Live At The Budokan* (Island 1978). With Gillan: *Gillan* (Eastworld 1978), *Mr. Universe* (Acrobat 1979), *Glory Road* (Virgin 1980), *Future Shock* (Virgin 1981), *Double Trouble* (Virgin 1982, double album), *Magic* (Virgin 1982), *Live At The Budokan* (Virgin 1983, double album), *What I Did On My Vacation* (Virgin 1986), *Child In Time* (Virgin 1990), *Live At*

Reading 1980 (Raw Fruit 1990). Compilations: *Very Best Of* (Music Club 1991), *Trouble: The Best Of* (Virgin 1991). With Black Sabbath: *Born Again* (Vertigo 1983). With Gillan/Glover: *Accidentally On Purpose* (Virgin 1988). As Garth Rockett: *Story Of* (Rock Hard 1990). As Ian Gillan: *Naked Thunder* (East West 1990), *Toolbox* (East West 1991), *The Japanese Album* (East West 1993). With the Javelins: *Raving...With The Javelins* (RPM 1994).

Videos: *Gillan Live At The Rainbow 1978* (1988), *Ian Gillan Band* (1990), *Ian Gillan Live* (1992). Garth Rockett And The Moonshiners: *Live* (1990).

Further reading: *Child In Time: The Life Story Of The Singer From Deep Purple*, Ian Gillan.

Girl

A band very much ahead of their time, Girl's lipstick and glam image portrayed on the cover of their debut, *Sheer Greed*, was quite a shock to the traditional British metal community during the rise of the New Wave Of British Heavy Metal, despite the existence of more outrageous glam bands in the preceding decade. Recorded with a line-up of Philip Lewis (vocals), Phil Collen (guitar), brothers Gerry (guitar) and Simon Laffy (bass), and Dave Gaynor (drums), *Sheer Greed* was an impressive slice of sleazy hard rock, but was overshadowed by the band's image and by publicity surrounding Lewis' relationship with actress Britt Ekland. Although the band were a capable live act, and were given great exposure by support slots on major UK tours with the Pat Travers Band and UFO (twice), they failed to capture the public's imagination. *Wasted Youth*, with Pete Barnacle taking over the drum stool, paled beside the debut, and the band, dispirited, dissolved as Collen was invited to join Def Leppard. A third, currently unreleased album, exists on tape. Lewis later became frontman for L.A. Guns, with whom he re-recorded 'Hollywood Tease', the opening track on *Sheer Greed*, and the success of this band along with the likes of Poison and Guns N'Roses suggests that Girl may have met a better fate had they appeared only a few years later.

Albums: *Sheer Greed* (Jet 1980), *Wasted Youth* (Jet 1982).

Girlschool

The all-female heavy metal band had its origins in Painted Lady, founded by teenagers Enid Williams (bass/vocals) and Kim McAuliffe (guitar/vocals). The remaining members of Painted Lady would form Tour De Force. After Kelly Johnson (guitar/vocals), and Denise Dufort (drums) had joined in 1978 the name became Girlschool and the independently-produced single, 'Take It All Away', for City Records, led to a tour with Motörhead. As a direct result of

Girlschool

Lemmy's sponsorship of the band they signed to the Bronze label in 1980, for whom Vic Maile produced the first two albums. There was a minor hit with a revival of Adrian Gurvitz' 'Race With The Devil', a 1968 success for Gun, before the group combined with Motörhead to reach the UK Top 10 as Headgirl with an EP entitled *St Valentine's Day Massacre*. The lead track was a frenetic version of Johnny Kidd's 'Please Don't Touch'. Girlschool had smaller hits later in 1981 with 'Hit And Run' and 'C'mon Let's Go', but soon afterwards a bored Williams was replaced by former Killjoys bass player Gill Weston (introduced to the band by Lemmy). Williams would subsequently form melodic rockers Framed, record two singles with Sham 69's Dave Parsons, and work on sessions with disco producer Biddu, before joining Moho Pack. Later she would sing, variously, country and opera (appearing in Fay Weldon's *The Small Green Space* and her own opera, *The Waterfall*) and teach performance and vocal skills. Girlschool persevered meanwhile with Slade's Noddy Holder and Jim Lea producing the glam-influenced *Play Dirty*, which found the group opting for a more mainstream rock sound. In 1984 Johnson left the band for an unsuccessful solo career (later abandoning music and taking up sign language to work with the deaf) and Girlschool added guitarist Chris Bonacci and lead singer Jacqui Bodimead from Canis Major. The group also switched visual style towards a more glam rock look as they recorded 'I'm The Leader Of The Gang' with Gary Glitter in 1986. After the departure of Weston in 1987 ex-Rock Goddess bass player Tracey Lamb was brought in, while McAuliffe left to work with punk singer Beki Bondage and present the cable show *Raw Power*. She also wrote an unpublished script for a rock show with Philthy Taylor of Motörhead. Later she formed Strange Girls with Toyah, Dufort and Williams. Girlschool persevered until splitting following a Russian tour supporting Black Sabbath. In the 90s McAuliffe brought the group back together with the addition of ex-Flatmates bass player Jackie Carrera.
Albums: *Demolition* (Bronze 1980), *Hit 'N' Run* (Bronze 1981), *Screaming Blue Murder* (Bronze 1982), *Play Dirty* (Bronze 1983), *Running Wild* (Mercury 1985), *Nightmare At Maple Cross* (GWR 1986), *Take A Bite* (GWR 1988). Compilations: *Race With The Devil* (Raw Power 1986), *Cheers You Lot* (Razor 1989), *Collection* (Castle 1991).
Videos: *Play Dirty Live* (1984), *Bronze Rocks* (1985).

Giuffria

This US band was formed in 1981 by Greg Giuffria (keyboards) when his previous band, Angel, split up.

His first step was to secure a good rhythm section; Chuck Wright (bass) and Alan Krigger (drums). Rough Cutt guitarist Craig Goldy joined after his former group fell apart. In 1984 Giuffria's self-titled debut album, released on MCA, demonstrated a melodic rock band which sounded symphonic in places and could have been mistaken for Angel on some tracks. Greg Giuffria referred to their music as 'cinema rock'. After the promotional tour for the album, Goldy left to join Driver and subsequently Ronnie James Dio, while Wright returned to session work. They were replaced by Lanny Cordola (guitar) and David Sikes (bass). Because of these personnel changes, the follow-up album, *Silk And Steel*, was not released until August 1986. This was very much a continuation of their first album - it did not sell in anything like sufficient quantities and in 1987 MCA dropped the group. Giuffria, Cordola, Wright, Ken Mary (drums) and David Glen Eisley (vocals) attempted to start again. They gained some support from Gene Simmons of Kiss, who had just set up his own record label. However, Simmons insisted that the name be changed to House Of Lords, and that James Christian replace Eisley on vocals.
Albums: *Giuffria* (MCA 1984), *Silk And Steel* (MCA 1986).

Glover, Roger

b. 30 November 1945, Brecon, Powys, Wales. Bassist Glover's professional musical career began when his group, the Madisons, amalgamated with fellow aspirants the Lightnings to form Episode Six. This popular act released nine singles between 1966 and 1969, but eclectic interests - including harmony pop, MOR and progressive rock-styled instrumentals - engendered a commercial impasse. Frustrated, both Glover and vocalist Ian Gillan then accepted an offer to join Deep Purple, where they enjoyed considerable international acclaim. However, clashes with guitarist Ritchie Blackmore led to Glover's sacking in 1973, although he remained nominal head of A&R at Purple Records, the group's custom-created label. Roger later embarked on a successful career in production with Nazareth, Status Quo, Judas Priest and Rory Gallagher. In 1974 Glover was commissioned to write the music to *The Butterfly Ball*, which in turn inspired a book, illustrated by Alan Aldridge, and film. The album included the services of David Coverdale, Glenn Hughes and Ronnie James Dio. He recorded a solo album, *Elements*, which again boasted the assistance of vocalist Dio, but Glover surprised several commentators in 1979 by rejoining Blackmore in Rainbow. Any lingering animosity was further

Godflesh

undermined in 1984 when both musicians were active in a rekindled Deep Purple which, although unable to recreate the halcyon days of the early 70s, remains a much in-demand live attraction.

Albums: *The Butterfly Ball* (Purple 1974), *Elements* (Polydor 1978), *Mask* (Polydor 1984). With Ian Gillan: *Accidentally On Purpose* (Virgin 1988).

Godflesh

The Godflesh partnership was inaugurated by Justin Broadrick (guitar, vocals) and G. Christian Green (bass) in 1988, when the former left the venerated (by John Peel at least) hardcore industrial trio, Head Of David. Green had formerly served time in industrialists Fall Of Because, and Godflesh were completed by the addition of a drum machine. An eponymous EP was released on the Swordfish label before moving to the more permanent home of Earache Records. By the advent of their debut album, the group had expanded to temporarily include guitarist Paul Neville (also ex-Fall Of Because). With strong critical reaction, they toured with Loop, and as part of the Earache Grindcrusher USA package, alongside Napalm Death. Broadrick had actually appeared with the latter as guitarist on side one of the legendary *Scum* album. 1991 produced three limited edition 12-inches (including one for the Sub Pop empire), which were eventually collected together as the *Slavestate* mini-album. With Neville opting to concentrate on his own project, Cabel Regime, Robert Hampson of Loop stepped in for additional guitar duties on the group's excellently-reviewed *Pure*. He would choose to stay at home, however, as the duo embarked on a promotional European tour. 1993 would see Broadrick branching out by providing guitar tracks for label mates Scorn (on their *Vae Solis* debut), and he also produced a 'biomechanical' remix of Pantera's 'Walk'. This 'biomechanical' method is described by Green as involving: 'stripping them (the tracks) down and reconstructing them from scratch with different drum patterns, different vocal lines etc.'. Meanwhile Godflesh's first own-name project in nearly two years, the *Merciless* EP, resurrected an eight-year old Fall Of Because song. October 1994 saw the introduction of a major new work, *Selfless*, a stunningly direct and brutal album from a band whose quality threshold has hardly wavered since their inception.

Albums: *Streetcleaner* (Earache 1989), *Slavestate* (Earache 1990; mini-album), *Pure* (Earache 1992), *Selfless* (Earache 1994).

Godz

Originating from Cleveland, Ohio, USA, the Godz

were a heavy metal band with a strong 'biker' image. Formed in 1977, they featured vocalist/bassist Eric Moore, guitarist Mark Chatfield, drummer Glen Cataline and guitarist/keyboard player Bob Hill. Their first album, produced by Grand Funk's Don Brewer, was an intensely powerful barrage with raw, gutsy vocals filtered through its core, which remains something of a metal minor-classic. *Nothing Is Sacred* was self-produced and featured Cataline on vocals, the most obvious contributory factor to the disappointment it brought on almost every level. The band split up soon after its release. In 1985 Moore and Chatfield resurrected the name and a new partnership was forged with former Outlaws guitarist Freddy Salem and drummer Keith Valentine. *I'll Get You Rockin'* materialized, but met a lacklustre reception. In 1987 most of the album was re-mixed and re-recorded, with three new tracks added and re-released as *Mongolians*. However hard they have tried, the Godz have never recaptured the energy and excitement generated by their debut release.

Albums: *The Godz* (Millenium 1978), *Nothing Is Sacred* (Millenium 1979), *I'll Get You Rockin'* (Heavy Metal 1985), *Mongolians* (Grudge 1987).

Gogmagog

This group was formed in 1985 in London, England, by Jonathan King, who wanted to create some sort of heavy metal theatre. At first he had Cozy Powell and John Entwhistle interested, but they had other projects taking off. So the line-up was finalized as Paul Dianno (vocals), Clive Burr (drums), Pete Willis (guitar), Janick Gers (guitar) and Neil Murray (bass): a line-up which saw Gogmagog being christened a New Wave Of British Heavy Metal 'supergroup'. To test the water to see if anybody was interested in the project, King put Gogmagog into a studio to record three songs that he had written with Russ Ballard. With these tracks in hand King went round to various major record companies to see if there was any support. All showed a genuine interest in the project. The only stumbling block was King's insistence on a substantial advance, which saw him universally turned away. The project subsequently fell apart, and the members of Gogmagog went their own way. After the group's demise a three-track single appeared on Music For Nations' subsidiary Food For Thought, entitled 'I Will Be There'. The group's music was nowhere near the heavy metal tag it was given, being closer to pop with a slight nod towards the musicians' rock roots.

Goodwin, Myles

When Canadian hard rockers April Wine

disintegrated in 1985, lead vocalist Goodwin embarked on a solo career. He immediately divorced himself from the style to which he was accustomed. Forsaking his blues-rock roots, he concentrated on MOR pop/rock with understated guitar and lightweight harmonies. Utilizing the services of session musicians, he recorded a self-titled debut on the Atlantic label in 1988. This failed to win a new audience, and at the same time alienated his former fan base. The album sank without trace and little has been heard of him since.

Album: *Myles Goodwin* (Atlantic 1988).

Gorefest

Formed in 1989, Dutch band Gorefest have managed to carve a niche for themselves in an increasingly overcrowded death metal genre, making their debut on the underground demo scene with two tapes, *Tangled In Gore* and *Horrors In A Retarded Mind*. After a sound if unspectacular 1991 debut, *Mindloss*, they sealed a deal with European extreme metal label Nuclear Blast and released the more self-assured *False*. Gorefest's material is morbidly metaphysical, and at their best they manage to combine melodic and inventive riffs with a decidedly abrasive edge. A popular live band, they released a recording of their performance at 1993's Dynamo Open Air Festival as *The Eindhoven Insanity*, which some argue is the first ever live death metal album. *Erase* represents their most confident outing to date, featuring the line up of Jan Chris De Koeijer (vocals/bass guitar), Frank Harthoorn (rhythm guitar), Boudewijn Bonebakker (lead/rhythm guitars), and Ed Warby (drums).

Albums: *Mindloss* (F2000 1991), *False* (Nuclear Blast/Relapse 1992), *The Eindhoven Insanity* (Nuclear Blast/Relapse 1993), *Erase* (Nuclear Blast/Relapse 1994).

Gramm, Lou

Vocalist Lou Gramm (b. Lou Grammatico, 2 May 1950, Rochester, New York, USA) possesses one of the great hard rock voices, and rose from small beginnings with Poor Heart and Black Sheep to fame and fortune with Foreigner. After the enormous success of *Agent Provocateur*, however, Gramm's desire for more upbeat guitar-based songs led him to write solo material with bassist friend Bruce Turgon. *Ready Or Not* was a satisfying solo debut, proving that Gramm could produce classy AOR material without Foreigner cohort Mick Jones, and produced a surprise hit in 'Midnight Blue'. Gramm returned to the Foreigner fold for *Inside Information*, but solo success had only increased the tension between Jones and the vocalist, and a split was inevitable. Gramm and

Turgon worked together again on *Long Hard Look*, producing another US hit in 'Just Between You And Me', and Gramm's departure from Foreigner was confirmed as he embarked on a solo US tour, with Jones drafting in former Wild Horses (USA) vocalist Johnny Edwards for *Unusual Heat*, which ironically returned to the harder style which Gramm had been missing. Gramm subsequently put together the ill-fated Shadow King with Turgon, drummer Kevin Valentine and ex-Dio/Whitesnake guitarist Vivian Campbell, which barely lasted beyond their first album and live show before Campbell left to replace the late Steve Clark in Def Leppard and Valentine joined Cinderella. However, Gramm and Jones eventually put their differences behind them, and the vocalist rejoined Foreigner, taking Turgon along with him.

Albums: *Ready Or Not* (Atlantic 1987), *Long Hard Look* (Atlantic 1989).

Grand Funk Railroad

Formed in 1968, Grand Funk Railroad were the first American heavy rock 'power trio' to reach massive fame, while alienating another large segment of the rock audience and critics at the same time. The group consisted of guitarist Mark Farner (b. 28 September 1948, Flint, Michigan, USA), bassist Mel Schacher (b. 3 April 1951, Owosso, Michigan, USA) and drummer Don Brewer (3 September 1948, Flint, Michigan, USA). The group was a spin-off of Terry Knight And The Pack, a popular soul-rock group in the Michigan area in the mid-60s. Farner and Brewer had both been members of that band (Brewer had also belonged to the Jazz Masters prior to the Pack). Following a single release on the small Lucky Eleven label, 'I (Who Have Nothin)', which reached number 46 in the US, the Pack were joined by Schacher, formerly of ? And The Mysterians. At this point Knight stopped performing to become the band's manager, renaming it Grand Funk Railroad (the name was taken from the Michigan landmark the Grand Trunk Railroad). The new trio signed with Capitol Records in 1969 and immediately began making its name by performing at several large pop festivals. Their first singles made the charts but Grand Funk soon proved its real strength in the album market. Their first, *On Time*, reached number 27 in 1969, followed by the number 11 *Grand Funk* in 1970. By the summer of that year they had become a major concert attraction, and their albums routinely reached the Top 10 for the next four years. Of those, 1973's *We're An American Band* was the biggest seller, reaching number 2. The group's huge success is often attributed to the public relations expertise of manager

Knight. In 1970, for example, Knight reportedly paid $100,000 for a huge billboard in New York City's Times Square to promote the group's *Closer To Home*, which subsequently became their first Top 10 album, reaching number 6 and spawning the FM radio staple title-track. That promotional campaign backfired with the press, however, which dismissed the band's efforts despite spiralling success with the public. In June 1971, for example, Grand Funk became only the second group (after the Beatles) to sell out New York's Shea Stadium. Their recordings sold in greater quantity even as many radio stations ignored their releases. 1970's *Live Album* reached number 5 and included another concert and radio favourite in Farner's 'Mean Mistreater'. The next year saw the release of *Survival* and *E Pluribus Funk*, the latter most notable for its round album cover. In 1972 the group fired Knight, resulting in a series of lawsuits involving millions of dollars. (they hired John Eastman, father of Linda McCartney, as their new manager). In 1973 the group shortened its name officially to Grand Funk, and added a fourth member, keyboardist Craig Frost (b. 20 April 1948, Flint, Michigan, USA). Now produced by Todd Rundgren, they finally cracked the singles market, reaching number 1 with album title-track 'We're An American Band', a celebration of its times on the road. In 1974 a major revision of Little Eva's 'Loco-motion' also reached the top (the first time in US chart history that a cover of a song that had previously reached number 1 also ascended to that position). In 1975, with their popularity considerably diminished, the group reverted to its original name of Grand Funk Railroad. The following year they signed with MCA Records and recorded *Good Singin', Good Playin'*, produced by Frank Zappa. When it failed to reach the Top 50, Farner left for a solo career. The others stayed together, adding guitarist Billy Elworthy and changing their name to Flint, a group who failed to derive commercial success with their solitary album. Grand Funk, this time consisting of Farner, Brewer and bassist Dennis Bellinger, reformed for two years in 1981-83 and recorded *Grand Funk Lives* and *What's Funk?* for the Full Moon label. Failing to recapture former glories, they split again. Farner returned to his solo career and Brewer and Frost joining Bob Seger's Silver Bullet Band.
Albums: *On Time* (Capitol 1969), *Grand Funk* (Capitol 1970), *Closer To Home* (Capitol 1970), *Live* (Capitol 1971), *Survival* (Capitol 1971), *E Pluribus Funk* (Capitol 1972), *Phoenix* (Capitol 1973), *We're An American Band* (Capitol 1973), *Shinin' On* (Capitol 1974), *All The Girls In The World Beware!!!* (Capitol 1975), *Caught In The Act* (Capitol 1975),

Born To Die (Capitol 1976), *Good Singin' Good Playin'* (Capitol 1976), *Grand Funk Lives* (Full Moon 1981), *What's Funk?* (Full Moon 1983). Selected Compilations: *Mark, Don & Mel 1969-71* (Capitol 1972), *Grand Funk Hits* (Capitol 1976), *The Best Of Grand Funk Railroad* (Capitol 1990), *More Of The Best Of Grand Funk Railroad* (Capitol 1991), *The Collection* (Castle 1992).

Great White

This Los Angeles-based outfit was formed in 1981 and comprised Jack Russell (vocals), Mark Kendall (guitar), Lorne Black (bass) and Gary Holland (drums). They adopted a no-frills approach from the start, relying on the music - earthy, honest blues-rock delivered with stunning precision - rather than gimmicks. The band attracted the attention of EMI Records with their self-financed mini-album, *Out Of The Night*, produced by their good friend Don Dokken. Unfortunately, the momentum was not maintained and *Stick It*, their EMI debut, was erratic and sold poorly, and the band was subsequently dropped. Far from disillusioned, they funded the recording of *Shot In The Dark* out of their own pockets, which eventually opened the door to a new deal with Capitol Records. Lorne Black and Gary Holland broke ranks at this stage and were replaced by Tony Montana and Audie Desbrow respectively. Michael Lardie was also added on keyboards to expand the group to a five-piece and add an extra dimension to their sound. Enjoying the benefits of a larger budget, *Once Bitten* received considerable critical acclaim with its more melodic, accessible sound. Sales of the album would surpass the million mark. *Recovery...Live* payed homage to their roots, being an inspired selection of blues-styled cover versions from the Who, Led Zeppelin, Humble Pie and Jimi Hendrix. *Twice Shy* and *Hooked* have consolidated their success with further platinum awards. *Sail Away* saw the introduction of new bass player, Teddy Cook, on an album influenced by Julian Barnes' novel, *The History Of The World In Ten And A Half Chapters*.
Albums: *Out Of The Night* (Aegan 1982, mini-album), *Stick It* (EMI 1984), *Shot In The Dark* (Telegraph 1986), *Once Bitten* (Capitol 1987), *Recovery...Live* (Enigma 1988), *Twice Shy* (Capitol 1989), *Live In London* (Capitol 1990), *Hooked* (Capitol 1991), *Psycho City* (Capitol 1992), *Sail Away* (RCA 1994).

Green Day

With alternative rock music going overground in the early 90s, few acts were better positioned to exploit

the commercial possibilities than Green Day - Billy Joe Armstrong (vocals/guitar), Mike Dirnt (bass/vocals) and Tre Cool (drums). Armstrong and Dirnt had been playing together since the age of 11 in the refinery town of Rodeo, California, originally titled Sweet Children. Two indie albums followed for Lookout, the first of which, *39/Smooth*, was recorded in a single day. Like the subsequent *Kerplunk*, however, it would sell 30,000 copies. That figure was dwarfed following their decision to move to Warner Brothers. Their major label debut, *Dookie*, gradually stalked the charts, going on to double platinum status in the band's native territory. Their arduous touring schedule was paramount in this rise, and was topped off by appearances on the 1994 Lollapalooza package and the revived Woodstock event. The other factor was the estimable quality of their songwriting, and a terrific simplicity of execution on numbers like 'Basket Case'. As Dirnt would concede: 'We just figured out a formula and Billie Joe writes real good songs, that's all'.
Albums: *39/Smooth* (Lookout 1990), *Kerplunk* (Lookout 1992), *Dookie* (Warners 1994).

Green Jelly

Pinpointed as 'this year's musical lowpoint' by *Rolling Stone* magazine in 1993, Green Jello ended that same year being forced to change their name to Green Jelly, in order to avoid a lawsuit from General Foods. Initially conceived as a 'video' band, they rose to fame largely through this medium. Their breakthrough hit certainly boasted excellent animation, but little musical substance, allied as it was to a sort of psychedelic heavy metal version of popular nursery rhyme, 'Three Little Pigs'. Like their follow-up, a cover version of the Sex Pistols' 'Anarchy In The UK', it was an exercise of limited merit.
Albums: *Cereal Killer* (Zoo/BMG 1993), *333* (Zoo/BMG 1994).

Green River

Seattle band Green River may go down in history as the first 'grunge' band, and were certainly the first to release a record on the Sub Pop label. They first came together in 1984 with Jeff Ament (ex-Deranged Diction) on bass, drummer Alex Shumway, guitarist/vocalist Mark Arm and former Mr Epp guitarist Steve Turner. Soon the line-up was expanded with the addition of ex-Ducky Boys/March Of Crimes guitarist Stone Gossard and they began to air their wares on the local north west scene. By 1985 they had appeared alongside the Melvins on the *Deep Six* compilation album on the C/Z label, released a six song EP, *Come On Down*, for Homestead, and were

playing the same clubs as another local band, Soundgarden. Both bands came to the attention of Sub Pop owner Bruce Pavitt, who decided to expand his cassette-based fanzine into a full record label and worked with them in producing the 12-inch EP, *Dry As A Bone*, which was released in June 1987. Turner left soon after and was replaced by another Deranged Diction member, Bruce Fairweather. In May 1988 they released the mini-album, *Rehab Doll* (cassette and CD vesions adended *Dry As A Bone*) but the band were already falling apart with musical differences between Arm and Ament which led to them splitting in June. Arm joined Turner with ex-Melvins' bassist Matt Lukin and drummer Dan Peters to form Mudhoney. Ament, Gossard and Fairweather regrouped with ex-Malfunkshun vocalist Andrew Wood and drummer Regan Hagar and formed Lords Of The Wasteland, who quickly evolved into Mother Love Bone. After the death of Wood in March 1990 that band fractured with Gossard and Ament forming the hugely successful Pearl Jam. Green River thus became an important footnote in the development of the 90s strongest rock movement, though their light was re-ignited temporarily on 30 November 1993 at the Aladdin Hotel in Las Vegas when Pearl Jam ended their live set early to make way for a one-off reformation of Green River with Gossard, Arm, Turner and Ament joined by Chuck Treece (bassist from Urge Overkill) playing drums.
Album: *Rehab Doll* (Sub Pop 1988, mini-album).

Grim Reaper

Formed in 1979, and featuring Steve Grimmet (vocals), Nick Bowcroft (guitars), Dave Wanklin (bass), and Lee Hams (drums), Grim Reaper are a typical example of the bands that formed the metal revival of the early 80s known as the New Wave Of British Heavy Metal. They characterised most of the movement's strengths (a fresh, down-to-earth approach, enthusiasm, and powerful but melodic guitar riffs) with the weaknesses that plagued it (bargain basement production values and daftly melodramatic lyrics delivered in an inappropriate falsetto). In 1994 one of their videos was dragged out of the crates by MTV cartoon characters *Beavis And Butthead* and introduced with an incredulous, 'Is this Spinal Tap?'. While they flirted with infernal imagery, Grim Reaper were never a Satanic band as has been claimed by some (including fundamentalist Christian preachers), and actually suffered from being a little bland. Their debut, *See You In Hell*, was probably Grim Reaper's finest moment, particularly the catchily anthemic title-track, and the band enjoyed some success on both sides of the Atlantic during the

Groundhogs

mid-80s. Ultimately they could neither replicate nor build on this, and in 1988 they broke up. Grimmet would join Onslaught then Lionsheart.

Albums: *See You In Hell* (Ebony 1983), *Fear No Evil* (Ebony 1985), *Rock You In Hell* (MCA 1987).

Groundhogs

The original Groundhogs emerged in 1963 when struggling UK beat group the Dollarbills opted for a more stylish name; Tony 'T.S.' McPhee (b. 22 March 1944, Humberstone, Lincolnshire, England; guitar), John Cruickshank (vocals/harp), Bob Hall (piano), Pete Cruickshank (b. 2 July 1945, Calcutta, India; bass) and Dave Boorman (drums) also adopted a 'John Lee' prefix in honour of mentor John Lee Hooker, whom the quintet subsequently backed in concert and on record. John Lee's Groundhogs recorded two singles before breaking up in 1966. McPhee completed several solo tracks with producer Mike Vernon before rejoining Pete Cruickshank in Herbal Mixture, a short-lived, pseudo-psychedelic group. In 1968 the two musicians formed the core of a reformed Groundhogs alongside Steve Rye (vocals/harmonica) and Ken Pustelnik (drums). The new unit made its debut with the rudimentary *Scratching The Surface*, but were then cut to a trio by Rye's departure. A second set, *Blues Obituary*, contained two tracks, 'Mistreated' and 'Express Man', which became in-concert favourites as the group embarked on a more progressive direction. This was confirmed with *Thank Christ For The Bomb*, the Groundhogs' powerful 1970 release which cemented a growing popularity. McPhee composed the entire set and his enthusiasm for concept albums was maintained with its successor, *Split*, which examined schizophrenia. Arguably the group's definitive work, this uncompromising selection included the stage classic, 'Cherry Red'. Pustelnik left the group following the release of *Who Will Save The World?* in 1972. Former Egg drummer Clive Brooks (b. 28 December 1949, London, England) was an able replacement, but although the Groundhogs continued to enjoy fervent popularity, their subsequent recordings lacked the fire of those early releases. The trio was also beset by managerial problems and broke up in 1975, although McPhee maintained the name for two disappointing releases, *Crosscut Saw* and *Black Diamond*. The guitarist resurrected the Groundhogs' sobriquet in 1984 in the wake of interest in an archive release, *Hoggin' The Stage*. Although Pustelnik was one of several musicians McPhee used for touring purposes, the most effective line-up was completed by Dave Anderson on bass, formerly of Hawkwind, and

drummer Mike Jones. McPhee has in recent years appeared as a solo performer as part of a 70s nostalgia tour together with various incarnations of his respected band. A fitting testament as the Groundhogs' story endures mainly through a live reputation second to none.

Albums: *Scratching The Surface* (Liberty 1968), *Blues Obituary* (Liberty 1969), *Thank Christ For The Bomb* (Liberty 1970), *Split* (Liberty 1971), *Who Will Save The World?* (United Artists 1972), *Hogwash* (United Artists 1972), *Solid* (WWA 1974), *Crosscut Saw* (United Artists 1976), *Black Diamond* (United Artists 1976), *Razor's Edge* (Conquest 1985), *Back Against The Wall* (Demi-Monde 1987), *Hogs On The Road* (Demi-Monde 1988). Compilations: *Groundhogs Best 1969-1972* (United Artists 1974), *Hoggin' The Stage* (Psycho 1984, double album), *Moving Fast, Standing Still* (Raw Power 1986, comprises McPhee solo album *2 Sides Of* plus *Razor's Edge*), *No Surrender* (Total 1990), *Classic Album Cuts 1968 - 1976* (1992). Tony McPhee solo: *2 Sides Of*.

GTR

This short-lived mid-80s UK supergroup was assembled from ex-members of Yes, Genesis, Bronz and Marillion. Featuring guitarists Steve Hackett and Steve Howe, alongside vocalist Max Bacon, bassist Phil Spalding and drummer Jonathon Mover, the line-up on paper was impressive. Considering the band's pedigree, it was no surprise to find them purveying sophisticated pomp-rock, with their roots firmly embedded in the early 70s progressive scene. 'When The Heart Rules The Mind' was a minor US hit, but the band split up soon after, following Steve Hackett's desire to re-vamp his solo career.

Album: *GTR* (Arista 1986).

Gun

A group who emerged in the summer of 1989 with a debut album, *Taking On The World*, which saw them acclaimed as one of Scotland's most invigorating modern rock bands. Gun comprised Mark Rankin (vocals), Scott Shields (drums) 'Baby' Stafford (guitar) and the Gizzi brothers, Giuliano 'Joolz' (guitar) and Dante (bass). Backed up by a spectacular live show, singles like 'Better Days', 'Money (Everybody Loves Her)' and 'Inside Out' all reached the UK charts when the *zeitgeist* was more geared to dance music than unrepentant rockers. Following their support to Simple Minds at Wembley Stadium, the group were also the personal choice of Mick Jagger and Keith Richards to support the Rolling Stones on their 1990 *Urban Jungle* UK tour. However, the sight of the Stones' intimidating

audience saw Stafford depart to go solo, believing he could never surpass his heroes. Gun recruited Alex Dixon (ex-Midnight Blue) in his stead and pressed on with a second album, *Gallus*, which arrived in 1992 (its title a Glaswegian term which loosely translates as 'dead cool'). Proffering three further hits in 'Steal Your Fire', 'Higher Ground' and 'Welcome To The Real World', it also boasted a tougher, more muscular songwriting approach. However, when *Swagger* was unveiled in 1994 the group had slimmed down to a four piece, replacing Shields on the drumstool with Mark Kerr. Recorded in the more rural setting of Wales over a two week period, it continued its predecessor's back to basics approach with its rock foundation shot through with the vigour and excitement of punk. Arguably the worst item contained on it, a rock version of Cameo's funk classic 'Word Up', was the first single to be lifted from *Swagger*. It rewarded the group with its biggest single success (Top 10), and at least opened up the group's more wholesome material for discovery by a new legion of fans. The best of which included 'Don't Say It's Over', co-written with Jim Vallance, and even a rap track, 'Something Worthwhile'.
Albums: *Taking On The World* (A&M 1989), *Gallus* (A&M 1992), *Swagger* (A&M 1994).

Guns N'Roses

The founder members of the most controversial heavy rock band of the late 80s included W. Axl Rose (an anagram of Oral Sex) (b. William Bailey, 6 February 1962, Lafayette, Indiana, USA) and Izzy Stradlin (b. Jeffrey Isbell, 8 April 1962, Lafayette, Indiana, USA). Vocalist Rose, who had first sung at the age of five in a church choir, met guitarist Stradlin in Los Angeles in 1984. He would change his name to Rose at age 17 when he discovered who his real father was, the Axl prefix coming from a band he had rehearsed with in Indiana. With Tracii Guns (guitar) and Rob Gardner (drums), they formed a rock band called in turn Rose, Hollywood Rose and L.A. Guns. Soon afterwards, Guns and Gardner left, to be replaced by two members of local band Road Crew, drummer Steven Adler (b. 22 January 1965, Cleveland, Ohio, USA) and guitarist Slash (b. Saul Hudson, 23 July 1965, Stoke-on-Trent, Staffordshire, England), the son of a clothes designer and an album cover artist. With bass player Duff Rose McKagan (b. Michael McKagan, 5 February 1964, Seattle, Washington, USA, ex-Fartz, Fastbacks, Ten Minute

Gun

Warning and approximately 30 other North-West outfits), the band was renamed Guns N'Roses. Following a disastrous US 'Hell Tour '85', Guns N'Roses released an EP, *Live?!*@ Like A Suicide* on the independent Uzi/Suicide label. This brought intense interest from critics and record companies and in 1986 the group signed to Geffen who reissued the EP the following year. During 1987 they toured extensively, though the group's appetite for self-destruction became readily apparent when Fred Coury of Cinderella was recruited to temporarily replace Adler after the latter had broken his hand in a brawl. February 1988 also saw the first internal rift when Rose was kicked out, then reinstated, within three days. Their debut album, *Appetite For Destruction*, produced by Mike Clink, would go on to sell 20 million copies worldwide and reach number 1 in America a year after its release date. 'Welcome To The Jungle' was used on the soundtrack of the Clint Eastwood film, *Dead Pool*, and reached the Top 30 in the UK. The group's regular live shows in the US and Europe brought frequent controversy, notably when two fans died during crowd disturbances at the Monsters Of Rock show in England in 1988. In 1989 the eight-song album *G N' R Lies* was issued, becoming a big hit on both sides of the Atlantic, as were the singles 'Sweet Child O' Mine' (written about Axl's girlfriend and later wife Erin Everly, daughter of Don Everly), 'Paradise City' and 'Patience'. However, Rose's lyrics for 'One In A Million' were widely criticised for their homophobic sentiments. Although Guns N'Roses appeared at the *Farm Aid IV* charity concert, their career was littered with incidents involving drugs, drunkenness and public disturbance offences in 1989/90. At times their excesses made the band seem like a caricature of a 60s supergroup, with headlines screaming of Stradlin urinating in public on an aeroplane, Slash and McKagan swearing live on television while collecting trophies for Favorite Heavy Metal/Hard Rock Artists and Album at the American Music Awards, and Rose's on-off relationship with Everly. In September 1990 Adler was replaced by Matt Sorum (b. 19 November 1960, Mission Viejo, California, USA) from the Cult. Apparently more restrained in their private life, Guns N'Roses added Dizzy Reed (b. Darren Reed; keyboards) for a 1991 world tour where their exciting and unpredictable performances brought favourable comparisons with the heyday of the Rolling Stones. In September the group released the highly-publicised pair of albums, *Use Your Illusion I* and *II*, preceded by a version of Bob Dylan's 'Knockin' On Heaven's Door' from the soundtrack of *Days Of Thunder*. Further hit singles, 'You Could Be Mine' (featured in the film *Terminator II*) and 'Don't Cry', followed. The *Illusion* brace immediately sat astride the top two album positions in the *Billboard* chart, the first occasion on which they had been thus dominated since Jim Groce enjoyed both number 1 sand 2 spots in 1974. Izzy Stradlin found the pressure too much and left late in 1991, going on to form the Ju Ju Hounds. He would be replaced by Gilby Clarke (ex-Kill For Thrills). Meanwhile Slash's growing reputation brought guest appearances on recordings by Dylan and Michael Jackson. He also contributed to tribute albums to Muddy Waters and Les Paul. Guns N'Roses' appearance at the 1992 Freddie Mercury AIDS Benefit concert prompted the reissue of 'Knockin' On Heaven's Door', and while Dylan fans groaned with disbelief the band's vast following were happy to see their heroes scale the charts shortly after its release. While both of their previous albums remained on the US chart, having sold more than 4 million copies each, it was not until the end of 1993 that any new material emerged. When it arrived it came in the form of *The Spaghetti Incident*, a much vaunted collection of covers with a punk foundation. A perfunctory affair, it was mainly notable for lining the pockets of several long-forgotten musicians (UK Subs, Nazareth, Misfits, Fear etc), and including a song written by mass murderer Charles Manson. The main inspiration behind the project, Duff McKagan, would see his debut solo album released at the same time. However, reports of an unhappy camp continued to filter through in 1994, leading to the dismissal of Gilby Clarke towards the end of the year, following his own, highly-public, outbursts about Rose. His replacement was Paul Huge, a former flatmate of Axl from his Indiana days. Huge's first recording with the band was a cover of the Rolling Stones' 'Sympathy For The Devil' for the soundtrack to Anne Rice's *Interview With A Vampire*.

Albums: *Appetite For Destruction* (Geffen 1987), *G N' R Lies* (Geffen 1989), *Use Your Illusion I* (Geffen 1991), *Use Your Illusion II* (Geffen 1991), *The Spaghetti Incident* (Geffen 1993).

Videos: *Use Your Illusion I* (1992), *Making Fuckin' Videos Vol 1* (1993), *Making Fuckin' Videos Vol 2* (1993).

Further reading: *In Their Own Words*, Mark Putterford, *Appetite For Destruction: The Days Of Guns N'Roses*, Danny Sugerman, *Guns N'Roses: The World's Most Outrageous Hard Rock Band*, Paul Elliot, *The Most Dangerous Band In The World*, Mick Wall, *The Pictures*, George Chin.

GWAR

This theatrical shock-rock quintet emerged from

Richmond, Virginia, USA. Assuming bizarre pseudonyms, they comprised Oderus Urungus (vocals), Balsac, The Jaws Of Death (guitar), Flattus Maximus (guitar), Beefcake The Mighty (bass) and Nippleus Erectus (drums). They are primarily renowned for an outrageous live show which involves the band adorning themselves in hideous papier mâché masks and blood- splattered torture implements, with set-pieces including the feigned buggery of a priest with a crucifix. Consequently their UK tour ground to a halt after just three dates due to the resulting moral panic. Taken to court in the US over allegedly displaying a penis as a stage-prop (the band suggested, bizarrely, that it was some form of fish), it would come as little surprise to learn that the origins of GWAR (apparently God What A Racket) lie in an art school collective. The music, which is no more than rudimentary thrash, complete with unintelligible vocals, takes second place to the visuals. Without the visual back-up, their albums are anti-climactic.

Albums: *Hell-O* (Shimmy Disc 1988), *Scumdogs Of The Universe* (Master 1990), *America Must Be Destroyed* (Zorro 1992), *This Toilet Earth* (Metal Blade 1994).

Videos: *The Movie* (1990), *Phallus In Wonderland* (1992), *Tour De Scum* (1994).

Gypsy Queen

This US heavy metal group hailing from Florida was fronted by twin sisters Pam and Paula Mattiola (formerly topless stars of *Playboy* magazine). Their debut album featured guitarists Pedro Riera and Bryan Le Mar, bassist Mars Cowling (ex-Pat Travers) and drummer Keith Daniel Cronin and was produced by Aerosmith supremo, Jack Douglas. Mid-paced pop-metal anthems and the occasional power-ballad were the order of the day, penned within a very limited musical framework. The album sold poorly and the Mattiola twins fired the entire band, recruiting Scott Migone (guitar), Joey O'Jeda (bass/keyboards) and Kenny Wendland (drums) in their place. A second album recorded in 1989 remains unreleased, delayed by legal complications which eventually saw the twins move to new home Scotti Bros (as Cell Mates).

Album: *Gypsy Queen* (Loop 1987).

GWAR

H

Hagar, Sammy

b. 13 October 1947, Monterey, California, USA.
Hagar is a singer, guitarist and songwriter whose
father was a professional boxer. Legend has it that
Elvis Presley persuaded him not to follow in his
father's footsteps, and instead he started out in 60s
San Bernardino bands the Fabulous Castillas, Skinny,
Justice Brothers and rock band, Dust Cloud. He
joined Montrose in 1973 (formed by ex-Edgar
Winter guitarist Ronnie Montrose) and became a
minor rock hero in the Bay Area of San Francisco, in
particular acquiring a reputation as a potent live
performer. After two albums with Montrose he left to
go solo, providing a string of semi-successful albums
and singles. He took with him Bill Church (bass), and
added Alan Fitzgerald (keyboards), and later Denny
Carmassi (also ex-Montrose; drums). The band
picked up good press on support tours with Kiss,
Boston and Kansas, but by 1979 Hagar had fashioned
a radically altered line-up with Gary Pihl (guitar),
Chuck Ruff (drums) and Geoff Workman
(keyboards) joining Hagar and Church. 1983's *Three
Lock Box* became their first Top 20 entry, including
'Your Love Is Driving Me Crazy', which made
number 13 in the singles chart. Hagar then took time
out to tour with Journey guitarist Neal Schon, Kenny
Aaronson (bass) and Mike Shrieve (ex-Santana;
drums), recording a live album under the band's
initials HSAS. Under this title they also cut a studio
version of Procol Harum's 'Whiter Shade Of Pale'.
Returning to solo work Hagar scored his biggest hit to
date with the *Voice Of America* out-take, 'I Can't
Drive 55'. In 1985 he surprised many by joining Van
Halen, from whom Dave Lee Roth had recently
departed. However, he has continued to pursue a
parallel, if intermittant solo career. His solo work
continues to be characterized by a refreshing lack of
bombast in a genre not noted for its subtlety.
Albums: *Nine On A Ten Scale* (Capitol 1976), *Red*
(Capitol 1977), *Musical Chairs* (Capitol 1978), *All
Night Long - Live* (Capitol 1978), *Street Machine*
(Capitol 1979), *Danger Zone* (Capitol 1979), *Live,
Loud And Clear* (Capitol 1980), *Standing Hampton*
(Geffen 1982), *Three Lock Box* (Geffen 1983), *Live
From London To Long Beach* (Capitol 1983), *VOA*
(Geffen 1983), *Sammy Hagar* (Geffen 1987), *Red*
(Geffen 1993), *Unboxed* (Geffen 1994).

Compilations: *Rematch* (Capitol 1983), *The Best Of*
(Geffen 1993). As Hagar, Schon, Aaronson and
Shrieve: *Through The Fire* (Geffen 1984).

Hallows Eve

The first incarnation of the heavy metal band
Hallows Eve dates back to 1984, when the nucleus of
Stacy Anderson (vocals), Tommy Stewart (bass) and
David Stuart (guitar), plus second guitarist Skellator
and drummer Tym Helton, recorded a demo which
was included on the *Metal Massacre IV* compilation.
Their music from the outset has been extreme,
representing one of the far outposts of the rock
spectrum via a turbulent, high-speed, wall-of-noise.
Lyrics dealt with death, reincarnation, torture and
mutilation, but the sentiments were usually
indecipherable through frantic background thrashing.
Tales Of Terror was recorded on a low budget, with a
dreadful production, but does feature the band's
strongest material. *Death And Insanity* and
Monument, although aesthetically more satisfying, are
more formularized. Stacy Anderson quit in 1988, and
the band have been inactive since.
Albums: *Tales Of Terror* (Roadrunner 1985), *Death
And Insanity* (Roadrunner 1986), *Monument*
(Roadrunner 1988).

Hamm, Stuart

This enormously talented bassist is perhaps better
known as a member of Joe Satriani's touring band,
but has also released a series of fine solo recordings.
Radio Free Albemuth displayed Hamm's virtuoso
abilities as he tackled Beethoven's 'Moonlight Sonata'
and a Debussy piece, but also aired some fine jazz-
rock-flavoured material, showing admirable restraint
in only adopting the lead role periodically,
concentrating on superb rhythm playing and song
integrity as guests Satriani and Allan Holdsworth
added colour. Hamm adopted a funkier flavour to his
playing on *Kings Of Sleep*, with the stunning 'Black
Ice' demonstrating a remarkable ability to both drive
and enhance a song through his dextrous rhythm-
playing. Shotgun Messiah's Harry K Cody added
some excellent lead guitar, and worked with Hamm
again, along with Eric Johnson, on *The Urge*.
Curiously, Hamm's career paralleled that of Satriani
in his addition of lead vocals to some tracks on his
third album, just as Satriani had done on *Flying In A
Blue Dream*, but the album's outstanding piece was a
live solo spot, 'Quahogs, Anyone?'. In addition to his
own albums and tours, he is a respected session
musician, having worked with the likes of Steve Vai.
He continues to work periodically with Satriani too.
Albums: *Radio Free Albemuth* (Relativity 1988), *Kings*

Of Sleep (Relativity 1989), *The Urge* (Relativity 1991).

Hand Of Glory

Hard rock band Hand Of Glory are dark Texan romantics with a strong dash of southern gothic. Though there are some musical similarities with the Cult and the Doors, Hand of Glory have a sound all of their own. Their 1989 debut, *Far From Kith and Kin*, had some strong moments, most notably the ironic revolutionary anthem, 'Ball and Chain', but lacked identity. With *Here Be Serpents* they really came into their own, blending the magical, the maudlin and the macabre with vitality and wit.
Albums: *Far From Kith and Kin* (Skyclad 1989), *Here Be Serpents* (Skyclad 1990).

Handsome Beasts

Hailing from Wolverhampton, England, the Handsome Beasts are the band responsible for launching the Heavy Metal Records label/company after their manager, Paul Birch, was unable to get them a deal. A thoroughly melodramatic band, perhaps typical of the New Wave Of British Heavy Metal, they were still able to grab the attention of the press thanks to humungous lead vocalist, Gary Dalloway. He would appear totally naked in a pig sty (complete with pig) for their first album cover. The rest of the band; Paul Robins (guitar), Steve Hough (bass) and Pete Malbassa (drums), were always overshadowed by Dalloway's image, yet they managed to produce some fine recordings which passed totally unmentioned. The only exception was the single, 'Sweeties', but again it was due to its cover that publicity was gained. Not surprisingly the band gave up. In 1990 Dalloway (now slimmer) revamped the band, utilizing the 'bad taste' sleeve angle one last time (a woman and a dog). This tawdry sensationalism was quite rightly given little press coverage and the band finally faded away.
Albums: *Beastiality* (Heavy Metal 1981), *The Beast Within* (FM Revolver 1990).

Hanoi Rocks

This Finnish heavy rock band were distinguished by their leaning towards 70s glam rock, which they carried off with more style and conviction than any of their peers. Initially the brainchild of Andy McCoy (b. Antti Hulkko) and Michael Monroe (b. Matti Fagerholm) back in 1976, they were not formed until 1980 when singer Monroe gathered up Nasty Suicide (b. Jan Stenfors; guitar), Stefan Piesmack (guitar), Pasi Sti (bass) and Peki Senola (drums). By September, when they cut their debut album, *Bangkok Shocks,*

Saigon Shakes, Hanoi Rocks (initially only released in Scandinavia), the line-up was Monroe, Suicide, McCoy (guitar), Sam Yaffa (b. Sami Takamaki; bass) and Gyp Casino (b. Jesper Sporre; drums). McCoy had previously played with two Finnish punk bands, Briard and Pelle Miljoona Oy. In addition Suicide had played in Briard, while Yaffa had also been a member of Pelle Miljoona Oy at various times. Hanoi Rocks' debut single - 'I Want You', was released on the Finnish Johanna label in 1980 and preceded the album. The band then travelled to London where they began recording *Oriental Beat*. Soon after it was finished Casino was sacked (and joined the Road Rats) and replaced by Razzle (b. Nicholas Dingley, Isle Of Wight, England), who had previously played with Demon Preacher and the Dark. In 1983 they were signed to CBS and started to attract attention in the British music press. They hit the UK charts for the first and only time in 1984 with a cover version of Creedence Clearwater Revival's 'Up Around The Bend', but the year ended in tragedy. The band were in the US when Razzle was killed in a car crash on 7 December. The car driver - Vince Neil of Mötley Crüe - was later found guilty of Vehicular Manslaughter. Former Clash drummer Terry Chimes was brought in as a replacement and when Yaffa left (to form Chain Gang then join Jetboy), Rene Berg (ex-Idle Flowers) also joined the group. However, Monroe never really accepted the loss of Razzle and in early 1985 he told the band he intended to quit. Hanoi Rocks played their final gig in May 1985. Monroe has since embarked on a solo career. Piesmack joined Pelle Miljoona Oy, then quit music, Sti and Senola also left the music scene, and McCoy (who had already formed a side project in 1983 - the Urban Dogs with Charlie Harper, Alvin Gibbs (UK Subs) and Knox (Vibrators), went on to form the Cherry Bombz with Suicide, Chimes and ex-Toto Coelo vocalist Anita Chellemah. The Cherry Bombz barely lasted a year and the members went on to play in various short-lived outfits, most notably Suicide (with Gibbs once more) in Cheap 'N' Nasty. A near reunion of Hanoi Rocks, featuring Monroe with Suicide and Sam Yaffa, emerged as Demolition 23 in 1994.
Albums: *Bangkok Shocks, Saigon Shakes, Hanoi Rocks* (Johanna 1981), *Oriental Beat* (Johanna 1982), *Self Destruction Blues* (Johanna 1982), *Back To Mystery City* (Lick 1983), *Two Steps From The Move* (CBS 1984). Compilations: *All Those Wasted Years* (Johanna 1985), *Rock 'N' Roll Divorce* (Lick 1985), *Best Of Hanoi Rocks* (Lick 1985), *Dead By Christmas* (Raw Power 1986), *Tracks From A Broken Dream* (Lick 1990).

Videos: *All Those Wasted Years* (1988), *The Nottingham Tapes* (1988).

Hansen, Randy

Raised in Seattle, Washington, USA, guitarist Hansen first attracted attention as a member of nightclub act Kid Chrysler And The Cruisers. The group's tongue-in-cheek repertoire encompassed several styles of popular music, but was marked by the musician's imperturbable pastiche of Jimi Hendrix. Having formed a trio, Machine Gun, in 1977, Hansen took his tribute on tour, but achieved a greater notoriety when he contributed Hendrix-influenced effects to the film soundtrack of *Apocalypse Now*. This in turn engendered a management deal with San Francisco-based entrepreneur David Rubinson who began promoting his client as an artist in his own right. *Randy Hansen* comprised original material which sadly paled in comparison to that of his mentor. Hendrix's songs still provided the focal point to the guitarist's live act and in 1984 he reverted completely to the role of imitator by joining drummer Buddy Miles in a revamped version of Band Of Gypsies. The 90s saw Hansen working as part of a tribute revue with original Hendrix bass player, Noel Redding.
Albums: *Randy Hansen* (EMI 1981), *Astral Projection Live* (Shrapnel 1983).

Hardline

This hard rock act evolved from a songwriting partnership between brothers Johnny and Joey Gioeli (vocals and guitar respectively, both ex-Brunette) and ex-Santana/Journey/Bad English guitarist Neal Schon. Bad English drummer Deen Castronovo joined, and completed the rhythm section by drafting in childhood friend Todd Jensen (ex-Dave Lee Roth; bass). *Double Eclipse* was classy American radio rock, with Schon unleashing some of the guitar firepower which had been restricted by Bad English's lighter AOR style, and the band spent some time touring, including US dates supporting Van Halen, before the debut was actually released. However, when Schon, Jensen and Castronovo took considerable time off to act as a backing band on Paul Rodgers' solo tour, the resulting friction split Hardline.
Album: *Double Eclipse* (MCA 1992).

Havohej

Profane black metal outfit formed in June 1993 and led by self-confessed New York Satanist, drum teacher and graphic artist, Paul Ledney. 'In the days when Venom first appeared there was something very personal about what was going on. You could relate to the music. Now there are just too many trendies jumping on a bandwagon and imitating what they perceive as being the atmosphere of the genre. They all put on make-up and sing about Satan. They believe that alone makes them evil'. Influenced equally by the early punk bands, Ledney put together Havohej as a studio project following the dissolution of his earlier band, Profanatica, when tapes of their first full album together were mysteriously destroyed in the studio (arguably a good thing, given its working title - *The Raping Of The Virgin Mary*). They had previously recorded a split album with Columbian band Massacre for the Osmose label, and a three track single, 'Unholy Darkness And Impurity'. Like Profanatica, Havohej benefited from the underground tape scene, particularly as many of the songs on the band's debut album were reconstructions of material from Ledney's former outfit. However, by the middle of 1994 Havohej too were no more.
Album: *Dethrone The God* (Candlelight 1993).

Hawkwind

Befitting a group associated with community and benefit concerts, Hawkwind was founded in the hippie enclave centred on London's Ladbroke Grove during the late 60s. Dave Brock (b. Isleworth, Middlesex, England; guitar/vocals), Nik Turner (b. Oxford, Oxfordshire, England; saxophone/vocals), Mick Slattery (guitar), Dik Mik (b. Richmond, Surrey; electronics), John Harrison (bass) and Terry Ollis (drums) were originally known as Group X, then Hawkwind Zoo, prior to securing a recording contract. Their debut, *Hawkwind*, was produced by Dick Taylor, former guitarist with the Pretty Things, who briefly augmented his new proteges on Slattery's departure. Indeed Hawkwind underwent many personnel changes, but by 1972 had achieved a core consisting of Brock, Turner, Del Dettmar (b. Thornton Heath, Surrey, England; synthesizer), Lemmy (b. Ian Kilmister, 24 December 1945, Stoke-on-Trent, Staffordshire, England; bass), Simon King (b. Oxford, Oxfordshire, England; drums), Stacia (b. Exeter, Devon, England; dancer) and poet/writer Robert Calvert (b. c.1945, Pretoria, South Africa; vocals). One part-time member was science fiction writer Michael Moorcock who helped organize some of Hawkwind's concert appearances and often deputized for Calvert when the latter was indisposed. This role was extended to recording credits on several albums. The group's chemically-blurred science-fiction image was made apparent in such titles as *In Search Of Space* and *Space Ritual*. They enjoyed a freak UK pop hit when the compulsive 'Silver Machine' soared to number 3, but this flirtation with a wider audience ended prematurely when a follow-

up single, 'Urban Guerilla', was hastily withdrawn in the wake of a terrorist bombing campaign in London. Hawkwind continued to shed personalities; Calvert left, and rejoined, Dettmar was replaced by Simon House (ex-High Tide), but the group lost much of its impetus in 1975 when Lemmy was fired on his arrest on drugs charges during a North American tour. The bassist subsequently formed Motörhead. Although the group enjoyed a period of relative stability following the release of *Astounding Sounds, Amazing Music*, it ended in 1977 with the firing of founder member Turner and two latter additions, Paul Rudolph (ex-Deviants and Pink Fairies) and Alan Powell. The following year Simon House left to join David Bowie's band before Brock, Calvert and King assumed a new name, the Hawklords, to avoid legal and contractual complications. The group reverted to using its former appellation in 1979, by which time Calvert had resumed his solo career. An undaunted Hawkwind pursued an eccentric path throughout the 80s. Dave Brock remained at the helm of a flurry of associates, including Huw Lloyd Langton, who played guitar on the group's debut album, Tim Blake (synthesizer) and drummer Ginger Baker. Nik Turner also reappeared in the ranks of a group which has continued to enjoy a committed following, despite the bewildering array of archive releases obscuring the group's contemporary standing. In 1990 they underwent a resurgence in popularity thanks primarily to the growth of the rave culture and their album, *Space Bandits*, reflected this new, young interest. It also saw the return of Simon House and the inclusion for the first time of a female vocalist, Bridgett Wishart (ex-Hippy Slags). However, when their next album started to copy rave ideas, it became obvious that they were running out of inspiration, with *Palace Springs* containing no less than five new versions of early tracks. In 1992 they set off to America for a very successful tour, but on their return fell apart. Eventually reduced to a three-piece they became totally dance/rave orientated and subsequent releases had little in common with the classic days gone by. Sad that a band celebrating 25 years in business had become so easily embroiled in current musical trends as opposed to setting them.
Albums: *Hawkwind* (Liberty 1970), *In Search Of Space* (United Artists 1971), *Doremi Fasol Latido* (United Artists 1972), *Space Ritual Alive* (United Artists 1973, double album), *Hall Of The Mountain Grill* (United Artists 1974), *Warrior On The Edge Of Time* (United Artists 1975), *Astounding Sounds Amazing Music* (Charisma 1976), *Quark, Strangeness And Charm* (Charisma 1977), *25 Years On* (Charisma 1978), *PXR 5* (Charisma 1979), *Live 1979* (Bronze 1980), *Levitation* (Bronze 1980), *Sonic Attack* (RCA 1981), *Church Of Hawkwind* (RCA 1982), *Choose Your Masques* (RCA 1982), *Zones* (Flicknife 1983), *The Chronicle Of The Black Sword* (Flicknife 1985), *The Xenon Codex* (GWR 1988), *Night Of The Hawk* (Powerhouse 1989), *Space Bandits* (GWR 1990), *Palace Springs* (GWR 1991), *Electric Tepee* (Essential 1992), *It Is The Business Of The Future To Be Dangerous* (Essential 1993), *The Business Trip* (Emergency Broadcast Systems 1994). Compilations: *Road Hawks* (United Artists 1976), *Masters Of The Universe* (United Artists 1977), *Repeat Performances* (Charisma 1980), *Friends And Relations* (Flicknife 1982), *Twice Upon A Time - Friends And Relations Vol. 2* (Flicknife 1983), *Text Of The Festival Live 70/72* (Illuminated 1983), *Independent Days* (Flicknife 1984, mini-album), *Bring Me The Head Of Yuri Gagarin* (Demi-Monde 1985), *In The Beginning* (Demi-Monde 1985, reissue of disc 1 of *Text Of Festival*), *Space Ritual Volume 2* (American Phonograph 1985, double album), *Anthology - Hawkwind Volumes 1, 2* and *3* (Samurai 1985-1986), *Live 70/73* (Dojo 1986), *The Collection* (Castle 1986, double album), *Angels Of Death* (RCA 1986), *Early Daze/Best Of* (Thunderbolt 1987), *Out And Intake* (Flicknife 1987), *Stasis: The UA Years* (EMI 1990), *Mighty Hawkwind Classics* (Anagram 1992).
Videos: *Night Of The Hawks* (1984), *Chronicle Of The Black Sword* (1986), *Live Legends* (1990), *Treworgy Tree Fayre* (1990), *The Academy* (1991), *Promo Collection* (1992), *Hawkwind: The Solstice At Stonehenge 1984* (1993).
Further reading: *This Is Hawkwind, Do Not Panic*, Kris Tate (1985).

Headgirl

A project conceived by British rock bands Motörhead and Girlschool, both of whom shared the same manager and record company, Bronze. The collaboration arose when Motörhead had to cancel a tour after their drummer, Taylor, broke his neck. They were at a Girlschool recording session when producer Vic Maile suggested that they work together. The result was an EP, *St. Valentine's Day Massacre*, spearheaded by 'Please Don't Touch', a cover of a Johnny Kidd And The Pirates song from 1960. This was recorded in December 1980 at the Jackson studio, Rickmansworth, Hertfordshire, and its success led to Headgirl (an amalgamation of the names of the two bands) appearing no less than three times on the UK television music programme, *Top Of The Pops*.

Hear 'N' Aid

The Hear 'N' Aid project came about after Jimmy Bain and Vivian Campbell of Dio had taken part in a Radiothon held over a weekend by KLOS of Los Angeles for the famine in Africa. They had noticed that there were not many rock stars taking part and this is when the whole idea was born. Initially, they got in touch with Ronnie James Dio, to tell him of the project. While Dio was ringing round to get support, Bain and Campbell wrote the score, and Dio produced the lyrics. 'Stars' was recorded over a four-month period in 1986. In addition to the single release, a video was planned and all the sessions were filmed. The most ambitious idea was to have an album released with each act writing a track for the record, but this never occurred. Instead, bands donated tracks, most of which were live recordings. Another idea was for a session to be held in London, so all the European rock stars could be included, but this had to be aborted due to lack of participants. Those that did take part included the following: Queensrÿche, Rough Cutt, Iron Maiden, Ted Nugent, Y&T, Spinal Tap, Night Ranger, Twisted Sister, Mötley Crüe, Vanilla Fudge, Dio, Blue Öyster Cult, Don Dokken, Yngwie Malmsteen, Quiet Riot, Judas Priest, King Cobra, W.A.S.P. and Journey.
Album: *Hear 'N' Aid* (Vertigo 1986).

Heart

This durable US rock band features the talents of sisters Ann (b. 19 June 1951, San Diego, California, USA) and Nancy Wilson (b. 16 March 1954, San Francisco, California, USA). The elder sister had released two singles as Ann Wilson And The Daybreaks on a local label in 1967. After a series of unreleased demos she took her sister to Vancouver, Canada, in search of a backing band. There they found bassist Steve Fossen (b. 15 November 1949) and guitarist Roger Fisher (b. 14 February 1950), and Heart was born (two initial monikers, the Army and White Heart, were rejected). After *Dreamboat Annie* emerged on Mushroom Records in 1976, their second single, 'Crazy On You', brought them to public attention. Michael Derosier (b. 24 August 1951, Canada) had previously become the band's first permanent drummer. They maintained their high profile when *Little Queen* and the single, 'Barracuda', became mainstays in the US charts. By the time *Dog And Butterfly* arrived in 1978, the professional relationships within the band had escalated to ones of a more personal nature, with Nancy Wilson dating guitarist Fisher, while sister Ann was involved with his brother, Mike. Mike Fisher, who had once been part of the group's embryonic line-up, had now become

their unofficial manager. However, before sessions for *Bebe Le Strange* on Epic were complete, the relationships had soured and Roger Fisher left the band, leaving the group bereft of the lead guitar which had previously been so prominent in the group's formula. The guitar parts were covered on tour by Nancy and multi-instrumentalist Howard Leese (b. 13 June 1953, Canada), who became a permanent member. By the time they resurfaced with *Private Audition* in 1983, Fossen and Derosier were also on the verge of departure. Their replacements were Mark Andes (b. 19 February 1948, Philadelphia, USA; ex-Spirit) and Denny Carmassi (ex-Montrose and Sammy Hagar), though their efforts on *Passionworks* were not enough to inspire any kind of revival in Heart's fortunes. Their confidence was bolstered, however, when Ann's duet with Mike Dean (Loverboy) produced 'Almost Paradise...Love Theme From Footloose', which rose to number 7 in the US charts. When Epic allowed their contract to lapse, Heart joined Capitol in 1985, seemingly with their career in its death throes. The new label brought about a transformation in the band's image, projecting them as a more rock-orientated concern, but could hardly have expected the turnaround in Heart's fortunes which resulted. *Heart* gave them a number 1 in the US, and highly lucrative singles 'What About Love' and 'Never', before 'These Dreams' finally achieved the equivalent number 1 slot in the singles chart. The follow-up, *Bad Animals*, was almost as successful, stalling at number 2. While both Wilson sisters continued to work on soundtrack cuts, the most profitable of which was Ann's duet with Robin Zander (Cheap Trick) 'Surrender To Me', Nancy married *Rolling Stone* writer Cameron Crowe. Heart's success continued with the long-conceived *Brigade* in 1990, from which 'All I Wanna Do Is Make Love To You' (written by Robert John 'Mutt' Lange) became a Top 10 hit in the UK and a number 1 in the US. Both Wilson sisters then became involved in solo projects, while former companions Fossen, Roger Fisher and Derosier embarked on a new dual career with Alias, who scored two big US single hits in 1990. The sisters returned as Heart in 1993, again backed by Fisher (guitar), Leese (keyboards), Fossen (bass) and Derosier (drums), and found themselves with another hit on their hands in 'Will You Be There (In The Morning)', which preceded *Desire Walks On*.
Albums: *Dreamboat Annie* (Mushroom 1976), *Little Queen* (Portrait 1977), *Dog And Butterfly* (Portrait 1978), *Bebe Le Strange* (Portrait 1980), *Greatest Hits/Live* (Portrait 1981, double album), *Private Audition* (Epic 1982), *Passionworks* (Epic 1983),

Heart

Heart (Capitol 1985), *Bad Animals* (Capitol 1987), *Brigade* (Capitol 1990), *Rock The House Live!* (Capitol 1991), *Desire Walks On* (Capitol 1993). Compilations: *Magazine* (Mushroom 1978), *Heart Box Set* (Capitol 1990).
Video: *If Looks Could Kill* (1988).

Heavy Metal Kids
Formed in London, England, in 1973, Heavy Metal Kids consisted of Gary Holton (vocals), Mickey Waller (guitar), Ron Thomas (bass) and Keith Boyce (drums). Signing to Atlantic Records the band released their self-titled debut album in 1974. Quickly gaining popularity on the live club circuit in and around the London area, playing brash street metal, the band followed up with *Anvil Chorus* in 1975. This featured keyboard player Danny Peyronel and the semi-legendary 'Cosmo' on guitar joining the quartet. The album also contained the utterly outrageous 'Call The Cops'. However, Holton's volatile nature got the band into trouble at various gigs, breaking his leg on an ill-fated American tour. Subsequently dropped by Atlantic Records, the band nevertheless released a third and final album. *Kitsch* appeared on RAK Records in 1977, and was again dominated by tough, street metal tunes. It still did not give the band the break it needed and they folded shortly after its release. Gary Holton went on to a short-lived solo career which saw him (very) briefly join the Damned, release a solo album in Europe and have a minor hit single with 'Catch A Falling Star' in 1984, before setting out to pursue an acting career. He will be best remembered for his role as Wayne, a streetwise cockney jack-the-lad in the hit television series, *Auf Wiedersehen Pet*. Sadly, he died of a drugs overdose during the filming of the series.
Albums: *Heavy Metal Kids* (Atlantic 1974), *Anvil Chorus* (Atlantic 1975), *Kitsch* (RAK 1977).

Heavy Pettin
This Scottish hard rock quintet formed in July 1981 when vocalist Steve 'Hamie' Hayman and guitarist Punky Mendoza merged with guitarist Gordon Bonnar, bassist Brian Waugh and drummer Gary Moat, who had been playing together as Weeper. Taking their name from a UFO album, the young band toured the UK heavily, and their impressive three-track demo led to a single, 'Roll The Dice', through Neat Records. This, coupled with a BBC Radio One *Friday Rock Show* session, led to a major

deal with Polydor. *Lettin' Loose*, produced by Brian May and Queen producer Mack, was a confident display of the band's talents, with their catchy melodic hard rock being favourably compared to Def Leppard, and Heavy Pettin made a big impression on UK tours with Kiss and Ozzy Osbourne. The domestic music press lauded a band who seemed set to follow in Leppard's footsteps, and *Rock Ain't Dead*'s mature songwriting sought to justify that opinion, as the band toured the US with Kiss, Ozzy, Mötley Crüe and AC/DC. However, it all went wrong for Heavy Pettin during the recording of *The Big Bang*. 'Romeo' was put forward as a candidate for the UK's Eurovision Song Contest entry by Polydor, albeit unsuccessfully, seriously damaging the band's credibility, which they salvaged to some extent on Magnum's UK tour. Polydor shelved the album as 'Romeo' failed to set the charts alight, and a dispirited Heavy Pettin, unhappy with their poppier new direction led by Bonnar's keyboards, split in early 1988. *The Big Bang* was released posthumously the following year.
Albums: *Lettin' Loose* (Polydor 1983), *Rock Ain't Dead* (Polydor 1985), *The Big Bang* (FM Revolver 1989).

Heir Apparent

Formed in Seattle, Washington, USA, in 1984, the band's original line-up consisted of Paul Davidson (vocals), Terry Gorle (guitar), Michael Jackson (keyboards), Derek Peace (bass) and Ray Black (drums). Via early demos they attracted the attention of the French based Black Dragon Records. This resulted in the band's debut, *Graceful Inheritance*, a worthy slice of Americanized melodic rock, released in 1986. After an uneventful European tour vocalist Paul Davidson left the band to be replaced by Steve Benito. They also briefly lost bassist Derek Peace to touring partners Savage Grace before he realized his mistake and rejoined. However, all this had taken its toll and the band were dropped by their record company. After several new demos they attracted the attention of Metal Blade Records, which resulted in *One Small Voice* being released in 1989. Shortly after both Black and Gorle left to be replaced by Gary McCormick and Klaus Derendorf respectively. However, little was heard from the band after that as they disappeared back into the Seattle club scene from whence they came.
Albums: *Graceful Inheritance* (Black Dragon 1986), *One Small Voice* (Metal Blade 1989).

Helix

Formed in Ontario, Canada, in 1978, the band's original line-up consisted of Brian Vollmer (vocals), Brent Doerner (guitar), Paul Hackman (guitar), Keith Zurbrigg (bass) and Brian Doerner (drums). Together they released *Breaking Loose* before swapping Brent Doerner and Zurbrigg for Leo Niebudek (guitar) and Mike Vzelac (bass). The resultant *White Lace & Black Leather* was an improvement on their basic hard rock approach, but again met with a less than enthusiastic reception. However, these releases did serve to gain the attention of Capitol Records who signed the band and released their third album, *No Rest For The Wicked*, in 1983. This featured a line-up bolstered by new drummer Greg Hinz (ex-Starchild), while Niebudek had departed to leave Hackman in sole charge of guitars. Widely judged to be their best album, this was a solid collection of rock songs which sold well. *Walkin' The Razors Edge*, released in 1984, introduced new bassist Daryl Gray. This, their most permanent line-up, went on to record two more albums for Capitol, *Long Way To Heaven* and *Wild In The Streets*, which demonstrated a much more commercial songwriting approach. However, they were dropped when neither managed to produce a breakthrough, though sadder still was Hackman's death in a tour bus accident during 1992.
Albums: *Breaking Loose* (H&S 1979), *White Lace & Black Leather* (H&S 1981), *No Rest For The Wicked* (Capitol 1983), *Walkin' The Razors Edge* (Capitol 1984), *Long Way To Heaven* (Capitol 1985), *Wild In The Streets* (Capitol 1987), *Back For Another Taste* (GWR 1990), *It's Business Doing Pleasure* (1993).

Hellanbach

Formed in Newcastle-upon-Tyne, England, in 1980, Hellanbach were one of the many groups to grow out of the New Wave Of British Heavy Metal. The band consisted of Jimmy Brash (vocals), Dave Patton (guitar), Kev Charlton (bass), and Steve Walker (drums). Instead of taking the usual route of making demos to secure a recording contract, the band went straight ahead with recording and releasing a four-track EP at their own expense. *Out To Get You* was a heavy yet melodic debut. Hellanbach then kept a low profile until re-emerging on the Neat Records label and releasing their debut album, *Now Hear This*, in 1983. It was given a mixed reaction by the press, however, and the comparisons to Van Halen were to dog them for the rest of their career. By the time *The Big H* was released in 1984, the band had obviously taken note of the criticisms levelled against them. Again, this was a worthy release from a dedicated band, deftly executed and full of melodic choruses. Due to a continued lack of media interest the band soon folded.

Albums: *Now Hear This* (Neat 1983), *The Big H* (Neat 1984).

Hellhammer

Formed in 1982, seminal Swiss extreme metal band Hellhammer toyed with Satanic imagery, but were chiefly concerned with generating morbid intensity. Generally considered to be formless noise at the time, Hellhammer attracted a cult following nonetheless. They appealed to the youthful grassroots of the heavy metal scene, who coveted the most bombastically abrasive sounds that could be committed to vinyl. Extreme metal cognoscenti often cite Hellhammer as the first true death metal band and their early demos are still regarded as underground classics by some. Nevertheless they undeniably lacked maturity and subtlety - take the band members' stage names: Satanic Slaughter (vocals); Savage Damage (bass); Bloodhunter (b. Bruce Day; drums). Satanic Slaughter and Savage Damage, under the names Thomas Gabriel Warrior and Martin Ain respectively, went on to form the better-realised thrash band Celtic Frost in 1984, having recorded only one mini-LP as Hellhammer.

Albums: *Apocalyptic Raids* (Noise 1984).

Hellion

From Los Angeles, California, Hellion came together in 1982 and quickly gained support from local radio stations and metal magazines worldwide. The band was the brainchild of vocalist Ann Boleyn who put together a series of formations before settling on a line-up of Alan Barlam (guitar), Sean Kelly (drums), Ray Schenck (guitar) and Bill Sweet (bass). After releasing their first album on Music For Nations their heavy approach based on Judas Priest and the Scorpions brought them to the attention of Ronnie James Dio, who used them as a support act and also produced their demos. His wife, Wendy, helped them gain a full time management deal. However the business side would take its toll and the band soon split up and parted from their new agency. Boleyn then convinced them to reform which they did with the exception of Sweet who was replaced by Dave Dutton. A second mini-album, *Postcards From The Asylum*, featured a cover of the Judas Priest standard, 'Exciter'. This revitalised the band and they took up a residency at the Troubadour Club in Los Angeles and toured in Europe. In 1987 Boleyn put together a new line-up with Alex Campbell (bass), Chet Thompson (guitar/sitar) and Greg Pecka (drums). Together they recorded *Screams In The Night*, but once more collapsed following release. After that Boleyn adopted an entirely different approach to her career and began

to work on a novel, *Black Dragon*, backed up by a mooted concept album. The book failed to land her a literary career though one final album, *The Black Book*, did surface to little residual interest.

Albums: *Hellion* (Music For Nations 1983, mini-album), *Postcards From The Asylum* (Music For Nations 1988, mini-album), *Screams In The Night* (Music For Nations 1988), *The Black Book* (Music For Nations 1990).

Helloween

Formed in 1984 in Hamburg, Germany, from of the ashes of local bands Second Hell and Iron Fist, their original line-up comprised Kai Hansen (guitar/vocals), Michael Weikath (guitar), Markus Grosskopf (bass) and Ingo Schwichenburg (drums). After having two tracks included on the *Death Metal* compilation album released by Noise Records in 1984, the label issued their self-titled debut mini-album in 1985. This was soon followed by *Walls Of Jericho* and an EP, *Judas*. The band gained a strong following with their unique blend of high speed power metal. Soon after its release, Helloween decided to add a vocalist/frontman, namely Michael Kiske, a charismatic 18-year-old. *Keeper Of The Seven Keys Part I*, released in 1987, showed the band to be taking a much more melodic approach and Kiske proved himself a worthy addition. Helloween then toured Europe relentlessly, building a sizeable following in the process. *Keeper Of The Seven Keys Part II* was released in 1988, together with a successful appearance at the Donnington Monsters Of Rock Festival that year. After which came an EP, *Dr. Stein*, but behind the scenes all was not well. The band had become increasingly unhappy with their record company and started to negotiate with several major labels who had previously shown an interest. As a stop-gap the band released *Live In The UK*, recorded at the Hammersmith Odeon in 1989. Kai Hansen then left to form his own outfit, Gamma Ray. His temporary replacement was Roland Grapow. A protracted legal battle with their record company ensured that it was not until 1990 that the band was back in action. They finally signed to EMI Records and gained major management in the form of the Smallwood/Taylor organization. The band's debut for their new label, *Pink Bubbles Go Ape,* released in 1990, depicted Helloween as a shadow of their former selves, sadly missing Kai Hansen and his songwriting skills. Shortly after the dismissal of Kiske, Ingo Schwichenberg was also given his marching orders due to personal health problems and a clash with Weikath, who was now the main force behind the band. Their replacements were Andi Deris (vocals;

ex-Pink Cream 69) and Ulli Kusch (drums), who were in place in time for their Castle/Raw Power debut, *Master Of The Rings*.

Albums: *Helloween* (Noise 1985, mini-album), *Walls Of Jericho* (Noise 1986), *Keeper Of The Seven Keys Part I* (Noise 1987), *Keeper Of The Seven Keys Part II* (Noise 1988), *Live In The UK* (Noise 1989), *Pink Bubbles Go Ape* (EMI 1990), *Chameleon* (EMI 1993), *Master Of The Rings* (Raw Power 1994).

Helmet

Moving to New York to pursue a Masters degree in jazz guitar, Page Hamilton 'discovered distortion' and new influences such as Big Black, Killing Joke and Sonic Youth during his tenure with Band Of Susans, leading him to form Helmet with fellow Oregon native Henry Bogdan (bass), Australian guitarist Peter Mengede and classically-schooled drummer John Stanier, a veteran of the Florida hardcore scene. The band's close-cropped, clean-cut anti-image contrasts with their brutally heavy music. Hamilton's lyrics draw from the atmosphere of his life in New York, and are delivered with an angry roar in economical song structures overlaid with an intense barrage of staccato riffing; the band play with rigid discipline, avoiding the high speed delivery of many thrash and hardcore bands and generating enormous power as a result. While selling modestly, *Strap It On* created considerable interest in Helmet, and the major label debut, *Meantime*, showed progression as the band established smoother rhythmic flows without compromising their sound. The band toured widely, with Faith No More in the USA and Ministry in Europe before undertaking headline dates of their own. Helmet subsequently parted company with Mengede, replacing him in mid-1993 with ex-postal worker Rob Echeverria. Before the release of a third album for new label Atlantic/East West, the group recorded 'Just Another Victim' with House Of Pain for the *Judgement Night* soundtrack. *Betty* featured co-production from Todd Ray, plus one track concocted with Butch Vig, 'Milquetoast', which also featured on a soundtrack, this time *The Crow*.

Albums: *Strap It On* (Amphetamine Reptile 1991), *Meantime* (Interscope 1992), *Betty* (East West 1994).

Helstar

Formed in 1982 in Houston, Texas, the band's original line-up consisted of James Rivera (vocals), Larry Barragan (guitar), Robert Trevin (guitar), Jerry Abarca (bass) and Rene Lima (drums). Through to an excellent four-track demo recorded in 1983 the band quickly became a favourite on the underground tape-trading scene. Attracting the attention of Combat Records, they released their debut album, *Burning Star*, in 1984. Produced by ex-Rods drummer Carl Canedy, it did not have the spark of the early demo but was still a worthy slice of power metal. Internal wrangles led to both guitarist Robert Trevin and drummer Rene Lima leaving the band to be replaced by André Corbin and Frank Ferreira respectively. A second album, *Remnants Of War*, was released in 1986 and followed closely in the footsteps of its predecessor. The band had been dissatisfied with their record label for some time and after due deliberation both parties parted amicably. Helstar then relocated to Los Angeles where they signed a new recording deal with Metal Blade, the first product of which was *A Distant Thunder* in 1988. The band had now developed their own distinctive sound and were picking up many new fans. They toured across America and Europe and on their return to America moved back to Houston. The next album, entitled *Nosferatu*, was a concept affair with vampires as its theme. However, this new approach towards their songwriting did not suit the now distinctive Helstar style and reactions were discouraging.

Albums: *Burning Star* (Music For Nations 1984), *Remnants Of War* (Noise/Combat 1986), *A Distant Thunder* (Restless/Metal Blade 1988), *Nosferatu* (Roadrunner 1989).

Hendrix, Jimi

b Johnny Allen Hendrix, 27 November 1942, Seattle, Washington, USA, d. 18 September 1970. (His father subsequently changed his son's name to James Marshall Hendrix). More superlatives have been bestowed upon Hendrix than any other rock guitarist. Unquestionably one of music's most influential figures, he brought an unparalleled vision to the art of playing electric guitar. Self-taught (and with the burden of being left-handed with a right-handed guitar) he spent hours absorbing the recorded legacy of southern-blues practitioners, from Robert Johnson to B.B. King. The aspiring musician joined several local R&B bands while still at school, before enlisting as a paratrooper in the 101st Airborne Division. It was during this period that Hendrix met Billy Cox, a bass player upon whom he would call at several stages in his career. Together they formed the King Kasuals, an in-service attraction later resurrected when both men returned to civilian life. Hendrix was discharged in July 1962 after breaking his right ankle. He began working with various touring revues backing, among others, the Impressions, Sam Cooke and the Valentinos. He enjoyed lengthier spells with the Isley Brothers, Little Richard and King Curtis, recording with each of these acts, but was unable to adapt to the discipline their performances required. The experience and stagecraft gained during this formative period proved essential to the artist's subsequent development. By 1965 Hendrix was living in New York. In October he joined struggling soul singer Curtis Knight, signing a punitive contract with the latter's manager, Ed Chaplin. This ill-advised decision would return to haunt the guitarist. In June the following year Hendrix, now calling himself Jimmy James, formed a group initially dubbed the Rainflowers, then Jimmy James And The Blue Flames. The quartet, which also featured future Spirit member Randy California, was appearing at the Cafe Wha? in Greenwich Village when Chas Chandler was advised to see them. The Animals' bassist immediately recognized the guitarist's extraordinary talent and persuaded him to come to London in search of a more receptive audience. Hendrix arrived in England in September 1966. Chandler became his co-manager, in partnership with Mike Jeffries (aka Jeffreys), and immediately began auditions for a suitable backing group. Noel Redding (b. 25 December 1945, Folkestone, Kent, England) was selected on bass, having recently failed to join the New Animals, while John 'Mitch' Mitchell (b. 9 July 1947, Ealing, Middlesex, England), a veteran of the Riot Squad and Georgie Fame's Blue Flames, became the trio's drummer. The new group, dubbed the Jimi Hendrix Experience, made its debut the following month at Evereux in France. On returning to England they began a string of club engagements which attracted pop's aristocracy, including Pete Townshend and Eric Clapton. In December the trio released their first single, the understated, resonant 'Hey Joe'. Its UK Top 10 placing encouraged a truly dynamic follow-up in 'Purple Haze'. The latter was memorable for Hendrix's guitar pyrotechnics and a lyric that incorporated the artist's classic line: "Scuse me while I kiss the sky'. On tour his trademark Fender Stratocaster and Marshall Amplifier were punished night after night, as the group enhanced its reputation with exceptional live appearances. Here Hendrix drew on black culture and his own heritage to produce a startling visual and aural bombardment. Framed by a halo of long, wiry hair, his slight figure was clad in a bright, rainbow-mocking costume. Although never a demonstrative vocalist, his delivery was curiously effective. Hendrix's playing technique, meanwhile, though still drawing its roots from the blues, encompassed an emotional range far greater than any contemporary guitarist. Rapier-like runs vied with measured solos, matching energy with ingenuity, while a plethora of technical possibilities - distortion, feedback and even sheer volume - brought texture to his overall approach. This assault was enhanced by a flamboyant stage persona in which Hendrix used the guitar as a physical appendage. He played his instrument behind his back, between his legs or, in simulated sexual ecstasy, on the floor. Such practices brought criticism from radical quarters, who claimed the artist had become an 'Uncle Tom', employing tricks to carry favour with a white audience - accusations which denied a similar showmanship from generations of black performers, from Charley Patton to 'T-Bone' Walker. Redding's clean, uncluttered bass lines provided the backbone to Hendrix's improvisations, while Mitchell's drumming, as instinctive as his leader's guitar work, was a perfect foil.

Their concessions to the pop world now receding, the Experience completed an astonishing debut album which ranged from the apocalyptic vision of 'I Don't Live Today', to the blues of 'Red House' and the funk of 'Fire' and 'Foxy Lady'. Hendrix returned to America in June 1967 to appear, sensationally, at the Monterey Pop Festival. During one number (Dylan's 'Like A Rolling Stone') he paused to inform the crowd that he was re-tuning his guitar, later in the same song admitting he had forgotten the words. Such unparalleled confidence only endeared him to the crowd. His performance was a musical and visual feast, topped off by a sequence which saw him playing the guitar with his teeth, and then burning the instrument with lighter fuel. He was now fêted in his homeland, and following an ill-advised tour supporting the Monkees, the Experience enjoyed reverential audiences in the country's nascent concert circuit. *Axis: Bold As Love* revealed a new lyrical capability, notably in the title-track, and the jazz-influenced 'Up From The Skies'. 'Little Wing', a delicate love song bathed in unhurried guitar splashes, offered a gentle perspective, closer to that of the artist's shy, offstage demeanour. Released in December 1967, the collection completed a triumphant year, artistically and commercially, but within months the fragile peace began to collapse. In January 1968 the Experience embarked on a gruelling American tour encompassing 54 concerts in 47 days. Hendrix was now tiring of the wild man image which had brought initial attention, but he was perceived as diffident by spectators anticipating gimmickry. An impulsive artist, he was unable to disguise below-par performances, while his relationship with Redding grew increasingly fraught as the bassist rebelled against the set patterns he was expected to play. *Electric Ladyland*, the last official Experience album, was released in October. This extravagant double set was initially deemed 'self-indulgent', but is now

Jimi Hendrix

recognized as a major work. It revealed the guitarist's desire to expand the increasingly limiting trio format, and contributions from members of Traffic (Chris Wood and Steve Winwood) and Jefferson Airplane (Jack Casady) embellished several selections. The collection featured a succession of virtuoso performances - 'Gypsy Eyes', 'Crosstown Traffic' - while the astonishing 'Voodoo Chile (Slight Return)', a posthumous number 1 single, showed how Hendrix had brought rhythm, purpose and mastery to the recently invented wah-wah pedal. *Electric Ladyland* included two UK hits, 'The Burning Of The Midnight Lamp' and 'All Along The Watchtower'. The latter, an urgent restatement of the Bob Dylan song, was particularly impressive, and received the ultimate accolade when the composer adopted Hendrix's interpretation when performing it live on his 1974 tour. Despite such creativity, the guitarist's private and professional life was becoming problematic. He was arrested in Toronto for possessing heroin, but although the charges were later dismissed, the proceedings clouded much of 1969. Chas Chandler had meanwhile withdrawn from the managerial partnership and although Redding sought solace with a concurrent group, Fat Mattress, his differences with Hendrix were now irreconcilable. The Experience played its final concert on June 29 1969; Jimi subsequently formed Gypsies Sons And Rainbows with Mitchell, Billy Cox (bass), Larry Lee (rhythm guitar), Juma Sultan and Jerry Velez (both percussion). This short-lived unit closed the Woodstock Festival, during which Hendrix performed his famed rendition of the 'Star Spangled Banner'. Perceived by some critics as a political statement, it came as the guitarist was being increasingly subjected to pressures from different causes. In October he formed an all-black group, Band Of Gypsies, with Cox and drummer Buddy Miles, intending to accentuate the African-American dimension in his music. The trio made its debut on 31 December 1969, but its potential was marred by Miles' comparatively flat, pedestrian drumming and unimaginative compositions. Part of the set was issued as *Band Of Gypsies*, but despite the inclusion of the exceptional 'Machine Gun', this inconsistent album was only released to appease former manager Chaplin, who acquired the rights in part-settlement of a miserly early contract. The Band Of Gypsies broke up after a mere three concerts and initially Hendrix confined his efforts to completing his Electric Ladyland recording studio. He then started work on another double set, the unreleased *First Rays Of The New Rising Sun*, and later resumed performing with Cox and Mitchell. His final concerts were largely

frustrating, as the aims of the artist and the expectations of his audience grew increasingly separate. His final UK appearance, at the Isle Of Wight festival, encapsulated this dilemma, yet still drew an enthralling performance.

The guitarist returned to London following a short European tour. On 18 September 1970, his girlfriend, Monika Danneman, became alarmed when she was unable to rouse him from sleep. An ambulance was called, but Hendrix was pronounced dead on arrival at a nearby hospital. The inquest recorded an open verdict, with death caused by suffocation due to inhalation of vomit. Eric Burdon claimed at the time to possess a suicide note, but this has never been confirmed. Two posthumous releases, *Cry Of Love* and *Rainbow Bridge*, mixed portions of the artist's final recordings with masters from earlier sources. These were fitting tributes, but many others were tawdry cash-ins, recorded in dubious circumstances, mispackaged, mistitled and serving only to dilute his outstanding career. This imbalance has been redressed of late with the release of fitting archive recordings, but the Hendrix legacy also rests in his prevailing influence on fellow musicians. Many guitarists have imitated his technique; few have mastered it, while none at all have matched him as an inspirational player. In November 1993 a tribute album, *Stone Free*, was released, containing a formidable list of performers including the Pretenders, Eric Clapton, Cure, Jeff Beck, Pat Metheny and Nigel Kennedy. A small testament to the huge influence Hendrix has wielded as rock's greatest guitarist.

Albums: *Are You Experienced?* (Track 1967), *Axis: Bold As Love* (Track 1967), *Electric Ladyland* (Track 1968), *Band Of Gypsies* (Track 1970). The rest of the extensive Hendrix catalogue was compiled after his death. *Cry Of Love* (Polydor 1971), *Experience* (Ember 1971), *Isle Of Wight* (Polydor 1971), *Rainbow Bridge* (Reprise 1971), *Hendrix In The West* (Polydor 1971), *More Experience* (Ember 1972), *War Heroes* (Polydor 1972), *Loose Ends* (Polydor 1974), *Crash Landing* (Polydor 1975), *Midnight Lightnin'* (Polydor 1975), *Nine To The Universe* (Polydor 1980), *The Jimi Hendrix Concerts* (CBS 1982), *Jimi Plays Monterey* (Polydor 1986), *Band Of Gypsies* (Polydor 1986), *Live At Winterland* (Polydor 1987), *Radio One* (Castle 1988), *Live And Unreleased* (Castle 1989). Compilations: *Smash Hits* (Track 1968), *The Essential Jimi Hendrix* (Polydor 1978), *The Essential Jimi Hendrix Volume Two* (Polydor 1979), *The Singles Album* (Polydor 1983), *Kiss The Sky* (Polydor 1984), *Cornerstones* (Polydor 1990), *Blues* (Polydor 1994). Videos: *Experience* (1987), *Jimi Plays Monterey*

(1986), *Isle Of Wight* (1989), *Rainbow Bridge* (1988), *Jimi Hendrix* (1994).

Further reading: *Hendrix - A Biography*, Chris Welch. *Jimi - An Intimate Biography Of Jimi Hendrix*, Curtis Knight. *Jimi Hendrix - Voodoo Child Of The Aquarian Age*, David Henderson. *Crosstown Traffic/Jimi Hendrix And Post-War Pop*, Charles Shaar Murray. *Jimi Hendrix - Electric Gypsy*, Harry Shapiro and Caesar Glebbeek. *The Hendrix Experience*, Mitch Mitchell and John Platt. *Are You Experienced*, Noel Redding and Carol Appleby, *In His Own Words*, Tony Brown.

Heretic

Formed in 1984 in Los Angeles, California, USA, the band's original line-up consisted of Julian Mendez (vocals), Brian Korban (guitar), Bobby Marquez (guitar), Dennis O'Hara (bass) and Rick Merrick (drums). Quickly gaining popularity on the club circuit in and around the Los Angeles area, the band attracted the attention of Metal Blade Records. Heretic's debut release for the label was a mini-album, *Torture Knows No Boundaries*, in 1987. This was a worthwhile serving of fast power metal, slightly marred because Julian Mendez's vocals were not really suited to the band's hard-hitting approach. To his credit the singer realized this and left the band, to be replaced by Mike Howe later the same year. On their second outing, the full-length *Breaking Point*, they sounded much more confident. However, when Howe left the band later that year to join Metal Church, a series of vocal replacements could not prevent Heretic folding in 1989.

Albums: *Torture Knows No Boundaries* (Metal Blade 1987, mini-album), *Breaking Point* (Metal Blade 1988).

Hirax

Hirax first formed in Los Angeles, California, USA, in 1984 - the band's original line-up consisting of Katon W. De Pena (vocals), Scott Owen (guitar), Gary Monardo (bass) and John Tabares (drums). Their promising demos attracted the attention of Metal Blade who included one of the band's tracks on the *Metal Massacre VI* compilation album, released in 1985. A debut album, *Raging Violence*, was released for the same label in 1985. Full of short and ultra-fast thrash metal, it hardly offered anything new. Shortly after its release Tabares left the band to be replaced by ex-DRI percussionist Eric Brecht. Their next release was a mini-album, *Hate, Fear And Power*, released in 1986. The material on offer was in the same vein as before but the production this time around had improved greatly. However, due to internal band

wrangles vocalist Katon W. De Pena left to be replaced by ex-Exodus vocalist Paul Baloff. He, in turn, did not stay long before being replaced himself by Billy Wedgeworth. Unable to maintain a stable line-up, the band folded after recording several further demos in 1988.

Albums: *Raging Violence* (Metal Blade 1985), *Hate, Fear And Power* (Metal Blade 1986).

Hole

US hardcore guitar band fronted by the effervescent Courtney Love (b. 1965, though this is a date some dispute; vocals/guitar). An ex-stripper and actress, who had small roles in Alex Cox's *Sid And Nancy* and *Straight To Hell*, she was born to hippy parents (including Grateful Dead associate Hank Harrison and Oregon therapist Linda Carroll) and even attended Woodstock as a baby. She spent the rest of her childhood years at boarding schools in England and New Zealand, where her parents had bought a sheep farm, before travelling around the world in her teens. She spent some time in San Francisco, joining ill-fated line-ups of Sugar Baby Doll (with L7's Jenifer Finch and Kat Bjelland, also participating in a formative line-up of the latter's Babes In Toyland). Returning to Los Angeles, Love appeared for a while as vocalist with Faith No More in an incarnation which only reached the rehearsal stage. Still in LA, she formed Hole with Caroline Rue (drums), Jill Emery (bass) and Eric Erlandson (guitar), following the suggestion of Sonic Youth's Kim Gordon. The band quickly produced a trio of fine singles; 'Retard Girl', 'Dicknail', and 'Teenage Whore', which were pointed and unsettling dirges, set in a grimly sexual lyrical environment. Favourable UK press coverage, in particular from the *Melody Maker*'s resident sycophant Everett True, helped make Hole one of the most promising new groups of 1991. Equally impressive was a debut album, produced by Don Fleming (Gumball etc.) and Kim Gordon (Sonic Youth), followed by massive exposure supporting Mudhoney throughout Europe. It was on this jaunt that Courtney achieved further notoriety by being the first woman musician to 'trash' her guitar on stage in the UK. In March 1992 Love married Nirvana singer/guitarist Kurt Cobain. That same month bassist Emery departed from the group line-up, with Rue following in short order. Love's domestic travails would continue to dominate coverage of her musical project, with Cobain's death on the eve of the release of *Live Through This* practically obliterating that album's impact. Which served to do the much-maligned Love a genuine disservice: this was another startling collection of songs written with intellect as well as invective. It included 'I Think That I Would Die', co-written with old friend and sparring partner Kat Bjelland, as well as a cover of the Young Marble Giants' 'Credit In The Straight World'. Replacements for Emery and Rue had been found in Kristen Pfaff (bass) and Patty Schemel (drums), though tragedy again followed Love when Pfaff was found dead from a heroin overdose in her bathtub, shortly after the album's release, and just two months after Cobain's death. Pfaff would be replaced by Melissa Auf Der Maur for Hole's 1994 tour

Albums: *Pretty On The Inside* (City Slang 1991), *Live Through This* (Geffen 1994).

Holocaust

Holocaust were formed in Edinburgh, Scotland, in 1978. The original line-up consisted of Gary Lettice (vocals), John Mortimer (guitar), Edward Dudley (guitar), Robin Begg (bass) and Paul Collins (drums). They were quickly signed by small independent, Phoenix Records, who released the band's debut single, 'Heavy Metal Mania', in 1980. The band's long playing debut, *The Nightcomers*, arrived a year later. The material on offer was basic hard rock fuelled by the enthusiasm that the New Wave Of British Heavy Metal had fired. It was to prove a very influential release, Metallica later covering one of its tracks on their *Garage Days Revisited* E.P. Come 1982 and the release of Holocaust's second single, 'Coming Through', the band was falling apart. A posthumous live album appeared in 1983, again on the Phoenix Records label, entitled *Live, Hot Curry & Wine*. Guitarist Edward Dudley left to form Hologram (who recorded one album, also for Phoenix, entitled *Steal The Stars*, in 1982). Hologram, however, proved short-lived as Holocaust reformed to release a third album, *No Mans Land*, in 1984. Soon after its release the band folded again. With the resurgence of interest in the N.W.O.B.H.M. bands (primarily owing to Metallica cover versions), the band started working together again in 1989.

Albums: *The Nightcomers* (Phoenix 1981), *Live, Hot Curry & Wine* (Phoenix 1983), *No Mans Land* (Phoenix 1984), *The Land Of Souls* (Chrome 1990), *Hypnosis Of Birds* (1993).

House Of Lords

This five-piece US heavy rock supergroup was put together by ex-Angel keyboardist Gregg Giuffria. Augmented by bassist Chuck Wright (ex-Quiet Riot), drummer Ken Mary (ex-Alice Cooper), vocalist James Christian (ex-Canata) and guitarist Lanny Cordola (ex-Giuffria) the line-up was impressive and promised much. With Giuffria in control, the band pursued an overstated melodic approach with swathes of keyboards, multi-phased harmonies and atmospheric arrangements redolent of mid-70s arena rock. Signing to RCA Records, their self-titled debut was recorded with the help of Andy Johns and long-time friend Gene Simmons (Kiss bassist) at the production desk. The result was well received, a state-of-the-art pomp-rock album with a powerful and sparkling sound. Apart from a few support slots on the Scorpions' European tour, the band did not commit themselves to touring in the way that was needed to stimulate album sales. Lanny Cordola quit as a result and was replaced by Michael Guy (ex-Fire) before the band entered the studio again. *Sahara* continued in the same musical vein, but the interest it generated (the album would go platinum) was once again allowed to ebb away as the band was still reluctant to tour. Guests included David Glen Eisley, the original Giuffria vocalist whom Simmons had advised they replace prior to them becoming House Of Lords. They split shortly thereafter, though they did reform to record a new album for the Japanese market.

Albums: *House Of Lords* (RCA 1988), *Sahara* (RCA 1990).

Howe II

After recording a solo instrumental album in 1988, guitarist Greg Howe decided to expand his musical horizons and incorporate his talents within a band framework. Brother Al stepped in as vocalist, with Vern Parsons and Joe Nevolo taking on bass and drum duties respectively. Released in 1989, their debut album was a highly accomplished work that combined elements of Van Halen and Rising Force; Al Howe's vocals were reminiscent of vintage Dave Lee Roth, while Greg's guitar style was not far removed from that of the Swedish guitarist, Yngwie Malmsteen. Their second album built on these solid foundations, but featured more melodic compositions.

Albums: *High Gear* (Roadrunner 1989), *Now Hear This* (Roadrunner 1991).

HSAS

This US group was formed in the early part of 1984 by Sammy Hagar (vocals) and Neil Schon (guitar). Both are from the San Francisco area and had planned a collaboration for some time. So when Hagar had finished promoting his latest solo record and Neil Schon had completed touring with Journey, HSAS was formed. They brought in Peter Schrieve (drums) and Kenny Aaronson (bass), primarily because they shared the same management. They wrote approximately 15 songs during one month and then decided to tour with the set. It was while they were on the road that they decided to record two dates in their hometown of San Francisco for their debut album, rather than in the studio. A deal was struck with Sammy Hagar's label, Geffen and *Through The Fire* was prepared for release. The only problem was that American radio was resistant to live records, so most of the crowd noise was taken out of the final mix, with the exception of two tracks where the audience actually participated in the songs. Because it was a Hagan/Schon project, it was never a permanent band so after the album's release, Sammy Hagar returned to his solo career and Neil Schon went back to Journey. Album: *Through The Fire* (Geffen 1984).

Hughes, Glenn

Glenn Hughes (b. 21 August 1952, Crannock, Staffordshire, England) quit school at the age of 15 to follow his dream of becoming a musician. He began playing lead guitar with the News in 1967, where he also sang, emulating his heroes Otis Redding and Wilson Pickett. Later he switched to bass guitar inspired by James Jamerson from the Tamla Motown 'house band'. These influences, added to a love of rock 'n' roll, led him to form Trapeze with Dave Holland (drums) and Mei Galley (guitar). Trapeze signed to the Moody Blues record label, Threshold, and released four albums up to 1973, when Hughes was offered a job with Birmingham band Electric Light Orchestra. He declined and in June joined Deep Purple instead. It is with Purple that Hughes made his mark in the UK with his superb singing on *Burn*, where he joined with, and some believe outclassed, their new vocalist David Coverdale. Hughes' influence over Purple became a contributing factor in Ritchie Blackmore deciding to quit, and his association with the band continued until 1976 when he reformed Trapeze with the original line-up, though this venture failed to tour or record. When they did finally begin a US tour Hughes walked out half way through. The band continued without him while their leader disappeared from public view. Two years later he surfaced with a solo album before again dropping out of sight. 1982 saw him join with Pat Thrall (guitar; ex-Pat Travers Band) and Quiet Riot drummer Frankie Banali to form Hughes/Thrall, who released one album to a poor reception (though this set would posthumously achieve 'legendary' status and become one of the most sought after rock albums of the 80s). After the project fell apart Hughes worked for a while with Gary Moore but nothing came of it. Then in 1985 he reunited with Mel Galley and a host of stars to record the concept album, *Phenomena*. Though considered obsolete by rock critics it did serve to put Hughes back on the map and Tony Iommi, looking for a replacement for Ian Gillan in Black Sabbath, contacted him. Hughes spent less than a year with the band but did record some fine vocals for *Seventh Star*. He then sank back into obscurity and personal problems but help from an unusual quarter was at hand. Bill Drummond of the KLF had always enjoyed the idea of blending rock with dance music (he had already obtained infamy in such matters with Extreme Noise Terror) so he coaxed Hughes back into the limelight in 1991 for the hit single, 'America - What Time Is Love?'. This success reanimated the vocalist's efforts and he set about forming a new band which has since enjoyed a small degree of concert success, and he has also renewed his partnership with Pat Thrall for a projected second album. A new band, World, was put together in 1993.

Albums: With Trapeze: *Trapeze* (Threshold 1970), *Medusa* (Threshold 1970), *You Are The Music...We're Just The Band* (Threshold 1972), *Final Swing* (Threshold 1973). With Deep Purple: *Burn* (Purple 1974), *Stormbringer* (Purple 1974), *Come Taste The Band* (Purple 1975), *Made In Europe* (Purple 1976). With Jon Lord: *Windows* (Purple 1974). With Roger Glover: *The Butterfly Ball* (Purple 1974). With Wizards Convention: *Wizards Convention* (RCA 1976). As Glenn Hughes: *Play Me Out* (Safari 1978). As Hughes/Thrall: *Hughes/Thrall* (Epic 1982). With Phenomena: *Phenomena* (Bronze 1985). With Black Sabbath: *Seventh Star* (Vertigo 1986).

Hunter, Ian

b. 3 June 1946, Shrewsbury, Shropshire, England. Having served a musical apprenticeship in several contrasting groups, Hunter was employed as a contract songwriter when approached to audition for a new act recently signed by Island Records. Initially known as Silence, the band took the name Mott The Hoople on his installation and Hunter's gravelly vocals and image-conscious looks - omnipresent dark glasses framed by long Dylanesque curly hair - established the vocalist/pianist as the group's focal point. He remained their driving force until 1974 when, having collapsed from physical exhaustion, he left the now-fractious line-up to begin a career as a solo artist. Late-period Mott guitarist Mick Ronson quit at the same time and the pair agreed to pool resources for particular projects. Ronson produced and played on *Ian Hunter*, which contained the singer's sole UK hit, 'Once Bitten Twice Shy'. Having toured together as Hunter/Ronson with Peter Arnesen (keyboards), Jeff Appleby (bass) and Dennis Elliott (drums), the colleagues embarked on separate paths. *All American Alien Boy* contained contributions from Aynsley Dunbar, David Sanborn and several members of Queen, but despite several promising tracks, the set lacked the artist's erstwhile passion. *Overnight Angels* continued this trend towards musical conservatism, although Hunter aligned himself with the punk movement following a period of seclusion by producing *Beyond The Valley Of The Dolls* for Generation X. *You're Never Alone With A Schizophrenic* marked his reunion with Ronson and subsequent live dates were commemorated on *Ian Hunter Live/Welcome To The Club* which drew material from their respective careers. Hunter's output during the 80s was mimimal, occasionally recording the odd song for film soundtracks and in 1990 he resumed his partnership with Mick Ronson on *YUI Otra*. Although he made an appearance at the 1992 Freddy Mercury Aids benefit, Hunter's reputation rests firmly on his contributions to 70s rock.

Albums: *Ian Hunter* (CBS 1975), *All American Alien Boy* (CBS 1976), *Overnight Angels* (CBS 1977), *You're Never Alone With A Schizophrenic* (Chrysalis 1979), *Ian Hunter Live/Welcome To The Club* (Chrysalis 1980, double album), *Short Back And Sides* (Chrysalis 1981), *All Of The Good Ones Are Taken* (Chrysalis 1983). With Mick Ronson *YUI Orta* (Mercury 1990). Compilation: *Shades Of Ian Hunter* (CBS 1979), *The Collection* (Castle 1991), *The Very Best Of* (CBS 1991).

Further reading: *Diary Of A Rock 'N' Roll Star*, Ian Hunter.

Hurricane

Formed in Los Angeles, California, USA, in 1983, this heavy metal band's original line-up consisted of Kelly Hanson (vocals), Robert Sarzo (guitar), Tony Cavazo (bass) and Jay Schellen (drums). Robert Sarzo is the brother of Whitesnake bassist Rudy Sarzo and Tony Cavazo is the brother of Quiet Riot guitarist Carlos Cavazo. Hurricane arrived via a mini-album released in 1986, entitled *Take What You Want*, on Roadrunner Records. It was a fine debut featuring hard-edged melodic rockers. The band then switched labels, signing to Enigma Records and releasing *Over The Edge*. It failed to sell and during 1989 Robert Sarzo left the band to be replaced by ex-Lion guitarist Doug Aldrich. This line-up went on to record the much improved *Slave To The Thrill*, released in 1990 to critical acclaim, followed by an ominous silence.

Albums: *Take What You Want* (Roadrunner 1986, mini-album), *Over The Edge* (Enigma 1988), *Slave To The Thrill* (Enigma 1990).

Hyperhead

When Gaye Bykers On Acid split, frontman Mary Mary (previously known as Mary Byker, though his real name is Ian Garfield Hoxley) began following a different musical path, working with the experimental industrial collective Pigface before forming Hyperhead with a long-time friend, American bassist Karl Leiker. Pigface colleagues Martin Atkins (drums, ex-PiL, Killing Joke) and guitarist William Tucker (My Life With The Thrill Kill Kult, Revolting Cocks) contributed along with guitarist Paul Dalloway to *Metaphasia*, showcasing an unpredictable hybrid style which drew from hard rock, soul, funk, indie pop and industrial for a diverse and interesting album. Mary, Leiker and Dalloway put together a touring band with guitarist Oscar, drummer Chin and percussionist Keith, and this line-up recorded the *Terminal Fear* EP, which actually preceded *Metaphasia*'s release. Hyperhead established an excellent live reputation, boosted by Keith's sometimes crazed behaviour on stage which added to the band's unpredictable air.

Album: *Metaphasia* (Devotion 1993).

Hypocrisy

One of Sweden's more extreme metal concerns, combining a musical intensity that borders on spite and unremittingly dark and violent lyrics. Comprising Peter Tägtgren (vocals/guitar and keyboards), Michael Hedlund (drums) and Lars Szöke (drums), their reputation was formed with the intimidating *Osculum Obscenum* and European tours with labelmates Brutality. Forthright exponents of black metal, the group's exposition of the mystical and diabolical was conveyed in tracks like 'Orgy In Blood' and 'The Arrival Of The Demons' on their 1994 opus, *Fourth Dimension*. This saw the trio concentrate on generating the maximum possible power from their riffs, sacrificing some velocity in the process. However, generally superior songwriting (particularly the title-track and 'Apocalypse') saw to it that they lost nothing in impact.

Albums: *Osculum Obscenum* (Nuclear Blast 1993), *Fourth Dimension* (Nuclear Blast 1994).

Hypocrisy

Icon

Heavy metal group formed in Phoenix, Arizona, USA, in 1981, by school friends Dan Wexler (guitar), Tracy Wallach (bass/backing vocals) and Stephen Clifford (lead vocals). Drummer Pat Dixon and John Aquilino (guitar) joined a couple of months later. Icon spent their first three years playing local bars and recording demo tapes, originally titled Schoolboys. Mike Varney heard the band and signed them to his Shrapnel label, soon after which Icon went into the studio to record their first album with Varney and Dan Wexler producing. After the sessions were finished Varney realized that he had a commercial record on his hands, and sold Icon's contract to Capitol Records. In late 1984 *Icon* was released, a dynamic record in the Don Dokken tradition of melodic heavy metal. Brushing poor sales aside Icon re-entered the studio in 1985 with producer Eddie Kramer to record the follow-up, *Night Of The Crime*. Capitol dropped them from their roster following a further disappointing sales curve and Icon returned to Phoenix. At this point Clifford, who had become a born again Christian, was replaced by Jerry Harrison. In 1987 Icon released a cassette album, which was only sold locally. Two years later Johnny Zazula heard the tape and signed them to his Megaforce label, which had just negotiated a worldwide distribution deal with Atlantic Records. In the middle of 1989 Icon were about to start recording when Aquilino left the band. His replacement was Drew Bollmann, a Phoenix native. With Dan Wexler again producing, *Right Between The Eyes* saw Icon come up with their best record yet - again in their familiar AOR/melodic heavy rock vein - with Alice Cooper guesting on two tracks. However, this was not to be Icon's triumphant return. After a short UK tour Dan Wexler announced their break-up.
Albums: *Icon* (Capitol 1984), *Night Of The Crime* (Capitol 1985), *A More Perfect Union* (Icon 1987; cassette only), *Right Between The Eyes* (Megaforce 1989).

Impelliteri, Chris

Impelliteri is one of the new-age guitarists influenced by a combination of rock and classical music styles. Utilizing a high-speed fretboard technique, his cramming of as many notes as possible into the shortest time-span is his most distinguishing feature. Moving to Los Angeles in 1986, he first recorded a self-financed mini-album of up-tempo instrumentals. The following year he formed Impelliteri, which featured vocalist Graham Bonnet (ex-MSG and Rainbow), drummer Pat Torpey (ex-Ted Nugent), bassist Chuck Wright (ex-Quiet Riot) and keyboardist Phil Wolfe. Together they recorded the stunning hard rock album, *Stand In Line*. Although it provoked unjust accusations of plàgiarism from Rainbow devotees, the music was powerful, exciting and melodic. The band disintegrated soon after the album's release; Chuck Wright joined House Of Lords and Pat Torpey teamed up with Mr. Big. Impelliteri himself would join forces with ex-Dio keyboard player Claude Schnell and vocalist Mark Weisz in 1990.
Albums: *Impelliteri* (Polytour 1986). As Impelliteri: *Stand in Line* (Music For Nations 1988).

Incubus Succubus

Incubus Succubus are a Cheltenham based rock band with strong English folk and gothic punk influences. Most of their lyrics revolve around one of two themes - vampirism and the pagan faith of Wicca. The vampiric strand accounts for much of their gothic feel. It is Wicca, however, which dominates their material, with its continuation of the Medieval witchcraft tradition of pre-Christian hunting gods and moon goddesses. Their Wiccan beliefs have attracted a strong following in the UK's pagan subculture, though his has yet to translate into mainstream success. The band (originally known as Children Of The Moon) has had a fluctuating line-up, but the core remains Tony McCormick (ex-Screaming Dead; guitars) and Candia (vocals).
Albums: *Beltaine* (Nightbreed 1992), *Belladonna and Aconite* (Nightbreed 1992), *Wytches* (Pagan Media 1994).

Infectious Grooves

This heavy funk-rock band was put together by the Suicidal Tendencies duo of vocalist Mike Muir and hugely talented bassist Robert Trujillo with guitarists Adam Siegel (from Excel) and Dean Pleasants and ex-Jane's Addiction drummer Stephen Perkins. The band was deemed more than a side project for Muir and Trujillo, given equal status with Suicidal, and the two bands often toured together, necessitating two exhausting sets per night for the pair. The debut established an entirely different groove from the parent band with a heavy, Red Hot Chilli Peppers-style funk attack, with Muir for once producing lighter lyrical fare, and stand-out track 'Therapy' featured guest backing vocals from Ozzy Osbourne, punctuating Muir's vocals with gleeful, manic roars of the title over furious riffing and a potent Trujillo-Perkins rhythm. Perkins left for Porno For Pyros the following year, and Josh Freese stepped in on *Sarsippius' Ark*, an odd collection of previously unreleased songs, live takes, covers and new numbers, with spoken interjections from a 'Sarsippius' character. *Groove Family Cyco* was a more conventional set of all-new material in the same hard funk vein, with Muir taking a satirical lyrical swipe at Rage Against The Machine on 'Do What I Tell Ya!', while adopting his more customary serious lyrical slant. With the break-up of Suicidal in early 1995, it seems likely that more time may be devoted to Infectious Grooves, although the industrious Muir has also formed a punk band, My Head, with Siegel.

Albums: *The Plague That Makes Your Booty Move...It's The Infectious Grooves* (Epic 1991), *Sarsippius' Ark* (Epic 1993), *Groove Family Cyco* (Epic 1994).

Inner City Unit

The weird and wonderful Inner City Unit were put together by Oxford-born English eccentric Nik Turner (saxophone/vocals) in 1979, along with Trev Thoms (guitar), Dead Fred Reeves (keyboards), Baz Magneto (bass) and Mick Stupp (drums). Nik's first non Hawkwind album was with Steve Hillage in 1977, entitled *Sphynx (Xitintoday)* - a set far removed from the punk sound then prevalent, which would become a major influence on Inner City Unit. A debut album, *Pass Out*, and two singles, 'Solitary Ashtray' and 'Paradise Beach', all appeared on his own Riddle label. In 1981 he moved the band to Avatar for *The Maximum Effect*, which also featured Captain Sensible and comedian Max Wall. Magneto reverted to his real name of Barry Downes to join Weapon and was replaced by Reeves who doubled up on bass and keyboards. The next album, *Punkadelic*, featured reworkings of earlier tracks, but soon after Nik rejoined Hawkwind. In 1984 Turner reformed Inner City Unit with Steve Pond replacing Stupp. Their first album together, *New Anatomy*, produced two firsts. It was the first album on ex-Hawkwind bassist Dave Anderson's new record label, Demi-Monde, and it was also the first album to feature a computer programme on vinyl for the Spectrum system. Inner City Unit then recorded the *Blood And Bone* 12-inch EP and backed it with a video which included the surreal 'Little Black Egg' and a guest appearance from Robert Calvert. A final album, *The Presidents Tapes*, was received with mass indifference and the band folded. Thoms then formed the Atom Gods and Turner the Fantastic All Stars, before journeying to

the US in 1993 and recording with Pressurehead. He has since worked on new projects with members of Psychic TV.

Albums: *Pass Out* (Riddle 1980), *The Maximum Effect* (Avatar 1981), *Punkadelic* (Flicknife), *New Anatomy* (Demi-Monde 1984), *The Presidents Tapes* (Flicknife 1985).

Video: *Blood And Bone* (1985).

Inner Sanctum

Formed in late 1979, Inner Sanctum surfaced at the time of the N.W.O.B.H.M. but also predated the rise of Metallica, Anthrax and thrash metal by combining traditional hard rock postures with the dark imagery of Black Sabbath. The group's early material like 'Streets And Alleys' and 'The Butcher' provided a discernible influence on prototype thrash metal bands Hellhammer, Testament and Coroner. Over the years the core membership of Inner Sanctum has remained two sets of brothers: Mick Pendergast (vocals), Rick Pendergast (guitar), Eric Barbasso (bass) and Adam Barbasso (guitar). The position of drummer has never been quite so secure, however. On the debut album percussion chores were completed by Mike Portnoy, now of Dream Theater. Two further drummers have also recorded with the band. *12 a.m.* comprised a selection of the 28 tracks the band had been perfecting since their formation, and was re-released as an 'undiscovered classic' by Rock The Nation Records in 1994.

Albums: *12 a.m.* (1985), *Revenge* (1986), *R.I.P. - Live* (1988).

Intrinsic

This California power metal quintet formed in 1983 with guitarists Mike Mellinger and Ron Crawford settling on the rhythm section of Joel Stern (bass) and Chris Binns (drums) in late 1984, with vocalist Garrett Graupner joining the following year. The band refined their fast, Iron Maiden-influenced style around the club scene, playing support slots with the likes of Megadeth and Armored Saint in San Francisco while conversely opening for glam bands in Los Angeles, before releasing *Intrinsic* to enormous critical acclaim. However, the band were held back while they searched for a new vocalist, with Graupner having departed by mutual consent, as both parties felt that his bluesy tones were unsuited to Intrinsic's more aggressive material. David Wayne (ex-Metal Church) stepped in as the band signed a deal with Important Records, who re-released the debut, but was ousted after only five live shows, and the band's continuing search for a vocalist prevented them capitalizing on their good press. A self-financed EP followed, demonstrating again the band's sophisticated guitar work but not quite reaching the heights of the debut, but no new deal ensued, and Intrinsic continued to shop their power demos around record labels.

Albums: *Intrinsic* (No Wimp 1987), *Distortion Of Perspective* (Cheese Flag 1991, mini-album).

Iron Butterfly

During the progressive music revolution in the late 60s one of the most surprising successes was that of Iron Butterfly. The band was formed by Doug Ingle (b. 9 September 1947, Omaha, Nebraska, USA; organ/vocals) who added Ron Bushy (b. 23 September 1941, Washington DC, USA; drums), Eric Brann (b. 10 August 1950, Boston, Massachusetts, USA; guitar), Lee Dorman (b. 19 September 1945, St. Louis, Missouri, USA; bass/vocals) and, briefly, Danny Weiss. Together they were arguably the first to amalgamate the terms 'heavy' and 'rock', following the release of their debut in 1968. Their second effort, *In-A-Gadda-Da-Vida* (In The Garden Of Eden), became a multi-million seller and was for a number of years the biggest selling item in Atlantic Records' catalogue. The album also became the record industy's first 'Platinum' disc. The 17-minute title-track contained everything a progressive rock fan could want - neo-classical organ with Far East undertones, a solid beat, screeching guitar parts, barbed-wire feedback and an overlong drum solo. Magnificently overwrought at the time, the intervening years have been less kind to its standing. The follow-up, *Ball*, was a lesser success, despite containing a better collection of songs, notably the invigorating 'It Must Be Love' and more subtle 'Soul Experience'. Brann departed after a poor live album and was replaced by two guitarists: Larry 'Rhino' Reinhardt (b. 7 July 1948, Florida, USA) and Mike Pinera (b. 29 September 1948, Florida, USA; ex-Cactus, Alice Cooper). No further success ensued. *Metamorphosis* was a confused collection recorded when the band was disintegrating. They reformed in the mid-70s with two disappointing albums but Iron Butterfly ultimately suffered from an identity crisis. Another reformation, this time in 1992, was masterminded by Mike Pinera. A new version of 'In-A-Gadda-da-Vida' was recorded and Pinera recruited Dorman and Bushy for extensive touring in the USA. By 1993 their legendary second album had sold an astonishing 25 million copies.

Albums: *Heavy* (Atco 1968), *In-A-Gadda-da-Vida* (Atco 1968), *Ball* (Atco 1969), *Iron Butterfly Live* (Atco 1970), *Metamorphosis* (Atco 1970), *Scorching Beauty* (MCA 1975), *Sun And Steel* (MCA 1976).

Compilations: *Evolution* (Atco 1971), *Star Collection* (1973), *Light And Heavy: The Best Of* (1993).

Iron Maiden

Formed in London, England, in 1976, Iron Maiden was from the start the brainchild of Steve Harris (b. 12 March 1957, Leytonstone, London, England; bass), formerly a member of pub rockers Smiler. Named after a medieval torture device, the music was suitably heavy and hard on the senses. The heavy metal scene of the late 70s was widely regarded as stagnant, with only a handful of bands proving their ability to survive and produce music of quality. It was just at this time that a new breed of young British bands began to emerge. This movement, which began to break cover in 1979 and 1980, was known as the New Wave Of British Heavy Metal, or N.W.O.B.H.M.. Iron Maiden were one of the foremost bands in the genre, and many would say its definitive example. Younger and meaner, the N.W.O.B.H.M. bands dealt in faster, more energetic heavy metal than any of their forefathers (punk being an obvious influence). There were several line-up changes in the Iron Maiden ranks in the very early days, and come the release of their debut EP, the group featured Harris, Dave Murray (b. 23 December 1958, London, England; guitar), Paul Di'anno (b. 17 May 1959, Chingford, London, England; vocals) and Doug Sampson (drums). The group made its live debut at the Cart & Horses Pub in Stratford, London, in 1977, before honing its sound on the local pub circuit over the ensuing two years. Unable to solicit a response from record companies, the group sent a three track tape, featuring 'Iron Maiden', 'Prowler' and 'Strange World', to Neal Kay, DJ at North London's hard rock disco, the Kingsbury Bandwagon Soundhouse. Kay's patronage of Iron Maiden won them an instant welcome, which translated itself finally into the release of *The Soundhouse Tapes* on the band's own label. November 1979 saw the group add second guitarist Tony Parsons to the line-up for two tracks on the *Metal For Muthas* compilation, but by the time the group embarked on sessions for their debut album, he had been replaced by Dennis Stratton (b. 9 November 1954, London, England), and Sampson by Clive Burr (b. 8 March 1957; drums). A promotional single, 'Running Free', would hit number 34 on the UK charts and brought an appearance on BBC programme *Top Of The Pops*. Refusing to mime, they became the first band since the Who in 1973 to play live on the show. *Iron Maiden* was a roughly produced album, but reached number 4 in the UK album listings on the back of touring stints with Judas Priest and enduringly popular material such as 'Phantom Of The Opera'. *Killers* boasted production superior to that of the first album, and saw Dennis Stratton replaced by guitarist Adrian Smith (b. 27 February 1957). In its wake Iron Maiden became immensely popular among heavy metal fans, inspiring fanatical devotion, aided by blustering manager Rod Smallwood and apocalyptic mascot Eddie (the latter had been depicted on the cover of 'Sanctuary' standing over PM Margaret Thatcher's decapitated body).

The release of *Number Of The Beast* was crucial to the development of the band. Without it, Iron Maiden might never have gone on to be such a force in the heavy metal arena. The album was a spectacular success, the sound of a band on the crest of a wave. It was also the debut of former infrantryman and new vocalist Bruce Dickinson (b. Paul Bruce Dickinson, 7 August 1958, Worksop, Nottinghamshire, England) replacing Paul Di'anno (who would go on to front Lone Wolf, Battlezone and Killers). Formerly of Samson, history graduate Dickinson would make his live debut with Maiden on 15 November 1981. Singles such as 'Run To The Hills' and 'The Number Of The Beast' were big UK chart hits, Iron Maiden

leaving behind their N.W.O.B.H.M. counterparts in terms of success, just as the movement itself was beginning to peter out. *Piece Of Mind* continued their success and was a major hit in the USA (number 14). Clive Burr was replaced by Nicko McBrain on the sessions, formerly drummer with French metal band Trust, who had supported Maiden on their 1981 UK tour (he had also played in Streetwalkers). *Piece Of Mind* was not dissimilar to the previous album, showcasing the strong twin guitar bite of Murray and Smith, coupled with memorable vocal lines and a sound which fitted their air-punching dynamic perfectly. Single offerings, 'Flight of Icarus' and 'The Trooper', were instant hits, as the group undertook two massive tours, the four month *World Piece* jaunt in 1983, and a *World Slavery* retinue which included four sellout dates at London's Hammersmith Odeon a year later. With the arrival of *Powerslave* in November some critics accused Iron Maiden of conforming to a self-imposed writing formula, and playing safe with tried and tested ideas. Certainly, there was no significant departure from the two previous albums, but it was nonetheless happily consumed by the band's core supporters, who also

Iron Maiden

purchased in sufficient quantities to ensure UK chart hits for 'Aces High' and 'Two Minutes To Midnight'. *Live After Death* was a double album package of all their best-loved material recorded live on their gargantuan 11 month world tour. By this time Iron Maiden had secured themselves an unassailable position within the metal hierachy, their vast popularity spanning all continents. *Somewhere In Time* was a slight departure. It featured more melody than before, and heralded the use of guitar synthesizers. Their songwriting still shone through and the now obligatory hit singles were easily attained in the shape of 'Wasted Years' and 'Stranger In A Strange Land'. Reaching number 11 in the US, this was another million plus seller. Since the mid-80s Maiden had been staging increasingly spectacular live shows, with elaborate lighting effects and stage sets. The *Somewhere In Time* tour (seven months) was no exception, ensuring their continued status as a live band, which had been the basis for much of their success. A period of comparitive inactivity preceded the release of *Seventh Son Of A Seventh Son,* which was very much in the same vein as its predecessor. A concept album, it still retained its commercial edge and yielded hit singles in 'Can I Play With Madness', the surprisingly sensitive 'Evil That Men Do' and 'The Clairvoyant'.

After another exhausting mammoth world trek, the band announced their intention to take a well-earned break of at least a year. Speculation abounded that this meant the dissolution of the band, exacerbated by Dickinson's solo project, *Tattooed Millionaire*, his book, *The Adventures Of Lord Iffy Boatrace*, and EMI's policy of re-releasing Maiden's single catalogue in its entirety (on 12-inch). After a considerable hiatus, news of the band surfaced again. Steve Harris felt that the direction pursued with the last two albums had been taken as far as was possible, and a return to the style of old was planned. Not wishing to pursue this game plan, Adrian Smith left to be replaced by Janick Gers (b. Hartlepool, Lancashire, England), once guitarist with White Spirit and Gillan (he had also contributed to Dickinson's solo release). The live show was also to be scaled down in a return to much smaller venues. *No Prayer For The Dying* was indeed much more like mid-period Iron Maiden, and was predictably well-received, bringing enormous UK hit singles with 'Holy Smoke' and 'Bring Your Daughter To The Slaughter'. The latter, previously released in 1989 on the soundtrack to *A Nightmare On Elm Street 5*, had already been granted the Golden Raspberry Award for Worst Song in that year. Yet it gave Iron Maiden their first ever UK number 1. The obligatory world tour followed. Despite being denounced as

'satanists' in Chile, 1992 also saw the band debut at number 1 in the UK charts with *Fear Of The Dark*, which housed another major single success in 'Be Quick Or Be Dead' (number 2). However, it was to be Dickinson's swan song with the band, who invited demo tapes to be sent to them following his announcement that he would permanently depart following current touring engagements. His eventual replacement would be Blaze Bayley from Wolfsbane.
Albums: *Iron Maiden* (EMI 1980), *Killers* (EMI 1981), *Number Of The Beast* (EMI 1982), *Piece Of Mind* (EMI 1983), *Powerslave* (EMI 1984), *Live After Death* (EMI 1985), *Somewhere In Time* (EMI 1986), *Seventh Son Of A Seventh Son* (EMI 1988), *No Prayer For The Dying* (EMI 1990), *Fear Of The Dark* (EMI 1992), *A Real Live One (Volume One)* (EMI 1993), *A Real Dead One* (EMI 1993), *Live At Donington '92* (EMI 1993).
Videos: *Live At The Rainbow* (1984), *Behind The Iron Curtain Video EP* (1986), *Live After Death* (1986), *Run To The Hills* (1987), *Twelve Wasted Years* (1987), *Maiden England* (1989), *First Ten Years (The Videos)* (1990).
Further reading: *Running Free: The Official Story Of Iron Maiden*, Garry Bushell & Ross Halfin (1985), *A Photographic History*, Ross Halfin (1988).

Ironhorse

This US group was founded by Randy Bachman, formerly the leader of the Canadian rock group Bachman Turner Overdrive. The initial line-up comprised Bachman (guitar/vocals), John Pierce (bass), Tom Sparks (guitar/vocals) and Mike Baird (drums). They scored a US Top 40 hit in 1979 with 'Sweet Lui-Louise' and by the time the second album was recorded, the line-up had undergone a few alterations with Ron Foos and Chris Leighton replacing Pierce and Baird respectively. This largely undistinguished outfit were to record one further album, the title of which summed up the attitude of their critics.
Albums: *Ironhorse* (Scotti Bros 1979), *Everything Is Grey* (Scotti Bros 1980).

J

Jackyl

This Atlanta, Georgia-based band were formed in 1990 by larger-than-life frontman Jesse James

Dupree, guitarists Jeff Worley and Jimmy Stiff, bassist Tom Bettini and drummer Chris Worley. The band created an enormous buzz with a basic AC/DC-ish style which transferred well to the live setting on a heavy touring schedule, and were quickly signed by John Kalodner to Geffen Records. *Jackyl* courted controversy from the start, enraging feminists with the ludicrously-titled 'She Loves My Cock', while Dupree's onstage antics kept the music press busy. During 'The Lumberjack', Dupree soloed on a chainsaw - his father had been so impressed by a club performance with a hired chainsaw that he bought his son a new one - and also regularly indulged his penchant for performing the latter part of the set naked, which resulted in an early departure from a Lynyrd Skynyrd support slot. However, tours with Damn Yankees and in particular Aerosmith proved more successful, and *Jackyl* achieved platinum status against the grunge-loaded odds. *Push Comes To Shove* continued in the vein of the debut, and added to the controversy when an advertising hoarding in Nashville had to be censored (Dupree was displaying his bare buttocks in the band photograph).
Albums: *Jackyl* (Geffen 1992), *Push Comes To Shove* (Geffen 1994).

Jade

The first working unit of Jade was formed in Winnipeg, Canada, in 1982. The original line-up consisted of Roxy Lyons (vocals), Pat Belrose (guitar), Terry Rudd (bass) and Dave Samson (drums). The band initially played on the local club circuit in the absence of a genuine rock scene. They decided to relocate to Ottawa where they quickly struck a one-off album deal with the small independent label, Zaphia Records. Their debut, *Teasing Eyes*, released in 1984, was a mediocre collection of tired pop rock. Realizing their mistake in choice of locale they relocated once again, this time to Toronto, where the rock community was much more active. Following disagreements on personal and professional matters, Lyons left the band to be replaced by ex-Agressor vocalist Sweet Marie Black. The band worked hard on their songwriting, taking a more rocky approach and subsequent demos led to them being signed by the Roadrunner label, who released *If You're Man Enough* in 1985. With more rock and less pop, the album nevertheless failed to attract any interest and the band sank back into obscurity in 1986.
Albums: *Teasing Eyes* (Zaphia 1984), *If You're Man Enough* (Roadrunner 1985).

Jag Panzer

Formed in Colorado, USA, in 1981, the band's original line-up consisted of the curiously-named The Tyrant (vocals), Mark Briody (guitar), John Tetley (bass) and Butch Carlson (drums). Quickly signing to the small independent Azra Records, their debut mini-album, *Jag Panzer*, was released in 1983. Basically a collection of demo tracks, it was a rough and ready affair of straight ahead power-metal inspired rock. The band decided to add an additional guitarist to give them an extra dimension, and with this in mind they decided to relocate to Los Angeles to seek young hopefuls. There they auditioned countless guitarists until Joey Tafolla was finally recruited. With Tafolla in place they promptly headed straight back to Colorado to record their first full-length album, *Ample Destruction*, released in 1984 (it was later re-released in 1990 on the Metalcore label). Unfortunately, the album still only established the band as a strong underground act with minimal cult status. Dissatisfied with this lack of success, Tafolla left the outfit for a solo career and later went on to play in Alice Cooper's touring band. Shortly after his departure both The Tyrant and Carlson also left the band. The Tyrant joined Riot, albeit briefly, before forming his own band, Titan Force. This left Briody and Tetley to pick up the pieces and reform the band. Joining them in this new incarnation of Jag Panzer were Bob Parduba (vocals), Christian Lasage (guitar) and Rikard Stjernqvist (drums). This line-up went on to record an impressive demo that secured them a new recording agreement with Auburn Records in 1987, resulting in *Chain Of Command* being released the same year.
Albums: *Jag Panzer* (Iron Works 1983, mini-album), *Ample Destruction* (Iron Works 1984), *Chain Of Command* (Auburn 1987).

Jagged Edge

This UK based quartet was formed in 1987 by guitarist Myke Gray, one of the few heavy metal musicians who is also a vegetarian. A series of personnel changes ensued before Andy Robbins (bass), Fabio Del Rio (b. Italy; drums) and Matti Alfonzetti (b. Sweden; vocals; ex-Bam Bam Boys) arrived to cement the line-up. Having been picked up by Polydor Records before a singer was even recruited, their debut five-track mini-album was rushed out in 1990. Although it featured some fine guitar work, complemented by Gray and Alfonzetti's spine-tingling vocals, the songs were weak. *Fuel For Your Soul*, released later the same year was in a different class. Intricate solos, power-ballads and hard driving rock 'n' roll combined with a dynamic production by

Jeff Glixman (Kansas etc.) to indicate a band who had come of age. However, it was not be be, with Jagged Edge splitting a year later. Gray and Del Rio would join Bruce Dickinson (Jagged Edge had previously been signed to Iron Maiden's management company, Sanctuary).

Albums: *Trouble* (Polydor 1990, mini-album), *Fuel For Your Soul* (Polydor 1990).

Jaguar

This band was formed in Bristol, England, in 1979, with an original line-up comprising Rob Reiss (vocals), Garry Pepperd (guitar), Jeff Cox (bass) and Chris Lovell (drums). Early demos led to the band having a track included on the *Heavy Metal Heroes* compilation album. The unit subsequently attracted the attention of Neat Records who released two Jaguar singles, 'Back Street Woman' and 'Axe Crazy', in 1981 and 1982 respectively. The band quickly gained popularity with their New Wave Of British Heavy Metal rooted speed metal. The single, 'Axe Crazy', was the first release to feature new vocalist Paul Merrell who replaced Reiss. Merrell's powerful melodic voice was in fine form for the band's debut album, *Powergames*, again released on Neat in 1983. This was well received with excellent vocal and guitar work complementing the high speed power-metal rhythms. The band quickly gained a strong following in Europe, especially in The Netherlands, where they toured extensively. However, this all changed with a drastic shift in musical style on their next album. After switching labels to Roadrunner Records, *This Time* was released in 1984. This saw the band slow down considerably, proffering instead melodic rock, accompanied by the guest keyboards of Larry Dawson. It was an ill-conceived gambit which lost the band a lot of fans. Shortly after its release drummer Lovell was replaced by Gary Davies. Owing to the adverse press reaction the album received, the band folded in 1985.

Albums: *Powergames* (Neat 1983), *This Time* (Roadrunner 1984).

Jane's Addiction

This innovative, art-rock quartet was formed in Los Angeles, USA, in 1986, by vocalist Perry Farrell. He had formerly starred in the Cure-influenced Psi Com, from whose ranks would also emerge Dino Paredes (Red Temple Spirits), while it is rumoured that two former members joined the Hare Krishna sect. With the addition of guitarist David Navarro, bassist Eric A. and drummer Stephen Perkins, Jane's Addiction incorporated elements of punk, rock, folk and funk into a unique and unpredictable soundscape. They debuted with a live album on the independent Triple X label, recorded at Hollywood's Roxy venue, which received widespread critical acclaim, despite a throwaway cover of Lou Reed's 'Rock 'n Roll' and Farrell's limited stage patter, largely consisting of profanities. Drawing inspiration from the Doors, PiL, Velvet Underground and Faith No More, they set about delivering a hypnotic and thought-provoking blend of intoxicating rhythms, jagged and off-beat guitar lines and high-pitched vocals of mesmeric intensity. *Ritual De Lo Habitual* is a work of depth and complexity, which requires repeated listening to reveal its hidden melodies, subtle nuances and enigmatic qualities. It included the video-friendly shoplifting narrative, 'Been Caught Stealing'. In the US, because of censorship of the album's provocative front cover (as with earlier work, featuring a Farrell sculpture), it was released in a plain envelope with the text of the First Amendment written on it. Farrell, meanwhile, helmed the 'Lollapalooza' concert series which for the first time filled large arenas with star-studded indie-rock/rap/alternative artists and events. Despite widespread media coverage, Jane's Addiction never made the commercial breakthrough that their talents deserved, and Farrell split the band in 1992. On his decision to defect to Porno For Pyros, taking drummer Perkins and bass player Martyn Le Noble with him, Farrell concluded: 'What it really boiled down to was, I wasn't getting along with them. I'm not saying whose fault it was. Even though I *know* whose fault it was'. The subject of such slurs, Navarro would go on to join the Red Hot Chili Peppers in 1994.

Albums: *Jane's Addiction* (Triple X 1987), *Nothing's Shocking* (Warners 1988), *Ritual De Lo Habitual* (Warners 1991).

Jerusalem Slim

When Michael Monroe began working on the follow-up to his *Not Fakin' It* solo album, songwriting work with ex-Billy Idol guitarist Steve Stevens metamorphosised into a full band with the recruitment of drummer Greg Ellis and Monroe's former Hanoi Rocks colleague, bassist Sam Yaffa. However, the guitarist's bombastic style never really gelled with Monroe's more straightforward rock 'n' roll approach, and the band dissolved when Stevens joined ex-Mötley Crüe vocalist Vince Neil's band; this did little to promote an amicable split, as Neil had been driving in the accident in which Monroe and Yaffa's late bandmate Razzle had died. Monroe and Yaffa formed the more satisfying Demolition 23, and disowned the posthumous release of *Jerusalem Slim*, which received universally poor reviews.

Album: *Jerusalem Slim* (Mercury 1993).

Jetboy

This UK glam/sleaze rock quintet featured ex-Hanoi Rocks bassist Sam Yaffa, with Mickey Finn (vocals), Fernie Rod (guitar), Billy Rowe (guitar) and Ron Tostenson (drums) completing the line-up. Applying cosmetic surgery to the riffs of AC/DC, Poison and Aerosmith, they leaned towards the bluesier end of this genre. However, Jetboy failed to add the necessary sparkle to make their material either memorable or commercially accessible. Yaffa quit in 1990 to join forces with former Hanoi Rocks vocalist Michael Monroe, and Jetboy have been inactive since. Albums: *Feel The Shake* (MCA 1988), *Damned Nation* (MCA 1990).

Jett, Joan, And The Blackhearts

b. Joan Larkin, 22 September 1960, Philadelphia, Pennsylvania, USA. Jett was one of the most successful US female singers to emerge from the rock scene of the 70s. She spent most of her childhood in the Baltimore, Maryland, area, where she learned guitar as a child, playing along to favourite rock 'n' roll records. In 1972 her family relocated to Los Angeles, where she became enamoured with artists including David Bowie, Suzi Quatro, T. Rex and Gary Glitter. At the age of 15 she began infiltrating the Los Angeles rock scene and formed her first band. Producer Kim Fowley took the group under his wing and named it the Runaways, procuring a record deal with Mercury Records. The group recorded three punk-tinged hard rock albums which were unsuccessful in the USA but hits in Japan, where they recorded a live album. Also successful in England, they recorded their swansong, *And Now...The Runaways*, in that territory in 1979. After the dissolution of the group, Jett moved to New York and teamed up with producer Kenny Laguna, who became her manager. Laguna had previously been involved with a number of 60s bubblegum hits. Laguna produced Jett's first solo album which was released on the European Ariola label. When no US label would pick it up they issued it themselves and the album sold well, becoming one of the best-selling US independent records of that time. That led to a deal with Neil Bogart's Boardwalk Records, who reissued it as *Bad Reputation* (a title inspired by the less than enthusiastic industry response to Jett after the Runaways) and saw it reach number 51 in the US charts. With her group the Blackhearts (guitarist Ricky Byrd, bassist Gary Ryan and drummer Lee Crystal), Jett recorded *I Love Rock 'N' Roll* in late 1981, produced by Laguna and Ritchie Cordell. The title-track, originally an obscure b-side for UK group the Arrows, became a major hit, largely owing to a big push from MTV, and spent seven weeks at number 1 in the USA in early 1982. The follow-up single, a cover of Tommy James And The Shondells' 'Crimson And Clover', was itself a Top 10 hit, reaching number 7 in 1982. Also housed on the album was an update of a Jett song from the Runaways era, 'You're Too Possessive'. With Bogart's death the group signed to MCA, which then distributed Blackheart Records. Subsequent outings on that label were not nearly as successful as the Boardwalk releases, although *Album* did collect a gold award. *Glorious Results Of A Misspent Youth* again retreated to Jett's past with the Runaways, this time on a revision of 'Cherry Bomb'. *Good Music* saw some intriguing collaborations, with members of the Beach Boys and Darlene Love guesting, and an unlikely rap duet with Scorpio of Grandmaster Flash And The Furious Five. The album also saw the departure of Lee Crystal and Gary Ryan, the former permanently replaced by Thommy Price. Jett meanwhile found time to make a second film appearance (following *We're All Crazy Now!*), playing Michael J. Fox's sister in *Light Of Day*. She would also sing the Bruce Springsteen-penned theme. *Up Your Alley* brought another hit with 'I Hate Myself For Loving You', before 1990's *The Hit List*, an album of cover versions, which included a duet with Ray Davies on 'Celluloid Heroes'. *Notorious* saw her hook up with Paul Westerburg of the Replacements for the co-written 'Backlash', but by the advent of *Pure And Simple* Byrd was no longer a permanent member of the band. This set saw a guest appearance from L7 on a track entitled 'Activity Grrrl', emphasising Jett's influence on a new generation of female rockers (by this time Jett had also produced Bikini Kill, in addition to late 70s LA punk band the Germs).
Albums: *Joan Jett* (Blackheart 1980), *Bad Reputation* (Boardwalk 1981, reissue of debut), *I Love Rock 'n' Roll* (Boardwalk 1981), *Album* (MCA/Blackheart 1983), *Glorious Results Of A Misspent Youth* (MCA/Blackheart 1984), *Good Music* (CBS/Blackheart 1986), *Up Your Alley* (CBS/Blackheart 1988), *The Hit List* (CBS/Blackheart 1990), *Notorious* (Epic/Blackheart 1991), *Pure And Simple* (Blackheart/Warners 1994). Compilation: *Flashback* (Blackheart 1993).

Johnny Crash

Following the break up of Tokyo Blade, vocalist Vicki James Wright became disillusioned with the British rock scene and moved to Los Angeles in search of compatible musicians. After a series of false starts, he finally stabilized a line-up of August Worchell and

Joan Jett And The Blackhearts

Christopher Stewart (guitars), Andy Rogers (bass) and Stephen Adamo (drums), under the name Johnny Crash. Blatantly parading traditional metal influences such as Mötley Crüe, AC/DC and Kiss, they delivered a high-energy blast of streetwise, blues-based rock 'n' roll on their Tony Platt-produced debut.

Album: *Neighbourhood Threat* (WTG 1990).

Joshua

This American band was formed by Joshua Pehahia (guitar/vocals) in 1981 after he had left Blind Alley. In the early days there was never a constant line-up save for singer Stephen Fontaine, who possessed a vocal range of four octaves. It was Perahia and Fontaine, plus two more acquaintances, who recorded the mini-album, *The Hand Is Quicker Than The Eye*, in 1982. The title was suggested by one of the studio engineers who saw Perahia's dexterity on the fret board. After the album's release Joshua attempted to tour, but frequent personnel changes made this impracticable, and no more than four dates were completed with the same line-up. In 1984 Joshua were signed to Polydor in America with Perahia (guitar/vocals), Ken Tamplin (guitar/vocals), Patrick Bradley (keyboards/vocals), Loren Robinson (bass/vocals), Jo Galletta (drums) and Jeff Fenholt (lead vocals). Perahia produced the album and wrote all the song arrangements. *Surrender* was released in 1985 and offered classy American hard rock, but the European arm of Polydor was not interested and its European release was handled by FM Revolver. Fenholt was not a permanent member of the band and left after the album's completion, while Gregory Valesco joined them as vocalist for touring. Tamplin went on to form his own unit, Shout. Joshua then signed to RCA with completely different personnel: Perahia (guitar/vocals), Bob Rock (lead vocals), Greg Schultz (keyboards/vocals), Emil Lech (bass) and Tim Gehrt (drums). This membership recorded *Intense Defence*, which was slightly more restrained. Bob Rock's input helped raise the standard of the songwriting and their future looked bright. However, Rock, Schultz and Lech left the band after the recording was finished, and formed their own outfit, Driver.

Albums: *The Hand Is Quicker Than The Eye* (Olympic 1982), *Surrender* (Polydor 1985), *Intense Defense* (RCA 1988).

Journey

This US rock group was formed in 1973 by ex-

Santana members Neil Schon (b. 27 February 1954, San Mateo, California, USA; guitar) and Greg Rolie (b. 1948; keyboards), with the assistance of Ross Valory (b. 2 February 1949, San Francisco, USA; ex-Steve Miller band; bass) and Prairie Prince (b. 7 May 1950, Charlotte, North Carolina, USA; ex-Tubes; drums). George Tickner was added later as rhythm guitarist and lead vocalist. On New Year's Eve the same year, they made their live debut in front of 10,000 people at San Fransisco's Winterland. The following day they played to 10 times as many at an open-air festival in Hawaii. In February 1974 Prince would return to the Tubes and be replaced by Aynsley Dunbar (b. 10 January 1946, Liverpool, Lancashire, England; ex-Jeff Beck, John Mayall, Frank Zappa, etc.). Initially they specialized in jazz-rock, complete with extended and improvised solo spots. This style can clearly be heard on their first three albums. In 1975 Tickner left (for medical school) and was eventually replaced by ex-Alien Project vocalist Steve Perry (b. 22 January 1953, Hanford, California, USA) following a brief tenure by Robert Fleischmann. The switch to highly sophisticated pomp-rock occurred with the recording of *Infinity*, when Roy Thomas Baker was brought in as producer to give the band's sound a punchy and dynamic edge. The album was a huge success, reaching number 21 on the *Billboard* charts and gaining a platinum award. Dunbar was unhappy with this new style and quit for Jefferson Starship, to be replaced by Steve Smith (b. 21 August 1954, Los Angeles, California, USA). *Evolution* followed and brought the band their first Top 20 hit, 'Lovin', Touchin', Squeezin''. *Captured* was a double live album that surprised many of the critics, being far removed from their technically excellent and clinically produced studio releases; instead, it featured cranked-up guitars and raucous hard rock, eventually peaking at number 9 in the US album chart. Founder member Rolie departed after its release, to be replaced by Jonathan Cain (b. 26 February 1950, Chicago, Illinois, USA), who had previously played with the Babys. Cain's arrival was an important landmark in Journey's career, as his input on the writing side added a new dimension to the band's sound. *Escape* was the pinnacle of the band's success, reaching number 1 and staying in the chart for over a year. It also spawned three US Top 10 hit singles in the form of 'Who's Crying Now', 'Don't Stop Believin'', and 'Open Arms'. The follow-up, *Frontiers*, was also successful, staying at number 2 on the *Billboard* album chart for nine weeks; 'Separate Ways', culled as a single from it, climbed to number 8 in the singles chart. After a series of internal disputes the band reduced to a three-man nucleus of

Schon, Cain and Perry to record *Raised On Radio* (though they were joined on live dates by Randy Jackson and Mike Baird on drums and bass). This was to become Journey's last album, before Schon and Cain joined forces with John Waite's Bad English in 1988. Smith would front a fusion band, Vital Information, before teaming up with ex-Journey members Rolie and Valory to form Storm in 1991. Perry would concentrate on his long-awaited second solo album. A *Greatest Hits* compilation was posthumously released to mark the band's passing, since when only a November 1991 reunion to commemorate the death of promoter Bill Graham has seen the core members regroup.

Albums: *Journey* (CBS 1975), *Look Into The Future* (CBS 1976), *Next* (CBS 1977), *Infinity* (CBS 1978), *Evolution* (CBS 1979), *Departure* (CBS 1980), *Dream After Dream* (CBS 1980), *Captured* (CBS 1981, double live album), *Escape* (CBS 1981), *Frontiers* (CBS 1983), *Raised On Radio* (CBS 1986). Compilations: *In The Beginning* (*CBS* 1979), *Greatest Hits/Best Of Journey* (CBS 1988), *Time3* (CBS 1992, triple-CD box set).

Judas Priest

This group was formed in Birmingham, England, in 1969, by guitarist K.K. Downing (b. Kenneth Downing) and close friend, bassist Ian Hill. As another hopeful, struggling young rock band, they played their first gig in Essington in 1971 with a line up completed by Alan Atkins (vocals) and John Ellis (drums). The name Judas Priest came from Atkins' previous band (who took it from a Bob Dylan song, 'The Ballad Of Frankie Lee And Judas Priest') before he joined up with Hill and Downing, but it was retained as the best choice. Consistent gigging continued with Alan Moore taking over on drums only to be replaced at the end of 1971 by Chris Campbell. 1972 was spent mostly on the road in the UK, and in 1973 both Atkins and Campbell departed leaving the nucleus of Hill and Downing once more (in 1991 Atkins would release a debut solo album, including 'Victim Of Changes', a song he co-wrote in Judas Priest's infancy). At this point their fortunes took a turn for the better. Vocalist and ex-theatrical lighting engineer Rob Halford (b. 25 August 1951, Walsall, England) and drummer John Hinch, both from the band Hiroshima, joined the unit. More UK shows ensued as their following grew steadily, culminating in the addition of second guitarist Glenn Tipton (b. 25 October 1948; ex-Flying Hat Band). In 1974 they toured abroad for the first time in Germany and the Netherlands, and returned home to a record deal with the small UK label, Gull. The band made their vinyl debut with *Rocka Rolla* in September 1974. Disappointed with the recording, the album failed to make any impact, and Hinch left to be replaced by the returning Alan Moore. In 1975 the band's appearance at the Reading Festival brought them to the attention of a much wider audience. *Sad Wings Of Destiny* was an improvement on the debut, with production assistance from Jeffrey Calvert and Max West. However, despite good reviews their financial situation remained desperate, and Alan Moore left for the second and final time. A worldwide contract with CBS saved the day, and *Sin After Sin* was a strong collection, with Simon Philips sitting in for Moore. The band then visited America for the first time with drummer Les Binks, who appeared on *Stained Class*, an album which showed Priest at a high watermark in their powers. *Killing Machine* yielded the first UK hit single, 'Take On The World', and featured shorter, punchier, but still familiar rock songs. *Unleashed In The East* was recorded on the 1979 Japanese tour, and in that year, Les Binks was replaced on drums by Dave Holland of Trapeze. After major tours with both Kiss and AC/DC, Priest's popularity was beginning to gather momentum. *British Steel* smashed into the UK album charts at number 3, and contained the hit singles 'Breaking The Law' and 'Living After Midnight'. After appearing at the 1980 Castle Donington Monsters Of Rock festival, they began recording *Point Of Entry*. It provided the hit single 'Hot Rockin', and was followed by sell-out UK and US tours. The period surrounding *Screaming For Vengeance* was phenomenally successful for the band. The hit single, 'You've Got Another Thing Comin'', was followed by a lucrative six month US tour with the album going platinum in the USA. *Defenders Of The Faith* offered a similar, potent brand of headstrong metal to *Screaming For Vengeance*. *Turbo*, though, proved slightly more commercial and was poorly received, Judas Priest's traditional metal fans reacting with indifference to innovations including the use of synthesized guitars. *Ram It Down* saw a return to pure heavy metal by comparison, but by this time their popularity had begun to wane. Dave Holland was replaced by Scott Travis (b. Norfolk, Virginia, USA; ex-Racer X) for the return to form that was *Painkiller*. Although not as universally popular as before, Priest were still a major live attraction and remained the epitome of heavy metal, with screaming guitars matched by screaming vocalist, with the protagonists clad in studs and black leather. The band were taken to court in 1990 following the suicide attempts of two fans (one successful) in 1985. Both CBS Records and Judas Priest were accused of inciting suicide

through the 'backwards messages' in their recording of the Spooky Tooth classic, 'Better By You, Better Than Me'. They were found not guilty in June 1993 after a long court battle, Downing admitting: 'It will be another ten years before I can even spell subliminal'. Soon after Halford became disheartened with the band and decided to quit and form his own outfit, Fight. He had temporarily fronted an Ozzy-less Black Sabbath and recorded 'Light Comes Out Of The Black' with Pantera for the *Buffy The Vampire Slayer* soundtrack. Apparently still reeling from the shock the rest of Judas Priest have not been able to get it back together and seem to be waiting for Halford's return.

Albums: *Rocka Rolla* (Gull 1974), *Sad Wings Of Destiny* (Gull 1976), *Sin After Sin* (CBS 1977), *Stained Class* (CBS 1978), *Killing Machine* (CBS 1978), *Unleashed In The East* (CBS 1979), *British Steel* (CBS 1980), *Point Of Entry* (CBS 1981), *Screaming For Vengeance* (CBS 1982), *Defenders Of The Faith* (CBS 1984), *Turbo* (CBS 1986), *Priest Live* (CBS 1987), *Ram It Down* (CBS 1988), *Painkiller* (CBS 1990). Compilations: *Best Of* (Gull 1978), *Hero Hero* (Telaeg 1987), *Collection* (Castle 1989), *Metal Works '73 - '93* (CBS 1993, double album). Videos: *Fuel Of Life* (1986), *Live* (1987), *Painkiller* (1990).

Further reading: *Heavy Duty*, Steve Gett.

Juggernaut

Formed in Texas, California, USA, in 1985, the band's original line-up consisted of Harlan Glenn (vocals), Eddie Katilius (guitar), Scott Womack (bass) and Bobby Jarzombek (drums). They signed to the Metal Blade Records label and had an early demo track included on the *Metal Massacre VII* compilation album. Their debut long player, *Baptism Under Fire*, was released in 1986. Their music was as the band's name suggested, traditional heavy metal, with emphasis on 'heavy'. The outfit received little attention from the media and Glenn soon left the band to be replaced by Steve Cooper in time for *Trouble Within*. Released in 1987, this also made little impact. With any degree of sustained success seemingly beyond them the band folded early in 1988.

Albums: *Baptism Under Fire* (Metal Blade 1986), *Trouble Within* (Metal Blade 1987).

Junkyard

This five-piece USA combo was made up of seasoned Los Angeles club circuit musicians. Formed in 1988, they comprised David Roach (vocals), Chris Gates and Brian Baker (guitars), Clay Anthony (bass) and

Patrick Muzingo (drums). Signing to Geffen Records, their debut offering featured 'trashy metallic boogie'. Two years later, *Sixes Sevens And Nines* emerged and the songwriting partnership of Roach and Gates had matured considerably, with the emphasis now on the music rather than image. Musically, Junkyard exist somewhere between Great White, Dokken and Z.Z. Top, dealing in abrasive raunch 'n' roll. For their second album producer Ed Stasium achieved a harder and bluesier sound (somewhat akin to Lynyrd Skynyrd), without pushing them in a blatantly commercial direction. The group were nevertheless dropped by Geffen in 1992, though they elected to persevere.

Albums: *Junkyard* (Geffen 1989), *Sixes, Sevens And Nines* (Geffen 1991).

K

Kansas

This US group was formed in 1972 after David Hope (b. c.1951, Kansas, USA; bass) and Phil Ehart (b. 1951, Kansas, USA; drums/percussion) changed the name of their band, White Clover, to Kansas, recruiting Kerry Livgren (b. 18 September 1949, Kansas, USA; guitar/vocals), Robert Steinhardt (b. c.1951, Michigan, USA; violin/strings/vocals), Steve Walsh (b. c.1951, St. Joseph, Missouri, USA; keyboards/vocals) and Richard Williams (b. c.1951, Kansas, USA; guitars). Although an American band, Kansas were heavily influenced from the outset by British rock of the time, such as Yes and Genesis, and this was evident in the lyrics of their primary songwriter, Walsh. Kansas released their debut in 1974, and the following two albums attained gold record status, guaranteeing the band a high profile in the USA (although no Kansas albums made the charts in the UK). By 1977 the band had tired of the progressive rock pigeon-hole into which the music press was forcing them, and decided to try a more commercial approach. Their popularity was confirmed on 27 June 1978 when they attended a ceremony at the Madison Square Gardens in New York at which the organization UNICEF named the band Deputy Ambassadors of Goodwill. In the early 80s Walsh decided to leave the band after he became unhappy with the increasingly commercial sound

they were producing. He released the solo set, *Schemer Dreamer*, which featured other members of Kansas. He was replaced by John Elefante (b. c.1958, Levittown, New York, USA; keyboards/vocals) who wrote four of the songs on *Vinyl Confessions*. The band split in 1983 following two unsuccessful albums. Livgren and Hope had become born-again Christians, the former releasing *Seeds Of Change*, a commercially disastrous solo effort based on his religious experiences. In October 1986 Walsh, Ehart and Williams re-formed Kansas with Steve Morse, lately of Dixie Dregs (guitar), and Billy Greer (bass). This reunion was celebrated with the release of *Power*, an album that rejected the jazz-rock feel of earlier releases in favour of a heavier sound.

Albums: *Kansas* (Kirshner 1974), *Songs For America* (Kirshner 1975), *Masque* (Kirshner 1976), *Leftoverture* (Kirshner 1977), *Point Of Know Return* (Kirshner 1977), *Two For The Show* (Kirshner 1978, double album), *Monolith* (Kirshner 1979), *Audio-Visions* (Kirshner 1980), *Vinyl Confessions* (Kirshner 1982), *Drastic Measures* (CBS 1983), *Power* (MCA 1986), *In The Spirit Of Things* (MCA 1988), *Live At The Whisky* (1993). Compilation: *The Best Of Kansas* (Epic 1984).

Kat

The self-proclaimed 'Great Kat' began her musical career as a classically trained violinist graduating from Juilliard. After six years of solid performance on the instrument, she switched to the guitar and began experimenting with a fusion of classical and rock music. Adopting a high-speed technique, she concentrated on short instrumentals. *Worship Me Or Die* was poorly received, despite Kat's proclamations that it represented 'the first real revolutionary music since Beethoven'. Undaunted she released *Beethoven On Speed*, which marked a considerable improvement in both musical and production terms. Promoting herself as a grotesque parody of a 'wild woman of rock', this contrivance fell flat with UK audiences and, despite her potential to produce an innovative metal/classical crossover album, little has been heard from the artist since.

Albums: *Worship Me Or Die* (Roadrunner 1987), *Beethoven On Speed* (Roadrunner 1990).

Katon, Michael

This acclaimed blues rock guitarist/vocalist grew up in Ipsilanti, Michigan, and his musical family background soon inspired him to pick up the guitar. Katon began playing with local bands in clubs and roadhouse bars around Detroit from the age of 15, and spent 20 years paying his dues in classic blues

fashion, working with a succession of blues and jazz bands, before the now Hell, Michigan-based guitarist released his solo debut, *Boogie All Over Your Head*, on his own Wild Ass label, with Swedish label Garageland picking up Katon in Eruope. The straightforward R&B boogie style, gravelly vocals and stylish blues guitar of *Proud To Be Loud* endeared Katon to both the blues and heavy metal crowds, and live shows with Ed Phelps (guitar/harmonica), Johnny Arizona (bass) and Gary Rasmussen (drums) proved to be wild affairs, particularly due to the guitarist's penchant for four and five hour sets acquired through his years of experience. Blues label Provogue were suitably impressed, offering Katon a European deal. Katon gave up drinking to concentrate on his guitar playing, resulting in the harder, more focused *Get On The Boogie Train*, and while his lyrics retained their customary humour, he also produced a fine slice of urban blues in 'Cadillac Assembly Line', a lament for Detroit's declining motor industry. *Rip It Hard* continued in the traditional blues-boogie vein, and while, like many bluesmen, major commercial success evades Katon, he remains a respected guitarist in the field.
Albums: *Boogie All Over Your Head* (Wild Ass 1985), *Proud To Be Loud* (Wild Ass 1988), *Get On The Boogie Train* (Wild Ass 1992), *Rip It Hard* (Wild Ass 1994).

Keel

Vocalist Ron Keel started his career in 1983 with Steeler, who also temporarily featured future guitar hero Yngwie Malmsteen. After one self-titled album on Shrapnel Records, he split the band to go solo. Forming a typical Kiss/Aerosmith styled band with musicians Brian Jay (guitar), Marc Ferrari (guitar), Kenny Chaisson (bass) and Dwain Miller (drums), Keel obtained the production services of Gene Simmons from Kiss for a second album which won them many fans. The follow-up, 1986's *The Final Frontier*, featured an all-star line-up including Joan Jett, Michael Des Barres (Silverhead/Detective) and Simmons. The album also spawned a hit single with a cover of Patti Smith's 'Because The Night'. Moving to MCA in 1987 proved less fruitful and after one album they switched to an indie label and sundered shortly after. In 1991 Keel talked in depth about getting a new act together with an all-female band. This has, so far, proved wishful thinking.
Albums: *Lay Down The Law* (Shrapnel 1984), *The Right To Rock* (Vertigo 1985), *The Final Frontier* (Vertigo 1986), *Keel* (MCA 1987), *Larger Than Live* (Mountain Castle 1989).

Kik Tracee

This US hard rock quintet was formed in 1990 by Stephen Shareux (vocals) and Michael Marquis (guitar). The line-up was completed by the addition of Rob Grad (bass), Gregory Hex (rhythm guitar) and Johnny Douglas (drums). Picked up by RCA Records, they debuted in 1991 with *No Rules*, a varied and uncompromising collection of mature rock numbers which, in an unusual choice of cover material, included a version of Simon And Garfunkel's 'Mrs. Robinson'.
Album: *No Rules* (RCA 1991).

Kill For Thrills

Hailing from Los Angeles, California, USA, this group delivered a trademark sound best described as 'sleaze rock'. Featuring the talents of Gilby Clarke (vocals/guitar), Jason Nesmith (guitar), Todd Muscat (bass) and David Scott (drums), their 1990 debut, *Dynamite From Nightmare Land*, was a prime example of no-nonsense standard chord hard rock. The album was produced by Vic Maile and Ric Browde who are renowned, respectively, for their work with Motörhead and Poison.
Album: *Dynamite From Nightmare Land* (MCA 1990).

Killdozer

This US rock group imbue their slow, menacing soundscapes with only the loosest imitations of song structure. Killdozer trace their origins back to Madison, Wisconsin, and their origins in hicksville USA are regularly celebrated in their primal country blues. Featuring Michael Gerald (bass/vocals), plus the brothers Dan and Bill Hobson (guitar and drums, respectively), the trio have released a steady stream of albums which often highlighted their distaste at what they saw as the social and political malaise of their native country. They were just as likely to turn the spotlight on smalltown weirdness, however, or their singer's rampant confusion about the state of the world. In a respite from this angst, *For Ladies Only* was a project dedicated to covers of classic songs of the 70s, including 'One Tin Soldier' and 'Good Lovin' Gone Bad'.
Albums: *Intellectuals Are The Shoeshine Boys Of The Ruling Elite* (Bone Air 1984), *Snakeboy* (Touch & Go 1985), *Burl* (Touch & Go 1986, mini-album), *Little Baby Buntin'* (Touch & Go 1987), *Twelve Point Buck* (Touch & Go 1988), *For Ladies Only* (Touch & Go 1989), *Uncompromising War On Art Under The Dictatorship Of The Proletariat* (Touch & Go 1994).
Video: *Little Baby Buntin' Live* (1990).

Killers

This UK quintet were founded in 1991 by former Iron Maiden vocalist Paul Di'Anno. Recruiting Steve Hopgood (drums), Cliff Evans (guitar), Gavin Cooper (bass) and Nick Burr (guitar), their approach is firmly rooted in the New Wave Of British Heavy Metal movement of the early 80s. *Murder One*, released in early 1992, was rather anachronistic, sounding virtually identical to early Iron Maiden, though the calibre of the protagonists guaranteed press and public interest.

Album: *Murder One* (RCA 1992).

King Diamond

When popular metal act Mercyful Fate split into two separate factions in March 1985, vocalist King Diamond (b. Kim Bendix Petersen, 14 June 1956, Copenhagen, Denmark), Michael Denner (guitar) and Timi Hansen (bass) decided to pursue their obsession with satanic heavy metal and the occult, while the others sought a more mainstream direction. King Diamond's music became characterized by supernatural storylines, high-pitched, banshee-like vocals and meandering guitar work. On live performances, their leader specialized in amateurish theatrical stunts to bring the songs to life. This included face make-up not dissimilar to that worn by Alice Cooper. Since 1985 there have been numerous line-up changes, but the most successful and long-lived personnel have included Andy Larocque (guitar, who would join Death, replaced by ex-Madison guitarist Mikael Myllynen, aka Mikael Moon), Pete Blakk (guitar), Hal Patino (bass) and Snowey Shaw (drums). Each successive album has offered ever more complex themes and sub-plots, resulting in the musical equivalent of a sinister version of Dungeons and Dragons. After the failure of *The Eye*, Diamond resurrected Mercyful Fate in 1993.

Albums: *Fatal Portrait* (Roadrunner 1986), *Abigail* (Roadrunner 1987), *Them* (Roadrunner 1988), *The Dark Sides* (Roadrunner 1988), *Conspiracy* (Roadrunner 1989), *The Eye* (Roadrunner 1990).

King Kobra

After departing the drum stool in Ozzy Osbourne's band in 1984, Carmen Appice decided to form his own outfit, under the King Kobra moniker. Enlisting the services of four relative unknowns, Mark Free (vocals), David Michael-Phillips (guitar), Mike Sweda (guitar) and Johnny Rod (bass), he negotiated a deal with EMI Records, which eventually resulted in *Ready To Strike* in 1985, a hard rock album full of infectious hooks and pyrotechnic guitar breaks. On the strength of this release they were offered the chance to write the theme music for the film, *Iron Eagle*. They changed styles at this juncture, switching to a more sophisticated and lightweight AOR approach. As a consequence of this album sales dried up and they were dropped by their label. Johnny Rod left to join W.A.S.P. and the band fell apart. A few months later, the nucleus of Appice and Michael-Phillips rebuilt the band with the addition of ex-Montrose vocalist Johnny Edwards, Jeff Northrup (guitar) and Larry Hart (bass). They returned to their hard rock origins and released *King Kobra III* on the Music For Nations label, but it was again poorly received. The band finally became obsolete when Appice left to join John Sykes's Blue Murder project in 1989.

Albums: *Ready To Strike* (Capitol 1985), *Thrill Of A Lifetime* (EMI 1987), *King Kobra III* (Music For Nations 1988).

King Of The Hill

This St. Louis, Missouri-based four-piece heavy metal outfit began life on the local club circuit as a covers band, with the line-up settling when bassist George Potsos joined Frankie Muriel (vocals), Vito Bono (drums) and Jimmy Griffin (guitar). Initially known as Broken Toyz, the band gradually introduced original material into their set, until the demand for their own songs allowed them to drop the cover versions entirely. They signed a recording contract in 1990, and, having adopted the name King Of The Hill, recorded their self-titled debut with Bang Tango producer Howard Benson. The album mixed party metal in the grand Van Halen style with funk influences, while also touching on AOR, with vocal harmonies which echoed Bon Jovi. The opening single, 'I Do U', did well on MTV, and with major backing from their record label the band spent much of 1991 on the road, touring with White Lion, Trixter, Lynch Mob and Steelheart in the US, and received a rapturous reception as Extreme's guests on their autumn UK tour. This, the band's first live work outside their own country, served to sharpen their performing abilities, with the charismatic Frankie becoming the visual focus of the band, drawing comparisons to both Dave Lee Roth and Prince, not least for his multiple costume changes throughout each show. However, despite the fact that King Of The Hill were due to record a second album in early 1992, they seemed to disappear almost overnight, and have not been heard from since.

Album: *King Of The Hill* (SBK 1991).

Kingdom Come

In 1984 German vocalist Lenny Wolf fronted the Led

Zeppelin-inspired Stone Fury, who released *Burns Like A Star* for MCA. After they split he returned to Germany and had a re-think. He moved back to America in 1987 with a new plan and found like-minded musicians Danny Stag (guitar), Rick Stier (guitar), Johnny Frank (bass) and James Kottack (drums). He then took his idea to ex-Gentle Giant vocalist Derek Shulman, now working in A&R, who ensured the new group signed to Polydor Records. What happened in 1988 was almost unheard of in heavy metal circles. The band had not so much been influenced by, but totally reproduced Led Zeppelin from the drum sound of John Bonham to the vocals of Robert Plant. It was a complete facsimile, yet such was the interest in America that the album went Gold on advanced orders alone. The rock world soon fell into two factions - those who hated it and those who didn't. Of their detractors, Robert Plant and John Paul Jones made less than flattering remarks and guitarist Gary Moore was prompted to write the song 'Led Clones' on his *After The War* album later that same year. Wolf lacked the ability to argue his case convincingly and even those who chose to support them began to change sides. Realising that all was not well they tried hard to be a little more original for the second album, *In Your Face*. This produced what DJ Tommy Vance described as a classic rock track for years to come in 'Do You Like It', a highly charged song that managed to avoid previous comparisons. However, their final single, 'Overrated', summed the whole project up and they disbanded. Wolf later returned as a solo artist and produced a fine single, 'Shouldn't I', but the ghost of *Kingdom Come* haunted his every move.
Albums: *Kingdom Come* (Polydor 1988), *In Your Face* (Polydor 1989).

Kinghorse

Based in Louisville, Kentucky, Kinghorse are a four-piece rock band featuring Sean Garrison (vocals), Kevin Brownstein (drums), Mark Abromavage (guitar) and Mike Bucayu (bass). They attracted a good deal of critical interest after their debut release, not least because they had secured cover artwork from legendary heavy metal artist Pushead (singer for Septic Death, but best known for his work with Metallica), and had Glenn Danzig (of Misfits and Danzig fame) on production duties. The resultant album was an exercise in heated nihilism and aggressive angst. Potent, painfully gritty and, at times, oddly poignant, Kinghorse were perhaps too unremittingly bleak for most tastes.
Album: *Kinghorse* (Caroline 1990).

Kings X

Initially known as the Edge and specializing in Top 40 cover versions, Doug Pinnick (bass/vocals), Ty Tabor (guitar) and Jerry Gaskell (drums) relocated to Houston, Texas, USA, in 1985, and were taken under the wing of Z.Z. Top video producer, Sam Taylor. Following Taylor's guidance, they concentrated on their own material and changed their name to Kings X. After recording demos and being turned down by several major record companies in the US, they finally secured a deal with the independent Megaforce label. *Out Of The Silent Planet*, with its unique sound and offbeat approach, emerged in 1988 to widespread critical acclaim. Fusing Beatles' style harmonies with hard rock and blues riffs, they encompassed a variety of genres that defied simple pigeon-holing. *Gretchen Goes To Nebraska* was an even greater triumph, building on previous strengths, but adding depth in both a technical and lyrical sense. Preferring the 'positive' tag to that of Christian rockers, *Faith, Hope, Love*, released in 1990, scaled even greater heights with its state-of-the-art production and inspired compositions.
Albums: *Out Of The Silent Planet* (Megaforce 1987), *Gretchen Goes To Nebraska* (Megaforce 1989), *Faith, Hope, Love* (Megaforce 1990).

Kiss

Following the demise of Wicked Lester, Kiss was formed in 1972 by Paul Stanley (b. Paul Eisen, 20 January 1950, Queens, New York, USA; rhythm guitar/vocals) and Gene Simmons (b. Chaim Witz, 25 August 1949, Haifa, Israel; bass/vocals), who went on to recruit Peter Criss (b. Peter Crisscoula, 27 December 1947, Brooklyn, New York, USA; drums/vocals) and Ace Frehley (b. Paul Frehley, 22 April 1951, Bronx, New York, USA; lead guitar/vocals). At their second show at the Hotel Diplomat, Manhattan, 1973, Flipside producer, Bill Aucoin, offered the band a management deal, and within two weeks they were signed to Neil Bogart's recently established Casablanca Records. In just over a year, Kiss had released their first three albums with a modicum of success. In the summer of 1975 their fortunes changed with the release of *Alive*, which spawned their first US hit single, 'Rock 'N' Roll All Nite'. The appeal of Kiss has always been based on their live shows: the garish greasepaint make-up, outrageous costumes, and pyrotechnic stage effects, along with their hard rocking anthems, combined to create what was billed as 'The Greatest Rock 'n' Roll Show On Earth'. Their live reputation engendered a dramatic upsurge in record sales, and *Alive* became their first certified platinum album in the USA.

Kiss

Destroyer proved just as successful, and also gave them their first US Top 10 single, earning Peter Criss a major songwriting award for the uncharacteristic ballad, 'Beth'. Subsequent releases, *Rock And Roll Over, Love Gun* and *Alive II*, each certified paltinum, confirmed the arrival of Kiss as major recording artists. By 1977 Kiss had topped the prestigious Gallup poll as the most popular act in the USA. They had become a marketer's dream. Kiss merchandise included: make-up kits, masks, board games, and pinball machines. *Marvel Comics* produced two super-hero cartoon books, and even a full length science-fiction film, *Kiss Meet The Phantom Of The Park*, was produced. The ranks of their fan club, the Kiss Army, had swollen to a six figure number. In 1978 all four group members each produced a solo album released on the same day, a feat never before envisaged, let alone matched. At the time this represented the biggest shipment of albums from one 'unit' to record stores in the history of recorded music. The albums enjoyed varying degrees of success; Ace Frehley's record came out on top and included the US hit single, 'New York Groove'. Gene Simmons, whose album featured an impressive line-up of guests including Cher, Donna Summer, Bob Seger and Janis Ian, had a hit single in the UK with 'Radioactive', which reached number 41 in 1978. After the release of *Dynasty* in 1979, which featured the worldwide hit single, 'I Was Made For Lovin' You', cracks appeared in the ranks. Peter Criss left to be replaced by session player Anton Fig, who had previously appeared on Ace Frehley's solo album. Fig played drums on the 1980 release *Unmasked* until a permanent replacement was found in the form of New Yorker Eric Carr (b. 12 July 1950), who made his first appearance during the world tour of 1980. A fuller introduction came on *Music From The Elder*, an album that represented a radical departure from traditional Kiss music and included several ballads, an orchestra and a choir. It was a brave attempt to break new ground but failed to capture the imagination of the record-buying public. Frehley, increasingly disenchanted with the musical direction of the band finally left in 1983. The two albums prior to his departure had featured outside musicians. Bob Kulick, who had contributed to the studio side of *Alive II* and played on Stanley's solo album, supplied the lead work to the four previously unreleased tracks on the *Killers* compilation of 1982 and Vincent Cusano (later to become Vinnie Vincent) was responsible for lead guitar on the 1982 release, *Creatures Of The Night*. By 1983 the popularity of the band was waning and drastic measures were called for. The legendary make-up which had concealed their

true identities for almost 10 years was removed on MTV in the US. Vinnie Vincent made his first official appearance on *Lick It Up*, an album which provided Kiss with their first Top 10 hit in the UK. The resurgence of the band continued with *Animalize*. Vincent had been replaced by Mark St. John (b. Mark Norton), a seasoned session player and guitar tutor. His association with the band was short-lived, however, as he was struck down by Reiters Syndrome. Bruce Kulick, the brother of long-time Kiss cohort Bob, was drafted in as a temporary replacement on the 1984 European Tour and subsequently became a permanent member when it became apparent that St. John would not be able to continue as a band member. Further commercial success was achieved with *Asylum* and *Crazy Nights*, the latter featuring their biggest UK hit single, 'Crazy, Crazy Nights', which peaked at number 4 in 1987 and was followed by a further two Top 40 hit singles, 'Reason To Live' and 'Turn On The Night'. *Hot In The Shade* succeeded their third compilation album, *Smashes, Thrashes And Hits,* and included their highest charting hit single in the US, 'Forever', which reached number 4 in 1990. Work on a new Kiss album with producer Bob Ezrin was delayed following Eric Carr's illness due to complications from cancer. He died on the 24th of November 1991, in New York, at the age of 41. Despite this setback, Kiss contributed a cover of Argent's classic, 'God Gave Rock 'N' Roll To You', to the soundtrack of the film, *Bill And Ted's Bogus Journey*, and brought in replacement drummer Eric Singer (ex-Black Sabbath, Badlands). 1994, meanwhile, brought the *Kiss My Ass* tribute album, with contributions from Lenny Kravitz, Stevie Wonder, Garth Brooks, Lemonheads, Faith No More, Dinosaur Jr., Rage Against The Machine and others. With a history spanning three decades, Kiss' impact on the consciousness of a generation of music fans, particularly in the US, remains enormous.

Albums: *Kiss* (Casablanca 1974), *Hotter Than Hell* (Casablanca 1974), *Dressed to Kill* (Casablanca 1975), *Alive* (Casablanca 1975), *Destroyer* (Casablanca 1976), *Rock And Roll Over* (Casablanca 1976), *Love Gun* (Casablanca 1977), *Alive II* (Casablanca 1977), *Dynasty* (Casablanca 1979), *Unmasked* (Casablanca 1980), *Music From The Elder* (Casablanca 1981), *Creatures Of The Night* (Casablanca 1982), *Lick It Up* (Vertigo 1983), *Animalize* (Vertigo 1984), *Asylum* (Vertigo 1985), *Crazy Nights* (Vertigo 1987), *Hot In The Shade* (Vertigo 1989), *Alive III* (Mercury 1993). Compilations: *The Originals* (Casablanca 1976, repackaging of first three albums), *Double Platinum* (Casablanca 1978), *Killers* (Casablanca 1982),

Smashes, Thrashes And Hits (Vertigo 1988), *Revenge* (Mercury 1992).
Videos: *Animalize* (1986), *Exposed* (1987), *Phantom Of The Park* (1987), *Crazy Nights* (1988), *Alive III* (1993), *Kiss My Ass* (1994).
Further reading: *Still On Fire*, Dave Thomas.

Kiss Of The Gypsy

This UK, melodic hard-rock quintet (formerly known as Fantasia) was formed in Blackpool, Lancashire, in 1990, by Tony Mitchell (vocals/guitar) and Martin Talbot (bass). With the addition of Darren Rice (guitar), George Williams (keyboards) and Scott Elliot (drums), they signed to Atlantic the following year. The band's music is blues-rock based, with a sense of energetic songwriting not dissimilar to that of Bad Company or Whitesnake. Following successful support slots to Winger, Magnum and Great White, the band released their self-titled debut album on the WEA/East West label in 1992, which saw them widely regarded as one of the most promising commercial British outfits to emerge since Def Leppard.
Album: *Kiss Of The Gypsy* (East West 1992).

Kix

This US group was formed by Donnie Purnell (bass) and Ronnie Younkins (guitar) in 1980. After experimenting with a number of line-ups, Steve Whiteman (vocals), Brian Forsythe (guitar) and Jimmy Chalfant (drums) were drafted in on a permanent basis. Their style was typical of America's east coast, a brash amalgam of influences that included Mötley Crüe, AC/DC and Kiss, while their live reputation within their native West Virginia was second to none. Securing a contract with Atlantic Records in 1981, their first two albums were a touch derivative and poorly promoted. *Midnight Dynamite* however, produced by Beau Hill (who had previously worked with Ratt) attracted some attention, and the band were given the support slot on Aerosmith's 1985 USA tour. *Blow My Fuse* and *Hot Wire* received a good reception on both sides of the Atlantic, with the band maturing as songwriters and starting to develop an identity of their own.
Albums: *Atomic Bomb* (Atlantic 1981), *Cool Kids* (Atlantic 1983), *Midnight Dynamite* (Atlantic 1985), *Blow My Fuse* (Atlantic 1988), *Hot Wire* (Atlantic 1991).

Kossoff, Paul

b. 14 September 1950, Hampstead, London, England, d. 19 March 1976. The son of English actor David Kossoff, Paul was an inventive, impassioned guitar player who was initially a member of Black Cat Bones, a nascent late-60s blues band which included drummer Simon Kirke. In 1968, both musicians became founder members of Free and later worked together in Kossoff, Kirke, Tetsu And Rabbit, a spin-off project which completed a lone album in 1971 during a hiatus in the parent group's career. Free was reconstituted in 1972, but Kossoff's tenure during this second phase was blighted by recurring drug and related health problems. Absent on portions of several tours, Kossoff finally left the group to pursue a solo career. *Back Street Crawler* contained several excellent performances, notably 'Molten Gold', but it was two years before the guitarist was well enough to resume live work. He accompanied John Martyn on a 1975 tour before assembling a new group, also entitled Back Street Crawler. The quintet completed one album but projected concerts were cancelled when Kossoff suffered a near-fatal heart attack. Specialists forbade an immediate return, but plans were hatched for a series of concerts the following year. However, in March 1976, Paul Kossoff died in his sleep during a flight to America. On Jim Capaldi's 1975 solo album, *Short Cut Draw Blood*, two songs were reputedly written in tribute to Kossof, 'Seagull' and 'Boy With A Problem'. Kossof played lead guitar on the latter, presumably oblivious to the poignant lyrics.
Album: *Back Street Crawler* (Island 1973).
Compilations: *Koss* (DJM 1977), *The Hunter* (Street Tunes 1983), *Leaves In The Wind* (Street Tunes 1983), *Croydon - June 15th 1975* (Street Tunes 1983), *Blue Soul* (Island 1986).

Kotzen, Richie

This highly gifted, new-age rock guitar god is very much in the Joe Satriani mould. By the time Kotzen had reached his seventh birthday, he had moved from piano to guitar lessons, and was playing live with his own band, Arthur's Museum, when he entered his teens. Taken under the wing of Mike Varney, he was introduced to bassist Stuart Hamm and ex-Journey drummer Steve Smith, with whom he recorded a solo instrumental album. This showcased Kotzen's inherent ability and feel for the electric guitar, but also highlighted the limitations of rock music without vocals. Realizing this, he formed Fever Dream, a power-trio comprising Danny Thompson (bass), Atma Anur (drums) and himself on guitar and vocals. Although the guitar breaks were excellent, there was a paucity of hooks and real tunes to latch onto. Kotzen would replace C.C. Deville in Poison's ranks in 1991.
Albums: *Richie Kotzen* (Roadrunner 1989), *Fever Dream* (Roadrunner 1990), *Electric Joy* (Roadrunner 1993).

Kreator

Formed in Essen, Germany, in 1984, originally under the name Tormentor, this heavy metal band comprised Mille Petroza (guitar/vocals), Rob (bass) and Ventor (drums). Their vicious thrash style was fired by the filth and industrial pollution problem that Essen, on the River Ruhr, was experiencing. After changing their name to Kreator, they signed with the Germany-based Noise label, and their debut album, *Endless Pain*, appeared in 1985. Despite roughshod production, it was eagerly received by fans of the then fast-growing thrash-metal scene. After the release of *Pleasure To Kill*, Kreator became one of the most popular bands of the genre, especially in Europe. Lyrically, they have always dealt with the darker side of life and have only recently wavered from their musical path, endearing them to fans who have helped maintain their place in the crowded and highly competitive field of thrash and death metal. They have gone through a number of second guitarists, eventually settling on Frank Blackfire, once with fellow German thrash metallers Sodom.
Albums: *Endless Pain* (Noise 1985), *Pleasure to Kill* (Noise 1986), *Terrible Certainty* (Noise 1988), *Out Of The Dark Into The Light* (Noise 1989), *Extreme Aggression* (Noise 1989), *Coma Of Souls* (Noise 1990), *Renewal* (Noise 1992).

Krokus

Hailing from Soluthurn, Switzerland, Krokus appeared in 1974 playing symphonic rock similar to Yes, Genesis and Emerson, Lake And Palmer. After four years and two rather lacklustre albums, they switched to a hard rock style and dropped the frills in favour of a back-to-basics approach in the mode of AC/DC. The group originally comprised Chris Von Rohr (vocals), Fernando Von Arb (guitar), Jurg Naegeli (bass), Tommy Kiefer (guitar) and Freddy Steady (drums). The songs were formulaic numbers based on simple riffs and predictable choruses that were chanted repeatedly. With Von Rohr's voice lacking the necessary vocal range, he stepped down to became the bass player in favour of new arrival 'Maltezer' Marc (b. Marc Storace, Malta; ex-Tea). Naegeli occasionally played keyboards and would subsequently take over the technical side of the band. *Metal Rendez-vous* was the turning point in the band's career; released in 1980, it was heavier than anything they had done before and coincided with the resurgence of heavy metal in Britain. They played the Reading Festival in 1980 and were well-received, and their next two albums continued with an aggressive approach, though they streamlined their sound to make it more radio-friendly. *Hardware* and *One Vice*

At A Time both made the UK album charts, at numbers 44 and 28 respectively. Before *Headhunter* materialized a series of personnel changes took place. The most important of these was the replacement of Kiefer with ex-roadie Mark Kohler (guitar), while Steve Pace stepped in on drums. Kiefer would subsequently return to replace Rohr. Produced by Tom Allom, *Headhunter's* high-speed, heavy-duty approach propelled it to number 25 in the *Billboard* album charts. Further line-up changes (the temporary addition of ex-Crown guitarist Patrick Mason and the exit then return of Pace) delayed the release of *The Blitz*, an erratic album, which reached number 31 on the US chart mainly on the strength of its predecessor. Since 1985 there has been a continuing downward trend in the band's fortunes, with their personnel in a constant state of flux (Kesier committing suicide in 1986, the introduction of guitarist Manny Maurer, etc.). Their music has progressed little during the last decade and relies heavily, even today, on the legacy of AC/DC and the Scorpions.
Albums: *Krokus* (Schmontz 1975), *To You All* (Schmontz 1977), *Painkiller* (Mercury 1978), *Pay It In Metal* (Mercury 1979), *Metal Rendez-vous* (Ariola 1980), *Hardware* (Ariola 1981), *One Vice At A Time* (Ariola 1982), *Headhunter* (Arista 1983), *The Blitz* (Arista 1984), *Change Of Address* (Arista 1985), *Alive And Screamin'* (Arista 1986), *Heart Attack* (MCA 1987), *Stampede* (Ariola 1990).

Kyuss

This Palm Springs, California quartet of school friends belied their origins in what seems a sedate community by mixing their differing tastes to provide a blues-based retro rock sound of stunning heaviness charged with a spiritual air. Vocalist John Garcia's mainstream tastes and bassist Nick Oliveri's metal background blended with guitarist Josh Homme and drummer Brant Bjork's penchant for Black Flag, the Misfits and the Ramones to produce music with the groove of classic Black Sabbath but with modern intensity and their own definite identity. Although their early efforts were unpopular in the hardcore-oriented late 80s, the band stuck doggedly with their music and were accepted as tastes broadened in the post-grunge 90s. *Wretch* was a decent debut, but the band found a kindred spirit in Master Of Reality leader Chris Goss to produce *Blues For The Red Sun*, where the looser atmosphere and mature material were given extra ambience as Goss captured the band's live power in the studio. Kyuss were suddenly hot property, touring the USA with Danzig and Faith No More, and in Australia with Metallica, although

Oliveri departed to be replaced by Scott Reeder from old touring partners the Obsessed. When their label collapsed, distributors Elektra offered Kyuss a deal, and the band collaborated with Goss again on the pounding sludge-rock of *Sky Valley*, with new drummer Alfredo Hernandez replacing the tour-weary Bjork, while the band continued to play live shows which one enthusiastic *Kerrang!* scribe rated as 'worth selling your legs to witness'.

Albums: *Wretch* (Dali-Chameleon 1991), *Blues For The Red Sun* (Dali-Chameleon 1992), *Sky Valley* (Elektra 1994).

L

L.A. Guns

This US group was formed by ex-Guns N'Roses guitarist Tracii Guns and Paul Black in Los Angeles in 1987, though the latter was soon replaced by ex-Girl/Bernie Tormé vocalist Phil Lewis. Working on material that was a hybrid of metal, glam and blues-based rock 'n' roll, they signed with Polygram Records in the US the following year. With the addition of Mick Cripps (guitar), Kelly Nickels (bass) and Steve Riley (drums; ex-W.A.S.P.) the line-up was complete. However, with Riley arriving too late to appear on their self-titled debut, the group used the services of Nickey Alexander (formerly 'Nicky Beat' of punk legends the Weirdos). *Cocked And Loaded* was a marked improvement over its predecessor; the band had matured as songwriters and Lewis' vocals were stronger and more convincing. *Hollywood Vampires* saw them diversifying musically, but retaining the essential energy and rough edges for which they had become renowned. Touring as support to Skid Row in Europe, it at last looked as though Guns' would no longer have to look longingly at the phenomenal success his former band had achieved in his absence. However, it was not to be. As the group disintegrated Guns would go on to put together an new outfit, Killing Machine, while Lewis formed Filthy Lucre.

Albums: *L.A. Guns* (Polygram 1988), *Cocked And Loaded* (Polygram 1989), *Hollywood Vampires* (Polygram 1991). Compilation: *Vicious Circle* (Polygram 1994).

Videos: *One More Reason* (1989), *Love, Peace & Geese* (1990).

L7

Guitarist/vocalists Donita Sparks (b. Chicago, Illinois, USA) and Suzi Gardner (b. Sacramento, California, USA) formed L7 in the mid-80s, linking with Jennifer Finch (b. Los Angeles, California, USA; bass/vocals) and trying several drummers, finally finding Dee Plakas (b. Chicago, Illinois, USA) after domestic touring to promote *L7*, supporting Bad Religion (drummer on their debut album was Roy Kolltsky). The band's raw punk-metal caught the interest of Sup Pop, who released *Smell The Magic*, a raucous grunge-flavoured blast which further enhanced the band's growing underground reputation. *Bricks Are Heavy* brought major success, with the surprisingly poppy 'Pretend We're Dead' becoming a major hit on both sides of the Atlantic. Subsequently the band became darlings of the music press with their multi-coloured hair and shock-tactic humour - at 1992's Reading Festival, Sparks retaliated against missile throwers by removing her tampon on stage and throwing it into the crowd, and later dropped her shorts during a live television performance on *The Word* - but the band's serious side led them to form Rock For Choice, a pro-abortion women's rights organisation which has gathered supporters from Pearl Jam to Corrosion Of Conformity for fund-raising concerts. L7 went on to appear as a band entitled Camel Lips in a John Waters' film, *Serial Mom*, before *Hungry For Stink* picked up where *Bricks Are Heavy* left off, blending serious and humorous lyrics against a still-thunderous musical backdrop.

Albums: *L7* (Epitaph 1988), *Smell The Magic* (Sup Pop 1990), *Bricks Are Heavy* (Slash/London 1992), *Hungry For Stink* (Slash/London 1994).

Last Crack

Last Crack, from Wisconsin, USA, specialized in schizophrenic 'acid-metal', a truly unique aural experience which revelled in the desecration of musical boundaries from thrash to blues, then back through funk, psychedelia and rock 'n' roll. Lead vocalist Buddo Buddo conveyed a mixture of gut-wrenching passion, flamboyance and deranged eccentricity in his caterwauling (his other claim to fame being his penchant for posing naked at photo sessions). The backbeat was equally unpredictable, with guitarists Pablo Schuter and Don Bakken switching and blending styles with consummate ease. Phil Buerstate (drums) and Todd Winger (bass) provided the necessary power in the rhythm section. The latter was replaced by Dave Truehardt in 1990.

Albums: *Sinister Funkhouse #17* (Roadracer 1989), *Burning Time* (Roadrunner 1991).

Lawnmower Deth

Lawnmower Deth were a thrash metal parody band from the north of England. Founded in 1987, the combined forces of Qualcast Mutilator (vocals), Mr Flymo (drums), Concorde Faceripper (guitars), Mightymo Destructimo (bass) and Scitzophrenic Sprintmaster (guitar) proved a timely antidote to the more ridiculous excesses of banal bloodlust and po-faced pretension in the thrash and death metal genres. With songs like 'Satan's Trampoline' and 'Can I Cultivate Your Groinal Garden', Lawnmower Deth were characterised by their schoolboy sense of humour. This same, somewhat infantile sense of fun, stretched to their live shows with 'gimmicks' like throwing around buckets of baked beans or dressing in third-rate Robin Hood costumes (a direct satire of the pagan Medieval thrash band Skyclad). Eventually the joke began to lose its edge, and Lawnmower Deth expanded musically by including snatches of ska and funk in their repertoire, finally winding the band up over the Christmas of 1994.

Albums: *Quack Em All* (Earache 1988), *Ooh Crikey Its...* (Earache 1990), *Return of The Fabulous Metal Bozo Clowns* (Earache 1992), *Billy* (Earache 1994).

Le Griffe

Despite using the French moniker Le Griffe (meaning 'The Claw') this band was formed in Stoke-On-Trent, Staffordshire, England, in 1980. Le Griffe's original line-up consisted of Chris Hatton (vocals/guitar), Paul Wood (guitar), Tim Blackwood (guitar), Kevin Collier (bass) and Martin Allen (drums). Quickly becoming popular on their local live circuit, the band signed to the (now defunct) Bullet Records label, who released a three-track EP entitled *Fast Bikes* in 1981. The EP was a worthy debut, featuring melodic rockers reminiscent of early Def Leppard coupled with 12-bar Status Quo-style boogie. The band gigged extensively throughout the UK and released a mini-album, *Breaking Strain,* again on the Bullet Records label, in 1984. At the time of its release guitarist Tim Blackwood left the band to be replaced by Amos Sanfillipo, but the band dissolved early in 1985 anyway. Bassist Collier went on to join Rogue Male.

Album: *Breaking Strain* (Bullet 1984, mini-album).

Lawnmower Deth

Leatherwolf

The origins of this Californian quintet date back to 1983 when Michael Olivieri (vocals/guitar), Geoff Gayer (guitar), Carey Howe (guitar), Matt Hurich (bass) and Dean Roberts (drums) were at high school together. Influenced by a range of styles from hard rock to jazz, they recorded a self-titled, five-track mini-album that attracted the attention of Island Records. Matt Hurich was replaced by Paul Carman before they left to record their second album in the Bahamas, under the guidance of REO Speedwagon producer Kevin Beamish. *Street Ready* avoided the pitfalls of their previous release, and saw the band developing their own identity, as they gingerly ventured into the pop-metal crossover market. Beamish achieved a harder and more powerful sound this time, but with an added dimension of accessibility and the potential for commercial success. Ultimately, however, this remained unrealised, with Leatherwolf dematerializing before the start of the new decade.

Albums: *Leatherwolf I* (Tropical 1986), *Leatherwolf II* (Island 1987), *Street Ready* (Island 1989).

Led Zeppelin

This pivotal quartet was formed in October 1968 by British guitarist Jimmy Page (b. James Patrick Page, 9 January 1944, Heston, Middlesex, England) following the demise of his former band, the Yardbirds. John Paul Jones (b. John Baldwin, 31 January 1946, London, England; bass/keyboards), a respected arranger and session musician, replaced original member Chris Dreja, but hopes to incorporate vocalist Terry Reid floundered on a contractual impasse. The singer unselfishly recommended Robert Plant (b. 26 August 1947, Birmingham, England), then frontman of struggling Midlands act Hobbstweedle, who in turn introduced drummer, John Bonham (b. 31 May 1947, Birmingham, England, d. 25 September 1980) when first choice B.J. Wilson opted to remain with Procol Harum. The quartet gelled immediately and having completed outstanding commitments under the name 'New Yardbirds', became Led Zeppelin following an off-the-cuff quip by the Who's Keith Moon, who remarked that they would probably go down like a lead Zeppelin when rating their prospects. Armed with a prestigious contract with Atlantic Records, the group toured the USA supporting Vanilla Fudge prior to the release of their explosive debut *Led Zeppelin*, which included several exceptional original songs, including; 'Good Times, Bad Times', 'Communication Breakdown', 'Dazed And Confused' - a hold-over from the Yardbirds' era,

and skilled interpretations of R&B standards 'How Many More Times?' and 'You Shook Me'. The set vied with Jeff Beck's *Truth* as the definitive statement of English heavy blues/rock, but Page's meticulous production showed a greater grasp of basic pop dynamics, resulting in a clarity redolent of 50s rock 'n' roll. His staggering dexterity was matched by Plant's expressive, beseeching voice, a combination that flourished on *Led Zeppelin II*. The group was already a headline act, drawing sell-out crowds across the USA, when this propulsive collection confirmed an almost peerless position. The introductory track, 'Whole Lotta Love', a thinly-veiled rewrite of Willie Dixon's 'You Need Love', has since become a classic, while 'Livin' Lovin' Maid' and 'Moby Dick', Bonham's exhibition piece, were a staple part of the quartet's early repertoire. Elsewhere, 'Thank You' and 'What Is And What Should Never Be' revealed a greater subtlety, a factor emphasized more fully on *Led Zeppelin III*. Preparation for this set had been undertaken at Bron-Y-Aur cottage in Snowdonia (immortalized in 'Bron-Y-Aur Stomp') and a resultant pastoral atmosphere permeated the acoustic-based selections, 'That's The Way' and 'Tangerine'. 'The Immigrant Song' and 'Gallow's Pole' reasserted the group's traditional fire and the album's release confirmed Led Zeppelin's position as one of the world's leading attractions. In concert, Plant's sexuality and Adonis-like persona provided the perfect foil to Page's more mercurial character, yet both individuals took full command of the stage, the guitarist's versatility matched by his singer's unfettered roar.

Confirmation of the group's ever-burgeoning strengths appeared on *Led Zeppelin IV*, also known as 'Four Symbols', the 'Runes Album' or 'Zoso', in deference to the fact that the set bore no official title. It included the anthemic 'Stairway To Heaven', a group *tour de force*. Arguably the definitive heavy-rock song, it continues to win polls and the memorable introduction remains every guitar novice's first hurdle. The approbation granted this ambitious piece initially obscured other contents, but the energetic 'When The Levee Breaks' is now also lauded as a masterpiece, particularly for Bonham's drumming. 'Black Dog' and 'Rock 'N' Roll' saw Zeppelin at their immediate best, while 'The Battle Of Evermore' was marked by a vocal contribution from Sandy Denny. However, the effusive praise this album generated was notably more muted for *Houses Of The Holy*. Critics queried its musically diverse selection - the set embraced folk ballads, reggae and soul - yet when the accustomed power was unleashed, notably on 'No Quarter', the effect was inspiring. A concurrent US

Jimmy Page and Robert Plant of Led Zeppelin reunited in 1994 for their *Unledded* **project**

tour broke all previous attendance records, the proceeds from which helped finance an in-concert film, issued in 1976 as *The Song Remains The Same*, and the formation of the group's own record label, Swan Song. Bad Company, the Pretty Things and Maggie Bell were also signed to the company, which served to provide Led Zeppelin with total creative freedom. *Physical Graffiti*, a double set, gave full rein to the quartet's diverse interests with material ranging from compulsive hard-rock ('Custard Pie' and 'Sick Again') to pseudo-mystical experimentation ('Kashmir'). The irrepressible 'Trampled Underfoot' joined an ever-growing lexicon of peerless performances while 'In My Time Of Dying' showed an undiminished grasp of progressive blues. Sell-out appearances in the UK followed the release, but rehearsals for a projected world tour were abandoned in August 1975 when Plant sustained multiple injuries in a car crash. A new album was prepared during his period of convalescence, although problems over artwork delayed its release. Advance orders alone assured *Presence* platinum status, yet the set was regarded as a disappointment and UK sales were noticeably weaker. The 10-minute maelstrom, 'Achilles Last Stand', was indeed a remarkable performance, but the remaining tracks were competent rather than fiery and lacked the accustomed sense of grandeur. In 1977 Led Zeppelin began its rescheduled US tour, but on 26 July news reached Robert Plant that his six-year-old son, Karac, had died of a viral infection. The remaining dates were cancelled amid speculation that the group would break up.

They remained largely inactive for over a year, but late in 1978 flew to Abba's Polar recording complex in Stockholm. Although lacking the definition of earlier work, *In Through The Out Door* was a strong collection on which John Paul Jones emerged as the unifying factor. Two concerts at Britain's Knebworth Festival were the prelude to a short European tour on which the group unveiled a stripped-down act, inspired, in part, by the punk explosion. Rehearsals were then undertaken for another US tour, but in September 1980, Bonham was found dead following a lengthy drinking bout. On 4 December, Swansong announced that the group had officially retired, although a collection of archive material, *Coda*, was subsequently issued. Jones later became a successful producer, notably with the Mission, while Plant embarked on a highly-successful solo career, launched with *Pictures At Eleven*. Page scored the film *Death Wish 2* and, after a brief reunion with Plant and the Honeydrippers project in 1984, he inaugurated the short-lived Firm with Paul Rogers. He then formed

the Jimmy Page Band with John Bonham's son, Jason, who in turn drummed with Led Zeppelin on their appearance at Atlantic's 25th Anniversary Concert in 1988. Despite renewed interest in the group's career, particularly in the wake of the retrospective *Remasters*, entreaties to make this a permanent reunion have been resisted. However, in 1994 Page and Plant went two thirds of the way to a reformation with their ironically-titled *Unledded* project, though John Paul Jones was conspicuous by his absence (for want of an invitation). Although their commercial success is unquestionable, Led Zeppelin are now rightly recognized as one of the most influential bands of the rock era and their catalogue continues to provide inspiration to successive generations of musicians.

Albums: *Led Zeppelin* (Atlantic 1969), *Led Zeppelin II* (Atlantic 1969), *Led Zeppelin III* (Atlantic 1970), *Led Zeppelin IV* (Atlantic 1971), *Houses Of The Holy* (Atlantic 1973), *Physical Graffiti* (Swan Song 1975), *Presence* (Swan Song 1976), *The Song Remains The Same* (Swan Song 1976, film soundtrack), *In Through The Out Door* (Swan Song 1979), *Coda* (Swan Song 1982). Compilations: *Led Zeppelin* (Swan Song 1991, 4-CD box set), *Remasters* (Swan Song 1991), *Remasters II* (Swan Song 1993). Page & Plant: *Unledded* (Fontana 1994).

Video: *The Song Remains The Same* (1986).

Further reading: *Hammer Of The Gods*, Stephen Davis. *Led Zeppelin: A Celebration*, Dave Lewis.

Legs Diamond

Deriving their name from an infamous 1920s gangster, Legs Diamond were formed by Michael Diamond (bass) and Jeff Poole (drums) in San Francisco, California, during 1977. Moving to Los Angeles, they recruited Rick Sanford (vocals), Michael Prince (guitar/keyboards) and Roger Romeo (guitar) to consolidate the line-up. Picked up by Mercury Records, their debut release was a classy hard rock album influenced by the traditions of Led Zeppelin and Deep Purple. The songs were well formed, but the album was let down by a weak production. The follow-up was every bit as strong, with the band alternating between brooding and intense power ballads and unabashed rockers. They toured as support to Ted Nugent, Kiss and Styx, but, to their surprise, were dropped by their label shortly afterwards. They subsequently negotiated a deal with the independent Cream label, releasing *Fire Power* in 1978. This marked a change in style to a more AOR-orientated approach, but it was poorly received. The band, disillusioned, decided to go their separate ways. Six years later Rick Sanford resurrected Legs Diamond, and after several personnel changes stabilized the line-up with Romeo and Prince joined by new members Dusty Watson (drums) and Mike Christie (bass). Signing to the independent metal specialists Music For Nations, they have delivered several albums of sophisticated hard rock and captured much of the excitement and promise that they never fulfilled the first time around.

Albums: *Legs Diamond* (Mercury 1977), *A Diamond Is A Hard Rock* (Mercruy 1977), *Fire Power* (Cream 1978), *Out On Bail* (Music For Nations 1984), *Land Of The Gun* (Music For Nations 1986), *Town Bad Girl* (Music For Nations 1990), *Captured Live* (Music For Nations 1992), *The Wish* (Music For Nations 1994).

Leviathan

US hard rock quintet Leviathan comprise Jack Aragon (vocals), Ron Skeen (guitar), John Lutzow (guitar), James Escobedo (bass) and Ty Tameus (drums). Formed in Colorado in 1992, they rose to public prominence in the same year with the release of a self-titled, self-financed 5-song debut CD. Afterwards the group accepted a deal with European label Rock The Nation and recorded its first full length album, *Deepest Secrets Beneath*. Aided by producer Jim Morris (Savatage, Crimson Glory), the group offered a technically precise demonstration of their songwriting skills and power riffs, with an emphasis on textual, neo-progressive structures.

Album: *Deepest Secrets Beneath* (RTN 1994).

Life Of Agony

Brooklyn, New York, USA-based quartet, formed in 1989 by Alan Robert (bass/vocals) and cousins Keith Caputo (vocals/keyboards) and Joey Z (guitar/vocals), eventually recruiting Sal Abruscato (drums). Together they began Life Of Agony (a choice of name emblematic of their downcast world view) as a simple hardcore act, all flaring nostrils and flying sweat, until diminutive lead singer Caputo sought out singing lessons from vocal coach Don Lawrence (who had previously worked with Mick Jagger, Sebastian Bach from Skid Row and Jon Bon Jovi). The result was a much greater level of dexterity employed in both songwriting and execution by the band, with Robert operating as chief lyricist behind Caputo's powerful delivery. Playing on the road in support of Agnostic Front, Biohazard, Fear Factory, Motörhead, Corrosion Of Conformity and Obituary, their debut set for Roadrunner saw a conscious attempt to pull in fans of more melodic metal (Stone Temple Pilots etc.).

Album: *River Runs Red* (Roadrunner 1994).

Life, Sex And Death

This trio were formed in Los Angeles, USA, during 1991 by demented vocalist and ex-Chicago street hobo Stanley. LSD, as they are often known, are completed by drummer Brian Michael Horak and ex-Enuff 'Z' Nuff guitarist Alex Kane. Signing to Warner Brothers, they debuted in July 1992 with *The Silent Majority*, which met with a mixed reception. Influences as diverse as Cheap Trick, Sex Pistols, Beatles and Guns N'Roses manifested themselves clearly, but Stanley's rasping yet inherently melodic vocal style gave the band some identity. LSD were certain to earn a degree of notoriety with their provocative album cover and Stanley's outrageous claim to having not washed for over a year, but their critical reception was hardly gleaming either.

Albums: *The Silent Majority* (Warners 1992).

Lillian Axe

This melodic rock quintet, originally from Michigan, USA, comprised Ron Taylor (vocals), Steve Blaze (guitar), Jon Ster (guitar/keyboards), Rob Stratton (bass) and Danny King (drums). Initially known as Stiff, the band were taken under the wing of Ratt guitarist Robbin Crosby before changing their name to Lillian Axe. Produced by Crosby, their debut was a fine amalgam of infectious rockers and hard-edged pop tunes. *Love And War* was even more impressive, featuring extended atmospheric compositions which were both anthemic and memorable. However, the record sold poorly and MCA dropped the band from their roster. In 1990 Danny King and Rob Stratton were replaced by Gene Barnett and Darren DeLatta respectively, after which the Music For Nations independent became their home for the early 90s.

Albums: *Lillian Axe* (MCA 1988), *Love And War* (MCA 1989), *Poetic Justice* (Music For Nations 1992), *Psychoschizophrenia* (Music For Nations 1994).

Limelight

This UK heavy metal trio, based in Mansfield, Nottinghamshire, was put together by the Scrimshaw brothers; Glen (guitar/keyboards) and Mike (bass/vocals), with Pat Coleman occupying the drum stool. Limelight specialized in extended melodic compositions of a progressive nature, featuring complex time changes and individual virtuoso sections (similar to that of Yes, yet also incorporating the contemporary style of the New Wave Of British Heavy Metal). Their one and only album contained admittedly strong material, but was let down by budget production and weak vocals. The Scrimshaw brothers returned to the pub rock scene, playing mainly pop-rock covers.

Leviathan

Album: *Limelight* (Future Earth 1980), *Limited Limelight* (Avatar 1981, remix/reissue of debut).

Lion

After the demise of the largely overlooked UK hard rock band Tytan, vocalist Kal Swan left England for Los Angeles to put together his own band. Formed in 1983, Lion consisted of Swan (vocals), Doug Aldrich (guitar), Jerry Best (bass) and ex-Steeler drummer Mark Edwards. The band quickly produced a self-financed EP, *Powerlove* (only available as a Japanese release), which gained them a strong following in the Far East. Due to the interest being shown towards them, primarily through their contributions to the soundtracks of two films, *The Wraith* and *Transformers*, they attracted the attention of the Scotti Brothers label. This resulted in the band's debut, *Dangerous Attraction*, released in 1987. This proved to be a strong, melodic hard rock effort, on which Swans' soaring vocals came to the fore. However, Scotti Brothers failed to promote the record fully and album sales suffered. The band signed a new recording agreement with Grand Slamm Records after disentangling themselves from their former employers, resulting in *Trouble At Angel City* being released in 1989. Unfortunately soon after release the band folded due to drummer Mark Edwards experiencing a debilitating accident and guitarist Doug Aldrich leaving to join Hurricane.

Albums: *Power Love* (Lion 1985, Japan only), *Dangerous Attraction* (Scotti Bros 1987), *Trouble At Angel City* (Grand Slam 1989).

Lionheart

Formed in 1980 by Dennis Stratton (guitar) on his exit from Iron Maiden, he was joined in this crusade by vocalist Jess Cox (Tygers Of Pan Tang), Frank Noon (Next Band/Def Leppard) on drums, Steve Mann (Liar) on guitar and Rocky Newton (Wildfire) on bass. They made their highly impressive debut one Saturday night at the Marquee, London, but suffered from bad press thanks to their opinions on Cox. This led to the cancellation of the next two appearances and saw Cox replaced by Reuben Archer (Lautrec). Noon quit in 1981 to join Paul Di'Anno's band before setting off for Waysted. The nucleus of Stratton/Mann and Newton continued with various line-ups that included drummers Les Binks (Judas Priest) and Clive Edwards (Grand Prix). In 1982 they signed to Heavy Metal Records but only managed to release one track, on the *Heavy Metal Heroes Vol 2* compilation. That track, 'Lionheart', remains the only representative recording of their early sound, as later they would significantly adapt their style. With

the addition of Chad Brown on vocals and session drummer Robert Jenkins, they went on to record an album with producer Kevin Beamish (REO Speedwagon). This was a slick, Americanized effort which failed to capture the old fans' interest or that of their target audience in the US. In 1985 they continued with drummer Andy Bierne and Phil Lanzon (keyboards) who had been playing with reformed glam rockers Sweet. After a while Lanzon also left and was replaced by Steve Mann from Stratus and new vocalist Keith Murrell. They split up finally in 1986, with Bierne going into management, Murrell to Mama's Boys and Newton and Mann joining MSG. Stratton later found fame in Japan as part of the British All Stars/Praying Mantis line-up which featured a number of ex-N.W.O.B.H.M. musicians.

Album: *Die For Love* (Epic 1984).

Lionsheart

Following his departure from UK thrashers Onslaught, ex-Grim Reaper vocalist Steve Grimmett set about forming a more melodic band to better suit his vocal abilities and musical inclinations, enlisting twin brothers Mark (guitar) and Steve Owers (bass), Graham Collet (keyboards) and Anthony Christmas (drums). Lionsheart signed to Music For Nations, but the Owers brothers departed before the release of their self-titled debut, with illness leaving Mark Owers unable to tour, and they were replaced by Nick Burr (guitar; ex-Killers/Idol Rich) and Zak Bajjon (bass). Lionsheart ignored grunge trends in favour of guitar-driven melodic hard rock with quality songwriting, and despite minimal reaction at home and in the USA, the band achieved deserved success in Europe and major status in Japan. *Pride In Tact* saw Lionsheart extending their approach from almost AOR balladry to harder blues-rock, with Burr proving equal to the task of following Mark Owers' performance on the debut.

Albums: *Lionsheart* (Music For Nation 1993), *Pride In Tact* (Music For Nations 1994).

Liquid Jesus

This experimental, Los Angeles-based quintet were formed in 1990 by bassist Johnny Lonely and guitarist Scott Tracey. Adding Todd Rigione (guitar), Buck Murphy (vocals) and John Molo (drums), they gigged incessantly on the LA bar and club circuit. Fusing psychedelic, blues, jazz and metal influences to bizarre extremes, they debuted with an independently released live album. Tipped by some as the next Jane's Addiction, they were signed by Geffen Records in 1991 and delivered *Pour In The Sky*. This pooled their

influences of Jimi Hendrix, Led Zeppelin, the Red Hot Chili Peppers and Queen, but accusations of plagiarism were sidestepped by virtue of their totally deranged and unpredictable delivery.
Albums: *Liquid Jesus Live* (Liquid Jesus 1990), *Pour In The Sky* (Geffen 1991).

Little Angels
This UK heavy rock quintet were formed in Scarborough, Yorkshire, during 1985, originally under the title Mr Thrud. Comprising Toby Jepson (vocals), Bruce John Dickinson (guitar), Mark Plunkett (bass), Jimmy Dickinson (keyboards) and Dave Hopper (drums) they were a youthful outfit, whose energy and enthusiasm in the live setting won them a loyal fan base in their native north east. Following a series of independent releases, notably the seven-track *Too Posh To Mosh*, they attracted the attention of Polydor Records. *Don't Prey For Me*, which featured new drummer Michael Lee, included a dozen gems of melodic, but rough-shod rock 'n' roll, characterized by Jepson's raucous and charismatic vocals. The big budget follow-up, mixed by the Steve Thompson/Michael Barbiero partnership, was a disappointment. Abandoning their roots, this set saw them made a concerted attempt to break into the American FM radio market. Internal disputes began to manifest themselves in 1991. Drummer Michael Lee secretly auditioned for the Cult, and was ejected from the band as a result. His replacement would be Mark Richardson. *Jam* regained much of the lost ground in 1993, entering the UK charts at number 1 and winning them the support slot on Van Halen's European tour. However, having found their niche, effectively refining it while still enlarging their fanbase, they nevertheless elected to go their separate ways in 1994. Several farewell gigs were played, with a final album release housed on Castle.
Albums: *Too Posh To Mosh* (Powerstation 1987), *Don't Prey For Me* (Polydor 1989), *Young Gods* (Polydor 1991), *Jam* (Polydor 1993), *Little Of The Past* (Polydor 1994). Compilation: *Too Posh To Nosh* (Castle 1994).
Video: *Big Bad Video* (1991).

Little Caesar
A highly underrated R&B-influenced rock band from Los Angeles, Little Caesar made their recorded debut with one track, 'Down To The Wire', on *Street Survivors*, a compilation showcasing the best unsigned local bands. With a line-up of Ron Young (vocals), Apache (guitar/steel guitar), Louren Molinaire (guitar), Fidel Paniagua (bass) and Tom Morris (drums), an EP, *Name Your Poison*, was recorded,

helping the band sign a major deal with Geffen. The self-titled debut, produced by Bob Rock, deservedly received excellent reviews. Packed with good material, from the basic rock 'n' roll of 'Down-N-Dirty' to the more soulful R&B of 'In Your Arms', plus two Motown covers in 'Chain Of Fools' and 'I Wish It Would Rain', the album displayed the band's strong songwriting talents and sense of melody, coupled with an emotive performance from the smoky-voiced Young. However, despite praise in the press for both live and recorded work, the album failed to take off. As it was released, Guns N'Roses were attaining enormous mass popularity, and the band's tattooed biker image, unpremeditated though it may have been, probably worked against them, allowing many to dismiss them as yet another Guns N'Roses clone band without hearing the evidence. Little was heard from the group for some time, although Young made a cameo appearance in *Terminator 2: Judgement Day*, and 'Down To The Wire' featured on the *Point Break* soundtrack, until they reappeared with ex-David Bowie/Dirty White Boy guitarist Earl Slick replacing the departed Apache for some live shows prior to recording *Influence*. Boasting a harder sound than the debut, the album was another high-quality outing, but despite further good press, sales were again disappointing. When Geffen failed to take up a third album option, the band split up, with Young going on to front the similarly ill-fated Manic Eden.
Albums: *Little Caesar* (Geffen 1990), *Influence* (Geffen 1992).

Little Egypt
Claiming their initial notoriety from the fact that lead guitarist/vocalist Nick Rossi is the son of Francis Rossi of Status Quo, Little Egypt formed in the early 90s as a similarly inclined metal/boogie affair. The nepotism extended further: the group supported Quo on their 1993 tour, while father, who wrote several of their early songs, also co-produced their debut album. Bob Young, famed for his harmonica contributions to the denim warriors, is their manager. The other members of Little Egypt include Duncan Turmain (guitar/vocals), Dan Eames (drums) and 'Flying' Dave Conti (bass).
Album: *Little Egypt* (1994).

Livgren, Kenny
The former Kansas guitarist (b. 18 September 1949, Kansas, USA) departed the fold in the early 80s to put on record his new-found religious beliefs as a born-again Christian. His debut solo effort saw him keeping a nucleus of Kansas personnel in support, adding the vocals of Ronnie James Dio on a

Living Colour

competent set. Afterwards Livgren indulged in some tepid AOR albums, often allied to grandiose orchestral concepts, both solo and with his spin-off project, AD.

Album: *Seeds Of Change* (Kirshner 1980).

Living Colour

This US rock band was originally formed by Vernon Reid (b. England; guitar), Muzz Skillings (bass) and William Calhoun (drums). Reid had studied performing arts at Manhattan Community College, having moved to New York at the age of two. His first forays were in experimental electric jazz with Defunk, before he formed Living Colour as a trio in 1984. Both Skillings and Calhoun were experienced academic musicians, having studied and received acclaim at City College and Berklee College Of Music respectively. The line-up was completed by the induction of vocalist Corey Glover, who had just finished his part in Oliver Stone's *Platoon* movie, and whom Reid had originally encountered at a friend's birthday party. Their first major engagement came when Mick Jagger caught them performing at CBGB's and invited them to the studio for his forthcoming solo album. Jagger's patronage continued as he produced two demos for the band, which would secure them a deal with Epic Records. Their debut, *Vivid*, earned them early critical favour and rose to number 6 in the US charts. Fusing disparate black musical formats like jazz, blues and soul, alongside commercial hard rock, its diversity was reflected in the support slots the band acquired to promote it; Cheap Trick, Robert Palmer and Billy Bragg among them. Musically, the band is aligned primarily to the first named of that trio of acts, although their political edge more closely mirrors the concerns of Bragg. In 1985 Reid formed the *Black Rock Coalition* pressure movement alongside journalist Greg Tate, and Living Colour grew to be perceived as their nation's most articulate black rock band. Two subsequent singles, 'Cult Of Personality' (which included samples of John F. Kennedy and won a Grammy award) and 'Open Letter (To A Landlord)' were both provocative but intelligent expressions of urban concerns. The ties with the Rolling Stones remained strong, with Reid collaborating on Keith Richards' solo album. They also joined the Stones on their *Steel Wheels* tour. After sweeping the boards in several Best New Band awards in such magazines as *Rolling Stone*, *Time's Up* was released in 1990, and afforded another Grammy Award. Notable contributions, apart from the omnipresent Jagger, included Little Richard on the controversial 'Elvis Is Dead'. 1991 saw worldwide touring establish them as

a highly potent force in the mainstream of rock. Bassist Doug Wimbish from Tackhead joined them for *Stain* which added a sprinkling of studio gimmickry on a number of tracks. The band announced its dissolution early in 1995. Vernon Reid issued a statement thus: '...Living Colour's sense of unity and purpose was growing weaker and fuzzier, I was finding more and more creative satisfaction in my solo projects. Finally it became obvious that I had to give up the band and move on'.

Albums: *Vivid* (Epic 1988), *Time's Up* (Epic 1990), *Stain* (Epic 1993).

Lizzy Borden

This theatrical rock outfit formed in Los Angeles in 1983, and took their name from the infamous axe murderess. Utilizing strong sexual and horror imagery, their visual deportment owed much to Alice Cooper. The group featured Lizzy Borden (vocals), his brother Joey Scott Harges (drums), Mike Kenny (bass) and Tony Matuzak (guitar). Their contribution to the *Metal Massacre IV* compilation impressed Metal Blade boss Brian Slagel enough to offer them a contract. The mini-album, *Give 'Em The Ax*, emerged in the summer of 1984, followed a year later by *Love You To Pieces*, their official full-length debut. Both were highly derivative of Rainbow/Iron Maiden, with Lizzy's vocals sounding similar to Geoff Tate's of Queensrÿche. Alex Nelson replaced Tony Matuzak on guitar at a juncture before the recording of *The Murderess Metal Roadshow*. This was a double live collection whose low-tech origins did little to flatter the band. Two more studio albums followed, including the abbreviated *Terror Rising*, which saw Betsy from Bitch duetting on a cover of the Tubes' kitsch classic, 'Don't Touch Me There'. Gene Allen was added as a second guitarist and Jesse Holmes and Mychal Davis replaced Nelson and Kenny respectively, before the recording of what is arguably the band's most enduring set, *Visual Lies*. Loosely based around a central theme of illusions, the album was varied and hard-hitting, characterized by infectious hooks, anthemic choruses and smouldering guitar breaks. They played the Reading Festival in 1987 to an indifferent reaction and Lizzy disbanded the group shortly afterwards (Holmes and Allen having already departed, with guitarist Ron Cerito replacing Mike Davis). Concentrating on a solo career he released the ambitious concept album, *Master Of Disguise*.

Albums: *Give 'Em The Axe* (Metal Blade 1984, mini-album), *Love You To Pieces* (Metal Blade 1985), *The Muderess Metal Roadshow* (Roadrunner 1986), *Menace To Society* (Roadrunner 1986), *Terror Rising*

(Metal Blade 1987, mini-album), *Visual Lies* (Roadrunner 1987). Compilation: *Best Of* (Metal Blade 1994). Lizzy Borden solo: *Master Of Disguise* (Roadrunner 1989).
Video: *Murdress Metal Roadshow* (1986).

Lone Star

This traditional hard rock quintet was formed in 1975 by Kenny Driscoll (lead vocals), Tony Smith (guitar), Paul 'Tonka' Chapman (guitar), Pete Hurley (bass) and Dixie Lee (drums). Specializing in dynamic heavy rock, they attracted considerable attention with their Roy Thomas Baker-produced debut, offering an approach and sound not dissimilar to early Queen's pomp/hard rock formula. Driscoll was replaced by John Sloman in 1977 before the release of *Firing On All Six*. This album pushed the dual guitars of Chapman and Smith to the forefront and concentrated on heavier material by dropping the delicate touches that appeared on their debut. Shortly after its release the band disintegrated, with Sloman joining Uriah Heep, Chapman replacing Michael Schenker in UFO and Dixie Lee teaming up with Wild Horses.
Albums: *Lone Star* (CBS 1976), *Firing On All Six* (CBS 1977), *BBC Radio 1 Live* (Windsong 1994).

Love/Hate

This Los Angeles, California-based quartet, formerly known as Data Clan, originally comprised Jizzy Pearl (lead vocals), Jon E. Love (guitar), Skid Rose (bass) and Joey Gold (drums). Proudly sub-titling themselves the 'stoopidest band in the world', the new name was first invoked in 1986. With a streetwise attitude and a highly talented frontman, their debut album, produced by Tom Werman, was released to widespread critical acclaim. A hybrid of Guns N'Roses and Mötley Crüe, their songs dealt with the well-worn themes of sex, drugs, drink and rock 'n' roll. It was in a live setting that the band truly excelled, however, playing with genuine commitment and generating real intensity with their brand of funk-infused, jitterbug rock. The visual spectacle of a cross constructed from empty Budwiser cans also appealed. *Wasted In America* confirmed their fan's faith in them and recruited many new converts, but nevertheless saw them dropped by Columbia. They regrouped for *Let's Rumble*, with Love replaced by Darren Housholder, but by this point some of the earlier momentum, if not their native talent, had dispersed.
Albums: *Blackout In The Red Room* (Columbia 1990), *Wasted In America* (Columbia 1992), *Let's Rumble* (1993).

Loverboy

Loverboy were formed in Toronto, Canada, in 1980, by Mike Reno (vocals), Paul Dean (guitar), Doug Johnston (keyboards), Scott Smith (bass) and Matthew Frenette (drums). Reno was formerly with Moxy, and Dean and Frenette had been members of Sweetheart, a melodic AOR/heavy rock band. With this pedigree Loverboy were signed by CBS Records as soon as they were formed. Producer Bruce Fairbairn helped them record a self-titled album that was to set Loverboy's standard for years to come. It was an American-styled melodic hard rock collection that also dipped into reggae and jazz moods. With the hit singles 'Turn Me Loose' and 'The Kid Is Hot Tonite', *Loverboy* went platinum. After touring the group re-entered the studio in 1981, with Fairbairn again producing, to record the follow-up, *Get Lucky*. The album lived up to its name by selling over two million copies, helped by the singles chart progress of 'Working For The Weekend'. The only territory where the band had failed to take off was Europe. After further touring Fairbairn produced the multi-platinum *Keep It Up* in 1983, from which 'Hot Girls In Love' charted. Loverboy's inviting blend of melodic AOR had now been honed to a fine art, the album's success keeping the band on the road for nearly two years. On *Lovin' Every Minute Of It* they were joined by Tom Allom, the best known for his work with Judas Priest. The result was a musically tougher album which proved to be the band's least successful, though it still sold well over a million copies. The title-track, released as a single, was written by Def Leppard producer, Robert John 'Mutt' Lange. Fairbairn had by now made his name as the producer of Bon Jovi, but returned to the helm for Loverboy's *Wildside*, released in 1987, and their most complete album to date. Bryan Adams, Richie Sambora and Jon Bon Jovi all co-wrote various tracks. 'Notorious' also proved the band's most successful single, achieving platinum status three times over. This was followed by a marathon two-year tour, their longest yet. They did, however, take a break for two months to record tracks with producer Bob Rock before they came over to support Def Leppard on their European tour in the spring of 1988. After this, Loverboy returned home to Canada and an uncertain future. Dean and Reno announced plans to record solo and this left the rest of the band in limbo. In 1989 a compilation album was released by CBS, *Big Ones*, which also contained three new tracks that had been recorded with Bob Rock. Later that year Dean released a solo effort assisted by Loverboy drummer Frenette and Jon Bon Jovi on harmonica. The parent band, meanwhile, have remained inactive.

Albums: *Loverboy* (CBS 1980), *Get Lucky* (CBS 1981), *Keep It Up* (CBS 1983), *Lovin' Every Minute Of It* (CBS 1985), *Wildside* (CBS 1987). Compilation: *Big Ones* (CBS 1989). Solo album: Paul Dean: *Hard Core* (CBS 1989).

Lynch Mob

Following Dokken's acrimonious split, guitarist George Lynch and drummer Mick Brown recruited bassist Anthony Esposito and tempted vocalist Oni Logan away from the embryonic Cold Sweat to complete Lynch Mob. *Wicked Sensation* was a decent hard rock debut, carried by Lynch's considerable ability, but youthful vocalist Logan's inexperience began to show through on the road. The band felt particularly uncomfortable when comparing Logan with Geoff Tate during a European tour with Queensrÿche, where the highlight of the set tended to be a rendition of 'Mr Scary', Lynch's Dokken-era instrumental guitar workout, and Logan was replaced by another relative unknown, Robert Mason, when touring was complete. *Lynch Mob* incorporated more R&B influences, moving further from the Dokken sound, and this suited Mason's bluesy tones, while the band paid tribute to their influences with a cover of Queen's 'Tie Your Mother Down'. However, neither album really took off, and Lynch split the band, opting to go solo while Brown rejoined Don Dokken. Albums: *Wicked Sensation* (Elektra 1990), *Lynch Mob* (Elektra 1992).

Lynott, Phil

b. 20 August 1951, Dublin, Eire, d. 4 January 1986. Having enjoyed considerable success in Thin Lizzy, Lynott first recorded solo in 1980, the same year that he married Caroline Crowther, daughter of the television celebrity, Leslie Crowther. Lynott's first single, 'Dear Miss Lonely Hearts', reached number 32 in the UK charts and was followed by an album, *Solo In Soho*. A tribute to Elvis Presley, 'King's Call' also reached number 35. Lynott had to wait until 1982 for his next hit, 'Yellow Peril', which reached the UK Top 20 after being used as the theme tune to television show *Top Of The Pops*. In the summer of 1983 Thin Lizzy broke up and it was widely anticipated that Lynott would go on to solo fame. A new group, Grand Slam, failed to develop and Lynott's subsequent solo single, 'Nineteen', did not sell. The last notable instalment in his career arrived in May 1985 when he partnered Gary Moore on the number 5 hit, 'Out In The Fields'. He played his last gig with Grand Slam at the Marquee in London on 3 December 1985. At the turn of the following year he suffered a drug overdose and, following a week in a coma, died of heart failure, exacerbated by pneumonia.
Albums: *Solo In Soho* (Vertigo 1981), *The Phillip Lynott Solo Album* (Vertigo 1992).
Further reading: *Phillip Lynott: The Rocker*, Mark Putterford. *Songs For While I'm Away*, Phillip Lynott.

Lynyrd Skynyrd

Formed in Jacksonville, Florida, in 1964, this US boogie/hard rock band took their (slightly corrupted) name from their Physical Education teacher, Leonard Skinner. The group initially comprised Ronnie Van Zant (b. 15 January 1948, Jacksonville, Florida, USA, d. 20 October 1977; vocals), Gary Rossington (b. 4 December 1951, Jacksonville, Florida, USA; guitar), Allen Collins (b. 19 July 1952, Jacksonville, Florida, USA, d. 23 January 1990; guitar; ex-Mods), Larry Jungstrom (bass) and Bob Burns (drums; ex-Me, You & Him), the quintet meeting through minor league baseball connections. Together they played under various names, including Noble Five, Wildcats, Sons Of Satan and My Backyard, releasing one single, 'Need All My Friends', in 1968, before switching to the Lynyrd Skynyrd moniker. After playing the southern states during the late 60s they released a second single, 'I've Been Your Fool', in 1971, after recording demos in Sheffield, Alabama. The group were discovered in Atlanta by Al Kooper in 1972 while scouting for new talent to place on his Sounds Of The South label. Signed for $9,000, the group's ranks were swollen by the addition of Leon Wilkeson (b. 2 April 1952; bass), who replaced Jungstrom (who would go on to work with Van Zant's brother, Donnie, in .38 Special). Kooper produced the group's debut album, *Pronounced Leh-Nerd Skin-Nerd*, which also featured former Strawberry Alarm Clock guitarist Ed King (originally standing in on bass for Wilkeson, who dropped out of the band for six months) and Billy Powell (b. 3 June 1952; keyboards). Their three-guitar line-up attracted a great deal of attention, much of it generated via support slots with the Who, and the combination of blues, honky tonk and boogie proved invigorating. Their momentous anthem, 'Free Bird' (a tribute to Duane Allman), included a superb guitar finale, while its gravity and durability were indicated by frequent reappearances in the chart years after. In 1974 the group enjoyed their biggest US hit with 'Sweet Home Alabama', an amusing and heartfelt response to Neil Young who had criticized the south in his compositions 'Southern Man' and 'Alabama'. After the release of parent album *Second Helping* drummer Bob Burns was replaced by Artimus Pyle (b. 15 July 1948, Spartanburg, South Carolina, USA). The group were by now renowned as much for their hard-living as their music, and Ed King became the first victim of excess when retiring from the band in May 1975 (Van Zant's name was also regularly to be found in the newspapers through reports of bar brawls and confrontations with the law). *Gimme Back My Bullets* arrived in March of the following year, with production expertise from Tom Dowd. In September 1976 Rossington was injured in a car crash, while Steve Gaines (b. 14 September 1949, Seneca, Missouri, d. 20 October 1977; guitar) became King's replacement. With their tally of gold discs increasing each year and a series of sell-out tours, the band suffered an irrevocable setback in late 1977. On 20 October, Van Zant, Gaines, his sister Cassie (one of three backing singers) and personal manager Dean Kilpatrick were killed in a plane crash *en route* from Greenville, South Carolina, to Baton Rouge, Louisiana. Rossington, Collins, Powell and Wilkeson were all seriously injured, but each would recover. That same month the group's new album, *Street Survivors*, was withdrawn as the sleeve featured an unintentionally macabre design of the band surrounded by flames. With their line-up devastated, the group dispersed and the remaining members went on to join the Rossington-Collins Band (with the exception of Pyle). In 1987 the name Lynyrd Skynyrd was revived for a 'reunion' tour featuring Rossington, Powell, Pyle, Wilkeson and King, with Ronnie's brother Johnny Van Zant (vocals) and Randell Hall (guitar). One of their performances was later issued as the live double set, *For The Glory Of The South*. Collins had earlier been paralysed, and his girlfriend killed, during an automobile accident in 1986. When he died in 1990 from pneumonia, this only helped to confirm Lynyrd Skynyrd's status as a 'tragic' band. However, members were still performing, and recording, in the early 90s, after disentangling themselves from legal complications over the use of the name caused by objections from Van Zant's widow. The most spectacular aspect of which was a 20th Anniversary performance live on cable television in February 1993, with Rossington, Powell, Wilkeson, King and Johnny Van Zant joined by guests including Peter Frampton, Brett Michaels (Poison), Charlie Daniels and Tom Kiefer (Cinderella), the latter having also written new songs with Rossington. Pyle was conspicuous by his absence, having been charged with a sexual assault on a four year old girl the previous year.

Albums: *Pronounced Leh-Nerd Skin-Nerd* (Sounds Of The South/MCA 1973), *Second Helping* (Sounds Of The South/MCA 1974), *Nuthin' Fancy* (MCA 1975), *Gimme Back My Bullets* (MCA 1976), *One More From The Road* (MCA 1976), *Street Survivors* (MCA 1977), *First And Last* (MCA 1978, rec. 1970-72), *For The Glory Of The South* (MCA 1987, double album), *The Last Rebel* (MCA 1993). Compilations: *Gold And Platinum* (MCA 1980, double album), *Best Of The Rest* (MCA 1982), *Legend* (MCA 1987), *Anthology* (Raw Power 1987), *Lynyrd Skynyrd 1991* (MCA 1991, 3-CD set), *Definitive* (MCA 1992).

M

M.A.R.S.

This short-lived supergroup project was assembled in 1987. Featuring Tony Macalpine (guitar), Tommy Aldridge (drums), Robert Rock (vocals) and Rudi Sarzo (bass), their collective pedigrees promised more than they delivered. Produced by Mike Varney, their sole album would have been indistinguishable from Vinnie Moore's, Tony Macalpine's, Marty Friedman's, Jason Becker's or Greg Howe's instrumental sets, were it not for the additional vocals of Rock. *Project Driver* seriously lacked identity, with the all-too transparent influences of Yngwie Malmsteen and Rainbow unbalancing the collection. The band dissolved soon after the release, with Sarzo and Aldridge joining Whitesnake, Rock taking over vocals in Joshua and Macalpine picking up his solo career once more.
Album: *Project Driver* (Roadrunner 1987).

Macabre

Chicago-based specialists in the field of sick rock, Macabre's chief obsession is with serial killers. The positive response to their mass murderer-fixated demos on the fanzine network, demonstrated the degree to which Macabre had tapped into a fascination of the heavy metal underground. During the late 80s serial killers were becoming the ultimate villains - icons of anti-sociability - and serial killer T-shirts, magazines and books were doing a brisk trade on the darker fringes of youth culture. In 1987 Macabre released their official debut, the self-financed EP, *Grim Reality*, which featured ditties about such deviants as German cannibal Fritz Haarmann, and Harvey Glatman 'the Want Ad killer'. Macabre's material often sounds like punk nursery rhymes: serial killer tributes which drip with black humour and kitsch crudity, delivered with frantic speed, minimal polish and a total disregard for any standards of good taste. As their career has progressed, their style has veered away from their more punkish roots to include a few death metal flourishes, but is still decidedly rough. With the stable line-up of Dennis the Menace (drums), Corporate Death (vocals, lead guitar) and Nefarious (bass guitar), Macabre remain a morbid gag of extravagant proportions.

Albums: *Gloom* (Vinyl Solution 1989), *Sinister Slaughter* (Nuclear Blast 1992)

Macalpine, Tony

Initially trained as a pianist, Tony Macalpine graduated to the electric guitar with an ambition to fuse rock and classical influences into a musical form that would have widespread appeal. Teaming up with ex-Journey drummer Steve Smith and ex-Dave Lee Roth bassist Billy Sheehan, he recorded *Edge Of Insanity*, which featured a set of classical-jazz-rock fusion instrumental numbers. The album was characterized by Macalpine's ability to improvise and imbue feeling and emotion into songs, even at break-neck speed. He experimented with the idea of forming a straightforward rock band as a consequence, and signed up Tommy Aldridge (drums), Rudi Sarzo (bass) and Robert Rock (vocals) to record *Project Driver* under the M.A.R.S. alias; a disappointing Rainbow-style collection of hard rock numbers. The band split soon after the release and Macalpine returned to solo status, forming his own Squawk label. He released another all-instrumental album but it was readily apparent, not least to the artist, that he had taken this particular format as far as it could go. On *Eyes Of The World* he added Alan Schorn on lead vocals, Mark Robertson (keyboards), Billy Carmassi (drums) and Mike Jacques (drums) to form Macalpine, the band, specializing in highly polished melodic rock, punctuated by fluid but economical guitar breaks.

Albums: *Edge Of Insanity* (Roadrunner 1986), *Maximum Security* (Vertigo 1987). As Macalpine: *Eyes Of The World* (Vertigo 1990).

Macc Lads

This trio from Macclesfield, Cheshire, England, comprised pseudonymous chancers The Beater (guitar/vocals), Muttley McLad (bass/vocals) and Chorley The Hord (drums). With a musical brief that incorporated elements of three-chord boogie, metallic riffs and punk, they insulted and entertained their audiences with a barrage of foul-mouthed one-liners and rock 'n' roll rugby songs. Lyrically, they extolled and exaggerated the virtues of the northern, macho, male-dominated pub scene: drinking real ale, 'pulling'

women, Chinese takeaways and homophobia. Sample song titles include: 'Now He's A Poof', 'Eh Up Let's Sup', 'Dan's Big Log' and 'No Sheep 'Til Buxton'. Releasing a series of albums full of schoolboy humour, they gradually ran out of ideas. Shunned by nearly every record company and live venue in the land, the Macc Lads' grim philosophy, if such a polysyllabic word is appropriate, remains.

Albums: *Beer & Sex & Chips 'N' Gravy* (FM Revolver 1985), *Bitter, Fit, Crack* (FM Revolver 1987), *Live At Leeds - The Who?* (FM Revolver 1988), *From Beer To Eternity* (Hectic House 1989), *The Beer Necessities* (Hectic House 1990), *Turtle's Heads* (Hectic House 1991), *Alehouse Rock* (Up Not Down 1994). Compilation: *20 Golden Crates* (1991).

Video: *Come To Brum* (1989), *Quality Of Mersey* (1990), *Three Bears* (1990), *Sex Pies And Videotape* (1992).

Machine Head

Formed in Oakland, California, USA, in June 1992, Machine Head comprise Robb Flynn (vocals/guitar; ex-Violence), Logan Mader (guitar), Adam Duce (bass) and Chris Kontos (drums). Specializing in angry, violent scenarios, their debut album relied heavily on Flynn's 'reflections about the self and some of my personal experiences'. These were accompanied by overdriven guitars in the tradition of a fresh-faced Anthrax, with a level of guile that few had anticipated. European touring with Slayer brought the band rave reviews the following year, before Roadrunner released 'Old', backed by cover versions of hardcore material by Poison Idea and the Cro-Mags. Meanwhile *Burn My Eyes* picked up third place in *Kerrang!* Magazine's critics lists for 1994, describing the band as 'the HM discovery of the year'.

Album: *Burn My Eyes* (Roadrunner 1994).

Madam X

One of Madam X's more distinctive songs, 'Come One, Come All', contained the line 'We're bad, we're good, that's all we ever wanted'. Sadly for them a critical majority denounced them as belonging to the former category. The group were formed in New York in 1983 by sisters Maxine and Roxy Petrucci on guitar and drums respectively, along with vocalist Bret Kaiser and bassist Christopher 'Godzilla' Doliber. They subsequently moved to Los Angeles where their brand of glam metal was better accepted. In February 1985 they released an anthemic single, 'High In High School', backed with a suitably grandiose video. The single was produced by Rick Derringer who also performed the same task on the album. Both, however, were very average affairs and live shows fell short of the expected excitement. In 1986 Roxy departed to form Vixen and Kaiser quit the scene with ego suitably deflated. Mark McConnell took over the drums whilst vocal duties were handled by Sebastian Bach. Within the year the band disintegrated with Doliber forming a wild and heavy band called Godzilla (which failed). Maxine remained in the shadow of her sister, but Bach found stardom with Skid Row.

Album: *We Reserve The Right* (Jet 1984).

Madball

Singer Freddy Cricien (b. Florida, USA), brother of Agnostic Front's Roger Miret, was unsurprisingly influenced by his imposing sibling. So much so that when he put his own band together after following the New York legends across the country, Madball would operate in a similar, all-out hardcore vein. In fact Cricien had made his debut at an Agnostic Front show at the age of seven, when visiting his New York-based brethren, getting up on stage to offer a rendition of the Animals' It's My Life'. Eventually he would move to the US capital, spending many of his evenings at the city's home for hardcore, CBGB's. In fact, it would be Vinnie Stigma of Agnostic Front who would give him his nickname, 'Madball', after harassing the young Cricien to the point at which his face resembled such an object, in the back of the tour van. When Madball was put together, it included Vinnie on guitar, with brother Roger on bass and Will Shepler on drums. Their first release, 'Ball Of Destruction', was unveiled in 1989 on In-Effect Records, and is now a genuine rarity. However, there was a three-year gap before a second 7-inch, 'Droppin' Many Suckers', this time for Wreck-age Records. It prefaced a switch to Roadrunner and a long-playing set which, predictably, accented machismo and power over subtlety, but was an energizing collection for all that. It saw the debut of the current line-up; Cricien (vocals), Shepler (drums), Stigma (guitar), Matt Henderson (guitar), Hoya (bass).

Album: *Set It Off* (Roadrunner 1993).

Magellan

Formed in Vacaville, California, USA, in the mid-80s, Magellan was originally a project put together by brothers Wayne (electric and acoustic guitar) and Trent (lead vocals/keyboards) Gardner. Together with Hal Stringfellow Imbrie (bass/vocals) they set out to reinstate the progressive rock tradition of the 70s which married riffs to jazz and classical flourishes. This combination was finely executed on their 1991 debut, *Hour Of Restoration*, which added modern, computer-generated possibilities to the equation. August 1993 saw the release of its follow-up, *Impending Ascension,* which earned comparisons to Dream Theater's crafted electro-rock. Opponents of grandiose musical statements were rewarded with much to scoff at, including quotes drawn from Shakespeare, Poe and Magellan, the historical explorer from whom the group took their name. The subject matter, however, was far from trite mysticism, and included topics like virtual reality and social alienation.

Albums: *Hour Of Restoration* (Magna Carta/Roadrunner 1991), *Impending Ascension* (Magna Carta/Roadrunner 1993).

Magnum

The Birmingham, England-based pomp rockers were formed in 1972 by Tony Clarkin (guitar), Bob Catley (vocals), Kex Gorin (drums) and Dave Morgan (bass). They remained unsigned, undertaking various engagements including acting as Del Shannon's backing band, until 1978, when they were picked up by Jet Records. By this time Morgan had departed, to be replaced by Colin 'Wally' Lowe, and Richard Baily had joined as keyboard player. Between 1978 and 1980, Magnum released three albums to a moderate degree of success, and toured relentlessly with Judas Priest, Blue Öyster Cult, and Def Leppard. *Chase The Dragon* was released in 1982, with new keyboard player Mark Stanway, and gave them their first Top 20 album; it featured the grandiose pomp of 'Sacred Hour' and 'The Spirit', both of which still appear in their current live set. Following the release of *Eleventh Hour* problems beset the band: Clarkin became ill, and a dispute with Jet Records ensued. These combined to cause the band to fragment. The troubles were soon resolved, and a number of low-key club dates persuaded them to continue. FM Revolver Records signed the band in 1985 for *On A StoryTeller's Night*. Its Top 40 success, along with a highly successful tour of the UK, prompted Polydor Records to offer a long-term contract. *Vigilante*, which featured new drummer Mickey Barker, was the first release under a new deal, and was produced by Queen's Roger Taylor. The backing of a major label paid immediate dividends with a Top 30 album and a sold-out UK tour. This success was taken one step further with *Wings Of Heaven* (1988), their first gold album and UK Top 10 hit. Top 40 single success came with 'Days Of No Trust', 'Start Talkin' Love', and 'It Must Have Been Love'. Numerous compilation albums, including *Mirador* and *Anthology*, were released, along with re-issues of their now extensive back-catalogue from Jet Records. A

Machine Head

two-year gap between official releases resulted in the Keith Olsen-produced *Goodnight L.A.* and again Top 40 success was achieved with a single, 'Rocking Chair', the album also enjoying Top 10 status. Extensive touring promoted *Goodnight L.A.* and several shows were recorded for a double live set, *The Spirit*. After years of struggle and setbacks, Magnum's popularity has been achieved the hard way, by dint of constant touring and a series of quality albums.

Albums: *Kingdom Of Madness* (Jet 1978), *Magnum II* (Jet 1979), *Marauder* (Jet 1980), *Chase The Dragon* (Jet 1982), *The Eleventh Hour* (Jet 1983), *On A StoryTeller's Night* (Polydor 1985), *Vigilante* (Polydor 1986), *Wings Of Heaven* (Polydor 1988), *Goodnight L.A.* (Polydor 1990), *Invasion - Magnum Live* (Receiver 1990), *The Spirit* (Polydor 1991, double album), *Sleepwalking* (Polydor 1992), *Rock Art* (EMI 1994). Compilations: *Anthology* (Raw Power 1986), *Collection* (Castle 1990), *Box Set* (Castle 1992), *Chapter And Verse - Best Of* (Polydor 1993), *Uncorked* (Jet 1994).

Videos: *The Sacred Hour Live* (1986), *On The Wings Of Heaven* (1988), *From Midnight To LA* (1990).

Mahogany Rush

Recovering in hospital from a bad drugs experience, Frank Marino claimed he was visited by an apparition of Jimi Hendrix. After leaving hospital he picked up a guitar for the first time and was able to play Hendrix riffs, or so the legend runs. The group was formed in Montreal during 1970 when Marino recruited bassist Paul Harwood and drummer Jim Ayoub to fulfil his desire to work in a power trio format. Their first three albums were derivative in the extreme; every component of Hendrix's unique style had been dismantled, adapted, then re-built under new song titles. Nevertheless, they were not condemned as copyists, but revered instead for paying tribute to the great man in such an honest and sincere fashion. By 1976 Marino had started to develop his own style, based on an extension of the Hendrix tricks he had already acquired. This is clearly evident on *Mahogany Rush IV* and *World Anthem*, released in 1976 and 1977 respectively. Eventually he outgrew the comparisons as his own style began to dominate the band's material. The name was amended to Frank Marino and Mahogany Rush, then to Frank Marino, following the release of *What's Next* and the departure of Ayoub.

Magnum

Albums: *Maxoom* (Kotai 1971), *Child Of The Novelty* (20th Century 1974), *Strange Universe* (20th Century 1975), *Mahogany Rush IV* (CBS 1976), *World Anthem* (CBS 1977), *Live* (CBS 1978), *Tales Of The Unexpected* (CBS 1979), *What's Next* (CBS 1980).

Malevolent Creation

Formed in Buffalo, New York, in 1987, it took Malevolent Creation four years to secure a deal and release their official debut. This gore-fixated recording, *The Ten Commandments*, was mixed at Morrisound Studios in Florida by Scott Burns. Burns' distinctive production more or less defined the death metal sound, and he was in great demand among death metal bands. But his work, like the genre, has become increasingly formulaic. Despite this, Malevolent Creation were an above average example of the genre, and attracted a degree of critical acclaim. They arrived on the death metal scene too late, however, to establish themselves among the front-runners and as its popularity waned, the band found themselves without a deal in 1994 and have since broken up.

Albums: *The Ten Commandments* (Roadrunner 1991), *Retribution* (Roadrunner 1992), *Stillborn* (Roadrunner 1993).

Malice

This Los Angeles band emerged from the local club scene of the early 80s with a sound influenced by European metal, particularly Judas Priest. Indeed Malice were widely described as Priest clones, not only for their twin guitar-based sound and James Neal's vocal similarities to Rob Halford, but also for their leather-clad image and guitarist Jay Reynolds' distinct resemblance to KK Downing. Malice, completed by Mick Zane (guitar), Mark Behn (bass) and Peter Laufman (drums), recorded a five-track demo with producer Michael Wagener of stunning quality, which had independent labels clamouring to release it in its own right, but the band instead signed to Atlantic Records. The demo formed half of *In The Beginning*, with the remaining five tracks produced by Ashley Howe, an excellent debut built on a solid base of power metal guitars, although the Priest comparison remained obvious. However, cracks were beginning to show by *License To Kill*, as internal conflicts began to divide the band, and the split came in late 1987, as Malice divided into two warring camps. Reynolds later joined Megadeth for a brief period.

Albums: *In The Beginning* (Atlantic 1985), *License To Kill* (Atlantic 1987).

Malmsteen, Yngwie

This Swedish-born guitar virtuoso was the originator of the high-speed, technically precise, neo-classical style that developed during the 80s. Influenced by Jimi Hendrix, Ritchie Blackmore and Eddie Van Halen, Malmsteen first picked up a guitar at the age of five and had formed his first band, Powerhouse, by the time he entered his teens. At age 14 he formed Rising, named after Rainbow's second album, and recorded a series of demo tapes. One of these was picked up by producer and guitar specialist Mike Varney. Malmsteen was persuaded by Varney to relocate to Los Angeles and join Ron Keel's Steeler as lead guitarist, and went straight into the studio to record the band's debut album. Following this he was approached by Kiss, UFO and Ozzy Osbourne, but declined their offers in favour of teaming up with Graham Bonnet in a new group called Alcatrazz. This association lasted for one studio album and a live set, recorded in Japan. After the dissolution of that band Malmsteen was immediately offered a solo deal by Polydor Records, just as his reputation and stature were beginning to escalate. He released the self-produced *Rising Force*, utilizing ex-Jethro Tull drummer Barriemore Barlow, vocalist Jeff Scott Soto and keyboardist Jens Johansson. This comprised a mixture of new songs and re-worked demo material that had been available for several years. Deciding to work within a band framework once more, but this time exercising tight control, Malmsteen formed Rising Force with Soto and Johansson, plus bassist Marcel Jacob and drummer Anders Johansson. This basic formation recorded two albums, the second of which, *Trilogy*, saw Soto replaced by ex-Ted Nugent vocalist Mark Boals, which showcased Malmsteen's amazing virtuosity and ability to combine speed with melody. Following an 18-month break after a serious road accident involving Malmsteen, Rising Force was resurrected again with ex-Rainbow vocalist Joe Lynn Turner. Produced by Jeff Glixman and mixed by the Thompson/Barbiero team, *Odyssey* was released in 1988 to widespread acclaim. At last Malmsteen's guitar pyrotechnics had been anchored within commercial hard rock structures. The guitar solos, for once, were economical, and did not detract from the songs. The album reached number 40 on the USA *Billboard* album chart and brought many new fans to the guitarist. Eager to capitalize on this success, Malmsteen then issued a disappointing and self-indulgent live album recorded in Leningrad. The momentum was lost and Joe Lynn Turner was dismissed, to be replaced with a Swedish vocalist, Goran Edman. *Eclipse* emerged in 1990 with weak vocals and an unusually restrained Malsteen on guitar, and it appeared that he was suppressing his real desires and ability in the search for commercial success. *Fire And Ice* debuted at number 1 in the Japanese charts, and introduced new vocalist Mike Vescera. He switched back to his old flamboyant style on *No Mercy*, however, which featured classical material and a string orchestra.

Albums: *Yngwie Malmsteen's Rising Force* (Polydor 1984), *Marching Out* (Polydor 1985), *Trilogy* (Polydor 1986), *Odyssey* (Polydor 1988), *Live In Leningrad* (Polydor 1989), *Eclipse* (Polydor 1990), *Fire & Ice* (Elektra 1992), *Seventh Sign* (Elektra 1994), *No Mercy* (CMC International 1994).

Videos: *Rising Force Live 85* (1989), *Trial By Fire* (1989), *Collection* (1992).

Mama's Boys

The three McManus brothers began their musical careers as folk musicians, playing the local dance hall and club circuit in their native Northern Ireland. After experiencing the Irish electric folk-rock outfit Horslips in concert in 1978, they decided to abandon their acoustic guitars and tambourines and become a hard rock power trio. John took on vocals and bass, Pat picked up lead guitar and Tommy occupied the drumstool. Merging traditional Irish influences with blues and heavy rock, they quickly developed a unique style that echoed Thin Lizzy. Their first two albums contained high-energy boogie and driving blues, but from *Turn It Up* onwards, they began to show a greater awareness of melody and veered towards AOR. Realizing the limitations of John as a vocalist, they expanded to a quartet in 1987, adding ex-Airrace singer Keith Murrell. *Growing Up The Hard Way* followed and was undoubtedly the band's most accomplished album, with a sophisticated approach reminiscent of Foreigner. After four years of recording inactivity, *Live Tonite* emerged. Recorded on their 1990 European tour, it featured latest vocalist Mike Wilson, plus four new songs. On 16 November 1994 Tommy McManus died of a lung infection following a bone marrow transplant, having for several years been plagued by leukaemia.

Albums: *Official Bootleg* (Pussy 1980), *Plug It In* (Albion 1982), *Turn It Up* (Spartan 1983), *Mama's Boys* (Jive 1984), *Power And The Passion* (Jive 1985), *Growing Up The Hard Way* (Jive 1987), *Live Tonite* (Music For Nations 1991), *Relativity* (CTM 1992).

Yngwie Malmsteen

Mammoth

The prerequisite for joining this appropriately titled outfit was, as legend has it, to weigh in excess of 20 stone. Consequently potential members were few and far between, but compensated for in girth what they lacked in number. Vocalist Nicky Moore (ex-Samson) and bassist John McCoy (ex-Gillan) eventually found guitarist Big Mac Baker and drummer 'Tubby' Vinnie Reid large enough for their requirements. The idea behind Mammoth was to present an alternative to 'pouting' rock bands like Poison and Bon Jovi, with the music, rather than the image, topping the agenda. Unfortunately, due to contractual problems with their record company Jive, their debut album was delayed for 10 months and the interest they generated had evaporated by the time it was released. It comprised a poorly produced but workmanlike selection of hard rock and R&B numbers, with guitarists Bernie Tormé and Kenny Cox guesting on a couple of tracks. The single, 'Can't Take The Hurt Anymore', was included on the soundtrack to *Nightmare On Elm Street 5, The Dream Child*. The band collapsed shortly after the album's release.
Album: *Mammoth* (Jive 1988).

Manic Street Preachers

These UK punk revivalists enjoyed a love-hate relationship with the music press which provided a bizarre story in 1991. The catalyst was Richey Edwards, who cut the words '4 Real' into his forearm to the amazement of *New Musical Express* critic Steve Lamacq, when he dared to call into question the band's authenticity. The group hails from Blackwood, Gwent, Wales, and is comprised of James Dean Bradfield (b. 21 February 1969; vocals/guitar), Richey Edwards (b. 27 December 1969; rhythm guitar), Nicky Wire (bass) and Sean Moore (b. 30 July 1970; drums). Their calculated insults at a wide variety of targets, particularly their peers, had already won them infamy following the release of their debut *New Art Riot* EP, and the Public Enemy-sampling 'Motown Junk' (a previous single, 'Suicide Alley', had been a limited pressing distributed to journalists only). Their personal manifesto was equally explicit: rock bands should cut down the previous generation, release one explosive album then disappear. Although the music press pointed out the obvious contradictions and naivete of this credo, the band polarized opinion to a degree which far outweighed their early musical proficiency. The singles, 'Stay Beautiful' and 'Love's Sweet Exile' (backed by the superior 'Repeat' - 'Repeat after me, fuck Queen and Country') were inconclusive, but the reissued version of 'You Love Us', with its taut, vicious refrain, revealed a band beginning to approach in power what they had always had in vision. Their debut album, too, was an injection of bile which proved perversely refreshing in a year of industry contraction and self-congratulation. Unfortunately, it never quite achieved its intention to outsell Guns N'Roses' *Appetite For Destruction*, nor did the band split immediately afterwards as stated. The polished, less caustic approach of *Gold Against The Soul* saw the Manics hitting a brick wall in expectation and execution, though as always there were moments of sublime lyricism (notably the singles 'Roses In The Hospital' and 'Life Becoming A Landslide'). *The Holy Bible* returned the group to the bleak worldview of yesteryear, notably on the haunting '4st 7lb', written by a near-anorexic Richey James before a nervous breakdown which saw him temporarily admitted to a mental facility. Other subject matter was drawn from prostitution, the holocaust and the penal system. Never easy listening at the best of times (despite the ability to write genuinely affecting songs like 'Motorcycle Emptiness'), the Manics have already produced enough inspired moments to justify their protracted early claims.
Albums: *Generation Terrorists* (Columbia 1992, double album), *Gold Against The Soul* (Columbia 1993), *The Holy Bible* (Columbia 1994).

Manowar

This traditionalist heavy metal quartet from the USA (whose motto is 'Death To False Metal') was formed in 1981 by bassist Joey Demaio (a former Black Sabbath roadie) and ex-Shakin' Street and Dictators' guitarist Ross The Boss (b. Ross Friedman). Recruiting vocalist Eric Adams and drummer Donnie Hamzik, they decided on an approach that was to be the total antithesis of melodic AOR. Dressed in animal skins, they delivered a brutal series of riffs that were characterized by Adam's barbaric vocals and the dense bass-work of Demaio. They debuted in 1982 with *Battle Hymns*, a milestone in the metal genre. With subject material firmly centred on fighting, bloodshed, death and carnage, they came over as a turbo-charged hybrid of Ted Nugent and Black Sabbath. The album was notable for an amazing version of the 'William Tell Overture', played as an electric bass solo, while the voice of actor Orson Welles appeared on 'Dark Avenger'. *Battle Hymns* failed to sell, however, and with the press treating the band as an absurd joke, they were dropped by Liberty Records in 1982. They subsequently signed to Megaforce (Music For Nations in the UK) using their own blood on the contract, their veins opened via a ceremonial dagger. Scott Columbus took over the

Manic Street Preachers

drumstool on *Into Glory Ride*, another intensely heavy, chest-beating collection of metal epics. They built up a small yet loyal cult following, but were generally panned by the rock mainstream. Their UK tours in 1983 and 1984 attracted poor audiences, but they had more success in Europe. *Sign Of The Hammer*, released in 1985, featured some excellent guitar work from Ross The Boss and contained the band's most accessible compositions to date, including the archetypal metal boast, 'All Men Play On 10'. Once again it flopped, and after a serious re-think they returned two years later with *Fighting The World* (in the meantime they had entered the *Guinness Book Of Records* for playing live at 160 decibels). On this album they incorporated elements borrowed from Kiss and Judas Priest into their songwriting, but although it was aimed at the rock mainstream, it failed to win many new fans. *Kings Of Metal* was released the following year and met with a similar fate. Disillusioned, Ross The Boss quit in 1988, with Scott Columbus following suit two years later (Ross was replaced by Death Dealer, aka Dave Shankel, Columbus by Rhino). The future of the group is still uncertain. Manowar are colourful, flamboyant and rather kitsch, but nevertheless an essential component in the music industry; the perfect antidote to the sometimes conservative rock fraternity.

Albums: *Battle Hymns* (Liberty 1982), *Into Glory Ride* (Megaforce 1983), *Hail To England* (Megaforce 1984), *Sign Of The Hammer* (Virgin 1985), *Fighting The World* (Atco 1987), *Kings Of Metal* (Atlantic 1988), *Triumph Of Steel* (Atlantic 1992).

Mantas

This short-lived hard rock quartet was formed by Mantas after quitting the demonic thrash metallers Venom. Enlisting the help of vocalist Pete Harrison, second guitarist Al Barnes and Keith Nichol on keyboards, their debut and only release comprised nine new originals penned by Mantas. Moving away from the one-dimensional approach of Venom, they straddled the ground between AOR and the more commercial slant of Rainbow, Saxon and Dio. *Winds Of Change* featured computerized drums and extensive use of keyboards, but Harrison's vocals lacked distinction and the material was ultimately dull. The album was ignored by mainstream record purchasers aside from diehard Venom fans. After a careful re-think, Mantas disbanded the group and re-joined Venom in 1989.

Album: *Winds Of Change* (Neat 1988).

Marillion

Frontrunners of the short-lived UK progressive rock revival of the early 80s, Marillion survived unfavourable comparisons with Genesis to become a popular melodic rock group, notching up several successful singles plucked from their grandiose concept albums. The group formed in Aylesbury, Buckinghamshire, originally as Silmarillion, a name taken from the novel by J.R.R. Tolkien. The group featured Doug Irvine (bass), Mick Pointer (b. 22 July 1956; drums), Steve Rothery (b. 25 November 1959, Brampton, South Yorkshire, England; guitar) and Brian Jelliman (keyboards). After recording the instrumental demo, 'The Web', the band recruited Fish (b. Derek William Dick, 25 April 1958, Dalkeith, Edinburgh, Scotland; vocals) and Diz Minnett (bass) and began building a strong following through almost continuous gigging. Before recording their debut, 'Market Square Heroes', Jelliman and Minnitt were replaced by Mark Kelly (b. 9 April 1961; keyboards) and Pete Trewavas (b. 15 January 1959, Middlesbrough, Cleveland, England; bass). Fish wrote all the lyrics for *Script For A Jester's Tear* and became the focal point of the group, often appearing on stage in garish make-up, echoing the style, both visually and vocally, of Genesis' singer Peter Gabriel. In 1983 Pointer was sacked and replaced for brief stints by Andy Ward of Camel, then John Marter and Jonathan Mover before the arrival of Ian Mosley (b. 16 June 1953, London, England), a veteran of many progressive rock bands, including Curved Air and the Gordon Giltrap band. Marillion's second album embraced a more straightforward hard rock sound and yielded two hits, 'Assassin' and 'Punch And Judy'. 1985's *Misplaced Childhood* was Marillion's biggest-selling album - surprisingly so, as it featured an elaborate concept, being virtually one continuous piece of music based largely on Fish's childhood experiences. 'Kayleigh', a romantic ballad extracted from this mammoth work, reached number 2 in the UK charts. By 1988 Fish was becoming increasingly dissatisfied with the group's musical development and left to pursue a solo career. The live double album, *Thieving Magpie*, was his last recorded contribution, and provided a fitting overview of the group's past successes. Marillion acquired Steve Hogarth (b. Doncaster, England), formerly of the Europeans, who made his debut on *Seasons End*, proving himself equal to the daunting task of fronting a well-established band. The 90s have found Marillion as popular as ever, with the ghost of Fish receding into the distance. With Hogarth fronting the band consistent success has continued to acrue, including chart status for 'Sympathy', 'The Hollow

Man' and 'Alone Again In The Lap Of Luxury'. Unusually for a band rooted in the progressive rock subculture, a genre dominated by the album, Marillion continue to be distinguished as much for their single output. That tradition looks likely to continue.

Albums: *Script For A Jester's Tear* (EMI 1983), *Fugazi* (EMI 1984), *Real To Real* (EMI 1984), *Misplaced Childhood* (EMI 1985), *Brief Encounter* (EMI 1986), *Clutching At Straws* (EMI 1987), *B Sides Themselves* (EMI 1988), *The Thieving Magpie* (EMI 1988), *Seasons End* (EMI 1989), *Holidays In Eden* (EMI 1991), *Brave* (EMI 1994). Compilation: *A Singles Collection* (EMI 1992).

Videos: *1982-1986 The Videos* (1986), *Live From Loreley* (1987), *From Stoke Row To Ipanema* (1990). Further reading: *Market Square Heroes*, Mick Wall.

Marilyn Manson

Controversial by design rather than accident, Florida group Marilyn Manson were formed in 1990 with the express intention of 'exploring the limits of censorship'. In keeping with this image, they were the first band to be signed to Trent Reznor (Nine Inch Nails) and John A. Malm Jr's Nothing label. Support slots with the likes of Suicidal Tendencies, Meat Beat Manifesto, Murphy's Law and the Genitorturers brought them considerable local recognition, in the form of the 1993 'Slammy' awards (taking the song of the year nomination for 'Dope Hat') and sundry other baubles (not least short-heading Gloria Estefan for the Best Local Musician category in *South Flordia* Magazine). Reznor also acted as guest musician and executive producer on the group's 1994 debut album, with half of the tracks mixed at the Sharon Tate house where NIN have also recorded. The group comprises Mr Manson (vocals, tape loops), Daisy Berkowitz (guitar), Twiggy Ramirez (bass), Madonna Wayne Gacy (Hammond organ, samples) and Sara Lee Lucas (drums).

Album: *Portrait Of An American Family* (Nothing/East West 1994).

Marino, Frank

This Canadian guitarist initially based his style obsessively on Jimi Hendrix. Forming Mahogany

Marillion

Rush in 1970 (later known as Frank Marino And Mahogany Rush), he decided to work solely under his own name from 1980 onwards. Playing the Heavy Metal Holocaust Festival in Port Vale during 1981, he was the surprise success of the day, upstaging headliners Triumph with a truly dazzling display of guitar pyrotechnics and showmanship. *The Power Of Rock 'N' Roll* was the first release under Marino's own name and featured a more aggressive style, coupled with lyrical references to sensitive social and political issues of the time. *Juggernaut* built on this success, but increased the tempo and introduced a greater degree of melody in the material. A four year break from recording ensued, owing to business and management setbacks, before *Full Circle* appeared in 1986. A stunning double live album was issued two years later, but nothing further appeared until a single track contribution to the *Guitar Speak Vol.2* album was released in 1990.

Albums: *The Power Of Rock 'N' Roll* (CBS 1981), *Juggernaut* (CBS 1982), *Full Circle* (Maze 1986), *Double Live* (Maze 1988).

Marionette

Formed in the early 80s in Islington, London, Marionette were a four-piece group in the tradition of the New York Dolls and Faces. The main strength of the band, fronted by vocalist Ray Zell along with Dave Veal on guitar, KK on bass and Pig on drums, was in their live performances - which at times recalled the punk gigs of the mid to late 70s. Their first release was *Provocatively Trashy*, a live cassette, soon after which they ventured into the recording studio for 'My Baby Sucks', which was a proposed single at the time, but did not materialise. By 1985 Zell was making a name for himself as a journalist in the music press, eventually working for *Kerrang!* magazine where he created the cartoon character, Pandora Peroxide, which is still a weekly feature today. Heavy Metal Records did release one album by them, but UK glam had long since given way to American imports. Zell has revived the band on occasions, but now seems content with writing.

Album: *Blonde Secrets And Dark Bombshells* (Heavy Metal 1985).

Marsden, Bernie

This masterly UK guitarist rose to prominence during his stints with Babe Ruth, UFO and Whitesnake. At the turn of the 70s Marsden took time out between Whitesnake projects to record solo material. He was assisted by several noteworthy musicians who included Ian Paice, Cozy Powell, Simon Phillips, Don Airey, Neil Murray and Jack Bruce. The albums

featured melodic hard rock, with Marsden successfully handling the vocals as well as some extended guitar workouts. He subsequently formed Bernie Marsden's S.O.S. which later became known as Alaska. Marsden remains an accomplished musician able to offer enormous variety and depth to heavy rock, though the solo trail was never his most rewarding enterprise.

Albums: *And About Time Too* (Sunburst 1979), *Look At Me Now* (Sunburst 1981).

Marseille

This band was formed in London, England, in 1976, ostensibly to record the soundtrack to the Jane Birkin film, *The French Way*. The original line-up consisted of Paul Dale (vocals), Neil Buchanan (guitar), Andy Charters (guitar), Steve Dinwoodie (bass) and Keith Knowles (drums). Signing to the now-defunct Mountain Records label, the band released their debut album in 1978. *Red, White And Slightly Blue* was a subtle blend of melodic rock and pop. A couple of tours followed, supporting UFO among others, who the band were later to model themselves on. This was most noticeable on *Marseille* where a more traditional hard rock sound was embraced. The group then ran into difficulties as Mountain Records went bankrupt. This left Marseille in limbo but they resurfaced in 1983 with new personnel and a record deal. The new line-up consisted of ex-Savage Lucy vocalist Sav Pearse, Mark Hays (guitar), Neil Buchanan (guitar), Steve Dinwoodie (bass) and Keith Knowles (drums). They went on to record the band's third and final album, *Touch The Night*, which appeared on the Ultra Noise Records label in 1984. Still failing to make any real impact with either press or public, the band folded soon after.

Albums: *Red, White And Slightly Blue* (Mountain 1978), *Marseille* (Mountain 1979), *Touch The Night* (Ultra Noise 1984).

Marshall Law

This Birmingham, England heavy metal quintet comprised Andy Pike (vocals), Dave Martin (guitar), Andy Southwell (guitar), Rog Davis (bass) and Mick Donovan (drums). Following in the tradition of UK rockers such as Judas Priest, Saxon and Iron Maiden, they transposed melody onto infectious, circular power-riffs, cleverly avoiding any monotony by the injection of twin lead guitar solos between rousing choruses. Signing to the Heavy Metal Records label, they released their self-titled debut in 1989 to considerable critical acclaim. Touted as the spearhead of a new revival in traditional British heavy rock, it all went a little quiet shortly thereafter.

Album: *Marshall Law* (Heavy Metal 1989).

Massacre

Formed in the US in the mid-80s, Massacre were one of the earliest extreme thrash metal bands, acting as pioneers of a style which was a popular underground phenomenon long before gaining public attention and widespread success. Founder members Kam Lee (vocals) and Rick Rozz (guitar) had been two thirds of the first Death line-up with Chuck Schuldiner. When Schuldiner relocated to California, the duo put together Massacre with Terry Butler (bass) and Bill Andrews (drums). Like other early thrash/death metal bands from Florida, they spread their name by recording demo tapes which were sent around the world and traded with various contacts. In the late 80s death metal and extreme thrash were becoming increasingly popular, and bands were much more widespread than when Massacre began. After a period of non-activity (with Rozz, Butler and Andrews again joining *Leprosy*-era Death), this new attention provided an opportunity for Massacre to begin work again, and they succeeded in gaining a record deal with UK label Earache, whose specialism in extreme music was now well established. Their debut album saw Lee and Rozz reunited with Butler and Andrews to record *From Beyond*, a set primarily based on original demo material which had never been given official release. Successful touring of the US preceded the April 1992 launch of a 12-inch, 'Inhuman Condition', which included a cover of the Venom standard, 'Warhead', with guest vocals from that band's Cronos. The recording of a second album introduced a new rhythm section in Pete Sison (bass) and Syrus Peters (drums),
Albums: *From Beyond* (Earache 1991), *Promise* (Earache 1995).

Masters Of Reality

This New York, USA-based quartet featured Chris Goss (vocals/guitar), Tim Harrington (guitar), Googe (bass) and Vinnie Ludovico (drums). Deriving their name from the title of Black Sabbath's third album, they fused a diverse array of rock styles into a form that clearly invoked names such as the Doors, Vanilla Fudge, Love and Deep Purple. The group originally formed as early as 1980, after which they embarked on a long-haul club touring policy which finally brought them serious attention. With the aid of producer Rick Rubin, who signed them originally to his Def Jam enterprise before it became Def American, they distilled their influences into a potent and powerful sound which had its roots in the 70s but was delivered with the technology of the present.

Their self-titled debut was released to widespread critical acclaim in 1989, but fans had to wait another four years for a follow-up, *Sunrise On The Sufferbus*. This featured the legendary Ginger Baker joining only surviving original member, Goss. The first line-up had imploded following disastrous touring engagements in support of their debut, and the intervening period had seen Masters Of Reality put on ice.
Album: *Masters Of Reality* (Def American 1989), *Sunrise On The Sufferbus* (Def American 1993).

Max And The Broadway Metal Choir

'The Devil gave us Death Metal and God gave us Max' - that's how the publicity introduced us to Maximilan Gelt - a Jewish delicatessen owner from Miami, Florida, in his late 40s. It seems that Max was contacted by a friend to come to London to see a band, the Broadway Metal Choir, featuring Jan Cyrka (guitar), Kevin Riddles (ex-Angelwitch/Tytan bass), Kevin Fitzpatrick (keyboards) and Andy Beirne (drums). As they lacked a vocalist Max put himself up for the job and got it, but after six weeks of touring he broke his leg and returned to Miami. Later he returned to London armed with new songs, and together with FM and guitarist Steve Boltz, backing singers Suzie O'List and Gillian O'Donovan, recorded 10 tracks of what can only be described as Led Zeppelin fronted by Mel Brooks. The press loved the story but not the finished product and, dejected, Max returned home to face a different type of music. His wife, Shirly, had launched divorce proceedings, claiming his recent obsession with heavy metal music had driven him 'insane'. The rest of the band split, returning to session work, or, in Cyrka's case, to minor guitar 'hero' status.
Album: *And God Gave Us Max* (Powerstation 1986).

Max Webster

Toronto, Canada-based group put together by guitarist Kim Mitchell, who had worked with various bands over the years including MC5 and Alice Cooper. Mitchell was very much the central figure due to his on-stage showmanship and guitar ability. He was backed by Dave Myles on bass, Terry Watkinson on keyboards and Gerry McCracken on drums. Their second album in particular is worthy of any record collection. The UK proved a hard nut to crack but they tried hard in 1979 with two albums and a single, 'Paradise Skies', that featured guest appearances from fellow Canadians, Rush. For some reason British audiences turned their back on the band and most of the tour was cancelled. 1980's *Universal Juveniles* did bring back some dignity but their career and songwriting was on the wane and by 1982 they had split up. Mitchell continued as a solo artist.

Albums: *Hangover* (Mercury 1976), *High Class In Borrowed Shoes* (Mercury 1977), *Mutiny Up My Sleeve* (Capitol 1978), *A Million Vacations* (Capitol 1979), *Live Magnetic Air* (Capitol 1979), *Universal Juveniles* (Mercury 1980).

May, Brian

b. 19 July 1947, Twickenham, Middlesex, England. Best known as the flamboyant and highly original guitarist in Queen, May has also recorded in his own right. In the summer of 1983 he teamed-up with Eddie Van Halen (guitar), REO Speedwagon's Alan Gratzer (drums), Fred Mandel (keybords) and Phil Chen (bass) for a supergroup session, which was released under the title *Star Fleet Project*. He subsequently produced the spoof heavy metal group Bad News as well as the recording of 'Anyone Can Fall In Love' by his actress/lover Anita Dobson. He also worked with Steve Hackett, completed a solo album and, in 1991, wrote and recorded the score for a production of Shakespeare's *Macbeth*. Following a commission for an advertisement by the Ford Motor Company in 1991, May released a further single, 'Driven By You', which became a sizeable hit at the end of 1991. He was also one of the prime movers behind the Freddy Mercury Aid Benefit in 1992, and he has sustained himself admirably as a solo artist in the wake of the latter's death.

Albums: *Star Fleet Project* (EMI 1983), *Back To The Light* (EMI 1992), *Live At Brixton* (EMI 1994).

Mayhem

Formed in Norway by Euronymous (real name Oystien Aarseth) who was a young fan of the Satanic black metal played by bands like Bathory and Venom, Mayhem made their first impact with the 1984 demo, *Pure Fucking Armageddon*, which is regarded as something of a classic of extreme metal in underground circles. The black metal genre was losing popularity however, along with the leather and chains imagery and Satanic lyrics that were its trademark. Rather than follow heavy metal fashion and adopt the hardcore punk or death metal genres that were becoming popular, Euronymous opted to preserve purist black metal. In order to do this he opened a record shop in Oslo named Helvete (Norwegian for Hell) and founded the Deathlike Silence label, both dedicated solely to black metal. In 1987 he released *Deathcrush*, Mayhem's official debut which featured six songs in seventeen and a half minutes of frenzied angst. Then, in 1991, the band's

vocalist shot himself (by way of black irony, he went under the stagename 'Dead'). Rather than halting Euronymous' black metal crusade, the tragedy only appeared to have redoubled his faith. Mayhem inspired a number of Scandinavian bands to readopt the musical style and imagery of black metal during the early 90s, while Euronymous became an increasingly melodramatic and popular spokesman on the extreme metal underground with his philosophies of cold hate and spite. A series of Norwegian church burnings in early 1993 were linked to the Black Metal Circle, a cult-like group centred around Euronymous' black metal crusade and dominated by members of bands like Emperor, Dark Throne and Burzum, all signed to Deathlike Silence. Euronymous revelled in the international publicity. Then, on August 10th 1993 he was found, stabbed 25 times, outside his Oslo apartment. Two weeks later Varg Vikernes (better known by his stagename of Count Grishnakh) of the band Burzum was arrested for the murder, and convicted the following year. Vikernes had been Euronymous' right-hand man, and it is not apparent whether the murder was committed because of a financial dispute over record royalties, over a woman, or because of darker doctrinal differences between the two. What does seem clear is that Euronymous was swallowed by the vivid world of pain and hate he had himself created, while the black metal revival he had inspired continues unabated. In 1994 *De Mysteriis Dom Sathanas*, Mayhem's last recording, was released posthumously. Sinisterly enough, it featured Grishnakh on bass guitar.

Albums: *Deathcrush* (Deathlike Silence 1987), *De Mysteriis Dom Sathanas* (Deathlike Silence 1994).

MC5

Formed in 1964 in Detroit, Michigan, USA, and originally known as the Motor City Five, the group was sundered the following year when its rhythm section left in protest over a new original song, 'Back To Comm'. Michael Davis (bass) and Dennis Thompson (drums) joined founder members Rob Tyner (b. Robert Derminer, 12 December 1944, Detroit, Michigan, USA, d. 18 September 1991; vocals), Wayne Kramer (guitar) and Fred 'Sonic' Smith (b. 1949, d. 4 November 1994; guitar) to pursue the radical direction this experimental composition offered. By 1967 their repertoire contained material drawn from R&B, soul and *avant garde* jazz, as well as a series of powerful original songs. Two singles, 'One Of The Guys'/'I Can Only Give You Everything' (1967) and 'Borderline'/'Looking At You' (1968), captured their nascent, high-energy sound as the group embraced the 'street' politics proselytized by mentor/manager John Sinclair. Now linked to this former DJ's Trans Love Commune and White Panther party, the MC5 became Detroit's leading underground act, and a recording deal with the Elektra label resulted in the seminal *Kick Out The Jams*. Recorded live at the city's Grande Ballroom, this turbulent set captured the quintet's extraordinary sound which, although loud, was never reckless. However, the Five were then dropped from their label's roster following several disagreements, but later emerged anew on Atlantic. Rock journalist Jon Landau, later manager of Bruce Springsteen, was invited to produce *Back In The USA* which, if lacking the dissolute thrill of its predecessor, showed a group able to adapt to studio discipline. 'Tonight', 'Shakin' Street' and a remade 'Lookin' At You' are among the highlights of this excellent set. A third collection, *High Time*, reasserted a desire to experiment, and several local jazz musicians added punch to what nonetheless remains a curiously ill-focused album on which each member, bar Davis, contributed material. A move to Europe, where the group performed and recorded under the aegis of Rohan O'Rahilly, failed to halt dwindling commercial prospects, while the departure of Davis, then Tyner, in 1972, brought the MC5 to an end. Their reputation flourished during the punk phenomenon, during which time each former member enjoyed brief notoriety. Davis later surfaced in Destroy All Monsters, and Sonic Smith married Patti Smith (and was heavily featured on the singer/poet's 'comeback' album, *Dream Of Life*, in 1988). Both Kramer and Tyner attempted to use the MC5 name for several unrelated projects. They wisely abandoned such practices, leaving intact the legend of one of rock's most uncompromising and exciting acts. In September 1991 Rob Tyner died of a heart attack at the seat of his parked car in his home town of Ferndale, Michigan. Smith also passed away three years later. Kramer, however, relaunched a solo career in the same year, enlisting several prominent members of the US underground/alternative scene so inspired by the original MC5 as his new cohorts.

Albums: *Kick Out The Jams* (Elektra 1969), *Back In The USA* (Elektra 1970), *High Time* (Elektra 1971). Compilation: *Babes In Arms* (ROIR 1983), *Looking At You* (Receiver 1994).

McDonald, Brian, Group

This melodic pop-rock outfit was put together in 1987 by keyboard wizard Brian McDonald. Enlisting the services of Will Hodges (guitar), Andrew G. Wilkes (bass), and D.W. Adams (drums), they signed to Capitol Records and released *Desperate Business* the same year. Influenced by Nightranger, Bryan Adams and Jeff Paris, the album was a solid musical statement, marred only by McDonald's vocals, which lacked both power and range. However, the set did feature singer/actress Fiona on backing vocals, which helped the cause.

Album: *Desperate Business* (Capitol 1987).

McKagan, Duff

b. Michael McKagan, 5 February 1964, Seattle, Washington, USA. Guns N'Roses' bass player who has served time in more *ad hoc* bands than anybody can care to remember. It was once said of McKagan that there were few punk/hard rock outfits in Seattle whose line-up he had not passed through at some point, including the Fartz, Ten Minute Warning, Thankless Dogs, Silly Killers and Wandering Bandeleros. However, in 1993 McKagan decided to take the big step up to a solo career. Writing and playing most of the instruments, his debut included guest appearances by a fine array of rock's glitterati, Jeff Beck, Lenny Kravitz, Sebastian Bach (Skid Row) among them. There were also appearances from his Guns N'Roses workmates Matt Sorum, Gilby Clarke and Slash, just to prove there were no bad feelings about his off-season foray. Despite the strength of the largely power-pop musical backing, McKagan's lyrics revealed only feint flashes of insight, notably on 'Man In The Meadow', dedicated to his former best friend, Todd Crew, who died of an overdose in 1987. It also disappointed those expecting him to return to his punk roots (he sang half of the tracks on Guns N'Roses punk tribute album, *The Sphaghetti Incident*).

Album: *Believe In Me* (Geffen 1993).

Meanstreak

Hailing from New York, Meanstreak were formed in 1985 by guitarists Marlene Apuzzo and Rena Sands. Recruiting vocalist Bettina France, bassist Martens Pace and drummer Diane Keyser, they were the first all-female thrash metal band to record an album. Signing to the independent Music For Nations label, they released *Roadkill*, produced by Alex Perialas and ex-Raven drummer Rob Hunter. Recorded within a week, the pressure resulted in a set which betrayed its origins by being both shambolic and ill-focused. The songs, meanwhile, were rigidly formularized and were further scuppered by weak vocals. The album remains of interest to thrash aficionados, but even then on a historical rather than musical level.

Album: *Roadkill* (Music For Nations 1988).

Meat Loaf

b. Marvin Lee Aday, 27 September 1947, Dallas, Texas, USA. The name Meat Loaf originated at school, when aged 13, he was christened 'Meat Loaf' by his football coach, owing to his enormous size and ungainly manner. Two years later his mother died of cancer, and fights with his alcoholic father grew worse. He moved to Los Angeles in 1967 and formed Popcorn Blizzard, a psychedelic rock outfit which toured the club circuit, opening for acts including the Who, Ted Nugent and the Stooges. In 1969 Meat Loaf successfully auditioned for a role in *Hair*, where he met soul vocalist Stoney. Stoney and Meat Loaf recorded a self-titled album in 1971, which spawned the minor *Billboard* chart hit, 'What You See Is What You Get'. *Hair* closed in New York in 1974, and Meat Loaf found new work in *More Than You Deserve*, a musical written by Jim Steinman, then took the part of Eddie in the film version of *The Rocky Horror Picture Show*. In 1976, he was recruited by Ted Nugent to sing lead vocals on his *Free For All*, after which he joined up with Jim Steinman again in the famous US satirical comedy outfit, the National Lampoon Roadshow. Meat Loaf and Steinman struck up a working musical relationship and started composing a grandiose rock opera. After a long search, they found Epic Records and producer Todd Rundgren sympathetic to their ideas and demo tapes. Enlisting the services of Bruce Springsteen's E Street Band, they recorded *Bat Out Of Hell* in 1978. This was pieced together around the high camp of the title-track, an operatic horror melodrama which saw Meat Loaf raging against nature, and 'Paradise By The Dashboard Lights', with Ellen Foley providing female accompaniment. The album was ignored for the first six months after release, although Meat Loaf toured extensively, supporting Cheap Trick, among others. Eventually the breakthrough came, and *Bat Out Of Hell* rocketed towards the top of the charts in country after country. It stayed in the UK and US album charts for 395 and 88 weeks respectively, and sold in excess of thirty million copies worldwide, the third biggest-selling album release of all time. However, with success came misfortune. Meat Loaf split with his manager, David Sonenberg, causing all manner of litigation. He was drinking heavily to cope with his new found but barely anticipated stardom, and lost his voice. He also lost his songwriter too, as Steinman split to release solo what had been mooted as a thematic follow-up to *Bat Out Of Hell* - *Bad For Good*: 'I spent seven months trying to make a follow-up with him, and it was an infernal nightmare. He had lost his voice, he had lost his house, and he was pretty much losing his mind'. After a three-year gap,

during which Meat Loaf declared himself voluntarily bankrupt, the eagerly anticipated follow-up, *Dead Ringer*, was released. Again it used Steinman's compositions, this time in his absence, and continued where *Bat Out Of Hell* left off, comprising grandiose arrangements, anthemic choruses and spirited rock 'n' roll. The title-song made the Top 5 in the UK and the album hit number 1, but it only dented the lower end of the Top 50 *Billboard* album chart. This was, seemingly, the last time Meat Loaf would be able to use Steinman's sympathetic songwriting skills, and the consequent weakening of standards undoubtedly handicapped the second phase of his career. Concentrating on Europe, relentless touring helped both *Midnight At The Lost And Found* and *Bad Attitude* to creep into the Top 10 UK album charts. Nevertheless, this represented a significant decline in popularity compared with his Steinman-penned albums. *Blind Before I Stop* saw Meat Loaf teaming up with John Parr for the single 'Rock'n'Roll Mercenaries', which, surprisingly, was not a hit. The album was, however, his strongest post-Steinman release and featured a fine selection of accessible, blues-based, hard rock numbers. With live performances, things had never been better; Meat Loaf's band included Bob Kulick (brother of Kiss guitarist Bruce Kulick, and now of Skull), and ex-Rainbow drummer Chuck Burgi. They delivered an electrifying show which ran for nearly three hours. Recorded at London's Wembley Stadium, *Meat Loaf Live* emerged in 1987, and featured raw and exciting versions of his finest songs. By now Meat Loaf was also a veteran of several films, including *Roadie*, *Americathon* and, in the 90s, *Wayne's World* and *Leap Of Faith*. Apart from re-releases and compilations, he maintained vinyl silence well into the 90s. However, he signed a new deal with Virgin Records in 1990, and as rumours grew that he was once again working with Steinman, the media bandwagon began to roll. *Bat Out Of Hell II - Back Into Hell*, from its title onwards, displayed a calculated, stylistic cloning of its precursor. The public greeted the familiarity with open arms, pushing lead-off single 'I'll Do Anything For Love (But I Won't Do That)' to number 1 in both the US and UK, its parent album performing the same feat. Though critics could point at the formulaic nature of their approach, Meat Loaf had no doubts that by working with Steinman again, he had recaptured the magic: 'Nobody writes like Jim Steinman. All these things - bombastic, over the top, self-indulgent. All these things are positives'.

Albums: *Bat Out Of Hell* (Epic 1978), *Dead Ringer* (Epic 1981), *Midnight At The Lost And Found* (Epic 1983), *Bad Attitude* (Arista 1985), *Blind Before I Stop*

(Arista 1986), *Meat Loaf Live* (Arista 1987), *Bat Out Of Hell II: Back Into Hell* (Virgin 1993), *Alive In Hell* (Pure Music 1994). Compilation: *Hits Out Of Hell* (Epic 1984). With Bonnie Tyler: *Heaven & Hell* (1993).

Videos: *Live At Wembley* (1984), *Bad Attitude Live* (1986), *Hits Out Of Hell* (1986), *Meat Loaf Live* (1991), *Bat Out Of Hell II - Picture Show* (1994).

Megadeth

This uncompromising and intense thrash metal quartet was founded in San Francisco, California, USA, by guitarist Dave Mustaine (b. 13 September) after leaving Metallica in 1983 (he co-wrote four songs on the latter's debut album, though he did not actually appear on this). Recruiting bassist Dave Ellefson, guitarist Chris Poland and drummer Gars Samuelson, Mustaine negotiated a deal with the independent Combat label. Working on a tight budget, Megadeth produced *Killing Is My Business...And Business Is Good* in 1985. This was a ferocious blast of high-energy thrash metal, weakened by a thin production. Nevertheless, Capitol Records, realizing the band's potential, immediately signed them up, even though Mustaine was beginning to acquire a reputation for his outspoken and provocative manner. *Peace Sells...But Who's Buying?* was a marked improvement over their debut, both technically and musically. It was characterized by incessant, heavy duty riffing, bursts of screaming guitar and lyrics which reflected Mustaine's outspoken perception of contemporary social and political issues. In 1988 Mustaine fired Poland and Samuelson, bringing in Jeff Young and Chuck Behler as replacements before the recording of *So Far, So Good...So What!* This built on their aggressive and vitriolic style, and included a cover of 'Anarchy In The UK', with Sex Pistols' guitarist Steve Jones making a guest appearance. Following two years of heroin-related problems, and the enforced departure of Poland and Behler, Mustaine re-appeared in 1990 with guitar virtuoso Marty Friedman and drummer Nick Menza. *Rust In Peace* was released to widespread critical acclaim, combining an anti-nuclear message with the explosive guitar pyrotechnics of Friedman. *Countdown To Extinction*, meanwhile, was a bruising encounter which entertained more melody in the execution of its theme - that of impending ecological disaster. Reports of Mustaine's drug problems again overshadowed sessions for their sixth album, *Youthanasia*, recorded in Phoenix, Arizona, where three quarters of the band now live. It was produced by Max Norman (who co-produced *Countdown To Extinction* and mixed *Rust In Peace*). Along with Slayer, Metallica and Anthrax, Megadeth remain at the forefront of the thrash metal genre, despite the vulnerability of their central creative force.

Albums: *Killing Is My Business...And Business Is Good* (Megaforce 1985), *Peace Sells...But Who's Buying?* (Capitol 1986), *So Far, So Good...So What!* (Capitol 1988), *Rust In Peace* (Capitol 1990), *Countdown To Extinction* (Capitol 1992), *Youthansia* (Capitol 1994). Video: *Rusted Pieces* (1991).

Melvins

The late Kurt Cobain of Nirvana rated the Melvins as his favourite group. Unsurprising, perhaps, as they are the only other band of note to originate from his hometown Aberdeen (though they have since relocated to San Francisco), and he did once roadie for them. Drummer Dale Crover also played with Nirvana for a spell, while Cobain would guest and co-produce *Houdini* for the band. The other members of the Melvins, formed in 1984, numbered Buzz Osbourne (vocals/guitar) and Lori Beck (bass). Matt Lukin (Mudhoney) was also a floating member. Reputed to be more influenced by the heavy rock angle than many who have fallen under the generic title 'grunge', the Melvins are big fans of Black Sabbath and even released three solo albums in a tribute to the Kiss strategy of similar pretensions. A cover of Flipper's 'Way Of The World' and 'Sacrifice' sat alongside Alice Cooper's 'Ballad Of Dwight Fry' on cover album, *Lysol*. *Stoner Witch*, their second album for Atlantic/East West, saw Crover and Osbourne joined by bass player Mark Deutrom, who had previously produced the band's first two albums. This time they were working with Garth Richardson of Red Hot Chili Peppers and L7 fame.

Albums: *Gluey Porch Treatments* (Alchemy 1986), *Ozma* (Boner 1987), *Bullhead* (Boner 1991), *Lysol* (Boner/Tupelo 1992), *Houdini* (Atlantic 1993), *Prick* (Amphetamine Reptile 1994), *Stoner Witch* (Atlantic 1994).

Mercyful Fate

This seminal black metal act was formed in Copenhagen, Denmark, in 1980 by vocalist King Diamond (b. Kim Bendix Petersen, 14 June 1956, Copenhagen, Denmark) and guitarist Hank Shermann with Michael Denner (guitar), Timi Grabber Hansen (bass) and Kim Ruzz (drums). The band's first vinyl appearance was with 'Black Funeral' on the *Metallic Storm* compilation, before *A Corpse Without Soul* (aka *Nuns Have No Fun*) saw the full debut of their heavy yet intricate guitar-based approach, and of King Diamond's unique vocal style, which ranged from deep bass growls to falsetto shrieks. *Melissa*, with a name taken from the human skull then owned by Diamond and used as a stage prop, fulfilled Mercyful Fate's promise, and the band became one of the mainstays of the black metal underground with their occult lyricism and theatrical approach (though Diamond's facial make-up later drew legal action from Kiss' Gene Simmons over alleged similarities to his 'God Of Thunder' persona). *Don't Break The Oath* was a more mature work as the band reaped the benefits of extensive touring with a tighter sound. However, when they regrouped after further successful live work to record a third album, Shermann's determination to pursue a surprising AOR direction saw the band split, with Diamond going on to a solo career with Hansen and Denner in tow while Shermann formed Fate. The posthumous release of *In The Beginning*, containing the debut mini-album plus BBC session tracks, seemed to be an epitaph for Mercyful Fate. However, the heavier approach of Shermann and Denner's Zoser Mez led to the reformation of the old band, with Ruzz replaced by Morten Nielsen on *In The Shadows*, and by Snowy Shaw on tour (the latter taking up the position permanently). The record harked back to *Don't Break The Oath*'s style, and also featured a guest appearance by Metallica's Lars Ulrich on 'Return Of The Vampire', a song resurrected form the band's second demo in 1982. Before 1994's *Time* Hansen would be replaced on bass by Sharlee D'Angelo, as the group toured the US with Flotsam & Jetsam and Cathedral (live recordings from which were released as *The Bell Witch* EP). When *Time* did emerge it provided unexpected diversions, with the Middle-Eastern flavour of 'The Mad Arab' and the serenity of 'Witch's Dance' rubbing shoulders with more traditional Mercyful Fate concerns ('Nightmare Be Thy Name', etc.).

Albums: *A Corpse Without Soul* (Rave-On 1982, mini-album), *Melissa* (Roadrunner 1983), *Don't Break The Oath* (Roadrunner 1984), *In The Shadows* (Metal Blade 1993), *Time* (Metal Blade 1994). Compilations: *In The Beginning* (Roadrunner 1988, rec. 1982/1983), *Return Of The Vampire* (Roadrunner 1992).

Messiah Force

Formed in Jonquire, Canada, in 1984, the band consisted of Lynn Renaud (vocals), Bastien Deschênes (guitar), Jean Tremblay (guitar), Eric Parisé (bass) and Jean-Francois Boucher (drums). The band was

Mercyful Fate

essentially formed from the ashes of two local power metal bands, Exode and Frozen. Utilizing a sound that was reminiscent of early Warlock, the band released their debut, *The Last Day*, on the small, independent Haissem Records label in 1987. Though a strong power metal release, the album passed largely unnoticed resulting in the band's demise soon after its release.

Album: *The Last Day* (Haissem 1987).

Metal Church

Formed in Seattle, USA, in 1982, Metal Church initially comprised David Wayne (vocals), Kurt Vanderhoof (guitar), Craig Wells (guitar), Duke Erickson (bass) and Kirk Arrington (drums). Their first album was a phenomenal debut, brimming with energy and promise. The style was the then-evolving thrash metal sound, and Metal Church executed their own brand with precision. *The Dark* was a strong follow-up, but failed to top the debut, and Wayne left at this point to be replaced by Mike Howe for the recording of *Blessing In Disguise*, another commendable effort. Kurt Vanderhoof then retired from the band's ranks through his dislike of touring, and was replaced by John Marshall, previously guitar technician for Metallica. Metal Church have proved to be a consistently excellent band, but have failed to rise to the level of success suggested by their first album. Personnel changes and short tenures with their record companies have undoubtedly contributed to their under-achievement.

Albums: *Metal Church* (Ground Zero 1985), *The Dark* (Elektra 1987), *Blessing In Disguise* (Elektra 1989), *The Human Factor* (Epic 1991), *Hanging In The Balance* (Blackheart 1994).

Metallica

The most consistently innovative metal band of the late 80s and early 90s were formed during 1981 in California, USA, by Lars Ulrich (b. 26 December 1963, Copenhagen, Denmark; drums) and James Alan Hetfield (b. 3 August 1963, USA; guitar/vocals) after each separately advertised for fellow musicians in the classified section of American publication, *The Recycler*. They recorded their first demo, *No Life Til' Leather*, with Lloyd Grand (guitar), who was replaced in January 1982 by David Mustaine, whose relationship with Ulrich and Hetfield proved unsatisfactory. Jef Warner (guitar) and Ron McGovney (bass) each had a brief tenure with the group, and at the end of 1982 Clifford Lee Burton (b. 10 February 1962, USA; bass), formerly of Trauma, joined the band, playing his first live performance on 5 March 1983. Mustaine departed to form Megadeth

and was replaced by Kirk Hammett (b. 18 November 1962; guitar). Hammett, who came to the attention of Ulrich and Hetfield while playing with rock band Exodus, played his first concert with Metallica on 16 April 1983. The Ulrich, Hetfield, Burton and Hammett combination endured until disaster struck the band in the small hours of 27 September 1987, when Metallica's tour bus overturned in Sweden, killing Cliff Burton. During those four years the group put thrash metal on the map with the aggression and exuberance of their debut, *Kill 'Em All*, the album sleeve of which bore the legend 'Bang that head that doesn't bang'. This served as a template for a whole new breed of metal, though the originators themselves were quick to dispense with their own rulebook. Touring with N.W.O.B.H.M. bands Raven and Venom followed, while Music For Nations signed them for European distribution. Although *Ride The Lightning* was not without distinction, notably on 'For Whom The Bell Tolls', it would be *Master Of Puppets* which offered further evidence of Metallica's appetite for the epic. Their first album for Elektra in the US (who had also re-released its forerunner), this was a taut, multi-faceted collection which both raged and lamented with equal conviction. After the death of Burton the band elected to continue, the remaining three members choosing to recruit Jason Newsted (b. 4 March 1963; bass) of Flotsam And Jetsam. Newsted played his first concert with the band on 8 November 1986. The original partnership of Ulrich and Hetfield, however, remained responsible for Metallica's lyrics and musical direction. The new line-up's first recording together would be *The $5.98 EP - Garage Days Revisited* - a collection of covers including material from Budgie, Diamond Head, Killing Joke and the Misfits, which also served as a neat summation of the group's influences to date. Sessions for *...And Justice For All* initially began with Guns N'Roses producer Mike Clink at the helm, before the group opted to return to Johnny Zazula, a realtionship they had begun with *Ride The Lightning*. A long and densely constructed effort, this 1988 opus included an appropriately singular spectuacular moment in 'One', also released as a single, while elsewhere the barrage of riffs somewhat obscured the usual Metallica artistry. Songs continued to deal with large themes - justice and retribution, insanity, war, religion and relationships, on 1991's *Metallica*. Compared to *Kill 'Em All* of nearly a decade previously, however, the group had grown from iconoclastic chaos to thoughtful harmony, hallmarked by sudden and unexpected changes of mood and tempo. The MTV-friendly 'Enter Sandman' broke the band on a stadium level.

Constant touring in the wake of the album ensued, along with a regular itinerary of awards ceremonies for their last album and single at Grammy, *Rolling Stone* and MTV ceremonies. There could surely be no more deserving recipients, Metallica having dragged mainstream metal, not so much kicking and screaming as whining and complaining, into a bright new dawn when artistic redundancy seemed inevitable.

Albums: *Kill 'Em All* (Megaforce 1983), *Ride The Lightning* (Megaforce 1984), *Master Of Puppets* (Elektra 1986), *...And Justice For All* (Elektra 1988), *Metallica* (Elektra 1991), *Live Shit: Binge & Purge* (Elektra 1993, 3 CD).

Videos: *Cliff 'Em All* (1987), *One The Video* (1988), *A Year In The Life Of Vols. 1 & 2* (1992), *Live Shit: Binge & Purge* (1993).

Further reading: *A Visual Documentary*, Mark Putterford (1993), *In Their Own Words*, Mark Putterford (1994).

Method Of Destruction

Following his work in legendary New York hardcore act Stormtroopers Of Death, vocalist Billy Milano formed M.O.D. (as they are commonly referred to) with Tim McMurtrie (guitar), Ken Ballone (bass) and Keith Davis (drums). The quality of the groove-based hardcore on *USA For MOD* was overshadowed by controversy over seemingly racist and near-fascist lyrics, although Milano later explained in an open letter to the press that his aim was to illustrate prejudice by writing from the bigot's perspective in the first person, thus stirring up truly negative reactions to these attitudes in the process; Milano subsequently noted that many of the most contentious lyrics were written by Anthrax's Scott Ian and had been part of the SOD set. The subsequent tour, while successful, proved unhealthy for MOD, with McMurtrie breaking his leg and continuing in a wheelchair, while Ballone broke his arm, and the line-up split after the tour. Milano was then joined by guitarist Louie Svitek, bassist John Monte (who had toured in place of the injured Ballone) and drummer Tim Mallare for the lyrically lighter *Surfin' MOD*, where Milano's sense of humour shone through, and the new band moved towards a metal/hardcore crossover style. *Gross Misconduct* maintained the quality, although Milano peppered the lyric sheet with explanations as he tackled serious subject matter once more. However, personal problems enforced Milano's departure from the music scene, with Svitek and Monte going on to form Mind Funk. MOD were revived as a trio in 1992 after the SOD reunion, with Milano (adopting the bassist role as he had in his days

with the Psychos), drummer Dave Chavarri and the returning McMurtrie on guitar for *Rhythm Of Fear*, sounding as if the band had never been away. Despite a rather fluid line-up thereafter, *Devolution* showed that Milano - now rhythm guitarist with Rob Moscheti on bass - was still producing strong and relevant hardcore to match the likes of Biohazard and Sick Of It All.

Albums: *USA For MOD* (Megaforce 1987), *Surfin' MOD* (Megaforce 1988, mini-album), *Gross Misconduct* (Megaforce 1989), *Rhythm Of Fear* (Megaforce 1992), *Devolution* (Music For Nations 1994).

Miller, Donnie

This American guitarist and singer/songwriter was most widely renowned for his leather-clad biker image. Influenced by Steve Earle, Bruce Springsteen and the old blues masters, he specialised in a laid-back, understated approach, with fluid but economical lead guitar breaks. Signed to Epic Records he released *One Of The Boys*, ably assisted by Vince Kirk (second guitar), Norman Dahlor (bass), Kurt Carow (keyboards) and Tim 'Kix' Kelly (drums). The album also featured guest appearances from Cyndi Lauper and Tommy Shaw (of Damn Yankees). 'The Devil Wears Lingerie' attracted some attention as a single, with its provocative and sordid promotional video, but that was effectively the last sighting of the artist.

Album: *One Of The Boys* (Epic 1989).

Mindfunk

This intense American thrash-funk quintet were formed in 1989 by vocalist Patrick R. Dubar and rhythm guitarist Jason Coppola. They had reportedly wanted the group to be called Mind Fuck, but re-thought this for obvious reasons. Adding John Monte (ex-MOD; bass), Reed St. Mark (ex-Celtic Frost; drums) and Louis J. Svitek (ex-MOD; guitar), they signed to Epic and debuted with an aggressive and confident self-titled album the same year. Slayer, Red Hot Chili Peppers and Anthrax were obvious reference points, as were the hardcore origins of several of their membership. However, they were dropped by Epic shortly afterwards (a fact bitterly recalled in their second album's title) and in came Jason Everman (ex-Nirvana, Soundgarden) and Shawn Johnson for Coppola and St Mark respectively.

Album: *Mindfunk* (Epic 1991), *Dropped* (Megaforce 1993).

Mindstorm

Mindstorm is the rock vision of vocalist Travis

Mitchell. Relying heavily on the Led Zeppelin legacy, the group is in essence the Canadian equivalent of Kingdom Come or Katmandu. Employing Al Rodgers (guitar), Bruce Moffet (drums), Russ Boswell (bass) and Gary Moffet (keyboards), the songs are immaculately constructed and delivered with aplomb. However, their credibility and creativity is compromised through the overwhelming sense of *deja-vu* their recordings invoke. With monstrously aching riffs and thunderous drumming, Mindstorm careers along a well-worn rock 'n' roll highway, with only the occasional musical detour. These include Eastern influences, simple acoustic bridges and brooding power ballads.

Albums: *Mindstorm* (Provogue 1987), *Back To Reality* (Provogue 1991).

Ministry

'The difference between Ministry and other bands is that we sold out before we even started.' Alain Jourgensen (b. Havana, Cuba) began producing music under the Ministry name in the early 80s in Chicago, but was most unhappy with the Euro-pop direction in which his record company pushed him for *With Sympathy*, later describing it as 'that first abortion of an album'. Ministry took on a more acceptable shape for Jourgensen after *Twitch*, with the addition of Paul Barker (b. Palo Alto, California, USA) on bass/keyboards and drummer Bill Rieflin to Jourgensen's guitar/vocals/keyboards. The band evolved their own brand of guitar-based industrial metal, considering *The Land Of Rape And Honey* to be their true debut, and employed a variety of guest musicians for both live and studio work, with regular contributions from ex-Rigor Mortis guitarist Mike Scaccia and ex-Finitribe vocalist Chris Connelly. Despite Jourgensen's dislike of touring, Ministry developed a stunning live show, with a backdrop of disturbing visual images to accompany the intense musical barrage, and the sinister figure of Jourgensen taking centre stage behind a bone-encrusted mike stand. *In Case You Didn't Feel Like Showing Up (Live)* displays the metamorphosis of the songs as the band extend themselves in concert. At this stage, Jourgensen and Barker were working on numerous other studio projects in a variety of styles, including Lard with Jello Biafra, but Ministry remained one of two main acts. The other, the outrageous Revolting Cocks, served as a more blatantly humorous outlet for the pair's creative talents, in contrast to the dark anger and socio-political themes of Ministry. As alternative culture became more acceptable to the mainstream,

Mindfunk

Ministry achieved major success with *Psalm 69* (subtitled *The Way To Succeed And The Way To Suck Eggs*), helped by the popularity on MTV of 'Jesus Built My Hotrod', featuring a guest vocal and lyric from Butthole Surfer Gibby Haynes. The band were a huge draw on the 1992 Lollapalooza tour, playing second on the bill, and their debut European tour later that year was also a resounding success. In 1994 Rieflin was replaced on the drumstool by former Didjits' drummer Ray Washam.

Albums: *With Sympathy* (Arista 1983), *Twelve Inch Singles 1981-1984* (Wax Trax 1984), *Twitch* (Sire 1986), *The Land Of Rape And Honey* (Sire 1988), *The Mind Is A Terrible Thing To Taste* (Sire 1989), *In Case You Didn't Feel Like Showing Up (Live)* (Sire 1990), *Psalm 69* (Sire/Warners 1992).

Misery Loves Co.

Formed in January 1993, Swedish duo Misery Loves Co. immediately picked up healthy press coverage with their blend of intelligent 90s metal and strong songwriting, *Kerrang!* stating 'the hottest new metal combo since the arrival of Machine Head'. Made up of Örjan Örnkloo (programming/guitar) and Patrik Wirén (vocals/guitar), the latter was formerly a member of thrash band Midas Touch (one album for Noise Records), while his partner played with female dance troupe the Bikinis. Putting their heads together, the group signed a Swedish deal with the MNW Zone label (also home to Clawfinger), and made their debut vinyl appearance on a compilation album, *Extreme Close Up*, before the release of a three track EP, *Private Hell*, in January 1994. Their debut album was licensed to Earache Records in the UK, while live appearances saw the duo augmented by the addition of Jim Edwards (guitar), Marre (bass) and Boss (drums).

Album: *Misery Love Co.* (MNW Zone 1994/Earache 1995).

Misfits

Like the 13th Floor Elevators in the 60s and the New York Dolls in the early 70s, this US punk band was swiftly surrounded in a cloak of mythology and cult appeal. Long after their demise (they played their last live gig in 1983), their obscure US-only records were fetching large sums of money in collecting circles, by those fascinated by the band's spine-chilling mix of horror-movie imagery and hardcore. The Misfits were formed in New Jersey, New York, in 1977 by Gerry Only (bass) and Glenn Danzig (vocals) and, like many aspiring new wave acts, played in venues like CBGBs, adding guitarist Bobby Steele and drummer Joey Image. Later that year, 'Cough Cool' became

their first single on their own Plan 9 label. A four-track EP, *Bullet* (in a sleeve showing J.F. Kennedy's assassination), was recorded before their debut album, and was followed by 'Horror Business'. A third single, 'Night Of The Living Dead', surfaced in 1979, the reference to the classic George A. Romero film revealing the Misfits' continued fascination with blood-and-guts horror. Then came an EP, *Three Hits From Hell*, recorded in 1980, but not issued until the following April, and a seasonal October single, 'Halloween'. Having now lost Steele to the Undead, replaced by Jerry's brother Doyle, Googy (aka Eerie Von) stepped in on drums during a European tour with the Damned as Joey's narcotic problems worsened. The Misfits rounded off 1981 by recording the seven-track mini-album *Evilive*, originally sold through the band's Fiend fan club, which also secured a German 12-inch release. The band's only original UK release was a 12-inch EP, *Beware*. Other Misfits releases included several patchy albums which failed to capture their live impact: 1982's *Walk Among Us*, *Earth A.D.* (aka *Wolfblood*) and the posthumous brace, *Legacy Of Brutality* and *Misfits*. Danzig issued his first solo single in 1981, 'Who Killed Marilyn?', later forming Samhain with Misfits' drummer Eerie Von. He was subsequently venerated in heavy metal magazines in the late 80s as his eponymous Danzig vehicle gained ground. The other Misfits mainstays, brothers Jerry and Doyle, formed the hapless Kryst The Conqueror, who releasd one five song EP with the help of Skid Row guitarist David Sabo.

Albums: *Beware* (Cherry Red 1979, mini-album), *Evilive* (Fiend 1981, mini-album), *Walk Among Us* (Ruby 1982), *Earth A.D.* (Plan 9 1983). Compilations: *Legacy Of Brutality* (Plan 9 1985), *The Misfits* (Plan 9 1986), *Evilive* (Plan 9 1987, expanded version of 1981 mini-album).

Mission

UK rock band who evolved from the Sisters Of Mercy, when Wayne Hussey (b. 26 May 1959, Bristol, England; ex-Walkie Talkies, Dead Or Alive) and Craig Adams split from Andrew Eldritch. They quickly recruited drummer Mick Brown (ex-Red Lorry, Yellow Lorry) and guitarist Simon Hinkler (ex-Artery). The original choice of title was the Sisterhood, which led to an undignified series of exchanges in the press between the band and Eldritch. In order to negate their use of the name, Eldritch put out a single under the name Sisterhood on his own Merciful Release label. Thus the title the Mission was selected instead. After two successful independent singles on the Chapter 22 label, they signed to Mercury in the autumn of 1986. Their major label

debut, 'Stay With Me', entered the UK singles charts while the band worked on their debut album. *God's Own Medicine* was the outcome, revealing a tendency towards straightforward rock, and attracting criticism for its bombast. A heavy touring schedule ensued, with the band's off-stage antics attracting at least as much attention as their performances. A particularly indulgent tour of America saw Adams shipped home suffering from exhaustion. His temporary replacement on bass was Pete Turner. After headlining the Reading Festival, they began work on a new album under the auspices of Led Zeppelin bass player John Paul Jones as producer. *Children* was even more successful than its predecessor, reaching number 2 in the UK album charts, despite the customary critical disdain. 1990 brought 'Butterfly On A Wheel' as a single, providing further ammunition for accusations that the band were simply dredging up rock history. In February, the long-delayed third album, *Carved In Sand,* was released, revealing a more sophisticated approach to songwriting. During the world tour to promote the album, both Hinkler and Hussey became ill because of the excessive regime. Hinkler departed suddenly when they reached Toronto, leaving Dave Wolfenden to provide guitar for the rest of the tour. On their return, Paul Etchells took over the position on a more permanent basis. Hussey had meanwhile joined with the Wonder Stuff in proposing a fund-raising concert in London under the banner The Day Of Conscience, but the event self-destructed with a barrage of allegations about commercial intrusion. In a similar vein over the Christmas period, members of the band joined with Slade's Noddy Holder and Jim Lea to re-record 'Merry Xmas Everybody' for charity. However, 1992 would bring numerous further personnel difficulties. Craig Adams returned to Brighton, while Hussey brought in Andy Hobson (bass), Rik Carter (keyboards) and Mark Gemini Thwaite (guitar). A reflective Hussey, promoting the *Sum And Substance* compilation, would concede: 'We had an overblown sense of melodrama. It was great - pompous songs, big grand statements. We've never attempted to do anything that's innovative'. A nation of rock critics found something to agree with Hussey on at last.
Albums: *God's Own Medicine* (Mercury 1986), *Children* (Mercury 1988), *Carved In Sand* (Mercury 1990), *Masque* (Mercury 1992). Compilations: *The First Chapter* (Mercury 1987), *Grains Of Sand* (Mercury 1990), *Sum And Substance* (Vertigo 1994). Videos: *South America* (1989), *Crusade* (1991), *Dusk To Dawn* (1991), *Waves Upon The Sand* (1991).
Further reading: *The Mission - Names Are Tombstones Baby*, Martin Roach with Neil Perry.

Mitchell, Kim

Having dissolved Max Webster in 1982 Mitchell quickly found inspiration to pursue a solo career. After inking a deal with Anthem Records he released a mini-album which followed closely in the Max Webster tradition. He then took a break from music until he signed with Bronze Records. His next release was the excellent and slightly offbeat *Akimbo Alogo* which also housed the single 'Go For Soda'. At times reminiscent of the excesses of Frank Soda And The Imps and Neil Merryweather (c.1974), Mitchell's approach was, at times, misunderstood by the press, but there was no mistaking his obvious talent as a guitarist. He finally achieved critical acclaim with *Rockland* though he has yet to produce a follow-up.
Albums: *Kim Mitchell* (Anthem 1982, mini-album), *Akimbo Alogo* (Bronze 1985), *Shakin' Like A Human Being* (Anthem 1987), *Rockland* (Atlantic 1989).

Moist

Vancouver, Canada-based band, featuring David Usher (vocals) and Mark Makowy (guitar), who met at a party hosted by mutual friend and keyboard player Kevin Young. Makowy brought in bass player Jeff Pearce, and eventually drummer Paul Wilcox completed the line-up. Following a demo cassette in early 1993, the band went on to release a debut album on their own label in February of the following year. Picked up by EMI Music Canada just one month later, the record would go platinum within their own country, mainly bolstered by a ferocious appetite for live appearances. Their most important early exposure in Europe came when they were invited on to the Annual *Smash Hits* Poll Winners' Party as a token rock presence (alongside that of Terrorvision).
Album: *Silver* (EMI 1994).

Molly Hatchet

This Lynyrd Skynyrd-style, blues-rock boogie outfit emerged from the USA's deep south. The name is taken from a lady who beheaded her lovers with an axe after sleeping with them in 17th-century Salem. The initial line-up comprised guitarists Dave Hlubek, Steve Holland and Duane Roland plus bassist Bonner Thomas, vocalist Danny Joe Brown and drummer Bruce Crump. Their debut album, produced by Tom Werman (of Cheap Trick and Ted Nugent fame), was an instant success, with its three-pronged guitar onslaught and gut-wrenching vocals. Brown was replaced by Jimmy Farrar in 1980, before the recording of *Beatin' The Odds*. Farrar's vocals were less distinctive than Brown's, and an element of their identity was lost while the former fronted the band. Nevertheless, commercial success ensued, with both

Beatin' The Odds and *Take No Prisoners* peaking on the *Billboard* album chart at number 25 and 36, respectively. In 1982 Danny Joe Brown rejoined the band, while Thomas was replaced by Riff West on bass. *No Guts...No Glory* emerged and marked a return to their roots: explosive guitar duels, heart-stopping vocals and steadfast rock 'n' roll. Surprisingly the album flopped and Hlubek insisted on a radical change in direction. Steve Holden quit and keyboardist John Galvin was recruited for the recording of *The Deed Is Done*. This was a lightweight pop-rock album, largely devoid of the band's former trademarks. Following its release the band retired temporarily to lick their wounds and reassess their future. In 1985 *Double Trouble Live* was unveiled, a triumphant return to former glories. It included stunning versions of their best-known songs plus a superb Skynyrd tribute in the form of 'Freebird'. Founder member Dave Hlubek departed, to be replaced by Bobby Ingram in 1989. They signed a new deal with Capitol Records and released *Lightning Strikes Twice*. This leaned away from their southern roots towards highly polished AOR. It featured covers of Paul Stanley's 'Hide Your Heart' and Miller/Burnette's 'There Goes The Neighbourhood',

but was poorly received by fans and critics alike. This despite the return of Danny Joe Brown, who had been plagued by illness due to diabetes.
Albums: *Molly Hatchet* (Epic 1978), *Flirtin' With Disaster* (Epic 1979), *Beatin' The Odds* (Epic 1980), *Take No Prisoners* (Epic 1981), *No Guts...No Glory* (Epic 1983), *The Deed Is Done* (Epic 1984), *Double Trouble Live* (Epic 1985), *Lightning Strikes Twice* (Capitol 1989).

Money, Eddie

Legend has it that Brooklyn native Eddie Mahoney was a New York police officer when first discovered by promoter Bill Graham (he was, in fact, a NYPD typist). Nevertheless, under Graham's managerial wing, Mahoney became Eddie Money and produced two hit singles in 'Baby Hold On' and 'Two Tickets To Paradise' from his self-titled debut, to begin a career which has seen him maintain arena headlining status in America with a series of consistently fine R&B-flavoured AOR records. *Life For The Taking* produced two more hits, 'Rock And Roll The Place' and 'Maybe I'm A Fool', as Money built a strong live following which set him free from the constraining need for radio or MTV airplay to sell albums or

Molly Hatchet

concert tickets, although the hits continued to come. *Where's The Party?* saw a slight dip in form, but Money stormed back with perhaps his best 80s album, *Can't Hold Back*, producing three huge hits in the title-track, 'I Wanna Go Back' and 'Take Me Home Tonight', where his warm, soulful vocals were augmented by Ronnie Spector's production. 1991's *Right Here* saw Money move away from the keyboard-dominated sound of preceding albums towards the rootsier feel of his early work, producing another hit in a cover of Romeo's Daughter's 'Heaven In The Backseat'. While European success continues to elude him, Money's future in his homeland seems secure.

Albums: *Eddie Money* (Columbia 1977), *Life For The Taking* (Columbia 1978), *Playing For Keeps* (Columbia 1980), *No Control* (Columbia 1982), *Where's The Party?* (Columbia 1984), *Can't Hold Back* (Columbia 1986), *Nothing To Lose* (Columbia 1988), *Right Here* (Columbia 1991). Compilation: *Greatest Hits: The Sound Of Money* (Columbia 1989).

Monroe, Michael

When Hanoi Rocks folded following the death of drummer Razzle in 1984, Monroe took several years off before deciding to start again and build a solo career. In 1988 *Nights Are So Long* emerged on the independent Yahoo label, featuring a mixture of originals and covers of songs by the Heavy Metal Kids, Johnny Thunders, MC5 and the Flamin' Groovies. This low-key comeback was a soul-cleansing process for Monroe, before he signed to Mercury Records, and threw himself back into the spotlight with all guns blazing. Recruiting Phil Grande (guitar), Tommy Price (drums), Kenny Aaronson (bass) and Ed Roynesdal (keyboards), he recorded *Not Fakin' It*, a streetwise selection of sleazy rock 'n' roll numbers, delivered in Monroe's inimitable, alley cat style. The album was well received and the tour to support it was a further triumph, proving easily the most successful of the Hanoi Rock spin-off projects.

Albums: *Nights Are So Long* (Yahoo 1988), *Not Fakin' It* (Polygram 1989).

Monster Magnet

This space-rock revivalist band was formed in New Jersey in 1989 by vocalist/guitarist David Wyndorf, with guitarist John McBain, bassist Joe Calendra and drummer Jon Kleinman. After a promising debut and the rather self-indulgent *Tab*, Monster Magnet suddenly found broad press and public support with *Spine Of God*, despite the back cover disclaimer that 'It's a satanic drug thing... you wouldn't understand'. The sound and songs drew on Wyndorf's obsession with late 60s psychedelia, music and culture, producing a hypnotic set which blended *Space Ritual*-era Hawkwind style with an MC5/Black Sabbath guitar barrage and a liberal sprinkling of drug references, all played with a 90s venom. The band were quick to capitalize, touring almost non-stop around Europe and the USA, and, following a US tour with Soundgarden, they lost McBain but gained a deal with A&M, who were happy to give the group creative freedom. The resultant *Superjudge*, with new guitarist Ed Mundell, was, if anything, more intense, and saw Monster Magnet pay tribute to Hawkwind with an affectionate blast through 'Brainstorm'. Their live shows remained an experience in themselves, with lighting engineer Tim Cronin's astral projection backdrop proving to be an essential component as the band whipped up a frenzy on stage, touring Europe with Paw and the US with Raging Slab.

Albums: *Monster Magnet* (Primo Scree 1991), *Tab* (Primo Scree 1991), *Spine Of God* (Primo Scree 1991), *Superjudge* (A&M 1993), *Dopes To Infinity* (A&M 1995).

Montrose

After working with Van Morrison, Boz Scaggs and Edgar Winter, guitarist Ronnie Montrose (b. Colorado, USA) formed Montrose in San Francisco in the autumn of 1973. Comprising vocalist Sammy Hagar, bassist Bill Church and drummer Denny Carmassi, they signed to Warner Brothers and released their self-titled debut the following year. Produced by Ted Templeman, *Montrose* was an album that set new standards in heavy metal; the combination of Hagar's raucous vocals with the guitarist's abrasive guitar sound was to become a blueprint against which new bands judged themselves for years to come. Including the classic recordings 'Bad Motor Scooter', 'Space Station No. 5' and 'Rock The Nation', the album still ranks as one of the cornerstones of the hard rock genre. Alan Fitzgerald replaced Bill Church on bass before the recording of the follow-up, *Paper Money*. Hagar was fired shortly after the tour to support it was completed. Bob James and Jim Alcivar were drafted in on vocals and keyboards, but they never recaptured the magic of the debut release. Hagar and Ronnie Montrose, the principal protagonists, would go on to solo careers, the latter joined by several ex-members of Montrose the band in Gamma. Carmassie would, in addition, re-emerge in the 90s as drummer for the Coverdale/Page project.

Albums: *Montrose* (Warners 1974), *Paper Money* (Warners 1975), *Warner Brothers Presents Montrose* (Warners 1975), *Jump On It* (Warners 1976).

Montrose, Ronnie

After rock guitarist Ronnie Montrose (b. Colorado, USA) dissolved his own band Montrose in 1976, he decided to pursue a solo career. Switching styles from hard to jazz-rock, he released *Open Fire*, an instrumental album that was unpopular with fans and critics alike. Disillusioned by this, he formed Gamma, who recorded three albums between 1979 and 1982. When Gamma ground to a halt in 1983, Ronnie recorded *Territory*, another low-key solo set. In 1987 he teamed up with vocalist Johnny Edwards (later Foreigner) and drummer James Kottak (later of Kingdom Come), both ex-Buster Brown and ex-Gamma bassist Glen Letsch. *Mean* was the result, an uncompromising hard rock record that had the guts and musical firepower of Montrose's debut, released 13 years earlier. This line-up was short-lived, with Johnny Bee Bedanjek replacing Edwards and the addition of synthesizer player Pat Feehan, before *The Speed Of Sound* was recorded. Adopting a more sophisticated, melody conscious approach, it lost much of the ground that had been recaptured by the previous album. Ronnie decided to go solo again, producing *The Diva Station* in 1990. This was a semi-instrumental affair and incorporated rock, metal, jazz and soul influences, including an astonishing version of the old Walker Brothers' hit, 'Stay With Me Baby'. Ronnie Montrose remains an extremely gifted guitarist, but as yet he has found it difficult to channel his energies in a direction which also brings commercial rewards. A situation which has seen him spend progressively more time on production work.
Albums: *Open Fire* (Warners 1978), *Territory* (Passport 1986), *Mean* (Enigma 1987), *The Speed Of Sound* (Enigma 1988), *The Diva Station* (Roadrunner 1990).

Moore, Gary

b. 4 April 1952, Belfast, Northern Ireland. This talented, blues-influenced singer and guitarist formed his first major band, Skid Row, when he was 16 years old - initially with Phil Lynott, who left after a few months to form Thin Lizzy. Skid Row continued as a three-piece, with Brendan Shields (bass) and Noel Bridgeman (drums). They relocated from Belfast to London in 1970 and signed a deal with CBS. After just two albums they disbanded, leaving Moore to form the Gary Moore Band. Their debut, *Grinding Stone*, appeared in 1973, but progress was halted the following year while Moore assisted Thin Lizzy after guitarist Eric Bell had left the band. This liaison lasted just four months before Moore was replaced by Scott Gorham and Brian Robertson. Moore subsequently moved into session work before joining Colosseum II in 1976. He made three albums with them, and also rejoined Thin Lizzy for a 10-week American tour in 1977 after guitarist Brian Robertson suffered a severed artery in his hand. Moore finally became a full-time member of Thin Lizzy, but he subsequently left midway through a US tour and formed a new band called G-Force, though this outfit soon floundered. Moore then resumed his solo career, cutting a series of commercially ignored albums until he scored hit singles in 1985 with 'Empty Rooms' and another collaboration with Phil Lynott, 'Out In The Fields'. His 1989 album, *After The War*, revealed a strong celtic influence, and also featured guest artists such as Ozzy Osbourne and Andrew Eldritch (Sisters Of Mercy). But his breakthrough to mainstream commercial acceptance came in 1990 with the superb, confident guitarwork and vocals of *Still Got The Blues*. Mixing blues standards and originals, Moore was acclaimed as one of the UK's foremost artists, a stature which the subsequent release of *After Hours* - featuring cameo appearances from B.B. King and Albert Collins - only confirmed.
Albums: *Back On The Streets* (MCA 1979), *Corridors Of Power* (Virgin 1982), *Rockin' Every Night - Live In Japan* (Virgin 1983), *Live* (Jet 1984), *Run For Cover* (10 1985), *Wild Frontier* (10 1988), *After The War* (Virgin 1989), *Still Got The Blues* (Virgin 1990), *After Hours* (Virgin 1992), *Blues Alive* (Virgin 1993). With Skid Row: *Skid Row* (CBS 1970), *Thirty Four Hours* (CBS 1971). Compilations: *Anthology* (Raw Power 1986), *The Collection* (Castle 1990, double album), *CD Box Set* (Virgin 1991), *Ballads + Blues 1982 - 1994* (Virgin 1994). With Gary Moore Band: *Grinding Stone* (CBS 1973). With Colosseum II: *Strange New Flesh Bronze* (MCA 1976), *Electric Savage* (MCA 1977), *War Dance* (MCA 1977). With Thin Lizzy: *Remembering Part 1* (Decca 1976), *Black Rose* (Vertigo 1979), *Live Life* (Vertigo 1983). With G-Force: *G-Force* (Jet 1979). With Greg Lake Band: *Greg Lake* (Chrysalis 1981), *Manoeuvers* (Chrysalis 1983).
Videos: *Emerald Aisles* (1986), *Live In Sweden* (1988), *Video Singles* (1988), *An Evening Of The Blues* (1991), *Ballads + Blues 1982-1994* (1994).

Moore, Vinnie

b. 1965. This jazz-trained virtuoso guitarist was playing the guitar competently by the age of 12. Picked up by talent scout Mike Varney, he was introduced to the techno-thrash band Vicious Rumours, with whom he recorded *Soldiers Of The Night* in 1985. He left the band as soon as the album was released to concentrate on a solo career. *Mind's

Gary Moore

Eye emerged in 1986, a self-written guitar instrumental collection. This combined a fusion of classical jazz, blues and hard rock that was heavily melodic and technically brilliant, earning comparisons to Joe Satriani's finest work. Two subsequent albums followed a similar pattern but were mellower still, after which he was employed by Alice Cooper as lead guitarist on his 1991 *Hey Stoopid* tour.

Albums: *Mind's Eye* (Shrapnel 1986), *Time Odyssey* (Squawk 1988), *Meltdown* (Squawk 1991).

Morbid Angel

Formed in Florida, USA, in 1984, the band's original line-up consisted of Stering Von Scarborough (bass/vocals), Trey Azagthoth (guitar), Richard Brunelle (guitar) and Pete Sandoval (drums). They quickly gained a following on the underground death metal scene because of their extreme, ultra-fast musical approach. The band recorded the self-financed *Abominations Of Desolation* in 1986. However, unhappy with the resulting recordings, they decided not to release them, as had originally been intended, on their own, now defunct Gorque Records label. They then underwent a personnel change replacing the departed Scarborough with David Vincent (ex-Terrorizer), who gave the band much more of an identity with his strong, charismatic presence (he had previously produced *Abominations Of Desolation*). Morbid Angel continued to gain momentum and eventually attracted the attention of the Earache Records label, resulting in the band's official debut, *Altars Of Madness*, released in 1989. This offered a relentless sheet of noise, punctuated by complex guitar riffs and ultra-fast rhythms. Death metal fans loved it and the band were soon elevated into the hierachy of that genre. By the release of *Blessed Are The Sick,* they had toured Europe extensively, building a strong following in the process. The album, like its forerunner produced by Tom Morris, was once again a marked improvement on previous efforts, and strengthened their position within a growing fan base. Owing to furious bootlegging and the band's burgeoning popularity, Earache Records released the original recordings of *Abominations Of Desolation* in 1991. For 1993's *Covenant*, released through Giant/Warner Bros. in the US, Flemming Rassmussen (Metallica etc.) was drafted in to produce, and their rising profile was cemented by a tour of that teritory supporting Black Sabbath and Motörhead. 1994 saw the replacement of Richard Brunelle by Eric Rutan (ex-Ripping Corpse).

Albums: *Altars Of Madness* (Earache 1989), *Blessed Are The Sick* (Earache 1991), *Abominations Of Desolation* (Earache 1991), *Covenant* (Earache 1993).

Mordred

Formed in San Francisco, USA, in 1985, Mordred were one of the first of a new breed of thrash metal bands that incorporated elements of funk into their high-speed onslaught. Comprising Scott Holderby (vocals), Danny White (guitar), James Sanguinetti (guitar), Art Liboon (bass) and Gannon Hall (drums), they signed to Noise Records and released *Fool's Game* in 1989. On their next album they recruited Aaron (Pause) Vaughn, a scratching disc jockey to give their sound a new dimension. This approach was thought to offer enormous crossover potential, combining elements of Faith No More, Megadeth and Parliament, but thus far the band have failed to gain a footing outside a strictly cult following.

Albums: *Fool's Game* (Noise 1989), *In This Life* (Noise 1991), *Vision* (Noise 1992).

More

This N.W.O.B.H.M. band was led by guitarist Kenny Cox with Paul Mario Day (vocals), Laurie Mansworth (guitar), Brian Day (bass) and Frank Darch (drums). Wild live shows which ended with most of the audience on stage, coupled with a promising session for BBC Radio One's *Friday Rock Show*, led to a deal with Atlantic as major N.W.O.B.H.M. acts such as Saxon and Iron Maiden began to make a serious impact. *Warhead* was a solid debut, but failed to match the live shows, and sales were poor despite a series of UK support performances which generally upstaged headliners Krokus, followed by an appearance in the opening slot of the 1981 Donington Festival. This lack of immediate success plus record company problems led to internal fighting, and by the release of *Blood And Thunder*, Cox had assembled an entirely new line-up of Nick Stratton (vocals), Andy John Burton (drums) and Barry Nicholls (bass). The album stuck faithfully to the riff-heavy style of *Warhead*, but without a UK release from a disinterested label, the band quickly faded.

Albums: *Warhead* (Atlantic 1980), *Blood And Thunder* (Atlantic 1982).

Morta Skuld

Milwaukee-based four-piece Morta Skuld specialize in a provocative cocktail of death metal and noise, brewed by Dave Gregor (vocals/guitar), Jason Hellman (bass), Jason O'Connell (guitar) and Kent Truckebrod (drums). Their debut for Deaf Records

Morbid Angel

was somewhat lacklustre, and several personnel difficulties erupted following its release, resulting in the band splitting in two. However, by the advent of a second long playing set the group had moved up a gear both in tempo and cohesion. The improvement was partially justified by the fact that, though their debut was released early in 1993, it had actually been written and recorded over a year previously. The newer material, akin to a skinnier Obituary sound, brought good reviews in the metal press.

Albums: *Dying Remains* (Deaf 1993), *As Humanity Fades* (Deaf 1994).

Mother Love Bone

This short-lived, Seattle-based quintet comprised Andrew Wood (vocals), Greg Gilmore (drums), Bruce Fairweather (guitar), Stone Gossard (guitar; ex-Green River) and Jeff Ament (bass; ex-Green River). Drawing influences from the Stooges, MC5 and the Velvet Underground they specialized in heavy-duty garage rock laced with drug-fuelled psychotic overtones. Signing to Polydor, they debuted with *Apple* in 1990 to widespread critical acclaim. Their promising career was curtailed abruptly by the untimely death of vocalist Andrew Wood in March, shortly after the album was released. Gossard and Ament would go on to enjoy further success with

Temple Of The Dog and, to a much greater extent, Pearl Jam.

Album: *Apple* (Polydor 1990). Compilation: *Stardog Champion* (Polydor 1992).

Mother's Finest

Despite the 90s fixation with funk rock, Mother's Finest have long been considered as the world's finest in this musical field. Led by vocalist Baby Jean (b. Joyce Kennedy) and hailing from Atlanta, Georgia, USA, the band boasts the talents of Moses Mo (b. Gary Moore; guitar), Glen Murdock (guitar/vocals), Mike (keyboards), Wizzard (b. Jerry Seay; bass) and B.B. Queen (b. B.B. Borden; drums). Formed in 1972, their music was basically funk with a metal edge and Baby Jean's vocals ranged from the sensual to all-out attack. The band never quite made the big league in their homeland and only gained a cult following in Europe, although they were successful in Holland. In 1983, following the release of *Iron Age*, probably their hardest and most enduring record, the band dissipated. B.B. Queen played with southern boogie merchants Molly Hatchet and then teamed up with former colleagues Moses Mo and B.B. Queen in Illusion. He would subsequently release two soul albums for A&M. Wizzard would hook up with Rick Medlocke's Blackfoot. The original line-up reformed in 1989 but the accompanying album failed to capture the fire and soul of earlier releases. Undaunted, they soldiered on and released a live recording, *Subluxation*, to critical acclaim. In its wake, and with a line-up now boasting just three original members; Baby Jean, Murdock and Wizzard, they provided the agenda-setting *Black Raido Won't Play This Record.*

Albums: *Mother's Finest* (RCA 1972), *Mother's Finest* (Epic 1976), *Another Mother Further* (Epic 1977), *Mother Factor* (Epic 1978), *Live Mutha* (Epic 1979), *Iron Age* (Epic 1982), *One Mother To Another* (Epic 1983), *Looks Could Kill* (Capitol 1989), *Subluxation* (Capitol 1990), *Black Radio Won't Play This Record* (Scotti Bros 1992).

Mötley Crüe

This heavy rock band were formed in 1980 by Nikki Sixx (b. Frank Faranno, 11 December 1958, California, USA; bass) and consisted of former members of several other Los Angeles-based groups. Tommy Lee (b. 3 October 1962, Athens, Greece; drums) was recruited from Suite 19; Vince Neil (b. Vince Neil Wharton, 8 February 1961, Hollywood, California, USA; vocals) from Rocky Candy; while Nikki himself had recently left London. Mick Mars (b. Bob Deal, 3 April 1956, USA; guitar) was added to the line-up after Sixx and Lee answered an advertisement announcing 'Loud, rude, aggressive guitarist available'. Their first single, 'Stick To Your Guns'/'Toast Of The Town', was issued in 1981 on their own Leathür label, followed by their self-produced debut, *Too Fast For Love*. The band signed to Elektra in 1982, and the album was remixed and reissued that August. The following year they recorded a new set, *Shout At The Devil*, with producer Tom Werman. He stayed at the helm for the two albums which broke them to a much wider audience in the USA, *Theatre Of Pain* (which sold more than two million copies) and *Girls, Girls, Girls*, which achieved the highest entry for a heavy metal album on *Billboard*'s album chart since *The Song Remains The Same* by Led Zeppelin in 1976. These albums refined the raw sound of earlier releases, without hiding the influence which Kiss and Aerosmith have exerted on their work. This change in style, which saw Mötley Crüe experimenting with organs, pianos and harmonicas in addition to their traditional instruments, has been described as a move from 'club-level metal glam' to 'stadium-size rock 'n' roll'. The band have not been without their setbacks: in 1984, Vince Neil was involved in a major car crash in which Hanoi Rocks drummer Razzle was killed. The subsequent *Theatre Of Pain* was dedicated to his

memory, and this grim incident helped inform the mood of the recording. Three years later, Nikki Sixx came close to death after a heroin overdose following touring with Guns N'Roses. Feuding with that same band, particularly that between Neil and Axl Rose, later provided the group with many of their column inches in an increasingly disinterested press. The band survived to appear at the Moscow Peace Festival in 1989 before more than 200,000 people, and then in 1991 to issue *Dr. Feelgood*, which gave them their first US number 1 chart placing. Vince Neil would be ejected from the band's line-up, unexpectedly, in 1992, starting the Vince Neil Band shortly thereafter. His replacement for 1994's eponymous album would be John Corabi (ex-Scream), though the band's problems would continue with a record label/management split and disastrous North American tour.

Albums: *Too Fast For Love* (Leathür 1981), *Shout At The Devil* (Elektra 1983), *Theatre Of Pain* (Elektra 1985), *Girls, Girls, Girls* (Elektra 1987), *Dr. Feelgood* (Elektra 1989), *Mötley Crüe* (Elektra 1994). Compilations: *Raw Tracks* (Elektra 1988), *Decade Of Decadence* (Elektra 1991).

Videos: *Uncensored* (1987), *Dr. Feelgood, The Videos* (1989), *Decade Of Decadence* (1991).

Motörhead

In 1975 Lemmy (b. Ian Fraiser Kilmister, 24 December 1945, Stoke, England; vocals/bass) was sacked from Hawkwind after being detained for five days at Canadian customs on possession charges. The last song he wrote for them was entitled 'Motörhead', and, after ditching an earlier suggestion, Bastard, this became the name of the band he formed with Larry Wallis of the Pink Fairies on guitar and Lucas Fox on drums. Together they made their debut supporting Greenslade at the Roundhouse, London, in July. Fox then left to join Warsaw Pakt, and was replaced by 'Philthy' Phil Taylor (b. 21 September 1954, Chesterfield, England; drums), a casual friend of Lemmy's with no previous professional musical experience. Motörhead was a four piece band for less than a month, with Taylor's friend 'Fast' Eddie Clarke (b. 5 October 1950, Isleworth, Middlesex, England) of Continuous Performance as second guitarist, until Wallis returned to the Pink Fairies. The Lemmy/Taylor/Clarke combination would last six years until 1982, in which time they became the most famous trio in hard rock. With a following made up initially of hell's angels (Lemmy had formerly lived with their president, Tramp, for whom he would write the biker epic 'Iron Horse'), the band made their debut with the eponymous 'Motörhead'/'City

Kids'. A similarly-titled debut album charted, before the group moved over to Bronze Records. *Overkill* and *Bomber* firmly established the group's *modus operandi*, a fearsome barrage of instruments topped off by Lemmy's hoarse invocations. They toured the world regularly and enjoyed hit singles with 'Ace Of Spades' (one of the most definitive heavy metal performances ever, it graced a 1980 album of the same name which saw the band at the peak of their popularity) and 'Please Don't Touch' (as Headgirl). Their reputation as the best live band of their generation was further enhanced by the release of *No Sleep 'Til Hammersmith*, which entered the UK charts at number 1. In May 1982 Clarke left, citing musical differences, and was replaced by Brian Robertson (b. 12 September 1956, Glasgow, Scotland), who had previously played with Thin Lizzy and Wild Horses. This combination released *Another Perfect Day*, but this proved to be easily the least popular of all Motörhead line-ups. Robertson was replaced in November 1983 by Wurzel (b. Michael Burston, 23 October 1949, Cheltenham, England; guitar) - so-called on account of his scarecrow-like hair - and Philip Campbell (b. 7 May 1961, Pontypridd, Wales; guitar; ex-Persian Risk), thereby swelling the Motörhead ranks to four. Two months later and, after a final appearance on television's *The Young Ones*, Taylor left to join Robertson in Operator, and was replaced by ex-Saxon drummer Pete Gill. Gill remained with the band until 1987 and played on several fine albums including *Orgasmatron*, the title-track of which saw Lemmy's lyric-writing surpass itself. By 1987 Phil Taylor had rejoined Motörhead, and the line-up remained unchanged for five years during which time Lemmy made his acting debut in the *Comic Strip* film, *Eat The Rich*, followed by other celluloid appearances including the role of taxi driver in *Hardware*. In 1992 the group released *March Or Die*, which featured the American Mikkey Dee (ex-King Diamond) on drums and guest appearances by Ozzy Osbourne and Slash (Guns N' Roses). The title-track followed on from '1916' and revealed a highly sensitive side to Lemmy's lyrical and vocal scope, both songs dealing with the horrors of war. The idiosyncratic Lemmy singing style, usually half-growl, half-shout, and with his neck craned up at 45 degrees to the microphone, remained as ever. On a more traditional footing they performed the theme song to the horror film *Hellraiser 3*, and convinced the film's creator, Clive Barker, to record his first promotional video with the band. Lemmy also hammed his way through insurance adverts, taking great delight in his press image of the unreconstructed rocker.
Albums: *Motörhead* (Chiswick 1977), *Overkill*

(Bronze 1979), *Bomber* (Bronze 1979), *On Parole* (United Artists 1979), *Ace Of Spades* (Bronze 1980), *No Sleep Till Hammersmith* (Bronze 1981), *Iron Fist* (Bronze 1982), *Another Perfect Day* (Bronze 1983), *What's Wordsworth* (Big Beat 1983), *Orgasmatron* (GWR 1986), *Rock'N'Roll* (GWR 1987), *Eat The Rich* (GWR 1987), *No Sleep At All* (GWR 1988), *1916* (Epic 1991), *March Or Die* (Epic 1992), *Bastards* (ZYX 1993). Compilations: *No Remorse* (Bronze 1984), *Anthology* (Raw Power 1986), *Dirty Love* (Receiver 1989), *From The Vaults* (Sequel 1990), *Best Of* (Action Replay 1990), *Collection* (Castle 1990), *Meltdown* (Castle 1991, 3-CD box set), *All The Aces* (Castle 1993).
Videos: *Deaf Not Blind* (1984), *Birthday Party* (1986), *Eat The Rich* (1988, film), *Toronto Live* (1989), *Best Of* (1991), *Everything Louder Than Everything Else* (1991).
Further reading: *Motörhead*, Alan Burridge, *Born To Lose*, Alan Burridge.

Mott

This short-lived group was founded in 1975. Morgan Fisher (keyboards), Overend Watts (bass, vocals) and Dale Griffin (drums), each formerly of Mott The Hoople, decided to drop the earlier suffix upon adding Nigel Benjamin (vocals) and Ray Major (guitar) to the line-up. Their albums proved sadly disappointing, invoking unfavourable comparison with their previous, highly-successful incarnation. The departure of Benjamin precipitated yet another change and, having invited ex-Medicine Head singer John Fiddler to join, the unit changed its name to British Lions.
Albums: *Drive On* (CBS 1975), *Shouting And Pointing* (CBS 1976).

Mott The Hoople

Having played in a number of different rock groups in Hereford, England, during the late 60s, the founding members of this ensemble comprised: Overend Watts (b. Peter Watts, 13 May 1947, Birmingham, England; vocals/bass), Mick Ralphs (b. 31 March 1944, Hereford, England; vocals/guitar), Verden Allen (b. 26 May 1944, Hereford, England; organ) and Dale Griffin (b. 24 October 1948, Ross-on-Wye, England; vocals/drums). After dispensing with their lead singer Stan Tippens, they were on the point of dissolving when Ralphs sent a demo tape to Island Records producer Guy Stevens. He responded enthusiastically, and after placing an advertisement in *Melody Maker* auditioned a promising singer named Ian Hunter (b. 3 June 1946, Shrewsbury, England; vocals/keyboards/guitar). In June 1969 Stevens

Lemmy of Motörhead with Wendy O'Williams

christened the group Mott The Hoople, after the novel by Willard Manus. Their self-titled debut album revealed a very strong Bob Dylan influence, most notably in Hunter's nasal vocal inflexions and visual image. With his corkscrew hair and permanent shades Hunter bore a strong resemblance to vintage 1966 Dylan and retained that style for his entire career. Their first album, with its M.C. Escher cover illustration, included pleasing interpretations of the Kinks' 'You Really Got Me' and Sonny Bono's 'Laugh At Me', and convinced many that Mott would become a major band. Their next three albums trod water, however, and it was only their popularity and power as a live act which kept them together. Despite teaming up with backing vocalist Steve Marriott on the George 'Shadow' Morton- produced 'Midnight Lady', a breakthrough hit remained elusive. On 26 March 1972, following the departure of Allen, they quit in disillusionment. Fairy godfather David Bowie convinced them to carry on, offered his assistance as producer, placed them under the wing of his manager, Tony De Fries, and even presented them with a stylish UK hit, 'All The Young Dudes'. The catchy 'Honaloochie Boogie' maintained the momentum but there was still one minor setback when Ralphs quit to form Bad Company. With new members Morgan Fisher and Ariel Bender (Luther Grosvenor) Mott enjoyed a run of further UK hits including 'All The Way From Memphis' and 'Roll Away The Stone'. During their final phase, Bowie's sideman Mick Ronson joined the group in place of Grosvenor (who had departed to join Widowmaker). Preparations for a European tour in late 1974 were disrupted when Hunter was hospitalized suffering from physical exhaustion, culminating in the cancellation of the entire tour. When rumours circulated that Hunter had signed a deal instigating a solo career, with Ronson working alongside him, the upheaval led to an irrevocable rift within the group resulting in the stormy demise of Mott The Hoople. With the official departure of Hunter and Ronson, the remaining members, Watts, Griffin and Fisher, determined to carry on, working simply as Mott.

Albums: *Mott The Hoople* (Island 1969), *Mad Shadows* (Island 1970), *Wild Life* (Island 1971), *Brain Capers* (Island 1971), *All The Young Dudes* (CBS 1972), *Mott* (CBS 1973), *The Hoople* (CBS 1974), *Live* (CBS 1974). Compilations: *Rock And Roll Queen* (Island 1972), *Greatest Hits* (CBS 1975), *Shades Of Ian Hunter - The Ballad Of Ian Hunter And Mott The Hoople* (CBS 1979, double album), *Two Miles From Heaven* (Island 1981), *All The Way From Memphis* (Hallmark 1981), *Greatest Hits* (CBS 1981, different to 1975 issue).

Further reading: *The Diary Of A Rock 'N' Roll Star*, Ian Hunter.

Mountain

Mountain were one of the first generation heavy metal bands, formed by ex-Vagrants guitarist Leslie West (b. Leslie Weinstein, 22 October 1945, Queens, New York, USA) and bassist Felix Pappalardi (b. 1939, Bronx, New York, USA, d. 17 April 1983) in New York in 1968. Augmented by drummer Corky Laing and Steve Knight on keyboards they played the Woodstock festival in 1970, releasing *Mountain Climbing* shortly afterwards. Featuring dense guitar lines from West and the delicate melodies of Pappalardi, they quickly established their own sound, although Cream influences were detectable in places. The album was an unqualified success, peaking at number 17 in the *Billboard* album chart in November 1970. Their next two albums built on this foundation, as the band refined their style into an amalgam of heavy riffs, blues-based rock and extended guitar and keyboard solos. *Nantucket Sleighride* (the title-track of which was used as the theme tune to television programme *World In Action*) and *Flowers Of Evil* made the *Billboard* charts at numbers 16 and 35, respectively. A live album followed, which included interminably long solos and was poorly received. The group temporarily disbanded to follow separate projects. Pappalardi returned to producing, while West and Laing teamed up with Cream's Jack Bruce to record as the trio (West, Bruce And Laing). In the autumn of 1974, Mountain rose again with Alan Schwartzberg and Bob Mann replacing Laing and Knight to record *Twin Peaks*, live in Japan. This line-up was short-lived as Laing rejoined for the recording of the disappointing studio album, *Avalanche*. The band collapsed once more and West concentrated on his solo career again. Pappalardi was shot and killed by his wife in 1983. Two years later, West and Laing resurrected the band with Mark Clarke (former Rainbow and Uriah Heep bassist) and released *Go For Your Life*. They toured with Deep Purple throughout Europe in 1985, but split up again soon afterwards.

Albums: *Mountain Climbing* (Bell 1970), *Nantucket Sleighride* (Island 1971), *Flowers Of Evil* (Island 1971), *The Road Goes On Forever-Mountain Live* (Island 1972), *Avalanche* (Epic 1974), *Twin Peaks* (CBS 1974), *Go For Your Life* (Scotti Bros 1985). Compilation: *The Best Of* (Island 1973).

Mourneblade

London band whose main claim to fame was that one member was a British skateboard champion. Formed

in late 1984 the group comprised Derek Jasnock (keyboards), Richard Jones (guitar), Dunken Mullet (vocals), Jeff Ward (drums) and Clive Baxter (bass). They blended the heavier qualities of Hawkwind with the bass driven power of Motörhead. In keeping with that tradition they took their name from a novel by Michael Moorcock, and signed to the Hawkwind-allied Flicknife Records. It was their tenuous links with the latter band which first got them noticed, and their debut album contained six excellent songs, though it failed to impress the Hawkwind fraternity or rock fans in general. They vanished off the music scene for a couple of years before regrouping in 1988, gaining a session on the *Friday Rock Show* in July of the following year. This saw them unveil a new sound, which had already been sketched more fully in January, when their second album had arrived. This contained further Hawkwind-inspired tracks like the 'Hall Of The Mountain King', but also, sadly, grim tales like 'Lolita' and 'Blonde Beautiful And Dead'. A few gigs and poor record sales later they returned to obscurity.
Albums: *Times Running Out* (Flicknife 1985), *Live Fast, Die Young* (Plastic Head 1989).

Mr. Big

Mr. Big (not to be confused with the 70s group of the same name) are a supergroup project, featuring bassist Billy Sheehan (ex-Dave Lee Roth), guitarist Paul Gilbert (ex-Racer X), drummer Pat Torpey (ex-Impelliteri and Robert Plant) and vocalist Eric Martin (ex-Eric Martin Band). Signing to Atlantic Records, their self-titled debut was a high-energy blast of sophisticated hard rock. *Lean Into It*, released two years later, marked a considerable progression; the band had evolved their own style and sounded more comfortable together. Drawing on influences from a wider musical spectrum, the album was well received by the critics and charted on both sides of the Atlantic. The exposition of AOR which has graced the charts remains, however, in sharp contrast to their reputation for strong live performances.
Albums: *Mr. Big* (Atlantic 1989), *Lean Into It* (Atlantic 1991), *Live* (Atlantic 1992), *Bump Ahead* (Atlantic 1993).

Mr. Bungle

Originating in Eureka, California, in the mid-80s, this bizarre punk-metal-jazz-*avant garde* amalgam was Mike Patton's first band prior to joining Faith No More, and the success of *The Real Thing* helped Patton find a record contract for his previous project. Patton and colleagues Trey Spruance (guitar), Trevor Dunn (bass) and Danny Heifetz (drums) adopted an oddly-costumed image to match their eclectic musical style, with Patton and Spruance adopting the respective pseudonyms Vlad Dracula and Scummy, enlisting jazz-noise experimentalist John Zorn to produce *Mr Bungle*. The album received surprisingly positive reviews considering its extreme, genre-hopping, improvisational format and strange lyrical themes, although Zorn's sympathetic production helped to focus the eccentricity. *Mr Bungle* sold respectably on the strength of Patton's name, but his Faith No More commitments kept live shows to a minimum. Spruance subsequently replaced Jim Martin in Faith No More for the recording of *King For A Day...Fool For a Lifetime*, although he departed shortly afterwards, while Patton hinted at the possibility of a further Mr Bungle album.
Album: *Mr Bungle* (Warners 1991).

MSG

After stints with UFO and the Scorpions, guitarist Michael Schenker (b. 10 January 1955, Savstedt, Germany) decided to step out into the spotlight on his own in 1980. Enlisting the services of Gary Barden (vocals), Simon Phillips (drums), Mo Foster (bass) and Don Airey (keyboards), the Michael Schenker Group (later shortened to MSG) was born. Their approach, characterized by Schenker's screaming guitar work, had much in common with both his previous bands. Schenker, now in complete control, hired and fired musicians at will, so the line-up of MSG has rarely been stable. Only Barden survived to record their second album; Cozy Powell (drums), Chris Glen (bassist, ex-Sensational Alex Harvey Band) and Paul Raymond (keyboards; ex-UFO) were the replacements. They enjoyed great success in the Far East, where they recorded a double live set at the Budokan Hall, Tokyo. This album finally helped to establish the band in Europe. Graham Bonnet replaced Barden on *Assault Attack* and ex-Rory Gallagher drummer Ted McKenna was also recruited. Bonnet insisted on making a significant contribution to the compositions and his influence can clearly be heard on the album, which is far more blues-orientated than previous releases. Schenker fired Bonnet shortly after the album's launch and welcomed back former vocalist Gary Barden. The next two album releases were rigidly formularized. Old ideas were simply re-hashed as the band remained stuck in a creative rut. Even the contribution of Derek St. Holmes (ex-Ted Nugent vocalist) could not elevate the very ordinary material. Barden left to form Statetrooper and MSG disintegrated. Schenker moved back to Germany and teamed up with singer Robin McCauley (ex-Grand

Prix) to form the McCauley Schenker Group, still retaining the acronym MSG. They completed the new-look band, with Steve Mann, Rocky Newton and Bobo Schopf on keyboards, bass and drums, respectively. They also concentrated on a more melodic direction, as McCauley's prolific writing skills were, for once, accepted by Schenker. With the release of *Perfect Timing* and *Save Yourself*, they began to re-establish a solid fan base once more, though 1992's confusingly titled *MSG* was universally despised.

Albums: *The Michael Schenker Group* (Chrysalis 1980), *MSG* (Chrysalis 1981), *One Night At Budokan* (Chrysalis 1982), *Assault Attack* (Chrysalis 1982), *Built To Destroy* (Chrysalis 1983), *Rock Will Never Die* (Chrysalis 1984), *Perfect Timing* (EMI 1987), *Save Yourself* (Capitol 1989), *MSG* (EMI 1992).

Mudhoney

Miraculously forged from a host of hobbyist bands, Seattle's Mudhoney can lay claim to the accolade 'godfathers' of grunge' more legitimately than most. The band comprises brothers Mark Arm (vocals) and Steve Turner (guitar), plus Matt Lukin (bass) and Dan Peters (drums). Arm and Turner were both ex-Green River, and 'fuck' band Thrown Ups. Lukin was ex-Melvins, Peters ex-Bundles Of Piss. Mudhoney were the band that first imported the sound of Sub Pop to the UK's shores. In August 1988 they released the fabulous 'Touch Me I'm Sick' single, followed shortly by their debut mini-LP. Contrary to popular belief, Turner chose the name *Superfuzz Bigmuff* after his favourite effects pedals rather than any sexual connotation. Early support included the admiration of Sonic Youth who covered their first a-side while Mudhoney thrashed through SY's 'Halloween' on the flip of a joint single. The first album proper was greeted as a comparitive disappointment by many, though there were obvious standout tracks ('When Tomorrow Hits'). The EP, *Boiled Beef And Rotting Teeth*, contained a cover of the Dicks' 'Hate The Police', demonstrating a good grasp of their heritage. Previously Spacemen 3's 'Revolution' had appeared on the b-side to 'This Gift'. The band also hold the likes of Celibate Rifles and Billy Childish is high esteem. Members of the former have helped in production of the band, while on trips to England they have invited the latter to join as support. It was their patronage which led to Chidlish' Thee Headcoats releasing material on Sub Pop. Their own shows, meanwhile, were becoming less eye-catching, and progressively close to eye-gouging. Early gigs in London saw Arm invite the audience, every last one of them, up on to the stage, with the resultant near

destruction of several venues. *Every Good Boy Deserves Fudge* was a departure, with Hammond organ intruding into the band's accomplished grunge formula. It demonstated their increasing awareness of the possibilities of their own songwriting. They are certainly not the wooden-headed noise dolts they are sometimes portrayed as: each comes from a comfortable middle class background, and while Arm is an English graduate, Turner has qualifications in anthropology. After much speculation Mudhoney became the final major players in the Sub Pop empire to go major when they moved to Warner Brothers, though many would argue that none of their efforts thus far have managed to reproduce the glory of 'Touch Me I'm Sick' or other highlights of their independent days.

Albums: *Superfuzz Bigmuff* (Sub Pop 1988, mini-album), *Mudhoney* (Sub Pop 1989), *Every Good Boy Deserves Fudge* (Sub Pop 1991), *Piece Of Cake* (Warners 1992), *Five Dollar Bob's Mock Cooter Stew* (Warners 1993). Compilation: *Superfuzz Bigmuff Plus Early Singles* (Sub Pop 1993).
Video: *Absolutely Live* (1994).

Murder Inc.

This *avant garde*/industrial metal band were formed in London during 1992 by ex-Killing Joke members and ex-Revolting Cocks' vocalist Chris Connelly. Utilizing two drummers in Martin Atkins and Paul Ferguson, their style was naturally dominated by a strong rhythmic element. Geordie Walker (guitar), Paul Raven (bass) and John Bechdel (guitar/keyboards) completed the line-up. Contracted to Music For Nations Records, the band debuted with a self-titled album in June 1992. This built on the brutal rhythms of Killing Joke's material, but, as with each of the spin-off projects, failed to inspire similar devotion to that enjoyed by the parent group.

Album: *Murder Inc.* (Music For Nations 1992).

My Dying Bride

From Bradford, Yorkshire, England, My Dying Bride proffer an intriguing blend of full-blooded doom metal, with more poise than most and a rare experimental streak. Vocalist Aaron's lyrics also depart somewhat from the herd - though he often concerns himself with biblical and religious matters, his stance is neither that of Christian or Satanist: 'The bible is a fantastic story...There's no heaven or hell as far as I'm concerned, it's just a nice story and I like to write about it because it affects so many people's lives'. After formation in 1990 they secured a deal with French label Listenable, through whom they provided their first official release, the 'God Is Alone' single. This

was enough to interest UK label Peaceville who released their debut EP, *Symphonaire Infernus Et Spera Empyrium*. Their 1992 album, *As The Flower Withers*, followed shortly afterwards, featuring artwork by popular cult artist Dave McKean. My Dying Bride were already making a name for themselves as innovators in the doom genre, with a sound that combined the morbid grind of death metal with orchestral flourishes and haunting refrains. The resultant effect was one of grandiose tragedy. After recording another EP, *The Thrash Of Naked Limbs*, they took their session violinist and pianist, Martin Powell, on as a full member of the band, confirming their dedication to a path which combined classical and contemporary influences. A second album, *Let Loose The Swans*, saw Aaron singing, rather than growling in the traditional death metal style, and is their most distinctive and accomplished work to date. The vitality and colour of the band was enshrined in their 1994 release, the *I Am The Bloody Earth* EP, with the a-side featuring guest vocals from Ghost (of G.G.F.H.), while the b-side, 'Transcending (Into The Exquisite)', featured a challenging remix from local dance gurus Drug Free America. November 1994 saw the release of a box set containing their previous EPs, which sold sold out almost immediately, reflecting My Dying Bride's growing popularity.
Albums: *As The Flower Withers* (Peaceville 1992), *Let Loose The Swans* (Peaceville 1993).

Myles, Alannah
Toronto-based vocalist Alannah Myles spent much of her early career unsuccessfully shopping for a recording deal in her native Canada, but when she and writing partner Christopher Ward changed tack, targeting an American deal with a David Tyson-produced demo and a video for 'Just One Kiss', they met with almost instant success. Tyson produced *Alannah Myles*, an excellent commercial hard rock debut on which the vocalist turned her deep, soulful voice to a variety of material, from gentle acoustic guitar-based ballads to raunchy rock 'n' roll with a power reminiscent of Heart's Ann Wilson. After the years of struggle, the debut ironically took off rapidly in Canada, with 'Love Is' helping Myles achieve major status in just three months, but the slow, steamy raunch of 'Black Velvet' brought much wider success. The raven-haired singer suddenly found herself topping the US singles chart and hitting the Top 3 in the UK as 'Black Velvet' became a worldwide hit. *Alannah Myles* subsequently became the most successful debut in Canadian music history, selling more than five million copies globally, and Myles proved that she was no mere studio songbird, taking

her band out on the road, supporting Robert Plant in the UK. *Rockinghorse* was a good second effort, but lacked material with the immediacy of her debut, and subsequently failed to repeat its enormous impact.
Albums: *Alannah Myles* (Atlantic 1989), *Rockinghorse* (Atalntic 1992).

Mythra
Judas Priest-influenced band from the north east of England who came together in 1979 at the height of the New Wave Of British Heavy Metal and released one of the most outstanding records of the era. Yet the band - Vince High (vocals), Mick Rundel (guitar), Barry Hopper (drums), Maurice Bates (rhythm guitar) and Pete Melsom (bass) - never achieved the greatness a band which sells 15,000 singles in 20 days deserves. The EP, *Death And Destiny*, first released on Guardian Records, was quickly re-issued on Street Beat Records to coincide with their appearance at the Bingley Hall festival with Motörhead. It too sold well and their battle cry of 'Death And Destiny' was sung by a thousand voices at said gig. Yet by 1981 their name was absent from the live listings, leaving the EP to command a high collectors' value and cult reputation. Metallica fans would do well to track it down to see how much *Kill 'Em All* owes to this band.

N.W.O.B.H.M.
(see New Wave Of British Heavy Metal)

Nailbomb
A side-project for Sepultura vocalist/guitarist Max Cavalera and Fudge Tunnel singer/guitarist Alex Newport, both now residents of Phoenix, Arizona. Nailbomb arrived with the public thus: 'It was right after the last show on the Ministry tour. It was in San Diego and we were having a party. Me and Alex were talking 'cause the tour was over, the rest of the guys in Sepultura were going to Brazil, and I wasn't going because it was close to the time my son (Zyon) would be born. But I didn't want to stay and just do nothing in Phoenix...So I told Alex, 'why don't we get together and do some songs, just for the hell of it'. We didn't even think of recording anything'. Originally titled Hate Project, then Sickman, they eventually settled

on Nailbomb because both partners wanted something 'real shocking'. A tape of the duo's demos reached Monte Conner at Roadrunner, who got them a studio budget to put together something a little more firm. The result was *Point Blank*, which improved on the quality of those demos but maintained the punk sound (a cross between Big Black and Discharge) which they had developed together. Contributions from Sepultura's lead guitarist Andreas Kisser and drummer Igor Cavalera were received, together with an appearance by Fear Factory's Dino Cazares on '24 Hour Bullshit'.

Album: *Point Blank* (Roadrunner 1994).

Naked Truth

This Atlanta, Georgia-based quartet originated in the local hardcore scene in 1988, although the individual band members arrived from far afield: vocalist Doug Watts came from Detroit, bassist Jeff from Harlem, New York, and drummer Bernard Dawson from Los Angeles, while Jimmie Westley was the only Georgia native, from Savannah. Life was initially tough for a black metal band in Georgia, but the dreadlocked group caught the interest of former Clash manager Bernie Rhodes, and he helped the band sign to Sony and relocate to London. *Green With Rage* introduced Naked Truth's raw, aggressive sound, which was given an individual slant by jazz and funk influences, but the homesick Jeff departed, and was replaced by London-born Kwame Boaten for the *Read Between The Lines* EP. The band were fortunate to pick up a UK tour with Little Angels after a Motörhead support slot was lost due to a tour cancellation, and despite the obviously different styles, Naked Truth went down well. The band built up a varied following, helped by a series of London residencies, before *Fight* appeared, showing the band's ability to mix styles as diverse as jazz and death metal seamlessly and convincingly, while Watts supplied varied vocals, from rap to all-out hardcore rage, and intelligent lyrics. The band were impressive as they supported Living Colour around the UK, but decided on a name change to Watts before releasing their second full album.

Albums: *Green With Rage* (Sony 1991, mini-album), *Fight* (Sony 1993).

Napalm Death

This quintet from Birmingham, England, was formed in 1981. Dispensing with their original style by the mid-80s, they then absorbed punk and thrash metal influences to create the new sub-genre of grindcore, arguably the most extreme of all musical forms. Side one of their debut album featured Justin Broadrick (guitar), Mick Harris (drums) and Nick Bullen (bass/vocals), but by side two this had switched to Bill Steer (guitar), Jim Whitely (bass) and Lee Dorrian (vocals), with Harris the only survivor from that first inception (though that too had been subject to numerous changes). Broadrick would go on to Head Of David and Godflesh. *Scum* largely comprised sub-two minute blasts of metallic white noise, over-ridden by Dorrian's unintelligible vocal tirade. The lyrics dealt with social and political injustices, but actually sounded like somebody coughing up blood. Their main advocate was Radio 1 DJ John Peel, who had first picked up on *Scum*, playing the 0.75 second-long track 'You Suffer' three times before inviting them to record a session for the programme in September 1987. This would come to be acknowledged as one of the 'Classic Sessions' in Ken Garner's 1993 book on the subject, and introduced new bass player Shane Embury (also Unseen Terror, who split after one album in 1988). Elsewhere Napalm Death were the subject of derision and total miscomprehension. They were, however, the true pioneers of the 'blast-snare' technique - whereby the tempo of a given beat is sustained at the maximum physical human tolerance level. They went on to attract a small but loyal cult following on the underground heavy metal scene. From *Enslavement To Obliteration*, consisting of no less than 54 tracks on the CD, was a state of the artless offering which easily bypassed pervious extremes in music. However, following a Japanese tour in 1989 both Dorrian and Steer elected to leave the band, the former putting together Cathedral, the latter Carcass. Despite the gravity of the split replacements were found in vocalist Mark 'Barney' Greenway (ex-Bendiction) and US guitarist Jesse Pintado (ex-Terrorizer). To maintain their profile the band embarked on the European *Grindcrusher* tour (in their wake grindcore had developed considerably and found mass acceptance among the rank and file of the metal world) with Bolt Thrower, Carcass and Morbid Angel, before playing their first US dates in New York. A second guitarist, Mitch Harris (ex-Righteous Pigs) was added in time for *Harmony Corruption*, which, along with the 12 inch 'Suffer The Children', saw Napalm Death retreat to a purer death metal sound. During worldwide touring in 1992 sole surviving original member Mick Harris became disillusioned with the band and vacated the drum stool for Danny Herrara, a friend of Pintado's from Los Angeles. A fourth album, *Utopia Banished*, celebrated the band's remarkable survival instincts, while the heady touring schedule continued unabated. By 1993 the band had played in Russia, Israel, Canada and South Africa in addition to the

Napalm Death

more familiar European and US treks. A cover of the Dead Kennedys' 'Nazi Punks Fuck Off', issued as a single, reinstated their political motives. As *Fear, Emptiness, Despair* confirmed, however, they remain the antithesis of style, melody and taste - the punk concept taken to its ultimate extreme, and a great band for all the difficulty of listening to them.

Albums: *Scum* (Earache 1987), *From Enslavement To Obliteration* (Earache 1988), *The Peel Sessions* (Strange Fruit 1989), *Harmony Corruption* (Earache 1990), *Utopia Banished* (Earache 1992), *Fear, Emptiness, Despair* (Earache 1994). Compilation: *Death By Manipulation* (Earache 1992).

Video: *Live Corruption* (1990).

Nasty Idols

This Swedish glam-metal quintet were formed in 1988 by vocalist Andy Pierce and guitarist Jonnie Wee, with Dick Qwarfort (bass), George Swanson (drums) and Roger White (keyboards) completing the line-up. They pursued a commercial hard rock direction in the style of Bon Jovi and Whitesnake, debuting with *Gigolos On Parole* to widespread indifference. Wee was soon replaced by Peter Espinoza on guitar, and his arrival marked a move towards a more glam-metal image, with Mötley Crüe and Hanoi Rocks influences taking over. *Cruel Intention* was the result, released in 1991. A marked improvement, it nevertheless failed to help them emulate this new set of influences in terms of commercial reward.

Albums: *Gigolos On Parole* (Black Mark 1989), *Cruel Intention* (Black Mark 1991).

Nasty Savage

This heavy metal/thrash quintet was formed in Brandigan, Florida, USA, during 1983 by vocalist and professional wrestler Nasty Ronnie and guitarist Ben Meyer. Assisted by David Austin (guitar), Fred Dregischan (bass) and Curtis Beeson (drums), they made their debut via demo tracks which subsequently appeared on the *Metal Massacre IV* and *Iron Tyrants* compilations in 1984. This led to a contract with Metal Blade Records, producing four albums over the ensuing five years. From an initial hard rock base of Iron Maiden and Judas Priest-styles, they gradually incorporated thrash elements into their music, drawing inspiration and ideas from Metallica, Anthrax and Slayer. They have been through four bass players in as many years, with the current guitarist Richard Bateman having taken up four string duties in 1988. Rob Proctor replaced Beeson on drums the following year. When they eventually sundered at the close of the decade they were chiefly lamented for a spectacular live show which featured their wild vocalist smashing television sets on stage and performing crude gymnastics.

Albums: *Nasty Savage* (Metal Blade 1985), *Indulgence* (Metal Blade 1987), *Abstract Reality* (Metal Blade 1988), *Penetration Point* (Metal Blade 1989).

Nazareth

Formed in 1968 in Dunfermline, Fife, Scotland, Nazareth evolved out of local attractions, the Shadettes. Dan McCafferty (vocals), Manny Charlton (guitar), Pete Agnew (bass) and Darrell Sweet (drums) took their new name from the opening line in 'The Weight', a contemporary hit for the Band. After completing a gruelling Scottish tour, Nazareth opted to move to London. *Nazareth* and *Exercises* showed undoubted promise, while a third set, *Razamanaz*, spawned two UK Top 10 singles in 'Broken Down Angel' and 'Bad Bad Boy' (both 1973). New producer Roger Glover helped focus the quartet's brand of melodic hard rock, and such skills were equally prevalent on *Loud 'N' Proud*. An unlikely rendition of Joni Mitchell's 'This Flight Tonight' gave the group another major chart entry, while the Charlton-produced *Hair Of The Dog* confirmed Nazareth as an international attraction. Another cover version, this time of Tomorrow's 'My White Bicycle', was a Top 20 entry and although *Rampant* did not yield a single, the custom-recorded 'Love Hurts', originally a hit for the Everly Brothers, proved highly successful in the US and Canada. Nazareth's popularity remained undiminished throughout the 70s but, having tired of a four-piece line-up, they added guitarist Zal Cleminson, formerly of the Sensational Alex Harvey Band, for *No Mean City*. Still desirous for change, the group invited Jeff 'Skunk' Baxter, late of Steely Dan and the Doobie Brothers, to produce *Malice In Wonderland*. While stylistically different from previous albums, the result was artistically satisfying. Contrasting ambitions then led to Cleminson's amicable departure, but the line-up was subsequently augmented by former Spirit keyboard player, John Locke. Baxter also produced the experimental *The Fool Circle*, while the group's desire to capture their in-concert fire resulted in *'Snaz*. Glasgow guitarist Billy Rankin had now joined the group, but dissatisfaction with touring led to Locke's departure following *2XS*. Rankin then switched to keyboards, but although Nazareth continued to enjoy popularity in the US and Europe, their stature in the UK was receding. Bereft of a major recording deal, Nazareth suspended their career during the late 80s, leaving McCafferty free to pursue solo ambitions (he had already released a solo album in 1975). A comeback album in 1992 with the addition of Billy Rankin produced the impressive *No Jive*, yet Nazareth's recent low profile in the UK will demand further live work to capitalize on this success.

Albums: *Nazareth* (Mooncrest 1971), *Exercises* (Mooncrest 1972), *Razamanaz* (Mooncrest 1973), *Loud 'N' Proud* (Mooncrest 1974), *Rampant* (Mooncrest 1974), *Hair Of The Dog* (Mooncrest 1975), *Close Enough For Rock 'N' Roll* (Mountain 1976), *Play 'N' The Game* (Mountain 1976), *Expect No Mercy* (Mountain 1977), *No Mean City* (Mountain 1978), *Malice In Wonderland* (Mountain 1980), *The Fool Circle* (NEMS 1981), *'Snaz* (NEMS 1981), *2XS* (NEMS 1982), *Sound Elixir* (Vertigo 1983), *The Catch* (Vertigo 1984), *Cinema* (Vertigo 1986), *Snakes & Ladders* (Vertigo 1990), *No Jive* (Mainstream 1992). Dan McCafferty: *Dan McCafferty* (1975). Compilations: *Greatest Hits* (Mountain 1975), *20 Greatest Hits: Nazareth* (Sahara 1985), *Anthology: Nazareth* (Raw Power 1988). Video: *Razamanaz* (1990).

Neil, Vince, Band

Following his surprise sacking from Mötley Crüe, frontman Vince Neil (b. Vincent Neil Wharton, 8 February 1961, Hollywood, California, USA) wasted no time in setting up his solo career, contributing 'You're Invited But Your Friend Can't Come' (co-written with Damn Yankees duo Jack Blades and Tommy Shaw) to the *Encino Man* (*California Man* outside the USA) soundtrack. After which he assembled a band with ex-Billy Idol guitarist Steve Stevens, ex-Fiona guitarist Dave Marshall, ex-Enuff Z'Nuff drummer Vikki Foxx, and bassist Robbie Crane, who had switched from rhythm guitar after original bassist Phil Soussan's departure. The Ron Nevison-produced *X-Posed* brought Neil a good deal of respect, demonstrating his songwriting ability on good-time arena metal which followed the direction in which he felt that Mötley Crüe should have moved. The Vince Neil Band picked up a high-profile opening slot with Van Halen, but throat problems for Neil held up subsequent live work, and Stevens departed with Brent Woods replacing him. Rumours abounded of a Mötley Crüe reunion while Neil and his band worked towards a second album, but the acrimony surrounding the split makes this seem unlikely.

Album: *X-Posed* (Warners 1993).

Nelson

The twin sons of early rock 'n' roll star Rick Nelson and wife Kris, Matthew and Gunnar Nelson were born on 20 September 1967, Los Angeles, California, USA. Musically-inclined as children, the boys learned to play bass and drums as well as singng. Their father booked studio time for them for their 12th birthday, and they recorded a self-penned song with vocal backing by the Pointer Sisters. By the early 80s the twins had joined a heavy metal band called Strange Agents, which later changed its name to the Nelsons. In 1990, now simply called Nelson, the twins, both sporting waist-length blond hair (which saw them nicknamed the 'Timotei Twins'), signed with David Geffen's new DGC record label and recorded a self-titled pop-rock album. The first single release, '(Can't Live Without Your) Love And Affection', reached number 1 in the US charts, while the album made the US Top 20. Afterwards, however, press reaction remained hostile towards any return.

Album: *Nelson* (DGC 1990).

Neon Cross

This Californian 'white metal' quartet was formed in 1984 by David Raymond Reeves (lead vocals) and Don Webster (guitar). Enlisting the services of Ed Ott (bass) and Michael Betts (drums), it took a further four years before the band made their debut with a track on 1988's *California Metal* compilation. A deal with Regency Records ensued and their self-titled debut album emerged as a competent amalgam of Stryper, Barren Cross and Bloodgood. It was, however, discredited somewhat by Reeves' limited vocal ability.

Album: *Neon Cross* (Regency 1988).

Neon Rose

This progressive rock group was formed in Sweden in 1973 by vocalist Roger Holegard and guitarist Gunnar Hallin. Augmented by Piero Mengarelli (guitar), Beno Mengarelli (bass/vocals) and Thomas Wilkund (drums), they signed to Vertigo the following year. Inspired by Iron Butterfly, Emerson, Lake And Palmer and Deep Purple, Neon Rose were an experimental quintet that indulged in long, esoteric and frequently blues-based workouts. They debuted with *A Dream Of Glory And Pride* in 1974, which showcased the band's instrumental capabilities, but also highlighted their vocal shortcomings. Two further albums were released, but the quality of material declined significantly. They disappeared from the scene in 1976, having only made an impact in their native Sweden.

Albums: *A Dream Of Glory And Pride* (Vertigo 1974), *Neon Rose Two* (Vertigo 1974), *Reload* (Vertigo 1975).

New England (UK)

This British hard rock quartet were formed in

Deptford, London, in 1990 by original Atom Seed member Chris Huxter (bass). Enlisting the services of Paul McKenna (lead vocals), Dave Cook and Ian Winters (drums), they secured a deal with the independent Street Link label. *You Can't Keep Living This Way* emerged in 1991 and confused the critics; the music was awkward to tie down and not easily pigeonholed, fusing influences as diverse as Led Zeppelin, Faith No More, the Doors and Van Halen, with the attitude of punk not lagging far behind. However, this was not enough to find them a place in metal's first division, and they collapsed soon afterwards.

Albums: *You Can't Keep Living This Way* (Street Link 1991).

New England (USA)

This American quartet comprised John Fannon (guitar/vocals), Jimmy Waldo (keyboards), Gary Shea (bass) and Hirsh Gardener (drums). Taken under the wing of Kiss's manager, Bill Aucoin, they purveyed sophisticated, melodic rock in a vein similar to Styx and Journey. In 1979 they were given the chance to impress on a major stage, landing the support slot on the American leg of the Kiss tour. Although competent, their music lacked individuality and the band themselves had a nondescript image. After a third album, produced by Todd Rundgren, the band disintegrated in 1981, with Waldo and Shea eventually going on to join Alcatrazz.

Albums: *New England* (Infinity 1979), *Explorer Suite* (Elektra 1980), *Walking Wild* (Elektra 1981).

New Frontier

This melodic US pop-rock group was formed in 1988 by ex-Billy Satellite vocalist Monty Byron and ex-Gamma bassist Glen Letsch. Adding David Neuhauser (keyboards) and Marc Nelson (drums), they successfully negotiated a deal with the newly-formed Mika label. Their debut album was produced by Ritchie Zito (of Heart and Cheap Trick fame) and featured a collection of hi-tech AOR numbers that were targeted at the *Billboard* charts. Failing to generate media interest, the band disintegrated shortly after the album's release. Letsch went on to play with Robin Trower.

Album: *New Frontier* (Mika 1988).

New Idol Son

Formed in the artistic hothouse of the Bay Area of San Francisco during 1991, New Idol Son immediately saw the press compare them to a '90s rebirth of MC5 meets Black Sabbath'. Vocalist/guitarist Matt Hizendragzer first met drummer Brent Hagin at a Mookie Blaylock (who later transmuted into Pearl Jam) show. Eventually Rich Carr (bass) and Mike Davis (guitar) were recruited via adverts in BAM magazine, with the band titled Difference Engine. Playing shows throughout the west coast as support to Downset, Fear Factory and others, they built a strong reputation among local press outlets until Pavement Music moved in for their signatures in 1994. However, at this point it was discovered that another band already held the rights to the name Difference Engine, and New Idol Son was born when Hizendragzer saw the legend on the back of a book in a second-hand store. Their debut album, *Reach*, offered crafted musical composition with emotive lyrics, sometimes imbued with quasi-religious overtones.

Album: *Reach* (Bulletproof 1994).

New Wave Of British Heavy Metal

The names speak for themselves - Iron Maiden, Def Leppard, Saxon, Samson, Venom, Diamond Head, Girlschool and Praying Mantis. Just a handful of the bands who made it during the period 1979 to 1981. The phrase was first coined by Geoff Barton at *Sounds*, but much credit is also due to DJ Neal Kay, whose help in giving bands like Iron Maiden and Praying Mantis (as well as many others) their first break was crucial. EMI Records were quick off the mark and with Kay's help they produced the compilation album, *Metal For Muthas*, which put many bands on the road to fame and others, like Toad The Wet Sprockett, on the road to obscurity. Well over 200 bands emerged during this period and many released records on their own labels - even more never got past the rehearsal stage, while others remained strictly 'bedroom' bands. This enthusiasm also helped to revitalise older bands and some, like Gillan and Motörhead, became spearheads for the movement. Yet by 1981 the corporate machine began to eat up the talent and American influences crept in to destroy the movement's identity. If, as has often been stated, the movement started with Iron Maiden's *Soundhouse Tapes* EP in 1979, then it would be equally true to say that the final nail in its coffin came in September 1981 when Paul Di'Anno left them. Just like punk in 1977, the ideas and attitude fell victim to clean living and commerciality.

Compilations: *Metal For Muthas Volume 1* (EMI 1980), *Metal For Muthas Volume 2 Cut Loud* (EMI 1980), *Brute Force* (MCA 1980), *New Electric Warriors* (Logo 1980), *The N.W.O.B.H.M. '79 Revisited* (Vertigo 1990).

New Idol Son

New World

New World were formed in February 1992 by guitarist Mike Polak, who completed the line-up with the addition of seasoned musicians Martin Koprax (vocals), Bernd Fuxa (bass) and Thomas Fend (drums). Polak had been featured on Mike Varney's 'Guitar On The Edge' series and teaches at the American Institute Of Music, Europe's biggest rock school, from where Fend was also drawn into the ranks. An eight-track demo, *The World We Created*, sold out quickly on the underground rock network, and as a consequence New World landed a deal with Rock The Nation Records. Their influences, ranging from jazz and classical to more conventional rock sources, saw comparisons to Dream Theater when their debut album was released in 1994.
Album: *Changing Times* (RTN 1994).

New York Dolls

One of the most influential rock bands of the last 20 years, the New York Dolls pre-dated the punk and sleaze metal movements which followed and offered both a crash course in rebellion with style. Formed in 1972, the line-up stabilized with David Johansen (vocals), Johnny Thunders (b. John Anthony Genzale Jnr., 15 July 1952, New York City, New York, USA,

d. 23 April 1991, New Orleans, Louisiana, USA; guitar), Arthur Harold Kane (bass), Sylvain Sylvain (guitar/piano) and Jerry Nolan (d. 14 January 1992; drums), the last two having replaced Rick Rivets and Billy Murcia (who died in November 1972). The band revelled in an outrageous glam-rock image: lipstick, high-heels and tacky leather outfits providing their visual currency. Underneath they were a first rate rock 'n' roll band, dragged up on the music of the Stooges, Rolling Stones and MC5. Their self-titled debut, released in 1973, was a major landmark in rock history, oozing attitude, vitality and controversy from every note. It met with widespread critical acclaim, but this never transferred to commercial success. The follow-up, *Too Much Too Soon*, was an appropriate title - and indicated that alcohol and drugs were beginning to take their toll. The album remains a charismatic collection of punk/glam-rock anthems, typically delivered with 'wasted' cool, that has yet to be equalled. Given a unanimous thumbs down from the music press the band began to implode shortly afterwards. Johansen embarked on a solo career and Thunders formed the Heartbreakers. The Dolls continued for a short time before eventually grinding to a halt in 1975, despite the auspices of new manager Malcolm McLaren. The link to the Sex Pistols and the UK punk movement is stronger than that fact alone, with the Dolls remaining a constant reference point for teen rebels the world over. Sadly for the band, their rewards were fleeting. Jerry Nolan died as a result of a stroke on 14 January 1992 whilst undergoing treatment for pneumonia and meningitis. Thunders had departed from an overdose, in mysterious circumstances, less than a year previously. *Red Patent Leather* is a poor quality and posthumously-released live recording from May 1975 - *Rock 'N' Roll* offers a much more representative collection.

Albums: *New York Dolls* (Mercury 1973), *Too Much Too Soon* (Mercury 1974), *Red Patent Leather* (New Rose 1984). Compilations: *Lipstick Killers* (ROIR 1983), *Rock 'N' Roll* (Mercury 1994).

Niagara

This melodic rock group was formed in Madrid, Spain, during 1987 by Angel Arias (bass) and V. M. Arias (guitar). The line-up was completed with the addition of Tony Cuevas (lead vocals), Joey Martos (drums) and Ricky Castaneda (keyboards). Using English lyrics and concentrating on a style that embodied elements of Europe and Whitesnake, they built up a sizeable following on the European heavy rock scene. Produced by Baron Rojo guitarist Carlos de Castro, *Now Or Never* was an impressive debut that featured abrasive guitar work, coupled with razor-sharp arrangements.

Album: *Now Or Never* (Avispa 1988).

Night Ranger

This talented and sophisticated American pomp-rock group released a string of first class albums between 1982 and 1988. Featuring Jack Blades (vocals/bass), Brad Gillis (guitar; ex-Ozzy Osbourne), Alan Fitzgerald (keyboards; ex-Montrose), Kelly Keagy (drums) and Jeff Watson (guitar), they gigged in and around their Californian hometown, San Francisco, as an extension of Gillis' club band, Ranger. They soon attracted the attention of promoter Bill Graham, who secured them support slots to Santana, Judas Priest and the Doobie Brothers. They also signed with Neil Bogart's short-lived Boardwalk label, though this decision would have a major impact on their later career when Boardwalk was swallowed up by MCA who had little sympathy for the band's rock roots. However, Night Ranger's first four albums made the *Billboard* Top 40 charts, with *Seven Wishes* reaching the Top 10 in June 1985. They also scored two Top 10 single hits in the USA with 'Sister Christian' and 'Sentimental Street' peaking at number 5 and 8, respectively. *Man In Motion* saw the departure of Fitzgerald as the band adopted a rockier direction. Produced by Keith Olsen, the album was their first commercial failure. The band split up shortly afterwards, with *Live In Japan*, featuring one of their 1988 concerts, emerging two years later. Jack Blades joined Damn Yankees with Ted Nugent, Tommy Shaw and Michael Cartellone. The name was resurrected in 1992 by Gillis and drummer/vocalist Kelly Keagy with new members, much to the disgust of Blades and Watson. It seems unlikely that this new formation can add much to the existing Nightranger legacy of solid US AOR.

Albums: *Dawn Patrol* (Boardwalk 1982), *Midnight Madness* (MCA 1983), *Seven Wishes* (MCA 1985), *Big Life* (MCA 1987), *Man In Motion* (MCA 1988), *Live In Japan* (MCA 1990). Compilation: *Greatest Hits* (MCA 1989).

Nightwing

After the demise of Strife in 1978, bassist/vocalist Gordon Rowley formed Nightwing, with Alec Johnson (guitar), Eric Percival (guitar), Kenny Newton (keyboards) and Steve Bartley (drums). They debuted in 1980 with *Something In The Air*, a grandiose AOR album in the style of Styx, Kansas or Journey. Percival quit shortly after it's release and the band continued as a four-piece to record *Black Summer*. This moved towards a more metallic style, in keeping with the New Wave Of British Heavy Metal which was in full swing at the time. The band expanded once more to a five-piece with the arrival of vocalist Max Bacon for the rawer *Stand Up And Be Counted*. Bacon's stay was short-lived as he moved on to Bronz, with Johnson also breaking ranks soon afterwards. Dave Evans and Glynn Porrino were swiftly recruited to fill in on vocals and guitar, but their compositional abilities failed to match those of Johnson. Consequently *My Kingdom Come* represented the nadir of the band's creative capabilities. Nightwing were in their death throes and finally resigned hope after the disappointing *Night Of Mystery, Alive!, Alive!*

Albums: *Something In The Air* (Ovation 1980), *Black Summer* (Gull 1982), *Stand Up And Be Counted* (Gull 1983), *My Kingdom Come* (Gull 1984), *Night Of Mystery, Alive!, Alive!* (Gull 1985).

Nine Inch Nails

Trent Reznor, the multi-instrumentalist, vocalist, and creative force behind Nine Inch Nails, trained as a classical pianist during his small-town Pennsylvania childhood, but his discovery of rock and early industrial groups, despite his dislike of the 'industrial' tag, changed his musical direction completely.

New York Dolls

Following a period working in a Cleveland recording studio and playing in local bands, Reznor began recording as Nine Inch Nails in 1988. The dark, atmospheric *Pretty Hate Machine*, written, played and co-produced by Reznor, was largely synthesizer-based, but the material was transformed on stage by a ferocious wall of guitars, and show-stealing Lollapalooza performances in 1991. Coupled with a major US hit with 'Head Like A Hole', it brought platinum status. Inspired by the live band, Reznor added an abrasive guitar barrage to the Nine Inch Nails sound for *Broken* (a subsequent remix set was titled *Fixed*), which hit the US Top 10, winning a Grammy for 'Wish'. 'Happiness In Slavery', however, courted controversy with an almost-universally banned video, where performance artist Bob Flanagan gave himself up to be torn apart as slave to a machine, acting out the theme of control common to Reznor's lyrics. Reznor also filmed an unreleased full-length *Broken* video which he felt 'makes 'Happiness In Slavery' look like a Disney movie'. By this time, Reznor had relocated to Los Angeles, building a studio in a rented house at 10050 Cielo Drive, which he later discovered was the scene of the Tate murders by the Manson Family (much to his disgust due to eternal interview questions thereafter about the contribution of the house's atmosphere to *The Downward Spiral*). Occupying the middle ground between the styles of previous releases, *The Downward Spiral*'s multilayered blend of synthesizer textures and guitar fury provides a fascinating soundscape for Reznor's exploration of human degradation through sex, drugs, violence, depression and suicide, closing with personal emotional pain on 'Hurt': 'I hurt myself today, To see if I still feel, I focus on the pain, The only thing that's real'. *The Downward Spiral* made its US debut at number 2, and a return to live work with Robin Finck (guitar), Danny Lohneer (bass/guitar), James Woolley (keyboards) and Reznor's long-time friend and drummer Chris Vrenna drew floods of praise, with Nine Inch Nails being one of the most talked-about acts at the Woodstock anniversary show. 1994 saw the first non-Nine Inch Nails releases on Reznor's Nothing label, and the band also found time to construct an acclaimed soundtrack for Oliver Stone's film, *Natural Born Killers*.
Albums: *Pretty Hate Machine* (TVT 1989), *Broken* (Nothing 1992, mini-album), *Fixed* (Nothing 1992, mini-album), *The Downward Spiral* (Nothing 1994).

1994

This US melodic-rock quartet was formed in 1977 by ex-L.A. Jets duo Karen Lawrence (vocals) and John Desautels (drums). With the addition of Steve Schiff (guitar) and Bill Rhodes (bass), they signed to A&M Records and released a self-titled debut the following year. This was characterized by Lawrence's powerful vocals and a style that incorporated elements of Heart, Aerosmith and Foreigner. Guitarist Steve Schiff was replaced by Rick Armand on *Please Stand By*, which lacked the rough edges of their debut, and saw them move towards mainstream AOR. Success eluded the band and Lawrence quit in 1980. After a decade of less than successful projects, which have included collaborations with Cheap Trick, Jeff Beck and Rod Stewart, it was rumoured that she may reform 1994. However, the only firm evidence of any such move was the guest appearance of Steve Schiff on her 1986 solo album.
Albums: *1994* (A&M 1978), *Please Stand By* (A&M 1979). Karen Lawrence solo: *Rip & Tear* (FM Revolver 1986).

Nirvana

Formed in Aberdeen, Washington, USA, in 1988, the Nirvana which the MTV generation came to love comprised Kurt Cobain (b. Kurt Donald Cobain, 20 February 1967, Hoquiam, Seattle, USA, d. 5 April 1994, Seattle; guitar/vocals), Krist Novoselic (b. 16 May 1965, Croatia, Yugoslavia; bass) and Dave Grohl (b. 14 January 1969; drums). Grohl was 'something like our sixth drummer', explained Cobain, and had been recruited from east coast band Dave Brammage, having previously played with Scream, who recorded for Minor Threat's influential Dischord label. Their original drummer was Chad Channing; at one point Dinosaur Jr's J. Mascis had been touted as a permanent fixture, along with Dan Peters from Mudhoney. Having been signed by the Seattle-based Sub Pop label, the trio completed their debut single, 'Love Buzz'/'Big Cheese', the former a song written and first recorded by 60s Dutch group, Shocking Blue. Second guitarist Jason Everman was then added prior to *Bleach*, which cost a meagre $600 to record. Though he was pictured on the cover, he played no part in the actual recording (going on to join Mindfunk, via Soundgarden and Skunk). The set confirmed Nirvana's ability to match heavy riffs with melody and it quickly attracted a cult following. However, Channing left the group following a European tour, and as a likely replacement proved hard to find, Dan Peters from labelmates Mudhoney stepped in on a temporary basis. He was featured on the single, 'Sliver', Nirvana's sole 1990 release. New drummer David Grohl reaffirmed a sense of stability. The revamped trio secured a prestigious deal with Geffen Records whose faith was rewarded with

Nine Inch Nails

Nevermind, which broke the band worldwide. This was a startling collection of songs which transcended structural boundaries, notably the distinctive slow verse/fast chorus format, and almost single-handedly brought the 'grunge' subculture overground. It topped the US charts early in 1992, eclipsing much-vaunted competition from Michael Jackson and Dire Straits and topped many Album Of The Year polls. The opening track, 'Smells Like Teen Spirit', reached the UK Top 10; further confirmation that Nirvana now combined critical and popular acclaim. In early 1992 the romance of Cobain and Courtney Love of Hole was sealed when the couple married (Love giving birth to a daughter, Frances Bean). It was already obvious, however, that Cobain was struggling with his new role as 'spokesman for a generation'. The first big story to break concerned an article in *Vanity Fayre* which alleged Love had taken heroin while pregnant, which saw the state intercede on the child's behalf by not allowing the Cobains alone with the child during its first month. Press interviews ruminated on the difficulties experienced in recording a follow-up album, and also Cobain's use of a variety of drugs in order to stem the pain arising from a stomach complaint. The recording of *In Utero*, produced by Big Black/Rapeman alumni Steve Albini, was not without difficulties either. Rumours circulated concerning confrontations with both Albini and record company Geffen over the 'low-fi' production. When the record was finally released the effect was not as immediate as *Nevermind*, though Cobain's songwriting remained inspired on 'Penny Royal Tea', 'All Apologies' and the evocative 'Rape Me'. His descent into self-destruction accelerated in 1994, however, as he went into a coma during dates in Italy (it was later confirmed that this had all the markings of a failed suicide attempt), before returning to Seattle to shoot himself on 5 April 1994. The man who had long protested that Nirvana were 'merely' a punk band had finally been destroyed by the success that overtook him and them. The wake conducted in the press was matched by public demonstrations of affection and loss, which included suspected copycat suicides. The release of *Unplugged In New York* offered some small comfort for Cobain's fans, with the singer's understated, aching delivery on a variety of covers and Nirvana standards one of the most emotive sights and sounds of the 90s. Grohl and Novoselic would play together again in the Foo Fighters, alongside ex-Germs guitarist Pat Smear (who had added second guitar to previous touring engagements and the band's *MTV Unplugged* appearance) following press rumours that Grohl would be working with Pearl Jam (much to Courtney

Love's chagrin) or Tom Petty.

Albums: *Bleach* (Sub Pop 1989), *Nevermind* (Geffen 1991), *In Utero* (Geffen 1993), *Unplugged In New York* (Geffen 1994). Compilation: *Incesticide* (Geffen 1992).

Video: *Live! Tonight! Sold Out!* (1994).

Further reading: *Come As You Are*, Michael Azerrad (1993), *Nirvana And The Sound Of Seattle*, Brad Morrell (1993), *Route 66: On The Road To Nirvana*, Gina Arnold (1993), *Never Fade Away*, Dave Thompson (1994), *Cobain - By The Editors Of Rolling Stone* (1994).

Nitzinger, John

b. Texas, USA. This energetic and highly talented guitarist/vocalist specializes in blues-based hard rock and boogie, and has worked with Bloodrock, Alice Cooper and Carl Palmer's P.M., supplying ferocious Ted Nugent-inspired guitar chords to each. Members of Bloodrock, for whom he also wrote songs, would return the favour by appearing on his solo material. His three albums on his own account are highly varied and explore a wider range of styles than might at first be imagined. Psychedelia, jazz, rock, blues and metal nuances have been integrated within his own extrovert approach, though since the mid-70s his recording career has taken a back seat to session work.

Albums: *Nitzinger* (Capitol 1971), *One Foot In History* (Capitol 1972), *Live Better...Electrically* (20th Century 1976).

No Exqze

This melodic rock quartet was formed by ex-Vandenberg bassist Dick Kemper in 1987. Recruiting Geert Scheigrond (guitar), Leen Barbier (vocals) and Nico Groen (drums), they signed to Phonogram and debuted with *Too Hard Too Handle* in 1988. No Exqze allowed Kemper to indulge his writing talents, which had previously been suppressed in Vandenberg. Not without good reason, it might be argued. Produced by Tony Platt, the album was dominated by Barbier's soulful vocals, which added depth and character to Kemper's rather average AOR-style compositions.

Album: *Too Hard Too Handle* (Phonogram 1988).

No Sweat

This Dublin-based, six-piece melodic rock group comprised Paul Quinn (lead vocals), Dave Gooding (guitar), Jim Phillips (guitar), P.J. Smith (keyboards), Jon Angel (bass) and Ray Fearn (drums). Together they impressed Def Leppard vocalist Joe Elliot, who took over production on their debut album and helped them secure a deal with London Records. The record company's public relations team subsequently launched an impressive and expensive campaign on their behalf. They supported Thunder on their 'Backstreet Symphony' tour in 1990 and were generally well-received by the press. Paul Quinn's voice oozed emotion, but their material failed to stamp its own identity. Accusations of hype followed, and the band quietly dissolved a year later.

Album: *No Sweat* (London 1990).

Nocturnus

This innovative American death metal band was formed by drummer and vocalist Mike Browning following his departure from an early incarnation of Morbid Angel. *The Key* showed an original approach, mixing the frenzied yet intricate riffing of guitarists Sean McNenney and Mike Davis with the atmospheric keyboard washes of Louis Panzer. Critical acclaim abounded, but the sound proved rather too radical for much of the death crowd, and Nocturnus struggled to rise above cult status. *Thresholds* was recorded with new vocalist Dan Izzo taking the pressure off Browning, with permanent bassist Emo Mowery being recruited after the sessions to replace touring bassist Jim O'Sullivan (Chris Anderson played on the album). However, with no upturn in the band's fortunes they parted company with Earache, re-emerging in 1994 with an EP for new label, Moribund.

Albums: *The Key* (Earache 1990), *Thresholds* (Earache 1992).

Nokemono

This Japanese hard rock quintet was formed in 1978. Inspired by fellow countrymen Bow Wow, Yukihiro 'Ace' Nakaya (vocals) and Shigeo 'Rolla' Nakano (guitar) decided to put a band together along similar lines. Recruiting Bunzo 'Bunchan' Satoh (guitar), Masaaki 'Cherry' Chikura (bass) and Tadashi 'Popeye' Hirota (drums), they were picked up by the local SMS label. The resultant *From The Black World* combined Van Halen, Deep Purple and UFO influences. It was an impressive debut somewhat marred by an inferior production. However, the band remained virtually unknown outside their own country and the album was to be their solitary contribution to Japanese metal.

Albums: *From The Black World* (SMS 1979).

Norum, John

Norum was formerly guitarist for Europe but quit just as the band were on the verge of worldwide recognition with 'The Final Countdown'. After completing the recording of the *Countdown* album,

he decided to break ranks because he was unhappy with the pop-metal direction that vocalist Joey Tempest was intent on pursuing. Turning to a solo career, he enlisted the help of Marcel Jacob (bass; ex-Yngwie Malmsteen), Peter Hermansson (drums; ex-220 Volts) and Goran Edman (vocals; ex-Madison) to record *Total Control* in 1987. Musically this followed a similar path to that of his former employers, but featured more prominent rock guitar work and less polished vocals. Following the release of a live album and a collaboration with Don Dokken, he moved to Los Angeles to work on sessions with Glenn Hughes (ex-Trapeze, Deep Purple) which became *Face The Truth*.

Albums: *Total Control* (CBS 1987), *Live In Stockholm* (CBS 1988), *Face The Truth* (Epic 1992).

Norum, Tone

Tone is the younger sister of former Europe guitarist, John Norum. She debuted in 1986 with *One Of A Kind*, an album written, arranged and played on by Joey Tempest (also of Europe) and her brother. Predictably, the musical direction was very close to that of her sibling's concern; melodic pop-metal, with the occasional power ballad. *This Time* followed a similar pattern, but used session musicians and the Billy Steinberg/Tom Kelly writing team who had previously penned hits for Madonna and Whitney Houston. The result was a highly polished melodic rock album in the style of Heart and Starship. *Red* saw Tone move away from AOR towards folk-rock.

Albums: *One Of A Kind* (Epic 1986), *This Time* (Epic 1988), *Red* (Epic 1989).

Notorious

This ill-fated pop-rock act seemed set to revive the careers of ex-Diamond Head singer Sean Harris and guitarist Robin George, but was aborted before it had a chance to get off the ground. With an expensively recorded debut for the relaunched Bronze label, with George contributing all instrumentation, the future seemed bright, but the duo were reluctant to recruit a touring band when pressed by the record company, as they viewed Notorious as a 'studio project'. The disagreement resulted in *Notorious* being deleted after only three weeks on release. The album itself was an under-rated effort, with Robert Plant's solo work an obvious influence, and produced an excellent single in 'The Swalk'. Denied any real chance of success, the duo parted company, with Harris returning to a revived Diamond Head.

Album: *Notorious* (Bronze 1990).

Nova, Aldo

b. Aldo Caparucio. Nova is a virtuoso guitarist of Italian descent. He arrived on the rock scene in 1982 with a self-titled debut of melodic AOR/pomp-rock that incorporated elements of Boston and Styx, with production offered by Blue Öyster Cult's Sandy Pearlman. Momentum was lost however, with *Subject*, a disjointed and ultimately disappointing concept album. *Twitch* made amends somewhat, with a return to smooth, sophisticated and melody-conscious symphonic rock. Disillusioned by the lack of media response and complex legal wrangles and contractual commitments, he left the music business in 1985. After a near six-year break, he was lured back into the studio by his good friend, Jon Bon Jovi (having guested on the latter's *Blaze Of Glory* solo project). Together they wrote the material for *Blood On The Bricks*, a stunning collection of hard rock songs, saturated with infectious hooks and inspired guitar breaks. The album was well-received in the music press and drew comparisons with Bryan Adams, Europe and, naturally enough, Bon Jovi. It may prove the launching pad for the second phase of Aldo Nova's career.

Albums: *Aldo Nova* (Portrait 1982), *Subject: Aldo Nova* (Portrait 1983), *Twitch* (Portrait 1985), *Blood On The Bricks* (Polygram 1991).

Nowherefast

This Californian melodic rock quartet was formed in 1981 by Steve Bock (vocals/bass) and Jeff Naideau (guitar/keyboards). Enlisting the services of Bob Frederickson (guitar) and Jimmy Hansen (drums), they soon struck a contract with the WEA/Scotti Brothers label. Incorporating elements of blues and funk into Kansas and Journey-like AOR, they delivered a self-titled debut in 1982. The album was unsuccessful and the band's name unfortunately proved a fair summation of the impact they had made.

Album: *Nowherefast* (Scotti Bros 1982).

Nuclear Assault

Formed in New York, USA, in 1985, this extreme and influential group consisted of John Conelly (guitar/vocals), Anthony Bramante (guitar), Dan Lilker (bass) and Glenn Evans (drums). Lilker formed Nuclear Assault while still a member of Anthrax, making them one of the earliest thrash metal outfits. The sound of Nuclear Assault proved much more aggressive, however, merging the styles of hardcore and thrash with socially aware lyrics. Becoming popular through constant touring and a refusal to compromise in their recorded work, their audience built steadily throughout the 80s. Lilker, however, would quit the band in 1993 to concentrate on a new project, Brutal Truth. Bramante was expelled around the same time, with the pair being replaced by Scott Metaxas and Dave DiPietro respectively, both formerly of Prophet. The transitional *Something Wicked* failed to provide any conclusive proof of artistic rejuvenation.

Albums: *Game Over* (Music For Nations 1986), *The Plague* (Music For Nations 1987), *Survive* (Music For Nations 1988), *Handle With Care* (Music For Nations 1989), *Out Of Order* (Music For Nations 1991), *Live At Hammersmith* (Music For Nations 1993), *Something Wicked* (Music For Nations 1993). Video: *Radiation Sickness* (1988).

Nuclear Valdez

This unconventional AOR act were based in Miami, Florida, but drew from their ethnic origins for both musical and lyrical inspiration. Vocalist/guitarist Froilan Sosa's family originated in the Dominican Republic, while Jorge Barcala (lead guitar), Juan Diaz (bass) and Robert Slade LeMont (drums) are all of Cuban descent, and the band incorporated the Latin influences in their backgrounds to give an unusual and unique flavour to their sound. Lyrically, the band were not content with the AOR conventions of love and heartache, but explored themes closer to their collective heart, such as the Castro regime and the feelings of the Cuban exiles who long to return home, while their choice of band name with its clever ecological overtones served to confirm their more cerebral approach. *I Am I* established their characteristic rhythmic sound with classy guitar work from Barcala and passionate, smoky vocals from Sosa, and also produced a US hit with 'Summer'. *Dream Another Dream* confirmed their abilities with further strong material, but Nuclear Valdez remain a cult act.

Albums: *I Am I* (Epic 1990), *Dream Another Dream* (Epic 1992).

Nudeswirl

This New Jersey band was formed by guitarist/vocalist Shane M Greene and guitarist Diz Cortright with drummer Woody Newland and bassist Christopher Vorga, specialising in an indie guitar-driven heavy rock style which brought comparisons to acts as diverse as Soundgarden, Nirvana, the Pixies and Trouble. This was rather different to Greene and Cortright's occasional They Might Be Giants tribute band, known as They Might Be Vaginas, which played locally with Greene on vocals and accordion and Cortright on bass. Nudeswirl signed to Megaforce on the strength of chaotic live shows

Aldo Nova

around the underground club circuit. *Nudeswirl* was a varied debut, with the band driving their weighty sound in a multitude of directions with unusual rhythms, with their use of Gretsch guitars lending the delivery a warm, earthy feel. However, the nuances of the album were rather lost in the live arena as the band toured Europe with Mind Funk and in the USA with Flotsam And Jetsam in addition to their own dates, producing some visually lifeless performances, and the band's future seems in doubt with the departure of Greene in mid-1994.

Album: *Nudeswirl* (Megaforce 1993).

Nugent, Ted

b. 13 December 1949, Detroit, Michigan, USA. Excited by 50s rock 'n' roll, Nugent taught himself the rudiments of guitar playing at the age of eight. As a teenager he played in the Royal Highboys and Lourds, but this formative period ended in 1964 upon his family's move to Chicago. Here, Nugent assembled the Amboy Dukes, which evolved from garage band status into a popular, hard rock attraction. He led the group throughout its various permutations, assuming increasing control as original members dropped out of the line-up. In 1974 a revitalized unit - dubbed Ted Nugent And The Amboy Dukes - completed the first of two albums for Frank Zappa's Discreet label, but in 1976 the guitarist abandoned the now-anachronistic suffix and embarked on a fully-fledged solo career. Derek St. Holmes (guitar), Rob Grange (bass) and Cliff Davies (drums) joined him for *Ted Nugent* and *Free For All,* both of which maintained the high-energy rock of previous incarnations. However, it was as a live attraction that Nugent made his mark - he often claimed to have played more gigs per annum than any other artist or group. Ear-piecing guitar work and vocals - 'If it's too loud you're too old' ran one tour motto - were accompanied by a cultivated 'wild man' image, where the artist would appear in loin-cloth and headband, brandishing the bow and arrow with which he claimed to hunt food for his family. Trapeze stunts, genuine guitar wizardry and a scarcely self-deprecating image ('If there had been blind people at the {my} show they would have walked away seeing') all added to the formidable Nugent persona. The aggression of a Nugent concert was captured on the platinum selling *Double Live Gonzo,* which featured many of his best-loved stage numbers, including 'Cat Scratch Fever', 'Motor City Madness' and the enduring 'Baby Please Don't Go'. Charlie Huhn (guitar) and John Sauter (bass) replaced St. Holmes and Grange for *Weekend Warriors,* and the same line-up remained intact for *State Of Shock* and *Scream*

Dream. In 1981 Nugent undertook a worldwide tour fronting a new backing group, previously known as the D.C. Hawks, comprising of Mike Gardner (bass), Mark Gerhardt (drums) and three guitarists; Kurt, Rick and Verne Wagoner. The following year the artist left Epic for Atlantic Records, and in the process established a new unit which included erstwhile sidemen Derek St. Holmes (vocals) and Carmine Appice (drums; ex-Vanilla Fudge). Despite such changes, Nugent was either unwilling, or unable, to alter the formula which had served him so well in the 70s. Successive solo releases offered little new and the artist drew greater publicity for appearances on talk shows and celebrity events. In 1989 Nugent teamed up with Tommy Shaw (vocals/guitar; ex-Styx), Jack Blades (bass; ex-Night Ranger) and Michael Cartellone (drums) to form the successful 'supergroup', Damn Yankees.

Albums: With the Amboy Dukes: *Amboy Dukes* (Mainstream 1967), *Journey To The Centre Of Your Mind* (Mindstream 1968), *Migrations* (Mainstream 1969), *Marriage On The Rocks* (Polydor 1969), *Survival Of The Fittest* (Polydor 1971), *Tooth, Fang And Claw* (Discreet 1974), *Call Of The Wild* (Discreet 1975). Solo: *Ted Nugent* (Epic 1975), *Free For All* (Epic 1976), *Cat Scratch Fever* (Epic 1977), *Double Live Gonzo* (Epic 1978), *Weekend Warriors* (Epic 1978), *State Of Shock* (Epic 1979), *Scream Dream* (Epic 1980), *Intensities In Ten Cities* (Epic 1981), *Nugent* (Atlantic 1982), *Penetrator* (Atlantic 1984), *Little Miss Dangerous* (Atlantic 1986), *If You Can't Lick 'Em...Lick 'Em* (Atlantic 1988). Compilations: *Great Gonzos: The Best Of Ted Nugent* (Epic 1981), *Anthology: Ted Nugent* (Raw Power 1986).

Video: *Whiplash Bash* (1990).

Nutz

This UK hard rock quintet was formed in 1973 by Dave Lloyd (vocals) and Mick Devonport (guitar). With the addition of Keith Mulholland (bass), Kenny Newton (keyboards) and John Mylett (drums), they gained a reputation as the ubiquitous support act. Playing competent, blues-based rock and boogie, their exuberant and high-energy live shows always overshadowed the drab and lifeless studio recordings. Their sexist album covers were typical of the genre, though less likely was Lloyd's contribution of a vocal to a *Crunchie* chocolate bar advertisement. Newton left to join Nightwing in 1978 while the band changed their name to Rage in a deliberate attempt to jump the N.W.O.B.H.M. bandwagon.

Albums: *Nutz* (A&M 1974), *Nutz Two* (A&M 1975), *Hard Nutz* (A&M 1976), *Live Cutz* (A&M 1977).

Nymphs

This band originated in the Los Angeles club scene around volatile vocalist Inger Lorre (b. Laurie Wenning), a former model from New Jersey, with a line-up which eventually stabilized with drummer Alex Kirst, guitarists jet freedom (who prefers to have his initials expressed in lower case) and Sam Merrick, completed by bassist Cliff D. The Nymphs signed to Geffen in 1989 bolstered by a wave of hype which suggested that the band were a female-fronted Guns N'Roses (in truth their sound owed more to Lou Reed, the Stooges and Patti Smith). A period of limbo ensued as the band fought to record a debut on their own terms. Tales of drug abuse, rehabilitation and mental hospitals escalated as the tension of being contractually prohibited from playing live took its toll. These problems were exacerbated when producer Bill Price was commandeered by Guns N'Roses to mix their *Use Your Illusion* albums. Lorre expressed the feelings of the Nymphs by crushing five poppies (to represent the band members) and urinating on them, all on top of the desk of her label's A&R chief. *Nymphs* eventually emerged in February 1992 to a fanfare of critical praise, a darkly enthralling set which mixed punk and grunge with Lorre's lyrical images of death, drugs and sex (often drawn from personal experience). Subsequent live shows were of variable quality, with internal tensions abounding due to Lorre's eccentric behaviour, and following *A Practical Guide To Astral Projection*, it was no surprise when the Nymphs disintegrated spectacularly on stage in Miami in September that same year. Lorre is reportedly currently concerned with writing children's stories.

Albums: *Nymphs* (Geffen 1992), *A Practical Guide To Astral Projection* (Geffen 1992, mini-album).

O

Obituary

This intense and disturbing death metal group hails from Brandon, Florida, USA, where they formed in 1985. After recording a single and contributing two tracks to *Metal Massacre* compilations as Xecutioner, they changed their name to Obituary. This was initiated by the appearance of another, inferior act, who also travelled under the Xecutioner banner. Signed to Roadrunner Records, the band comprised John Tardy (vocals), Allen West (guitar), Trevor Peres (guitar), David Tucker (bass) and Donald Tardy (drums). *Slowly We Rot*, unveiled in 1989, was characterized by their vocalist's gurgling, sewer-like vocals, primarily employed as a musical instrument rather than a means of imparting lyrics, over a maelstrom of crashing powerchords and demonic drumming. Indeed, the indecipherable nature of John Tardy's outbursts helped insure them against some of the hysterical criticisms levelled at other death metal pioneers. *Cause Of Death* saw the band refine their unique style with ex-Death guitarist James Murphy and bassist Frank Watkins in place of West and Tucker respectively. Obituary, however, continued to specialize in a hideous and brutal musical carnage, taking the death metal concept to its ultimate conclusion. The release of *World Demise*, again recorded with long-time producer Scott Burns, did reveal a more considered approach, with the occasional snatch of audible lyric from Tardy (a press statement from Peres noted 'We're serious people, and we wanna be taken seriously'). By this time Tucker had been replaced by Frank Watkins, while Allen West was also enjoying his own side-project, Six Feet Under, with Cannibal Corpse's Chris Barnes.

Albums: *Slowly We Rot* (Roadracer 1989), *Cause Of Death* (Roadracer 1990), *The End Complete* (Roadracer 1992), *World Demise* (Roadrunner 1994).

Obsessed

Spawned by the Washington DC underground of the early 80s, the Obsessed were ranked alongside Minor Threat and Bad Brains in the vicinity, yet never made the immediate transition to nationwide renown which those two outfits achieved. Though more obviously metal-inclined than either, notwithstanding odes to mysticism and Black Sabbath riffs, the Obsessed (Scott 'Wino' Weinrich, vocals/guitar, Mark

Laue, bass, Ed Gulli, drums) proved influential to two rival camps of supporters, who could be delineated by the length of their hair. They made their debut with a three-track EP (*Sodden Jackyl*) for their own Invictus label, but otherwise relied on live shows and the circulation of demo tapes to establish their reputation. After several years of attrition, Weinrich hooked up with Saint Vitus, replacing vocalist Scott Reagers (on the latter's request), and moving to Los Angeles. The group would go on to cut several albums of ultra-heavy hardcore together between 1986 and 1991. Towards the end of this stint Saint Vitus' German label, Hellbound, approached Weinrich about the now legendary Obsessed demos, and an eponymous album was released in 1990 (also referred to as *The Purple Album*). A fine collection which overcame the obvious budget limitations, it immediately drew the kind of attention deprived the band in its infancy, but put Weinrich's tenure with Saint Vitus into question. Forced to choose by guitarist Dave Chandler, he elected to reform the Obsessed with Scott Reeder (bass) and Greg Rogers (drums; ex-Poison 13). The raging *Lunar Womb* revealed a rejuvenated and ferocious band back at the peak of its powers. However, problems with Hellbound delayed progress, until Columbia stepped in to offer the Obsessed a recording contract, while Reeder (going on to join Kyuss) was replaced by part-time B.A.L.L./Scream member, Guy Pinhas. Despite landing with a major, however, the Obsessed, and Weinrich in particular, maintained an enviable status amongst their peers, the more high profile of their supporters including L7's Jennifer Finch, Corrosion Of Conformity's Pepper Keenan, Fugazi's Ian MacKaye, Pantera's Phil Anselmo, and Henry Rollins.
Albums: *The Obsessed* (Hellbound 1990), *Lunar Womb* (Hellbound 1991), *The Church Within* (Columbia 1993).

Obsession

This Connecticut, USA-based outfit was formed in 1983 by vocalist Mike Vescara and guitarist Bruce Vitale. Adding Art Maco (guitar), Matt Karugas (bass) and Jay Mezias (drums), they made their debut with a track on the *Metal Massacre* compilation album in 1983. Combining Judas Priest, Venom and Anvil influences, they subsequently recorded the *Marshall Law* mini-album; a high-speed, dual guitar onslaught, accentuated by Vescara's piercing howl. A contract with Enigma ensued and the two albums that resulted showed the band diversifying into more melodic territory. In mid-1988 Maco and Mezias quit, but the band finally folded when Vescara accepted the position of frontman with Japanese rockers,

Loudness.
Albums: *Marshall Law* (Metal Blade 1984), *Scarred For Life* (Enigma 1986), *Methods Of Madness* (Enigma 1987).

Obus

This Spanish melodic metal band was formed in 1980 by vocalist Fortu, guitarist Francisco Laguna, Fernando Sanches (drums) and Juan Luis Serrano. Though restricting their potential audience by insisting on singing in their native tongue, this undoubtedly helped the authenticity of their sound, which was otherwise unoriginal. Signing to the local Chapa Discos label, they recorded three amateurish albums lacking in fresh ideas before dissolving in the mid-80s.
Albums: *Preparato* (Chapa Discos 1981), *Podoroso Como El Trueno* (Chapa Discos 1982), *El Que Mas* (Mausoleum 1984).

Of Perception

Between 1979 and 1984 Deviant (b. Stuart Powell, Enfield, England; vocals/guitar/keyboards) and Jellyfish (b. Kevin Nicholson, Tottenham, London, England; bass/vocals/keyboards), were the mainstay of the New Wave Of British Heavy Metal band Tooth. After playing in various other groups the two reunited in 1989 for a jam session with various friends and session men. Within a year they had put together a stable line-up with ex-Swamp Angels guitarist Dave Williams and former lighting engineer Pete Smith. After a few gigs and two demos they found ex-Neil Christian bassist Arthur Anderson to record/produce and mix an entire album in 24 hours. The resulting *So Join Mr Dreams* offered a marriage of Doors, Motörhead and Hawkwind influences. It found little favour in the UK but an audience emerged in Europe. Dejected after a tour of Holland fell through at the last moment in 1992 they headed off to the studio to record a new album with producer Brian Martin. The resultant *Lords So Strange R* was a much more ambitious project, with the debut of female backing vocalist Jazz J. Soon after they split up, which turned out to be a blessing in disguise. Absent from the music scene, they picked up a cult following in Spain and Germany as well as 'underground' magazines from around the world. The group reformed late in 1994 minus Jazz J and Smith, and after initial studio work were joined by session drummer 'Chops'.
Albums: *So Join Mr Dreams* (Hawke Park 1991), *Lords So Strange R* (Hawke Park 1992).
Video: *Of Perception* (1991).

Obituary

Omen

This Los Angeles, USA-based, melodic power-metal outfit formed in 1984. Comprising J.D. Kimball (vocals), Kenny Powell (guitar; ex-Sacred Blade), Jody Henry (bass) and Steve Wittig (drums), they debuted with a track on the *Metal Massacre V* compilation. This led to a contract with Metal Blade and the release of *Battle Cry* the same year. This was a competent, if uninspired, collection of Iron Maiden-style rockers, which lacked distinction due to Kimball's weak vocals. Three more albums followed a similar pattern, with 1987's mini-opus *Nightmares* being the most interesting (it featured a strong cover of AC/DC's 'Whole Lotta Rosie'). Coburn Pharr replaced Kimball in 1988 and helped the band produced *Escape From Nowhere,* their finest recorded work. Adding Rush-styled dynamics to their basic metal framework, it was characterized by Pharr's powerful and high-pitched vocals. Surprisingly, it failed to sell and Pharr left to join Annihilator in 1990.

Albums: *Battle Cry* (Roadrunner 1984), *Warning Of Danger* (Roadrunner 1985), *The Curse* (Roadrunner 1986), *Nightmares* (Roadrunner 1987), *Escape From Nowhere* (Roadrunner 1988).

One Hit Wonder

Hailing from Long Beach, Orange County, California, and led by singer and principal songwriter Dan Root, One Hit Wonder additionally comprise Randy Bradbury (bass), Trey Pangborn (guitar) and Chris Webb (drums). Their self-titled debut EP in 1995, produced by alternative rock team the Robb brothers (Lemonheads, Buffalo Tom), consolidated the impression laid by an initial batch of underground 7-inch singles for Lethal Records. The material on offer ('Break Your Heart', 'After Her Disasters') provided down at heel takes on life backed by focused metal riffing with power pop flourishes.

Only Child

This rock group was put together by the multi-talented songwriter, vocalist and guitarist Paul Sabu in 1988. Featuring Tommy Rude (keyboards), Murril Maglio (bass) and Charles Esposito (drums), their self-titled debut consisted of melodic rock which partially justified the critical acclaim it received. The praise heaped upon the album by *Kerrang* magazine, in particular, was rather premature, as the overtly commercial riffs and obvious hooks soon wore thin. This was borne out by the shortfall in anticipated sales. Esposito was replaced by Tommy Amato in 1989 and they were signed by Geffen Records to start work on new material, but thus far Only Child have remained ominously quiet.

Album: *Only Child* (Rampage 1988).

Onslaught

This UK thrash quintet, originally conceived as a punk/metal hybrid, was formed in Bristol in 1983 by guitarist Nige Rockett and drummer Steve Grice. With the addition of vocalist Paul Mahoney and bassist Jason Stallord, they recorded *Power From Hell* on the independent Cor label in 1985. This opened the doors to a contract with Under One Flag, the thrash subsidiary of Music For Nations. *The Force* saw the band expand to a quintet, with the arrival of new vocalist Sy Keeler; Mahoney was relegated to bass and Stallord switched to rhythm guitar. The album was heavily reliant on the styles of Slayer, Metallica and Anthrax, with little original input of their own. Mahoney was replaced by James Hinder on bass shortly after the album was released. Moving to London Records, *In Search Of Sanity* was their make or break album. Before it was completed Steve Grimmett (ex-Grim Reaper) and Rob Trottman replaced Keeler and Stallord respectively. After a series of delays, the album finally surfaced in early 1989. Producer Stephan Galfas had watered down their aggressive sound in an attempt to court commercial success. Even the cover of AC/DC's 'Let There Be Rock' proved less strong than expected, and the material generally lacked distinction. They had moved away from hard-line thrash towards mainstream metal with negative results. The album was slated by the metal media and Grimmett quit in 1990. A replacement was found in the form of Tony O'Hara, but the band were dropped by their label soon after. Disillusioned, they went their separate ways in 1991.

Albums: *Power From Hell* (Music For Nations 1985), *The Force* (Music For Nations 1986), *In Search Of Sanity* (London 1989).

Oral

A rather sad four-piece all female band comprising 'glamour' models and Stripagram girls, the line-up of Oral (a suitably childish reference point) was filled out by Bev (vocals), Monica (guitar), Dee (drums) and Candy (bass). Candy had quit by the time their only album was released and as they played no gigs it is questionable whether any of them could play at all. Evidently the whole thing was done to further their day jobs and they gained a little publicity thanks to song titles like 'I Need Discipline' and 'Gas Masks Vicars And Priests'. Their debut album was entitled *Sex*, written so that anyone glancing at the sleeve would read simply 'Oral Sex'. Even the group's

version of the Sex Pistols' 'Black Leather' was ill-advised.
Album: *Sex* (Conquest 1987).

Orange

This Yugoslavian hard rock quintet was formed in 1981 by Zlato Magdalenic (vocals), Nijo Popovic (guitar), Tomaz Zontar (keyboards), Marko Herak (bass) and Franc Teropic (drums). Together they secured a contract with the local RTB label. Musically, they incorporated elements of AC/DC, Deep Purple and Accept, but added little creative input of their own. The band were known as Pomeranca in Yugoslavia and attracted a small but loyal cult following after the release of their debut album in 1982. This featured native lyrics and consequently closed down a large section of their potential audience. *Madbringer* saw the band using English lyrics for the first time, but their crude enunciation failed to enhance their appeal.
Albums: *Peklenska Pomeranca* (RTB 982), *Madbringer* (RTB 1983).

Organization

Formed from the remnants of Death Angel, the Organization are Rob Cavestany (vocals/guitar), Andy Galeon (drums/vocals), D. Pepa (bass) and Gus Pepa (guitar). The former band, while on tour supporting *Act III*, endured a bus crash with seriously injured drummer and youngest member Andy Galeon. When singer Mark Osegueda decided he was unable to wait for him to make a full recovery, Cavestany took over as singer and front man and the Organization was born. Marking their arrival with an appearance at the Dynamo Festival in Europe in 1992, the members had learned enough about the music industry to act in a more independent fashion, setting up their own Unsafe Unsane Recordings for the release of *Free Burning* (licensed to Bulletproof/Music For Nations in the UK).
Album: *Free Burning* (Unsafe Unsane Recordings 1993).

Orphan

This Canadian melodic rock quartet was formed in 1982 by ex-Pimps duo Chris Burke Gaffney (vocals/bass) and Brent Diamond (keyboards). Enlisting the services of guitarist Steve McGovern and drummer Ron Boivenue, they negotiated a contract with the Portrait label the following year. Drawing inspiration from commercial rockers like Bryan Adams and Queen, they debuted with *Lonely At Night*, a sophisticated collection of accessible AOR anthems. *Salute* saw Boivenue succeeded by Terry Norman Taylor and the guest appearance of guitarist Aldo Nova, but the songs lacked the impact of those on their debut release and the band's progress dissipated.
Albums: *Lonely At Night* (Portrait 1983), *Salute* (Portrait 1985).

Osbourne, Ozzy

b. John Osbourne, 3 December 1948, Birmingham, England. In 1979 this highly individual and by now infamous vocalist and songwriter left Black Sabbath, a band whose image and original musical direction he had helped shape. His own band was set up with Lee Kerslake, formerly of Uriah Heep, on drums, Rainbow's Bob Daisley (bass) and Randy Rhoads, fresh from Quiet Riot, on guitar. Rhoads' innovative playing ability was much in evidence on the debut, *Blizzard Of Oz*. By the time of a second album, Daisley and Kerslake had left to be replaced by Pat Travers drummer Tommy Aldridge, and Rudy Sarzo (bass). Throughout his post-Black Sabbath career, Osbourne has courted publicity, most famously in 1982 when he had to undergo treatment for rabies following an on-stage incident when he bit the head off a bat. In the same year his immensely talented young guitarist, Rhoads, was killed in an air crash. In came Brad Gillis, former guitarist in Night Ranger, but, so close was Rhoads' personal as well as musical relationship to Osbourne, many feared he would never be adequately replaced. *Speak Of The Devil* was released later in 1982, a live album which included Sabbath material. Following a tour which saw Sarzo and Gillis walk out, Osbourne was forced to re-think the line-up of his band in 1983 as Daisley rejoined, along with guitarist Jake E. Lee. Aldridge left following the release of *Bark At The Moon*, and was replaced by renowned virtuoso drummer Carmine Appice. This combination was to be short-lived, however, Randy Castillo replacing Appice, and Phil Soussan taking on the bass guitar. Daisley appears on *No Rest For The Wicked*, although Sabbath bassist Geezer Butler played on the subsequent live dates. The late 80s were a trying time for Osbourne. He went on trial in America for allegedly using his lyrics to incite youngsters to commit suicide; he was eventually cleared of these charges. His wife, Sharon (daughter of Don Arden), also became his manager, and has helped Osbourne to overcome the alcoholism which was the subject of much of his work. His lyrics, though, continue to deal with the grimmest of subjects like the agony of insanity, and *The Ultimate Sin* is concerned almost exclusively with the issue of nuclear destruction. In later years Osbourne has kept to more contemporary issues, rejecting to a certain

Ozzy Osbourne

extent the satanic, werewolf image he constructed around himself in the early 80s. He embarked on a farewell tour in 1992, but broke four bones in his foot which inhibited his performances greatly. He also donated $20,000 to the Daughters Of The Republic Of Texas appeal to help restore the Alamo, and performed his first concert in the city of San Antonio since being banned for urinating on a wall of the monument in 1982. Predictably neither retirement nor atonement sat too comfortably with the man, and by late 1994 he was announcing the imminent release of a new solo album, recorded in conjunction with Steve Vai. He also teamed up with Therapy? to sing lead vocals on 'Iron Man' for the Black Sabbath tribute album, *Black Nativity*. Less likely was his pairing with Miss Piggy on 'Born To Be Wild', for a Muppets compilation album. He also confesssed that his original partner on his 1992 Don Was-produced duet with Kim Basinger, 'Shake Your Head', was Madonna, though he hadn't actually recognised her. Other bizarre couplings had included one with Billy Connolly and boxer Frank Bruno on the 'Urpney Song', written by Mike Batt for cartoon series, *Dreamstone*.

Albums: With Black Sabbath: *Black Sabbath* (Vertigo 1970), *Paranoid* (Vertigo 1970), *Master Of Reality* (Vertigo 1971), *Black Sabbath Vol. IV* (Vertigo 1972), *Sabbath Bloody Sabbath* (World Wide Artists 1974), *Sabotage* (NEMS 1975), *Technical Ecstasy* (Vertigo 1976), *Never Say Die* (Vertigo 1978). Solo: *Blizzard Of Oz* (Jet 1980), *Diary Of A Madman* (Jet 1981), *Talk Of The Devil* (Jet 1982), *Bark At The Moon* (Jet 1983), *The Ultimate Sin* (Epic 1986), *Tribute* (Epic 1987), *No Rest For The Wicked* (Epic 1988), *Just Say Ozzy* (Epic 1990), *No More Tears* (Epic 1991), *Live & Loud* (Epic 1993, double album).

Videos: *Ultimate Ozzy* (1987), *Wicked Videos* (1988), *Bark At The Moon* (1992), *Don't Blame Me* (1992).

Further reading: *Diary Of A Madman*, Mick Wall, *Ozzy Osbourne*, Garry Johnson.

Ostrogoth

This Belgian hard rock outfit was formed in Gent, Belguim, during 1983, by guitarist Rudy Vercruysse and drummer Mario Pauwels. After a series of false starts, the line-up stabilized with the addition of Marc Debrauwer (vocals), Marnix Vandekauter (bass) and Hans Vandekerckhove (guitar). They debuted with a mini-album, *Full Moon's Eyes*, a competent if predictable re-hash of Iron Maiden and Judas Priest riffs. This line-up recorded two further collections in the same vein, but received little recognition outside their native Belgium. The band splintered in 1985, with only the nucleus of Vercruysse and Pauwels

remaining. They re-built Ostrogoth with Peter de Wint (vocals), Juno Martins (guitar), Sylvain Cherotti (bass) and Kris Taerwe (keyboards). In 1987 they produced *Feelings Of Fury*, which added a melodic slant to their previous enterprises. The group subsequently disbanded with Pauwels moving on to Shellshock and Hermetic Brotherhood.

Albums: *Full Moon's Eyes* (Mausoleum 1983, mini-album), *Ecstasy And Danger* (Mausoleum 1983), *Too Hot* (Mausoleum 1985), *Feelings Of Fury* (Ultraprime 1987).

Outside Edge

Formerly known as Blackfoot Sue and Liner, this band switched to the name Outside Edge in 1984 to pursue an AOR direction. Comprising Tom Farmer (vocals/bass), Eddie Golga (guitar), Pete Giles (keyboards) and Dave Farmer (drums), they signed to Warner Bros. and released a self-titled debut in 1985. This was Americanized melodic rock, but featured rough and ragged vocals from Farmer, in contrast to the musical stylisation. *Running Hot* followed in 1986 and was produced by Terry Manning (of Z.Z. Top fame), but Outside Edge were still unable to break through on a commercial level. The Farmer brothers left in 1989 and the remaining duo recruited new members to become Little Wing.

Albums: *Outside Edge* (Warners 1985), *Running Hot* (10 1986).

Overdose

First sighted contributing a track to the *Metal Massacre 9* compilation, Brazilian thrash band Overdose actually started their career alongside the better known Sepultura, each band supplying one side to the *Brutal Devastation/Seculo XX* album in 1985. Afterwards the fortunes of the two bands diverged, and Overdose looked like becoming merely a footnote in the Sepultura story (Overdose vocalist B.Z., a graphic artist, also designed their logo). Claudio David (guitar), Sergio Cichovicz (guitar), Eddie Weber (bass), Andre Marcio (drums) and B.Z. kicked their heels while contractual problems were sorted out. They sustained themselves with a rigorous South American touring schedule which helped define their bombastic and potent sound. They also recorded profusely. 1994's *Progress Of Decadence* would prove to be their sixth album, but the first to be released in Europe, the group having previously sustained themselves with a staunch following in their native territory.

Selected album: *Progress Of Decadence* (Under One Flag 1994).

Overkill

This New York thrash metal quartet was formed in 1984 by vocalist Bobby Ellsworth, guitarist Bobby Gustafson, bassist D.D. Vernie and drummer Sid Falck. Together they self-financed the recording of a mini-album. Desperately short of cash and exposure, they sold the rights to the small Azra label and made a net loss. They were soon picked up by Megaforce, however, and released their full debut album in 1985. *Feel The Fire* was a brutal speed-metal riff assault, but lacked the variation in light and shade to compete with groups such as Metallica and Anthrax. Three more albums followed a similar pattern, with *Under The Influence* elevating their profile and courting comparisons with Testament. Following *The Years Of Decay*, Gustafson quit and was replaced by Rob Cannavino and Merrit Gant (ex-Faith Or Fear). Expanded to a quintet, the band recorded *Horrorscope,* their finest work to date. Unlike their earlier releases, they varied their approach and only switched to hyperspeed at crucial moments, in order to maximize the impact of their delivery. The album also featured an incredible cover of Edgar Winter's 'Frankenstein'. Their reputation has continued to increase, following successful support slots on Helloween and Slayer tours, and a second excellent album in *I Hear Black*.

Albums: *Overkill* (Azra 1984, mini-album), *Feel The Fire* (Megaforce 1985), *Taking Over* (Megaforce 1987), *Under The Influence* (Megaforce 1988), *The Years Of Decay* (Megaforce 1989), *Horrorscope* (Megaforce 1991), *I Hear Black* (Megaforce 1993).

Oz

This Finnish heavy metal outfit was formed by The Oz (vocals) and Eero Hamalainen (guitar) in 1977. Complemented by Kari Elo (bass) and Tauno Vajavaara (drums), they adopted an approach that fused elements of Black Sabbath and Motörhead into a violent power chord frenzy. It took five years before the band made their debut with *The Oz,* a heavy rock album, which suffered from a budget production and weak vocals. Elo and Hamalainen were fired shortly after the album's release, with bassist Jay C. Blade and guitarists Speedy Foxx and Spooky Wolff recruited as replacements. The band relocated to Sweden and produced *Fire In The Brain*, a collection of tough and uncompromising power-metal songs not dissimilar to the work of Judas Priest. It served to bring them to the attention of RCA Records who offered them a European deal. The two albums that followed, however, were disappointing. Oz had moved away from their metallic roots and experimented with a greater use of melody, and this approach did not suit.

Overdose

It came as no surprise when they lost their contract. Disillusioned, the band split up in 1987 before reforming two years later (with no original members). Comprising Ape De Martini (vocals), Mark Ruffneck (drums), T.B. Muen (bass), Michael Loreda (guitar) and Mike Paul (guitar), they entered the studio to start work on new material in vain pursuit of former glories.

Albums: *The Oz* (Kraf 1982), *Fire In The Brain* (Wave 1983), *III Warning* (RCA 1984), *Decibel Storm* (RCA 1986).

Ozz

This American hard rock project was founded by vocalist Alexis T. Angel and guitarist Gregg Parker. Using session musicians to complete the band they debuted with *Prisoners* in 1980. Produced by Andy Johns, Parker's guitar work proved exemplary and provided the perfect foil for Angel's vocal acrobatics (comparisons to prime Led Zeppelin were frequently mooted). Parker then relocated to London in 1982 to form the short-lived Ninja, but interest remained high enough in his former project to generate the release of *Exploited*, a compilation of live material and studio out-takes.

Albums: *Prisoners* (Epic 1980), *Exploited* (Streamline 1983).

P

Page, Jimmy

b. James Patrick Page, 9 January 1944, Heston, Middlesex, England. One of rock's most gifted and distinctive guitarists, Page began his professional career during the pre-beat era of the early 60s. He was a member of several groups, including Neil Christian's Crusaders and Carter Lewis And The Southerners, the last of which was led by the popular songwriting team, Carter And Lewis. Page played rousing solos on several releases by Carter/Lewis proteges, notably the McKinleys' 'Sweet And Tender Romance', and the guitarist quickly became a respected session musician. He appeared on releases by Lulu, Them, Tom Jones and Dave Berry, as well as scores of less-renowned acts, but his best-known work was undertaken for producer Shel Talmy. Page appeared on sessions for the Kinks and the Who, joining an elite band of young studio musicians which included Nicky Hopkins, John Paul Jones and Bobby Graham. The guitarist completed a solo single, 'She Just Satisfies', in 1965, and although it suggested a frustration with his journeyman role, he later took up an A&R position with Immediate Records, where he produced singles for Nico and John Mayall. Having refused initial entreaties, Page finally agreed to join the Yardbirds in 1966 and he remained with this groundbreaking attraction until its demise two years later. The guitarist then formed Led Zeppelin, with which he forged his reputation. His propulsive riffs established the framework for a myriad of tracks - 'Whole Lotta Love', 'Rock 'N' Roll', 'Black Dog', 'When The Levee Breaks' and 'Achilles Last Stand' - now established as rock classics, while his solos have set benchmarks for a new generation of guitarists. His acoustic technique, featured on 'Black Mountain Side' and 'Tangerine', is also notable, while his work with Roy Harper, in particular on *Stormcock* (1971), was also among the finest of his career. Page's recordings since Led Zeppelin's dissolution have been ill-focused. He contributed the soundtrack to Michael Winner's film *Death Wish II*, while the Firm, a collaboration with Paul Rodgers, formerly of Free and Bad Company, was equally disappointing. However, a 1988 release, *Outrider*, did much to re-establish his reputation with contributions from Robert Plant, Chris Farlowe and Jason Bonham, the son of Zeppelin's late drummer, John. The guitarist then put considerable effort into remastering that group's revered back catalogue. *Coverdale/Page* was a successful but fleeting partnership with the former Whitesnake singer in 1993, but it was his reunion with Robert Plant for the ironically-titled *Unledded* project which really captured the public's imagination.

Albums: *Death Wish II* (Swan Song 1982, film soundtrack), *Outrider* (Geffen 1988). Compilations: *Jam Session* (Charly 1982), *No Introduction Necessary* (Thunderbolt 1984), *Smoke And Fire* (Thunderbolt 1985). With Roy Harper: *Whatever Happened To Jugula* (Beggars Banquet 1985). With David Coverdale: *Coverdale/Page* (EMI 1993). With Robert Plant: *Unledded/No Quarter* (Fontana 1994).

Pallas

This UK progressive rock outfit was formed in Aberdeen, Scotland, in 1975, by Evan Lawson (vocals), Neil Mathewson (guitar), Ronnie Brown (keyboards), Graeme Murray (bass) and Derek Forman (drums). They toured the British club circuit for many years, receiving constant rejections from A&R departments. Undeterred, they decided to self-finance the recording of a demo album. This materialized in 1983 as *Arrive Alive*, a quality collection of melodic songs. The set's modest success led to a deal with EMI, the services of Yes producer, Eddie Offord, and a large budget to record *The Sentinel* in Atlanta, Georgia, USA. This was an ambitious and intricate concept album which betrayed the group's Marillion and Yes influences. Lawson split at this juncture, to be replaced by Alan Reed. *The Wedge* followed and represented the pinnacle of the group's creativity. However, its commercial failure led to EMI severing links. Despite this the band remained together, but finally split when unable to find a new label sympathetic to their cause.

Albums: *Arrive Alive* (Kigg Cool 1983), *The Sentinel* (Harvest 1984), *The Wedge* (EMI 1986).

Pandemonium

Alaskan heavy metal band formed by the Resch brothers; Chris (vocals), Eric (bass) and David (guitar), in 1981. They relocated to Los Angeles, California, and teamed up with Chris Latham (guitar) and Dave Graybill (drums) the following year. Making their debut on the first *Metal Massacre* compilation with 'Fighting Backwards', it opened the door to a full contract with Metal Blade Records. Three albums followed over the next five years, with each successive release becoming less formularized (despite displaying the continually strong influence of Van Halen) but to little commercial advantage.

Albums: *Heavy Metal Soldiers* (Metal Blade 1984), *Hole In The Sky* (Metal Blade 1985), *The Kill* (Metal Blade 1988).

Pandora's Box

This one-off project was put together by US producer Jim Steinman to record his rock opera, *Original Sin*. The band featured Roy Bittan (piano), Jeff Bova (synthesizers), Jim Bralower (drums), Eddie Martinez (guitar) and Steve Buslowe (bass). Utilizing a series of guest vocalists, which included Elaine Caswell, Ellen Foley, Gina Taylor, Deliria Wild, Holly Sherwood and Laura Theodore, *Original Sin* was a grandiose concept album themed on sex. Featuring classical interludes, spoken introductions, atmospheric ballads and breathtaking rock 'n' roll, it was almost too ambitious. Despite state-of-the-art production (courtesy of Steinman) it never received the sort of recognition afforded his Meat Loaf projects.

Album: *Original Sin* (Virgin 1989).

Paradise Lost

Pantera

Texan heavy metal quartet formed in 1981, initially comprising Terry Glaze (guitar/vocals), Darrell Abbott (guitar), Vince Abbott (drums) and Rex Rocker (bass). Drawing musical inspiration from Kiss, Aerosmith and Deep Purple, they debuted with *Metal Magic* in 1983. This well-received set led to prestigious support slots to Dokken, Stryper and Quiet Riot. *Projects In The Jungle* indicated that the band were evolving quickly and starting to build a sound of their own. The Kiss nuances had disappeared and the band sounded similar to early Def Leppard, with anthemic cuts likes 'Heavy Metal Rules' and 'Out For Blood' leading the charge. The membership altered names at this juncture with Glaze becoming Terence Lee, Darrell Abbott switching to Diamond Darrell and brother Vince emerging as Vinnie Paul. *Power Metal* saw Phil Anselmo take over on vocals, but the album lacked the depth and polish of previous efforts, and had yet to make the full conversion to extant thrash which would become their new trademark. Diamond Darrell turned down the offer to join Megadeth at this point in order to concentrate on new Pantera material. The decision proved crucial, as a return to form was made with 1990's *Cowboys From Hell*. This was an inspired collection of infectious hard rock, played with unabashed fervour, with Anselmo growing as a creative and visual force. *Vulgar Display Of Power*, meanwhile, belied half of its title by invoking a sense of genuine songwriting prowess to augment the bone-crushing arrangements. Building up a fierce reputation, it surprised few of the group's supporters when *Far Beyond Driven* entered both the UK and US album charts at number 1. Rock music had found powerful new ambassadors in the brutally honest and savagely executed thrash metal of Pantera.

Albums: *Metal Magic* (Metal Magic 1983), *Projects In The Jungle* (Metal Magic 1984), *I Am The Night* (Metal Magic 1985), *Power Metal* (Metal Magic 1988), *Cowboys From Hell* (Atco 1990), *Vulgar Display Of Power* (Atco 1992), *Far Beyond Driven* (East West 1994).
Video: *Vulgar Video* (1994).

Paradise Lost

This Halifax, Yorkshire, England-based death metal quintet was formed in 1988, taking their name from Milton's famous composition (though vocalist Nick Holmes would concede that the poem 'doesn't half go on'). Together with Gregor Mackintosh (guitar), Aaron Aedy (guitar), Stephen Edmondson (bass) and Matthew Archer (drums), they were signed to the independent Peaceville label on the strength of two impressive demos. They debuted in 1990 with *Lost Paradise*, which was heavily influenced by Napalm Death, Obituary and Death. It featured indecipherable grunting from Holmes, over a barrage of metallic white noise. *Gothic* saw a major innovation in the 'grindcore' genre; with female vocals, keyboards and guitar lines that for once, were not lost in the mix. Importantly, the tempo had also dropped: 'We started to play more slowly because all the others were playing as fast as possible'. Many, notably Asphyx and Autopsy, followed suit. With indications in the early 90s of the metal sub-genres becoming accepted within the mainstream, it came as no surprise when Paradise Lost found a wider audience with *Shades Of God*, their first effort for Music For Nations. Recorded with producer Simon Efemey (Diamond Head, Wonder Stuff), and with artwork from cult cartoonist Dave McKean, this release was heralded in the press as a 'coming of age'. Sold out shows in Europe followed, before the group returned to Longhome studios in the UK, with Effemy once again in attendance. The *As I Die* EP gained a strong foothold on MTV, with approving glances from peers including Metallica, before *Icon* was released in September 1993. If previous offerings had seen the band's fan base expand, *Icon* brought about an explosion of interest, and acclaim usually reserved for the US gods of death metal. Reactions to the band's live shows in the US with Sepultura were just as strong. However, before sessions for a fifth album could begin Archer amicably departed.
Albums: *Lost Paradise* (Peaceville 1990), *Gothic* (Peaceville 1991), *Shades Of God* (Music For Nations 1992), *Icon* (Music For Nations 1993).
Videos: *Live Death* (1990), *Harmony Breaks* (1994).

Paradox

German thrash-metal outfit formed in 1986 by ex-Warhead duo Charly Steinhauer (vocals/guitar) and Axel Blaha (drums). After a series of false starts and a track included on the *Teutonic Invasion Part 1* compilation, the line-up stabilized with the addition of Markus Spyth (guitar) and Roland Stahl (bass). Signing to UK label Roadrunner, they delivered *Product Of Imagination* in 1987, a collection of formulaic speed-metal material. *Heresy* saw a major personnel reshuffle and a marked improvement in their conversion of Metallica and Anthrax riffing. Stahl and Spyth had been replaced by Dieter Roth (guitar), Manfred Springer (guitar) and Armin Donderer (bass), with the expanded line-up allowing a degree of flexibility and more depth to their sound.
Albums: *Product Of Imagination* (Roadrunner 1987), *Heresy* (Roadrunner 1989).

Pariah (UK)

Formerly known as Satan, this Newcastle-Upon Tyne, England group became Pariah in 1988, feeling that their original name may have led to misconceptions concerning their style. They were never a true black metal outfit as their original moniker suggested, but part of the New Wave Of British Heavy Metal scene instead. Pariah comprised Michael Jackson (vocals), Steve Ramsey (guitar), Russ Tippins (guitar), Graeme English (bass) and Sean Taylor (drums). They debuted with *The Kindred* in 1988, an album of hard, fast metal, characterized by the dual guitar onslaught of Ramsey and Tippins. Following *Blaze Of Obscurity*, Jackson quit and was replaced by Mark Allen, but there was to be no further significant progress. Along with Demon, Pariah passed into history as one of the most talented metal acts of their generation to be lost to obscurity.

Albums: *The Kindred* (Steamhammer 1988), *Blaze Of Obscurity* (Steamhammer 1989).

Pariah (USA)

This Florida, USA-based speed-metal quartet were formed in 1987 by the Egger brothers, with the full line-up comprising Garth Egger (vocals), Shaun Egger (guitar), Chris Egger (drums) and Wayne Derrick (guitar). Unable to secure a record deal in the US they were finally signed to the Dutch Moshroom label in 1988, for whom they debuted with *Take A Walk*, a mixture of styles that alternated between derivative Anthrax/Metallica thrash and the characterless pop-metal of Europe and Bon Jovi. The album failed commercially and nothing has been heard from the group since.

Album: *Take A Walk* (Moshroom 1988).

Paris

This US power-trio was put together in 1975 by former Fleetwood Mac guitarist Bob Welch and ex-Jethro Tull bassist Glenn Cornick. Adding Thom Mooney on drums, they signed to Capitol Records in 1976 and released their self-titled debut album. Weaving mystical lyrical tapestries, within psychedelic, blues-based progressive rock, their strange and tormented style was ignored at the time of release, and remains an odd curio even today. Hunt Sales replaced Mooney on *Big Towne 2061* and the band adopted a more mainstream approach, with the lyrics taking on a religious emphasis. This also failed to find an audience and the band went their separate ways after its release. Welch embarked on a highly successful solo career while Sales joined Tin Machine.

Albums: *Paris* (Capitol 1975), *Big Towne 2061* (Capitol 1976).

Paris, Jeff

This American vocalist/guitarist started his career in the jazz-rock group Pieces. He subsequently played with a number of similar bands on a short-term basis, and built up a reputation as a quality backing vocalist and talented songwriter. He worked with Cinderella, Y&T, Vixen and Lita Ford in this capacity and was offered a solo recording deal by Polygram in 1986. He debuted with *Race To Paradise* the same year, a highly polished and melodic collection of AOR anthems, similar in style to Michael Bolton and Eric Martin. *Wired Up* saw Paris toughen up his approach. The album was typical North American rock and drew comparisons with Bruce Springsteen and Bryan Adams. However, both sets failed commercially and Polygram terminated his contract in 1988.

Albums: *Race To Paradise* (Polygram 1986), *Wired Up* (Polygram 1987).

Parr, John

This vocalist, guitarist, composer and producer specializes in highly melodic AOR. Though British his success had been drawn largely from the US where his recordings for the Atlantic label have been compared to Rick Springfield and Eddie Money. Parr composed the themes for the movies *American Anthem* and *St. Elmo's Fire*, the second of which made the UK Top 10 singles chart in 1985. The follow-up, 'Naughty Naughty', achieved a paltry number 58. He also duetted with Meat Loaf on 'Rock 'N' Roll Mercenaries', but this failed to embellish either artist's profile, stopping just short of the Top 30. Producing two solo albums, his self-titled debut in 1985 and *Running The Endless Mile* in 1986, both fared poorly with the critics. His finest moment remains the energetic 'St. Elmo's Fire (Man In Motion)', to give it its full title.

Albums: *John Parr* (Atlantic 1985), *Running The Endless Mile* (Atlantic 1987).

Partners In Crime

This short-lived supergroup was put together by ex-Status Quo drummer John Coghlan. Enlisting the services of Noel McCalla (vocals; ex-Moon), Mark de Vanchque (keyboards; ex-Wildfire), Ray Major (guitar; ex-Mott) and Mac Mcaffrey (bass), they specialized in Americanized melodic rock. Debuting with *Organised Crime* in 1985, it was obvious that this set of seasoned musicians gelled together well. Produced by John Eden (Status Quo) and James Guthrie (Pink Floyd, Queensrÿche) it was a strong album in many respects, yet failed to stand out fom a plethora of other acts offering similar material. The band sundered soon after the album was released.

Album: *Organised Crime* (Epic 1985).

Paw

This Lawrence, Kansas quartet formed in 1990 with brothers Grant (guitar) and Peter Fitch (drums) and bassist Charles Bryan, recruiting vocalist Mark Hennessy (b. Mark Thomas Joseph Brendan Hennessy, 6 May 1969, Kansas, USA) from local art-noise band King Rat, which Hennessy described as a period when 'I thought I was Nick Cave'. Paw were the leading local band, and picked up support gigs with Nirvana and the Fluid before recording their first seven-song demo at Butch Vig's Smart Studios in Wisconsin, which led to an enormous major label bidding war, won by A&M Records. *Newsweek* described Paw as 'the next Nirvana', but Hüsker Dü, Dinosaur Jr and the Replacements were perhaps better reference points for *Dragline*'s marriage of melody and raw guitar power, with a distinctive small-town storytelling aspect to the songs. 'Sleeping Bag' was perhaps the most poignant, telling the childhood story of a car crash which hospitalised the seriously injured Peter Fitch, and when older brother Grant feared the worst, he slept in Peter's sleeping bag, 'as corny as it sounds, just to be a little closer to him'. *Dragline* deservedly received universal acclaim,

and the band toured exhaustively, earning an excellent live reputation, touring Europe with Therapy? and Hammerbox, the UK with Tool, and both the UK and USA with Monster Magnet, as singles 'Sleeping Bag, and 'Couldn't Know' brought them a wider audience. The band returned to the studio in late 1994, but without Bryan, who had tired of the endless touring.
Album: *Dragline* (A&M 1993).

Pearl Jam

This revisionist (or, depending on your viewpoint, visionary) rock quintet were formed in Seattle, USA, in the early 90s, by Jeff Ament (bass) and Stone Gossard (rhythm guitar). Gossard had played with Steve Turner in the Ducky Boys, the latter moving on to perform with Ament in Green River. Gossard would also become a member of this band when Mark Arm (like Turner, later to join Mudhoney) switched from guitar to vocals. Gossard and Ament, however, elected to continue working together when Green River washed up, and moved on to Mother Love Bone, fronted by local 'celebrity' Andrew Wood. However, that ill-fated group collapsed when, four weeks after the release of its debut album, *Apple*, Wood was found dead from a heroin overdose. Both

Pearl Jam

Gossard and Ament would subsequently participate in Seattle's tribute to Wood, Temple Of The Dog, alongside Chris Cornell of Soundgarden who instigated the project, Soundgarden drummer Matt Cameron, plus Gossard's schoolfriend Mike McCready (guitar) and vocalist Eddie Vedder (ex-Bad Radio), from San Diego. He had been passed a tape of demos recorded by Ament, Gossard and McCready by Red Hot Chili Peppers' drummer Jack Irons. Both Vedder and McCready would eventually hook up permanently with Ament and Gossard to become Pearl Jam, with the addition of drummer Dave Krusen (having originally dabbled with the name Mookie Blaylock). The band signed to Epic Records in 1991, debuting the following year with the powerful, yet melodic *Ten*. A bold diarama, it saw the band successfully incorporate elements of their native traditions (Soundgarden, Mother Love Bone, Nirvana) with older influences such as the Doors, Velvet Underground, the Stooges and the MC5. The self-produced recording (together with Rick Parashar) showed great maturity for a debut, particularly in the full-blooded songwriting, never better demonstrated than on hit single 'Alive'. Dynamic live performances and a subtle commercial edge to their material catapulted them from obscurity to virtual superstars overnight, as the Seattle scene debate raged and Kurt Cobain accused them of 'jumping the alternative bandwagon'. In the USA *Ten* was still in the Top 20 a year and a half after its release, having sold over 4 million copies in that country alone. The touring commitments which followed, however, brought Vedder to the verge of nervous collapse. He struggled back to health in time for the Lollapalooza II tour, an appearance on *MTV Unplugged*, and Pearl Jam's cameo as Matt Dillon's 'band', Citizen Dick, in the Cameron Crowe film, *Singles*. Vedder would also front a re-united Doors on their induction into the Rock 'n' Roll Hall Of Fame in Los Angeles at the Century Plaza hotel, performing versions of 'Roadhouse Blues', 'Break On Through' and 'Light My Fire'. The eagerly awaited 'difficult' follow-up was announced in October 1993, close on the heals of Nirvana's latest offering. Whilst reviews were mixed the advance orders placed the album on top of charts on both sides of the Atlantic. *Vitalogy* seemed overtly concerned with re-establishing the group's grass roots credibility, a strong clue to which arrived in the fact that the album was available for a week on vinyl before a CD or cassette release (a theme revisited on 'Spin The Black Circle'). There were also numerous references, some oblique, others not, to the death of Nirvana's Kurt Cobain. Ironically 1994 also saw drummer Dave Abbruzzese dispensed with, amid

unfounded rumours that former Nirvana sticksman Dave Grohl would be invited in to the ranks.
Albums: *Ten* (Epic 1991), *Vs.* (Epic 1993), *Vitalogy* (Epic 1994).
Further reading: *Pearl Jam: The Illustrated Biography*, Brad Morrell.

Pell, Axel Rudi

This German heavy metal guitar virtuoso left Steeler in 1988 to concentrate on a solo career. Influenced by Ritchie Blackmore, Yngwie Malmsteen and Tony Macalpine, he offered explosive guitar pyrotechnics within a traditional metal framework. *Wild Obsession* featured vocalist Charlie Huhn (vocals), Bonfire member Joerg Deisinger (bass) and Jorg Michael (drums; ex-Rage). It was well-received by the music press, but this was not translated into sales, partly due to Pell's reluctance to take the band out on the road. *Nasty Reputation* represented a major leap forward in songwriting. The heart of the music was still in the early 70s, but the guitar work and the sheer energy of the delivery was quite remarkable. Bob Rock, now on vocals, gave the music great authority, with the expanded quintet also including two more new faces, Volker Krawczak (bass) and Kai Raglewski (keyboards).
Albums: *Wild Obsession* (Steamhammer 1989), *Nasty Reputation* (Steamhammer 1991), *The Ballads* (Steamhammer 1993).

Pentagram

Amongst the best of the bands continuing the seminal heavy metal tradition of early Black Sabbath, the core of Pentagram was formed by Bobby Liebling (vocals) and Joe Hasselvander (drums) in the US in 1978. Like Sabbath, their roots were in the lively white blues bands of the early 70s, which they translated into ominous, crunching riffs and dark, devilish lyrics. However, unlike Black Sabbath, who treat the infernal with ambivalence, Pentagram have always seemed much more comfortable with their Satanic themes. Their first album, *Pentagram*, was released in 1985, but by this time Hasselvander had left, dismayed at lack of label support, and joined Raven. Hasselvander (replaced by Stuart Rose) however had already laid down most of the tracks for their next album, *Day of Reckoning*. Strong local and cult support was not enough to sustain Pentagram's, increasingly unfashionable, approach and they split in 1990. But this same cult appeal saw the rights for their first two albums (with their debut retitled as *Relentless*) bought by UK label Peaceville and re-released in 1993. Inspired by this renewed interest Liebling reformed the band with the classic line up of

Hasselvander (drums), Martin Swaney (bass), and Victor Griffin (guitar and keyboards) and released the new album *Be Forewarned*. While it would be difficult to call Pentagram original, their sinisterly infectious riffs and fidelity to metal's darker roots certainly justify the band's enduring appeal.

Albums: *Pentagram* (1985), *Day of Reckoning* (Peaceville 1987), *Be Forewarned* (Peaceville 1994).

Perry, Joe, Project

b. 10 September 1950, Boston, Massachusetts, USA. Having severed an apprenticeship in the aspiring Jam Band, guitarist Perry then became a founder member of Aerosmith. This durable hard rock act became one of USA's leading attractions during the 70s, principally through the artist's exciting, riffing style and vocalist Steve Tyler's charismatic performances. Tension between the group's leading figures led to the former's departure in 1979. He subsequently formed the Joe Perry Project with Ralph Mormon (vocals), David Hull (bass) and Ronnie Stewart (drums) but neither *Let The Music Do The Talking* nor *I've Got The Rocks 'N' Rolls Again*, which featured new singer Charlie Farren, captured the fire of the guitarist's previous group. Perry then established a new line-up around Mach Bell (vocals), Danny Hargrove (bass) and Joe Pet (drums) for *Once A Rocker, Always A Rocker*, but once again the combination failed to generate commercial approbation. Former Aerosmith colleague Brad Whitford (guitar) was then added to the group, but it was disbanded in 1984 when a full-scale reunion of Aerosmith was undertaken. The ensuing *Done With Mirrors* featured the title-song of the Project's debut album, but Aerosmith's successful rebirth brought Perry's external aspirations to a premature close.

Albums: *Let The Music Do The Talking* (CBS 1980), *I've Got The Rocks 'N' Rolls Again* (CBS 1981), *Once A Rocker, Always A Rocker* (MCA 1984).

Perry, Steve

Following the success of *Escape* and *Frontiers*, the members of Journey took an extended break in order to pursue solo projects. Vocalist Steve Perry (b. 22 January 1953, Hanford, California, USA) put together a team of respected session players to produce *Street Talk*, which displayed soul and R&B influences in both Perry's vocals and songwriting, and proved a superb showcase for his talents. *Street Talk* proved to be the most successful of the Journey solo efforts, producing an enormous US hit in 'Oh Sherrie', an emotive tribute to Perry's girlfriend, and its influence on the style of *Raised On Radio*, Journey's final album, was obvious. However, amid rumours of

Pet Lamb

up to three follow-up records being scrapped, it was not until 1994 that *For The Love Of Strange Medicine* saw the resumption of Perry's career, with a more straightforward AOR style than on the previous album. Any doubts over the viability of the project after such a protracted absence were dispelled when the album made its US chart debut at number 15, and produced a US Top 10 hit with 'You Better Wait'.

Albums: *Street Talk* (Columbia 1984), *For The Love Of Strange Medicine* (Columbia 1994).

Persian Risk

The line-up of this heavy metal outfit, based in the north of England, was in a constant state of flux during their formative period in the early 80s. At one time Phil Campbell and Jon Deverill, later of Motörhead and the Tygers Of Pan Tang respectively, were involved. They debuted with a track on the *Heavy Metal Heroes Vol. 2* compilation, and later recorded a single for Neat Records. It took a further three years to record an album because of the regular line-up shuffles. *Rise Up* finally saw the light of day in 1986 with the team now comprising Carl Sentance (vocals), Phil Vokins (guitar), Graham Bath (guitar), Nick Hughes (bass) and Steve Hopgood (drums). Formularized and rather out-dated, the songs were rooted in the early phase of the New Wave Of British Heavy Metal, which, unlike Persian Risk, had matured and progressed considerably since its inception. The album was unsuccessful and the band disintegrated when Bath and Hopgood left to join Paul Di'anno's Battlezone.

Album: *Rise Up* (Razor 1986).

Pestilence

This German speed/thrash metal quartet was put together by guitarists Randy Meinhard and Patrick Mameli in 1986. Enlisting the services of Marco Foddis (drums) and Martin van Drunen (vocals/bass), they debuted with a track on the *Teutonic Invasion II* compilation (1987) on the Rock Hard label. A deal with Roadrunner ensued and they cut *Mallevs Maleficarum*, a high speed metallic blur reminiscent of Slayer and Testament. Meinhard quit soon after the album was released to form Sacrosanct. Ex-Theriac guitarist Patrick Uterwijk stepped in as replacement and the band entered the studio to record *Consuming Impulse*. This marked a distinct technical and musical improvement over their enthusiastic, but slightly amateurish debut. Produced by Harris Johns, the album took off in the USA and Pestilence toured extensively with Death and Autopsy during 1990. However, van Drunen left shortly afterwards to front his own band, Asphyx

(subsequently forming Submission and acting as guest vocalist on the second Comecon album), with Mameli taking over vocal duties. Pestilence finally split in 1994 with Mameli becoming increasingly hostile to the death metal fraternity which had devoured the band's work. Rumours abounded that Roadrunner were on the verge of dropping them anyway.

Albums: *Mallevs Maleficarum* (Roadrunner 1988), *Consuming Impulse* (Roadrunner 1989), *Testimony To The Ancients* (Roadrunner 1991), *Spheres* (Roadrunner 1993).

Pet Lamb

Formed in Dublin in 1991, the four members of Pet Lamb are Dylan Philips (guitar/vocals), Brian Mooney (guitar/vocals), Kevin Talbot (bass) and James Lillis (drums). Influenced by the hardcore assault of the Butthole Surfers and Jesus Lizard, with the songwriting shared between Phillips and Mooney, they admitted to their central inspiration being: 'a mixture of lust, beer, frustration and boredom'. The group were first adopted by small independent imprint Blunt, a liaison which produced two EPs, and brought about support slots to the musically sympathetic Therapy?, No Means No, Babes In Toyland and others. After a session for the John Peel programme Roadrunner snapped the band up, packing them off to Dublin's Sonic Studios to record their debut for the label, 'Black Mask' - 'a kind of teenage sex and death fantasy, featuring Satan'. In its wake came a debut album, *Sweaty Handshake*, propelled by songs like the defiant 'Insult To Injury' and self-loathing 'Fun With Maggots'.

Album: *Sweaty Handshake* (Roadrunner 1995).

Peterik, Jim

This US keyboardist/composer started his career as a session musician. His first taste of success came with 'Ides Of March' at the end of the 60s. It was 1977, however, before he actually got round to recording a solo album; *Don't Fight The Feeling* was a mature, melodic rock album, that drew comparisons with Bob Seger, Bruce Springsteen and Michael Bolton. However, it made little headway and Peterik returned to session work, guesting on Sammy Hagar and .38 Special albums. In 1978 he formed AOR band Survivor with guitarist Frankie Sullivan with whom he went on to multi-platinum success.

Album: *Don't Fight The Feeling* (Scotti Bros. 1977).

Petra

One of the first US Christian hard rock bands, Petra are an excellent musical unit who have never been swayed by passing trends and have stuck fast to their own ideals and beliefs. The group was formed in 1972 by vocalist Greg Volz and guitarist Bob Hartman, recruiting Mark Kelly (bass), John Slick (keyboards) and Louie Weaver (drums) to their cause. Petra specialized in a varied musical approach that incorporated elements of the Eagles, Joe Walsh, Kansas and Deep Purple. They have released well over a dozen quality albums to date, with their popularity having gradually waned from its peak in 1984. At this time, they appeared in the US Top 12 best-attended bands list in *Performance* magazine, while *Not Of This World* sold in excess of a quarter of a million units. John Schlitt (ex-Head East) replaced Volz after 1986's *Back To The Street* and the band adopted a heavier direction thereafter. John Lawry and Ronnie Cates replaced Slick and Kelly on keyboards and bass respectively in 1988. Their two most recent releases owe much to Kiss and Stryper and are more aggressive than their earlier material.

Albums: *Petra* (Myrrh 1974), *Come And Join Us* (Myrrh 1977), *Washes Whiter Than* (Star Song 1979), *Never Say Die* (Star Song 1981), *More Power To Ya* (Star Song 1982), *Not Of This World* (Kingsway 1983), *Beat The System* (Kingsway 1985), *Captured In Time And Place* (Star Song 1986), *Back To The Street* (Star Song 1986), *This Means War* (Star Song 1987), *On Fire* (Star Song 1988), *Petra Means Rock* (Star Song 1989), *Petra Praise - The Rock Cries Out* (Dayspring 1989), *Beyond Belief* (Star Song 1990).
Video: *Captured In Time And Space* (1989).

Pez Band

This melodic US pop-rock outfit was formed in 1976 by vocalist Mimi Betinis and guitarist Tommy Gawenda. Enlisting the services of Mike Gorman (bass) and Mick Rain (drums), they made their debut with a self-titled album on the Passport label. The accent on the commercial dynamic was overt, with thin melodies and lightweight guitar work. The album flopped and the band changed direction to hard-driving, blues-based rock. *Laughing In The Dark* was a remarkable improvement and featured highly engaging lead guitar, reminiscent of Gary Moore and Pat Travers. This too failed to find favour (perhaps because the band were already labelled as an unsuccessful pop act). Disillusioned by the lack of media response, they bowed out with a live mini-album, *30 Seconds Over Schaumberg*. The group reformed temporarily in 1981, releasing *Cover To Cover*, but then disbanded for a final time.
Albums: *Pezband* (Passport 1977), *Laughing In The Dark* (Passport 1978), *30 Seconds Over Schaumberg* (Passport 1978), *Cover To Cover* (Passport 1981).

Phantom Blue

This guitar-orientated melodic rock outfit hailed from Los Angeles, California, USA. The all-female line-up, comprising vocalist Gigi Hangach (vocals), guitarists Nicole Couch (guitar), Michelle Meldrum (guitar), Kim Nielsen (bass) and Linda McDonald (drums), was impressive on a technical, visual and musical level. Under the guiding hand of Shrapnel Records' guitar supremo, Mike Varney, the girls were introduced to Steve Fontano and Marty Friedman (later of Megadeth), who became responsible for producing and arranging their debut album. Comprising nine originals, *Phantom Blue* was a credible and rewarding bout of mature, inividual rock which, with a sheen of production gloss to temper the screaming guitars, impressed widely. A second, long-delayed album, *Built To Perform*, saw Friedman guest once more, and included a cover of Thin Lizzy's 'Bad Reputation', but much of the momentum had been lost. In 1994 Rana Ross replaced Nielson on bass as the band attempted to recapture lost ground.
Album: *Phantom Blue* (Roadrunner 1989), *Built To Perform* (Roadrunner 1993).

Phenomena

This ambitious video and musical project was co-ordinated by Tom Galley (brother of former Whitesnake guitarist, Mel Galley) - the albums are concept affairs, centred on the theme of supernatural phenomena. However, utilizing an impressive list of guest musicians has not always guaranteed a good result, and Phenomena went some way towards proving this truism. With Neil Murray (bass), Cozy Powell (drums), Mel Galley (guitar) and Glenn Hughes (vocals) among the starting line-up, great things were evidently expected for *Phenomena*. However, the songs were often overtly complex and lacked a central melody line. *Dream Runner* released two years later suffered from similar problems, but the music was less of a disappointment. It featured an impeccable array of guests once more, with Ray Gillen, Max Bacon, Scott Gorham, Kyoji Yamamoto and John Wetton contributing in one form or another. The album received good reviews in the music media, but sold poorly. As a result, plans to make the Phenomena projects into films were aborted.
Albums: *Phenomena* (Bronze 1985), *Phenomena II - Dream Runner* (Arista 1987).

Phoenix

This UK group rose from the ashes of Argent in 1975. A trio, the band comprised John Verity (vocals/guitar), Robert Henrit (drums) and Jim

Rodford (keyboards/bass). They continued in much the same vein as before; hard-rock infused with melody and a keen sense of dynamics, and debuted with a self-titled album in 1976, before landing the support slot to Ted Nugent's UK tour. The band proved an excellent live proposition, but this was never translated into album sales, and they split up after just 12 months together. In 1979 Verity and Henrit reformed Phoenix with Russ Ballard (keyboards/vocals), Bruce Turgon (bass), Ray Minnhinnett (guitar) and Michael Des Barres (vocals). This short-lived collaboration produced *In Full View*, a non-descript melodic rock album that sold poorly. The band disintegrated shortly afterwards, with Verity and Henrit joining Charlie and then later forming Verity, under the vocalist's own surname.

Albums: *Phoenix* (CBS 1976), *In Full View* (Charisma 1980).

Picture

This Dutch heavy metal quartet was formed in 1979 by Ronald van Prooyen (lead vocals) and Jan Bechtum (guitar). With the addition of bassist Rinus Vreugdenhil and drummer Laurens 'Bakkie' Bakker, they modelled themselves on British bands, most noticeably Uriah Heep, Deep Purple and Motörhead. They went through numerous line-up changes during their seven-year, seven-album career, but produced consistently high quality material throughout. Vocalists included Pete Lovell, Shmoulik Avigal and Bert Heerink (ex-Vandenberg) while Chris van Jaarsueld, Henry van Manen and Rob van Enhuizen were responsible for six-string duties at one time or another. The band folded in 1987, but played a one-off reunion concert the following year.

Albums: *Picture* (Backdoor 1980), *Heavy Metal Ears* (Backdoor 1981), *Diamond Dreamer* (Backdoor 1982), *Eternal Dark* (Backdoor 1984), *Traitor* (Backdoor 1985), *Every Story Needs Another Picture* (Backdoor 1986), *Marathon* (Touchdown 1987)

Pitch Shifter

Nottingham, England-based quartet comprising Jonathan Clayden (vocals), Jonathan Carter (guitar/programming), D (drums) and Mark Clayden (bass). In early 1991 they signed to Peaceville Records and lanched their career with the release of *Industrial*.

Pitch Shifter

Among those impressed with the group's visceral guitar assault (at that time also featuring second guitarist Stuart Toolin, and no drummer) was DJ John Peel, who invited them to perform three tracks on his show in May 1991. Moving over to Earache Records, they recorded their debut for the label in January of the following year, with the *Submit* mini-album. For its full length follow-up the group increased the ratio of technology, though its application remained studiously intense. The lyrics built on the themes of oppression and social injustice, while the use of samplers and sequencers offered an extra aural dimension. Touring with Treponem Pal, Consolidated, Neurosis and Biohazard ensued - and this musical melting pot produced the germ of an idea within the band. The resultant *The Remix Wars* saw the band revisiting their back catalogue, allowing access also to other sympathetic hands, including Therapy?, Biohazard and rappers Gunshot.

Albums: *Industrial* (Peaceville 1991), *Submit* (Earache 1992, mini-album), *Desensitized* (Earache 1993), *The Remix Wars* (Earache 1994).

Video: *Deconstruction* (1992).

Plant, Robert

b. 20 August 1948, Birmingham, West Midlands, England. Plant's early career was spent in several Midlands-based R&B bands, including the New Memphis Bluesbreakers and Crawling King Snakes, the last of which featured drummer and future colleague, John Bonham. In 1965 Plant joined Lee John Crutchley, Geoff Thompson and Roger Beamer in Listen, a Motown-influenced act, later signed to CBS Records. A cover version of 'You Better Run', originally recorded by the (Young) Rascals made little headway, and Plant was then groomed for a solo career with two 1967 singles, 'Laughing, Crying, Laughing' and 'Long Time Coming'. Having returned to Birmingham, the singer formed Band Of Joy in which his growing interest in US 'west coast' music flourished. This promising group broke up in 1968 and following a brief association with blues veteran Alexis Korner, Plant then joined another local act, Hobstweedle. It was during this tenure that guitarist Jimmy Page invited the singer to join Led Zeppelin. Plant's reputation as a dynamic vocalist and frontman was forged as a member of this highly-influential unit, but he began plans for a renewed solo career following the death of John Bonham in 1980. *Pictures At Eleven* unveiled a new partnership with Robbie Blunt (guitar), Paul Martinez (bass) and Jezz Woodruffe (keyboards) and while invoking the singer's past, also showed him open to new musical directions. *The Principle Of Moments* contained the restrained UK/US Top 20 hit, 'Big Log' (1983), and inspired an ambitious world tour. Plant then acknowledged vintage R&B in the Honeydrippers, an *ad hoc* group which featured Page, Jeff Beck and Nile Rodgers, whose mini-album spawned a US Top 3 hit in 'Sea Of Love'. Having expressed a desire to record less conventional music, Robert fashioned *Shaken 'N' Stirred*, which divided critics who either lauded its ambition or declared it too obtuse. The singer then disbanded his group, but resumed recording in 1987 on becoming acquainted with a younger pool of musicians, including Phil Johnstone, Dave Barrett, Chris Blackwell and Phil Scragg. *Now And Zen* was hailed as a dramatic return to form and a regenerated Plant now felt confident enough to include Zeppelin material in live shows. Indeed one of the album's standout tracks, 'Tall Cool One', featured a cameo from Jimmy Page and incorporated samples of 'Black Dog', 'Whole Lotta Love' and 'The Ocean', drawn from their former group's extensive catalogue. The singer's artistic rejuvenation continued on the acclaimed *Maniac Nirvana* and the excellent *Fate Of Nations*, before hooking up with Jimmy Page for the *Unledded/No Quarter* project, which at last satisfied those who would never have the vocalist forget his past.

Albums: *Pictures At Eleven* (Swan Song 1982), *The Principle Of Moments* (Swan Song 1983), *Skaken 'N' Stirred* (Esparanza 1985), *Now And Zen* (Esparanza 1989), *Maniac Nirvana* (Atlantic 1990), *Fate Of Nations* (Fontana 1993). With Jimmy Page: *No Quarter* (Fontana 1994).

Videos: *Knebworth 90* (1990), *Mumbo Jumbo* (1991).

Pleasure Elite

Pleasure Elite were formed in winter 1990 in Seattle, USA, around pseudonymous musicians V. Blast (vocals), Lord Hoop De' Luv (guitar/vocals/sequencer), the Deacon (keyboards), Razor Monkey (drums) and Father Shark (guitar). Boasting a frenetic live show which won them early supports with KMFDM, Rage Against The Machine, Jesus Jones and Alien Sex Fiend, the band's lyrical concerns included media manipulation, lust and corruption. They made their debut with *Bad Juju* in May 1994, an album which delighted in crossing sundry musical frontiers including industrial metal and more traditional rock structures. With production by Pearl Jam associate Don Gilmore, the collection was promoted by the release of a strong attendant single, 'Media Feed'.

Album: *Bad Juju* (Music For Nations 1994).

Point Blank

Essentially from the same mould as Texan blues boogie supremos, Z.Z. Top, Point Blank's first two releases were produced by Bill Ham who had also masterminded the latter's rise to fame. Point Blank's line-up has been somewhat fluid but in the main featured John O'Daniel (vocals), Rusty Burns (guitar), Kim Davis (guitar), Bill Randolph (bass), Mike Hamilton (keyboards) and Buzzy Gren (drums). Their third venture into the recording studio resulted in *Airplay* which saw a slightly less intensive boogie stance, but this was rectified on *The Hard Way*, a part-live release which saw the band in blistering form. Bobby Keith replaced John O'Daniel in 1981 and their last two albums reflected a more radio-friendly approach to their sound, but without commercial success.

Albums: *Point Blank* (Arista 1976), *Second Season* (Arista 1977), *Airplay* (MCA 1979), *The Hard Way* (MCA 1980), *American Excess* (MCA 1981), *On A Roll* (MCA 1982).

Poison

This heavy metal band was formed in Pennsylvania, USA, in the spring of 1983 by Bret Michaels (b. Bret Sychalk, 15 March 1962, Harrisburg, Pennsylvania, USA; vocals) and Rikki Rockett (b. Richard Ream, 8 August 1959, Pennsylvania, USA; drums). They were soon joined by Bobby Dall (b. Kuy Kendall, 2 November 1958, Miami, Florida, USA; bass) and Matt Smith (guitar). Legendarily, Slash from Guns N'Roses would also audition at one point. The quartet played local clubs as Paris, before moving to Los Angeles and changing their name. It was at this point that Smith left the band and was replaced by C.C. Deville (b. 14 May 1963, Brooklyn, New York, USA; guitar). They were signed by Enigma Records in 1985 and released their first album in 1986, which went double platinum in America and produced three hits. *Open Up And Say...Ahh!* gave them their first US number 1, 'Every Rose Has Its Thorn'. Four other singles were also released, including a cover of 'Your Mama Don't Dance' which was a major US hit for Loggins And Messina in 1972. Poison were originally considered a 'glam band' because of the make-up they wore, but by the release of *Flesh And Blood*, in 1990, this image had been toned down dramatically. That year they also played their first UK shows, and fans declared their love of songs like 'Unskinny Bop' and 'Talk Dirty To Me' when the band made their official UK debut in front of 72,500 people at the Donnington Monsters of Rock Festival on 18 August 1990. The following year saw Deville replaced on guitar by the much-travelled Richie Kotzen. *Native Tongue* also had the addition of brass with the Tower Of Power Horns and eastablished the band alongside Bon Jovi as purveyors of image-conscious hard melodic rock. As well as many supporters, this naturally also saw them pilloried by more purist elements in heavy metal fandom. 1994 saw Michaels' face on the newstands once more as he dated *Baywatch* star Pamela Anderson, before being unceremoniously 'dumped' when it was decided that Michaels' press image did not fit with hers.

Albums: *Look What The Cat Dragged In* (Enigma 1986), *Open Up And Say...Ahh!* (Capitol 1988), *Flesh And Blood* (Capitol 1990), *Native Tongue* (Capitol 1993).

Video: *A Sight For Sore Ears* (1990).

Poison Idea

These hardcore heavyweights' broad appearance (nearly all members of the band could look on the term obese as a description of kindness) gave little credence to the harsh, speedy rock path they pursued. Formed in Portland, Oregon, USA, in late 1980, their first incarnation featured Jerry A. (vocals), Pig Champion (guitar), Chris Tense (bass) and Dean Johnson (drums). They debuted with the unwieldy EP *Pick Your King* which contained no less than 13 tracks, packaged in a sleeve featuring Elvis Presley on one side and Jesus Christ on the other. By the time of *Kings Of Punk* they were slightly more tuneful, but no less belligerent. However, Johnson and Tense were both fired and replaced by Steve 'Thee Slayer Hippy' Hanford (drums) and Tim Paul (ex-Final Warning, now Gruntruck; bass). The sound was also filled out with additional guitarist Vegetable (ex-Mayhem). However, Tim Paul only lasted one abortive gig (just one song, in fact) before being replaced by the returning Tense. His tenure, though slightly longer, lasted only until the release of *War All The Time*, after which Mondo (also ex-Mayhem) joined. The line-up wars continued after 'Getting The Fear' was released, with Vegetable sacked on New Year's Eve, replaced by Kid Cocksman (ex-Gargoyle; guitar), and Mondo quit after the appropriately titled 'Discontent'. Myrtle Tickner (ex-Oily Bloodmen) then became the band's fourth bass player. Aldine Striknine (guitar; ex-Maimed For Life) stepped in for the next casualty Kid Cocksman (apparently kicked out for being too thin) to record *Feel The Darkness*, after which Mondo returned once more, this time on second guitar. Despite the line-up confusions and obvious gimmickry, they produced a body of work of some substance, characterized by a lyrical preference for matters alcoholic and sexual, with some of the world's great song titles ('Record Collectors Are Pretentious

Assholes', etc.). Live they were both enormously impressive, and impressively enormous. After *We Must Burn* Poison Idea disbanded with Tense and Johnson going on to form Apartment 3G.

Albums: *Kings Of Punk* (Pusmort 1986), *War All The Time* (Alchemy 1987), *Record Collectors Are Pretentious Assholes* (Bitzcore 1989), *Poison Idea* (In Your Face 1989), *Feel The Darkness* (Vinyl Solution 1990), *Pajama Party* (Vinyl Solution 1992), *Blank, Blackout, Vacant* (Vinyl Solution 1992), *We Must Burn* (Vinyl Solution 1993).

Porno For Pyros

This theatrical rock act was formed by Jane's Addiction frontman Perry Farrell in 1992, following the demise of his previous act. Enlisting former bandmate Stephen Perkins (drums), bassist Martyn Lenoble and guitarist Peter DiStephano, Farrell began developing his new band's direction during their low-key live debut on the Lollapalooza II second stage. With Farrell's creative input and Perkins' rhythmic talents, similarities between Porno For Pyros and Jane's Addiction's recorded output were inevitable, but the subtle shift in musical direction became more obvious in the live setting. Porno For Pyros' shows were closer in character to a carnival, with Farrell as ringmaster, than a traditional rock show, with the band augmented not only by Matt Hyde's keyboards but also by a cast of dancers and performance artists, from the ballerina pirouetting to 'Orgasm', to the sharp contrast of the fire-breathing stripper who appeared during 'Porno For Pyros'. The band subsequently headlined at the 1993 Reading Festival in spectacular fashion, and also appeared at the Woodstock Anniversary show in 1994.

Albums: *Porno For Pyros* (Warners Bros 1993).

Possessed

Formed in San Francisco, California, USA, in 1983, this heavy metal band consisted of Jeff Beccarra (bass/vocals), Mike Tarrao (guitar), Larry Lalonde (guitar) and Mike Sus (drums). Through early demos and their inclusion on the *Metal Massacre VI* compilation album, released on Metal Blade Records in 1984, the band attracted the attention of Combat Records who promptly signed the band. This resulted in their debut, *Seven Churches*, released in 1985. Growling vocals and ultra-fast Slayer-influenced riffs were the order of the day and the band quickly made their mark on the death metal underground. The next album, produced by ex-Rods drummer Carl Canedy, entitled *Beyond The Gates* released in 1986 the band had toured throughout Europe building a strong following. On their return to America the band

recorded and released a mini-album entitled *The Eyes Of Terror*. Produced by guitar maestro Joe Satriani, the album was, as expected, heavily guitar-oriented but due to internal band wrangles the band folded soon after its release.

Albums: *Seven Churches* (Roadrunner 1985), *Beyond The Gates* (Under One Flag 1986), *The Eyes Of Terror* (Under One Flag 1987, mini-album).

Powell, Cozy

b. Colin Powell, 29 December 1947, England. Powell is a virtuoso drummer who has played with the likes of Jeff Beck, Rainbow and Emerson, Lake And Powell. His musical career began in 1965 when he was a member of the Sorcerers, before working with Casey Jones And The Engineers for a couple of months, then returning to his first band, who would change their name first to Youngblood, and then to Ace Kefford Stand. Powell then moved on to Big Bertha. In 1971 Jeff Beck founded a new group consisting of Robert Tench (vocals), Max Middleton (keyboards), Clive Chaman (bass), and Powell. The Jeff Beck group were among the premier exponents of R&B jazz-rock, and Powell appears on two of their albums. It was after his work with Bedlam, the band he formed in 1972 with Frank Aiello (vocals), Dennis Ball (bass) and Dave Ball (guitar), that Powell came to the attention of producer Micky Most. This gave Powell the opportunity to release hit singles such as 'Dance With The Devil' and 'The Man In Black'. This latter single was recorded whilst Powell was in Cozy Powell's Hammer, a group with Bedlam's Aiello as vocalist, along with newcomers Don Airey (keyboards), Clive Chaman (bass) and Bernie Marsden (guitar). This project came to an end in April 1975 when Powell decided to take a break and spend three months motor racing. Strange Brew was formed in July 1975, with Powell on drums, but this project lasted for little more than a month. He then joined Ritchie Blackmore's Rainbow, with whom he played until 1980, his farewell concert with them being at the first Donington Rock festival. In 1981 Powell appeared on the Michael Schenker Group's *MSG*, and in the mid-80s replaced Carl Palmer, becoming the third member of Emerson, Lake And Powell. He also released three solo sets in the early 80s, working with Gary Moore among other name musicians. The album he recorded with Emerson, Lake And Powell had little chart success and his tenure with the group was short, as was now becoming customary for the artist (he also played for two years in Whitesnake). In 1990 Powell appeared on and produced Black Sabbath's *Headless Cross*.

Albums: With Jeff Beck: *Rough And Ready* (Epic

1971), *The Jeff Beck Group* (Epic 1972). With Bedlam: *Bedlam* (Chrysalis 1973). With Rainbow: *Rising* (Polydor 1976), *On Stage* (Polydor 1977), *Long Live Rock 'N' Roll* (Polydor 1978), *Down To Earth* (Polydor 1979). With the Michael Schenker Group: *MSG* (Chrysalis 1981). With Whitesnake: *Saints 'N' Sinners* (Liberty 1982), *Slide It In* (Liberty 1983). With Emerson, Lake And Powell: *Emerson, Lake And Powell* (Polydor 1985). With Forcefield: *Forcefield* (President 1987), *Forcefield II* (President 1988), *Forcefield III* (President 1989). With Black Sabbath: *Headless Cross* (IRS 1990). Solo: *Over The Top* (Ariola 1979), *Tilt* (Polydor 1981), *Octopus* (Polydor 1983), *The Drums Are Back* (1992).

Power

US quartet hailing from New Jersey, built on the skills of Alan Tecchio (ex-Hades, Watchtower; vocals), Daniel Dalley (ex-solo; guitar), Mike Watt (drums) and Bill Krohn (bass). Watt had previously attended Boston's Berklee College Of Music, while acclaimed guitarist Dalley had released a solo instrumental album in 1989 as well as being a regular interviewee in musician's magazines.. However, frontman Tecchio was the best known member, in addition to his previous activities being concurrently part of Non-Fiction. Power signed to European label Rock The Nation Records for the release of *Justice Of Fire* in 1994, which typically addressed its thematic constructs against a background of riffing and power surges.
Album: *Justice Of Fire* (RTN 1994).

Praying Mantis

Formed in London, England, in 1977, Praying Mantis were at the forefront of the New Wave Of British Heavy Metal. The original line-up consisted of Tino 'Troy' Neophytou (guitar/vocals), Robert Angelo (guitar), Tino's brother Chris 'Troy' Neophytou (bass/vocals) and Mick Ransome (drums). Through early demo recordings the band attracted the attention of heavy metal club DJ Neal Kay, who helped them release an independent three-track EP, *The Soundhouse Tapes Vol. 2*, a title also used by Iron Maiden for their first release. The band's career can be closely linked with Iron Maiden during those early years as in addition to both bands appearing on the *Metal For Muthas* compilation released by EMI Records in 1980, they also toured England together. Signing to Arista Records and replacing Robert Angelo (who joined Weapon in July 1981) and Mick Ransome with guitarist/vocalist Steve Carroll and ex-Ten Years After drummer Dave Potts, the band's debut, *Time Tells No Lies*, was

released in 1981. It was not well received due to the lacklustre production and basic melodic rock sound. The band decided a line-up change was needed, replacing the departed Steve Carroll with ex-Grand Prix vocalist Bernie Shaw, and they also recruited keyboard player Jon Bavin. This line-up went on to record 'Turn The Tables' for a compilation album released on the Yet Records label in the mid-80s. Through a lack of media interest the band metamorphosised into Stratus, who specialized in standard melodic rock and also featured ex-Iron Maiden drummer Clive Burr. To celebrate the 10th anniversary of the N.W.O.B.H.M. the band reformed early in 1990 to tour Japan as part of the British All Stars. This new line-up consisted of founder members Tino and Chris Troy, ex-Iron Maiden vocalist Paul Di'anno, ex-Iron Maiden guitarist Dennis Stratton and ex-Weapon drummer Bruce Bisland.
Albums: *Time Tells No Lies* (Arista 1981), *Predator In Disguise* (1993).

Precious Metal

This US glam-metal rock group were formed in Los Angeles, California, in the mid-80s. They came to the public's attention via their 1985 debut, *Right Here, Right Now*, which was produced by AOR producer and guitar-hero, Paul Sabu. An all-female outfit, they featured Leslie Wasser (vocals), Janet Robin (guitar), Mara Fox (guitar), Alex Rylance (bass) and Carol Control (drums). Unfairly categorized alongside 70s female outfit the Runaways, Precious Metal set about forging an original style. They were hampered in this by the inability of the hard rock press to critically engage with female bands above and beyond obvious comparisons and cosmetic factors. Their second and third album releases demonstrated that, at the very least, there was more potential at work than they were being given credit for.
Albums: *Right Here, Right Now* (Polygram 1985), *That Kind Of Girl* (Chameleon 1988), *Precious Metal* (Chameleon 1990).

Pretty Maids

This Danish heavy metal quintet was formed in 1981 by vocalist Ronnie Atkins and guitarist Ken Hammer. Taking their musical brief from British acts Deep Purple, Judas Priest and UFO, their style was such that enthusiasm often outweighed originality. The band have been through numerous line-up changes, with the current outfit comprising Atkins and Hammer along with Ricky Marx (guitar), Allan Delong (bass) and Phil Moorhead (drums). Although competent musicians, at times their delivery, image, and song titles provoked Spinal Tap comparisons in

Primus

the press. *Future World* from 1987 is the band's strongest release to date. The more recent Roger Glover-produced *Jump The Gun* failed to offer anything new, aside from affording the band the opportunity of working with one of their obvious heroes.

Albums: *Pretty Maids* (Bullet 1983), *Red, Hot And Heavy* (CBS 1984), *Future World* (CBS 1987), *Jump The Gun* (CBS 1990).

Primus

The vast majority of reviewers can generally agree on one word to describe Primus - weird. Formed in San Francisco in 1984 by former Blind Illusion bassist Les Claypool, seven drummers passed through before Tim 'Herb' Alexander settled in, with Claypool's Blind Illusion colleague, ex-Possessed man Larry Lalonde replacing original guitarist Todd Huth shortly before the band recorded their debut. Musically, the band are highly talented and original, mixing funk, punk, thrash, metal and rock in their own intense manner, once described by Claypool as 'psychedelic polka'. Claypool and Alexander produce quirky, sometimes hypnotic rhythms, accentuating each other's playing, while former Joe Satriani pupil Lalonde creates and colours within the framework, although his playing owes more to Frank Zappa than to that of his old teacher. Claypool's vocals lean towards cartoonish narrative, with lyrics of a suitably abstract and humorous nature, drawing from both life and his film and literary influences. A common theme to all their albums is marine life, reflecting the band's passion for sea-fishing (they have played with fish-shaped covers on their vocal microphones). Their debut, *Such On This*, was a self-financed live set successfully released on their own Prawn Song label, and much of the material was to feature on *Fizzle Fry*, an independent studio release which won a Bay Area Music Award and, helped by touring with Faith No More, Jane's Addiction, 24-7 Spyz and Living Colour, a major record deal. *Sailing The Seas Of Cheese* further raised their profile, with their reworking of 'Tommy The Cat' from the debut (with a Tom Waits guest vocal) featuring in hit movie *Bill & Ted's Bogus Journey*. A lengthy world tour in support of Rush was then followed by stadium dates with U2. Any doubts as to the band being a sufficient draw for the closing (effectively headlining) slot on the 1993 Lollapalooza tour were dispelled when *Pork Soda* debuted in the US charts at number 7, producing a hit in 'My Name Is Mud'. Claypool would also hook up with Huth and former Primus drummer Jay Lane to form side-project Sausage, recording *Riddles Are Abound Tonight* for Interscope in 1994.

Albums: *Suck On This* (Prawn Song 1990), *Frizzle Fry* (Caroline 1990), *Sailing The Seas Of Cheese* (Interscope 1991), *Pork Soda* (Interscope 1993).

Princess Pang

This New York-based rock quintet was formed in 1986 around the nucleus of Jeni Foster (vocals), Ronnie Roze (bass) and Brian Keats (drums). The line-up was finally completed a year later by the addition of guitarists Jay Lewis and Andy Tyernon. Signing to Metal Blade Records, they were introduced to Ron St. Germain (of Bad Brains fame) who eventually handled the production of their debut. Released in 1989, it was a gutsy hard rock album, full of tales of New York's low-life. Foster, with her aggressive delivery, drew comparisons to Guns N' Roses' Axl Rose, though the band failed to capitalise on the attentive press they initially received.

Album: *Princess Pang* (Roadrunner 1989).

Prism

This Canadian rock group has always proved difficult to categorize in terms of musical style, and major commercial success has proven similarly elusive. Their most stable line-up comprised Ron Tabak (vocals - replaced by Henry Small in 1981), Lindsay Mitchell (guitar), Al Harlow (bass) and Rocket Norton (drums). Their first two releases on the Ariola label were lightweight pop rock workouts with layered keyboards fills, while *Armageddon* saw the band, now signed to the Capitol label, move towards a heavier, grandiose style. with several lengthy compositions. Their next two recordings saw further line-up changes and resulted in a more typical American rock sound, ideal for radio consumption. In the process they found considerable success as a live act on the US circuit. However, just as long-term rewards seemed within reach, Ron Tabak was killed in a car crash during 1984. Prism died with him.

Albums: *Prism* (Ariola 1977), *See Forever Eyes* (Ariola 1978), *Armageddon* (Ariola 1979), *Young And Restless* (Capitol 1980), *Small Change* (Capitol 1981), *Beat Street* (Capitol 1983). Compilation: *The Best Of Prism* (Phonogram 1988).

Pro-Pain

This New York hardcore outfit was assembled by the former Crumbsuckers rhythm section of Gary Meskil (bass/vocals) and Dan Richardson (drums) after the demise of their old band. Tom Klimchuck provided the guitars on *Foul Taste Of Freedom*, a full-blooded and aggressive hardcore blast given a brutally heavy sound by producer Alex Perialas, and matched by typically challenging lyrics, an approach which drew Pantera and Biohazard comparisons. It also impressed Roadrunner Records sufficiently to gain the band a deal. However, Klimchuck departed shortly after the release to be replaced by Nick St Dennis, with a second guitarist in Mike Hollman (ex-Possessed) added later. Pro-Pain ran into problems over the original cover for *The Truth Hurts*, which depicted a stitched-up female torso after an autopsy, while the inner artwork featured a series of disturbing police photographs of street crime victims from the early 90s. Despite the fact that the cover was from an art exhibit in a prominent Indiana gallery and that the police photos were public domain, the cover was obscured by a large sticker in the USA, while it was replaced entirely in the UK, with the original available by mail order. The music, meanwhile, had acquired a new groove from the band's touring experience, while Meskil's lyrics remained true to his roots, with the social decay in his Long Island home a favourite subject.

Albums: *Foul Taste Of Freedom* (Energy 1992), *The Truth Hurts* (Roadrunner 1994).

Prong

This US thrash-hardcore rock trio was formed in the mid-80s. Hailing from New York's Manhattan lower east side, the band comprised Tommy Victor (vocals/guitar), Mike Kirkland (vocals/bass) and Ted Parsons (drums), and caused an immediate stir with their first release on the independent Spigot label. Emotionally angry, lyrically brutal, Prong partnered a relentless assault with some fierce guitar-riffing. Their second album for Epic, *Prove You Wrong*, in 1991, was their most significant work to date. By the advent of *Cleansed* the group had expanded to a four-piece. First they had added ex-Flotsam & Jetson bass player Tony Gregory, before recruiting Killing Joke musician Raven, who had previously worked with the band on their *Whose Fist Is It Anyway* remix EP. John Bechdel of Murder Inc. additionally expanded the band's sound with his programming and sampling skills.

Albums: *Primitive Origins* (Spigot 1987), *Force Fed* (Spigot 1988), *Beg To Differ* (Epic 1990), *Prove You Wrong* (Epic 1991), *Cleansed* (Epic 1994).

Pungent Stench

A Viennese death metal band, Pungent Stench began as a musical project in February 1988. In this form they released a split album with the Disharmonic

Orchestra and an EP entitled *Extreme Deformity* in 1989. Their increasing popularity among fans of extreme, grotesque music soon convinced them to become a permanent unit, comprising Alex Wank (drums), Jacek Perkowski (bass) and bositerous frontman Martin Schirenc (vocals/guitar). After an undistinguished first album they released *Been Caught Buttering*, a strong development in Pungent Stench's distinctive style. The death metal genre has always been fixated with blood and guts, but Pungent Stench took things further with a level of sickness which showed a certain morbid panache. They also have a rampant sense of humour which runs throughout their gross lyrics and nauseating artwork, while touring committments with Type O Negative, Brutal Truth and Soldom helped spread their warped messages around the world. Later releases, such as the 1993 EP *Dirty Rhymes and Psychotronic Beats*, highlighted the funk or even dance-related elements in their death metal cocktail. *Club MONDO BIZARRE For Members Only* revealed an increasing tendency towards material concerning sexual deviance (fitting, perhaps, for a band hailing from the same city as Freud).
Albums: *For God Your Soul... For Me Your Flesh* (Nuclear Blast 1990, remixed and re-released in 1993), *Been Caught Buttering* (Nuclear Blast 1991), *Club MONDO BIZARRE For Members Only* (Nuclear Blast 1994).
Video: *La Muerte* (1993).

Q5

This US group was formed in Seattle, Washington, in 1983 by the innovative guitarist Floyd Rose. He is otherwise best known for being the inventor of the locking tremelo system, the now indispensable device that ensures the guitar stays in tune even after the heaviest of tremelo use. Joining Floyd Rose in Q5 were Jonathan K (vocals), Rick Pierce (guitar), Evan Sheeley (bass/keyboards) and Gary Thompson (drums), all previously with TKO. Signing to the small independent label Albatross Records, the band released their debut, *Steel The Light*, in 1984. It was later released in Europe on the Roadrunner Records label in 1985. The album was typically Americanized

melodic hard rock and in a glut of such releases passed largely unnoticed. Floyd Rose built his own recording studio at his home which the band then used for the recording of a second album. With virtually unlimited studio time available, *When The Mirror Cracks* was released on the Music For Nations label in 1986. Full of strong, melodic compositions, it did, however, tend to sound slightly over-produced. The band fell apart in 1987, and Floyd Rose will be remembered more for his contribution to guitar technology than his recordings with Q5.
Albums: *Steel The Light* (Albatross 1984), *When The Mirror Cracks* (Music For Nations 1986).

Quartz

Quartz were formed in Birmingham, England, in 1974 by ex-Idle Race guitarist Mike Hopkins and local singer Mike Taylor, initially taking the name Bandylegs. Two years later they joined forces with Geoff Nicholls (guitar/keyboards), Dek Arnold (bass/vocals) and Mal Cope (drums) to become Quartz. It was their friendship with Black Sabbath's Tony Iommi that helped get them a deal with Jet Records, and Iommi agreed to produce their first album as well as taking them on Sabbath's 1977 tour. *Quartz* should have been a stepping stone to stardom but the group were deluged by press accusations of plagiarism of their sponsors. By 1978 they had been dropped by Jet, and found themselves moving from label to label in search of commercial success. Indie imprint Reddingtons Rare Records offered a new bolthole in 1980 as Quartz had a crack at the singles market with their version of Mountain's classic, 'Nantucket Sleighride', which was used as the theme to UK television's *Weekend World* current affairs programme. The band soldiered on, releasing a 12-inch red vinyl single, 'Satan's Serenade', also on Reddingtons, and had a track featured on EMI's *Mutha's Pride* EP showcase after becoming caught up in the New Wave Of British Heavy Metal. Jet reissued their debut album in a large brown paper bag with a competition which allowed the winning entrant to fill said recepticle at a famous record shop. This promotion was backed up with a mini-tour followed by support slots to Gillan on his UK tour. MCA finally picked up their contract and released *Stand Up And Fight*, which contained one of their best-loved numbers in 'Stoking Up The Fires Of Hell'. Nicholls began to moonlight by playing keyboards for Black Sabbath and later joined them on a full-time basis when Quartz ground to a halt in 1984.
Albums: *Quartz* (Jet 1977), *Live Songs* (Logo 1980), *Stand Up And Fight* (MCA 1980), *Against All Odds* (Heavy Metal 1983).

Queen

Arguably Britain's most consistently successful group of the past two decades, Queen began life as a glam rock unit in 1972. Brian May (b. 19 July 1947, Twickenham, Middlesex, England; guitar) and Roger Taylor (b. Roger Meddows-Taylor, 26 July 1949, Kings Lynn, Norfolk, England; drums) had been playing in a college group called Smile with bassist Tim Staffell. When the latter left to join Humpty Bong (featuring former Bee Gees drummer Colin Petersen), May and Taylor elected to form a new band with vocalist Freddie Mercury (b. Frederick Bulsara, 5 September 1946, Zanzibar, Africa, d. 24 November 1991). Early in 1971 bassist John Deacon (b. 19 August 1951, Leicester, England) completed the line-up. Queen were signed to EMI late in 1972 and launched the following spring with a gig at London's Marquee club. Soon after the failed single, 'Keep Yourself Alive', they issued a self-titled album, which was an interesting fusion of 70s glam and late 60s heavy rock (it had been preceded by a Mercury 'solo' single, credited to Larry Lurex). Queen toured extensively and recorded a second album which fulfilled their early promise by reaching the UK Top 5. Soon after, 'Seven Seas Of Rhye' gave them their first hit single, while *Sheer Heart Attack* consolidated their commercial standing. The title-track from the album was also the band's first US hit. The pomp and circumstance of Queen's recordings and live act were embodied in the outrageously camp theatrics of the satin-clad Mercury, who was swiftly emerging as one of rock's most notable showmen during the mid-70s. 1975 was to prove a watershed in the group's career. After touring the Far East, they entered the studio with producer Roy Thomas Baker and completed the epic 'Bohemian Rhapsody', in which Mercury succeeded in transforming a seven-minute single into a mini-opera. The track was both startling and unique in pop and dominated the Christmas charts in the UK, remaining at number 1 for an astonishing nine weeks. The power of the single was reinforced by an elaborate video production, highly innovative for its period and later much copied by other acts. An attendant album, *A Night At The Opera*, was one of the most expensive and expansive albums of its period and lodged at number 1 in the UK, as well as hitting the US Top 5. Queen were now aspiring to the superstar bracket. Their career thereafter was a carefully marketed succession of hit singles, annual albums and extravagantly produced stage shows. *A Day At The Races* continued the bombast, while the catchy 'Somebody To Love' and anthemic 'We Are The Champions' both reached number 2 in the UK. Although Queen seemed in danger of being stereotyped as over-produced glam rock refugees, they successfully brought eclecticism to their singles output with the 50s rock 'n' roll panache of 'Crazy Little Thing Called Love' and the disco-influenced 'Another One Bites The Dust' (both US number 1s). Despite this stylistic diversity, each Queen single seemed destined to become an anthem, as evidenced by the continued use of much of their output on US sporting occasions. The group's soundtrack for the movie *Flash Gordon* was another success, but was cited by many critics as typical of their pretentious approach. By the close of 1981, Queen were back at number 1 in the UK for the first time since 'Bohemian Rhapsody' with 'Under Pressure' (a collaboration with David Bowie). After a flurry of solo ventures, the group returned in fine form in 1984 with the satirical 'Radio Gaga', followed by the histrionic 'I Want To Break Free' (and accompanying cross-dressing video). A performance at 1985's Live Aid displayed the group at their most professional and many acclaimed them the stars of the day, though there were others who accused them of hypocrisy for breaking the boycott of apartheid-locked South Africa. Coincidentally, their next single was 'One Vision', an idealistic song in keeping with the spirit of Live Aid. Queen's recorded output lessened during the late 80s as they concentrated on extra-curricular ventures. The space between releases did not affect the group's popularity, however, as was proven in 1991 when *Innuendo* entered the UK chart at number 1. By this time they had become an institution. Via faultless musicianship, held together by May's guitar virtuosity and the spectacular Mercury; Queen were one of the great theatrical rock acts. The career of the group effectively ended with the death of lead singer Freddie Mercury on 24 November 1991. 'Bohemian Rhapsody' was immediately reissued to raise money for AIDS research projects, and soared to the top of the British charts. A memorial concert for Mercury took place at London's Wembley Stadium in the spring of 1992, featuring an array of stars including Liza Minnelli, Elton John, Guns N'Roses, George Michael, David Bowie and Annie Lennox (Eurythmics). Of the remaining members Brian May's solo career would enjoy the highest profile, while Roger Taylor would work with the Cross.

Albums: *Queen* (EMI 1973), *Queen II* (EMI 1974), *Sheer Heart Attack* (EMI 1974), *A Night At The Opera* (EMI 1975), *A Day At The Races* (EMI 1976), *News Of The World* (EMI 1977), *Jazz* (EMI 1978), *Live Killers* (EMI 1979), *The Game* (EMI 1980), *Flash Gordon* (EMI 1980), *Hot Space* (EMI 1982), *A Kind Of Magic* (EMI 1986), *Live Magic* (EMI 1986), *The Miracle* (EMI 1989), *Queen At The Beeb* (Band Of Joy

Quiet Riot

1989), *Innuendo* (EMI 1991). Compilations: *Greatest Hits* (EMI 1981), *The Works* (EMI 1984), *The Complete Works* (EMI 1985), *Greatest Hits Vol. 2* (EMI 1991).

Videos: *Greatest Flix* (1981), *We Will Rock You* (1984), *Live In Rio* (1985), *Live In Budapest* (1987), *Magic Years* (1987), *Rare Live - A Concert Through Time And Space* (1989), *The Miracle EP* (1989), *Queen At Wembley* (1990), *Greatest Flix II* (1991), *Box Of Flix* (1991).

Selected further reading: *Queen*, George Tremlett. *Official Biography*, Larry Pryce.

Queensrÿche

Queensrÿche were formed in Seattle, USA, by Geoff Tate (vocals), Chris DeGarmo (guitar), Michael Wilton (guitar), Eddie Jackson (bass), and Scott Rockenfield (drums), from the ashes of club circuit band the Mob and, in Tate's case, the Myth. Immediately Tate offered them a distinctive vocal edge, having studied opera but turned to hard rock because of the lyrical freedom it offered. A four track demo tape recorded in the basement of Rockenfield's parents house in June 1982 led to record store owners Kim and Diana Harris offering to manage the band. The tape itself took on a life of its own, circulating throughout the north west of America, and in May 1983 the band launched their own 206 Records label to house the songs on a self-titled 12-inch EP (lead track, 'Queen Of The Reich', had long since given them their name). The EP caused quite a stir in rock circles and led to EMI offering them a seven album deal. The record was quickly re-released and grazed the UK Top 75, although the band's sound was still embryonic and closer to Britain's N.W.O.B.H.M. than the progressive rock flavour which would become their hallmark. Their first full album for EMI, *The Warning*, was comparatively disappointing, failing to live up to the promise shown on the EP, particularly in the poor mix which was the subject of some concern for both the record company and band. Only 'Road To Madness' and 'Take Hold Of The Flame', two perennial live favourites, met expectations. *Rage For Order* followed in 1986 and saw the band creating a more distinctive style, making full use of modern technology, yet somehow the production (this time from Neil Kernon) seemed to have over-compensated. Although a dramatic improvement, and the first genuine showcase for Tate's incredible vocal range and the twin guitar sound of DeGarmo and Wilton, the songs emerged as clinical and neutered. 1988 saw the Peter Collins-produced *Operation Mindcrime*, a George Orwell-inspired concept album which was greeted with enthusiastic critical acclaim on its release. With some of the grandiose futurism of earlier releases dispelled, and additional orchestration from Michael Kamen, worldwide sales of over one million confirmed this as the album to lift the band into rock's first division. In the wake of its forerunner, there was something positively minimal about *Empire*, which boasted a stripped-down but still dream-like rock aesthetic best sampled on the single, 'Silent Lucidity', a Top 5 US hit, which was also nominated for a Grammy. The album itself earned Top 10 placings on both sides of the Atlantic. Only single releases broke a four year recording gap between *Empire* and 1994's *Promised Land*, the most notable of which was 1993's 'Real World', included on the soundtrack to the Arnold Schwarzenegger flop *Last Action Hero*. Though a more personal and reflective set, *Promised Land* continued the band's tradition of dramatic song structures, this time without Kamen's arranging skills. Over a decade into a career which at first seemed of limited appeal, Queensrÿche's popularity continues to grow.

Albums: *The Warning* (EMI 1984), *Rage For Order* (EMI 1986), *Operation Mindcrime* (EMI 1988), *Empire* (EMI 1990, double album), *Promised Land* (EMI 1994). Compilation: *Queensrÿche* (EMI 1988; includes *Queensrÿche* and *Prophecy* EPs).

Videos: *Live In Tokyo* (1985), *Video Mindcrime* (1989), *Building Empires* (1993).

Quicksand

This band grew from roots in the 80s New York hardcore scene, but evolved towards an intense, cerebral delivery akin to that of Prong, Tool and Helmet. The line-up of Walter Schriefels (guitar/vocals), Sergio Vega (bass), Tom Capone (guitar) and Alan Cage (drums) made their debut with an independently released EP, stimulating enough interest to gain both major recording and management deals. *Slip* was a strong full debut, built on Quicksand's ability to blend melodic songwriting with dense riffing, and drew Fugazi comparisons amid considerable music press acclaim. The band's low-key approach and anti-image made a major breakthrough difficult, however, despite an extensive touring schedule which included dates with Rage Against The Machine.

Album: *Slip* (Polygram 1993).

Quiet Riot

Heavy metal band Quiet Riot had their 'five minutes' of fame in 1983 with a remake of a Slade song, 'Cum On Feel The Noize', and a US number 1 album, *Metal Health* - the first metal album to reach that position in the US charts. However, they were unable to maintain that momentum with subsequent releases. The band formed in 1975 with lanky vocalist Kevin DuBrow (b. 1955), Randy Rhoads (guitar), Drew Forsyth (drums) and Kelly Garni (bass), taking their name from a suggestion made by Status Quo's Rick Parfitt. They recorded two albums with that line-up, released only in Japan, which are now collector's items. Rudy Sarzo then replaced Garni. Rhoads left in 1979 to join Ozzy Osbourne and was later tragically killed in a plane crash in March 1982. At that point the band briefly split up, with some members joining the vocalist in a band called DuBrow, Sarzo also working with Ozzy. Quiet Riot regrouped around DuBrow, Sarzo, guitarist Carlos Cavazo and drummer Frankie Banali and signed to the Pasha label for their breakthrough album and single in 1983, their musical and visual style fashioned after the harder rocking glam acts of the 70s. Friction within the group followed their quick success and resultant publicity affected sales of the follow-up, *Condition Critical*, which reached number 15 in the US charts but was considered disappointing. After several personnel changes Quiet Riot recorded another album in 1986, which reached number 31 but showed a marked decline in the group's creativity. DuBrow was subsequently ejected from the band and a self-titled 1988 album, with new vocalist Paul Shortino (ex-Rough Cutt), barely made the charts. The group then disbanded, with DuBrow going on to form Little Women. Banali would later work with W.A.S.P.

Albums: *Quiet Riot* (Columbia Japan 1977), *Quiet Riot II* (Columbia Japan 1978), *Metal Health* (Epic 1983), *Condition Critical* (Epic 1984), *QRIII* (Epic 1986), *Quiet Riot* (Pasha 1988). Compilation: *Wild Young And Crazee* (Raw Power 1987).

Quireboys

After violent incidents at early live shows, this UK band altered their name from Queerboys to Quireboys, to avoid further trouble. Comprising Spike (vocals), Nigel Mogg (bass; brother of Phil Mogg of UFO), Chris Johnstone (keyboards), Guy Bailey (guitar), Ginger (guitar) and Coze (drums), they were originally all drinking buddies in London pubs. Drawing musical inspiration from the Faces, Rolling Stones and Mott The Hoople, they specialized in bar-room boogie, beer-soaked blues and infectious raunch 'n' roll. Spike's rough-as-a-gravel-path vocal style, closely resembling Rod Stewart's, added fuel to accusations of the band being little more than Faces copyists. After releasing two independent singles they signed to EMI and

immediately underwent a line-up re-shuffle. Coze and Ginger were removed and replaced by Ian Wallace and Guy Griffin, respectively. They recorded *A Bit Of What You Fancy* in Los Angeles, under the production eye of Jim Cregan (former Rod Stewart guitarist). It was an immediate success, entering the UK album charts at number 2. 'Hey You', lifted as a single, also met with similar success, peaking at number 14 in January 1990. An eight-track live album followed, which duplicated most of the numbers from their first album, as a stop-gap measure to bridge the long period between successive studio releases. However, when *Bitter Sweet & Twisted* failed to ignite Spike would leave to form his own band, God's Hotel, denying rumours that he had been invited to replace Axl Rose in Guns N'Roses (after having contributed to Slash's solo album). The Quireboys had come to a natural conclusion, or, as Spike prefers to put it - 'we were past our sell-by-date'. Bassist Nigel Mogg put together his own project, the Nancy Boys, in New York.

Albums: *A Bit Of What You Fancy* (Parlophone 1989), *Live Around The World* (Parlophone 1990), *Bitter Sweet & Twisted* (Parlophone 1992). Compilation: *From Tooting To Barking* (Castle 1994). Video: *A Bit Of What You Fancy* (1990).

R

Rabin, Trevor

b. 1955, South Africa. Trevor Rabin learned classical piano and guitar from an early age, forming his first band, Rabbit, when he was aged only 14. Rabbit were a short-lived teenybop sensation in South Africa during the early 70s, releasing two albums which reached gold status. Moving to England in 1977, he signed to Chrysalis Records and polished up some demos he had previously recorded in South Africa for release as his first solo album. This featured a mixture of styles, and included jazz, rock, blues and AOR numbers. Future releases pursued a more mainstream melodic rock approach, with *Wolf*, released in 1981, being his *tour-de-force*. He also ventured into production with Wild Horses and Manfred Mann. He accepted the invitation to join Yes in 1983, and it was not until there was a major conflict in this camp that he managed to find enough time to record another solo effort. *Can't Look Away*, surfacing in 1989, had more in common with Yes than with his previous solo work. In 1990 he helped contribute to Seal's big-selling debut album.

Albums: *Trevor Rabin* (Chrysalis 1978), *Face To Face* (Chrysalis 1979), *Wolf* (Chrysalis 1981), *Can't Look Away* (Elektra 1989).

Racer X

This Los Angeles, California, USA band earned a reputation for guitar-orientated melodic rock, delivered with precision despite the blurring speed. Featuring Jeff Martin (vocals; ex-Surgical Steel), Paul Gilbert (guitar), John Alderete (bass) and Harry Gschoesser (drums; ex-Nobros) they released *Street Lethal*, a high-tech fusion of relentless guitar work and some memorable songs. Scott Travis (ex-Hawk) took over the drum stool and Bruce Bouillet was added as a second guitarist in 1986. By the time *Second Heat* was issued the following year the band had matured considerably, with the music more accomplished on several levels, most notably in arrangement and production. Paul Gilbert left in 1988 to join Mr. Big, and was replaced by Chris Arvan. Jeff Martin broke ranks shortly afterwards and Scott Travis understandably accepted the offer to join his heroes, Judas Priest. The band ground to a halt in 1990.

Albums: *Street Lethal* (Roadrunner 1986), *Second Heat* (Roadrunner 1987), *Extreme Volume...Live* (Roadrunner 1988), *Live...Extreme Vol. 2* (Roadrunner 1992).

Rage

Formerly known as Avenger, this German power trio changed their name to Rage in 1985, to avoid confusion with the British Avenger (and thereby get confused with the British band Rage). A series of line-up changes ensued before the combination of vocalist Peavey Wagner, guitarist Manni Schmidt and drummer Chris Efthimiadis gelled. Their first two albums were rather one-dimensional, being competent, but uninspiring techno-thrash affairs. With the recording of *Perfect Man*, they experimented more with song structures and had improved considerably as musicians. Future releases combined the technical prowess and subtle melodies of Rush, with the unbridled aggression of Megadeth. Their reputation in Germany has grown rapidly, but they have yet to make any significant impression outside their homeland.

Albums: *Reign Of Fear* (Noise 1986), *Execution Guaranteed* (Noise 1987), *Perfect Man* (Noise 1988), *Secrets In A Weird World* (Noise 1989), *Reflections Of A Shadow* (Noise 1990), *Beyond The Wall* (Noise 1992), *Saviour* (Noise 1993).

Rage Against The Machine

The name says everything about Rage Against The Machine. The aggressive musical blend of metal guitar and hip-hop rhythms is an appropriate background to the rap-styled delivery of angry, confrontational, political lyrics, addressing the band's concerns over inner city deprivation, racism, censorship, propaganda, the plight of Native Americans and many other issues as the band strive to be more than mere entertainment. Formed in Los Angeles in 1991 by former Lock Up guitarist Tom Morello and ex-Inside Out vocalist Zack de la Rocha, with bassist Timmy C and drummer Brad Wilk, Rage Against The Machine signed a major record deal with, importantly, creative control on the strength of a demo tape and some impressive early live shows. Further live work with Pearl Jam, Body Count, Tool and Suicidal Tendencies ensued, with the band encountering trouble with the French government during the Suicidal tour over t-shirts which showed a genuine CIA instructional cartoon on how to make a Molotov cocktail, taken from documents made for the Nicaraguan Contra rebels. The t-shirts were confiscated and destroyed by French Customs. The band subsequently released a self-titled debut, with a stunning cover photograph of a Buddhist monk burning himself to death in protest at the Vietnam War, and rose rapidly to fame, Henry Rollins describing them as 'the most happening band in the US'. The album was a hit on both sides of the Atlantic, and Rage Against The Machine scored single success with 'Killing In The Name', although de la Rocha was distinctly unhappy with a radio edit which removed all expletives and 'completely shut down the whole purpose of that song'. A sell-out UK tour in 1993 was followed by further powerful performances on the Lollapalooza festival tour in the USA.

Album: *Rage Against The Machine* (Epic 1992).

Raging Slab

Greg Strzempka (vocals/guitar) and Elyse Steinman (bottleneck guitar) formed Raging Slab in 1983, picking up lead guitarist Mark Middleton and bassist Alec Morton while going through numerous drummers, including ex-Whiplash/Slayer percussionist T.J. Scaglione and future Warrior Soul frontman Kory Clarke. The three-guitar frontline gave a definite Southern rock flavour to the Slab's basic rock 'n' roll, but gigging around the New York hardcore scene of the 80s also added a hard, contemporary edge. The band made their debut with *Assmaster*, which was elaborately packaged with a comic drawn by friends at *Marvel Comics*, and was followed by *True Death* as the band supported themselves with constant touring before a major deal emerged. *Raging Slab*, with latest drummer Bob Pantella, was excellent, with 'Geronimo', a sensitive lament to the fall of the Native American nation, as its centrepiece,. However, despite support tours with everyone from Mötley Crüe to the Butthole Surfers, it sold poorly. The band at last found a spiritual home and more creative freedom at Def American, and moved to a Pennsylvania farm where they built their own studio to record the acclaimed *Dynamite Monster Boogie Concert*. This was Raging Slab's most consistent work as they freely extended their talents in new directions, and finally felt at home with their 14th drummer, Paul Sheenan. The live shows were as hot as ever as the Slab toured America with Monster Magnet and undertook their first European tour.

Albums: *Assmaster* (Buy Our Records 1987), *True Death* (Buy Our Records 1988, mini-album), *Raging Slab* (RCA 1989), *Dynamite Monster Boogie Concert* (Def American 1993).

Rainbow

In 1975 guitarist Ritchie Blackmore (b. 14 April 1945, Weston-Super-Mare, England; guitar) left Deep Purple, forming Rainbow the following year. His earlier involvement with American band Elf led to his recruitment of the latter's Ronnie James Dio (vocals), Mickey Lee Soule, (keyboards), Craig Gruber on bass and Gary Driscoll as drummer. Their debut, *Ritchie Blackmore's Rainbow*, was released in 1975, and was undeservedly seen by some as a poor imitation of Deep Purple. The constant turnover of personnel was representative of Blackmore's quest for the ultimate line-up and sound. Dissatisfaction with the debut album led to new personnel being assembled. Jimmy Bain took over from Gruber, and Cozy Powell replaced Driscoll. With Tony Carey on keyboards, *Rainbow Rising* was released, an album far more confident than its predecessor. Shortly after this Bain and Carey left, being replaced by Bob Daisley and David Stone respectively. It was when Rainbow moved to America that difficulties between Dio and Blackmore came to a head, resulting in Dio's departure from the band in 1978. His replacement was Graham Bonnet, whose only album with Rainbow, *Down To Earth*, saw the return as bassist of Roger Glover, the man Blackmore had forced out of Deep Purple in 1973. The album was a marked departure from the Dio days, and while it is often considered one of the weaker Rainbow collections, it

Ratt

did provide an enduring single, 'Since You've Been Gone', written and originally recorded by Russ Ballard. Bonnet and Powell soon became victims of another reorganization of Rainbow's line-up. Drummer Bobby Rondinelli and particularly new vocalist Joe Lynn Turner brought an American feel to the band, a commercial sound introduced on *Difficult To Cure*, the album which produced their biggest hit in 'I Surrender'. Thereafter the group went into decline as their increasingly middle-of-the-road albums were ignored by fans (former Brand X drummer Chuck Burgi replaced Rondinelli for 1983's *Bent Out Of Shape*). In 1984 the Rainbow project was ended following the highly popular Deep Purple reunion. The group played its last gig on 14 March 1984 in Japan, accompanied by a symphony orchestra as Blackmore, with a typical absence of modesty, adapted Beethoven's 'Ninth Symphony'. A compilation, *Finyl Vinyl*, appeared in 1986, and (necessarily) featured several different incarnations of Rainbow as well as unreleased recordings.

Albums: *Ritchie Blackmore's Rainbow* (Oyster 1975), *Rainbow Rising* (Polydor 1976), *Live On Stage* (Polydor 1977), *Long Live Rock And Roll* (Polydor 1978), *Down To Earth* (Polydor 1979), *Difficult To Cure* (Polydor 1981), *Straight Between The Eyes* (Polydor 1982), *Bent Out Of Shape* (Polydor 1983). Compilations: *Best Of* (Polydor 1983), *Finyl Vinyl* (Polydor 1986, double album), *Live In Germany* (Connoisseur 1990, rec. 1976). Videos: *The Final Cut* (1986), *Live Between The Eyes* (1988).

Ram Jam

Formed in the mid-70s, Ram Jam was an east coast group best known for its one Top 20 single, 'Black Betty', in 1977. That song was the focus of a boycott by several groups who considered it offensive to black women, even though it had originally been written by Huddie 'Leadbelly' Ledbetter, the legendary black folk and blues singer. The group consisted of guitarist Bill Bartlett (b. 1949), bassist Howie Blauvelt (formerly a member of Billy Joel's early group the Hassles), singer Myke Scavone and drummer Pete Charles. Bartlett had earlier been lead guitarist with the Lemon Pipers. After leaving that group, Bartlett retired from music for some time, before recording a demo of the Leadbelly song. Released on Epic Records, it reached number 18, but the group never had another hit. In the UK they succeeded twice, in 1977 (number 7) and in 1990 a re-mix version made number 13 making them a quite extraordinary one-hit-wonder.

Albums: *Ram Jam* (Epic 1977), *Portrait Of An Artist As A Young Ram* (Epic 1978).

Ratt

This heavy metal group formed in Los Angeles, California, USA, and featured Stephen Pearcy (vocals), Robbin Crosby (guitar), Warren DeMartini (guitar), Juan Croucier (bass) and Bobby 'The Blotz' Blotzer (drums). They evolved out of 70s band Mickey Ratt, transmuting into their present form in 1983, with a hint of pop about their brand of metal similar to Cheap Trick or Aerosmith. They released a self-titled mini-album in 1983 on a local label, and struck up a close personal friendship with members of Mötley Crüe which no doubt helped them to sign to Atlantic the following year. They made their breakthrough with their first full album, *Out Of The Cellar*, which stayed in the *Billboard* Top 20 for six months. They toured with Ozzy Osbourne before joining a Billy Squier jaunt where they were apparently 'thrown off' because they were more popular than the headline act. Their subsequent output has seen them follow a familiar heavy metal route with accusations over sexist videos contrasting with their ability to sell out concert halls and produce recordings that regularly received gold discs. *Decimater* featured several songs co-written with Desmond Child and proved their most adventurous recording to date, though Crosby would depart after *Rat 'n' Roll*. In 1993 Pearcy unveiled his new outfit, Arcade, confirming the dissolution of the band.

Albums: *Ratt* (Time Coast 1983, mini-album), *Out Of The Cellar* (Atlantic 1984), *Invasion Of Your Privacy* (Atlantic 1985), *Dancing Undercover* (Atlantic 1986), *Reach For The Sky* (Atlantic 1988), *Decimater* (Atlantic 1990), *Rat 'n' Roll* (East West 1991). Video: *The Video* (1986).

Rattlesnake Kiss

Birmingham, UK-based heavy metal quintet, formed in 1990 by vocalist Sean Love and guitarists Ralph Cardall and Bill Carroll. Influenced by American bands such as Queensrÿche, Van Halen and Rush, their speciality was in highly sophisticated and technically accomplished hard rock. The songs, which came over more powerfully in a live setting than in the studio, combined power with musical precision. Picked up by the independent Sovereign label they released a self-titled debut album in early 1992, though this did not fully reflect the band's musical prowess or energy due to thin production. Album: *Rattlesnake Kiss* (Sovereign 1992).

Raven

Formed in 1980, Raven were one of the first bands to

Raven

be associated with the New Wave Of British Heavy Metal movement. Hailing from Newcastle, the group comprised the Gallagher brothers; John (vocals/bass) and Mark (guitar), plus drummer Rob 'Wacko' Hunter. Unleashing a three-component wall of noise punctuated by searing guitar work and shattering vocals, they signed to local independent label, Neat Records. Their reputation grew with the release of a single, 'Don't Need Your Money', and the ensuing live shows which promoted it. John Gallagher's trademark high-pitched vocals and the group's before-its-time speed metal were heard to best effect on four albums for Neat Records, including the excellent *Live At The Inferno*. They then relocated to America and secured a deal with Atlantic Records. Adopting a more melodic approach, *Stay Hard* emerged in 1985 and sold well, but only in their adopted territory - the home-grown fan base was left somewhat aghast. Since then the band has reverted back to its former blitzkrieg style, releasing a string of competent, but rather dated and pedestrian albums. Drummer Rob Hunter moved into production work in 1988, to be replaced by Joe Hasselvander.

Albums: *Rock Until You Drop* (Neat 1981), *Wiped Out* (Neat 1982), *All For One* (Neat 1983), *Live At The Inferno* (Neat 1984), *Stay Hard* (Atlantic 1985), *The Pack Is Back* (Atlantic 1986), *Life's A Bitch* (Atlantic 1987), *Nothing Exceeds Like Excess* (Under One Flag 1989). Compilation: *The Devil's Carrion* (Castle 1985, double album).

Re-Animator

Formed in Hull, England, in 1987, Re-Animator consisted of Kevin Ingleson (guitar/vocals), Mike Abel (guitar), John Wilson (bass) and Mark Mitchell (drums). Strongly influenced by the legacy of the New Wave Of British Heavy Metal, and armed with the new thrash metal musical attitude this had helped to inspire, the band signed to the Music For Nations subsidiary label, Under One Flag. They released their debut mini-album, *Deny Reality*, in 1989, a harsh barrage of guitars that stood them in good stead for their full album debut, *Condemned To Eternity*. This offered no great departure in musical style but was still regarded as a solid statement. The release of *Laughing* in 1991 saw a major change in direction for the band. Gone were the guitar set-pieces as the band incorporated funk elements in a manner approximating Red Hot Chili Peppers. Added to other stylistic experiments it resulted in an album which was neither one thing nor another. However, the new approach gelled better on 1993's agenda-setting *That Was Then, This Is Now*.

Albums: *Deny Reality* (Under One Flag 1989, mini-album), *Condemned To Eternity* (Under One Flag 1990), *Laughing* (Under One Flag 1991), *That Was Then, This Is Now* (Under One Flag 1993).

Real Kids

This American quartet, originally from Boston, gained recognition amid the punk-rock explosion in New York during the late 70s. Formed by vocalist/guitarist and part-time Modern Lover John Felice in 1975, they pre-dated the punk movement, but jumped on the bandwagon as soon as it started to roll. With bassist Allen 'Alpo' Paulino, Billy Borgioli (guitar) and Howard Ferguson (drums) completing the line-up, they were nevertheless a talented outfit. Delivering a varied and classy selection of predominantly high-energy rockers, they infused reggae, rock 'n' roll and pop influences into their songs, making them instantly memorable. Their self-titled debut, released in 1978, is one of the great unheralded classics of this genre. However, a big-seller it was not, and Felice moved over to a career as a Ramones roadie. He also worked as part of the Taxi Boys back in Boston. Borgioli and Ferguson departed to be replaced by Billy Cole and Robby 'Morocco' Morin before the recording of a second album. *Outta Place* was a disappointment, for Felice's new compositions lacked the infectious sparkle that made their debut so special. A shambolic live album, recorded in Paris in 1983, was their final offering before disbanding. Paulino and Borgioloi would form the Primitive Souls (one EP), while their former leader would resurface with John Felice And The Lowdowns.

Albums: *The Real Kids* (Red Star 1978), *Outta Place* (Star-Rhythm 1982), *All Kindsa Jerks Live* (New Rose 1983), *Hit You Hard* (New Rose 1983). Compilation: *Girls! Girls! Girls!* (Lolita 1983; comprises Real Kids and Taxi Boys recordings).

Realm

This Milwaukee, USA-based hi-tech thrash metal quintet was formed by guitarists Takis Kinis and Paul Laganowski in 1985. By a process of trial and error they finally completed the line-up with Mark Antoni (vocals), Steve Post (bass) and Mike Olson (drums). Following a string of successful club shows they landed support slots to Wendy 'O' Williams and Megadeth tours in 1986. Signing to Roadracer Records they released *Endless War* in 1988. This was a complex fusion of hard rock, thrash and jazz influences and included a remarkable cover of the Beatles' 'Eleanor Rigby'. Their second album saw them becoming arguably too complex with a multitude of unnecessary time-changes, rendering much of the material incoherent and unmelodic.

Albums: *Endless War* (Roadracer 1988), *Suiciety* (Roadracer 1990).

Reckless

This Canadian pop-metal act was formed by guitarist Steve Madden with Jan Melanson (vocals), Gene Stout (bass) and Gil Roberts (drums), originally under the name Harlow. *Reckless* emerged to a generally positive reception, with commercial guitar-led metal in a Van Halen vein given individual identity by Melanson's quirky vocal delivery. Coupled with the frontwoman's striking blond looks, this seemed to give Reckless a chance to stand out from the crowd. However, the album bombed, and the band broke up. Madden tried again with a new line-up featuring Doug Adams (vocals), Todd Pilon (bass) and Steve Wayne Lederman (drums), but while *Heart Of Steel* was another good effort based around Madden's stylish guitar work, it lacked the distinctive qualities of its predecessor, and the band faded.

Albums: *Reckless* (EMI 1981), *Heart Of Steel* (Heavy Metal America 1984).

Red Dogs

This blues-based UK rock 'n' roll quintet was formed in 1989 by Mickey 'The Vicar' Ripley (vocals) and Chris John (guitar). Enlisting the services of Mick Young (bass), Paul Guerin (guitar) and Stow (drums), the band signed to Episode Records the following year. They debuted with *Wrong Side Of Town*, a six-track offering which took the Rolling Stones as its primary influence. The Red Dogs raised their profile by supporting Cheap And Nasty and UFO on their 1991 UK tours. Taking their infectious brand of bar-room boogie to a larger stage proved initially successful, though afterwards they failed to heighten their profile significantly.

Album: *Wrong Side Of Town* (Episode 1989, mini-album).

Red Fun

A band from Stockholm, Sweden, formed in 1992, consisting of four veterans of that country's metal scene. Thomas Persson (vocals), whose mane of red hair gives the band their name, was formerly part of Alien. Tobbe Moen (bass) is an experienced session player, while Freddy von Gerber (drums) had appeared in a number of groups including Intermezzo, Bam Bam Boys, Rat Bat Blue and Easy Action. Kee Marcello (guitar) was also a member of the last-named band, as well as, more famously,

Red Hot Chili Peppers

Dan Reed Network

Europe. Having been built around Marcello and Persson's lifelong friendship, Red Fun recorded a self-titled debut album during the winter of 1992 as well as a promotional single, 'My Baby's Coming Back'. With press statements about putting some of the hedonism back in to hard rock following grunge's domination, and support slots to Guns N'Roses and Neil Young in the summer of 1993, Red Fun were set firm to appeal to traditionalists.

Album: *Red Fun* (Cheiron/Music For Nations 1993).

Red Hot Chili Peppers

These engaging Hollywood ruffians mixed funk and punk in the mid-80s and encouraged a legion of other bands to regurgitate the formula. Led by 'Antwan The Swan' (b. Anthony Kiedis; vocals), the band's original line-up also featured 'Flea' (b. Michael Balzary, Melbourne, Australia), Hillel Slovak (b. Israel; guitar, d. 25 June 1988) and Jack Irons (b. California, USA; drums). They began life as garage band Anthem before Balzary departed for seminal 80s punks Fear. When Irons and Slovak moved on to join the less notable What Is This?, the nails appeared to be firmly in place on the Anthem coffin. However, under their new name, the Red Hot Chili Peppers acquired a speculative recording deal with EMI America.

Unfortunately, as Irons and Slovak were under contract with their new band, their debut album had to be recorded with Jack Sherman on guitar and Cliff Martinez (ex-Captain Beefheart, Weirdos) on drums. Production was handled, somewhat surprisingly, by the Gang Of Four's Andy Gill. The results were disappointing. Nevertheless the band set about building their considerable reputation as a live outfit, much of which was fuelled by their penchant for appearing semi-naked or worse. Slovak returned to guitar duties for the second album, this time produced by George Clinton. Also featured was a horn section comprising Maceo Parker and Fred Wesley, veterans of James Brown among others. Martinez returned shortly after to reinstate the original Anthem line-up, and their third album saw a shift back to rock from the soul infatuation of its predecessors. 1988 brought the release of their renowned *Abbey Road* EP, featuring a pastiche of the famous Beatles album pose on the cover (the band were totally naked save for socks covering their genitalia). However, the mood was darkened when Slovak took an accidental heroin overdose and died in June. Deeply upset, Irons left, while the band recruited John Frusciante (guitar) and Chad Smith (drums). After the release of *Freaky Styley* the single,

'Knock Me Down', was released as a tribute to Slovak. Of their most commercially successful excursion, 1991's *Blood, Sex, Sugar, Magik*, they accurately diagnosed their motivation, and much of their attraction: 'Just recognizing that I was a freak, but knowing that was a cool place to be.' Producer Rick Rubin, usually associated with the harder end of the metal and rap spectrum (Slayer, Danzig), nevertheless brought out the Peppers' first ballads. Such sensitivity has done little to deter the vanguard of critics who have long since raged at what they saw as the band's innate sexism. Frusciante was replaced in June 1992 by Arik Marshall, who in turn was sacked one year later. 1994 saw new guitarist Dave Navarro (ex-Jane's Addiction) perform his live UK debut as the band headlined the Reading Festival, before joining the Rolling Stones on their US tour.

Albums: *Uplift Mofo Party Plan* (EMI 1988), *Mother's Milk* (EMI 1989), *The Red Hot Chili Peppers* (EMI 1990), *Freaky Styley* (EMI 1990), *Blood, Sex, Sugar, Magik* (Warners 1991). Compilations: *What Hits!?* (EMI 1992), *Plasma Shaft* (Warners 1994, double album).

Video: *What Hits!?* (1992).

Further reading: *True Men Don't Kill Coyotes*, Dave Thompson.

Reed, Dan, Network

Along with Living Colour, this band led the way in the late 80s growth of funk-rock. Hailing from Oregon, USA, the Network featured Dan Reed (vocals), Melvin Brannon II (bass), Brion James (lead guitar), Daniel Pred (drums), and Blake Sakamoto (keyboards). Signed to Mercury Records, they released their first, self-titled album in 1988, which contrasted the commercial rock of artists such as Bon Jovi with the funk rhythms of Prince. The album was enthusiastically received by those craving rock music with a difference, as tracks such as 'Get To You' and 'Ritual' soon became dance floor hits at rock club bastions. That debut was followed by *Slam*, produced by Nile Rodgers of Chic fame, who gave the album a slightly harder edge while still retaining the funk element of its predecessor. A single, 'Rainbow Child', provided the band with its first minor UK hit single, briefly entering the Top 40 in 1989. Prestigious support slots were gained in 1990 in Europe with Bon Jovi and the Rolling Stones, which helped to raise their profile and bring their music to much larger audiences. In 1991 *The Heat* was released, which saw them reunited with Bruce Fairburn, producer of their first album. This included a highly original version of Pink Floyd's 'Money' as well as the singles 'Mix It Up' and 'Baby Now I', both of which failed to make an impression in the charts. Despite critical acclaim, support slots on major tours and a fair degree of radio exposure, Dan Reed Network have yet to achieve their big commercial break and have had to watch contemporaries such as Living Colour and Faith No More achieve platinum status. That situation seems unlikely to change in the near future.

Albums: *Dan Reed Network* (Mercury 1988), *Slam* (Mercury 1989), *The Heat* (Mercury 1991). Compilation: *Mixing It Up - The Best Of* (Mercury 1993)

Reef

Kenwyn (guitar), Gary (vocals), Dominic (drums) and Jack (bass) came to fame via an advert for the Mini-Disc portable stereo system. This depicted them as a heavy metal band touting for a deal, presenting their song, 'Naked', to an unimpressed A&R man, who throws the offending demo out of the window only for it to be retrieved and played by a passing skateboarder. Despite the impression given of them being a US band (the video was filmed in New York), Reef actually hail from Bath, England. Signed to the Sony empire, their first release was 'Good Feeling' in late 1994. The group, anxious to avoid a 'Stiltskin situation', were keen not to be perceived as a one-horse operation and to this end declined to offer 'Naked' as a single release, often not even playing it live.

REO Speedwagon

Formed in Champaign, Illinois, USA, in 1970 when pianist Neil Doughty (b. 29 July 1946, Evanston, Illinois, USA) and drummer Alan Gratzer (b. 9 November 1948, Syracuse, New York, USA) were joined by guitarist and songwriter Gary Richrath (b. 10 October 1949, Peoria, Illinois, USA). Although still in its embryonic stage, the group already had its unusual name which was derived from an early American fire-engine, designed by one Ransom E. Olds. Barry Luttnell (vocals) and Greg Philbin (bass) completed the line-up featured on *REO Speedwagon*, but the former was quickly replaced by Kevin Cronin (b. 6 October 1951, Evanston, Illinois, USA). The quintet then began the perilous climb from local to national prominence, but despite their growing popularity, particularly in America's mid west, the band was initially unable to complete a consistent album. Although *REO Two* and *Ridin' The Storm Out* eventually achieved gold status, disputes regarding direction culminated in the departure of their second vocalist. Michael Murphy took his place in 1974, but when ensuing albums failed to generate new interest, Cronin rejoined his former colleagues. Bassist Bruce

REO Speedwagon

Hall (b. 3 May 1953, Champaign, Illinois, USA) was also brought into a line-up acutely aware that previous releases had failed to reflect their in-concert prowess. The live summary, *You Get What You Play For*, overcame this problem to become the group's first platinum disc, a distinction shared by its successor, *You Can Tune A Piano, But You Can't Tuna Fish*. However, sales for *Nine Lives* proved disappointing, inspiring the misjudged view that the band had peaked. Such impressions were banished in 1980 with the release of *Hi Infidelity*, a crafted, self-confident collection which topped the US album charts and spawned a series of highly-successful singles. An emotive ballad, 'Keep On Lovin' You', reached number 1 in the US and number 7 in the UK, while its follow-up, 'Take It On The Run', also hit the US Top 5. However, a lengthy tour in support of the album proved creatively draining and *Good Trouble* is generally accepted as one of REO's least worthy efforts. Aware of its faults, the quintet withdrew from the stadium circuit and, having rented a Los Angeles warehouse, enjoyed six months of informal rehearsals during which time they regained a creative empathy. *Wheels Are Turning* recaptured the zest apparent on *Hi Infidelity* and engendered a second US number 1 in 'Can't Fight This Feeling'.

Life As We Know It and its successor, *The Earth, A Small Man, His Dog And A Chicken*, emphasized the group's now accustomed professionalism, by which time the line-up featured Cronin, Doughty, Hall, Dave Amato (b. 3 March 1953; lead guitar; ex-Ted Nugent), Bryan Hitt (b. 5 January 1954; drums; ex-Wang Chung) and Jesse Harms (b. 6 July 1952; keyboards). Too often lazily dubbed 'faceless', or conveniently bracketed with other in-concert 70s favourites Styx and Kansas, REO Speedwagon have proved the importance of a massive, secure, grass roots following.

Albums: *REO Speedwagon* (Epic 1971), *REO Two* (Epic 1972), *Ridin' The Storm Out* (Epic 1973), *Lost In A Dream* (Epic 1974), *This Time We Mean It* (Epic 1975), *REO* (Epic 1976), *REO Speedwagon Live/You Get What You Play For* (Epic 1977), *You Can Tune A Piano But You Can't Tuna Fish* (Epic 1978), *Nine Lives* (Epic 1979), *Hi Infidelity* (Epic 1980), *Good Trouble* (Epic 1982), *Wheels Are Turning* (Epic 1984), *Life As We Know It* (Epic 1987), *The Earth, A Small Man, His Dog And A Chicken* (Epic 1990). Compilations: *A Decade Of Rock 'N' Roll 1970-1980* (Epic 1980), *Best Foot Forward* (Epic 1985), *The Hits* (Epic 1988), *A Second Decade Of Rock 'N' Roll 1981-1991* (Epic 1991).

Videos: *Wheels Are Turnin'* (1987), *REO Speedwagon* (1988).

Revolting Cocks

Endearingly titled industrial funk metal band, the name occasionally shortened to RevCo when propriety demands. The Revolting Cocks history stretches back to the mid-80s when Al Jourgenson (also Ministry) met Belgians Richard 23 and Luc Van Acker in a Chicago pool hall. Legend has it that a drunken Van Acker stumbled in to Jourgenson when the latter was attempting to make a winning shot in a $500 game. However, Jourgenson recovered his composure to win, and the three celebrated by wrecking the club. On their exit the manager was heard to remark 'Get out, you revolting cocks!'. The group's first single under their new moniker would be 'No Devotion', housed on Chicago's infamous Wax Trax label. When it made the PMRC's 'Naughty 9' list for its blasphemy something of a noble tradition was born. The lyrical scope of the group's debut offered no respite. Subject matter included rioting soccer fans, sitcom junkies and industrial accidents. Joined in 1987 by multi-instrumentalist William Rieflin, the next single, 'You Often Forget', featured both 'malignant' and 'benign' versions in tribute to the prevalent media fascination with Betty Ford's breasts. Richard 23 then departed for Front 242, to be replaced by Chris Connelly of Finitribe fame. Paul Barker of Ministry was also on hand to guest and co-produce the half-live *You Goddamned Son Of A Bitch*, recorded at a Chicago show in September 1987. However, *Beers, Steers And Queers* would be the group's second album proper, its title-track a hilarious machismo pile-up of cowboy kitsch and dialogue stolen from the homo-erotic scenes of *Deliverance*. A 'cover' of Olivia Newton John's '(Let's Get) Physical' was also on hand to startle the casual browser - basically consisting of a loop of someone screaming the title. Afterwards the band would move away from Wax Trax (as had Ministry, from whom RevCo would now additionally absorb Roland Barker, Mike Scaccia and Louie Svitek). The madness continued unabated at their new label, with *Linger Ficken' Good* this time seizing Rod Stewart's 'Do You Think I'm Sexy' and righteously deflowering it with additional lyrics from Connelly concerning dentistry. Afterwards RevCo took a break from inflaming moral umbrage while Jourgenson concentrated on Ministry activities.

Albums: *Big Sexy Land* (Wax Trax 1986), *You Goddamned Son Of A Bitch* (Wax Trax 1988), *Beers, Steers + Queers* (Wax Trax 1990), *Linger Ficken' Good*

Revolting Cocks

And Other Barnyard Oddities (Devotion 1993).

Rhoads, Randy

Possibly one of the greatest hard rock guitarists America ever produced, Randy Roads (b. Randall William Rhoads, 6 December 1956, Santa Monica, California, USA, d. 19 March 1982) would, had his life not been so tragically curtailed in a freak aeroplane accident, be talked about in the same breath as Eddie Van Halen or even Jimmy Page. Certainly, there are many sterile technicians in the metal world whose celebrated virtuosity offers no match to Rhoads' flair. At an early age Rhoads began to study the guitar and in 1972 formed his first band, Quiet Riot, who, by 1975, with vocalist Devin Dubrow and drummer Drew Forsyth, began to earn a good live reputation. By 1978 (when they were joined by bassist Rudy Sarzo), this had earned them a recording contract with Columbia Records, who pushed them (successfully) into the Japanese market. In October 1979 Sarzo joined American legends Angel and Rhoads became a guitar tutor. With Ozzy Osbourne finally free of Black Sabbath he began to put together a new band called Blizzard Of Ozz, having recruited a bassist and drummer. Ozzy then held auditions for a guitarist in Los Angeles. At the end of a day spent listening to rehashed Sabbath riffs he fell asleep. Later that evening he awoke to hear a gripping and original style. Half-conscious, he turned to his manager/wife Sharon and asked who the girl with the guitar was. From out of his mass of long blonde hair Rhoads appeared to take the post. It is with Ozzy that Rhoads is best remembered for his stunning live performances and excellence in the studio. The first Ozzy album contained his powerful signature on tracks like 'Crazy Train' and 'Suicide Solution', as well as the more sensitive 'Dee', a track written by Rhoads for his mother. The title-track to the second album, *Diary Of A Madman*, contains a superb mixture of acoustic and electric guitar, while 'You Can't Kill Rock And Roll' moved one reviewer to say that 'Randy is at his most eloquent, spacey and rich'. Not satisfied with being merely a rock guitarist, Rhoads also concentrated on his masters degree in classical guitar, eventually hoping to melt the two styles to create new wonders. It was not to be. Whilst *en route* to Florida for further live shows the tour bus made an unscheduled stop where the driver's friend had a small aeroplane. After taking up a couple of band members for a joy ride Rhoads and a make-up girl were persuaded to enlist. The pilot, high on cocaine, seemingly aimed the aircraft at the empty tour bus and all passengers were killed. Ozzy and his wife have never fully recovered from the tragedy. Nor, for that matter, has his music. In 1987 Ozzy and Rhoads' mother put together a tribute album containing live recordings and a studio outtake of 'Dee'.

Albums: With Quiet Riot: *Quite Riot* (Columbia 1978), *Quiet Riot 2* (Columbia 1979). With Ozzy Osbourne: *Blizzard Of Ozz* (Jet 1980), *Diary Of A Madman* (Jet 1981). *Randy Rhoads Tribute Album* (Epic 1987).

Riff Raff

Featuring Doug Lubahn (vocals/bass), Ned Lubahn (guitar/keyboards), Werner Fritzching (guitar) and Mark Kaufman (drums), this group from New York, USA, released just one album of above-average melodic heavy rock. *Vinyl Futures* represents a mixture of styles, the closest approximation of which might be early Rush crossed with Foreigner. They are not to be confused with the Finnish band of the same title. Lubahn would go on to work with Billy Squier when Riff Raff bit the dust.

Album: *Vinyl Futures* (Atco 1981).

Riggs

This Californian quartet was founded by vocalist/guitarist Jerry Riggs in 1981. With Jeremy Graf (guitar), David Riderick (bass) and Stephen Roy Carlisle (drums) completing the line-up, they specialized in hard-edged, metallic pop, with considerable crossover potential. Riggs on vocals was particularly distinctive, sounding not dissimilar to Bryan Adams. Their debut and only release remains an undiscovered gem of infectious and classy AOR. They were unfortunate in that they lacked a strong visual image and, without a strong promotional push, the project was doomed. Disillusioned, they disbanded, with Jerry Riggs later going on to play with Pat Travers.

Album: *Riggs* (Full Moon 1982).

Riot

Riot's career has forever been dogged by record company problems and a general lack of interest from press quarters - a surprising epitaph for a New York band who formed in 1976 and were the subject of a petition to get one of their albums released in Europe. Signed in 1977 to Ariola, the band comprised L.A. Kouvaris (guitar), Mark Reale (guitar), Peter Bitelli (drums), Jimmy Iommi (bass) and vocalist Speranza. Constant touring brought them little success and by 1979 Kouvaris was replaced by Rick Ventura. Capitol Records signed them and released *Narita* - still hailed as a hard rock classic, it brought them widespread attention in the UK which led to an appearance at the

Donington Festival in 1980. The following year they returned to the studio and recorded *Fire Down Under.* Capitol refused to release it and fans in the UK started the aforementioned petition to force their hand. Capitol stuck fast and dropped them, but Elektra were quick to see their potential. The album was eventually released to critical acclaim. However, Iommi and Bitelli quit, to be replaced by Kip Leming and Sandy Slavin, while former Rachel vocalist Rhett Forrester replaced Speranza. The next album, *Restless Breed,* was a mixed affair, but contained an excellent version of Eric Burden's 'When I Was Young'. After a badly produced live album they were dropped by Elektra. They released one final album to a total absence of industry or fan interest in 1984. A brief but unsuccessful reformation with most of the original line-up ensued in 1986, before Reale emerged with an all-new band, featuring Tony Moore (vocals), Don Van Stavern (bass) and Bobby Jarzombek (drums) and made an acclaimed comeback with *Thundersteel,* although *Privilege Of Power* and *Nightbreaker,* with new vocalist Michael Dimeo and guitarist Mike Flyntz, saw the band's sound fail to progress with the times. Forrester had a short-lived solo career before he too disappeared from view. Later it emerged he was murdered during an attempted robbery in January 1994.

Albums: *Rock City* (Ariola 1977), *Narita* (Capitol 1979), *Fire Down Under* (Elektra 1981), *Restless Breed* (Elektra 1982), *Riot Live* (Elektra 1982), *Born In America* (Grand Slam 1984), *Thundersteel* (CBS 1988), *Privilege Of Power* (CBS 1989), *Riot Live* (CBS 1989, rec. 1980), *Nightbreaker* (Rising Sun 1994).

Roadhouse

This melodic UK hard rock quintet was assembled in 1991 around former Def Leppard guitarist Pete Willis. Utilizing the talents of Wayne Grant (bass), Richard Day (guitar), Paul Jackson (vocals) and Trevor Brewis (drums), the band were signed by Phonogram largely on the strength of the guitarist's connections. Their self-titled debut album was a major disappointment, however, featuring an average collection of commercial AOR-styled songs. The band lacked identity and have so far been unable to inject drive or spontaneity into their uptempo numbers, while the ballads lacked sincerity, emotion or class.

Album: *Roadhouse* (Phonogram 1991).

Roberts, Kane

Kane Roberts first came to prominence as machismo lead guitarist in Alice Cooper's band, during his mid-80s comeback, when he was lured from Lone Justice to add musical and visual muscle to Cooper's theatrical live show. With the help of Cooper's management he secured a solo deal with MCA Records in 1987. His debut release, however, was somewhat at odds with his tough-guy image, featuring a collection of AOR and ballads. He quit Cooper's band the following year to concentrate fully on his solo career. Playing down the muscleman image, he teamed up with Desmond Child to write material for *Saints And Sinners.* This was a highly polished melodic rock album in a Bon Jovi meet Kiss vein, with John McCurry (guitar), Steven Steele (bass), Myron Grombacher (drums) and Chuck Kentis (keyboards) being recruited as permanent band members.

Albums: *Kane Roberts* (MCA 1987), *Saints And Sinners* (Geffen 1991).

Rock City Angels

This blues-based hard rock quintet from the US were formed by vocalist Bobby Durango and bassist Andy Panik in 1982. After a series of false-starts under the names the Abusers and the Delta Rebels, they settled on the title Rock City Angels, adding guitarists Doug Banx and Mike Barnes and drummer Jackie D. Jukes to complete the line-up. *Young Man's Blues* was an impressive debut. Utilizing full digital technology, it was a double album which featured a superb amalgam of earthy rockers and honest blues numbers. Durango's vocals have a southern twang to them, while the songs themselves combined elements of Lynyrd Skynyrd, Little Feat and the Georgia Satellites. Despite this the album failed commercially and, disillusioned, the band broke-up in 1989. Durango immediately started a new outfit under his own name.

Album: *Young Man's Blues* (Geffen 1988, double album).

Rock Goddess

Formed by sisters Jody and Julie Turner at the tender age of 13 and nine respectively, even in such infancy Jody proved a good guitarist and Julie showed considerable promise as a drummer. Their father, John, ran a music shop in Wandsworth, London, which had a rehearsal room next to it. The sisters, along with school friend and budding bassist Tracey Lamb, soon started to put a set together. By 1981 they had recorded their first demo tape and began to play clubs in London, earning a reputation as schoolgirl rockers who could hold their own against more established outfits. They soon attracted the attention of Karine, singer with indie band Androids Of Mu, who invited them to contribute one track,

'Make My Night', which she produced, to the all-female compilation album, *Making Waves*. They then set out on tour with Androids Of Mu and the Gymslips, with their father now managing them. Through his efforts they acquired a deal with A&M Records, and spent most of 1982 writing songs and playing live. The following year they released their debut album, and a single entitled 'My Angel'. With Girlschool running out of steam they picked up much of their following and boosted their line-up with Kate Burbela on second guitar. Their follow-up album the same year was a better received product, yet Lamb decided to leave and was replaced by Dee O'Malley, who departed herself in 1986 to start a family. The final album was a good effort but interest in the band had long gone and Jody left to pursue a solo career. In 1988 Lamb joined Girlschool.

Albums: *Rock Goddess* (A&M 1983), *Hell Hath No Fury* (A&M 1983), *Young And Free* (Just In 1987).

Rockhead

Rockhead were put together by producer Bob Rock (b. Robert Jens Rock, 19 April 1954, Winnipeg, Canada), famed for his work with Bon Jovi, Aerosmith, Mötley Crüe and Metallica, with Steve Jack (vocals), Jamey Kosh (bass) and Chris Taylor (drums). Rockhead (the producer/guitarist's nickname) had little difficulty in finding a recording deal, with Richie Sambora and the Cult's Billy Duffy guesting on their debut, and landed a prestigious European tour support slot with Bon Jovi. All this made the band an easy target for sniping critics, but although *Rockhead* was hardly innovative, it was a solid and, naturally, superbly-produced collection of stadium hard rock which translated well to the stage. The band proved to be a capable live act too, clearly enjoying themselves and providing Bob Rock with a pleasant diversion from studio work.

Album: *Rockhead* (EMI 1993).

Rods

This New York power-trio exploded onto the heavy metal scene in 1980. Formed by ex-Elf guitarist David Feinstein, the line-up was completed by drummer Carl Canedy and bassist Stephen Farmer. Although heavily influenced by Kiss, Ted Nugent and Deep Purple, they transformed these influences into a unique sound that was at once aggressive, powerful and uncompromising. *Rock Hard*, released on the independent Primal label, was a terse and anthemic debut, which eventually led to the inking of a deal with Arista. Gary Bordonaro replaced Farmer before their first major label release (a re-mixed version of *Rock Hard*, with three additional tracks). *Wild Dogs*

was a disappointing follow-up and sold poorly, which ensured the band would be dropped by their label. Consigned once more to the independent sector, *In The Raw* was a poorly-produced collection of demos, while the live album suffered from muddy sound and uninspired performances. By this stage the band had largely alienated their original fan base. *Let Them Eat Metal*, although a marked improvement, still failed to sell and they branched into more melodic rock, recruiting Andy McDonald (guitar), Rick Caudle (vocals), and Emma Zale (keyboards). In 1987 the band returned to a three-piece format again, with Craig Gruber (ex-Elf) replacing Bordonaro, before ex-Picture vocalist Shmoulic Avigal was added to record *Heavier Than Thou*. A third successive release to fail to make any impact, this increased existing internal pressures and the band imploded shortly thereafter.

Albums: *Rock Hard* (Primal 1980), *The Rods* (Arista 1981), *Wild Dogs* (Arista 1982), *In The Raw* (Shrapnel 1983), *Live* (Music For Nations 1983), *Let Them Eat Metal* (Music For Nations 1984), *Heavier Than Thou* (Zebra 1987).

Rogue Male

Formed in London, England, in 1984, the band's original line-up consisted of Jim Lyttle (vocals/guitar), John Fraser Binnie (guitar), Kevin Collier (bass; ex-Le Griffe) and Steve Kingsley (drums). Signing to the Music For Nations label their debut, *First Visit*, was released in 1985, an album full of fast, tough, punk-influenced metal. With live gigs revealing mainman Jim Lyttle to be a charismatic bandleader they embarked on an ill-fated American tour. Blaming their American label Elektra Records for a lack of promotion, the band returned to England to begin work on a second album. At this point Steve Kingsley left to be replaced by session drummer Charlie Morgan, who played on the album recordings, but was replaced soon after by Danny Fury. *Animal Man* was released in 1986 but the band dissolved soon after release in the face of public indifference.

Albums: *First Visit* (Music For Nations 1985), *Animal Man* (Music For Nations 1986).

Rollins, Henry

Vocalist Henry Rollins (b. Henry Garfield, 13 February 1961, Washington DC, USA) quickly returned to action following the break-up of Black Flag, releasing *Hot Animal Machine*, followed by the *Drive-By Shooting* EP (under the pseudonym Henrietta Collins and the Wifebeating Childhaters). The Rollins Band was eventually formed in 1987

with Chris Haskett (guitar), Andrew Weiss (bass) and Sim Cain (drums). The group developed their own brand of hard rock, with blues and jazz influences, over several studio and live albums, building a considerable following with their heavy touring schedule. Rollins' lyrics dealt with social and political themes, often unashamedly exorcising personal demons from a troubled childhood. The sight of the heavily-muscled and tattooed frontman on stage, dripping sweat and roaring out his rage, is one of the most astonishing, memorable sights in hard rock music, topping off an enthralling live act. Their commercial rise began with the opening slot on the first Lollapalooza tour, exposing the band to huge audiences for the first time. *The End Of Silence* was a deserved success, and contained some of Rollins' most strikingly introspective lyrics. 'Just Like You' narrated his difficulty in dealing with his similarities to an abusive father: 'You should see the pain I go through, When I see myself I see you'. Rollins' spoken word and publishing activities (his regime is one which allows for little more than a few hours sleep each night) also drew major media interest. An accomplished and experienced spoken word performer with several albums to his credit, Rollins' often hilarious style is in distinct contrast to his musical persona, and has drawn comparisons to Lenny Bruce and Denis Leary (though, in contrast, he implores his audiences not to destroy themselves with 'poisons' like alcohol and tobacco). Despite the humour, there is a serious edge to his words, best animated in the harrowing story of the murder of his best friend, Joe Cole, within feet of him. Rollins' workaholic frame also levers his own publishing company, 2.13.61 (after his birthdate), which has grown from very small beginnings in 1984 to publish a wide range of authors, including Rollins' own prolific output. He also has a music publishing enterprise, Human Pitbull, and co-owns a record label with Rick Rubin, dedicated to classic punk reissues - Rollins himself having graduated from the infamous late 70s Washington DC 'straight edge' scene and bands like SOA. He has additionally broken into film acting, appearing in *The Chase* and *Johnny Mnemonic*. Back with the Rollins Band, *Weight*, produced by long-time soundman Theo Van Rock, saw the first personnel change since the band's inception, with Melvin Gibbs replacing Weiss, and adding a funkier spine to the band's still intense core.
Albums: Henry Rollins: *Hot Animal Machine* (Texas Hotel 1986). Rollins Band: *Life Time* (Texas Hotel 1988), *Do It* (Texas Hotel 1988), *Hard Volume* (Texas Hotel 1989), *Turned On* (Quarterstick 1990), *The End Of Silence* (Imago 1992), *Weight* (Imago 1994).

Spoken word: *The Boxed Life* (Imago 1993).
Further reading: all titles by Henry Rollins: *High Adventure In The Great Outdoors* aka *Bodybag*, 1985, *Pissing In The Gene Pool* 1986, *Art To Choke Hearts* 1986, *Bang!* 1987, *One From None* 1987, *See A Grown Man Cry* 1991, *Black Coffee Blues* 1993, *Now Watch 'Em Die* 1993, *Get In The Van: On The Road With Black Flag* 1994.

Romeo's Daughter

Above-average AOR band fronted by female vocalist Leigh Matty and expertly backed by songwriter and guitarist Craig Joiner, Tony Mitman on keyboards, Ed Poole on bass and drummer Andy Wells. The band came together under the direction of producer Robert 'Mutt' Lange in what seemed to be an attempt to recreate a similar project from the late 70s with his wife's band, Night. Lange, along with John Parr and Joiner, worked hard on the songs and production and armed with a deal with Jive Records issued the single, 'Heaven In The Back Seat', a minor hit that brought together elements of both Heart and Belinda Carlisle whilst retaining an 'English' sound. 1989's self-titled album sold well and the band proved a popular live attraction, receiving much attention from Radio 1's *Rock Show* who broadcast live concerts and an exclusive session. 'Heaven In The Back Seat', meanwhile, also turned up on the soundtrack to *Nightmare On Elm Street 5: The Dream Child*. The band went to ground but resurfaced in 1993 with another single, 'Attracted To The Animal', followed by a major tour and an album on Music For Nations. By this time they had lost much of their earlier impact and by 1994 had left both management and label in search of new ideas, and were said to be toying with the idea of a name change.
Albums: *Romeos Daughter* (Jive 1989), *Delectable* (Music For Nations 1993).

Rose Tattoo

This legendary Australian band was formed by former Buster Brown members Angry Anderson (vocals) and Mick 'Geordie' Leech (bass) with Peter Wells (slide guitar/vocals), Michael Cocks (lead guitar) and Dallas 'Digger' Royall (drums) in Sydney in 1977. They released their classic self-titled debut (known as *Rock 'N' Roll Outlaws* outside Australia) the following year. *Rose Tattoo* was an aggressive blues-rock masterpiece packed with excellent songs, and the band's electric live performances and tough tattooed image drew support from punks and rockers alike. Their European debut in 1981, supporting Rainbow, and an appearance at the Reading Festival caused quite a stir, but a poor sound on *Assault & Battery* rather dulled their impact. This was despite the quality of the material, with Anderson characteristically offering political comment and true story narrative against a straightforward boogie background. *Scarred For Life*, with Robin Riley replacing Cocks, had a stronger production and yet more quality songs, but the band fell apart on their first US tour with Aerosmith and Pat Travers over numerous personal problems. Anderson and Leech assembled a new line-up with Greg Jordan (slide guitar), Robert Bowron (drums) and John Meyer (guitar) for *Southern Stars*, but the band later split. *Beats From A Single Drum* was released for contractual reasons under the name Rose Tattoo, but was in fact Anderson's solo debut as he expanded his horizons into film and television. However, the legend remained strong, and Rose Tattoo were persuaded to reform the original line-up (sadly without Royall, who had died in 1990) for an Australian support slot with Guns N'Roses (who had covered the group's 'Nice Boys' on their debut EP) in 1993, plus a small tour of their own, culminating in a biker festival headline slot. Despite an average age around 45, Rose Tattoo proved that the old fire still burned brightly with dazzling performances.

Albums: *Rose Tattoo* (Albert 1978), *Assault & Battery* (Albert 1981), *Scarred For Life* (Albert 1982), *Southern Stars* (Albert 1984), *Beats From A Single Drum* (Mushroom 1987). Compilation: *Nice Boys Don't Play Rock 'N' Roll* (Albert 1992).

Rossington Collins

This US rock band was formed in 1979 by the four surviving members of the 1977 Lynyrd Skynyrd plane crash; Gary Rossington (guitars), Allen Collins (guitars), Billy Powell (keyboards) and Leon Wilkerson (bass), who joined with Dale Krantz (vocals), Barry Harwood (guitars) and Derek Hess (drums). They continued in the best traditions of Skynyrd, though the female lead vocals gave them a different sound. They broke up in 1983 after just two albums. Powell later joined the Christian rock band Vision, while Collins was paralysed from the waist down in a car accident in the mid-80s, and died of pneumonia on 23 January 1990. Krantz married Rossington and both they and Powell took their place in the Lynyrd Skynyrd reunion tour of 1987.

Albums: *Anytime, Anyplace, Anywhere* (MCA 1980), *This Is The Way* (MCA 1982).

Roth, Dave Lee

Dave Lee Roth (b. 10 October 1955, Bloomington, Indeanapolis, USA), former lead vocalist with Van Halen, first expressed his desire to go solo during a period of band inactivity during 1985. He subsequently recorded a mini-album, *Crazy From The Heat*, featuring a varied selection of material that was a departure from the techno-metal approach of Van Halen. The album was favourably reviewed and after much speculation, he finally broke ranks in the autumn of 1985. Roth soon found himself in the US Top 3 with an unlikely version of the Beach Boys' 'California Girls' (complete with a suitably tacky video) and an even stranger cover of 'I Ain't Got Nobody'. This bizarre change must have baffled and bemused his fans, but he soon assembled an impressive array of musicians, notably guitar virtuoso Steve Vai (ex-Zappa and Alcatrazz), bassist Billy Sheehan (ex-Talas) and drummer Greg Bissonette to record *Eat 'Em And Smile*. This featured an amazing selection of blistering rockers and offbeat, big production numbers. It proved that Roth was still a great showman; the album was technically superb and infused with an irreverent sense of 'Yankee' humour. *Skyscraper*, released two years later, built on this foundation, but focused more on an elaborately produced hard rock direction. Billy Sheehan departed shortly after its release to be replaced by Matt Bissonette. Brett Tuggle on keyboards was also recruited to expand the line-up to a five piece and add an extra dimension to their sound. Steve Vai left in 1989 to pursue a solo career, but was only temporarily missed as Jason Becker stepped in, a new six-string whizz kid of the Yngwie Malmsteen school of guitar improvisation. *A Little Ain't Enough* emerged in 1991 and, although technically faultless, it tended to duplicate ideas from his previous two albums. *Your Filthy Little Mouth* saw him relocate to New York. This time, amid the histrionics about girls and cars, were odes to the Los Angeles riots, and the unutterably horrible pseudo reggae of 'No Big 'Ting'.

Albums: *Crazy From The Heat* (Warners 1985), *Eat 'Em And Smile* (Warners 1986), *Skyscraper* (Warners 1988), *A Little Ain't Enough* (Warners 1991), *Your Filthy Little Mouth* (Warners 1994).

Video: *David Lee Roth* (1987).

Rough Cutt

Typical of its kind mid-80s Los Angeles, California, USA rock band following in the footsteps of Ratt and Quiet Riot but lacking originality. Led by vocalist Paul Shortino, they were proficient enough to gain support slots on American tours with Accept and Krokus, but generated little interest in the UK. Warner Brothers decided to take a chance on them in 1985 and released the first of two average albums. In 1986 they were dropped by the company and Shortino left to join Quiet Riot leaving the rest of the band - Amir Derakh (guitar), David Alford (drums),

Dave Lee Roth

Matt Thor (bass) - to form Jailhouse to similar disappointing results.
Albums: *Rough Cutt* (Warners 1985), *Wants You* (Warners 1986).

Rough Diamond

This highly-touted supergroup was formed to considerable fanfare in 1976. Dave Clempson (ex-Bakerloo, Colosseum, Humble Pie; guitar), Damon Butcher (keyboards; ex-Steve Marriot's All Stars), Willie Bath (bass) and Geoff Britton (ex-Wings; drums) joined former Uriah Heep singer David Byron, but their launch was undermined by a court case brought by another group claiming the same name. The delay undermined the quintet's confidence and the ensuing album proved disappointing. Its appearance during the punk explosion exacerbated problems and although the band looked to the USA for solace, friction between Byron and his colleagues proved insurmountable. The singer embarked on a solo career in October 1977 while the remaining members added Garry Bell and adopted a new name, Champion, releasing an album on Epic in 1978.
Album: *Rough Diamond* (Island 1977).

Rox

Hailing from Manchester, England, Rox were a glam rock band heavily influenced by Kiss and Angel, who sprang to life in 1981 (as Venom) with Mark Anthony (vocals), Red Hot Red (b. Ian Burke; guitar), Paul Diamond (b. Paul Hopwood; guitar), Gary Maunsell (bass) and Tony Fitzgerald (drums). They soon built up a loyal following and received a great deal of attention from *Sounds*. A year later Fitzgerald left and was replaced by Bernie Emerald (b. Bernard Nuttall). With the departure of Anthony they recruited their roadie, Kevin Read, who took on the name of 'Kick Ass' Kevin Kozak. After reported threats from Newcastle's black metal merchants of the same name they decided to change theirs to Rox. Maunsell was then replaced by Billy Beaman before they set out on tour. After the release of the EP, *Hot Love In The City*, in August 1992 they signed to Music For Nations. The group released a 12-inch EP, *Krazy Kutz*, a year later, before a higher profile tour and album, *Violent Breed*. Soon after Kozak was replaced by Anthony again, this time using the name Mark Savage. Despite the fact that there were no new records to promote they managed to hitch a ride on the Quiet Riot tour of the UK in 1984. The following year Diamond quit and the band split up (Diamond later turning up in a new group, Torino).
Album: *Violent Breed* (Music For Nations 1983).

Royal Court Of China

This Nashville, Tennessee quartet were formed in 1984 by Joe Blanton (vocals, rhythm guitar), Chris Mekow (drums), Robert Logue (bass) and Oscar Rice (guitar), taking their name from a reference to the highest form of Chinese opium, which had originally been the name chosen by Jimmy Page and Paul Rodgers for the group which became the Firm. Impressive local gigging and the self-financed *Off The Beat 'n' Path* EP led to a contract with A&M, but with Logue and Rice's penchant for a folkier sound, the album tended more towards REM in style than the hard rock direction which the other two preferred, and following a tour with REO Speedwagon, the band split. Blanton and Mekow retained both name and deal, and recruited bassist Drew Cornutt and guitarist Josh Weinberg, although the latter was replaced by Jeff Mays when he failed to live up to expectations in the studio. *Geared And Primed*, produced by Vic Maile, was an impressively diverse album, following a harder direction while retaining the more rootsy guitar elements of their previous release, particularly on the lighter material. However, the album lacked the depth of quality material to make it a success, and the band faded from sight.
Albums: *The Royal Court Of China* (A&M 1987), *Geared And Primed* (A&M 1989).

RPLA

RPLA sprang to fame when they starred on an unlikely front cover of *Kerrang!* magazine, who marketed them as a 'Pretty Boy' band *a la* Poison and Mötley Crüe. Not long after this appearance they emerged with a different image and admitted that they were a 'gay' rock band. While this should have made no difference at all it knocked the macho metal press off its stride and suddenly the rave write-ups and gig reviews disappeared, with the band suffering as a result. They became the subject of a news item on Channel 4 TV about sexism/homophobia in rock and *Kerrang!* were singled out. Within a few weeks a small piece on them became conspicuous by its appearance in said magazine. Whatever their press relationship was, the band did themselves no favours because the music content was never strong enough to overcome even the mildest prejudice.
Album: *Metal Queen Hijack* (EMI 1992).

Rub Ultra

Dub metal crossover artists formed in London in August 1993, comprising Will (vocals), Steve (guitar), Charlie (bass), Sarah (vocals/percussion; sister of Will) and Pete (drums). Together they released two EPs in 1994, *Combatstrengthsoap* and *Cosmyk Fynger*

Tactik, the latter's cover featuring a holiday snap of a camel's posterior. Following support slots with Headswim, S*M*A*S*H* and Therapy? (whose Michael McKeegan was prepared to roadie for the band) rumours began to circulate that their debut album for Virgin indie subsidiary Hut would have none other than John Leckie as producer.

Runaways

Formed in 1975, the Runaways were initially the product of producer/svengali Kim Fowley and teenage lyricist Kari Krome. Together they pieced together an adolescent female-group following several auditions in the Los Angeles area. The original line-up consisted of Joan Jett (b. Joan Larkin, 22 September 1960, Philadelphia, Pennsylvania, USA; guitar/vocals), Micki Steele (bass - later of the Bangles) and Sandy West (drums), but was quickly bolstered by the addition of Lita Ford (b. 23 September 1959, London, England; guitar/vocals) and Cherie Currie (vocals). The departure of Steele prompted several replacements, the last of which was Jackie Fox (b. Jacqueline Fuchs) who had failed her first audition. Although originally viewed as a vehicle for compositions by Fowley and associate Mars Bonfire (b. Dennis Edmonton), material by Jett and Krome helped assert the quintet's independence. *The Runaways* showed a group indebted to the 'glam-rock' of the Sweet and punchy pop of Suzi Quatro, and included the salutary 'Cherry Bomb'. *Queens Of Noise* repeated the pattern, but the strain of touring - the quintet were highly popular in Japan - took its toll on Jackie Fox, who left the line-up and abandoned music altogether becoming an attorney practicing in intellectual property law. Personality clashes resulted in the departure of Cherie Currie, whose solo career stalled following the failure of her debut, *Beauty's Only Skin Deep*. Guitarist/vocalist Vicki Blue and bassist Laurie McAllister completed a revitalized Runaways, but the latter was quickly dropped. Subsequent releases lacked the appeal of the group's early work which, although tarred by novelty and sexual implication, nonetheless showed a sense of purpose. The Runaways split in 1980 but both Jett and Ford later enjoyed solo careers, the former engendering considerable commercial success during the 80s. In 1985 the mischievous Fowley resurrected the old group's name with all-new personnel. This opportunistic concoction split up on completing *Young And Fast*. 1994 brought reports that Fowley was being sued by Jett, Ford, Currie and West over unpaid royalties. Fox was not involved in the action, presumably because she is now herself a practising lawyer.

Albums: *The Runaways* (Mercury 1976), *Queens Of Noise* (Mercury 1977), *Live In Japan* (Mercury 1977), *Waitin' For The Night* (Mercury 1977), *And Now...The Runaways* (Phonogram 1979), *Young And Fast* (Allegiance 1987). Compilations: *Rock Heavies* (Mercury 1979), *Flamin' Schoolgirls* (Phonogram 1982).

Running Wild

This quartet from Hamburg, Germany, were strongly influenced by the New Wave Of British Heavy Metal Movement of the early 80s. Formed in 1983 by guitarist/vocalist Rockin' Rolf, a plethora of personnel changes occurred before Majik Moti (guitar), Jens Becker (bass) and Iain Finlay (drums) were recruited and a degree of stability was achieved. They initially pushed a black-metal image, but made little impact with their rigidly formularized, one-paced rantings. They changed course musically with their third album and tried to emulate the style of Iron Maiden, and also adopted a rather unfortunate swashbuckling pirate's image. However, Rolf's weak vocals and the repetitiveness of their material always hindered their chances of promotion to rock's upper echelons.

Albums: *Gates Of Purgatory* (Noise 1984), *Branded And Exiled* (Noise 1985), *Under Jolly Roger* (Noise 1987), *Ready For Boarding* (Noise 1988), *Port Royal* (Noise 1988), *Death Or Glory* (Noise 1990), *Blazin' Stone* (Noise 1991). Compilation: *The First Years Of Piracy* (Noise 1992).

Video: *Death Or Glory* (1992).

Rush

This Canadian heavy rock band comprised Geddy Lee (b. 29 July 1953, Willowdale, Toronto, Canada; keyboards/bass/vocals), Alex Lifeson (b. 27 August 1953, British Columbia, Canada; guitar) and John Rutsey (drums). From 1969-72 they performed in Toronto playing a brand of Cream-inspired material, honing their act on the local club and bar circuit. In 1973 they recorded a version of Buddy Holly's 'Not Fade Away' as their debut release, backing it with 'You Can't Fight It', for their own label, Moon Records. Despite failing to grab the attention as planned, the group pressed ahead with the recording of a debut album, which was remixed by Terry 'Broon' Brown. Brown would continue to work with the band until 1984's *Grace Under Pressure*. With no bite from the majors, once again this arrived via Moon, with distribution by London Records. However, at least the quality of the group's live appointments improved, picking up support slots with the New York Dolls in Canada and finally crossing the US border to play gigs with Z.Z. Top. Eventually Cliff

Burnstein of Mercury Records (who would later also sign Def Leppard) heard the band, and his label would reissue the group's debut. At this point Neil Peart (b. 12 September 1952, Hamilton, Ontario, Canada; drums; ex-Hush), who was to be the main songwriter of the band, replaced Rutsey, and Rush undertook their first full tour of the USA. Rush's music was typified by Lee's oddly high-pitched voice, a tremendously powerful guitar sound, especially in the early years, and a recurrent interest in science fiction and fantasy from the pen of Neil Peart. Later he would also conceptualise the work of authors like John Barth, Gabriel Garcia Marquez and John Dos Passos. This approach reached its zenith in the group's 1976 concept album, *2112*, based on the work of novelist/philosopher Ayn Rand, which had as its central theme the concept of individual freedom and will. Including a 20-minute title-track which lasted all of side one, it was a set which crystalised the spirit of Rush for both their fans and detractors. However, the band's most popular offering, *A Farewell To Kings*, followed by *Hemispheres* in 1978, saw Peart finally dispense with his 'epic' songwriting style. By 1979 Rush were immensely successful worldwide, and the Canadian Government awarded them the title of official Ambassadors of Music. As the 80s progressed Rush streamlined their image to become sophisticated, clean-cut, cerebral music-makers. Some early fans denigrated their determination to progress musically with each new album, though in truth the band had thoroughly exhausted its earlier style. They enjoyed a surprise hit single in 1980 when 'Spirit Of Radio' broke them out of their loyal cult following, and live shows now saw Lifeson and Lee adding keyboards for a fuller sound. Lee's vocals had also dropped somewhat from their earlier near-falsetto. The best recorded example of the band from this period is the succinct *Moving Pictures* from 1981, a groundbreaking fusion of technological rock and musical craft which never relied on the former at the expense of the latter. However, their career afterwards endured something of a creative wane, with the band at odds with various musical innovations. Despite this, live shows were still exciting events for the large pockets of fans the band retained all over the world, and in the powerful *Hold Your Fire* in 1987 they proved they were still able to scale former heights. Often criticised for lyrical pretension and musical grandstanding - unkind critics have suggested that Rush is exactly what you get if you let your drummer write your songs for you, they nevertheless remain Canada's leading rock attraction.
Albums: *Rush* (Moon 1974), *Fly By Night* (Moon 1975), *Caress Of Steel* (Mercury 1975), *2112* (Mercury 1976), *All The World's A Stage* (Mercury 1976, double album), *A Farewell To Kings* (Mercury 1977), *Hemispheres* (Mercury 1978), *Permanent Waves* (Mercury 1980), *Moving Pictures* (Mercury 1981), *Exit: Stage Left* (Mercury 1981, double album), *Signals* (Mercury 1982), *Grace Under Pressure* (Mercury 1984), *Power Windows* (Mercury 1985), *Hold Your Fire* (Mercury 1987), *A Show Of Hands* (Mercury 1989, double album), *Presto* (Atlantic 1989), *Roll The Bones* (Atlantic 1991), *Counterparts* (Mercury 1993). Compilations: *Archives* (Mercury 1978, triple set comprising first three albums), *Rush Through Time* (Mercury 1980), *Chronicles* (Mercury 1990).
Videos: *Grace Under Pressure* (1986), *Exit Stage Left* (1988), *Thru' The Camera's Eye* (1989), *A Show Of Hands* (1989), *Chronicles* (1991).

S

S.A.D.O.

This German group achieved a degree of notoriety during the mid-80s with their Tubes-like stage show which incorporated a selection of scantily-clad females in sado-masochistic uniform. Vocalist Andre Cook has been the only permanent member since the band's inception in 1983, losing original collaborators Matti Kaebs (drums), Wolfgang Eicholz (guitar), Matthias Moser (guitar) and Stepan Neumann (bass) - all of whom left to form V2 after the release of the erroneously-titled *Circle Of Friends*. Cook attempted to jump the thrash-metal bandwagon with *Dirty Fantasy*, attracting minimal attention, then adopted a more melodic AOR approach for *Sensitive*. Their final line-up included Cook, a returning Moser (guitar), Duncan O'Neill (bass) and Danny (drums), but all to little avail as the band disbanded shortly after release. Albums: *Shout* (Noise 1984), *Circle Of Friends* (Noise 1987), *Dirty Fantasy* (Noise 1988), *Another Kind Of...*(Noise 1989, mini-album), *Sensitive* (Noise 1990).

Sabbat

Formed in England in 1986, this group comprised Martin Walkyier (vocals), Andy Sneap (guitar), Frazer Craske (bass) and Simon Negus (drums). It was a demo tape, *Fragments Of A Faith Forgotten*, which first brought Sabbat to the attention of the press and public in 1986. Part of a new wave of thrash metal bands, Sabbat stood out for their skillful live displays and musical flair, and earned a two-page spread in *Kerrang!* magazine before releasing any vinyl. Lyrically they were preoccupied with pagan arts, witchcraft and the dark ages, elements of which were incorporated into a bizarre and theatrical stageshow. Their brand of thrash, meanwhile, was complex but forceful, and they quickly became a cult attraction on the metal circuit. *History Of A Time To Come* emerged soon afterwards and was well-received, reflecting the promise of earlier recordings. Its successor, *Dreamweaver*, was based on Brian Bates' novel *The Way Of Wyrd*, and demonstrated considerable musical development. After this Walkyier and Craske left, to replaced by Ritchie Desmond (vocals), Wayne Banks (bass) and extra guitarist Neil Watson. This line-up recorded the less taxing and ultimately inconsequential *Mourning Has Broken*. It was immediately followed by the break-up of Sabbat. Martin Walkyier has since formed Skyclad, while Sneap launched Godsend.

Albums: *History Of A Time To Come* (Noise 1988), *Dreamweaver (Reflections Of Our Yesterdays)* (Noise 1989), *Mourning Has Broken* (Noise 1991).

Sabu

The son of actor Selar Sabu, vocalist/guitarist Paul Sabu (b. Burbank, California, USA) has carved out a successful career as a songwriter, producer/engineer and guitarist for a variety of major acts. He has also contributed to numerous film soundtracks, but his solo projects have been dogged by bad luck. The Sabu band, featuring bassist Rick Bozzo and drummer Dan Holmes, found some success with their soulful hard rock debut, but the album was lost in America in confusion with a disco album released by Sabu on the Ocean label: 'basically....for the money'. Sabu turned to studio work, putting the band on ice until Motown subsidiary Morocco offered him a deal. As Kidd Glove, the band adopted a harder style, showcasing Sabu's excellent vocals, reminiscent of a smokier Sammy Hagar, and rivetting guitar work. However, the album didn't take off, and when Morocco folded the band followed suit. Sabu was joined by Bozzo, Dan Ellis (keyboards) and Charles Esposito (drums) for the critically-acclaimed *Heartbreak*, which did well until the label went into liquidation, and Sabu supported himself with an Arista songwriting contract while he put together his next project, Only Child.

Albums: *Sabu* (MCA 1980, mini-album), *Heartbreak* (Heavy Metal America 1985). Kidd Glove: *Kidd Glove* (Morocco 1984).

Sacred Reich

This Phoenix, Arizona, USA thrash band formed in 1985, with Jason Rainey (rhythm guitar) joined by Phil Rind (bass/vocals) and Greg Hall (drums), with Wiley Arnett replacing original lead guitarist Jeff Martinek in 1987. The band stuck together despite Flotsam And Jetsam wooing Arnett and Rind (who was also offered the Dark Angel vocal slot) and Slayer offering Greg Hall Dave Lombardo's then vacant drumstool, appearing on *Metal Massacre 8* before making a fine debut with *Ignorance*. This displayed considerable maturity and musicianship with hardcore political lyrics to match the ironic band name. Rind continued to work on political themes on *Surf Nicaragua*, while the band toured heavily, and the *Live At The Dynamo* EP followed an acclaimed 1989 performance at the Dutch festival. *The American Way* reaped the benefits of Scared Reich's experience, with Hall's performance particularly outstanding, while Rind's lyrics ranged across ecology (on the brilliant 'Crimes Against Humanity', the original album title), intolerance, apartheid and the ills of US society ('Lady Liberty rots away, No truth, no justice, The American way'). The band also preached musical tolerance with '31 Flavors', the funk-rock album closer. Hall, however, found the constant touring hard, and was later replaced by Dave McClain, who made his recording debut on *Independent*, ironically the band's first major label outing, which saw them stretch their musical abilities beyond straight thrash boundaries.

Albums: *Ignorance* (Metal Blade/Enigma 1987), *Surf Nicaragua* (Metal Blade/Enigma 1988, mini-album), *The American Way* (Metal Blade/Enigma 1990), *Independent* (Hollywood 1993).

Saga

Drawing on a variety of influences from Rush to Emerson, Lake And Palmer, multi-talented musician Mike Sadler and drummer Steve Negus put together their first line-up in Toronto, Canada, in 1977, with the guitar/keyboard playing brothers Jim and Ian Crichton. A self-financed album was then released on their own label. In 1980 they signed to Polydor Records and, with additional musicians, produced *Images At Twilight*, which continued the science fiction themes of their debut. A 12-inch EP was released in the UK to promote the album and, receiving a good deal of positive reaction, they set out on tour, supported for many shows by Magnum. Later that year they added another keyboard player, Jim Gilmore, and began work on the next album. Released in 1981, this elevated them into the major concert circuit where they proved a big attraction in

America. Their record company lost interest, but Epic came to the rescue until a more lasting deal was set up with Portrait Records. However, the band lost direction and the founder members became disillusioned and soon left to pursue a new band under their own name. The rest of the group continued to little interest, but in one final attempt to recapture the imagination they returned to the sci-fi concept for their final album in 1989.

Albums: *Saga* (Maze 1978), *Images At Twilight* (Polydor 1980), *Silent Knight* (Polydor 1980), *Worlds Apart* (Polydor 1981), *In Transit* (Polydor 1982), *Head Or Tails* (Epic 1983), *Behaviour* (Portrait 1984), *Wildest Dreams* (Atlantic 1987), *The Beginners Guide To Throwing Shapes* (Bonaire 1989).

Salas, Stevie, Colorcode

Guitarist/vocalist Stevie Salas was working in a Los Angeles recording studio when George Clinton turned him into a hot property by asking him to play on his 1986 album, *R&B Skeletons In The Closet*. Salas subsequently found himself in demand for his guitar and production skills, working with acts such as Was (Not Was), Andy Taylor, the Tubes and Eddie Money, and contributing to the *Bill & Ted's Excellent Adventure* soundtrack. A lucrative and enjoyable stint in Rod Stewart's touring band ensued before Salas was able to concentrate on his own project with bassist C.J. deVillar and drummer Winston A. Watson. *Stevie Salas Colorcode* was a sparkling debut, fusing raw hard rock and funk into excellent songs, from the anthemic 'Stand Up' to 'Indian Chief', a sensitive tribute to Salas' father. With airplay success for opening single 'The Harder They Come', the band were hotly tipped by the rock press. Live shows with Joe Satriani in the US and 24-7 Spyz in the UK further enhanced Colorcode's reputation, but the momentum was lost, along with their recording deal, during the sale of Island Records to Polygram, when the majority of Island's hard rock acts were dropped. However, the band retained a Japanese deal, and released two further albums: *Stuff*, a collection of demo and live tracks with a superb acoustic reworking of 'Blind' from the debut, and the *Bootleg Like A Mug!!* live set, which displayed a distinct Hendrix influence with covers of 'Little Wing' and 'Hey Joe'. Salas went on to work with old friend Bootsy Collins and ex-Band Of Gypsys drummer Buddy Miles, releasing *Hardware* in 1992 under the Third Eye name (conversely packaged in the UK as *Third Eye Open* on Rykodisc by Hardware), before reuniting with the Colorcode band and a host of guest stars to record *Stevie Salas Presents The Electric Pow Wow*, a mixture of original material and largely obscure covers. The adaptable guitarist also played as part of Terence Trent D'Arby's live band. Salas then put Colocode on ice for a time to work more closely with Sass Jordan on her *Rats* album, the pair having aleady collaborated on *Racine* and Salas' *Electric Pow Wow* set. Another Colorcode album, *Back From The Living Dead*, then emerged with the original line-up augmented by bassist T.M. Stevens, Pride And Glory/ex-Sass Jordan drummer Brian Tichy, and 24-7 Spyz bassist Rick Skatore, and the material and performances matched the quality of the debut.

Albums: *Stevie Salas Colorcode* (Island 1990), *Stuff* (Polystar 1991), *Bootleg Like A Mug!!* (Polystar 1992), *Stevie Salas Presents The Electric Pow Wow* (Polystar 1993), *Back From The Living Dead* (Polystar 1994).

Salem, Kevin

Prominent New York-based rock singer/songwriter Kevin Salem (guitar/vocals) made best use of his dramatic surname by recruiting Dave Dunton (keyboards), Keith Levreault (drums; ex-Blood Oranges, Roscoe's Gang), Todd Novak (guitar/vocals; ex-Dragsters) and Scott Yoder (bass; ex-Blue Chieftains) to provide a 'going concern' rock group. Salem himself hailed from Johnstown, Pennsylvania, before moving to Boston where he joined Dumptruck for their acclaimed 1987 album, *For The Country*. He would stay with that band until the dawn of the 90s, when frustrations and legal complications saw him depart. Relocating to New York, Salem performed with his own *ad-hoc* band, also working as a sideman for Freedy Johnston and Yo La Tengo. His session contributions included tracks on Johnston's *Can You Fly*, the Pooh Sticks' *Million Seller* and Chris Harford's *Be Headed*. As well as recording with Miracle Legion Salem also took the production mantle for Madder Rose's debut album. His first album under his own name was actually completed in 1992, after he had recorded 11 songs in a variety of New York studios, sneaking in after-hours to lay down the tracks when cash flow problems arose. The resulting *Keep Your Crosses Fingered* would have to be postponed however. Instead Salem concentrated on putting together the current line-up of his band, who recorded *Soma City* in five days at Hoboken's Water Music studios. It was helped in no small part by the production tutelage of Niko Bolas (best known for his work with Neil Young) who fitted Salem in for free between commissions from Billy Joel and Rod Stewart. It included one song, 'Forever Gone', co-written with Nirvana/Urge Overkill producer Butch Vig.

Album: *Soma City* (Roadrunner 1994).

Salty Dog

This Los Angeles-based band were put together in late 1986 by bassist Mike Hannon (b. Columbus, Ohio, USA) and drummer Khurt Maier (b. Sacramento, California, USA), enlisting Youngstown, Ohio-born vocalist Jimmi Bleacher and replacing their original guitarist (Scott Lane) with Canadian Pete Reveen in early 1987. The band developed a blues-based style which drew immediate Led Zeppelin comparisons, but owed more to a mixture of influences from old bluesmen like Memphis Slim, 'Sonny Boy' Williamson and Willie Dixon to the more contemporary sounds of Black Flag and Motörhead. *Every Dog Has Its Day*, recorded in Rockfield Studios in Wales with producer Peter Collins, demonstrated that the Zeppelin references were most apt due to the sheer variety of styles within Salty Dog's bluesy framework, from straightforward opener, 'Come Along', through the smouldering 'Slow Daze', to the tongue-in-cheek acoustic blues of 'Just Like A Woman'. The album received a flurry of good reviews, but Salty Dog were unable to capitalize, as Bleacher departed shortly after its release. The band struggled to find a replacement, locating Dallas native Darrel Beach (ex-DT Roxx) in late 1991, but the loss of momentum proved crucial and Salty Dog faded.
Album: *Every Dog Has Its Day* (Geffen 1990).

Samhain

Samhain were Glenn Danzig's second major project and formed a bridge between the macabre exuberance of punk legends the Misfits and the seductively menacing rock of his current band, Danzig. The core of Samhain consisted of Glenn Danzig (vocals), ex-Misfits drummer Eerie Von (now bass), Steve Zing (drums), and Peter 'Damien' Marshall (guitars), with Lyle Preslar (ex-Minor Threat) and London May (drums) also recording under the banner. In Samhain Danzig stripped away a lot of the kitsch grotesquerie that had characterized the Misfits, and replaced it with a starker, less comic book approach. Sinister and predatory, Samhain's music was an exercise in lean, evocative rhythm and bleak mood. As with the Misfits, the production is very uneven, and the sound often feels too thin to sustain the bite the material demands. Nevertheless, at their best, most notably on their strongest album, *November Coming Fire*, Samhain could be hauntingly hungry and morbidly resonant. Their last recording, *Final Descent*, features a remastered version of the *Unholy Passion* material compiled with another session from 1987 with future Danzig band guitarist John Christ.
Albums: *Initium* (Plan 9 1984), *Unholy Passion* (Plan 9 1985, mini-album), *November Coming Fire* (Plan 9 1986). Compilation: *Final Descent* (Plan 9 1990).

Samson

This UK heavy metal group were formed in 1978 by guitarist Paul Samson, and have since been dogged by line-up changes, management disputes and record company problems. These have occurred at critical points in their career, just as major success seemed imminent. The first incarnation of the band comprised Paul Samson (guitar), Chris Aylmer (bass), Bruce Bruce (vocals) and Clive Burr (drums), the latter soon moving on to Iron Maiden and being replaced by the masked Thunderstick. Samson specialized in high energy blues-based rock and were among the leading lights of the New Wave Of British Heavy Metal movement, with each of their first four albums becoming minor classics of the genre. In 1981 Bruce Bruce and Thunderstick departed, the former assumed his real name, Bruce Dickinson, and joined Iron Maiden as vocalist. Thunderstick formed a new group under his own name. Nicky Moore (ex-Tiger) and Mel Gaynor (ex-Light Of The World) stepped in on vocals and drums respectively, but Gaynor soon moved on to Simple Minds, with Pete Jupp filling in as replacement (he would later join FM). *Before The Storm* and *Don't Get Mad, Get Even* are Samson's most accomplished works, with Moore's gritty and impassioned vocals giving the band a sound that was both earthy and honest. Chris Aylmer left in 1984 and was replaced by ex-Diamond Head bassist, Merv Goldsworthy, before the recording of an excellent live album, *Thank You And Goodnight*. Samson split soon after, with *Head Tactics* a posthumous release comprising remixes of tracks from *Head On* and *Shock Tactics*. Nicky Moore went on to form Mammoth, while Paul Samson released a solo effort, *Joint Forces,* in 1986. The band reformed in 1988, and released *Refugee* two years later, a classy if slightly dated collection of blues-based hard rock numbers.
Albums: *Survivors* (Lazer 1979), *Head On* (Gem 1980), *Shock Tactics* (RCA 1981), *Before The Storm* (Polydor 1982), *Don't Get Mad, Get Even* (Polydor 1984), *Thank You And Goodnight* (Metal Masters 1984), *Refugee* (Communique 1990), *Live At Reading* (Raw Fruit 1991), *Joint Forces* (1993). Compilations: *Head Tactics* (Capitol 1986), *Pillars Of Rock* (Connoisseur 1990).
Video: *Biceps Of Steel* (1985).

Sanctuary

Formed in Seattle, Washington, USA, in 1985, Sanctuary consisted of Warrel Dane (vocals), Lenny Rutledge (guitar/vocals), Sean Blosl (guitar/vocals), Jim Sheppard (bass) and Dave Budbill (drums/vocals). Through two early demo tracks included on a low budget compilation, *Northwest Metal Fest*, the band attracted the attention of Megadeth guitarist Dave Mustaine, who offered to oversee their next recordings. With this recommendation behind them the band signed to CBS/Epic Records and Mustaine was duly drafted as producer. *Refuge Denied* introduced Sanctuary's somewhat basic thrash sound, one of great intensity but little direction or scope. After extensive touring with Megadeth the band offered the slightly superior *Into The Mirror Black*, but broke up shortly afterwards.

Albums: *Refuge Denied* (CBS 1987), *Into The Mirror Black* (CBS 1990).

Santers

Canadian heavy metal trio with a strong blues influence formed in 1980 by guitarist and vocalist Rick Santers and his brother Mark on drums together with their friend, Rick Lazaroff, on bass. Aside from playing numerous concerts and recording their debut album in 1981, Rick Santers was in demand as a session player and, in particular, helped fellow Canadian Lee Aaron with her demos and first album. In 1982 Santers the band picked up a European licensing deal with Heavy Metal Records who released *Racing Time* in December. This featured some fine guitar work, especially on the tracks 'Mistreatin' Heart' and 'Hard Time Loving You'. Their last album was released two years later before Rick decided to return to session work.

Albums: *Shot Down In Flames* (Ready 1981), *Racing Time* (Ready/Heavy Metal 1982), *Guitar Alley* (Ready/Heavy Metal 1984).

Saraya

Formed in 1987 by vocalist Sandi Saraya and keyboard player Gregg Munier, this US rock band originally travelled under the title Alsace Lorraine. With the addition of Tony Rey (guitar), Gary Taylor (bass) and Chuck Bonfarte (drums), they changed their name to Saraya. Fusing influences such as Heart, the Pretenders and Pat Benatar, they recorded a self-titled debut for Polygram; a melodic and highly polished collection of AOR numbers characterized by Sandi's hammy but infectious vocal style. Following internal disputes Rey and Taylor quit in 1990 and were replaced by Tony Bruno and Barry Dunaway respectively. *When The Blackbird Sings*, released in 1991, built on their former style but again failed to find success.

Albums: *Saraya* (Polygram 1989), *When The Blackbird Sings* (Polydor 1991).

Sarkoma

Alternative metal band from the mid west of America staffed by 'a brotherhood of musicians' who include Brian Carter (vocals), Tony Chrisman (bass), Mike Hilleburg (guitar), Aaron Ingram (drums) and Stuart Johnson (guitar). Sarkoma made their debut in 1992 with the *Completely Different* EP, before regional and national touring. Lyrical content derived from the personal and imagined experiences of Johnson, including one song, 'Blue Horizon', written from a female perspective. Other issues explored on the group's debut album, *Integrity*, included evolution ('Universal Footsteps') and celebrity ('Mortamer'). With strong all-round songwriting it may not prove too long before the band are forced to become better acquainted with the latter sentiment.

Album: *Integrity* (Bulletproof 1994).

Satan

Formed from the ashes of Blitzkrieg in Newcastle-upon-Tyne, England, in 1981, the original line-up of Satan comprised Trevor Robinson (vocals), Russ Tippins (guitar), Steve Ramsey (guitar), Graeme English (bass) and Andy Reed (drums). In 1981 the band recorded two tracks for a compilation, *Roxcalibur*, and a self-financed single entitled 'Kiss Of Death'. Soon after its release vocalist Robinson left the band to be replaced by Ian Swift who himself was soon supplanted by Brian Ross. Through numerous demos and a name built for themselves via the underground tape-trading scene, they attracted the attention of Noise Records. Their debut album, *Court In The Act*, followed in 1984. Typified by speed-metal riffs and strong lead guitar work, this was again well-received. However, the name of the band did not work to their advantage, and was atypical of their lyrical dimension. Not only did they alter the name to Blind Fury but once again changed vocalists, replacing the departed Ross with Lou Taylor. This line-up recorded one album using the Blind Fury appellation, *Out Of Reach*, in 1985. The band changed vocalists yet again replacing Taylor with Michael Jackson and reverted to the name Satan shortly thereafter. A new demo attracted the interest of the German-based Steamhammer Records and *Into The Future* was released in 1986. The album's poor production was parried by the power and quality of the material. *Suspended Sentence* followed in 1987. However, once again the name was causing problems and record company and managerial pressure now saw it changed to Pariah. After two further albums, *The Kindred* and *Blaze Of Obscurity*, the band in all its myriad guises folded in 1990.

Albums: *Court In The Act* (Neat 1984), *Into The*

Future (Steamhammer 1986), *Suspended Sentence* (Steamhammer 1987).

Satriani, Joe

Joe Satriani grew up in Long Island, New York, USA, and is a skilled guitarist responsible for teaching the instrument to, among others, Kirk Hammett of Metallica, and Steve Vai. After travelling abroad extensively in his youth he returned to the USA to form the Squares. This project folded in 1984 through an abject lack of commercial recognition, giving Satriani the opportunity to concentrate on his experimental guitar playing. The outcome of this was the release of an EP, *Joe Satriani*. Following a spell with the Greg Kihn band, appearing on *Love And Rock 'N' Roll*, Satriani released *Not Of This Earth*, an album which was less polished than its successor, *Surfing With The Alien*. Despite offering no vocal accompaniment, this set was a major seller and brought mainstream respect to an artist often felt to be too clinical or technical for such reward. In 1988 he was joined more permanently by Stu Hamm (bass) and Jonathan Mover (drums), also working for a spell on Mick Jagger's late-80s tour. Never afraid to push his considerable musical skills to the limit, Satriani has played the banjo and harmonica on his albums, as

well as successfully attempting vocals on *Flying In A Blue Dream*. In 1993 he released *Time Machine*, a double CD which contained a mixture of new and previously unreleased tracks dating back to 1984, and also live material from his 1993 Extremist world tour. The guitarist then replaced Ritchie Blackmore in Deep Purple in 1994.

Albums: *Not Of This Earth* (Relativity 1986), *Surfing With The Alien* (Relativity 1987), *Dreaming 11* (Relativity 1988), *Flying In A Blue Dream* (Relativity 1990), *Time Machine* (1993, double album).

Savage

Formed in Mansfield, England, in 1978, Savage's line-up consisted of Chris Bradley (bass/vocals), Andy Dawson (guitar), Wayne Redshaw (guitar) and Mark Brown (drums). Their debut album, *Loose 'N' Lethal*, won critical acclaim for its ultra-heavy riffs and was firmly rooted in the New Wave Of British Heavy Metal. The band then toured Europe where they quickly gained popularity, especially in Holland. Similar success in their homeland was not so forthcoming. In 1984 the band signed a new recording agreement with Zebra Records who released an EP, *We Got The Edge*. This revealed an amended approach with a mellower, more cultured

Savatage

sound. Restraint was also in evidence on 1985's *Hyperactive*. After this, Savage seemed to lose both momentum and direction and they disbanded in 1986.

Albums: *Loose 'N' Lethal* (Ebony 1983), *Hyperactive* (Zebra 1985).

Savage Grace

No relation to the early 70s group who recorded for Reprise Records, this US power-metal quartet, originally titled Maquis De Sade, were formed in Los Angeles, California, in 1981. Since then they have enjoyed a chequered career hindered by unstable line-ups, the first of which featured Mike Smith (vocals), Chris Logue (guitar/vocals), Brian East (bass) and Dan Finch (drums). They were signed on the strength of a track included on the *Metal Massacre* series of compilations and a self-financed EP, *The Dominatress*, which the band had released in 1983. *Master Of Disguise*, their full debut from 1985, preceded their first line-up changes; ex-Agent Steel guitarist Mark Marshall was added, while Mike Smith's departure left Chris Logue to handle the lead vocals. Drummer Dan Finch also quit to be replaced by Mark Markum.

This incarnation of the band managed to stay together long enough to record 1986's *After The Fall From Grace*. Savage Grace then toured Europe with Heir Apparent and swapped bassist Brian East for that band's Derek Peace before beginning work on recordings for a projected third album. However, the continual line-up shuffles had taken their toll and Peace rejoined Heir Apparent as Savage Grace disappeared late in 1988.

Albums: *Master Of Disguise* (Metal Blade 1985), *After The Fall From Grace* (Black Dragon 1986).

Savatage

Previously known as Metropolis and Avatar, Savatage, a melodic, heavy rock quintet, were formed in Florida, USA, in 1983 by the Oliva brothers. The full band line-up comprised Jon Oliva (vocals/keyboards), Criss Oliva (guitar), Steve 'Doc' Wacholz (drums) and Keith Collins (bass), the latter eventually replaced by Johnny Lee Middleton. Their initial approach was strongly influenced by Judas Priest and Iron Maiden, a style demonstrated by their *City Beneath The Surface* EP from their year of formation. Savatage's first three albums also clearly reflect their influences, with a

Saxon

high-energy fusion of power-riffs and high-pitched vocals. *Fight For The Rock* marked a detour towards more melodic AOR, which was poorly received by their fans, before returning to their roots for the next album. Chris Caffery was added as a second guitarist in 1989, before the recording of *Gutter Ballet*. This, and *Streets*, represented the band's finest work to this point. Both were elaborate rock operas, featuring a mixture of dynamic hard rock and atmospheric ballads. Utilizing an orchestra and state-of-the-art production techniques, they also found themselves with a minor hit single on their hands in the shape of 'Jesus Saves'. Jon Oliva was then relegated to nominal backing vocals behind new frontman Zachary Stevens - having elected instead to concentrate on penning rock operas full time and working as part of Doctor Butcher. Stevens was ex-White Witch, and joined in time for 1993's *Edge Of Thorns*. That year also brought tragedy when founding member and guitarist Criss Oliva was killed in October in a car crash near his home in Clearwater, Florida. For *Handful Of Rain* the group recruited ex-Testament guitarist Alex Skolnick, whose former band had toured with Savatage in support of Dio in 1989. The set included one notable tribute to the late guitarist, 'Alone I Breathed'. 'Watching You Fall', meanwhile, discussed the war in Bosnia.

Albums: *Sirens* (Music For Nations 1985), *The Dungeons Are Calling* (Music For Nations 1985, mini-album), *Power Of The Night* (Atlantic 1985), *Fight For The Rock* (Atlantic 1986), *Hall Of The Mountain King* (Atlantic 1987), *Gutter Ballet* (Atlantic 1990), *Streets* (Atlantic 1991), *Edge Of Thorns* (Bullet Proof 1993), *Handfull Of Rain* (Bullet Proof 1994).

Saxon

Formed in the north of England in the late 70s, Saxon were originally known as Son Of A Bitch and spent their early days paying dues in clubs and small venues up and down the UK, with Peter 'Biff' Byford (vocals), Graham Oliver (guitar), Paul Quinn (guitar), Steve Dawson (bass) and Pete Gill (drums) building a strong live reputation. After the name switch they signed a deal with French label Carrere, better known for its disco productions than its work with heavy metal bands. During the late 70s many young metal bands were emerging in a UK scene which became known as the New Wave Of British Heavy Metal. These bands challenged the supremacy of the old guard of heavy metal bands, and Saxon were at the head of this movement along with Iron Maiden and Diamond Head. The first album was a solid, if basic heavy rock outing, but the release of *Wheels Of Steel* turned the tide. Saxon's popularity soared, earning themselves two UK Top 20 hits with 'Wheels Of Steel' and '747 (Strangers In The Night)'. They capitalized on this success with the release in the same year of *Strong Arm Of The Law*, another very heavy, surprisingly articulate, metal album. A further Top 20 hit arrived with 'And The Bands Played On', drawn from the following year's *Demin And Leather*, which also produced 'Never Surrender'. They toured the USA to great acclaim and appeared at the Castle Donington 'Monsters Of Rock' festival. By the time of 1982's *The Eagle Has Landed*, which gave Saxon their most successful album, reaching the UK Top 5, the group were at their peak. That same year, Pete Gill was replaced by drummer Nigel Glockler, who had previously worked with Toyah. At this point Saxon counted among their rivals only the immensely popular Iron Maiden. The release of *Power And The Glory* enforced their credentials as a major rock band. The follow up, *Innocence Is No Excuse*, was a more polished and radio-friendly production but it stalled just inside the Top 40. It heralded an uncertain time for the band and a resulting slide in their popularity. The departure of Steve Dawson contributed to their malaise. *Rock The Nations* was as punishing as old, but the chance to recapture former glories had now expired. In 1990 Saxon returned to the public eye with a UK tour that featured a set-list built on their popular older material. *Solid Ball Of Rock* was their most accomplished album for some time, but any return to their previous status seems unlikely.

Albums: *Saxon* (Saxon Carrere 1979), *Wheels Of Steel* (Saxon Carrere 1980), *Strong Arm Of The Law* (Carrere 1980), *Denim And Leather* (Carrere 1981), *The Eagle Has Landed* (Carrere 1982), *Power And The Glory* (Carrere 1983), *Crusader* (Carrere 1984), *Innocence Is No Excuse* (Parlophone 1985), *Rock The Nations* (EMI 1986), *Destiny* (EMI 1988), *Rock 'N' Roll Gypsies* (Roadrunner 1990), *Solid Ball Of Rock* (Virgin 1991). Compilations: *Anthology* (Raw Power 1988), *Back On The Streets* (Connoisseur 1990), *Greatest Hits Live* (Essential 1990), *Best Of* (EMI 1991).

Videos: *Live Innocence* (1986), *Power & The Glory - Video Anthology* (1989), *Saxon Live* (1989), *Greatest Hits Live* (1990).

Scanner

This German rock quintet rose from the ashes of Lion's Breed in 1987. Comprising Tom S. Sopha (guitar), Michael Knoblich (vocals), Wolfgang Kolorz (drums), Axel A.J. Julius (guitar) and Martin Bork (bass), their brand of metal-thrash identified them with fellow countrymen, Helloween. Signing to Noise Records in 1988, Scanner released *Hypertrace*, a

science-fiction concept album. The storyline revolved around extra-terrestrial robots preventing war between the superpowers and, although far from original, it found an appreciative and appreciable audience. Knoblich quit the group in 1989 and was replaced by ex-Angel Dust vocalist S.L. Coe. They recorded *Terminal Earth*, another concept album, centred this time on the aforementioned robots' concern for planet Earth, and the damage that the human race has inflicted upon it. Not suprisingly, it bore a strong musical resemblance to its predecessor.
Albums: *Hypertrace* (Noise 1988), *Terminal Earth* (Noise 1990).

Scat Opera

Formed in the late 80s around Ernie Brennan (vocals), Steve Yates (guitar), John O'Reilly (bass) and Mark Diment (drums), Scat Opera recorded several well-received demos before picking up prestigious support slots with Faith No More in the autumn of 1989. Though comparisons to that band followed, in truth Scat Opera played at greater velocity and with more precise musical definition. The pieces, however, were not entirely in place until they signed a contract with Music For Nations in the spring of 1990. They made their debut a year later with *About Time*,

recorded at Slaughterhouse Studios and produced by Colin Richardson. A UK tour as support to Gaye Bykers On Acid ensued, before returning to the studio (this time Windings Studio in Wales) with Richardson for a second set, *Four Gone Confusion*, to be released in October 1992. Again the music incorporated elements drawn from funk (particularly apparent in bass player O'Reilly's slapping technique), jazz and metal.
Albums: *About Time* (Music For Nations 1991), *Four Gone Confusion* (Music For Nations 1992).

Scatterbrain

A New York, USA band who have experienced at first hand the swings and roundabouts of the modern music industry, Scatterbrain drew original members Tommy Christ (vocals) and Paul Nieder (guitar) from hardcore outfit Ludichrist. This group, who released two albums for Relativity, *Immaculate Deception* in 1987 and *Powertrip* in 1989, were never accepted by the hardcore community, whose low tolerance threshold for humour militated against Ludichrist's flippancy. Scatterbrain was consequently invoked as the duo's new home, featuring additional members Guy Brogna (bass) and Mike Boyko (drums). However, early songs like 'Goodbye Freedom, Hello

Scat Opera

Mom' indicated that their sense of fun had not deserted them in the transition. Their debut, *Here Comes Trouble*, boasted two minor hits, 'Down With The Ship' and 'Don't Call Me Dude', both of which also had memorable videos. Touring the US and Europe, Scatterbrain discovered a rich vein of support for their efforts in Australia, where 'Don't Call Me Dude' would go Top 10. *Scumbuggery* followed in 1991, though this would be their last tenure with their label. For *Mundis Intellectuals* the group moved over to Music For Nations' subsidiary Bulletproof Records, with opening track 'Write That Hit' addressing the group's problems with industry executives (some of the lyrics, including 'How about hip hop?', were legendarily taken from real suggestions made to them by their former record company).

Albums: *Here Comes Trouble* (In-Effect 1990), *Scumbuggery* (In-Effect 1991), *Mundis Intellectuals* (Bulletproof 1994).

Schenker, Michael

b.10 January 1955, Savstedt, Germany. Schenker began his musical career in 1971 at the age of 16, when, along with brother Rudolf, he formed the Scorpions. After contributing impressive guitarwork on the band's *Lonesome Crow* debut, he was offered the chance to replace Bernie Marsden in UFO. Schenker joined the group in June 1973 and their resultant musical direction swung to hard rock. *Phenomenon*, released in 1974, featured the metal classics 'Doctor, Doctor' and 'Rock Bottom', with Schenker's performance on his Gibson 'Flying V' hammering home the band's new identity. A series of excellent albums followed before Schenker eventually quit in 1978 after the recording of *Obsession*. The split had been predicted for some time following personal conflicts between Schenker and vocalist Phil Mogg. The guitarist moved back to Germany and temporarily rejoined the Scorpions, contributing to *Lovedrive*, released in 1979. Soon afterwards he formed his own band, the Michael Schenker Group, which was later abbreviated to MSG. MSG's personnel has remained in a constant state of flux, with Schenker hiring and firing musicians seemingly at will. In 1991 Schenker also took time out between MSG albums to contribute to the Contraband project, a one-off collaboration between members of Shark Island, Vixen, Ratt and L.A.Guns.

Albums: With the Scorpions: *Action/Lonesome Crow* (Brain 1972), *Lovedrive* (EMI 1979). With UFO: *Phenomenon* (Chrysalis 1974), *Force It* (Chrysalis 1975), *No Heavy Pettin'* (Chrysalis 1976), *Lights Out* (Chrysalis 1977), *Obsession* (Chrysalis 1978),

Strangers In The Night (Chrysalis 1979, double album). With MSG: *The Michael Schenker Group* (Chrysalis 1980), *MSG* (Chrysalis 1981), *One Night At Budokan* (Chrysalis 1982), *Assault Attack* (Chrysalis 1982). *Built To Destroy* (Chrysalis 1983), *Rock Will Never Die* (Chrysalis 1984), *Perfect Timing* (EMI 1987), *Save Yourself* (Capitol 1989), *MSG* (EMI 1992). With Contraband: *Contraband* (Impact/EMI 1991).

Schon And Hammer

This was a short-lived partnership between Journey's Neal Schon (b. 27 February 1954, San Mateo, California, USA; guitar/vocals) and Jan Hammer (b. 17 April 1948, Prague, Czechoslovakia; keyboards/drums). The fusion of styles between Schon's AOR and Hammer's jazz-rock produced *Untold Passion*, a record which largely consisted of virtuoso performances from both musicians duelling against each other. The innovative British electric jazz bassist Colin Hodgkinson, previously with Back Door, accompanied the duo in the studio on the first album and Schon's vocal contributions proved to be particularly satisfying. By the time of the second release many of Schon's comrades from Journey had been enlisted, resulting in a lighter collection of songs and a departure from Schon And Hammer's *raison d'être*. The partnership was soon dissolved, with Schon returning full-time to Journey and Hammer moving to television work, enjoying particular success with the *Miami Vice* series.

Albums: *Untold Passion* (CBS 1981), *Here To Stay* (CBS 1982).

School Of Violence

This New York hardcore quartet was formed in 1985 by Stegmon Von Heintz (guitar), Karl Axell (vocals), Rick Stone (bass) and M.S. Evans (drums). Their recorded debut came on a compilation album, *The People Are Hungry*. This led to a contract with Metal Blade Records and the release of *We The People* in 1988. Assimilating influences drawn from punk and thrash bands like Bad Brains, Anthrax and D.O.A., it featured vitriolic lyrics addressing social and political injustices. The production was very ragged however, and the messages were swamped beneath the drum and bass-laden tumult.

Album: *We The People* (Metal Blade 1988).

Scorn

A synthesis of new technology and the traditional grindcore logarithms of pounding bottom end drums and bass, Scorn are a UK duo of ex-Napalm Death personnel Mick Harris (drums; also a member of

Scorpions

Painkiller) and Nick Bullen (bass/vocals) - initially helped out by a further former member of that band, Justin Broadrick (guitar). A debut album and attendant single, *Vae Solis* and 'Lick Forever Dog', were produced by John Wakelin at Rhythm Studios in Birmingham. Setting out on the road with Cancer and Pitch Shifter to promote this primeval slab of white noise, the group were joined by Candiru guitarist Pat McCahan, who replaced Broadrick (now fully occupied with Godflesh). A five-track, 40-minute 12-inch single emerged in October 1992, 'Deliverance', followed by the *White Irises Blind* E.P. *Colossus* was the group's second full length affair and once more saw them working with Wakelin. If anything, *Evanescence* surpassed previous exercises in extremity, with a bass sound so deep that the term dub was widely invoked. This sonic marginalism led them in to contact with musicians outside of their own tribe, and 1995 saw the release of a remix album, with contributors including Coil, Scanner, Meat Beat Manifesto and Bill Laswell among others.
Albums: *Vae Solis* (Earache 1992), *Colossus* (Earache 1993), *Evanescence* (Earache 1994).

Scorpions

This German hard rock group was formed by guitarists Rudolf and Michael Schenker in 1971. With Klaus Meine (vocals), Lothar Heinberg (bass) and Wolfgang Dziony (drums), they exploded onto the international heavy rock scene with *Lonesome Crow* in 1972. This tough and exciting record was characterized by Schenker's distinctive, fiery guitarwork on his Gibson 'Flying V' and Klaus Meine's dramatic vocals. Soon after the album was released Heinberg, Dziony and Schenker left, the latter joining UFO. Francis Buchholz and Jurgen Rosenthal stepped in on bass and drums respectively for the recording of *Fly To The Rainbow*. Ulrich Roth was recruited as Schenker's replacement in 1974 and Rudy Lenners took over the drum stool from Rosenthal the following year. The following releases, *Trance* and *Virgin Killer*, epitomized the Scorpions new-found confidence and unique style; a fusion of intimidating power-riffs, wailing guitar solos and melodic vocal lines. Produced by Dieter Dierks, the improvements musically were now matched technically. Their reputation began to grow throughout Europe and the Far East, backed up by exhaustive touring. *Taken By Force* saw Herman

Rarebell replace Lenners, with the band branching out into anthemic power-ballads, bolstered by emotive production, for the first time. Although commercially successful, Roth was not happy with this move, and he quit to form Electric Sun following a major tour to support the album. *Tokyo Tapes* was recorded on this tour and marked the end of the first phase of the band's career. This was an electrifying live set populated by top form renditions of their strongest numbers. Mathias Jabs was recruited as Roth's replacement, but had to step down temporarily in favour of Michael Schenker, who had just left UFO under acrimonious circumstances. Schenker contributed guitar on three tracks of *Lovedrive* and toured with them afterwards. He was replaced by Jabs permanently after collapsing on stage during their European tour in 1979. The band had now achieved a stable line-up, and shared the mutual goal of breaking through in the USA. Relentless touring schedules ensued and their albums leaned more and more towards sophisticated hard-edged melodic rock. *Blackout* made the US *Billboard* Top 10, as did the following *Love At First Sting* which featured the magnificent 'Still Loving You', a fine and enduring hard rock ballad. *World Wide Live* was released in 1985, another double live set, but this time only featuring material from the second phase of the band's career. Superbly recorded and produced, it captured the band at their melodic best, peaking at number 14 in a four month stay on the US chart. The band took a well-earned break before releasing *Savage Amusement* in 1988, their first studio album for almost four years. This marked a slight change in emphasis again, adopting a more restrained approach. Nevertheless it proved a huge success, reaching number 5 in the USA and number 1 throughout Europe. The band switched to Phonogram Records in 1989 and ended their 20-year association with producer Dieter Dierks. *Crazy World* followed and was to become their most successful album to date. The politically poignant 'Wind Of Change', lifted as a single, became their first million-seller as it reached the number 1 position in country after country around the world. Produced by Keith Olsen, *Crazy World* transformed the band's sound, ensuring enormous crossover potential without radically compromising their identity or alienating their original fanbase. Buchholz was sacked in 1992, at which time investigators began to look into the band's accounts for alleged tax evasion. His replacement would be classically trained musician Ralph Heickermann, who had previously provided computer programming for Kingdom Come, as well as varied soundtrack work.

Albums: *Action/Lonesome Crow* (Brain 1972), *Fly To The Rainbow* (RCA 1974), *In Trance* (RCA 1975), *Virgin Killers* (RCA 1976), *Taken By Force* (RCA 1978), *Tokyo Tapes* (RCA 1978), *Lovedrive* (EMI 1979), *Animal Magnetism* (EMI 1980), *Blackout* (EMI 1982), *Love At First Sting* (EMI 1984), *World Wide Live* (EMI 1985), *Savage Amusement* (EMI 1988), (1990), *Crazy World* (Vertigo 1990), *Face The Heat* (Vertigo 1993). Compilations: *The Best Of The Scorpions* (RCA 1979), *The Best Of The Scorpions, Volume 2* (RCA 1984), *Gold Ballads* (Harvest 1987), *CD Box Set* (EMI 1991). Herman Rarebell solo: *Nip In The Bud* (Harvest 1981).

Videos: *World Wide Live* (1985), *Crazy World Tour* (1991).

Scream

Not to be confused with the Washington, DC punk band of the same name, this group took shape from the ashes of LA favourites Racer X when in-demand Philadelphian vocalist/guitarist John Corabi joined Bruce Bouillet (lead guitar) and John Alderete (bass) in that band's final line-up. With the departure of Scott Travis to Judas Priest, the drumstool was filled by Walt Woodward III (ex-Americade and Shark Island), and the band became the Scream. In contrast to the complex guitar-orientated metal of the old act, the Scream played in a variety of styles, from the gentle ballad, 'Father, Mother, Son' and the witty acoustic blues of 'Never Loved Her Anyway' to the electric hard rock of 'Outlaw' and the atmospheric 'Man In The Moon'. They even tackled funk-rock with 'Tell Me Why', revealing influences as diverse as the Rolling Stones, Van Halen, Led Zeppelin, Humble Pie and Aerosmith. However, the resultant debut, *Let It Scream*, was a highly cohesive work with a powerful Eddie Kramer production and a charismatic performance from Corabi. The album and subsequent live work were well-received, and with priority backing from Hollywood Records, the Scream seemed set for stardom, until Corabi was tempted away to replace Vince Neil in Mötley Crüe. A lengthy search for a new singer ensued, with Billy Scott eventually being recruited, but the band subsequently changed their name to Stash, with a new direction reportedly in the vein of Sly And The Family Stone.

Album: *Let It Scream* (Hollywood 1991).

Screaming Trees

Hard-drinking rock band from the rural community of Ellensburg, near Seattle, USA. The Screaming Trees blend 60s music (the Beach Boys being an obvious reference point) with psychotic, pure punk

rage. Not to be confused with the Sheffield, England, synthesizer group of the same name who were also operational in the mid-80s, the Connor brothers (Gary Lee; guitar and Van; bass) are among the largest men in rock, rvialled in their girth only by fellow Seattle heavyweights Poison Idea. The rest of the line-up comprises Mark Lanegan (vocals) and Barrett Martin (drums - replacing original encumbent Mark Pickerell in 1991). *Even If And Especially When*, the best of three strong albums for SST Records, included notable compositions like the live favourite, 'Transfiguration', which typified the group's blend of punk aggression and 60s mysticism. Major label debut *Uncle Anaesthesia* brought production from Terry Date and Soundgarden's Chris Cornell. By the time Screaming Trees moved to Epic Records they had embraced what one *Melody Maker* journalist called 'unashamed 70s Yankee rock', straddled by bursts of punk spite. Lanegan had by now released a solo, largely acoustic album, *The Winding Sheet*, for Sub Pop in 1990. This affecting, intensely personal collection included a cover of Leadbelly's 'Where Did You Sleep Last Night', which Kurt Cobain would later employ as the trump card in Nirvana's *MTV Unplugged* session. Other extra-curricular activities included Gary Lee Conner's Purple Outside project, and his brother Van fronting Solomon Grundy (one album each in 1990).
Albums: *Clairvoyance* (Velvetone 1986), *Even If And Especially When* (SST 1987), *Invisible Lantern* (SST 1988), *Buzz Factory* (SST 1989), *Uncle Anaesthesia* (Epic 1991), *Sweet Oblivion* (Epic 1992), *Change Has Come* (Epic 1993). Compilation: *Anthology* (SST 1991).

Sea Hags

Purveyors of all things degenerate and of definite 'wrong side of the tracks' orientation, Sea Hags were formed in San Francisco, California, in 1985. With a line-up comprising ex-rock photographer Ron Yocom (guitar/vocals), Frankie Wilsey (guitar), Chris Schlosshardt (bass) and Adam Maples (drums), their own manager would famously describe their trajectory thus: 'there's only so far you can get with three junkies and one alcoholic'. Their first and only album was recorded for Chrysalis by Guns N' Roses producer, Mike Clink (after the Cult's Ian Astbury had expressed an interest). This collection, which aped the group's obvious inspiration, Aerosmith, riff for riff, caught the attention of the press, a situation exacerbated by the media-friendly antics of the subjects. However, the sadly predictable death of Chris Schlosshardt from a suspected drug overdose killed the band's momentum. Maples was briefly

rumoured to be replacement for Steven Adler in Guns N'Roses, while Wilsey joined Arcade.
Album: *Sea Hags* (Chrysalis 1989).

2nd Heat

Drawn together in Bremerhaven, Germany, by Kai Braue (guitar), Marcel Robbers (vocals), Mathias Gonik (bass) and Frank Hoogestraat (guitar), 2nd Heat were formed in 1992 and soon earned their spurs on bills with Phantom Blue, Tigertailz, Lee Aaron and Saga. Soon after the group, who specialise in guitar-intensive traditional metal, raised their profile by recording a self-financed cassette, which would sell over 800 copies. This came to the attention of Rock The Nation Records, who signed the band and re-released the tape with the addition of a bonus track, 'Cyan Eyes', to generally strong reviews.
Album: *Shreddervision* (RTN 1994).

Seducer

This hard rock group was formed in Amsterdam, Netherlands, in 1980 by vocalists/guitarists Frans Phillipus and Jerry Lopies. After a series of false starts, the line-up stabilized with the recruitment of bassist Eppie Munting and drummer Rene van Leersum. Specializing in blues-based hard rock and boogie, the band contributed their first tracks to a compilation, *Holland Heavy Metal Vol. 1*, in 1982. A deal with the independent Universe label followed and a self-titled debut appeared in 1983. This was poorly received, and a line-up re-shuffle ensued with Van Leersum and Lopies departing in favour of ex-Hammerhead guitarist Erik Karreman, drummer Jan Koster and vocalist Thijs Hamelaers. They contributed two further numbers to the *Dutch Steel* compilation in 1984, but the group disbanded shortly afterwards as Koster and Karreman formed Highway Chile, while Hamelaers went on to Germane and later the Sleez Beez.
Album: *Seducer* (Universe 1983).

Sentinel Beast

This thrash metal group was formed in Sacramento, California, USA, in 1984 by bassist Mike Spencer, vocalist Debbie Gunn and drummer Scott Awes. Adding guitarists Barry Fischel and Mark Koyasako, they debuted with their theme tune, 'Sentinel Beast', on the *Metal Massacre VII* compilation in 1986. This opened the door to a full contract with Metal Blade Records and the emergence of *Depths Of Death* the same year. This was standard Anthrax-style heavy metal, poorly produced and notable only for the high-speed cover of Iron Maiden's 'Phantom Of The Opera'. The album was a commercial flop and

Sepultura

founder member Spencer left to join Flotsam And Jetsum soon after its release. The band subsequently disintegrated, with Debbie Gunn re-appearing later in Znowhite and Ice Age.
Albums: *Depths Of Death* (Metal Blade 1986).

Sepultura

Formed in Belo Horizonte, Brazil, in 1984 by brothers Igor (b. 24 September 1970, Brazil; drums) and Max Cavalera (b. 4 August 1969, Brazil; vocals/guitar), with Paulo Jnr. (b. 30 April 1969, Brazil; bass) and guitarist Jairo T, who was replaced in April 1987 by Andreas Kisser (b. 24 August 1968) of fellow Brazilian metal act Pestilence. Sepultura is the Portuguese word for grave, and this is a strong clue as to the nature of a music which deals with themes of death and destruction, originally influenced by bands such as Slayer and Venom. In 1985 Sepultura recorded an album with Brazilian band Overdose (whom Sepultura had supported on their very first gig), but this debut, *Bestial Devastation*, was of poor quality and had limited circulation. Their first solo effort, *Morbid Visions*, was released in 1986, followed a year later by *Schizophrenia*. The music on both was typified by speed, aggression and anger, much of which stemmed from the band's preoccupations with the poor social conditions in their native land. It was Monte Conner of American record label Roadrunner who brought the band to international notice in 1989 when they released *Beneath The Remains*, which had been recorded in Rio with Scott Burns as producer. In 1990 Sepultura played at the Dynamo Festival in Holland where they met Gloria Bujnowski, manager of Sacred Reich; their relationship with her led to the re-release of *Schizophrenia*. Despite European and American success, Sepultura have not deserted Brazil, and they played at the Rock in Rio festival in 1990. *Arise*, released in 1991, proved the best selling album in the history of the Roadrunner label. The sessions for *Chaos A.D.* saw the group strip down their music in a more minimalist approach, which mirrored the punk ethos, especially evident on a cover of New Model Army's 'The Hunt' (they had previously cut the Dead Kennedys' 'Drug Me' for an Altnerative Tentacles compilation). 1994, meanwhile, would see Cavalera branch out to release the *Point Blank* CD, working alongside Fudgetunnel's Alex Newport under the name Nailbomb.
Albums: *Bestial Devastation* (Cogumelo 1985, split LP with Overdose), *Morbid Visions* (Cogumelo

1986), *Schizophrenia* (Cogumelo 1987), *Beneath The Remains* (Roadracer 1989), *Arise* (Roadracer 1991), *Chaos A.D.* (Roadrunner 1993). Max Cavalera in Nailbomb: *Point Blank* (Roadrunner 1994).

Sergeant

This predominantly Swiss, six-piece group was formed from the ashes of the Steve Whitney Band. Comprising Pete Prescott (vocals), Rob Seales (guitar), Chrigi Wiedemeier (guitar), Urs Amacher (keyboards), Rolf Schlup (bass) and Geri Steimer (drums) they specialized in Americanized hard-rock with melodic undercurrents. Signing to Mausoleum Records, they debuted in 1985 with *Sergeant*, a workman-like rock record that paid respect to Van Halen, Kiss and Foreigner. *Streetwise*, released the following year, was a major disappointment, as it merely regurgitated and reprocessed the riffs of their debut. Disillusioned by the media and public response, the band went their separate ways shortly after the album was released. In 1988 Seales and Amacher re-formed the band with new members Romy Caviezel (vocals), Harry Borner (bass) and Urs Rothenbuhler (drums), but this collaboration has yet to release any new material.
Albums: *Sergeant* (Mausoleum 1985), *Streetwise* (Mausoleum 1986).

707

US melodic pomp-rock group formed in 1979 by Kevin Russell (guitar/vocals), Jim McLarty (drums) and Phil Bryant (bass/vocals). However, the band's line-up was always in a constant state of flux. Tod Howarth (keyboards/guitar/vocals) and Felix Robinson (bass; ex-Angel) made important contributions during the group's lifetime. 707 debuted with a radio-friendly self-titled album, characterized by strong musicianship and instantly contagious hooklines and choruses. Their next two albums adopted a more metallic approach, with *2nd Album* deservedly reaching the lower reaches of the US *Billboard* chart. *Megaforce*, produced by Keith Olsen, also provided the theme tune for the film of the same name. Unfortunately, the creative ideas had started to run dry by this stage, while the songs duplicated earlier ideas and were generally less immediate. Internal disputes became more and more common, and the band finally fell apart in 1983. Howarth went on to play with Frehley's Comet.
Albums: *707* (Casablanca 1980), *2nd Album* (Casablanca 1981), *Megaforce* (Broadwalk 1982).

Sex, Love And Money

Formed in Greenville, North Carolina, USA, by Chuck Manning (vocals/guitar), John Bateman (guitar), Jim Bury (bass) and Jon Chambliss (drums), this metal outfit took its name from a local expression. 'It's a term that people call other people around here - SLAM babies - their primary concerns are Sex, Love and Money. To us it's a deeper, darker, and more realistic view of what we think everybody's invisible engine is'. Bateman graduated from Greenville's highly regarded Art School, after spending much of his life in Columbia, South America. This bred an early interest in both metal and flamenco. He hooked up with the remaining members who were participating in a Ramones-influenced punk band in April 1991. Songwriting within the band is arranged on a democratic principle with each member writing their own parts in isolation, Manning adding the lyrics. A creative process which first saw fruition in January 1995 with the release of a self-titled debut album for Music For Nations' subsidiary Bulletproof Records.
Album: *Sex, Love And Money* (Bulletproof 1995).

Shadow King

Following Lou Gramm's departure from Foreigner in 1988 he pursued a relatively less successful solo career for three years. In 1991 his desire to be part of a band once more led to the formation of Shadow King. Named after one of the band's songs, and based on the description of a huge, decadent and apocalyptic city; the band is completed by Vivian Campbell (guitar; ex-Dio and Whitesnake), Bruce Turgon (bass) and Kevin Valentine (drums). Signing to Atlantic Records, they debuted with a self-titled album in 1991. This was a strong collection of hi-tech, hard-edged AOR characterized by Gramm's soulful vocal delivery. Campbell's guitar work was surprisingly economical and restrained, marking a distinct change from his previous flamboyant output. Superbly produced by Keith Olsen, it was one of the year's most accomplished and mature rock releases. Afterwards Campbell would move on to join Def Leppard
Album: *Shadow King* (Atlantic 1991).

Shah

Formed in Moscow, Russia, in 1985, Shah comprise Antonio Garcia (vocals/guitar), Anatoly Krupnov (bass) and Andrei Sazanov (drums). The group were pioneers of thrash metal in the USSR and attracted the attention of Velerie Gaina, guitarist with fellow Soviet band, Kruiz. Gaina helped Shah record their first demo, which he then took to the West and German independent label Atom H Records. Suitably impressed, the label signed the band, resulting in a

Dave Sharman

debut collection, *Beware*, which betrayed the obvious influence of Anthrax. Bearing in mind the cultural and political hurdles the band had to overcome, it was a considerable achievement. In 1990 Shah played at the Public Against Violence Festival in Ostava, Czechoslovakia, along with German melodic rockers Bonfire and UK thrash metal band Talion and was a huge success. They continue to perform regularly and extensively in their own country.

Albums: *Beware* (Atom H 1989).

Shakin' Street

This rock 'n' roll quintet was influenced by the Stooges, Rolling Stones and Blue Öyster Cult, and took their name from a song by the MC5. Formed in Paris in 1975 by Fabienne Shine (b. Tunisia; vocals) and her songwriting partner, Eric Lewy (guitar/vocals), the group was completed by Mike Winter (bass), Armik Tigrane (guitar) and Jean Lou Kalinowski (drums). Signing to CBS, they debuted with the average *Vampire Rock*, a selection of predominantly uptempo rockers, notable only for Shine's unusual vocals. Ross The Boss (ex-Dictators) replaced Tigrane for the second album. This was a vast improvement, with a denser sound and more abrasive guitar work brought through in the final mix. Ross The Boss subsequently left to form Manowar with Joey De Maio in 1981, but Shakin' Street carried on for a short time with ex-Thrasher guitarist Duck McDonald, before finally disbanding. Their second album proved an undiscovered classic of the metal genre and is much sought after by collectors.

Albums: *Vampire Rock* (CBS 1978), *Shakin' Street* (CBS 1980).

Shark Island

This five-piece, melodic hard rock group was formed in 1986 from the ashes of Los Angeles glam rockers, the Sharks. Comprising Richard Black (vocals), Spencer Sercombe (guitar), Tom Rucci (bass), Michael Guy (guitar) and Walt Woodward (drums; ex-Americade), they recorded an album of demos in 1987 which saw A&M Records step in with a development deal. As a result of which, two of the band's songs were aired on the soundtrack to *Bill And Ted's Excellent Adventure*. Losing second guitarist Guy and replacing their rhythm section with Chris Heilman (ex-Bernie Tormé; bass) and Gregg Ellis (drums), they then moved over to Epic Records for a second album and first release proper in 1988. This showed the band to have matured considerably, with the material displaying new-found confidence in better production surroundings. Black had developed into an accomplished vocalist and songwriter, with a

style that married the best elements of Jon Bon Jovi and David Coverdale (Whitesnake). It is an oft-repeated rumour that Axl Rose of Guns N'Roses leaned heavily on his style in developing his own delivery. Black was also involved in the Contraband project of 1991, which featured Michael Schenker and members of L.A. Guns, Ratt and Vixen. This one-off collaboration recorded an album of cover versions, including Shark Island's 'Bad For Each Other'. Sercombe would also work on various MSG dates.

Albums: *S'Cool Bus* (Shark 1987), *Law Of The Order* (Epic 1989).

Sharman, Dave

b. c.1970, England. Dave Sharman first rose to prominence in 1989 when he featured on a session for BBC Radio 1 DJ Tommy Vance's *Friday Rock Show*. Comprising four instrumental selections, this proved such a success that producer Tony Wilson was allegedly alerting labels during recording. His debut album, titled after its year of release, saw rave reviews from both the metal and musician fraternities, with US magazine *Guitar For The Practising Musician* declaring Sharman 'Guitar God In Waiting'. Later, he was invited on the 'Night Of The Guitars' tour, where he shared a stage with Rick Derringer, Ronnie Montrose and others. A second album, *Exit Within*, was conceived when the guitarist met ex-Whitesnake bass player Neil Murray at an Ian Gillan audition, the duo linking with German vocalist Thomas Brache. The resultant 'Trucker' and 'Frantic' tracks were utilized by Radio 1's *Rock Show* and used as theme music. A more solid band aggregation was sought for *Here 'N' Now*, with Sharman joined by Steve Wood (drums), Tom Jeffreys (bass) and a retained Brache on vocals. Titling the new band Graphic, they debuted with a set which comprised seven band compositions and three instrumentals.

Albums: *1990* (1990), *Exit Within* (1992). With Graphic: *Here 'N' Now* (Bleeding Hearts 1995).

Shaw, Tommy

After Styx broke up in 1983 former vocalist Tommy Shaw embarked on a solo career. Signing to A&M Records, he released *Girls With Guns* the following year. This proved a big disappointment to Styx fans, who had high hopes for Shaw, and were not impressed with the strictly average melodic pop-rock on offer. The pomp and ceremony of old appeared to have vanished overnight. *What If* followed the same pattern and was another commercial disappointment. Moving to Atlantic Records, Shaw teamed up with ex-Charlie vocalist/guitarist Terry Thomas. This produced *Ambition* and marked a return to form, both in the standard of songwriting and the singer's delivery. Rather than build on this and develop a successful solo career, he declared his intention to become part of a band set-up once more. Teaming up with guitarist Ted Nugent, bassist Jack Blades (ex-Night Ranger) and drummer Michael Cartellone, he would go on to multi-platinum success as part of Damn Yankees.

Albums: *Girls With Guns* (A&M 1984), *What If* (A&M 1985), *Ambition* (A&M 1987).

Sherriff

This Canadian melodic rock quintet was formed in 1981 by Arnold Lanni (vocals/keyboards) and bassist Wolf Hassel (bass). With the addition of Freddy Curci (vocals), Steve De Marchi (guitar) and Rob Elliot (drums), they signed to Capitol Records and released a self-titled debut the following year. Their approach was characterized by grandiose sweeping melodies, which drew inspiration from Kansas, Foreigner and Styx, but with a smattering of their own ideas to authenticate the songs. The album failed to attract the media's attention and the band parted company. Lanni and Hassel later formed Frozen Ghost, while Curci and De Marchi teamed up in Alias. In 1988, quite unexpectedly, 'When I'm With You' from the debut Sherriff album became a number 1 US hit 5 years after it first charted (at number 61). The album was re-released and also did well; resulting in pressure to re-form Sherriff. Lanni and Hassel declined as they retained rights to the name and wanted to continue with Frozen Ghost.

Album: *Sherriff* (Capitol 1982).

Shire

This American hard rock quartet was formed in 1983 by David Anthony (vocals), Alan St. Lesa (guitar), Mick Adrian (bass) and Steve Ordyke (drums). They secured a record deal with Enigma the following year. Influenced by Dokken, Kiss and Van Halen, their debut was a somewhat formularized collection of mid-paced rockers that ultimately lacked distinction. Produced by Don Dokken and Michael Wagner, the album was eagerly anticipated, but proved a major disappointment when it arrived. Little more was heard of Shire in its wake.

Album: *Shire* (Enigma 1984).

Shiva

This UK rock trio, which combined both progressive rock and metal traditions, was formed in 1981 by multi-instrumentalist John Hall (vocals/guitar/keyboards). Adding Andy Skuse

(bass/keyboards) and Chris Logan (drums) they signed to Heavy Metal Records in 1982. Together they debuted with *Fire Dance*, a complex and inventive album which brought to mind memories of Rush, Deep Purple and Uriah Heep to its generally sympathetic reviewers. Instrumentally, the album was faultless, but the vocals were less impressive. Phil Williams replaced Logan in 1984, but this new line-up failed to record.

Album: *Fire Dance* (Heavy Metal 1982).

Shok Paris

Hailing from Ohio State, USA, Shok Paris were formed in 1982 by the three-man nucleus of drummer Bill Sabo and guitarists Eric Manderwald and Ken Erb. With vocalist Vic Hix and bassist Kel Bershire completing the line-up, they debuted with 'Go Down Fighting' on the *Cleveland Metal* compilation. This opened the door to a deal with Auburn Records and they recorded *Go For The Throat* in less than two days. Musically, with their high-energy, aggressive songs they were very much in the Riot, Kiss and Accept mould. Jan Roll took over the drumstool on *Steel And Starlight*, but this proved to be simply a repeat performance, played under different titles with less conviction than the debut.

Albums: *Go For The Throat* (Auburn 1984), *Steel And Starlight* (Auburn 1987).

Shortino, Paul

Former Quiet Riot vocalist Shortino found musical ambition early in life, coming from a talented family and taking vocal lessons before his teens. Later came a series of bands on Hollywood's Sunset Strip playing club gigs. It was in this scene that he first encountered Wendy and Ronnie Dio (of Dio), through whose auspices Shortino was engaged as vocalist for Rough Cutt. After that band sundered he would join Quiet Riot in 1989, but not before he had written songs for the television series *Fame*, and played the part of Duke Fame in *Spinal Tap*. The 90s saw him elect to pursue a solo career, joining with guitarist Jeff Northrup. The first results of this collaboration would arrive with the release of the agenda-setting *Back On Track* in March 1994.

Album: *Back On Track* (Bulletproof 1994).

Shotgun Messiah

This Swedish act began life as Kingpin, with Harry K. Cody (guitar), Tim Skold (bass) and Stixx Galore (drums) joined by ex-Easy Action vocalist Zinny J. San, releasing *Welcome To Bop City* in 1988. A subsequent relocation to Los Angeles, USA, saw a name change for both band and (remixed) album.

Shotgun Messiah was set apart from other glam albums by the quality of musicianship, Cody evoking Steve Vai and Joe Satriani with his fluid soloing. San departed after touring was complete, with Skold taking the vocalist slot while Bobby Lycon joined as bassist for *Second Coming*, which offered promising songwriting progression and gruff, powerful vocals from Skold. However, the band failed to expand beyond their cult status despite enthusiastic press support, and both Lycon and Stixx left after *I Want More*, an EP of covers (Ramones, New York Dolls, Iggy Pop) and acoustic reworkings of older material. Cody and Skold (now bassist/vocalist) took the bold step of industrializing Shotgun Messiah, using drum machines, synthesizers and samples on *Violent New Breed*, and creating a new sound by blending commercial songwriting with abrasive delivery for an excellent album, although the transformation was viewed with cynicism in some quarters. However, this effort still could not enhance Shotgun Messiah's fortunes, and Cody and Skold called it a day soon after.

Albums: *Shotgun Messiah* (Relativity 1989), *Second Coming* (Relativity 1991), *I Want More* (Relativity 1992, mini-album), *Violent New Breed* (Relativity 1993).

Shy

This quintet were founded in Birmingham, England, and specialized in Americanized, melodic heavy rock. Formed in 1982, they released their debut album the following year on the independent Ebony label. The songs were excellent, characterized by the silver-throated purr of Tony Mills, but the album was let down by a slight production. New bassist Roy Stephen Davis joined in 1984, and along with vocalist Mills, guitarist Steve Harris, drummer Alan Kelly and keyboard player Pat McKenna, they secured a new deal with RCA Records. Two quality albums of sophisticated pomp-metal followed, with 1987's *Excess All Areas* being the band's finest work. This included a melodramatic version of Cliff Richard's 'Devil Woman' given a true heavy metal revision. They gained the support slot on Meat Loaf's 1987 UK tour, but the album still failed to sell in large quantities. RCA dropped the band, but they were rescued by MCA Records, which allocated a large budget to record *Misspent Youth*, with Roy Thomas Baker as producer. This album was a major disappointment as the band's naturally aggressive approach had been tempered. The songs were geared for Stateside FM-radio consumption and the group's identity was suffocated in the clinically sterile production. In 1993 new vocalist, Los Angeles-based,

Birmingham-born John 'Wardi' Ward, replaced Tony Mills, who had departed in 1990. The new line-up played at the White Knights Festival in Russia in 1992, and signed to Parachute Records. They launched their comeback in 1994 with a cover of the Rolling Stones' 'It's Only Rock 'n' Roll'.

Albums: *Once Bitten, Twice...* (Ebony 1983), *Brave The Storm* (RCA 1985), *Excess All Areas* (RCA 1987), *Misspent Youth* (MCA 1989).

Sieges Even

This German 'techno-thrash' quartet was put together by vocalist Franz Herde and guitarist Markus Steffen in 1986. After recording three demos they were picked up by the Steamhammer label in 1988. They debuted with *Life Cycle*, a complex and inventive speed-metal fusion of jazz, rock and classical styles. The material was characterized by a multitude of quick-fire time changes, that ultimately fragmented the songs and made them difficult to distinguish from one another. The album was generally well-received, but made little impact outside Germany.

Album: *Life Cycle* (Steamhammer 1988).

Silent Rage

This Californian hard rock quartet was formed in 1986 by Mark Hawkins (vocals/guitar/synthesizer), Timmy James Reilly (vocals/guitar), E.L. Curcio (bass) and Jerry Grant (drums). They debuted with 'Make it Or Break It' on the *Pure Metal* compilation. This led to producer/guitarist Paul Sabu taking an interest in the band. He produced *Shattered Hearts* and co-wrote three numbers on the album. This collection followed a direction similar to Y&T, Kiss and Van Halen but featured extensive use of keyboards, which added a strong melodic undercurrent to the songs. Moving to Kiss bassist Gene Simmons' self-titled label, a subsidiary of RCA Records, *Don't Touch Me There* materialized in 1990. This built on the strong foundations of their debut and was immaculately produced, but blatantly geared for Stateside FM radio playlists.

Albums: *Shattered Hearts* (Chameleon 1987), *Don't Touch Me There* (Simmons/RCA 1990).

Silver Mountain

This melodic heavy metal group was formed in Malmo, Sweden, in 1978, taking their name from a song on Rainbow's debut album, 'Man On The Silver Mountain'. Not surprisingly, the band's sound proved to be an amalgam of Deep Purple, Rainbow and Judas Priest influences. Silver Mountain have been through an endless series of line-up changes, with the only constant being founder member Jonas Hansson (guitar/vocals). It took almost five years before the band secured a record deal, with Roadrunner Records. They went on to release four quality, if slightly dated metal albums, and built up strong followings in Scandinavia, Greece and Japan. The most recent line-up comprised Johan Dahlstrom (vocals), Jonas Hansson (guitar/vocals), Erik Bjorn Nielsen (keyboards), Per Stadin (bass) and Kjell Gustavson (drums).

Albums: *Shakin' Brains* (Roadrunner 1983), *Universe* (Roadrunner 1985), *Live In Japan '85* (SMS 1986), *Roses And Champagne* (Hex 1988).

Silverhead

The first real band to be fronted by actor/singer Michael Des Barres, Silverhead formed in 1971 with Steve Forest (guitar), Rod Davies (guitar), Nigel Harrison (bass) and Pete Thompson (drums). They were signed to Deep Purple's record label in 1982 by Tony Edwards and their debut album soon followed. Although quite mild on record their stage presence and raucous glam rock style won them a lewd reputation. This did little to help and Forest quit. Adopting a heavier approach they enlisted Robbie Blunt as Forest's replacement and recorded an album, *16 & Savaged*, and toured, mainly in America. By 1974 they had found an audience in Japan and in New York where glam had its home with the New York Dolls. It was during this time that Des Barres met up with 'super groupie' Pamela Miller. Not long after the band split. While Des Barres married Miller, Harrison joined Ray Manzarek form the Doors for his solo outings before they both formed Nite City (Harrison later found fame with Blondie), Blunt joined the reformed Chicken Shack but would later be remembered for playing guitar on Robert Plant's hit single, 'Big Log'. Des Barres went on to Detective and a solo career. A little insight in to Silverhead circa 1974 can be discovered in Pamela Des Barres' book, *I'm With The Band*.

Albums: *Silverhead* (Purple 1972), *16 & Savaged* (Purple 1973).

Simmons, Gene

One of the most charismatic characters in the world of heavy rock, Simmons (b. Chaim Witz, 25 August 1949, Haifa, Israel) is bass player with Kiss. Indeed, he was a founder member of the band in 1971 along with Paul Stanley. Simmons's first involvement with the music industry was in producing radio jingles, but it was not long before Kiss became a worldwide phenomenon. Simmons, along with his band mates, donned complete make-up (in his case a blood dripping, fire eating demon) and it was not until

1983 when Kiss unmasked that the 'real' Gene Simmons was revealed. Simmons has recorded some 20 albums with Kiss and has penned a great deal of the material either solely or in partnership with Paul Stanley. In 1978, while still in full demonic make-up, he released a credible solo album as did all his then band mates. A star-studded number of guest stars featured, including Bob Seger, Cher, Donna Summer, Helen Reddy and Cheap Trick guitarist Rick Neilsen and it reached number 22 on the US chart. A single was released at the same time, 'Radioactive' which was marketed in red vinyl together with a free Gene Simmons Kiss mask. It reached number 41 in the UK charts. During the 80's Simmons expanded his talents into production, films and set up his own record label, Simmons Records. In 1989 he took rock vocalist King Diamond to court for using facial make-up similar to what he had worn in Kiss. Simmons won the case. The 90s sees Kiss still recording under the guidance of Simmons and Stanley while the former's other music business activities continue.

Album: *Gene Simmons* (1978).

Simple Aggression

Formed on the first day of October 1989 in the hills of Independence, Kentucky, USA, Simple Aggression subsequently relocated to Cincinnati to establish their reputation. Comprising Doug Carter (vocals), James Carr (guitar), Darrin McKinney (guitar), Dave Swart (bass) and Kenny Soward (drums), the group took a name which prophesied a high velocity metal attack. However, the quintet were more than a simple 'thrash' band, preferring instead to work a steady groove at the core of their sound (the influence of the Red Hot Chili Peppers was certainly at work). A latent commercial instinct was also unveiled on their long playing debut by the inclusion of a strong ballad, 'Of Winter'.

Album: *Formulations In Black* (Bulletproof 1994).

Sinner

This German hard rock/thrash metal group was formed by Matthias Lasch in 1980. Lasch later became known as Mat Sinner, adding guitarists Wolfgang Werner and Calo Rapallo, drummer Edgar Patrik (later of Bonfire) and keyboardist Franky Mittelbach to complete the band's initial line-up. Influenced by Accept, Judas Priest, Iron Maiden and later Metallica, they released six workman-like, but ultimately uninspiring albums between 1982 and 1987. The personnel was in a constant state of flux, with Sinner the only constant. Their early career was dominated by New Wave Of British Heavy Metal style material, reminiscent of Angelwitch and Tygers

Of Pan Tang, then moved towards a thrashier direction as Slayer and Anthrax arrived on the scene. The band have never made any impression outside Germany and after *Dangerous Charm* in 1987 they lost their record deal.

Albums: *Wild 'n' Evil* (SL 1982), *Fast Decision* (Noise 1983), *Danger Zone* (Noise 1984), *Touch Of Sin* (Noise 1985), *Comin' Out Fighting* (Noise 1986), *Dangerous Charm* (Noise 1987).

Six Feet Under

This Swedish power-metal quintet modelled themselves on Deep Purple, Rainbow and Whitesnake. The band were formed in 1982 by vocalist Bjorn Lodin and guitarist Thomas Larsson. Recruiting Peter Ostling (keyboards), Kent Jansson (bass) and Claus Annersjo (drums), they signed to the Europa Film label the following year. This contract resulted in two albums which featured few original ideas. Larsson's guitar style was based almost exclusively on Ritchie Blackmore's, which imbued the songs with too strong a sense of *deja vu*. Marcus Kallstrum took over the drumstool on *Eruption*, which sold fewer copies than their debut. Disillusioned, the band went their separate ways in 1985.

Albums: *Six Feet Under* (Europa Film 1983), *Eruption* (Europa Film 1984).

Skagarack

This Danish melodic hard rock quintet were formed in 1985 by vocalist Torben Schmidt and guitarist Jan Petersen. With the addition of Tommy Rasmussen (keyboards), Morten Munch (bass) and Alvin Otto (drums), they incorporated elements of Whitesnake, Night Ranger and Boston into their music. From AOR beginnings, they have gradually evolved into a heavier and more powerful group than their self-titled debut might have suggested. Schmidt's vocals are reminiscent of David Coverdale's: melodic, powerful and emotive, and Skagarak remain a fine band whose obvious potential has yet to cross the Scandinavian frontier.

Albums: *Skagarack* (Polydor 1986), *Hungry For A Game* (Polydor 1988), *A Slice Of Heaven* (Medley 1990).

Skid Row (Eire)

This blues-based rock band was put together by Gary Moore in Dublin, Eirre, in 1968, when the guitarist was only 16 years old. Recruiting Phil Lynott (vocals/bass), Eric Bell (guitar) and Brian Downey (drums) the initial line-up only survived 12 months. Lynott, Bell and Downey left to form Thin Lizzy, with Brendan Shiels (bass/vocals) and Noel Bridgeman (drums) joining Moore as replacements in a new power-trio. The group completed two singles, 'New Places, Old Faces' and 'Saturday Morning Man' - only released in Ireland - before securing a UK deal via CBS Records. Skid Row was a popular live attraction and tours of the US and Europe, supporting Canned Heat and Savoy Brown, augered well for the future. Their albums were also well-received, but Moore's growing reputation as an inventive and versatile guitarist outstripped the group's musical confines. He left in 1971 to work with the folk-rock band Dr. Strangely Strange and later on to the Gary Moore Band. Although Paul Chapman proved an able replacement, Skid Row's momentum now faltered and the trio was disbanded the following year. Sheils has, on occasion, revived the name for various endeavours, while Chapman later found fame with UFO.

Albums: *Skid Row* (CBS 1970), *34 Hours* (CBS 1971), *Alive And Kicking* (CBS 1978). Compilation: *Skid Row* (CBS 1987).

Skid Row (USA)

Hailing from New Jersey, USA, Skid Row were formed in late 1986 by Dave 'The Snake' Sabo (guitar) and Rachel Bolan (bass). Sebastian Bach (b. 3 April 1968, Canada; vocals; ex-Madam X), Scotti Hill (guitar) and Rob Affuso (drums) were soon added and the line-up was complete. Influenced by Kiss, Sex Pistols, Ratt and Mötley Crüe, the band's rise to fame was remarkably rapid. The break came when they were picked up by Bon Jovi's management (Sabo was an old friend of Jon Bon Jovi) and offered the support slot on their US stadium tour of 1989. Bach's wild and provocative stage antics established the band's live reputation. Signed to Atlantic Records, they released their self-titled debut album to widespread critical acclaim the same year. It peaked at number 6 on the *Billboard* album chart and spawned two US Top 10 singles with '18 And Life' and 'I Remember You'. *Slave To The Grind* surpassed all expectations, debuting at number 1 in the US charts. Their commercial approach had been transformed into an abrasive and uncompromising barrage of metallic rock 'n' roll, delivered with punk-like arrogance. Afterwards, however, progress was halted by a period of inter-band squabbling which threatened to break the group. As Bach admitted to the press: 'I know I can be overbearing. But that's all changed now. Now people are in my face, giving their two cents' worth, making sure that everybody's vision is realised'. 1994 found them working on a new album, *Subhuman Race*, with production by Bob Rock.

Albums: *Skid Row* (Atlantic 1989), *Slave To The Grind* (Atlantic 1991), *Subhuman Race* (Atlantic 1994).
Video: *Oh Say Can You Scream?* (1991).

Skin

The collapse of Jagged Edge led Myke Gray (b. 12 May 1968, Fulham, London, England) to form Taste with Jagged Edge bassist Andy Robbins, ex-Kooga vocalist/guitarist Neville MacDonald and drummer Dickie Fliszar, previously with Bruce Dickinson's live band, in 1991. Rory Gallagher's previous use of the Taste name soon led to a name-change to Skin. The band were content to ignore grunge trends and instead developed a more traditional melodic hard rock style, at times reminiscent of mid-80s Whitesnake, but with a fresh contemporary edge both musically and lyrically. Near-constant touring, including support stints with Thunder and Little Angels, helped the band develop a strong UK fan base, and Skin built on this, with the *Skin Up* EP and 'House Of Love' both doing well before 'Money' pushed them into the UK Top 20. Their self-titled debut album displayed the band's songwriting and musicianship to the full, with strong, bluesy vocals from MacDonald, and it deservedly hit the UK Top 10. The band successfully transferred their electric live show to the second stage at Donington in 1994, and scored another Top 20 single with 'Tower Of Strength', confirming their status as one of Britain's most popular rising rock bands.
Album: *Skin* (Parlophone 1994).

Skrew

Once described by *Alternative Press* magazine as 'the soundtrack to the Apocalypse', Texan industrial metal crew Skrew's unsettling take on atavism is concocted by Adam Grossman (vocals/guitar), Opossum (guitar), Brandon Workman (bass), Mark Dufour (drums), Jim Vollentine (keyboards) and Doug Shappuis (guitar). The band's origins can be traced back to the city of Austin in 1991 where they originally emerged as a duo, before expanding the group after the first album for live commitments. Singer, guitarist and lyricist Grossman remained the core of both incarnations. Tours with Corrosion Of Conformity and Prong in Europe followed, before a domestic jaunt prefaced studio work on a second album, this time as the full sextet. *Dusted* thus arrived with a three-guitar frontal assault, with outstanding tracks including the sharpened hardcore stance of 'Jesus Skrew Superstar', while the equally disturbing 'Godsdog' took a more experimental route.
Albums: *Burning In Water, Drowning In Flame* (Devotion 1992), *Dusted* (Devotion 1994).

Skull

This hard rock quartet was put together by ex-Meat Loaf guitarist Bob Kulick in 1991. Recruiting vocalist Dennis St. James, bassist Kjell Benner and drummer Bobby Rock, they adopted an approach that bridged the musical styles of Kiss and Styx. Signing to the independent Music For Nations label, they released *No Bones About It* to a mixed reception. The songs were strong and adequately performed, but were ultimately too derivative in their musical approach.
Album: *No Bones About It* (Music For Nations 1991).

Skyclad

This innovative UK thrash-folk-rock crossover group were put together in 1991 by former Sabbat vocalist Martin Walkyier. Enlisting the services of Steve Ramsey (guitar), Graeme English (bass) and Keith Baxter (drums), they were signed by European label Noise. The debut, *Wayward Sons Of Mother Earth*, combined pagan lyrics, crashing powerchords and electric violin (curtesy of Fritha Jenkins) to startling effect. Press descriptions included citing them as the 'heavy metal equivalent of Fairport Convention', but they certainly offered a welcome alternative to run of the mill trad-rock.
Albums: *The Wayward Sons Of Mother Earth* (Noise 1991), *A Burnt Offering For The Bone Idol* (Noise 1992), *Jonah's Ark* (Noise 1993).

Slade

Originally recording as the 'N Betweens, this UK quartet comprised Noddy Holder (b. Neville Holder, 15 June 1946, Walsall, West Midlands, England; vocals/guitar), Dave Hill (b. 4 April 1952, Fleet Castle, Devon, England; guitar), Jimmy Lea (b. 14 June 1952, Wolverhampton, West Midlands, England; bass) and Don Powell (b. 10 September 1950, Bilston, West Midlands, England; drums). During the spring of 1966 they performed regularly in the Midlands, playing an unusual mixture of soul standards, juxtaposed with a sprinkling of hard rock items. A chance meeting with producer Kim Fowley led to a one-off single, 'You Better Run', released in August 1966. Two further years of obscurity followed until their agent secured them an audition with Fontana Records' A&R head Jack Baverstock. He insisted that they change their name to Ambrose Slade and it was under that moniker that they recorded *Beginnings*. Chaff on the winds of opportunity, they next fell into the hands of former Animals' bassist turned manager, Chas Chandler. He abbreviated their name to Slade and oversaw their new incarnation as a skinhead group for the stomping 'Wild Winds Are Blowing'. Their image as 'bovver boys', complete with cropped hair and Dr Marten boots, provoked some scathing press from a media sensitive to youth culture violence. Slade persevered with their skinhead phase until 1970 when it was clear that their notoriety was passé. While growing their hair and cultivating a more colourful image, they retained their aggressive musicianship and screaming vocals for the bluesy 'Get Down Get With It', which reached number 20 in the UK. Under Chandler's guidance, Holder and Lea commenced composing their own material, relying on distinctive riffs, a boot-stomping beat and sloganeering lyrics, usually topped off by a deliberately misspelt title. 'Coz I Luv You' took them to number 1 in the UK in late 1971, precipitating an incredible run of chart success which was to continue uninterrupted for the next three years. After the average 'Look Wot You Dun' (which still hit number 4) they served up a veritable beer barrel of frothy chart-toppers including 'Take Me Bak 'Ome', 'Mama Weer Al Crazee Now', 'Cum On Feel The Noize' and 'Skweeze Me Pleeze Me'. Their finest moment was 1977's 'Merry Xmas Everybody', one of the great festive rock songs. Unpretentious and proudly working class, the group appealed to teenage audiences who cheered their larynx-wrenching singles and gloried in their garish yet peculiarly masculine forays into glam rock. Holder, clearly no sex symbol, offered a solid, cheery image, with Dickensian side whiskers and a hat covered in mirrors, while Hill took tasteless dressing to marvellous new extremes. Largely dependent upon a young, fickle audience, and seemingly incapable of spreading their parochial charm to the USA, Slade's supremacy was to prove ephemeral. They participated in a movie, *Slade In Flame*, which was surprisingly impressive, and undertook extensive tours, yet by the mid-70s they were yesterday's teen heroes. The ensuing punk explosion made them virtually redundant and prompted in 1977 the appropriately titled, *Whatever Happened To Slade*. Undeterred they carried on just as they had done in the late 60s, awaiting a new break. An appearance at the 1980 Reading Festival brought them credibility anew. This performance was captured on the *Slade Alive At Reading '80* EP which pushed the group into the UK singles chart for the first time in three years. The festive 'Merry Xmas Everybody' was re-recorded and charted that same year (the first in a run of seven consecutive years, subsequently in it's original form). Slade returned to the Top 10 in January 1981 with 'We'll Bring The House Down' and they have continued to gig extensively, being rewarded in 1983

with the number 2 hit, 'My Oh My', followed the next year with 'Run Run Away', a UK number 7 and their first US Top 20 hit, and the anthemic 'All Join Hands' (number 15). Slade are one of the few groups to have survived the heady days of glitter and glam with their reputation intact and are regarded with endearing affection by a wide spectrum of age groups. Which makes it seem churlish to point out that their creative peak is behind them.

Albums: As Ambrose Slade: *Ambrose Slade - Beginnings* (Fontana 1969). As Slade: *Play It Loud* (Polydor 1970), *Slade Alive* (Polydor 1972), *Slayed* (Polydor 1972), *Old, New, Borrowed And Blue* (Polydor 1974), *Stomp Your Hands, Clap Your Feet* (Warners 1974, US title), *Slade In Flame* (Polydor 1974, film soundtrack), *Nobody's Fools* (Polydor 1976), *Whatever Happened To Slade?* (Barn 1977), *Slade Alive Vol. 2* (Barn 1978), *Return To Base* (Barn 1979), *We'll Bring The House Down* (Cheapskate 1981), *Till Deaf Us Do Part* RCA (1981), *Slade On Stage* (RCA 1982), *Slade Alive* (Polydor 1983, double album), *The Amazing Kamikaze Syndrome* (RCA 1983), *On Stage* (RCA 1984), *Rogues Gallery* (RCA 1985), *Crackers - The Slade Christmas Party Album* (Telstar 1985), *You Boyz Make Big Noize* (RCA 1987). Compilations: *Sladest* (Polydor 1973), *Slade Smashes* (Barn 1980), *Story Of* (Polydor 1981, double album), *Slade's Greats* (Polydor 1984), *Keep Your Hands Off My Power Supply* (CBS 1984, US title), *Wall Of Hits* (Polydor 1991), *Slade Collection 81-87* (RCA 1991). Videos: *Slade In Flame* (1990), *Wall Of Hits* (1991).

Slaughter

When Vinnie Vincent's Invasion disintegrated in 1988, vocalist Mark Slaughter and bassist Dana Strum decided to start a new group under the name Slaughter. Recruiting guitarist Tim Kelly and drummer Blas Elias, they soon secured a deal with Chrysalis Records and recorded *Stick It To Ya*. With an approach that fused elements of Kiss, Mötley Crüe and Bon Jovi, their style was ultimately derivative, yet distinctive due to the stratospheric-like vocals of Mark Slaughter. Three minute blasts of memorable metallic pop, complete with rousing anthemic choruses was the usual recipe. Following support slots to Kiss on their American tour, the album took off and peaked at number 18, during its six-month residency on the *Billboard* album chart. A live mini-album followed, which featured live versions of songs from their debut release.

Albums: *Stick It To Ya* (Chrysalis 1990), *Stick It To Ya Live* (Chrysalis 1990), *The Wild Life* (Chrysalis 1992). Video: *From The Beginning* (1991).

Slayer

Slave Raider

Formed in America in 1987 around the antics of vocalist Chainsaw Caine and his cohorts Nicci Wikkid (guitar), Letitia Rae (bass), Lance Sabin (guitar) and a drummer who called himself The Rock. At best they could be described as a poor man's Twisted Sister but lacked the talent to move off the bottom rung. Having recorded their debut album to be used as a demo Jive Records picked them up and Caine set his sights on taking the UK by storm. This included live performances where he would 'chainsaw' a large cardboard cut-out of Rick Astley in half. As a stage *coup de grace* it was neither particularly funny nor particularly original. Jive however pushed them hard with promotional videos and press coverage to little avail. They then put them in a London recording studio with Chris Tsangarides, but even the legendary producer could do little to help them and soon after the release of their second album Jive dropped them and they broke up.

Albums: *Take The World By Storm* (Jive 1988), *What Do You Know About Rock 'N' Roll* (Jive 1989).

Slayer

This intense death/thrash metal quartet was formed in Huntington Beach, Los Angeles, USA, during 1982. Comprising Tom Araya (bass/vocals), Kerry King (guitar), Jeff Hanneman (guitar) and Dave Lombardo (drums) they made their debut in 1983, with a track on the compilation *Metal Massacre III*. This led to Metal Blade signing the band and releasing their first two albums. *Show No Mercy* and *Hell Awaits* were undiluted blasts of pure white metallic noise. The band played at breakneck speed with amazing technical precision, but the intricacies of detail were lost in a muddy production. Araya's lyrics dealt with death, carnage, satanism and torture, but were reduced to an indecipherable guttural howl. Rick Rubin, producer and owner of the Def Jam label teamed up with the band in 1986 for the recording of *Reign In Blood*. Featuring 10 tracks in just 28 minutes, it took the concept of thrash to its ultimate conclusion. The song 'Angel Of Death' became notorious for its references to Joseph Mengele, the Nazi doctor who committed atrocities against humanity (ironic, given that Araya has obvious non-Aryan origins). They themselves admitted to a right wing stance on matters of society and justice, despite being the subject of virulent attacks from that quarter over the years. *Hell Awaits* saw Rubin achieve a breakthrough in production with a clear and inherently powerful sound, and opened the band up to a wider audience. *South Of Heaven* was Slayer applying the brakes and introducing brain-numbing

bass riffs similar to Black Sabbath, but was delivered with the same manic aggression as before. The guitars of Hanneman and King screamed violently and Araya's vocals were clearly heard for the first time. *Seasons In The Abyss* pushed the band to the forefront of the thrash metal genre, alongside Metallica. A state-of-the-art album in every respect, although deliberately commercial it is the band's most profound and convincing statement. A double live album followed, recorded in London, Lakeland and San Bernadino between October 1990 and August 1991. It captured the band at their brutal and uncompromising best and featured definitive versions of many of their most infamous numbers. However, it saw the permanent departure of Lombardo after many hints of a separation, with ex-Forbidden drummer Paul Bostaph stepping in. Lombardo would on to form Grip, working with Death mainman Chuck Shuldiner. 1994 saw the group work alongside Ice-T on a cover of the Exploited's 'Disorder' for the *Judgement Night* soundtrack, before the unveiling of their long-anticipated sixth studio album, *Divine Intervention*.

Albums: *Show No Mercy* (Metal Blade 1984), *Hell Awaits* (Metal Blade 1985), *Reign In Blood* (Def Jam 1986), *Live Undead* (Enigma 1987), *South Of Heaven* (Def American 1988), *Seasons In The Abyss* (Def American 1990), *Decade Of Aggression-Live* (Def American 1991), *Divine Intervention* (American 1994).

Sledgehammer

Formed in Slough by former school teacher Mike Cooke (guitar/vocals) in 1978, with Terry Pearce (bass) and Ken Revell (drums), the trio's first live appearance came as support to Motörhead. In 1979 they recorded the single, 'Sledgehammer', which proved to be their only hit and was reissued at least three times on different labels. To promote the single they toured with April Wine and Budgie and played the Reading Festival. They re-recorded the track for the *Metal For Muthas* compilation album and then spent much of the year on the road with Def Leppard and various New Wave Of British Heavy Metal packages. Their debut album, released in 1984, had been recorded during 1981 with help from John McCoy (Gillan). This failed to sell, as did the single, 'In The Queue'. Again, both suffered from comparisons to 'Sledgehammer', with the band unable to shake off the 'one hit wonder' syndrome. They soon faded away from the landscape, though they turned to matters more serious a couple of years later with 'Porno Peat' (an anti-pornography single) and concentrated on raising both money and awareness for women's rape centres and child abuse groups.

Album: *Blood On Their Hands* (Illuminated 1984).

Sleep

This San Jose, California doom trio draw from 60s and 70s influences like Black Sabbath, Jimi Hendrix and Pink Floyd to produce their own retro-styled brand of 'stoner' metal, a term derived from the band's smoking habits, even using suitably ancient amplifiers for an authentic early Sabbath sound. Al Cisneros (bass/vocals), Mat Pike (guitar) and Chris Hakius (drums) made their recorded debut with a cover of 'Snowblind' on the *Masters Of Misery* Sabbath tribute. After which they produced an awesomely heavy debut in *Sleep's Holy Mountain*, built on intense, weighty riffs and slow, lengthy song structures similar to early Sabbath, although, like contemporaries such as Monster Magnet and Cathedral, the delivery had a distinctly modern edge. Sleep's live performances continued the tradition of fearsomely heavy guitars as they toured the UK and Europe with Cathedral, Cannibal Corpse and Fear Factory, and played US dates with Nik Turner's Hawkind Experience. A second album, *Dope Smoker*, was slated for release in Spring 1995, and remarkably comprises a single 37 minute long track.

Albums: *Sleep's Holy Mountain* (Earache 1993), *Dope Smoker* (Earache 1995).

Sloan

This Canadian grunge band originated at the Nova Scotia College Of Art in Halifax, where drummer Andrew Scott and bassist Chris Murphy linked with Northern Ireland-born guitarist Patrick Pentland and guitarist/vocalist Jay Ferguson. Sloan developed their own sound from a mixture of hardcore and grunge influences, producing a guitar-fuelled battery of short, sharp songs, releasing the *Peppermint* EP, recorded at a friend's house in Halifax, through their own Murderecords label. A lively performance at Canada's East Coast Music Conference brought the band to the attention of Geffen Records, who liked the EP and promptly signed Sloan. *Smeared* impressed reviewers and public alike, with the pop songwriting and vocal melodies counterpointed by Pentland's raw, aggressive guitar work. In spite of a low-key promotional approach, the record performed well as North American college radio picked up on 'Underwhelmed'.

Album: *Smeared* (Geffen 1992).

Smashing Pumpkins

Smashing Pumpkins

Once widely viewed as poor relations to Nirvana's major label alternative rock, Chicago, USA's Smashing Pumpkins, led by vocalist/guitarist Billy Corgan (b. 17 March 1967, Chicago, Illinois, USA) have persevered to gradually increasing acceptance and press veneration. Corgan's inspirations, the Beatles, Led Zeppelin, Doors and Black Sabbath, as well as a professional jazz musician father, add up to a powerful musical cocktail over which his lyrics, which frequently cross the threshold of normality and even sanity, float unsettlingly. The rest of the band comprises D'Arcy Wretzky (bass), James Iha (guitar) and Jimmy Chamberlain (drums). Smashing Pumpkins made their official debut with a drum machine at the Avalon club in Chicago. Chamberlain was then drafted in from a ten-piece showband (JP And The Cats) to fill the percussion vacancy (Corgan had previously played in another local band, the Marked). The group made its debut in early 1990 with the release of 'I Am The One' on local label Limited Potential Records. Previously they had included two tracks on a Chicago compilation, *Light Into Dark*. This led the band to the attention of influential Seattle label Sub Pop, with whom they released 'Tristess'/'La Dolly Vita' in September 1990, before moving to Caroline Records. *Gish*, produced by Butch Vig, announced the group to both indie and metal audiences, and went to number 1 on the influential Rockpool College Radio Chart. Ironically, given the Nirvana comparisons, this came before Vig had produced *Nevermind*. However, it was *Siamese Dream* which launched the band to centre stage with its twisted metaphors and skewed rhythms. A Top 10 success in the US *Billboard* charts, it saw them joined by mellotron, cello and violin accompaniment to give the sound extra depth. However, these remained secondary to the pop hooks and rock atmospherics which have defined the band's sound.
Albums: *Gish* (Caroline 1991), *Siamese Dream* (Virgin 1993).

Sniper

This Japanese heavy metal group was formed in 1981 by guitarist Mansanori Kusakabe. Enlisting the services of Shigehisa Kitao (vocals), Romy Murase (bass) and Shunji Itoh (drums), their brand of heavy metal drew strongly on the styles of UFO and Deep Purple. Debuting with the single 'Fire' in 1983, they contributed 'Crazy Drug' to the *Heavy Metal Forces* compilation album the following year. Their first album was recorded live at the Electric Ladyland Club in Nagoya in 1984 and featured new recruit Ravhun Othani (ex-Frank Marino Band) as a second guitarist.

The album was a limited edition of 1,000, which sold out, only to be re-pressed twice, with similar success. The band disintegrated shortly after its release, but was resurrected in 1985 by Kusakabe. The new line-up included Noburu Kaneko (vocals), Takeshi Kato (keyboards), Tsukasa Shinohara (bass) and Toshiyuki Miyata (drums). They produced *Quick And Dead*, but it made little impact outside Japan. A proposed tour of Holland to support it was cancelled and the band have been inactive since.
Albums: *Open The Attack* (Electric Ladyland 1984), *Quick And Dead* (Megaton 1985).

Snowblind

This UK melodic hard rock quintet was formed in 1982 by guitarist Andy Simmons. With Tony Mason (vocals), Ross Bingham (guitar/keyboards), Geoff Gilesoie (bass) and Kevin Baker (drums) completing the line-up, they were one of the few non-speed metal/thrash bands signed to the Belgian Mausoleum label. Using Magnum, Rush and Grand Prix as their musical blueprint, they debuted with a self-titled album in 1985. This comprised grandiose epics, punctuated by explosive guitar runs in places. The only drawback was Mason's vocals, which lacked the necessary warmth and range to give the songs real distinction. The album fared badly and little has been heard from them since.
Album: *Snowblind* (Mausoleum 1985).

Soda, Frank

This eccentric Canadian vocalist/guitarist is widely known for his warped sense of humour. He appeared on stage kitted out in strange outfits and the climax of the show usually involved making a television set explode on his head, Backed by the Imps, a two-piece rhythm section comprising Charles Towers (bass) and John Lechausser (drums), they recorded two hard rock albums characterized by frenzied, Frank Zappa-like guitar and Soda's shallow vocals. *Saturday Night Getaway* used session musicians instead of the Imps and featured four cuts from *In The Tube*, with the remaining new songs sounding second-rate in comparison. He built up a small but loyal cult following in Canada, but failed to make an impression elsewhere. He did, however, help singer Lee Aaron launch her career in 1982.
Albums: *In The Tube* (Quality 1979), *Frank Soda And The Imps* (Quality 1980), *Saturday Night Getaway* (Quality 1981), *Adventures Of Sodaman* (Visual 1983).

Sodom

This black metal/thrash trio was formed in 1983 by

Angel Ripper (bass/vocals), Aggressor (vocals/guitar) and Witchhunter (drums). They drew inspiration from bands such as Motörhead, Anvil and Venom, making their debut with an agenda-setting EP, *Sign Of Evil*. By the time *Obsessed By Cruelty* emerged in 1986, Aggressor had quit to be replaced firstly by the similarly-pseudonymous Grave Violator, then Destructor and finally Blackfire. *Persecution Mania* followed in 1987 and marked a vast improvement over their debut, though lyrics had not moved on from obsessions with war, bloodlust and the black arts. Produced by Harris Johns, it had a crisp and powerful sound and was to become their best-selling release. They toured Europe in 1988 with Whiplash and recorded *Mortal Way Of Life*, the first ever double live thrash album. *Agent Orange* followed in 1989 and they landed the support slot on Sepultura's European tour to help promote it. Michael Hoffman was recruited as the new guitarist when Blackfire left for Kreator in 1990.

Albums: *Obsessed By Cruelty* (Steamhammer 1986), *Persecution Mania* (Steamhammer 1987), *Mortal Way Of Life* (Steamhammer 1988, double album), *Agent Orange* (Steamhammer 1989), *Ausgebombt* (Steamhammer 1990), *Better Off Dead* (Steamhammer 1991), *Tapping The Vein* (Steamhammer 1993).

Sojourn

This US melodic rock quintet was formed in 1983 by Kevin Bullock (vocals/guitar/keyboards) and Doug Robinson (guitar/vocals). Enlisting the services of Kevin Stoker (keyboards), Doug Pectol (bass) and Dane Spencer (drums), they secured a deal with the Mad Cat label in 1985. They debuted with *Lookin' For More*, a melodic rock album with rough edges. It incorporated abrasive guitar work within a pomp-rock framework, and drew comparisons with Triumph, Journey and UFO. *Different Points Of View* consolidated their style before they went out on tour with Mr. Mister to promote the work, but nothing was heard from them afterwards.

Albums: *Lookin' For More* (Mad Cat 1985), *Different Points Of View* (Mad Cat 1988).

Solitude

Solitude were formed by Mike Hostler (drums) and Dan Martinez (guitar) in Delaware, USA, in 1985. With the addition of Keith Saulsbury (vocals/guitar) and Rodney Cope (bass) they released their first demo, *Focus Of Terror*, in 1987, their second, *Sickness*, following a year later. Increasingly strong reviews were maintained by their third and final demo, *Fall Of Creation*. Red Light then stepped in and signed the

band in 1993 (Music For Nations offering a UK deal). *From This Life*, their debut album, saw them combine diverse influences, taking Black Sabbath, Slayer and Pantera as a traditional metal foundation, but adding also elements of blues and progressive rock. Lyrically, targets included the death of communism ('After The Red'), betrayal ('In This Life') and growing old ('The Empty'), all dealt with in bold, primary colours and language. Touring with Death Angel, Sacred Reich, Forbidden, Celtic Frost and other death metal/thrash bands has not helped them escape the death metal category which somewhat inadequately describes their sound.

Album: *From Within* (Red Light 1994).

Solitude Aeturnus

Formed in 1988 by Texan guitarist John Perez, Solitude Aeturnus set out to revive the 'heavy groove orientated' style of Black Sabbath. The results were slow, epic, guitar-based heavy metal with a definite ethereal edge. Solitude Aeturnus secured a deal in 1991 and released *Into the Depths of Sorrow*. This established them as a part of the doom metal movement, which was a more atmospheric, grinding counterpart to the frantic aggression of death metal. While many of the bands in the doom genre were interested in creating sweeping vistas of tragic horror, Solitude Aeturnus have a more grandiose, dreamlike quality. Much of this is due to the semi-operatic vocals of Robert Lowe which contrast effectively with the maudlin power of the lumbering guitar riffs of John Perez and Edgar Rivera (the rhythm section comprises Lyle - bass, and Wolf - drums). Unfortunately, while they are good at what they do, Solitude Aeturnus have a tendency to be somewhat one-dimensional. Their third album, *Through the Darkest Hour*, followed a label change and has seen the band's material develop a little more punch.

Albums: *Into the Depths of Sorrow* (Roadracer 1991), *Beyond The Crimson Horizon* (Roadracer 1992), *Through The Darkest Hour* (Bullet Proof 1994).

Sortilege

This French heavy metal band was formerly known as Blood Wave. Sortilege were formed in 1981 by vocalist Christian Augustin and guitarist Stephanne L'Anguille Dumont. Adding Didier Dem (guitar), Daniel Lapp (bass) and Bob Snake (drums) they secured a contract with the Dutch Rave On label in 1983. They specialized in a persistent metallic boogie which recalled other French acts such as Trust and Telephone. *Metamorphose* was also released as *Metamorphosis*, complete with English lyrics, but it still failed to make any impact outside France. *Hero*

Tears saw the band running short of ideas. They broke up shortly after it's release.

Albums: *Sortilege* (Rave On 1983), *Metamorphose* (Steamhammer 1984), *Hero Tears* (Steamhammer 1985).

Soul Asylum

Originally a Minneapolis, Minnesota, USA, garage hardcore band, Soul Asylum spent their early years under the yoke of comparisons to the more feted Replacements and Husker Du. Indeed, Bob Mould has been known to fondly describe Soul Asylum as 'our little brothers', and was on hand as producer for their first two long playing sets. Their roots in hardcore are betrayed by the choice of their original name, Loud Fast Rules. Their first formation in 1981 centred around the abiding creative nucleus of Dave Pirner (b. c.1965; vocals, guitar) and Dan Murphy (b. c.1963; guitar), alongside Karl Mueller (b. c.1965; bass) and Pat Morley (drums). Together they specialised in sharp lyrical observations and poppy punk. Morley left in December 1984 to be replaced, eventually, by Grant Young (b. c.1965), who arrived in time for *Made To Be Broken*. As their music progressed it became easier to trace back their heritage to the 60s rather than 70s. *Hang Time*, their third album proper, was their first for a major. It saw them move into the hands of a new production team (Ed Stasium and Lenny Kaye), with a very apparent display of studio polish. The mini-album which was meant to have preceded it (but didn't), *Clam Dip And Other Delights*, included their dismantling of a Foreigner song, 'Jukebox Hero', and a riotous reading of Janis Joplin's 'Move Over'. When playing live they have been known to inflict their renditions of Barry Manilow's 'Mandy' and Glen Campbell's 'Rhinestone Cowboy' on an audience. Though *The Horse They Rode In On* was another splendid album, the idea of Soul Asylum breaking into the big league was becoming a progressively fantastic one (indeed band members had to pursue alternative employment in 1990, during which time Pirner suffered a nervous breakdown). However, largely thanks to the MTV rotation of 'Somebody To Shove', that was about to change. In its aftermath they gained a prestigious slot on the *David Letterman Show* before support billing to Bob Dylan and Guns N'Roses, plus a three way headlining package with Screaming Trees and the Spin Doctors on a three-month Alternative Nation Tour. Soon they were appearing in front of a worldwide audience of 400 Million at the 1993 MTV Awards ceremony, where they were joined by REM's Pete Buck and Victoria Williams for a jam of their follow-up hit, 'Runaway Train'. With Pirner dating film starlet Winona Ryder, the profile of a band who seemed destined for critical reverence and public indifference could not have been more unexpectedly high.

Albums: *Say What You Will* (Twin Tone 1984), *Made To Be Broken* (Twin Tone 1986), *While You Were Out* (Twin Tone 1986), *Hang Time* (Twin Tone/A&M 1988), *Clam Dip And Other Delights* (What Goes On 1989, mini-album), *Soul Asylum And The Horse They Rode In On* (Twin Tone/A&M 1990), *Grave Dancers Union* (A&M 1993). Compilations: *Time's Incinerator* (Twin Tone 1984, cassette only), *Say What You Will Clarence, Karl Sold The Truck* (Twin Tone 1989).

Sound Barrier

Formerly known as Colour, Sound Barrier were a black heavy metal band formed in 1980 by Spacey T. (guitar), Bernie K (vocals), Stanley E. (bass) and Dave Brown (drums), who signed to MCA Records in 1982. They debuted with *Total Control*, a highly complex fusion of metal, soul, funk and blues influences that defied simple pigeon-holing. Despite or because of this it sold poorly and they were subsequently dropped by their label. They bounced back with a mini-album on the independent Pitbull label, which consolidated the style laid down on their debut release. This led to a contract with Metal Blade, but the resulting *Speed Of Light* was very disappointing. It adopted a simpler, more mainstream approach and proved an unsuccessful attempt to widen their appeal. Emil Lech had taken over on bass by this stage, but the band splintered shortly after the album's release. Bernie K. went on to Masi, Spacey T. and Stanley E. joined Liberty, while Emil Lech teamed up with Joshua.

Albums: *Total Control* (MCA 1983), *Born To Rock* (Pit Bull 1984), *Speed Of Light* (Metal Blade 1986).

Soundgarden

This Seattle-based US quartet fused influences as diverse as Led Zeppelin, the Stooges, Velvet Underground and most particularly early UK and US punk bands into a dirty, sweaty, sexually explicit and decidedly fresh take on rock 'n' roll. The group; Chris Cornell (b. Seattle, Washington, USA; vocals/guitar), Kim Thayil (guitar), Hiro Yamamoto (bass) and Matt Cameron (drums), proffer a sound characterized by heavy-duty, bass-laden metallic riffs that swings between dark melancholia and *avant garde* minimalism. Cornell's ranting vocal style and articulate lyrics complete the effect. The group's first recording, the *Screaming Life* EP, was the second release on the hugely influential Sub Pop label, and marked out their territory. Indeed, Thayil had

brought together the label's owners Bruce Pavitt and Jonathan Poneman in the first place. After signing to SST Records and releasing *Ultamega OK*, they attracted the attention of A&M Records and eventually released *Louder Than Love*, one of the most underrated and offbeat rock albums of 1989. This also meant that they were the first of the Sub Pop generation to sign to a major. After its release Cameron and Cornell would also participate in the two million selling Temple Of The Dog album, which co-featured Pearl Jam members Eddie Vedder, Stone Gossard and Jeff Ament laying tribute at the door of deceased Mother Love Bone singer Andrew Wood. However, following the recording sessions for *Louder Than Love* Yamamoto would be replaced by Jason Everman (ex-Nirvana), though he would record on only one track, a cover of the Beatles' 'Come Together', before departing for Mindfunk via Skunk. His eventual replacement would be band friend Ben 'Hunter' Shepherd. *Badmotorfinger* built on the group's succesful formula but added insistent riffs, the grinding but melodious guitar sound which would come to define 'grunge', and their own perspectives on politics, religion and society. Among its many absorbing moments was the MTV friendly single, 'Jesus Christ Pose'. Landing the support slot to Guns N'Roses' US *Illusions* tour deservedly opened Soundgarden up to a much wider audience. This was capitalized on by their fourth long player, which debuted at number 1 on the *Billboard* chart on 19 March 1994. Produced by Michael Beinhorn (Soul Asylum, Red Hot Chili Peppers etc.) and the band themselves, it was a magnum opus clocking in at more than 70 minutes and featuring 15 songs. Eventually selling over three million copies, it was promoted by an Australasian tour in January 1994, headlining the 'Big Day Out' festival package above the Ramones, Smashing Pumpkins and Teenage Fanclub, before moving on to Japan.
Albums: *Ultemega O.K.* (SST 1989), *Louder Than Love* (A&M 1990), *Badmotorfinger* (A&M 1991), *Superunknown* (A&M 1994). Compilation: *Screaming Life/FOPP* (Sub Pop 1990).
Video: *Motorvision* (1993).

Spanos, Danny

This American vocalist/composer performed and recorded under his own name, always preferring the services of hired hands to a conventional band set-up. He recorded three albums during the early 80s, using a variety of session musicians, including Earl Slick, Rick Derringer, Carmine Appice, Dana Strum and Frankie Banali. His style fell somewhere between Jimmy Barnes and Bryan Adams; easily accessible

hard rock with gritty vocals and infectious hooklines. Ultimately, the songs lacked real character and he failed to break into the big time.
Albums: *Danny Spanos* (Windsong 1980), *Passion In The Dark* (Epic 1983), *Looks Like Trouble* (Epic 1984).

Spartan Warrior

This UK heavy metal group was formed in 1983 by Dave Wilkinson (vocals) Neil Wilkinson (guitar), Paul Swaddle (guitar), Tom Spencer (bass) and Gordon Webster (drums), making their debut with two cuts on the *Guardian* compilation in 1984. This opened the door to a contract with Roadrunner Records, which resulted in two non-descript, poorly produced metal albums. These incorporated elements of Rush, Deep Purple and Led Zeppelin, but few original ideas of their own. Failing to make any impact, the band returned to their day jobs in 1986.
Albums: *Spartan Warrior* (Roadrunner 1984), *Steel 'N' Chains* (Roadrunner 1985).

Speedway Boulevard

This short-lived US group featured a *pot-pourri* of musical styles. Formed in 1979, the band comprised Ray Herring (vocals/piano), Gregg Hoffman (guitar/vocals), Jordan Rudes (keyboards), Dennis Feldman (bass/vocals) and Glenn Dove (drums). They signed to Epic Records and debuted in 1980 with a self-titled album that defied simple categorization. It featured a solid foundation of heavy-duty symphonic rock, modified by blues, funk, soul and Carribbean influences. In places, it courted comparisons with Led Zeppelin's more experimental phases. Sadly, the band broke up before their true potential could be realized. Feldman went on to play with Balance and later Michael Bolton. Rudes guested on Vinnie Moore's *Time Odyssey*.
Album: *Speedway Boulevard* (Epic 1980).

Spellbound

This Swedish metal quintet was assembled in 1984 by Hans Froberg (vocals), J.J.Marsh (guitar), Al Strandberg (guitar/keyboards), Thompson (bass) and Ola Strandberg (drums), marking their debut with a track on Sonet's *Swedish Metal* compilation. This led to a full contract with Sonet, with the band delivering *Breaking The Spell* in 1984. Their style, based on an amalgam of Van Halen, Led Zeppelin and Europe, was given some degree of distinction by Froberg's powerful vocals. *Rockin' Reckless* followed, a virtual carbon copy of their debut, and suggested that the band were running out of ideas after just one album. Their association with Sonet ended in 1987, and nothing has been heard from them since.

Albums: *Breaking The Spell* (Sonet 1984), *Rockin' Reckless* (Sonet 1986).

Spider (UK)

This British boogie group was formed on Merseyside in 1976 by the Burrows brothers. The band comprised bassist/vocalist Brian Burrows, drummer Rob E. Burrows and guitarists Sniffa and Col Harkness. After incessant gigging around the north west, they relocated to London and were eventually signed by RCA Records in 1983. They debuted with *Rock 'N' Roll Gypsies*, a fuel-injected collection of boogie-based rockers, identical in almost every respect to the style of Status Quo. From then on, they were regarded as a poor-man's 'Quo. The album sold miserably and RCA dropped them. Picked up by A&M Records, they released *Rough Justice*, a semi-concept affair concerning a courtroom trial. Spider were the defendants, being accused of playing heavy metal rock 'n' roll. Another flop, it left the band without a label once more. Undaunted they plodded on, with Stu Harwood replacing Sniffa on guitar in 1986. Moving to the Mausoleum label, they produced *Raise The Banner* the same year. Musically they had not progressed, and the market for low-tech, three-chord boogie proved an ever contracting one. Out-dated, and out of luck, they broke up shortly after the album was released. Brian Burrows is now a cartoonist and record sleeve designer.

Albums: *Rock 'N' Roll Gypsies* (RCA 1983), *Rough Justice* (A&M 1984), *Raise The Banner* (Mausoleum 1986).

Spider (USA)

Prior to the formation of Spider in New York during 1978, Amanda Blue (vocals), Keith Lentin (guitar) and Anton Fig (drums) had worked together six years previously in the South African based Hammak. Adding keyboardist Holly Knight and ex-Riff Raff bassist Jimmy Lowell, they soon negotiated a contract with the Dreamland label. This was made possible by Ace Frehley's (Kiss guitarist) recommendation, following Anton Fig's appearance on the guitarist's solo album. Specializing in commercial American rock, with pop-rock overtones, they released two classy albums and scored minor US single successes with 'New Romance' and 'Better Be Good To Me'. They changed name to Shanghai in 1982 to avoid confusion with the British group of the same name.

Albums: *Spider* (Dreamland 1980), *Between The Lines* (Dreamland 1981).

Spin Doctors

This four-piece group came together in 1989 when vocalist Christopher Barron and guitarist Eric Schenkman met drummer Aaron Comess at the New School of Jazz in New York. With the line-up completed by bassist Mark White, the band signed a record deal the following year. *Pocket Full Of Kryptonite* was a varied collection of well-crafted, tuneful rock songs flavoured with funk rhythms and witty, intelligent lyrics, and displayed the band's considerable musical ability, playing in a wide range of styles from the light, jazzy feel of the more balladic numbers to hard funk reminiscent of the Red Hot Chili Peppers, with almost nonchalant ease, while retaining a recognisable sound of their own. Undeterred by the album's lack of initial success, the Spin Doctors took to the road in the US, touring to the point of physical and financial exhaustion. When a Vermont radio station began to plug the album heavily, others soon followed, and the band's popularity spiralled upwards. *Pocket Full Of Kryptonite* became a major hit, producing a US Top 10 single in 'Little Miss Can't Be Wrong', despite the small storm caused by the track's opening line, 'Been a whole lot easier since the bitch left town' (the lyric was in fact aimed satirically at Barron's former step-mother rather than an exercise in rock misogyny). A live set, *Homebelly Groove*, was released to satisfy the new demand. By this time, comparisons were being drawn between the rise of the Spin Doctors and that of Nirvana, both being the people's choice, but the band simply stayed on the road, maintaining their impressive live reputation, while another single, 'Two Princes', led to worldwide success. However, late 1994 saw their first major setback, when news filtered through that guitarist Eric Shenkman had been ousted in favour of Anthony Krizan (b. New Jersey, USA).

Albums: *Pocket Full Of Kryptonite* (Epic 1991), *Homebelly Groove* (Epic 1992), *Turn It Upside Down* (Epic 1994).

Spinal Tap

The concept for Spinal Tap - a satire of a fading British heavy metal band - was first aired in a late 70s' television sketch. Christopher Guest, formerly of parody troupe *National Lampoon*, played the part of lead guitarist Nigel Tufnell, while Harry Shearer (bassist Derek Smalls) and actor Michael McKean (vocalist David St. Hubbins) had performed with the Credibility Gap. Their initial sketch also featured Loudon Wainwright and drummer Russ Kunkel, but these true-life musicians dropped out of the project on its transformation to full-length film. *This Is*

Spinal Tap, released in 1984, was not a cinematic success, but it has since become highly popular through the medium of video. Its portrayal of a doomed US tour is ruthless, exposing incompetence, megalomania and sheer madness, but in a manner combining humour with affection. However, rather than incurring the wrath of the rock fraternity, the film has been lauded by musicians, many of whom, unfathomably, claim inspiration for individual scenes. The contemporary UK comedy team, the Comic Strip, used elements of Spinal Tap's theme in their second film, *More Bad News*. Spinal Tap reunited as a 'real' group and undertook an extensive tour in 1992 to promote *Break Like The Wind*, which featured guest appearances by Jeff Beck, Nicky Hopkins and Slash (Guns N'Roses). At this stage it seems Spinal Tap's jokes at metal's expense are too deep rooted in truth to ever wear thin.

Albums: *This Is Spinal Tap* (Polydor 1984), *Break Like The Wind* (MCA 1992).

Video: *This Is Spinal Tap* (1989).

Split Beaver

This somewhat offensively titled heavy metal quartet was formed in Wolverhampton, England, during 1982 by Darrel Whitehouse (vocals), Mike Hoppet (guitar), Alan Rees (bass) and Mick Dunn (drums). They signed to the local Heavy Metal Records label the same year. The band specialized in plodding and clichéd British rock, influenced by Deep Purple and Thin Lizzy but without either the wit nor technique. They debuted with *When Hell Won't Have You*, a pedestrian and disappointing collection of uptempo rockers, after which they split up. It seems Hades was not the only place unwilling to entertain Split Beaver.

Album: *When Hell Won't Have You* (Heavy Metal 1982).

Spread Eagle

This New York metal band came together when vocalist Ray West joined Paul DiBartolo (guitar), Rob DeLuca (bass) and Tommi Gallo (drums), who had previously been together in a Boston band. The band were signed at a very early stage, and were forced to complete their songwriting in the studio while recording their debut. *Spread Eagle* comprised wonderfully raucous and raw metal built on vicious chainsaw guitar, although some typically sex-orientated lyrics provoked criticism, despite their tongue-in-cheek nature. The band tended to be slow starters live, taking time to build up a real head of steam, but otherwise their raw power and aggression transferred well to the stage. *Open To The Public* was more refined, as the band had matured and were able

to spend more time on songwriting and recording, although much of the drumming was provided by session players as Gallo flitted in and out of the band. However, Spread Eagle have yet to improve upon their minor league status.

Albums: *Spread Eagle* (MCA 1990), *Open To The Public* (MCA 1993).

Spy

This six-piece symphonic US rock group was formed in 1979 by David Nelson (guitar), John Vislocky (vocals), Danny Seidenberg (violin), Michael Visceglia (bass), Dave Le Bolt (keyboards) and Rob Goldman (drums). Spy were a highly versatile and talented band in the Boston, Styx and Kansas vein. Their self-titled debut, released in 1980, was an undiscovered classic of the pomp-rock genre. Saturated with keyboards, stunning vocal harmonies and fluid guitar work it is still difficult to explain why the album sold so poorly. They had more songs in preparation, but CBS dropped them before they could be fully completed. Spy disintegrated as most of the band members returned to session work.

Album: *Spy* (Kirshner 1980).

Spys

This US pomp-rock quintet was formed in 1981 by ex-Foreigner duo Al Greenwood (keyboards) and Ed Gagliardi (bass). Enlisting the services of John Blanco (vocals), John Digaudio (guitar) and Billy Milne (drums), they signed to EMI the following year. They debuted with a self-titled album, produced by Neil Kernon (of Dokken and Michael Bolton fame). This featured some upfront, punchy guitar work amid the sophisticated, keyboard dominated arrangements. On *Behind Enemy Lines*, they became a little self-indulgent, utilizing a Russian male voice choir on several tracks. The album flopped and with growing legal and contractual problems, SPys disintegrated in 1983. Greenwood went on to work with Joe Lynn Turner and later N.Y.C.

Albums: *Spys* (EMI 1982), *Behind Enemy Lines* (EMI 1983).

Squier, Billy

Having gained valuable experience as guitarist in the power-pop group Sidewinders, Billy Squier (b. Boston, USA), who had also appeared in the less-celebrated Magic Terry and the Universe, formed his own band under the name of Piper and recorded two albums for A&M during the late 70s. He dissolved Piper in 1979 and signed a solo deal with Capitol Records thereafter. *Tale Of The Tape* was released the following year and helped establish Squier's reputation as a sophisticated and talented songwriter/guitarist. Drawing inspiration from Led Zeppelin, Queen, Fleetwood Mac and Genesis amongst others, he has continued to release quality albums of hard rock/pop crossover material. In the UK Squier has largely been ignored, even though he toured with Whitesnake in 1981 and played the Reading Festival. The story in the US is entirely different. There he has scored major successes with *Don't Say No* and *Emotions In Motion*, both of which made number 5 in the *Billboard* album chart. The former also produced hit singles in 'The Stroke' and 'My Kinda Lover'. By the time he released his eighth studio album, *Tell The Truth*, in 1993, Squier could reflect on worldwide sales of over 11 million records.

Albums: *Tale Of The Tape* (Capitol 1980), *Don't Say No* (Capitol 1981), *Emotions In Motion* (Capitol 1982), *Signs Of Life* (Capitol 1984), *Enough Is Enough* (Capitol 1986), *Hear And Now* (Capitol 1989), *Creatures Of Habit* (Capitol 1991), *Tell The Truth* (Capitol 1993).

Video: *Live In The Dark* (1986).

St. Paradise

This short-lived US hard rock group was formed in 1978 by ex-Ted Nugent band duo Derek St. Holmes (vocals/guitar) and Rob Grange (bass/vocals). Recruiting ex-Montrose drummer Denny Carmassi, the line-up looked very promising. Signed by Warner Brothers, they released a self-titled debut in 1979. Comprising Americanized power-metal, the album lacked both drive and individuality and compared unfavourably with everything that the band's members had been associated with before. Following a European tour supporting Van Halen, which failed to win new fans for St. Paradise, the band disintegrated. Carmassi joined Gamma and St. Holmes worked with Aerosmith's Brad Whitford for a short time, before rejoining Nugent once more.

Album: *St. Paradise* (Warners 1979).

Stage Dolls

This melodic power-trio emerged from Trondheim, Norway. Formed in 1983, the original line-up comprised Torstein Flakne (vocals/guitar; ex-Kids), Terje Storli (bass) and Erlend Antonson (drums; ex-Subway Sect), the latter eventually replaced by Steinar Krokstad. Their three albums combine high-tech production with superbly crafted AOR, the songs heavily infused with melody and a keen sense of dynamics. 'Love Cries', lifted as a single from their self-titled 1988 album, became a minor Stateside hit in 1989. On the strength of this, they secured the support slots on the Blue Murder and Warrant USA tours the same year, but failed to build on the initial momentum.

Albums: *Soldier's Gun* (Polygram 1985), *Commandoes* (Polygram 1986), *Stage Dolls* (Polydor 1988).

Stampede

This melodic UK hard rock concern was formed in 1981 by ex-Wild Horses trio Reuben Archer (vocals), Laurence Archer (guitar) and Frank Noon (drums). Recruiting bassist Colin Bond, they signed to Polydor Records the following year. Noon left for Tormé and was replaced by Eddie Parsons before they debuted with *The Official Bootleg*, recorded live at the Reading Festival. Their music at this point incorporated elements of Deep Purple and UFO, particularly the guitar style of Laurence Archer which appeared to be a composite of the techniques of Michael Schenker and Ritchie Blackmore. *Hurricane Town* followed, but was a disappointment. It featured disposable, mid-paced rockers reminiscent of Thin Lizzy. Unable to attract media attention, Stampede split up in 1983. Laurence Archer joined Grand Slam and later recorded a solo album, *L.A.*

Albums: *The Official Bootleg* (Polydor 1982), *Hurricane Town* (Polydor 1983).

Starcastle

This US melodic pomp-rock group was formed in Illinois, USA, in 1972 by Stephen Hagler (guitar/vocals), Herb Schildt (keyboards) and Gary Strater (bass). The six-piece line-up was completed by ex-REO Speedwagon vocalist Terry Luttrell, guitarist Matt Stuart and drummer Steve Tassoer. After being championed by the local WGPU Radio Station in Champaign, Illinois, they were signed by Epic Records in 1974. Their music, which incorporated elements of Yes, Emerson, Lake And Palmer and Rush, was characterized by multi-vocal harmonies and complex, but carefully executed time-changes. They released four albums before splitting up, but never achieved the recognition their talents so evidently deserved.

Albums: *Starcastle* (Epic 1975), *Fountains Of Light* (Epic 1977), *Citadel* (Epic 1978), *Reel To Reel* (Epic 1979).

Starchild

This Canadian hard rock quartet, formed in 1977 by Richard Whittie (vocals), Robert Sprenger (guitar), Neil Light (bass) and Gregg Hinz (drums), debuted with *Children Of The Stars* the following year. Influenced by Triumph, Rush and Styx, the album was characterized by Sprenger's inventive guitar work and Whittie's distinctive vocals. Hinz quit to join

Helix shortly after the album's release, with ex-Lone Star drummer Dixie Lee stepping in as replacement. The band continued for a short time, but split up before any further recordings were made.

Album: *Children Of The Stars* (Axe 1978).

Starfighters

This UK hard rock/boogie quintet was formed in 1980 by ex-Suburban Studs' vocalist Steve Burton and guitarist Stevie Young (cousin of AC/DC's Angus Young). With Pat Hambly (guitar), Doug Dennis (bass) and Steve Bailey (drums; ex-Holly And The Italians) completing the line-up, they were picked up by Jive Records in 1981, after having toured with AC/DC. Produced by Tony Platt, their debut album was characterized by raunchy rock 'n' roll, with abrasive, up-front guitar work from Young. However, at best they were a poor man's AC/DC, specializing in second-hand riffs, hackneyed vocals and a predictable backbeat. On *In Flight Movie*, they tried desperately to move away from this approach, concentrating instead on more traditional blues-based hard rock. Unfortunately this new style had even less to commend it, and they broke up soon after its release.

Albums: *Starfighters* (Jive 1981) *In Flight Movie* (Jive 1983).

Starr, Jack

After quitting the heavy metal band Virgin Steele in 1984, guitarist Jack Starr teamed up with ex-Riot vocalist Rhett Forrester and former Rods' rhythm section Gary Bordonaro and Carl Canedy. They delivered *Out Of The Darkness* in 1984, a subtle combination of aggression, melody and dynamics. Starr dissolved the band soon after the album came out, preferring instead to use a new set of backing musicians on each subsequent release. Over the next four albums he moved away from his metallic roots, towards more commercial, arena-style rock typified by Bon Jovi and Dokken. Starr is one of the more original new-style, techno-wizard guitarists, but has yet to receive the recognition his talents undoubtedly deserve. He has recently opted to record under the band name of Burning Starr.

Albums: *Out Of The Darkness* (Music For Nations 1984), *Rock The American Way* (Passport 1985), *No Turning Back* (US Metal 1986), *Blaze Of Glory* (US Metal 1987), *Burning Starr* (US Metal 1989).

Start

This Icelandic pop-rock group was formed in 1980 by vocalist Petur Kristjansson and guitarist Kristjan Edelstein. Enlisting the services of Eirikur Haukson (guitar/vocals), Nikulas Robertson (keyboards), Jon Olafsson (bass/vocals) and David Karlsson (drums), they signed to the Steinar label the following year. They debuted with *En Hun Snyst Nu Samt*, a predictable collection of soft-rock anthems with Icelandic vocals. They disappeared into oblivion, after representing Iceland in the Eurovision Song Contest.

Album: *En Hun Snyst Nu Samt* (Steinar 1981).

Starz

New York band formed in 1975 by guitarist Brendan Harkin, drummer Joey X Dube and bassist Peter Sweval. Whilst looking for musicians to complete their line-up they worked as session men and also recorded a soundtrack to the porn film, *Divine Obsession*. The following year they recruited guitarist Richie Ranno and vocalist Michael Lee Smith and signed to Capitol Records, who released the hit single, 'She's Just A Fallen Angel', and the album, *Starz*. Two more albums followed in 1977 before Harkin and Sweval left to be replaced by Bobby Messano and Orville Davies respectively. This line-up recorded the monumental *Coliseum Rock* set which took them to a worldwide audience. What followed was two years of touring but no new recordings. After a farewell tour they split in 1980. Ranno and Dube formed a new band with bassist Oeter Scance. A year later Ranno and Scance reunited with Smith and together with ex-Prism drummer Doug Madick, formed Hellcats. This band continued in the Starz vein of anthemic rock with melody. Indeed, they even included much Starz material in their live set, their success leading to a series of Starz live albums and compilations being released. Messano had spent his time working with various bands associated with Atlantic Records including Fiona, and in 1989 formed his own band.

Albums: *Starz* (Capitol 1976), *Violation* (Capitol 1977), *Attention Shoppers* (Capitol 1977), *Coliseum Rock* (Capitol 1978). Compilations: *Live In America* (Violation 1983), *Live In Canada* (Heavy Metal 1985), *Piss Party* (Heavy Metal 1985), *Brightest Starz* (Heavy Metal 1985), *Starz To Coliseum Rock* (Heavy Metal 1985), *Do It With The Lights On* (Performance 1987), *Live In Action* (Roadrunner 1989). Hellcats: *Hellcats* (King Klassic 1982), *Hellcats Kids* (King Klassic 1987). Bobby Messano: *Messano* (Strategic 1989).

Statetrooper

After leaving MSG vocalist Gary Barden formed Statetrooper in 1986 with Martin Bushell (guitar), Jeff Summers (guitar; ex-Weapon), Steve Glover (keyboards), Jeff Brown (bass; ex-Wildfire) and Bruce Bisland (drums; ex-Wildfire/Weapon). They debuted the following year with a self-titled album of melodic

AOR, which featured extensive keyboards with a production from Phil Chilton. It courted comparisons with Foreigner, Styx and Thin Lizzy, but lacked consistency in terms of songwriting. The album sold poorly and following a short period with Brian Robertson (ex-Motörhead and Thin Lizzy) on guitar, the band broke up.

Album: *Statetrooper* (FM Revolver 1987).

Status Quo

The origins of this durable and now-legendary attraction lie in the Spectres, a London-based beat group. Founder members Mike (later Francis) Rossi (b. 29 May 1949, Peckham, London, England; guitar/vocals) and Alan Lancaster (b. 7 February 1949, Peckham, London, England; bass) led the act from its inception in 1962 until 1967, by which time Roy Lynes (organ) and John Coughlan (b. 19 September 1946, Dulwich, London, England; drums) completed its line-up. The Spectres' three singles encompassed several styles of music, ranging from pop to brash R&B, but the quartet took a new name, Traffic Jam, when such releases proved commercially unsuccessful. A similar failure beset 'Almost But Not Quite There', but the group was nonetheless buoyed by the arrival of Rick Parfitt aka Rick Harrison (b. 12 October 1948, Woking, Surrey, England; guitar/vocals), lately of cabaret attraction, the Highlights. The revamped unit assumed their 'Status Quo' appellation in August 1967 and initially sought work backing various solo artists, including Madeline Bell and Tommy Quickly. Such employment came to an abrupt end the following year when the quintet's debut single, 'Pictures Of Matchstick Men', soared to number 7. One of the era's most distinctive performances, the song's ringing guitar pattern and *de rigueur* phasing courted pop and psychedelic affectations. A follow-up release, 'Black Veils Of Melancholy', exaggerated latter trappings at the expense of melody, but the group enjoyed another UK Top 10 hit with the jaunty 'Ice In The Sun', co-written by former 50s singer, Marty Wilde. Subsequent recordings in a similar vein struggled to emulate such success, and despite reaching number 12 with 'Down The Dustpipe', Status Quo was increasingly viewed as a *passé* novelty. However, the song itself, which featured a simple riff and wailing harmonica, indicated the musical direction unveiled more fully on *Ma Kelly's Greasy Spoon*. The album included Quo's version of Steamhammer's 'Junior's Wailing', which had inspired this conversion to a simpler, 'boogie' style. Gone too were the satin shirts, frock coats and kipper ties, replaced by long hair, denim jeans and plimsolls. The departure of Lynes *en route* to Scotland - 'He just got off the train and that was the last we ever saw of him' (Rossi) - brought the unit's guitar work to the fore, although indifference from their record company blighted progress. Assiduous live appearances built up a grass roots following and impressive slots at the Reading and Great Western Festivals (both 1972) signalled a commercial turning point. Now signed to the renowned Vertigo label, Status Quo scored a UK Top 10 hit that year with 'Paper Plane' but more importantly, reached number 5 in the album charts with *Piledriver*. A subsequent release, *Hello*, entered at number 1, confirming the group's emergence as a major attraction. Since that point their style has basically remained unchanged, fusing simple, 12-bar riffs to catchy melodies, while an unpretentious 'lads' image has proved equally enduring. Each of their 70s albums reached the Top 5, while a consistent presence in the singles' chart included such notable entries as 'Caroline' (1973), 'Down Down' (a chart topper in 1974), 'Whatever You Want' (1979) and 'Lies'/'Don't Drive My Car' (1980). An uncharacteristic ballad, 'Living On An Island' (1979), showed a softer perspective while Quo also proved adept at adapting outside material, as evinced by their version of John Fogerty's 'Rockin' All Over The World' (1977). That song was later re-recorded as 'Running All Over The World' to promote the charitable *Race Against Time* in 1988. The quartet undertook a lengthy break during 1980, but answered rumours of a permanent split with *Just Supposin'*. However, a dissatisfied Coughlan left the group in 1981 in order to form his own act, Diesel. Pete Kircher, (ex-Original Mirrors), took his place, but Quo was then undermined by the growing estrangement between Lancaster and Rossi and Parfitt. The bassist moved to Australia in 1983 - a cardboard cut-out substituted on several television slots - but he remained a member for the next two years. Lancaster's final appearance with the group was at *Live Aid*, following which he unsuccessfully took out a High Court injunction to prevent the group performing without him. Rossi and Parfitt secured the rights to the name 'Status Quo' and reformed the act around John Edwards (bass), Jeff Rich (drums) and keyboard player Andy Bown. The last-named musician, formerly of the Herd and Judas Jump, had begun his association with the group in 1973, but only now became an official member. Despite such traumas Quo continued to enjoy commercial approbation with Top 10 entries 'Dear John' (1982), 'Marguerita Time' (1983), 'In The Army Now' (1986) and 'Burning Bridges (On And Off And On Again)' (1988), while *1+9+8+2* was their fourth chart-topping album. Status Quo celebrated its silver anniversary in October 1991 by entering *The Guinness Book Of Records* having completed four charity concerts in four UK cities in the space of 12 hours. This ambitious undertaking, the subject of a television documentary, was succeeded by a national tour which confirmed the group's continued mass-market popularity. 1994 brought another number 1 single with 'Come On You Reds', a musically dubious project recorded with the league football champions, Manchester United. The much-loved Status Quo have carved a large niche in music history by producing uncomplicated, unpretentious and infectious rock music. Their track-record is staggering - just two statistics worthy of consideration are: worldwide sales of over 100 million, and 45 British hit singles (more than any other band).

Albums: *Picturesque Matchstickable Messages* (Pye 1968), *Spare Parts* (Pye 1969), *Ma Kelly's Greasy Spoon* (Pye 1970), *Dog Of Two Head* (Pye 1971), *Piledriver* (Vertigo 1972), *Hello* (Vertigo 1973), *Quo* (Vertigo 1974), *On The Level* (Vertigo 1975), *Blue For You* (Vertigo 1976), *Status Quo Live!* (Vertigo 1977, double album), *Rockin' All Over The World* (Vertigo 1977), *If You Can't Stand The Heat* (Vertigo 1978), *Whatever You Want* (Vertigo 1979), *Just Supposin'* (Vertigo 1980), *Never Too Late* (Vertigo 1982), *1+9+8+2* (Vertigo 1982), *Back To Back* (Vertigo 1983), *In The Army Now* (Vertigo 1986), *Ain't Complaining* (Vertigo 1988), *Perfect Remedy* (Vertigo 1989), *Rock 'Til You Drop* (Vertigo 1991), *Live Alive Quo* (Vertigo 1992). Compilations: *Status Quo-tations* (Marble Arch 1969), *The Best Of Status Quo* (Pye 1973), *The Golden Hour Of Status Quo* (Golden Hour 1973), *Down The Dustpipe* (Golden Hour 1975), *The Rest Of Status Quo* (Pye 1976), *The Status Quo File* (Pye 1977, double album), *The Status Quo Collection* (Pickwick 1978, double album), *Twelve Gold Bars* (Vertigo 1980), *Spotlight On Status Quo Volume 1* (PRT 1980, double album), *Fresh Quota* (PRT 1981), *100 Minutes Of Status Quo* (PRT 1982), *Spotlight On Status Quo Volume 2* (PRT 1982), *From The Makers Of...* (Phonogram 1983, triple album), *Works* (PRT 1983), *To Be Or Not To Be* (Contour 1983), *Twelve Gold Bars Volume 1 & 2* (Vertigo 1984, double album), *Na Na Na* (Flashback 1985), *Collection: Status Quo* (Castle 1985), *Quotations, Volume 1* (PRT 1987), *Quotations, Volume 2* (PRT 1987), *From The Beginning* (PRT 1988), *C.90 Collector* (Legacy 1989), *B-Sides And Rarities* (Castle 1990), *The Early Works 1968 - '73* (Essential 1990, CD box set).

Videos: *Live At The NEC* (1984), *Best Of Status Quo, Preserved* (1986), *End Of The Road* (1986), *Rocking All Over The Years* (1987), *The Anniversary Waltz* (1991), *Rock Til You Drop* (1991).

Further reading: *Status Quo: The Authorised Biography*, John Shearlaw.

Steel Forest

This Dutch quintet was formed in Amsterdam during 1981 by Sunny Hays (vocals), Fred Heikens (guitar), Appie van Vliet (keyboards), Ron Heikens (bass) and Joop Oliver (drums). They negotiated a deal with the Dureco label the following year. They made their debut with *First Confession*, a clichéd and formularized Euro-rock opus, which failed to find an audience. Hays was replaced by Thijs Hamelaers (later of Sleez Beez) and William Lawson (ex-Angus) took over the drumstool after the album was released, but this line-up disintegrated before entering the studio.

Album: *First Confession* (Dureco 1982).

Steele, Chrissy

This Canadian 'heavy metal goddess' linked up with former Headpins guitarist, songwriter and producer Brian MacLeod to concoct *Magnet To Steele* in 1991. The album was recorded on MacLeod's power yacht whilst cruising along the coast of British Columbia. Steele has a powerful and characteristic style, but the derivative and commercial structure to the material did her no favours. The bravado and sexual imagery of the press releases appeared more interesting than the actual music.

Album: *Magnet To Steele* (Chrysalis 1991).

Steeler (Germany)

This German heavy metal quintet, formerly known as Sinner, emerged as Steeler in 1981. The band were formed in Bochum, Westphalia, by Peter Burtz (vocals) and virtuoso guitarist Axel Rudi Pell. With the addition of Volher Krawczak (bass), Bertram Frewer (backing vocals) and Volker Jakel (drums), they signed to the independent Earthshaker label in 1984. They debuted the same year with a self-titled album of uptempo hard-rockers which recalled the Scorpions. However, the strong material was discredited somewhat by the budget production. After *Rulin' The Earth*, the band moved to Steamhammer Records and replaced Krawczak with new bass player Herve Rossi. *Strike Back* saw the band move towards an Americanized arena-rock approach, typical of Ratt, Dokken and Kiss. After *Undercover Animal* a series of line-up changes ensued, with Pell leaving to build a solo career. In consequence the future of the band was sealed, and no further releases accrued.

Albums: *Steeler* (Earthshaker 1984), *Rulin' The Earth* (Earthshaker 1985), *Strike Back* (Steamhammer

1986), *Undercover Animal* (Steamhammer 1988).

Steeler (USA)

This US hard rock quartet was formed in Nashville, Tennessee, in 1982 by vocalist Ron Keel. Recruiting Rik Fox (bass) and Mark Edwards (drums), the line-up was completed when Shrapnel label boss, Mike Varney, introduced Swedish guitarist Yngwie Malmsteen to the band. They relocated to Los Angeles and gigged incessantly on the bar and club circuit. Varney offered them a deal and they delivered a self-titled debut the following year. It was pure Americana bar-rock; chest-beating anthems, punctuated by shrill guitar work. Malmsteen quit just as the album was released, joining Alcatrazz and later forming his own outfit, Rising Force. Keel formed a new outfit under his own name, while Fox formed Sin.
Album: *Steeler* (Shrapnel 1983).

Steeplechase

This non-descript melodic US rock quartet was formed in 1980 by Joe Lamente (vocals), Tony Sumo (guitar), Bob Held (bass) and Vinny Conigliaro (drums). They were signed to the local BCR label the following year. Drawing inspiration from the mid-west rock scene, their music incorporated elements of Petra, Starz and Spy. Their debut and sole album failed to take off and the band disintegrated soon after its release. Lamente joined Shelter and later recorded the solo set, *Secrets That You Keep*, in 1986.
Album: *Steeplechase* (BCR 1981).

Steinman, Jim

American songwriter/producer/musician Steinman first came to the public's attention in 1975 as musical arranger for the comedy company National Lampoon. He was also a playwright and it was at an audition that he first met Dallas singer/actor Meat Loaf. Together they conceived one of the biggest rock albums of all time, *Bat Out Of Hell*. Steinman's unique Wagnerian production technique was later to grace countless other artists from Bonnie Tyler to Barry Manilow. With Meat Loaf unable to record a follow-up Steinman grew impatient and decided to record the album himself. Released in 1981, *Bad For Good* lacked the vocal impact of Meat Loaf and was not a best-seller - it was, however, still a superb album featuring Todd Rundgren as guitarist and co-producer. Many of the songs would later appear on the *Bat Out Of Hell 2* album which heralded a reunion with Meat Loaf, having parted company after the latter's *Deadringer* set, also from 1981. Perhaps the most stunning track from *Bad For Good* was a

spoken-word piece titled 'Love And Death And An American Guitar', where Steinman proclaims in a style reminiscent of Jim Morrison's 'Horse Latitudes', that 'I once killed a Fender guitar'. He was also the mastermind for the 1990 double album project, *Original Sin*, a concept piece based on sexuality - at times almost operatic in construction it would not be taken seriously and so he returned to production work where he remains most in demand.
Albums: *Bad For Good* (Epic 1981), *Original Sin* (Virgin 1990, double album).

Steppenwolf

Although based in southern California, Steppenwolf evolved out of a Toronto act, the Sparrow(s). John Kay (b. Joachim F. Krauledat, 12 April 1944, Tilsit, Germany; vocals), Michael Monarch (b. 5 July 1950, Los Angeles, California, USA; lead guitar), Goldy McJohn (b. 2 May 1945; keyboards), Rushton Moreve (bass) and Jerry Edmonton (b. 24 October 1946, Canada; drums) assumed their new name in 1967, inspired by the novel of cult author Herman Hesse. John Morgan replaced Moreve prior to recording. The group's exemplary debut album included 'Born To Be Wild' which reached number 2 in the US charts. This rebellious anthem was written by Dennis Edmonton (Mars Bonfire), guitarist in Sparrow and brother of drummer Jerry. It was featured in the famous opening sequence of the film, *Easy Rider*, and has since acquired classic status. Steppenwolf actively cultivated a menacing, hard rock image, and successive collections mixed this heavy style with blues. 'Magic Carpet Ride' and 'Rock Me' were also US Top 10 singles yet the group deflected any criticism such temporal success attracted by addressing such contemporary issues as politics, drugs and racial prejudice. Newcomers Larry Byrom (guitar) and Nick St. Nicholas (b. 28 September 1943, Hamburg, Germany; bass), former members of Time, were featured on *Monster*, Steppenwolf's most cohesive set. A concept album based on Kay's jaundiced view of contemporary (1970) America, it was a benchmark in the fortunes of the group. Continued personnel changes undermined their stability, and later versions of the band seemed content to further a spurious biker image, rather than enlarge on earlier achievements. John Kay dissolved the band in 1972, but his solo career proved inconclusive and within two years he was leading a reconstituted Steppenwolf. The singer has left and reformed his creation several times over the ensuing years, but has been unable to repeat former glories.
Albums: *Steppenwolf* (Dunhill 1968), *The Second* (Dunhill 1968), *Steppenwolf At Your Birthday Party*

(Dunhill 1969), *Early Steppenwolf* (Dunhill 1969 - Sparrow recordings from 1967), *Monster* (Dunhill 1969), *Steppenwolf 'Live'* (Dunhill 1970), *Steppenwolf 7* (Dunhill 1970), *For Ladies Only* (Dunhill 1971), *Slow Flux* (Mums 1974), *Hour Of The Wolf* (Epic 1975), *Skullduggery* (Epic 1976), *Live In London* (Attic 1982), *Wolf Tracks* (Attic 1982), *Rock & Roll Rebels* (Qwil 1987), *Rise And Shine* (IRS 1990). Compilations: *Steppenwolf Gold* (Dunhill 1971), *Rest In Peace* (Dunhill 1972), *16 Greatest Hits* (Dunhill 1973), *Masters Of Rock* (Dunhill 1975), *Golden Greats: Steppenwolf* (MCA 1985).

Sterling Cooke Force

This Jimi Hendrix-inspired US group was put together by guitarist/vocalist Sterling Cooke in 1983. Recruiting Gino Cannon (vocals), Harry Shuman (bass) and Albie Coccia (drums), they recorded two unspectacular albums during the mid-80s. *Force This* saw Cooke rescind the vocals to Cannon and the music adopted a more melodic and restrained style. Second-hand riffs, bridges and solos were the order of the day, which left the band with a serious identity crisis. After losing their recording contract they were consigned to the status of minor club circuit band from then on.
Albums: *Full Force* (Ebony 1984), *Force This* (Ebony 1986).

Stevens', Steve, Atomic Playboys

Steve Stevens first attracted attention as lead guitarist in Billy Idol's band, where his flash and fiery style brought Idol's hard rock to life. Stevens also accompanied Michael Jackson on 'Dirty Diana' and has worked with Ric Ocasek of the Cars, Steve Lukather of Toto and the Thompson Twins. He broke ranks from Idol's band in 1988 to form Steve Steven's Atomic Playboys with vocalist Perry McCarty, drummer Thommy Price and keyboard player Phil Ashley. Released in 1989, their self-titled debut was a major disappointment. With the exception of the title-cut, the songs were derivative and overtly commercial. Following an unsuccessful US club tour in 1990, the band split up.
Album: *Steve Steven's Atomic Playboys* (Warners 1989).

Steve Whitney Band

This Euro-rock group was formed in 1975 by Chrigi Wiedemeier (guitar), Rolf Schlup (bass), Mick Hudson (vocals), Andy Lindsay (guitar) and Pete Leeman (drums) - with absolutely no sign of a Steve Whitney. They debuted in 1980 with *Hot Line*, an overtly commercial melodic rock album that lacked conviction. Gary Steimer and Rob Seales replaced Leeman and Lindsay, respectively, on *Night Fighting*, which marked a distinct change in direction. This saw them drop the poppy harmonies and switch to blues-based hard rock in the classic AC/DC mould. Mick Hudson then quit and the remaining four members continued as Sergeant.
Albums: *Hot Line* (EMC 1980), *Night Fighting* (EMC 1982).

Stiltskin

Authors of the most distinctive riff of 1994, few knew who Stiltskin were at the time, yet millions recognised the instrumental section of 'Inside' which accompanied a lavish Levi's television advertisement. Picked up by the jeans manufacturer when it was overheard playing at the group's publishers, 'Inside' shot to number 1 in the UK charts when finally released as a single in the summer of 1994. The band had actually formed in 1989 when Peter Lawlor (guitar) and James Finnigan (bass) met for the first time in London. Finnigan had previously spent two years working alongside the Kane brothers in Hue And Cry, before electing to pursue a rockier direction. His new partner, meanwhile, had just returned from New York, dismayed with the dominance of dance and rap music. The duo began working on songs together in Lawlor's demo studio, recruiting an old friend of Finnigan's, Ross McFarlane, as drummer. However, unable to find a suitable singer or arouse record company interest, McFarlane relocated to Glasgow to drum with several bands, including Slide and Fireball. There were few further developments until the summer of 1993, when Lawlor and Finnigan were driving along the M8 between Edinburgh and Glasgow and passed a figure 'frantically retrieving objects which resembled guitars from a van engulfed in flames on the motorway's hard shoulder'. That distressed figure would turn out to be Ray Wilson, who accepted an offer of a lift from the pair in order to make the gig he was playing that night. When he walked off stage, Lawlor and Finnigan offered him the job as Stiltskin vocalist. The new formation persuaded McFarlane to return to the fold, shortly after which they were approached to use 'Inside'. Their management team set up White Water records to house their releases, with a second single, 'Footsteps', also charting, before a debut album in late 1994.
Album: *The Mind's Eye* (White Water 1994).

Stingray

This South African melodic rock group was formed in 1978 by Dennis East (vocals), Mike Pilot (guitar), Danny Anthill (keyboards), Allan Goldswain (keyboards), Eddie Boyle (bass) and Shaun Wright (drums). Together they based their style firmly on American rock giants such as Styx, Boston, Kansas and Journey. They released two technically excellent albums, characterized by the heavy use of keyboards and multi-part vocal harmonies, but failing to attract attention outside their native South Africa, the band broke up in 1981.

Albums: *Stingray* (Carrere 1979), *Operation Stingray* (Nitty Gritty 1980).

Stone Fury

Moving from Hamburg, Germany, to Los Angeles, USA, in 1983, vocalist Lenny Wolf teamed up with Bruce Gowdy (guitar) to form Stone Fury. Adding Rick Wilson (bass) and Jody Cortez (drums), they signed to MCA Records and debuted the following year with *Burns Like A Star*. The album offered traditional blues-based hard rock, similar in construction to Led Zeppelin. Wolf's vocals were modelled very closely on Robert Plant's, both in pitch and phrasing, which provoked accusations of imitation. *Let Them Talk* was more restrained and employed a greater use of melody and atmospherics. Unable to make a breakthrough in the USA, Wolf went back to Germany and later formed Kingdom Come on his return to the States in 1987. Gowdy, in the meantime, formed World Trade.

Albums: *Burns Like A Star* (MCA 1984), *Let Them Talk* (MCA 1986).

Stone Temple Pilots

The Stone Temple Pilots are the result of a chance meeting between vocalist Scott Weiland (who prefers to be known by his surname only) and bassist Robert DeLeo at one of Black Flag's final shows in Los Angeles. After discovering that they both went out with the same girl, a songwriting partnership led to the formation of a full band, originally known as Mighty Joe Young, and later renamed Stone Temple Pilots, with drummer Eric Kretz and DeLeo's guitarist brother Dean joining the duo. Moving away from the Guns N'Roses-crazed Los Angeles scene of the time to San Diego, the band were able to play club shows and develop hard rock material given an alternative edge by their varied influences. Although the sound of the band brought many others to mind, from Led Zeppelin to Seattle bands such as Pearl Jam and Alice In Chains, and Weiland's deep voice bore a passing resemblance to that of Eddie Vedder, it was very much Stone Temple Pilots' own sound, and there was no denying the quality of *Core*. The dense wall of muscular guitar over a tight, precise rhythm section provides a powerful setting for Weiland's emotive vocals and challenging lyrics. 'Sex Type Thing', perhaps the band's best-known song, deals with sexual harassment from the viewpoint of a particularly brutish male, and the singer was initially concerned that the message would be misinterpreted. His fears proved unfounded and, helped by heavy touring, *Core* would reach the US Top 20 by the summer of 1993, eventually selling over four million copies in the US. The follow-up, *Purple*, would debut at number 1 in the US album charts, staying there for three weeks. This time the band purposely avoided any material which could be construed as derivative of Pearl Jam, having tired of the unfair criticism, and their second effort proved to be an atmospheric and rewarding experience as STP produced a quasi-psychedelic sound which confirmed their own identity and talents.

Albums: *Core* (Atlantic 1992), *Purple* (Atlantic 1994).

Storm

This Los Angeles-based quartet, formed in 1978 by Jeanette Chase (vocals), Lear Stevens (guitar), Ronni Hansen (bass) and David Devon (drums), played hi-tech hard-rock, characterized by Lear's Brian May-like guitar sound and the powerful vocals of Chase. They incorporated elements of Queen, Van Halen and Styx within complex, and at times classically styled arrangements. Their second album moved more towards AOR, with the inclusion of more lightweight material and even folk influences.

Albums: *Storm* (MCA 1979), *Storm* (Capitol 1983).

Stormbringer

This Swiss quintet was formed in 1984 by Dave Barreto (vocals), Angi Schilero (guitar), Fabian Emmenger (keyboards), Urs Hufschmid (bass) and Laurie Chiundinelli (drums). Taking their name from Deep Purple's 1974 album, they specialized in melodic power-metal, evidently based on the works of the latter group. However, it proved to be a rather non-descript tribute, and attracted few supporters. Disillusioned by the lack of media and public response, they split up soon after the album was released. Schilero went on to play with China for a short time, before starting his own band.

Album: *Stormbringer* (Musk 1985).

Stormtroopers Of Death

More commonly known as S.O.D., this band initially came into existence as a one-off side project for Anthrax musicians Scott Ian (guitar) and Charlie Benante (drums). Taking time out during the recording of Anthrax's *Spreading The Disease* in 1985, they asked Nuclear Assault bassist Dan Lilker and roadie Billy Milano (vocals; ex-Psychos) to join them, to make use of three day's free studio time. The result was *Speak English Or Die*, a manic fusion of thrash and hardcore styles, that had both humour and considerable crossover appeal. Milano went on to form Method Of Destruction, using exactly the same musical blueprint (indeed, some of Scott Ian's S.O.D. lyrics would be re-used in this project). A posthumous release, *Live From Budokan*, emerged in 1992, while sporadic reunions have also occurred over recent years.

Albums: *Speak English Or Die* (Megaforce 1985), *Live From Budokan* (Megaforce 1992).

Stormwitch

This German heavy metal quintet, who employed a strong satanic/gothic horror image, were formed by guitarist Lee Tarot (b. Harold Spengler) in 1981, together with Andy Aldrian (vocals), Steve Merchant (guitar), Ronny Pearson (bass) and Pete Lancer (drums). These were all fellow Germans, who nevertheless altered their names in order to sound American. Their first three albums offered undistinguished Euro-metal, reminiscent of Running Wild, and made little impact outside Germany. A lack of success saw them change direction on 1987's *The Beauty And The Beast*, adopting a more straightforward hard rock approach. All to little avail, however, with the band disintegrating shortly afterwards.

Albums: *Walpurgis Night* (Powerstation 1984), *Tales Of Terror* (Powerstation 1985), *Stronger Than Heaven* (Powerstation 1986), *The Beauty And The Beast* (Gama 1987).

Stradlin, Izzy, And The Ju Ju Hounds

Tired of the pressures of working with one of the world's high-profile acts, Stradlin left Guns N'Roses in the autumn of 1991 to work on a solo project. With himself on guitar and lead vocals, and the former Burning Tree rhythm section of Mark Dutton and Doni Grey, Stradlin added a Ju Ju Hounds line-up of former Georgia Satellites guitarist Rick Richards, ex-Broken Homes bassist Jimmy Ashhurst, and drummer Charlie Quintana, for the band's 1992 recording debut. Axl Rose's description of the band as 'Izzy's Keith Richards thing' was apt, as the influence of the Rolling Stones guitarist on Stradlin's songwriting and vocal style was obvious, even incorporating their shared taste for reggae with a furious cover of Toots And the Maytals' 'Pressure Drop'. However, far from being a mere homage, the album was excellent, and generally well-received. Subsequent live shows were electric affairs, with

Stradlin appearing more relaxed, and Richards, in particular, contributing some stunning slide/lead guitar work, and vocals. Somewhat surprisingly, Stradlin made a brief return to the Guns N'Roses camp for some open-air European shows in the summer of 1993, ironically standing in for his replacement, Gilby Clarke, after the latter broke his wrist.

Album: *Izzy Stradlin And The Ju Ju Hounds* (Geffen 1992).

Stranger

This melodic pop-rock quartet was formed in Florida, USA, during 1981 by Greg Billings (vocals), Ronnie Garvin (guitar), Tom Cardenas (bass) and John Price (drums). With the line-up stabilized, they signed to CBS Records the following year. Produced by Tom Werman (of Ted Nugent and Mötley Crüe fame), their debut album was a highly impressive collection of anthemic rockers, punctuated by some fiery guitar work from Garvin. Despite its seemingly obvious commercial potential the album failed to make an impact, and little was heard of the band until a second album, a full nine years later.

Albums: *Stranger* (Epic 1982), *No Rules* (Thunderbay 1991).

Strangeways

This Scottish quartet was put together in 1985 by brothers Ian (guitar) and David Stewart (bass). With Jim Drummond (drums) and Tony Liddell (vocals), they debuted with a self-titled album in 1985. This offered a blend of Americanized, melodic AOR comparable with the work of Boston, Journey or Kansas. Produced by Kevin Elson (of Journey fame), it surpassed many expectations, but was ignored by the British public. Terry Brock (from Atlanta, USA) replaced Liddell on *Native Sons*, which saw the band consolidate their style and progress significantly as songwriters. It remains one of the sadly neglected albums of the pomp-rock/AOR genre. *Walk In The Fire* was not as immediate, with Brock's vocals sounding hoarse and less sophisticated. He left to audition for Deep Purple in 1989, but was unsuccessful. Strangeways have been inactive since.

Albums: *Strangeways* (Bonaire 1986), *Native Sons* (RCA 1987), *Walk In The Fire* (RCA 1989).

Strapps

This UK hard rock quartet was formed in 1975 by Ross Stagg (vocals/guitar), Noel Scott (keyboards), Joe Read (bass) and Mick Underwood (drums), and were picked up by EMI Records the following year. Drawing their inspiration from Deep Purple, Thin

Stryper

Lizzy and Uriah Heep, they released four albums over a five-year period. These met with very limited success, except in Japan, where they maintained a cult following. Strapps never graduated from support act status in Europe, which was a fair summation of their true potential. The band finally disintegrated in 1979, when Underwood joined Gillan.

Albums: *Strapps* (EMI 1976), *Secret Damage* (EMI 1977), *Sharp Conversation* (EMI 1978), *Ball Of Fire* (EMI 1979).

Stratus

When former Iron Maiden drummer Clive Burr joined Praying Mantis in 1985 the new band became known as Stratus - the remaining personnel comprising Bernie Shaw (vocals), Tino Troy (guitar), Alan Nelson (keyboards), and Chris Troy (bass). Moving away from the formularized New Wave Of British Heavy Metal approach, Stratus employed the extensive use of keyboards and multi-part vocal harmonies. They debuted with *Throwing Shapes*, a lacklustre pomp-rock album lacking in both in energy and quality songs. The album fared badly and the band split up soon after it was released. Bernie Shaw went on to join Uriah Heep.

Album: *Throwing Shapes* (Steeltrax 1985).

Stray Dog

This blues-based US heavy metal group started life as a power-trio in 1973. Formed by the nucleus of Snuffy Walden (vocals/guitar), Alan Roberts (bass/vocals) and Leslie Sampson (b. 1950; drums), their style incorporated elements of Grand Funk, Jimi Hendrix and Led Zeppelin. Timmy Dulaine (guitar/vocals) and Luis Cabaza (keyboards) were added in 1974, with rather negative results. The aggression and power of the three-piece had been dissipated amongst needlessly intricate arrangements. *While You're Down There* was a major disappointment and following management and contractual problems, the band went their separate ways in 1975. Walden later reappeared as theme composer to popular US television soap opera *30 Something*.

Albums: *Stray Dog* (Manticore 1973), *While You're Down There* (Manticore 1974).

Streets

This melodic heavy rock quartet was formed in 1982 by ex-Kansas vocalist Steve Walsh and Mike Slamer (guitar; ex-City Boy). Drafting in Billy Greer (bass) and Tim Gehrt (drums), they adopted a much more straightforward AOR approach than their former employers, concentrating on infectious hooklines and

memorable choruses, rather than intricate keyboard fills and complex arrangements. Their self-titled debut was received very favourably by the music media, but failed to win over a large audience, partly due to poor promotion. *Crimes In Mind* saw the band maturing as songwriters, but Atlantic Records were guilty of indifference once more, and the album failed to take off. Disillusioned, Streets broke up in 1986, with Walsh and Greer joining the re-vamped Kansas.
Albums: *Streets* (Atlantic 1983), *Crimes In Mind* (Atlantic 1985).

Stressball

New Orleans sludge metal specialists, formed in 1989, whose name is derived from drummer and part-time chef Joe Fazzio's own 'stressball' - 'it takes batteries and it's supposed to be like a paper-weight or something, and when you get pissed off, you throw it at the wall and it sounds like glass breaking'. The rest of the group comprises Lennon Laviolette (guitar), Steven Gaille (vocals) and Eddy Dupuy (bass). Fazzio is also a good friend of Pantera's Phil Anselmo, and the two play together in the side-band, Both Legs Broken (along with Kirk Windstein from Crowbar and Mark Schultz from Eyehategod). Stressball was inaugurated while Fazzio and friends practised at a 100 year old warehouse in the centre of New Orleans, where bands such as Graveyard Rodeo (who practically invented the slow, torturous sound associated with the scene), Eyehategod and stablemates Crowbar also emerged. Fazzio himself had previously played in a band called Crawlspace with Mike Williams from Eyehategod, with whom they have toured widely.
Album: *Stressball* (Pavement 1993).

Strife

Blues-based British hard rock trio who formed in 1972. The band - John Reid (vocals/guitar), Gordon Rowley (bass/vocals) and David Williams (drums/vocals) - gigged incessantly and earned a reputation as a perennial support act, but lacked the individuality to reach headline status. Strife built up a small but loyal cult following during the mid-70s, with their honest, no-frills, good-time rock 'n' roll. They released two average rock albums, with *Back To Thunder* featuring Don Airey on keyboards and Paul Ellison in place of Williams on drums. After one last stab at success with the EP, *School,* the band gave up in 1979. Rowley went on to form Nightwing.
Albums: *Rush* (Chrysalis 1975), *Back To Thunder* (Gull 1978).

Striker

This versatile hard rock quartet was formed in 1977 by the multi-talented Rick Randle (vocals/keyboards/guitar). Enlisting the services of Scott Roseburg (vocals/bass/guitar), Rick Ramirez (guitar) and Rick Taylor (drums/vocals), Striker signed with Arista Records the following year. Their music incorporated rock, funk, boogie, blues and soul influences, and although this eclecticism avoided press pigeon-holing, it also served to severely limit their potential audience. A debut album featured impressive guitar and vocal harmonies, but ultimately lacked identity because of the varied styles employed. Failing to win an appreciative audience, Randle dissolved the band in 1979. Rick Ramirez went on to join Bruzer.
Album: *Striker* (Arista 1978).

Stryper

Christian heavy metal quartet from Los Angeles, California, formed by the Sweet brothers in 1981. Originally known as Roxx Regime, this group featured Michael Sweet (vocals), Robert Sweet (drums), Timothy Gaines (bass) and Oz Fox (guitar), playing standard, Americanized hard rock. Devising a carefully constructed image and marketing strategy, they subsequently changed their name to Stryper and dressed in matching yellow and black outfits. They were now a band with a mission - to spread the word of God through rock music, and become the total antithesis of the satanic metal movement. Signing to Enigma Records, they attracted widespread media attention which generally focused on the 'novelty' factor of their spiritual inclinations. A debut mini-album, *Yellow And Black Attack,* featured standard hard rock, with simple lyrics and high-pitched harmonies, while live shows climaxed with the band throwing bibles into the audience. By their third album they had built up a loyal army of fans and the excellently-produced melodic rock contained within widened their appeal. *To Hell With The Devil* peaked at number 32 on its three month stay on the *Billboard* album charts. *In God We Trust* saw the band mellow with more emphasis on pop-rock singalong numbers and the resultant exclusion of driving rock. The album was a commercial disappointment, failing to build on the success of the previous release. It did reach number 32, but only stayed on the *Billboard* chart for five weeks. The band took time off for a radical re-think, before entering the studio again. Oz Fox ventured into production during this time and oversaw the recording of the debut album by fellow Christian-rockers Guardian. *Against The Law* emerged in 1990, marking a return to a more

aggressive style. The yellow and black stage costumes had been jettisoned and the lyrics were considerably less twee. However, by this time, most of their original fans had moved on and the album sold poorly. When Michael Sweet quit in 1992 it seeemed only divine intervention could rescue Stryper's career.
Albums: *The Yellow And Black Attack* (Enigma 1984), *Soldiers Under Command* (Enigma 1985), *To Hell With The Devil* (Enigma 1986), *In God We Trust* (Enigma 1988), *Against The Law* (Enigma 1990).
Video: *Live In Japan* (1988).

Styx

This Chicago-based quintet are widely believed to be responsible for the development of the term pomp-rock (pompous, overblown arrangements, with perfect-pitch harmonies and a very full production). Styx evolved from the bands Tradewinds and T.W.4, but re-named themselves after the fabled river from Greek mythology, when they signed to Wooden Nickel, a subsidiary of RCA Records, in 1972. The line-up comprised Dennis De Young (vocals/keyboards), James Young (guitar/vocals), Chuck Panozzo (bass), John Panozzo (drums) and John Curulewski (guitar). Combining symphonic and progressive influences they released a series of varied and highly melodic albums during the early 70s. Success was slow to catch up with them; *Styx II*, originally released in 1973, spawned the Top Ten *Billboard* hit 'Lady' in 1975. The album then made similar progress, eventually peaking at number 20. After signing to A&M Records in 1975, John Curulewski departed with the release of *Equinox*, to be replaced by Tommy Shaw. This was a real turning point in the band's career as Shaw took over lead vocals and contributed significantly on the writing side. From here on Styx albums had an added degree of accessibility and moved towards a more commercial approach. *The Grand Illusion*, released in 1977, was Shaw's first major success, peaking at number 6 during its nine-month stay on the *Billboard* album chart. It also featured the number 8-peaking single, 'Sail Away'. *Pieces Of Eight* and *Cornerstone* consolidated their success, with the latter containing 'Babe', the band's first number 1 single in the USA. *Paradise Theater* was the Styx's *tour de force*, a complex, laser-etched concept album, complete with elaborate and expensive packaging. It generated two further US Top 10 hits in 'The Best Of Times' and 'Too Much Time On My Hands'. The album became their most successful ever, and also stayed at number 1 for three weeks on the album chart. *Kilroy Was Here* followed, yet another concept album, which brought them close to repetition. A watered down pop-rock

album with a big-budget production, its success came on the back of their previous album rather than on its own merits. *Caught In The Act* was an uninspired live offering. They disbanded shortly after its release. Styx re-formed in 1990 with the original line-up, except for pop-rock funkster Glenn Burtnick, who replaced Tommy Shaw (who had joined Damn Yankees). *Edge Of The Century* indicated that the band still had something to offer, with a diverse and classy selection of contemporary AOR. As one of the tracks on the album stated, the group were self-evidently 'Not Dead Yet'.
Albums: *Styx* (Wooden Nickel 1972), *Styx II* (Wooden Nickel 1973), *The Serpent Is Rising* (Wooden Nickel 1973), *Man Of Miracles* (Wooden Nickel 1974), *Equinox* (A&M 1975), *Crystal Ball* (A&M 1976), *The Grand Illusion* (A&M 1977), *Pieces Of Eight* (A&M 1978), *Cornerstone* (A&M 1979), *Paradise Theater* (A&M 1980), *Kilroy Was Here* (A&M 1983), *Caught In The Act* (A&M 1984), *Edge Of The Century* (A&M 1990). Compilation: *The Best Of Styx* (A&M 1979).
Video: *Caught In The Act* (1984).

Sugar

In the aftermath of Nirvana's commercial breakthrough unhinging a flood of loud, powerful and uncompromising USA-based music, Bob Mould (guitar/vocals) has found himself subject to the somewhat unflattering representation 'Godfather of Grunge'. The ex-Hüsker Dü songwriter has earned this accolade on the back of his former group's considerable influence, but with Sugar he seems set to continue to justify the critical plaudits which have followed his every move. Joined by David Barbe (ex-Mercyland; bass/vocals), and Malcolm Travis (ex-Zulus; drums), he has found another powerful triumvirate to augment his own muse. Barbe has proved particularly complementary, a talented songwriter in his own right, his presence as a forthright and intelligent counterpoint mirrors the contribution Grant Hart made to Hüsker Dü. Sugar's breakthrough, most visibly in the UK, came with the arrival of *Copper Blue* in 1992. Populated by energetic, evocative, and determinedly melodic pop noise, the album found critics grasping for superlatives. The Hüsker Dü comparisons were inevitable, but Mould was now viewed as an all-conquering prodigal son. Singles like 'Changes' tied the band's musical muscle to a straightforward commercial skeleton, and daytime radio play became an unlikely but welcome recipient of Sugar's crossover appeal. The historically contrary Mould responded a few months later with *Beaster*, in which the melodies and hooks, though still present, were buried under layers of harsh feedback and noise. Ultimately as rewarding as previous work, its appearance nevertheless reminded long-term Mould watchers of his brilliant but pedantic nature. *F.U.E.L.* offered a hybrid of the approaches on the two previous albums, and again saw Mould venerated in the press, if not with the same fawning abandon that *Copper Blue* had produced.

Albums: *Copper Blue* (Creation 1992), *Beaster* (Creation 1993), *F.U.E.L. (File Under Easy Listening)* (Creation 1994).

Sugarcreek

This top class pomp-rock group emerged from North Carolina, USA. The band were formed in 1981 by vocalist Tim Clark and guitarist Jerry West. Recruiting Rick Lee (keyboards), Robbie Hegler (bass) and Lynn Samples (drums), they drew inspiration from the popular AOR rock artists of the day (Journey, Styx and Kansas). They made a significant breakthrough with *Fortune*, a highly melodic album swathed in keyboards and silky-smooth vocal harmonies. Michael Hough was added as a second guitarist for *Rock The Night Away*, which marked a more commercial slant to the band's songwriting. He quit shortly after the album was released and the band subsequently shortened their name to Creek in 1986.

Albums: *Live At The Roxy* (Beaver 1981), *Fortune* (Beaver 1982), *Rock The Night Away* (Ripete 1984), *Sugarcreek* (Music For Nations 1985).

Suicidal Tendencies

Vocalist Mike Muir formed Suicidal in the early 80s in the Venice Beach area of Los Angeles, enlisting Grant Estes (guitar), Louiche Mayorga (bass) and Amery Smith (drums). Despite an inauspicious start, being voted 'worst band and biggest assholes' in *Flipside* magazine's 1982 polls, the band produced a hardcore classic in *Suicidal Tendencies*, and although they initially fell between hardcore punk and thrash stools, MTV's support of 'Institutionalized' helped the group take off. *Join The Army* was recorded with respected guitarist Rocky George and drummer R.J. Herrera replacing Estes and Smith, and the skateboarding anthem, 'Possessed To Skate', kept the group in the ascendancy. *How Will I Laugh Tomorrow...When I Can't Even Smile Today?* marked the debut of Mike Clark (rhythm guitar) as the group's sound exploded, extending from a balladic title-track to the furious 'Trip At The Brain'. This progression continued on *Controlled By Hatred/Feel Like Shit...Deja Vu*, but as the band's stature increased, so did their problems. Their name and image were easy targets for both the PMRC and the California police, with the former blaming teenage suicides on a band who were unable to play near their home town due to performance permit refusals from the latter, who feared Suicidal Tendencies were an LA gang. Naturally, the outspoken Muir fought vehemently against these bizarre accusations and treatment. Talented bassist Robert Rujillo, with whom Muir formed Infectious Grooves in tandem with Suicidal, made his debut on the excellent *Lights...Cameras...Revolution*, which produced hits in the defiant 'You Can't Bring Me Down' and 'Send Me Your Money', a vitriolic attack on televangelist preachers. The band also re-recorded their debut during these sessions for release as *Still Cyco After All These Years*. The Peter Collins-produced *The Art Of Rebellion*, with new drummer Josh Freece, was a more ambitious, diverse work, and rather more lightweight than previous albums. Any fears that the band were mellowing were dispelled by furious live shows. *Suicidal For Life*, with Jimmy DeGrasso (ex-White Lion/Y&T) replacing Freece, emphasized the point as the band returned in fast-paced and profanity-peppered style, while continuing to extend individual talents to the full. Shortly after its release news filtered through that the band were no more, and a chapter in hardcore history slammed shut behind them.

Albums: *Suicidal Tendencies* (Frontier 1983), *Join The Army* (Caroline/Virgin 1987), *How Will I Laugh Tomorrow...When I Can't Even Smile Today* (Epic 1988), *Controlled By Hatred/Feel Like Shit...Deja Vu* (Epic 1989), *Lights...Camera...Revolution* (Epic 1990), *The Art Of Rebellion* (Epic 1992), *Still Cyco After All These Years* (Epic 1993), *Suicidal For Life* (Epic 1994). Compilation: *FNG* (Virgin 1992).

Surface

This Birmingham, England-based hard rock group was formed in 1986 by Gez Finnegan (vocals), Mark Davies (guitar), Loz Rabone (guitar), Dean Field (keyboards), Ian Hawkins (bass) and Jamie Hawkins (drums). They styled themselves on the successful US AOR formula of groups such as Journey, and signed to the independent Killerwatt label, where they debuted with *Race The Night*, which was recorded live. The album failed and the band returned to their former part-time status.

Album: *Race The Night* (Killerwatt 1986).

Surgin

This US melodic hard rock group was founded in 1984 by former Rest members Tommy Swift (drums) and Jack Ponti (guitar/vocals). Enlisting the services

Survivor

of Russel Arcara (vocals), John Capra (keyboards), Gay Shapiro (keyboards) and Michael King (bass/vocals), they debuted in 1985 with *When Midnight Comes*. This featured the Bon Jovi track, 'Shot Through The Heart', which was written by Ponti and Jon Bon Jovi, while they were both part of Rest. Elsewhere the album comprised infectious hard rock anthems, underscored by strong melody lines, and was critically acclaimed at the time of release. In spite of tours supporting Aerosmith and Ratt, Surgin failed to achieve commercial success. As Ponti concentrated on session work and composing for other artists, Surgin became redundant.
Album: *When Midnight Comes* (Music For Nations 1985).

Surrender

This Canadian hard rock quintet was formed in 1978 by Alfie Zappacosta (vocals/guitar), Steve Jenson (guitar), Peter Curry (keyboards), Geoff Waddington (bass) and Paul Delaney (drums). Incorporating elements of Rush, Triumph and Yes in their music over the course of two excellent albums characterized by extended guitar-keyboard interplay, they nevertheless failed to find an appreciative audience. Curry and Waddington quit in 1983 and the remaining trio continued as Zappacosta.
Albums: *Surrender* (Capitol 1979), *No Surrender* (Capitol 1982). As Zappacosta: *Zappacosta* (Capitol 1984), *A To Z* (Capitol 1987).

Survivor

This sophisticated melodic US rock group was put together by guitarists Jim Peterik (formerly of Ides Of March) and Frankie Sullivan in 1978. Recruiting vocalist Dave Bickler, they recorded their self-titled debut as a three-piece. This featured a *pot-pourri* of ideas that had no definite direction or style. They expanded the band to a quintet in 1981, with the addition of Marc Doubray (drums) and Stephen Ellis (bass). From this point on, the band were comparable in approach to the AOR rock styles of Styx, Foreigner and Journey, but never achieved the same degree of recognition or success. Their first short-lived affair with glory came with the song 'Eye Of The Tiger', used as the theme to the *Rocky III* film. The single, with its heavy drum beat and rousing chorus, became a worldwide number 1 hit, and is still a staple of FM radio and various advertising campaigns. Unfortunately, the rest of the songs on the album of the same name were patchy in comparison. Nevertheless, the work succeeded on the strength of the title cut, peaking at number 2 and 12 on the US and UK album charts, respectively. *Caught In The Game*, released the following year, was a more satisfying album. It adopted a heavier approach and featured a more up-front guitar sound from Sullivan, but did not find favour with the record-buying public. Bickler was fired at this stage and replaced by ex-Cobra vocalist Jimi Jamison, whose vocals added an extra, almost soulful dimension to the band. The resulting *Vital Signs* gave the band their second breakthrough. It enjoyed a six-month residency on the *Billboard* album chart, attaining number 16 as its highest position, and also spawned two Top 10 hits with 'High On You' and 'The Search Is Over'. They recorded 'Burning Heart' (essentially a re-tread of 'Eye Of The Tiger') as the theme song to *Rocky IV* in 1986 and achieved another international hit, reaching number 5 on the UK singles chart. Surprisingly, the song was not included on *When Seconds Count*, which pursued a heavier direction once more. The band had contracted to a three-piece nucleus of Jamison, Sullivan and Peterik at this juncture and had used session musicians to finish the album. *Too Hot To Sleep* was probably the most consistent and strongest album of the band's career, featuring a magnificent collection of commercially-minded, hard rock anthems. The album made little commercial impact and the band finally disbanded in 1989.

Albums: *Survivor* (Scotti Bros 1979), *Premonition* (Scotti Bros 1981), *Eye Of The Tiger* (Scotti Bros 1982), *Caught In The Game* (Scotti Bros 1983), *Vital Signs* (Scotti Bros 1984), *When Seconds Count* (Scotti Bros 1986), *Too Hot To Sleep* (Scotti Bros 1988). Compilation: *Best Of* (Scotti Bros 1989).

Sven Gali

This Toronto, Canada-based group was formed in 1988 by guitarists Dee Cernile and Andy Frank, vocalist Dave Wanless (b. London, England), and bassist Shawn Maher after the members had accumulated professional experience as backing musicians for a number of Canadian acts, but had tired of their anonymous status. Enlisting New York session drummer Gregg Gerson, the band spent their formative years on the domestic club circuit, honing an accessible, yet raw metal sound which would serve them well. Their self-titled debut and ensuing live shows, including a UK tour with Wolfsbane, drew comparisons to Skid Row (USA) in terms of style, delivery and stage performance, and the band's ability and genuine enthusiasm suggests that they may be able to overcome the difficulties facing traditional metal in post-grunge times.

Album: *Sven Gali* (Ariola/BMG 1993).

Sweaty Nipples

Unattractively-titled heavy metal band, whose name legendarily arrived from the following scenario: 'The temperature was 198 degrees in a bakery. Olga, a 240lb dominating boss, had just finished chastising Davey, Brian and Dave for make bread loaves in a phallic form when her shirt sleeve got caught in a mixer'. This hapless mysognist tale continues until it results in Dave (rechristened Davey Nipples; bass) burrowing his head into the lady's mammaries to disengage her from the machine. An inauspicious start for the band, which also featured the aforementioned Brian Lehfeldt (vocals/percussion) and Dave Merrick (vocals/samples), as well as Ryan Moore (guitar). The group have built a healthy following in their native North West America on the back of compulsive live performances not seen in that region since the heyday of Poison Idea. In the process they have picked up awards at the 1991 Portland Music Association ceremony (best alternative/metal act) and the 1992 PMA equivalent for best live show. With this behind them they joined the North West leg of the 1992 Lollapalooza tour, sharing a stage with Faith No More, Bad Brains and others. Their debut album was recorded for Nastymix (predominantly a rap outlet) with Rick Parashar (Alice In Chains, Pearl Jam) and Kelly Gray (Candlebox) at the controls. Scheduled for release in October 1991, Nastymix subsequently entered receivership and the resulting mire of lawyers and officialdom placed Sweaty Nipples in stasis. They persevered by playing live and adding two new members, Scott Heard (vocals/guitar) and Hans Wagner (drums), eventually gaining a new deal with Megaforce (Music For Nations in the UK). After an eponymous single, the group made their long-playing debut with *Bug Harvest*. This, despite the group's grisly moniker, weighed in with a highly effective, and somewhat fearsome three guitar/two drummers attack.

Album: *Bug Harvest* (Megaforce 1994).

Sweet Savage

This melodic hard rock quartet was formed in Belfast, Northern Ireland, in 1979 by guitarists Vivian Campbell and Trevor Fleming. Recruiting bassist David Haller and drummer David Bates, they achieved their first break by landing the support slots on 1981 tours by Motörhead and Wishbone Ash. Debuting the same year with 'Take No Prisoners'/'Killing Time', the future looked very bright for the band. A UK tour supporting Thin Lizzy was followed by an impressive session on UK DJ Tommy Vance's *Friday Rock Show* ('Eye of The Storm' appeared on the compilation, *Friday Rock*

Show II). Two further singles, 'Straight Through The Heart' (1981) and 'The Raid' (1981), were released, before Campbell accepted the offer to join Ronnie James Dio. Four re-written Sweet Savage tracks appeared on Dio's *Holy Diver*. The band continued for a short time with Ian Wilson as Campbell's replacement. However, he proved an inadequate substitute and the band folded in 1984, after the re-release of 'Straight Through The Heart'.

Sweet Sister

Spanish heavy metal band formed in 1990 with a line-up of Tete (vocals/guitar), Pedro (guitar/keyboards), Toni (bass) and Jordi (drums). They recorded their first demo in 1992. Two others followed before they entered the studio in 1994 to record 22 tracks of which 12 were selected for their debut album with Music For Nations' subsidiary Under One Flag. Reflecting varied musical tastes running from the Cure to Guns N'Roses via U2, the album attracted a degree of press support but sales were limited outside their native territory.
Album: *Flora And Fauna* (Under One Flag 1994).

Sword

This Canadian heavy metal quartet was formed in Montreal in 1981 by vocalist Rick Hughes and drummer Dan Hughes. Augmented by Mike Plant (guitar) and Mike Larock (bass), it took the band five years to secure a record deal. Finally signing to Aquarius in 1986, in the same year they released *Metalized*, which paid respect to both the early 80s British scene and older groups such as Black Sabbath and Rainbow. Sword then secured support slots on the Alice Cooper and Metallica tours of 1987, regaling audiences with a primal example of early power metal. *Sweet Dreams*, released in 1988, consolidated this approach: monstrously aching riffs and gut-wrenching guitar breaks, encased within dynamic and melodic arrangements. Sword were an excellent unit, but through a lack of image and record company backing, their commercial prospects were ultimately compromised, and they broke up in 1991.
Albums: *Metalized* (Aquarius 1986), *Sweet Dreams* (Aquarius 1988).

Sye

This Canadian hard rock group was formed in 1981 by Phillipino-born vocalist/guitarist Bernie Carlos. Based in Toronto, Carlos joined forces with bassist and fellow countryman Phillipino Gunner San Augustin. The duo joined the Metal Blade label and debuted with *Turn On The Night* in 1985. Session musician Ray Cincinnato played drums on the album, but Steve Ferguson was recruited as a permanent addition after the work was released. Sye's music featured some impressive guitar parts, but was ultimately hampered by the weak and indistinct vocals. It would be four years before a follow-up appeared, by which time their name had largely been forgotten.
Albums: *Turn On The Fire* (Metal Blade 1985), *Winds Of Change* (Loudspell 1989).

T

T-Ride

This innovative trio originated in Santa Clara, California, where childhood friends Eric Valentine (drums) and Dan Arlie (bass/vocals) linked up with guitarist Jeff Tyson to produce an effective blend of musical influences and styles. Signed to Hollywood Records, the band rejected the label's offers of major production names like Eddie Kramer in favour of their drummer, who had already amassed considerable production experience with a variety of acts, in addition to producing the excellent demo which clinched their deal. Valentine duly made a sterling job of *T-Ride*. The band were compared most obviously to Queen and Van Halen due to the sheer variety of the material, quality musicianship and songwriting, and stunning vocal harmonies, but the delivery also had sufficient humour and individuality to give the band their own identity. The debut attracted a succession of positive reviews, moving Joe Satriani to describe the band as the future of metal, and T-Ride were equal to the task of transferring their songs to the live arena, but the album simply disappeared, and the band have been quiet since.
Album: *T-Ride* (Hollywood 1992).

Taffola, Joey

Beginning his career on the guitar at the age of 14, Joey Taffola served his apprenticeship with the unremarkable speed-metal outfit Jag Panzer. In 1987 he left the band and returned to California to take instruction from guitar guru Tony Macalpine. Moving to the Guitar Institute Of Technology, Taffola studied jazz, rock and classical styles alongside Paul Gilbert (later of Racer X). After recording a series of demos, Shrapnel boss Mike Varney signed Taffola

to produce a guitar instrumental album. With the help of former Jag Panzer drummer Reynold Carlson and ex-Rising Force bassist Wally Voss, *Out Of The Sun* appeared in 1987. Although the album featured guest appearances by Paul Gilbert (guitar) and Tony Macalpine (keyboards), it lacked both direction and individuality. Taffola's style proved a characterless hybrid of Yngwie Malmsteen's, Macalpine's and Vinnie Moore's styles. After an aborted band project featuring ex-Rising Force vocalist Mark Boals, Taffola started work on his second album, *Infa Red.*
Album: *Out Of The Sun* (Roadrunner 1987), *Infa Red* (Roadrunner 1991).

Talas

This US hard rock outfit was masterminded by bass virtuoso Billy Sheehan. Enlisting the services of former Chain Reaction vocalist Phil Naro, guitarist Mitch Perry and drummer Mark Miller, they specialized in melodic, guitar-orientated rock with a strong commercial edge. After the release of a self-financed debut album in 1980 the band began to build up a small, but loyal fanbase. This attracted the attention of Food For Thought Records. Enjoying a larger budget, Talas delivered *Sink Your Teeth Into That* in 1982. This was a showcase for Sheehan's amazing bass work and featured 'Shyboy', which he later re-recorded with Dave Lee Roth. At this point the band were put on hold, as Sheehan helped out UFO on their European tour. After an unfruitful association with Steve Stevens, Sheehan put Talas back on the road and recorded *Live Speed On Ice* in 1983. The album did not sell and the band became redundant as Sheehan then left to join Dave Lee Roth's band and later formed Mr. Big.
Albums: *Talas* (Relativity 1980), *Sink Your Teeth Into That* (Food For Thought 1982), *Live Speed On Ice* (Important 1983). Compilation: *The Talas Years* (Combat 1990).

Talion

This UK speed-metal quartet, formerly known as Trojan, formed in 1988, the line-up comprising Graeme Wyatt (vocals), Pete Wadeson (guitar), Phil Gavin (bass) and Johnny Lee Jackson (drums). Influenced by Metallica, Megadeth and Judas Priest, their niche was uninspired and at times amateurish speed metal. Signed to the independent Major Records, they debuted with *Killing The World* in 1989. This was a fairly lacklustre recording which ensured that the band did not progress beyond pub-rock status.
Album: *Killing The World* (Major 1989).

Talisman

This Swedish melodic metal outfit was founded in 1989 by ex-Rising Force bassist Marcel Jacob. Recruiting vocalist Jeff Scott Soto and guitarist Christopher Stahl, they joined Airplay Records and made their debut the following year with a self-titled album, incorporating elements of Europe, Yngwie Malmsteen and TNT. High-pitched vocal harmonies and bursts of fiery guitar were the band's trademarks, but they failed to make an impression outside Sweden.
Album: *Talisman* (Airplay 1990).

Tall Stories

This cult AOR act was formed in New York in 1988 by vocalist/guitarist Steve Augeri. The Tall Stories line-up settled with the addition of lead guitarist Jack Morer and the experienced rhythm section of Tom DeFaria (drums) and Kevin Totoian (bass). The latter had replaced Anthony Esposito (bass), who would join Lynch Mob, while numerous early drummers included the Damn Yankees' Michael Cartellone. The band's abilities developed as they played the clubs around the tri-state area of New York, New Jersey and Connecticut, and they were signed by Epic. The Frank Fillipetti-produced *Tall Stories* was universally hailed as an AOR classic, with an artful guitar-based delivery reminiscent of Tyketto. Augeri's vocals evoked Journey's Steve Perry and Strangeways' Terry Brock in addition to Tyketto's Danny Vaughn. However, like many good 90s AOR albums, *Tall Stories* remains an undiscovered gem, and the band have been quiet since.
Album: *Tall Stories* (Epic 1991).

Tangier

This US hard rock outfit have adopted a different style on each of their albums to date. Formed in 1984 by vocalist Bill Matson and guitarist/songwriter Doug Gordon, they initially played blues-based hard rock, which paid respect to Free, Molly Hatchet and Bad Company. With Rocco Mazella (guitar), Mike Kost (bass) and Mark Hopkins (drums) completing the line-up, they toured frequently but failed to make a breakthrough. Five years after formation, Matson and Gordon returned with Gari Saint (guitar), Garry Nutt (bass) and Bobby Bender (drums) to record *Four Winds*. The first act to be signed to Atco, the band offered a sophisticated sound which leaned towards mainstream AOR with blues undercurrents. Matson and Saint quit in 1990, with Mike Le Compte taking over vocal duties and the band contracting to a four-piece in the process. *Stranded* emerged the following year and saw the band diversifying their approach and toughening their act. The hybrid was a little awkward at times, but more often achieved the desired end result of producing radio-friendly material with memorable choruses.

Albums: *Four Winds* (Atco 1989), *Stranded* (Atco 1991).

Tank

This band, led by Algy Ward (bass/vocals, ex-Damned) with brothers Peter (guitar) and Mark Brabbs (drums), were dogged throughout their career by a reputation as Motörhead copyists stemming from their *Filth Hounds Of Hades* debut. The band's early power trio stance obviously owed much to Motörhead, although their songwriting style and sense of humour set them apart, and they were given a very hot reception by the notoriously intolerant Motörhead crowd on the *Iron Fist* tour. *Power Of The Hunter* showed distinct progression and included a fun cover of the Osmonds' 'Crazy Horses', but the collapse of Kamaflage Records shortly after the release was a setback. Undaunted, Tank emerged as a quartet with ex-White Spirit guitarist Mick Tucker on *This Means War*, an impressive concept album inspired by the Falklands conflict, but this too was unsuccessful, and the Brabbs brothers departed. Tank recorded two further albums, adding Cliff Evans (guitar) and drummers Graeme Crallan (on *Honour And Blood*) and Gary Taylor (on *Tank*) without any upturn in their fortunes. Tucker departed prior to the release of the latter, and the band split in 1989 after an ill-fated US club tour.

Albums: *Filth Hounds Of Hades* (Kamaflage 1982), *Power Of The Hunter* (Kamaflage 1982), *This Means War* (Music For Nations 1983), *Honour And Blood* (Music For Nations 1985), *Tank* (GWR 1988).

Tankard

Formed in 1982, prolific German thrash metal band Tankard are determined to live up to their country's reputation as a nation of beer drinkers. To drink heavily while on tour, relaxing, or in the studio is hardly uncommon in the rock world, but Tankard's interest in alcohol borders on the obsessive. Always light-hearted and loud, typical Tankard song titles include 'The Morning After' and 'Beermuda', which are delivered in a drunken assault of punk-influenced thrash guitars. While they are something of a beery institution on the European mainland, this has never translated into acceptance in the UK or US markets. *Tankwart* is an oddity, released only in their domestic market, consisting of covers of traditional German drinking songs. The previous year's *Two Faced* had seen the band take a more conventional approach to their craft with the intention of producing 'serious' music. It was not a happy compromise.

Albums: *Zombie Attack* (Noise 1985), *Chemical Invasion* (Noise 1987), *The Morning After* (Noise 1988), *Hair Of The Dog* (Noise 1990), *The Meaning Of Life* (Noise 1990), *Fat, Ugly, Live* (Noise 1991), *Stone Cold Sober* (Noise 1992), *Alien* (Noise 1993), *Two Faced* (Noise 1993), *Tankwart* (Noise 1994).

T.A.S.S.

Industrial metal trio formed in Berlin, Germany, in the summer of 1992 by ex-Voodoo Club members The Voodoo and Dr. Rabe. With the addition of American singer/lyricist Collier they set about following in Nine Inch Nails' wake by producing a fusion of guitar riffs with aggressive technology and sampling. Their debut album raised critical expectations and it was no surprise when February 1995's single, 'Snakedance', became a club hit.

Album: *Maniafesto* (Gun 1994).

Tattooed Love Boys

This streetwise UK rock quartet were formed in 1987 by vocalist Gary Mielle and drummer Mick Ransome (ex-Praying Mantis). With Cris C.J. Jagdhar (guitar) and Darayus Z. Kaye (bass) completing the line-up, they drew inspiration from the New York Dolls, Ramones and Hanoi Rocks. Debuting with *Bleeding Hearts And Needle Marks* in 1988, they proved they could write instant if ultimately disposable sleazy rock anthems, which possessed a degree of naive charm. The album sold poorly and the band disintegrated in 1989. They were resurrected in 1991 with the nucleus of Ransome and Mielle plus new recruits Dean Marshall (bass), Nick Singleton (guitar) and Chris Danby (rhythm guitar). *No Time For Nursery Rhymes'* attempt at a more sophisticated approach backfired totally. The result was an amateurish affair, which hinted at plagiarism of Guns N' Roses.

Albums: *Bleeding Hearts And Needle Marks* (Razor 1988), *No Time For Nursery Rhymes* (Music For Nations 1990).

Temple Of The Dog

This one-off project involved members of Seattle, USA-based bands Mother Love Bone and Soundgarden, and was recorded as a tribute to the late Andrew Wood, former Mother Love Bone vocalist. The 'band' comprised Chris Cornell (vocals), Matt Cameron (drums), Mike McCready (guitar), Stone Gossard (rhythm guitar) and Jeff Ament (bass). Signed to A&M Records, the album received widespread critical acclaim immediately following its release. The music fused the Doors/Joy

Terrorvision

Testament

Division/Stooges fixation of Mother Love Bone with the harder, dirtier and at times funkier rhythms of Soundgarden. It was a moving, powerful and genuine tribute to the first casualty of the 90s Seattle scene. Gossard and Ament later formed Pearl Jam.
Album: *Temple Of The Dog* (A&M 1991).

Terraplane

Terraplane evolved in the early 80s in south London as Nuthin' Fancy, the post-school band of Danny Bowes (vocals) and Luke Morley (guitar). By 1983 they had evolved into Terraplane with the addition of Nick Linden (bass) and Gary James (drums). The band soon became fixtures on the London circuit, playing at the Reading Festival before releasing an independent single, 'I Survive'. Suitably impressed, Epic Records signed Terraplane, but the young band perhaps took too much notice of advice about image and style from their label and management, who chose to emphasize a poppier direction, away from the band's melodic hard rock roots. When the debut finally emerged, the humorous original title of *Talking To God* (later You) *On The Great White Telephone* had been replaced by the bland *Black & White*. While the quality of Morley's songwriting was obvious, the production resulted in a slick pop sound in contrast to the band's rockier live approach, given a heavier edge with the addition of rhythm guitarist Rudi Riviere (ex-Sapphire). *Black & White* was only a moderate success but failed to break the lucrative pop market, and *Moving Target*, recorded without the departed Riviere (to America and session work), was rather directionless, with the band folding a year later. Morley, Bowes and James regrouped with much greater success in Thunder, perhaps demonstrating what might have been for Terraplane had the band been left to develop in their own right.
Albums: *Black & White* (Epic 1986), *Moving Target* (Epic 1987).

Terrorizer

This American quartet were more of a project than a real band, featuring the Morbid Angel rhythm section of Pete Sandoval (drums) and David Vincent (bass, vocals), in collaboration with the Californian-based duo of Oscar Garcia (vocals) and Jesse Pintado (guitar). Terrorizer broke up when Morbid Angel's emergence from the underground death metal scene meant that Sandoval and Vincent no longer had time to spare. *World Downfall*, however, was a definitive grindcore album, given a fierce sound by producer Vincent and engineer Scott Burns. Sandoval and Vincent produced their customary tight performance to ensure effective delivery of often highly paced

material, while Pintado showed the ability and aggression which was to lead to his subsequent recruitment to the Napalm Death ranks. Which just left Garcia to growl and spit outrage through largely politicised, hardcore-influenced lyrics. A second album remains unreleased.
Album: *World Downfall* (Earache 1989).

Terrorvision

This Bradford, England, quartet formed in 1986 as Spoilt Brats, and quickly fused rock, funk and thrash influences into an infectiously upbeat pop-metal style. Singer Tony Wright, guitarist Mark Yates, bassist Leigh Marklow and drummer Shutty were signed by EMI on the strength of their 'Pump Action Sunshine' demo, and negotiated their own label name, Total Vegas. Two remixed demo tracks, 'Urban Space Crime' and 'Jason', appeared on the *Thrive* EP as Terrorvision followed a hectic touring schedule prior to the release of *Formaldehyde*. The debut produced minor hits in 'American TV' and 'New Policy One', and was backed by UK and European tours with the Ramones and Motörhead respectively, while Def Leppard frontman Joe Elliott was sufficiently impressed to invite Terrorvision to open Leppard's 1993 show at Sheffield's Don Valley Stadium. 1994 proved to be quite a year for Terrorvision, beginning with their UK Top 30 breakthrough with 'My House'. *How To Make Friends And Influence People* emerged to rave reviews and entered the UK Top 20, bringing the band their first silver disc, and produced four more Top 30 singles in 'Oblivion', 'Middleman', 'Pretend Best Friend' and 'Alice, What's The Matter?', the greatest number by any single band in 1994. They also played both the Reading and Donington Festivals, in addition to two sold-out UK tours and a series of European dates, before moving on to work on a new album in 1995.
Albums: *Formaldehyde* (Total Vegas 1992), *How To Make Friends And Influence People* (Total Vegas 1994).

Tesla

Originally known as City Kid, Tesla are a five-piece, blues-based, hard rock quintet from Sacramento, California, USA. Named after the scientist Nikola Tesla, the current line-up came together in 1985. The band comprises Jeff Keith (vocals), Tommy Skeoch (guitar/vocals), Frank Hannon (guitar/keyboards/vocals), Brian Wheat (bass/vocals) and Troy Lucketta (drums; ex-Eric Martin Band, Breathless). They signed to Geffen Records in 1986 and recorded *Mechanical Resonance*, a universally acclaimed debut that ranks alongside that of Montrose's first album in terms of setting new

Therapy?

standards. The title was taken from one of Tesla's theories and combined raunchy metallic rock with blues and rock 'n' roll influences. Jeff Keith's impassioned vocals gave the material an added dimension, as the songs alternated between passionate, gut-wrenching ballads and crazy, fuel-injected rockers. The album eventually took off in the US, reaching number 32 on the *Billboard* chart. *The Great Radio Controversy* saw the band rapidly maturing, with a highly polished, but no-less energetic collection of songs that were saturated with infectious riffs and subtle hook-lines. The ballad, 'Love Song', became a Top 10 hit, while the album climbed to number 18 on the US charts. Tesla's third collection created something of a precedent, a live album that was totally acoustic and included a number of inspired cover versions. It highlighted the band's humour, technical excellence and ability to entertain. *Psychotic Supper* showed they could easily switch back to power-mode, with a near 70-minute onslaught of high-energy hard rock numbers. Tesla defy convention and have no gimmicks, nor do they conform to any particular image, choosing instead to tour relentlessly (for over a year to support *Psychotic Supper*, playing over 138 shows in the process). *Bust A Nut*, meanwhile, included a cover of Joe South's 'Games People Play', and offered a further blast of superbly declaimed traditional, neo-purist, heavy metal.

Albums: *Mechanical Resonance* (Geffen 1986), *The Great Radio Controversy* (Geffen 1989), *Five Man Acoustical Jam* (Geffen 1990), *Psychotic Supper* (Geffen 1991), *Bust A Nut* (Geffen 1994).
Video: *Five Man Video Band* (1991).

Testament

This thrash act was one of the first to emerge from San Francisco's Bay Area in Metallica's wake in the 80s. Originally formed as Legacy in 1983, becoming Testament two years later, the line-up included vocalist Steve Souza alongside Alex Skolnick (lead guitar, replacing original guitarist Derek Ramirez), Eric Peterson (rhythm guitar), Greg Christian (bass), and Louie Clemente (drums). However, Souza soon departed for Exodus and was replaced by giant frontman Chuck Billy. *The Legacy* was a ferocious introduction, quickly establishing Testament at the forefront of the burgeoning thrash scene. Following a live mini-album recorded at Holland's Dynamo Festival, *The New Order* consolidated their popularity with improved songwriting, producing one certifiable classic in 'Disciples Of The Watch'. Skolnick, however, was losing interest in pure thrash, extending his undoubted talents by moonlighting in Stuart

Hamm's touring band at one point, and his influence brought a more considered melodic power metal approach to *Practice What You Preach*, which worked superbly. However, *Souls Of Black* was rushed to coincide with the European Clash Of The Titans tour with Slayer, Megadeth and Suicidal Tendencies, and was consequently disappointing. After *The Ritual*, Skolnick joined Savatage and Clemente also departed. *Return To Apocalyptic City* introduced Glen Alvelais (guitar, ex-Forbidden) and John Tempesta (drums, ex-Exodus), but Alvelais' tenure was short-lived, with journeyman guitarist James Murphy (ex-Death/Obituary/Disincarnate/Cancer) stepping in for *Low*, which saw a return to the glorious thrashing style of yore. Tempesta subsequently joined White Zombie, and was replaced by John Dutte (ex-Evil Dead).

Albums: *The Legacy* (Megaforce 1987), *Live At Eindhoven* (Megaforce 1987, mini-album), *The New Order* (Megaforce 1988), *Practice What You Preach* (Megaforce 1989), *Souls Of Black* (Megaforce 1990), *The Ritual* (Atlantic 1992), *Return To Apocalyptic City* (Atlantic 1993, mini-album), *Low* (East West 1994).

Therapy?

Northern Irish hard rock/indie metal trio comprising Andy Cairns (guitar/vocals), Michael McKeegan (bass) and Fyfe Ewing (drums). Cairns and Ewing first met by chance at a charity concert in the late 80s. At that time both were playing in covers bands, but decided to begin writing together. McKeegan was drafted in for live support (having originally lent his bass to the duo's bedroom sessions) and the enduring Therapy? line-up was in place. They played their first gig supporting Decadence Within at Connor Art College in the summer of 1989, by which time they had already composed some 30 songs. After two demos failed to ignite attention from suitable labels, the band released their debut single, 'Meat Abstract'/'Punishment Kiss', on their own Multifuckingnational imprint. Following approving plays from John Peel the group found their way on to Wiiija Records, via the intervention of Silverfish's Leslie. Their debut single was then added to new material for a mini-album, *Baby Teeth*. This was followed in short order by a second abbreviated set, *Pleasure Death*. Both these collections went to number 1 in the UK indie charts, but the band remained hamstrung by lack of finance from their record company. Therapy? signed to A&M in 1992, and collected a much bigger budget for a new album, *Nurse*, and touring. However, at best the press were neutral about the record, which featured more complex arrangements and themes than the punk-descended speed burnouts of earlier releases. The band's career was revitalized in March 1993 when 'Screamager' made the UK Top 10. Almost a year later *Troublegum* was unveiled, which returned to more familiar Therapy? elements - buzzsaw guitar, harsh but persistent melodies and musical adrenalin - aided by a cleaner, leaner production than had previously been the case. Nominated for the Mercury Prize - alongside the Prodigy easily the most extreme record to be offered as a candidate - it enshrined Therapy?'s progress as the most commercially successful British band working in their territory.

Albums: *Baby Teeth* (Wiiija 1991, mini-album), *Pleasure Death* (Wiiija 1992, mini-album), *Nurse* (A&M 1992), *Troublegum* (A&M 1994).

Thin Lizzy

Formed in Dublin, Eire, in 1969, this fondly remembered hard-rocking group comprised Phil Lynott (b. 20 August 1951, Dublin, Eire, d. 4 January 1986; vocals/bass), Eric Bell (b. 3 September 1947, Belfast, Northern Ireland; guitar) and Brian Downey (b. 27 January 1951, Dublin, Eire; drums). After signing to Decca Records, they issued two albums, neither of which charted. A change of fortune occurred after they recorded a novelty rock version of the traditional 'Whiskey In The Jar'. The single reached the UK Top 10 and popularized the group's blend of Irish folk and strident guitar work. The group then underwent a series of line-up changes during early 1974. Bell was replaced by Gary Moore and two more temporary guitarists were recruited, Andy Gee and John Cann. The arrival of guitarists Brian Robertson (b. 12 September 1956, Glasgow, Scotland) and Scott Gorham (b. 17 March 1951, Santa Monica, California, USA) stabilized the group as they entered their most productive phase. A series of UK concerts throughout 1975 saw the group make considerable headway. 1976 was the breakthrough year with the acclaimed *Jailbreak* hitting the charts. The driving macho celebration of 'The Boys Are Back In Town' reached the UK Top 10 and US Top 20 and was voted single of the year by the influential *New Musical Express*. In early 1977 Robertson was forced to leave the group due to a hand injury following a fight and was replaced by the returning Moore. Another UK Top 20 hit followed with the scathing 'Don't Believe A Word', drawn from *Johnny The Fox*. Moore then returned to Colosseum and the recovered Robertson took his place. Both 'Dancin' In The Moonlight' and *Bad Reputation* were UK Top 10 hits and were soon followed by the excellent double album, *Live And Dangerous*. 1979 saw the group scaling new commercial heights with such Top 20

singles as 'Waiting For An Alibi' and 'Do Anything You Want To', plus the best-selling *Black Rose*. The torturous line-up changes continued apace. Robertson again left and joined Wild Horses. Moore returned, but within a year was replaced by Midge Ure (formerly of Slik and the Rich Kids). By late 1979, the peripatetic Ure had moved on to Ultravox and was replaced by Snowy White. In early 1980, Lynott married Caroline Crowther, daughter of the television personality Leslie Crowther. After recording some solo work, Lynott reunited with Thin Lizzy for *Chinatown*, which included the controversial Top 10 single, 'Killer On The Loose'. The heavily-promoted *Adventures Of Thin Lizzy* maintained their standing, before White bowed out on *Renegade*. He was replaced by John Sykes, formerly of the Tygers Of Pan Tang. One more album, *Thunder And Lightning*, followed before Lynott split up the group in the summer of 1984. A posthumous live album, *Life-Live*, was issued at the end of that year. Its title took on an ironically macabre significance two years later when Lynott died of heart failure and pneumonia after a drugs overdose. Four months later, in May 1986, Thin Lizzy reformed for the Self Aid concert organized in Eire by Bob Geldof, who replaced Lynott on vocals for the day. The 90s found Brian Robertson touring with tribute band, Ain't Lizzy, while the original group's name remained on the lips of many young groups as a primary influence.

Albums: *Thin Lizzy* (Decca 1971), *Shades Of Blue Orphanage* (Decca 1972), *Vagabonds Of The Western World* (Decca 1973), *Night Life* (Vertigo 1974), *Fighting* (Vertigo 1975), *Jailbreak* (Vertigo 1976), *Johnny The Fox* (Vertigo 1976), *Bad Reputation* (Vertigo 1977), *Live And Dangerous* (Vertigo 1978, double album), *Black Rose* (Vertigo 1979), *Renegade* (Vertigo 1981), *Thunder And Lightning* (Vertigo 1983), *Life-Live* (Vertigo 1983, double album), *BBC Radio 1 Live In Concert* (Windsong 1992, rec 1983). Compilations: *Remembering - Part One* (Decca 1976), *The Continuing Saga Of The Ageing Orphans* (Decca 1979), *Rockers* (Decca 1981), *Adventures Of Thin Lizzy* (Vertigo 1981), *Lizzy Killers* (Vertigo 1983), *The Collection* (Castle 1985, double album), *The Best Of Phil Lynott And Thin Lizzy* (Telstar 1987), *Dedication - The Best Of Thin Lizzy* (Vertigo 1991). Videos: *Live And Dangerous* (1986), *Dedication* (1991).

Further reading: *Phil Lynott: Dancing In The Moonlight*, Pamela McCleeve.

38 Special

38 Special were formed in 1977 by guitarist and vocalist Donnie Van Zant (brother to Johnny of the

Van Zant Band and Lynyrd Skynyrd's Ronnie), with Jeff Carlisi (guitar), Don Barnes (guitar), Larry Junstrom (bass) and drummers Steve Brookins and Jack Grodin. In keeping with fraternal tradition the band proffered Southern boogie/rock, though their sound later slipped in to AOR. Signed to A&M Records they had little impact outside of the southern states but in 1979 scored a minor hit with 'Rocking Into The Night', which was followed by an album and major tour. With fame eluding them (despite a further single success in 1980 with 'Hang On Loosely') they dropped out of the scene in 1984 but made a comeback in 1986 and recorded the film theme, *Revenge Of The Nerds 2*. Barnes left soon after as did Brookins, both in an attempt to launch their own bands. Danny Clancy joined on guitar while Brookins was replaced by keyboard player Max Carol. 1988's *Rock N Roll Strategy* earned strong reviews, but after release the group lost their contract with A&M. B*one Against Steel*, meanwhile, saw them return to a southern boogie framework without the AOR trappings and won many new supporters.

Albums: *38 Special* (A&M 1977), *Special Delivery* (A&M 1978), *Rockin' Into The Night* (A&M 1979), *Wild-Eyed Southern Boys* (A&M 1980), *Special Forces* (A&M 1982), *Tour De Force* (A&M 1983), *Strength In Numbers* (A&M 1987), *Rock N Roll Strategy* (A&M 1988), *Bone Against Steel* (Charisma 1991).

Thor

b. Jon-Mikl Thor. This body builder turned singer who took his name from a Marvel comic character, was a former Mr. Teenage USA, Mr. Canada and Mr. North America. His band consisted of vocalist Pantera (b. Rusty Hamilton, a former model), Steve Price (guitar), Keith Zazzi (bass) and Mike Favata (drums). Their debut release, *Keep The Dogs Away*, appeared on the Three Hats Record label in 1978. This album was an uneventful affair of basic hard rock/heavy metal which, even at the time of its release, sounded dated. Thor then took quite a long break until returning with the release of a mini-album, *Unchained*, in 1984. Then came Thor's most successful album, *Only The Strong*, released on Roadrunner in 1985. Much attention was paid to Thor's live party-piece - where, by blowing into it, he expanded and burst a rubber hot-water bottle (often with the claim 'let's see Michael Jackson do this'). Other 'theatricals' included staged clashes between Norse gods, with Thor replendent in spiked body armour, wielding a mighty (plastic) sword or bearded axe. All conducted without the tiniest trace of irony, and an almost camp machismo from the group's frontman. 1985 proved an eventful year for Thor as

not only did he have two singles, 'Let The Blood Run Red' and 'Thunder On The Tundra' (both from *Only The Strong*), released, but also a live album, *Live In Detroit*. That year also saw him enter the film world appearing in and writing the soundtrack for *Recruits*. Part of the soundtrack formed the basis for Thor's next release, *Recruits: Wild In The Streets*. That marked the end of Thor's musical aspirations as he once again turned his attention to the movie business by appearing in *Zombie Nightmare* alongside original *Batman* star, Adam West.

Albums: *Keep The Dogs Away* (Three Hats 1978), *Unchained* (Ultra Noise 1984, mini-album), *Only The Strong* (Roadrunner 1985), *Live In Detroit* (Raw Power 1985), *Recruits: Wild In The Streets* (Roadrunner 1986).

Video: *Live In London* (1985).

Thought Industry

From Michigan, USA, Thought Industry comprise Brent Oberlin (vocals/bass), Dustin Donaldson (drums), Paul Enzio (guitar) and Chris Lee (guitar). Though often wrongly classified within the 'industrial' metal fraternity (the result not just of their name but also tours with Godflesh and Skinny Puppy), Thought Industry's sound is too relentlessly individual for either that or another pigeonhole, metal: 'To me most 'metal' bands rehash cliched musical/lyrical ideas and are very conservative in their output and viewpoints. We use the power of metal or punk without it's parody or redundancy'. Any satisfactory description of the band's music would be hard pressed to deny the strong metallic undercurrent, however, which their dual guitar approach epitomises. Critical guesses over *Songs For Insects* spanned the Jesus Lizard, Voivod and Primus, with lyrics which dealt with hallucinogenic drugs, violence and social alienation. For the lugubriously titled follow-up subjects would be dealt with inside a more personal framework, but the musical onslaught continued unabated.

Albums: *Songs For Insects* (Music For Nations 1993), *Mods Carve The Pig: Assassins, Toads And God's Flesh* (Music For Nations 1994).

Thrasher

In June and July 1984 the US heavy metal label Combat funded a super session and enlisted Carl Canedy (drums) to write and produce an album's worth of material. Canedy formed a writing partnership with guitarist Andy MacDonald and they put the 'Thrasher' band together at the Music America Studios in New York. An impressive line-up was amassed: Kenny Aaronson (Derringer/HSAS;

bass), Dickie Peterson (Blue Cheer; vocals), Billy Sheehan (Talas; bass), Mars Cowling (Pat Travers Band; bass), Maryann Scandiffio (Black Lace; vocals), Dan Spitz (Anthrax; guitar), Jack Starr (Virgin Steel; guitar), Rhett Forrester (Riot; vocals), Kim Simmonds (Savoy Brown; guitar), Gary Bordonaro (Rods; bass) and additional vocalists James Rivera, Leslie Dunn and Jackie Kenyon.
Album: *Thrasher* (Music For Nations 1985).

Throbs

This short-lived band took shape in mid-1988 when Canadian vocalist Ronnie Sweetheart moved to New York to link up with Danny Nordahl (bass), Ronnie Magri (drums) and Swedish guitarist Roger Ericson. The Throbs were signed by Geffen Records after only their third live show in New York, and experimented with adding a second guitarist to the line-up, including one show with future Wildhearts mainman Ginger shortly after his departure from the Quireboys, before recording their debut as a quartet. The production team of one-time Alice Cooper collaborators Bob Ezrin and Dick Wagner were highly suited to the project, as the band clearly drew influences from the sleazier US rock of the early 70s along with later contemporaries such as Hanoi Rocks, although they lacked Cooper's sly lyrical wit. However, despite some enthusiastic reviews for the record, the ensuing live shows, which included a UK tour with Mr. Big, were poor, with the Throbs' performances failing to live up to their image. The band continued to work on the road for a while after losing their recording deal, but eventually disintegrated, with Ericson and Nordahl going on to form the Vibes.
Album: *The Language Of Thieves And Vagabonds* (Geffen 1991).

Thunder

This British hard rock quintet was heavily influenced by Bad Company and the Rolling Stones. Thunder evolved from the ashes of Terraplane, with the surviving nucleus of Danny Bowes (vocals), Luke Morley (guitar) and Gary James (drums) recruiting Mark Luckhurst (bass) and Ben Matthews (guitar) to complete the line-up. Moving away from the melodic power-pop of their former incarnation, they teamed up with producer Andy Taylor (ex-Duran Duran) to record *Backstreet Symphony*, a stunning album of bluesy rockers and atmospheric ballads, which received widespread critical acclaim. Their style is characterized by a dual guitar attack of alternating riffs and lead breaks, with Bowes' gritty and emotional vocals adding charisma and distinction.

Live the icing on the cake is drummer Gary James' erratic behaviour, which has included appearing in a tutu or offering impromptu Frank Sinatra impersonations. They landed the opening slot at Donington in 1990 and were the surprise success of the day. In 1991 they concentrated on the American market, touring extensively in an attempt to make the all important breakthrough. However, though another strong collection, *Laughing On Judgement Day* was not the album to do it. 1993 saw Luckhurst (who would go on to join the Coverdale/Page touring band) depart in acrimony to be replaced by Mikael Hoglund (ex-Great King Rat). The title of their quite excellent third album, *Behind Closed Doors*, proved appropriate as the group had spent over 12 months recording the set in the US with the aid of Aerosmith/AC/DC producer Mike Fraser.
Albums: *Back Street Symphony* (EMI 1990), *Laughing On Judgement Day* (EMI 1992), *Behind Closed Doors* (EMI 1995).

Thunderhead

After an unsuccessful audition with Victory, American vocalist Ted Bullet met ex-Viva guitarist Henrik Wolter and ex-Talon bassist Ole Hempleman in a Hanover bar, and with the addition of drummer Alex Scotti to complete this German-based band, recorded a demo which quickly produced a deal with Intercord. *Behind The Eight Ball* was recorded when the band had hardly played a live date, but was a reasonable debut in a basic metal style similar to the Almighty's early work, and sold well on the German market as the group played with Victory and Uriah Heep in the US and in the UK and Europe with Motörhead. *Busted At The Border* and *Crime Pays* followed in the traditional metal footsteps of the debut, although Thunderhead became a more cohesive band as a result of their live work, with more power metal overtones to their heavily guitar-based sound. They sustained a level of success in Germany, undoubtedly helped by their frontman's on-stage demeanour, but remained a minor act in global terms.
Albums: *Behind The Eight Ball* (Intercord 1989), *Busted At The Border* (Intercord 1990), *Crime Pays* (Intercord 1991).

Thunderstick

Barry Graham, aka Thunderstick, began drumming for Iron Maiden in 1977, a year later joining Samson where he spent the next three years as the New Wave Of British Heavy Metal's most controversial figure - the man in the rapist's mask. The image was indeed offensive and did little to elevate either his or Samson's career, but he was still a powerful drummer in the Keith Moon mould. Aside from appearing on Samson's three albums, *Survivors*, *Head On* and *Shock Tactics*, he also appeared on the Gillan set, *For Gillan Fans Only*. After Samson he teamed up with Gillan guitarist Bernie Tormé in the Electric Gypsies, where he remained until forming Thunderstick the band in 1982. Adopting a more theatrical mask and outfit, he put together this Screaming Lord Sutch/Alice Cooper-styled outfit with Neil Hay (bass), Ben K. Reeve (guitar), Colin Heart (guitar) and Vinnie Monroe (vocals). In November 1983 they released a 12-inch EP entitled *Feel Like Rock 'N' Roll*, with a line-up featuring American singer Jodee Valentine and guitarists Wango Wiggins and Cris Martin replacing Heart, Monroe and Hay (the latter joining Julia Fordham's backing band), while Reeve switched to bass. Most press interest seemed to revolve around Valentine who played the 'pin up' role. The music was consequently largely forgotten and when their album came out in 1984, there was more concern about the pending marriage between Valentine and Graham. The band hacked away for another two years before splitting up (which was also what happened to the newly-weds). Graham later rejoined Paul Samson on a couple of projects but he is more concerned these days with music management.

Album: *Beauty & The Beasts* (Thunderbolt 1984).

Tigertailz

Tigertailz are a band renowned for their outrageous glam-rock looks as much as their music, which is also strongly influenced by 70s glam-rockers such as T. Rex and the Sweet. Formed in South Wales during 1984, they built up a loyal and vociferous following throughout the UK with a line-up featuring Stevie James (aka Steevi Jaimz; vocals), Jay Pepper (guitar), Pepsi Tate (bass) and Ace Fincham (b. USA; drums). The last named pair had both worked in N.W.O.B.H.M. act Treason, and also Crash KO. Their first release, *Young And Crazy*, met with little critical acclaim although their eternally loyal fans lapped it up. Stevie James departed soon after in somewhat acrimonious circumstances. He would form St Jaimz. His replacement was Kim Hooker (ex-Rankelson) who provided vocals on the much stronger *Bezerk*. This release showcased Tigertailz as an equal to American acts such as Mötley Crüe in terms of penning instantly memorable glam-rock anthems. Continuing to develop a loyal following, particularly in Japan, the writing was nonetheless on the wall when Finchum departed in 1992. The remaining trio (Tate, Pepper and Hooker) re-emerged a year later with a new band, Wazbones.

Albums: *Young And Crazy* (Music For Nations 1987), *Bezerk* (Music For Nations 1990).

Tool

One of the leading new metal acts of the 90s, Tool were formed in Los Angeles, USA in 1990 by guitarist Adam Jones, vocalist Maynard James Keenan, bassist Paul D'Amour and drummer Danny Carey. All four band members are Lachrymologists, and the influence of this very personal and cathartic religion is evident in both the pained intensity of their music and lyrics based on personal experience and feelings. *Opiate* was a powerful introduction to Tool's densely rhythmic style, with 'Hush' helping establish a buzz for the band; the accompanying video graphically displayed the song's anti-censorship slant of 'I can't say what I want to/Even if I'm not serious' as the band appeared naked with their mouths taped shut. European dates with friends Rage Against The Machine and a US tour with the Rollins Band helped sharpen Tool's live performances. Their increased confidence was evident on *Undertow*, which featured a guest vocal from Henry Rollins on 'Bottom'. While the band retained their angry intensity and penchant for difficult lyrical subjects, their songwriting became more adventurous, culminating in the experimental ambient closer, 'Disgustipated' - lyrically, however, the track displayed a sense of humour which belied Tool's miserable image by protesting about a carrots' right to life, satirizing the politically correct movement. *Undertow* reached platinum status as the band toured extensively, including a stint on the 1993 Lollapalooza tour.

Albums: *Opiate* (Zoo 1992, mini-album), *Undertow* (Zoo 1993).

Tormé, Bernie

Irish guitarist who formed punk band Urge in 1976, came to London a year later to join Scrapyard and subsequently put together the Bernie Tormé band. In 1978 he appeared on the NEMS punk compilation, *Live At The Vortex*, which helped raise his profile, and later he earned himself a solo deal with Jet Records. After three solo singles and numerous live appearances it was announced that he was to join the Ian Gillan Band where he remained until 1981, playing on three albums - *Mr Universe* (Acrobat 1979), *Glory Road* (Virgin 1980) and *Future Shock* (Virgin 1981). After Gillan he formed the Electric Gypsies with drummer Frank Noon (Def Leppard/Next Band) and Everton Williams on bass (formerly of punk group Bethnal). After one single, 'Shoorah Shoorah', Noon left and was briefly replaced by Thunderstick (Samson and his own, eponymous band). In March 1982 he flew to America to join

Ozzy Osbourne's band as a replacement for the recently deceased Randy Rhoads. Two months later he returned to the UK and reformed the Bernie Tormé band with Ron Rebel (Iron Maiden/McCoy) on drums, and bassist James C. Bond (Stampede). This line-up lasted until 1984 when he formed 'Tormé' with ex-Girl vocalist Phil Lewis. After a number of records the band split having gained little ground, and both Tormé and Lewis relocated to America. Lewis collaborated with members of W.A.S.P. and Guns N'Roses in L.A. Guns while Tormé joined ex-Twisted Sister vocalist Dee Snider in Desperados, where he remained for a year, eventually quitting due to the band's inactivity. Since then he has worked on various projects, though none have proved fruitful.

Albums: *Turn Out The Lights* (Kamaflage 1982), *Electric Gypsies* (Zebra 1983), *Live* (Zebra 1984), *Back To Babylon* (Zebra 1985), *Die Pretty Die Young* (Heavy Metal 1987), *Official Bootleg* (Onsala International 1987), *Are We There Yet* (Heavy Metal 1991).

Toronto

By 1979 guitarist Brian Allen and drummer Jim Fox had broken away from the Canadian band Rose, with whom they had been with since 1976, together with American bassist Nick Costello from Centaurus. This formed the nucleus of a band whose locality also lent them their name. The line-up was soon completed with Scott Kreyer (keyboards), Sheron Alton (guitar) and vocalist Holly Woods. Although they produced solid AOR material they never made it outside of their home country, despite both A&M and MCA releasing their albums in Europe. Costello and Fox had left by 1983 and the band were now more often billed as Holly Woods & Toronto. A final album was very much in the Lee Aaron vein and saw a marked improvement, but with falling sales, even at home, they folded.

Albums: *Lookin' For Trouble* (Solid Gold 1980), *Head On* (Solid Gold 1981), *Get It On Credit* (Solid Gold 1982), *Girls Night Out* (Solid Gold 1983), *Assault And Flattery* (Solid Gold 1984).

Touch

This cult AOR/pomp rock act evolved from American Tears, an obscure band who released three albums in the USA in the mid-70s, when bassist/vocalist Doug Howard joined Craig Brooks (vocals/guitar), Glenn Kithcart (drums) and songwriter Mark Mangold (keyboards/vocals). Their self-titled debut has long been regarded as a neglected classic of the genre, featuring a strong collection of songs and a sound dominated by superb vocal harmonies and Mangold's impressive keyboard work. The band opened the bill for the inaugural Donington Monsters Of Rock festival in 1980, and passed into Donington folklore when Howard accidentally swallowed a bee while having a drink at the end of the set. Their best-known track, 'Don't You Know What Love Is', appeared on the compilation of live recordings from that day, *Monsters Of Rock*, but despite all the good press, the debut failed to sell significantly. A follow-up effort was recorded, with Todd Rundgren at the production helm, but the band split before it could be released, disenchanted with their record company and management. Two tracks from these sessions were included on a 1990 reissue of *Touch*. Mangold became a session musician, working with Brooks on Michael Bolton's early solo albums, before forming Drive, She Said with Al Fritsch.

Album: *Touch* (Ariola 1980).

Travers, Pat, Band

Canadian guitarist Pat Travers began his career playing in his brother's band. Having moved to London, he set up a group of his own consisting of Peter 'Mars' Cowling (bass) and drummer Roy Dyke (of Ashton, Gardner And Dyke). In 1976 they played at the Reading Rock Festival, and this led to greater recognition of their debut, *Pat Travers*. In 1977 Nicko McBrain, who subsequently joined Iron Maiden, replaced Roy Dyke. Travers himself turned his talents to songwriting, his music taking a more experimental turn, and being aided by other artists, including Scott Gorham. During their 1977 tour, Clive Edwards replaced McBrain, and Michael Dycke added another guitar. Guitarist Pat Thrall, who had been a member of Automatic Man, and Tommy Aldridge (drums), formerly of Black Oak Arkansas, were recruited to work on *Heat In The Street*, an extremely powerful album. Their relationship with the band was short-lived, however; Thrall left and Aldridge departed in order to work with Ozzy Osbourne. Subsequent recordings featured Sandy Gennaro (drums) and Michael Shrieve (ex-Santana), and were notable for their solid, blues-like sound. In 1984 the line-up of Pat Marchino (drums), Barry Dunaway (bass), Jerry Riggs (guitar) and Travers released *Hot Shot*, an album which was not a commercial success. There was then a lengthy break in Travers' recording career until 1990 when he released *School Of Hard Knocks*. The following year Travers was working again with Thrall, Aldridge and Cowling, touring Japan along with Jerry Riggs and Scott Zymowski, and planning a reunion album. After which came a series of blues-orientated albums, including the well-received *Blues Trackcv* .

Albums: *Pat Travers* (Polydor 1976), *Makin' Magic* (Polydor 1977), *Putting It Straight* (Polydor 1977), *Heat In The Street* (Polydor 1978), *Go For What You Know* (Polydor 1979), *Crash And Burn* (Polydor 1980), *Radio Active* (Polydor 1981), *Black Pearl* (Polydor 1982), *Hot Shot* (Polydor 1984), *School Of Hard Knocks* (Razor 1990), *Boom Boom* (Essential 1991), *Just A Touch* (1993), *Blues Tracks* (1993), *Blues Magnet* (Provogue 1994). Compilations: *Anthology Volume 1* (Polydor 1990), *Anthology Volume 2* (Polydor 1990).
Video: *Boom Boom* (1991).

Trespass

Suffolk band formed in 1976 by the Sutcliffe brothers, Mark (guitar) and Paul (drums). It was during 1979 that, along with Steve Mills (vocals), Cris Linscott (bass) and Dave Crawte (rhythm guitar), they released 'One Of These Days', on their own Trial label. The single remains one of the undiscovered classics of the era and the band should have made a more lasting impression with their blend of traditional hard rock and 'new' heavy metal. A second single, 'Jealousy', passed by without comment, but live they were getting noticed. In 1981 Linscott left to be replaced by Robert Irving and Mark took over vocal duties from Mills. Later a new vocalist, Robert Ekland, joined, and they then recorded an album and the *Bright Lights* EP. Receiving a degree of critical acclaim the major labels remained blind to their talents and the band faded away. In 1988 Crawte, now playing bass, and the brothers formed Blue Bludd, with Phil Kane (vocals) and Robert Ariss (keyboards). They adopted an American sound drawing comparisons to White Lion or Ratt, and signed with Music For Nations for two albums, *The Big Noise* and *Universal Language*.
Album: *Trespass* (Trial 1981).

Tribe After Tribe

This 'African acid rock' trio developed from vocalist/guitarist Robbi Robb's Asylum Kids, who were major pop stars in their native South Africa. However, a lyrical move towards anti-apartheid politics meant trouble for the band - bassist Robby Whitelaw's left cheek and jaw were left permanently paralysed after a vigilante beating - and Robb and Whitelaw were forced to flee the country with the help of Amnesty International, relocating to Los Angeles in 1987. Recruiting drummer PK, Tribe After Tribe created an innovative and atmospheric sound, mixing rock with traditional African styles and Robb's emotive political lyricism. An uncompromising outfit, they had difficulty in finding a sympathetic ear at a record company until Megaforce signed them in 1990, when the band were on the verge of releasing their debut independently. In the event further studio time with producer Bob Johnston enhanced the basic tracks. *Tribe After Tribe* was a haunting debut, attracting many admirers, including Pearl Jam's Eddie Vedder, who invited Tribe After Tribe to support on their 1992 US tour. *Love Under Will*, with new drummer Chris Frazier (ex-Steve Vai), continued the development of the band's uniquely spiritual style as they persisted in ignoring the marketing men. They also extended their political stance by campaigning in support of the Rock The Vote movement in their adopted country, their own background adding considerable weight to the argument.
Albums: *Tribe After Tribe* (Megaforce 1991), *Love Under Will* (Megaforce 1993).

Triumph

This Canadian power-trio formed in Toronto during 1975. The band share many similarities to Rush other than geographical location, as they are all highly accomplished musicians who have experimented with many facets of high-tech melodic rock. Comprising Rik Emmet (guitar/vocals), Gil Moore (drums) and Mike Levine (bass/keyboards), they nevertheless follow a rockier road than their fellow countrymen. Interest built slowly, but the band finally made a breakthrough with *Progressions Of Power*, their fourth album, released in 1980. *Allied Forces* and *Never Surrender* saw the pinnacle of their success, with both albums attaining gold status in the USA. Their music is characterized by Emmet's high-pitched vocals and intricate guitar work, supplemented by keyboard fills and a thunderous rhythm section. *Thunder Seven*, a CD-only release was a disjointed collection, while the live album that followed suffered from a wooden sound and flat production. In live settings the band frequently used Rick Santers as an extra guitarist to overcome the limitations of a three-man line-up. Again like Rush, their concerts were renowned for their sophisticated special effects rather than the actual music, and featured every conceivable pyrotechnic device available, plus the ultimate in computerised, laser-lighting rigs. *The Sport Of Kings* saw the band move in a blatantly commercial direction, but *Surveillance* marked a return to their roots: an aggressive and well-produced hard rock album. Emmett left the band in 1988 and was replaced by guitarist Phil Xenides. The vocals were taken over by Moore, but much of the group's character left with Emmett.
Albums: *Triumph* (Attic 1976), *Rock 'N' Roll Machine*

(Attic 1977), *Just A Game* (RCA 1979), *Progressions Of Power* (RCA 1980), *Allied Forces* (RCA 1981), *Never Surrender* (RCA 1982), *Thunder Seven* (RCA 1984), *Stages* (MCA 1985), *The Sport Of Kings* (MCA 1985), *Surveillance* (MCA 1987), *Edge Of Excess* (1993). Compilations: *Triumph* (RCA 1976, comprising original *Triumph* and *Rock 'N' Roll Machine*), *Classics* (RCA 1989).

Videos: *Night Of Triumph Live* (1988), *Triumph At The US Festival* (1988).

Trojan

Formed in Wigan, England, in 1982, Trojan's original line up consisted of Dave Kenyon (vocals), Pate Wadeson (guitar), Andy J. Halliwell (guitar), Brian Bentham (bass) and Mick Taylor (drums). The band first became noticed on the heavy metal underground scene with a hastily recorded five-track cassette. This credible offering was a blend of high speed thrash metal with a punk attitude. The band contributed a track to a budget compilation, *Metal Maniaxe*, released on Ebony Records in 1982. However, due to a relative lack of record company promotion, coupled with a yearning by various members of the band to pursue other musical directions, they dissolved. Determined to carry on, Wadeson underwent lengthy auditions to re-form the band. By 1984 a new line-up was confirmed, featuring Graeme Wyatt (vocals), Eddie Martin (bass) and Sam Hall (drums). *Chasing The Storm* was released on Roadrunner Records in 1985 and was well received, with its sound firmly rooted in the N.W.O.B.H.M. The group toured extensively at home and abroad culminating in an appearance at the Whiplash Festival in Belgium in 1986. Through managerial and personal problems the band split up for a final time in 1988 at which time Wadeson and Wyatt went on to form the melodic thrash band, Talion.

Album: *Chasing The Storm* (Roadrunner 1985).

Trouble

This influential Chicago quintet formed in 1979, with vocalist Eric Wagner and guitarists Bruce Franklin and Rick Wartell joined by Sean McAllister (bass) and Jeff Olson (drums). Trouble's early material drew strong Black Sabbath comparisons with a doom-laden, riff-heavy approach, and *Trouble* (later renamed *Psalm 9* to prevent confusion with their fourth album) was a stunning debut. However, the biblical imagery and positive lyrical approach brought a white metal label which hindered their rise from underground status into the metal mainstream, where white metal was identified with the sickly-sweetness of Stryper rather than Trouble's powerful hippie-metal. *The Skull* added a darker air to their epic doom style, but personnel problems ensued. McAllister was fired and Olson left to become a minister, while Ron Holzner (bass) and Dennis Lesh (drums) came in for *Run To The Light*, where the shorter, punchier material was let down by weak production. Lesh was subsequently replaced by ex-Zoetrope drummer Barry Stern. A deserved major deal with Def American followed, and Trouble duly reached new creative heights, incorporating Beatles and Pink Floyd influences for a broader, more psychedelic yet still heavy sound on *Trouble*. The superb *Manic Frustration* continued the progression as Trouble's most mature and accessible work to date, but despite colossal critical praise, the band remained a cult phenomenon. Parting company with their label, Trouble returned to their underground roots, touring heavily and selling self-financed recordings on the road before re-merging with a Bulletproof/Music For Nations deal in late 1994.

Albums: *Trouble/Psalm 9* (Metal Blade 1984), *The Skull* (Metal Blade 1985), *Run To The Light* (Metal Blade/Enigma 1987), *Trouble* (Def American 1990), *Manic Frustration* (Def American 1992).

Trout, Walter, Band

This highly talented and experienced blues guitarist finally formed and recorded with his own band in 1989 after a lengthy spell with John Mayall. With the help of Jim Trapp (bass), Leroy Larson (drums) and Dan Abrams (keyboards) he debuted with *Life In The Jungle* in 1990. This showcased Trout's remarkable feel and dexterity and courted Jimi Hendrix, Robin Trower and Gary Moore comparisons. Klas Anderhill took over the drumstool on *Prisoner Of A Dream* and saw the band move in a more commercial direction. Much of the soulful passion was replaced for a heavier approach more akin to bands such as Europe, Whitesnake and Bon Jovi. Trout moved away from his blues roots with *Transition* although his remarkable ability as a guitarist shone through an album of patchy songs.

Albums: *Life In The Jungle* (Provogue 1990), *Prisoner Of A Dream* (Provogue 1991), *Transition* (Provogue 1992), *Live, No More Fish Jokes* (Provogue 1992), *Tellin' Stories* (Silvertone 1994).

Trower, Robin

b. 9 March 1947, London, England. Guitarist Trower spent his early career in the Paramounts, a popular Southend, Essex-based R&B/beat group which completed five singles between 1963 and 1965. Having briefly worked with a trio dubbed the Jam, he joined several colleagues from his earlier act in Procol

Harum. Trower remained in this much-praised unit until 1971, when his desire to pursue a tougher musical style proved incompatible with their well-established grandiose inflections. He initially formed the short-lived Jude with Frankie Miller (vocals), Jim Dewar (bass/vocals) and Clive Bunker (drums; ex-Jethro Tull), but having retained Dewar (formerly with Lulu and Stone The Crows), founded the Robin Trower Band with drummer Reg Isidore. *Twice Removed From Yesterday* and *Bridge Of Sighs* explored a melodic, guitar-based path, redolent of the late-period Jimi Hendrix, whom Robin was often criticized for merely aping. His lyrical technique, offset by Dewar's gritty delivery, nonetheless proved highly popular and the trio achieved considerable success in the USA. Although ex-Sly And Family Stone drummer Bill Lordan replaced Isidore in 1974, *For Earth Below* and *Long Misty Days* maintained the same musical balance. However, Trower's desire for a purer version of R&B resulted in his inviting black producer Don Davis to collaborate on *In City Dreams* and *Caravan To Midnight*. The new style alienated the guitarist's rock audience, while the rock-based *Victims Of The Fury* was bedevilled by weaker material. In 1981 he and Lordan formed BLT with bassist Jack Bruce, but within two years Trower had reconvened the Robin Trower Band with Dewar, David Bronze (bass), Alan Clarke and Bobby Clouter (both drums). *Back It Up* failed to repeat former glories and the artist was then dropped by longtime label, Chrysalis Records. The well-received *Passion*, released independently, engendered a new deal with Atlantic Records, for whom a new line-up of Trower, Bronze, Davey Pattison (vocals) and Pete Thompson (drums) completed *Take What You Need*. Trower is also heavily involved in record production.

Albums: *Twice Removed From Yesterday* (Chrysalis 1973), *Bridge Of Sighs* (Chrysalis 1974), *For Earth Below* (Chrysalis 1975), *Robin Trower Live* (Chrysalis 1976), *Long Misty Days* (Chrysalis 1976), *In City Dreams* (Chrysalis 1977), *Caravan To Midnight* (Chrysalis 1978), *Victims Of The Fury* (Chrysalis 1980), *Back It Up* (Chrysalis 1983), *Beyond The Mist* (Music For Nations 1985), *Passion* (Gryp 1987), *Take What You Need* (Atlantic 1988), *In The Line Of Fire* (Atlantic 1990). Compilation: *Portfolio* (Chrysalis 1987).

Trust

This French metal band were formed in the late 70s by vocalist Bernard Bonvoisin and guitarist Norbert 'Nono' Krief, with drummer Jean-Emile 'Jeannot' Hanela and bassist Raymond Manna. The band were musically influenced by AC/DC, but their lyrics reflected the anti-establishment punk ethos. *Trust* was an enormous domestic success, and the outstanding 'L'Elite' stimulated international interest. Yves 'Vivi' Brusco replaced Manna and guitarist Mohammed 'Moho' Chemlekh was added shortly after the recording of *Repression*, a superb effort which caused controversy in France due to the sympathetic treatment of infamous French criminal Jaques Mesrine in 'Instinct De Mort' and 'Le Mitard', the latter using Mesrine's lyrics. An English language version, with lyrics translated by Sham 69's Jimmy Pursey, brought a good reaction from outside France, although Bonvoisin sounded slightly uncomfortable and much of the lyrical edge was lost. Trust were a popular support to Iron Maiden on their *Killers* UK tour, subsequently appearing at the 1981 Reading Festival. *Marche Ou Creve* saw Nicko McBrain take over on drums, and was another solid release, featuring a tribute to late AC/DC vocalist Bon Scott in 'Ton Dernier Acte'. However, the band lost some credibility when 'Misere', which attacked the Thatcher government, was omitted from the English language version (retitled *Savage*). A drummer 'swap' with Iron Maiden saw Clive Burr replace McBrain for 1983's *Trust*, before Farid replaced him. Inner tensions broke Trust apart after the disappointing *Rock 'N' Roll*, with Bonvoisin recording two solo albums while Krief worked with Johnny Halliday. Renewed interest following Anthrax's covers of 'Antisocial' and 'Sects' stimulated a reformation, with Brusco on rhythm guitar and new bassist Frederick, a union which produced a live album.

Albums: *Trust* (CBS 1979), *Repression/Repression Version Anglaise* (CBS 1980), *Marche Ou Creve* (Epic 1981), *Trust* (Epic 1983), *Man's Trap* (Epic 1984), *Rock 'N' Roll* (Epic 1984), *Live - Paris By Night* (Celluloid 1989). Compilation: *Best Of* (Premier 1988).

Tuff

This US rock quartet were formed in 1990 by Stevie Rachelle (vocals), Jorge Desaint (guitar), Todd Chase (bass) and drummer Michael Lean. They signed to Atlantic Records and debuted with *What Comes Around, Goes Around* in 1991. The influences here were evidently Poison, Warrant and Bon Jovi, yet they displayed just enough energy to maintain a level of credibility. However, reviews were not kind and afterwards the group remained quiet.

Album: *What Comes Around, Goes Around* (Atlantic 1991).

Tungsten

Duo formed in Chalmette, Louisiana, USA, a small

Twisted Sister

town on the edge of New Orleans, in the early 90s. Al Hodge (guitar/bass/vocals) and Mark Talamo (drums/electronics) became friends in high school a decade previously, sharing interests in both traditional heavy metal and technology. However, unlike many of the groups caught in its nets by the diversity of the 90s, Tungsten were unafraid of the term metal: 'There are so many bands out there that are almost embarrassed to say that. I'd rather be called a metal band than be a 60s hippie-wanna-be band that hails from the trend land of Seattle'. Lyrically their debut articulated Hodge's frustrations with failed relationships and a sense of betrayal, particularly virulent on tracks like 'Born XY' or 'Just Fades Away'. It was recorded at Talamo's own 16-track digital studio, where he has also engineered albums for Crowbar and Down.

Album: *183.85* (Music For Nations 1994).

Turner, Joe Lynn

American vocalist who first came to prominence in 1977 with the band Fandango, who played typical AOR music. The band also featured a guitarist called Rick Blakemore which, with hindsight, may have been a good omen. Turner's radio-friendly vocals

graced all four of their albums - *Fandango* (RCA 1977), *One Night Stand* (RCA 1978), *Last Kiss* (RCA 1979) and *Cadillac* (RCA 1980). In 1981 he was invited by guitarist Ritchie Blackmore to replace Graham Bonnet in Rainbow. Blackmore was looking to change the sound of the band and aim it squarely at the American market. Turner's vocals were perfect for this and helped to get the band further airplay with singles 'I Surrender' and 'Street Of Dreams', but Rainbow still remained more popular in the UK and the rest of Europe. Consequently, after three excellent albums - *Difficult To Cure* (Polydor 1981), *Straight Between The Eyes* (Polydor 1982) and *Bent Out Of Shape* (Polydor 1983) - Blackmore finished the band and reformed Deep Purple. Turner then obtained a deal with Elektra Records and released one underrated album in 1985. Through lack of publicity the album flopped and Turner took a rest until he teamed up with Swedish guitar hero Yngwie Malmsteen and Rising Force. In 1988 a single, 'Heaven Tonight', became a hit and Turner looked like he was back on track, but a degree of criticism about his live performance from some quarters damaged sales of *Odyssey* (Polydor 1988). The band set out on a world tour and played to packed halls in

Russia where they recorded and filmed concerts in Leningrad released in 1989 as *Trial By Fire* (Polydor). Turner was replaced later in 1989 and returned to writing new material and guesting with various other artists. A year later Ritchie Blackmore contacted him again and suggested that he replace Ian Gillan in the reformed Deep Purple. Turner accepted and appeared on *Slaves And Masters* (BMG 1990) and toured with them. Things quietened down with the band and by 1993 he had been replaced by Gillan again. If rumours that Blackmore is reforming Rainbow prove true there is every possibility that Turner may return as their vocalist.
Album: *Rescue You* (Elektra 1985).

21 Guns

This melodic hard rock quartet were assembled in 1991 by ex-Thin Lizzy guitarist Scott Gorham. Recruiting fellow Americans Leif Johansen (bass), Michael Sturgis (drums) and Tommy La Verdi (vocals) to complete the line-up, they were soon offered a contract by RCA Records. They debuted in the summer of 1992 with *Salute*, a highly polished melodic rock album which met with positive reviews in the press. Influences such as Foreigner, White Lion and Journey were prevalent throughout the album, though Gorham's distinctive style held any accusations of plagiarism in check.
Album: *Salute* (RCA 1992).

24-7 Spyz

This multi-faceted South Bronx, New York, hardcore quartet formed in 1986, playing a mixture of ska, punk and funk until they began to incorporate hardcore aggression in the manner of Fishbone and Bad Brains, progressing like the former in particular towards an eclectic but accessible sound. Founder Jimi Hazel (guitar), Peter Fluid (vocals), Rick Skatore (bass) and Anthony Johnson (drums) made their debut with *Harder Than You*, mixing rap and reggae into their funk and thrash melting pot, with stunning performances from the Jimi Hendrix-worshipping Hazel and the energetic Fluid. *Gumbo Millenium* continued in similar genre-blending fashion as the band began to attract press attention for their wild live act, but musical differences saw both Fluid and Johnson depart as touring ended. Jeff Brodnax (vocals) and Joel Maitoza (drums) made their debut on *This Is...24-7 Spyz*, with the band surprisingly maintaining a continuity of style both live and in the studio, despite the drastic line-up change. *Strength In Numbers* contained 24-7 Spyz's most consistent material, but like Fishbone, the band's diversity seemed to hold them back, and commercial success remained distant. A reunion of the original line-up seemed to be on the cards in mid-1994, but was never confirmed.
Albums: *Harder Than You* (In-Effect 1989), *Gumbo Millenium* (In-Effect 1990), *This Is...24-7 Spyz* (East West 1991, mini-album), *Strength In Numbers* (East West 1992).

Twisted Sister

Formed in 1976, this New York quintet's original purpose was to provide the antidote to the disco music that was saturating the airwaves during the mid-70s. Featuring Dee Snider (vocals), Eddie Ojeda (guitar), Mark 'The Animal' Mendoza (bass; ex-Dictators), Jay Jay French (guitar) and Tony Petri (drums) they had a bizarre image that borrowed ideas from Kiss, Alice Cooper and the New York Dolls. Musically they combined sexually provocative lyrics and dumb choruses with heavy-duty, metallic rock 'n' roll. A.J. Pero (ex-Cities) took over on drums before the recording of their debut, *Under The Blade*. This was picked up from the independent Secret label by Atlantic Records, following a successful UK appearance at the Reading Festival and a controversial performance on *The Tube* television show in 1982. They never lived up to their initial promise, with successive albums simply regurgitating earlier ideas. Their greatest success was *Stay Hungry*, which cracked the Top 20 album charts on both sides of the Atlantic. It also included the hit single, 'I Am, I'm Me', which peaked at number 18 in the UK. Their audience had become bored with them by the time *Come Out And Play* was released and the tour to support it was also a flop. Pero quit and returned to his former outfit, Cities; Joey 'Seven' Franco (ex-Good Rats) was drafted in as replacement. Snider steered the band in a more melodic direction on *Love Is For Suckers*. The album was still-born, Atlantic terminated their contract, and the band imploded in 1987. Snider went on to form Desperado, with ex-Gillan guitarist Bernie Tormé (subsequently evolving, more permanently, into Widowmaker). Looking back on his days dressing up with his old band, Snider would conclude: 'All that flash and shit wears thin. There's gotta be something beyond it. And there wasn't with Twisted Sister'.
Albums: *Under The Blade* (Secret 1982), *You Can't Stop Rock 'N' Roll* (Atlantic 1983), *Stay Hungry* (Atlantic 1984), *Come Out And Play* (Atlantic 1985), *Love Is For Suckers* (Atlantic 1987), *Live* (Music For Nations 1994).

2 Tribes

Funk metal crossover aggregation formed in London

Tyketto

during 1990, the mixed-race line-up giving them their name. The band, who, predictably, were often said to represent the UK's answer to Living Colour, comprised Ashton Liburd (vocals), Paul Gold (bass), Rod Quinn (b. Dublin, Eire; drums) and John McLoughlin (guitar). The group's efforts were spearheaded by a single, 'The Music Biz', which had that same legend scrawled over a pig on its jacket. Their uncompromising live sets, meanwhile, included a cover of Public Enemy's '911 Is A Joke', the American rap stars' vicious attack on emergency response times in black communities, borrowed after a relative of the band died waiting three hours for an ambulance. Signed to Chrysalis subsidiary Compulsion, they made their long playing debut with a self-titled album in early 1992 which met with a degree of enthusiasm from the rock press. Especially notable was the agenda-setting 'File Under Rock (Bite The Hand That Bleeds Us)' single, which bemoaned the fact that their records were always housed under the 'black' sections in stores, despite 2 Tribes being an authentic rock act. It included the lines: 'This ain't Soul II Soul, It's rock 'n' roll'. However, despite earning a Single Of The Week plaudit in the *New Musical Express*, it was not enough to avert their descent into obscurity, with the band splitting soon after its release.

Album: *2 Tribes* (Compulsion 1992).

Tygers Of Pan Tang

This hard rock band was formed in Whitley Bay, Newcastle-upon-Tyne, England, in 1978, as part of the New Wave Of British Heavy Metal. The four-piece line-up comprised Jess Cox (vocals), Rob Weir (guitar), Rocky (bass) and Brian Dick (drums). Their debut EP was the first rock release on Newcastle's Neat label, and it quickly topped all the metal charts. On the back of their first flush of success they moved to MCA Records. However, after one album Cox departed to be replaced by John Deverill (from Cardiff, Wales; vocals) and John Sykes (guitar). Sykes later left (to join Thin Lizzy and then Whitesnake) and was replaced by former Penetration guitarist Fred Purser. *The Cage* broke the band in the USA, before two years of disputes with MCA held up their career, and only compilation albums were released during this period. Steve Lamb joined as guitarist in 1985, and a year later former vocalist Cox formed Tyger

Type O Negative

Tyger in order to try and recapture past glories.

Albums: *Wild Cat* (MCA 1980), *Spellbound* (MCA 1981), *Crazy Nights* (MCA 1981), *The Cage* (MCA 1982), *The Wreck-Age* (Music For Nations 1985), *First Kill* (Neat 1986), *Burning In The Shade* (Zebra 1987). Compilation: *The Best Of The Tygers Of Pan Tang* (MCA 1983). Jess Cox solo: *Third Step* (Neat 1983).

Tyketto

Following the demise of Waysted in 1987, American vocalist Danny Vaughn set about forming his own band, with drummer Michael Clayton, bassist Jimi Kennedy and guitarist Brooke St. James, with Vaughn's former Waysted colleague Jimmy Dilella (guitar/keyboards) also involved briefly. Taking the name Tyketto from some 'tagging' on a graffiti-covered Brooklyn wall, the band were signed by Geffen Records in 1989. The Richie Zito-produced *Don't Come Easy* was a classic slice of melodic hard rock, with Vaughn's immaculate vocals enhancing an already strong collection of songs, which were given a rootsy flavour by the mix of acoustic and electric guitars. Conditions were difficult for the band in their recession-hit homeland, but they proved themselves on a UK tour with White Lion, and seemed to be destined for stardom. However, the album title proved somewhat prophetic. Kennedy departed, with James Lomenzo (ex-White Lion) filling in before a permanent replacement was found in Jaimie Scott. *Strength In Numbers* was recorded in 1992, but the release was delayed by over a year when Geffen surprisingly dropped Tyketto, despite the fact that the label had already sent out advance tapes and prepared two possible sleeves. Retaining only a Japanese deal, the band signed to Music For Nations in Europe in December 1993, and the album was finally released, albeit to a cooler reaction than that afforded to the debut. However, excellent live performances dispelled any doubts, and with American label interest, the future again seems bright for this genuinely talented band.

Albums: *Don't Come Easy* (Geffen 1991), *Strength In Numbers* (Music For Nations 1994).

Type O Negative

From the carcass of controversial nihilist New York act Carnivore, vocalist and bass guitarist Peter Steele formed Type O Negative in 1988. Fusing elements of heavy metal, gothic rock, industrial music and psychedelia, Type O Negative are a four-piece that explore the darker edges of the human soul with caustic irony. Their second release, The *Origin Of The Feces*, was a typical act of media terrorism. Mixed by the band to sound like a live recording from hell, it features chants of 'You Suck' and slow-handclapping from the audience, while Steele cynically drawls to the band 'Let's get this over with'. The sleeve featured a close up of a sphincter, while the band photos inside each have a 'turd' lovingly laid upon them. Despite such truculence, success beckoned as Type O Negative secured tours with influential bands such as Nine Inch Nails, Jackyl, Danzig and Mötley Crüe. *Bloody Kisses* proved a surprise success, with its effective blend of musical velvet and razor blades, leading to the re-release of *Origin Of Feces* (in less offensive packaging). The current line-up consists of Peter Steele (vocals/bass), Josh Silver (keyboards), Kenny Hickey (guitar) and Johnny Kelly (drums).

Albums: *Slow, Deep, Hard* (Roadrunner 1991), *Origin Of Feces* (Roadrunner 1992), *Bloody Kisses* (Roadrunner 1993).

U

UFO

This well regarded UK rock band formed in 1969 when drummer Andy Parker joined Phil Mogg (b. 1951, London, England; vocals), Pete Way (bass) and Mick Bolton (guitar) in Hocus Pocus. With a name change to UFO and a musical style that fused progressive space-rock and good-time boogie, they released three albums that were successful only in Germany and Japan. In 1974 Bolton quit, to be replaced by Larry Wallis (ex-Pink Fairies), followed by Bernie Marsden (later of Whitesnake) and finally Michael Schenker. Securing a contract with Chrysalis Records they recorded *Phenomenon*, a stunning hard rock album that featured the all-time heavy metal classics 'Rock Bottom' and 'Doctor, Doctor'. Schenker's presence helped to forge their new sound, as he strangled the hard-edged metallic riffs out of his trusty Flying V. A series of excellent albums followed, and the band expanded to a five-piece in 1976, with the addition of a keyboardist, initially Danny Peyronel (ex-Heavy Metal Kids) and later Paul Raymond (formerly of Savoy Brown). *Lights Out* and *Strangers In The Night* consolidated the band's success, the latter a superb double live album recorded on their sell-out US tour of 1977. After long-running internal disagreements, Schenker quit in 1978 to rejoin the Scorpions and later form MSG. Paul Chapman (ex-Lone Star) was offered the guitarist's vacancy, having played with the band for short periods on two previous occasions. From this point on, they never recaptured the level of success and recognition they had attained with Schenker. A string of uninspiring albums followed, which lacked both aggression and the departed guitarist's riffs. Paul Raymond joined MSG in 1980, with Neil Carter (ex-Wild Horses) taking his place. Pete Way left after the release of *Mechanix*, eventually forming Waysted and ex-Eddie And The Hot Rods/Damned bassist Paul Gray took over his position. *Making Contact* represented the nadir of the band's creativity, being dated and devoid of the old energy. A farewell UK tour was undertaken in 1983, but it was a sad end for what was originally a fine band. Two years later Mogg resurrected the name with Raymond and Gray, plus ex-Magnum drummer Jim Simpson and the Japanese guitarist Atomic Tommy M. They recorded *Misdemeanor*, which unsuccessfully rekindled the old flame, with forceful guitars and hard and insistent melodies. Success eluded them and they disbanded again. In 1991, UFO were reborn once more. This time the line-up featured the nucleus of Mogg and Way, plus guitarist Lawrence Archer (ex-Grand Slam) and drummer Clive Edwards (ex-Wild Horses). *High Stakes And Desperate Men* attempted to recapture the halcyon days of 1974-78, with limited success, but talk in 1995 of a full-scale reunion, including Schenker, was what really fueled fan interest.

Albums: *UFO 1* (Beacon 1971), *UFO 2 - Flying* (Beacon 1971), *UFO Lands In Tokyo - Live* (1972, Japan only), *Phenomenon* (Chrysalis 1974), *Force It* (Chrysalis 1975), *No Heavy Pettin'* (Chrysalis 1976), *Lights Out* (Chrysalis 1977), *Obsession* (Chrysalis 1978), *Strangers In The Night* (Chrysalis 1979), *No Place To Run* (Chrysalis 1980), *The Wild, The Willing And The Innocent* (Chrysalis 1981), *Mechanix* (Chrysalis 1982), *Making Contact* (Chrysalis 1983), *Misdemeanor* (Chrysalis 1985), *Ain't Misbehavin'* (FM Revolver 1988), *High Stakes And Desperate Men* (Essential 1992), *BBC Live In Concert* (Windsong 1992), *Lights Out In Tokyo: Live* (Castle 1993). Compilations: *Headstone - The Best Of UFO* (Chrysalis 1983), *The Collection* (Castle 1985), *The Decca Years* (Decca 1993).

Video: *Misdemeanor Live* (1985).

Ugly Kid Joe

Formed in Isla Vista, California, USA, in 1989 by Whitfield Crane (vocals), Klaus Eichstadt (guitar) and drummer Mark Davis, adding second guitarist Roger Lahr, and bringing in bassist Cordell Crockett in early 1991, the band flirted with several names before settling on Ugly Kid Joe, coined for a support slot in order to satirise headliners Pretty Boy Floyd. The band made their debut with a mini-album, *As Ugly As They Wanna Be*, which was an almost instant success, selling over 2 million copies in the USA on the back of the poppy hit, 'Everything About You', a humorous number featured in the enormously popular *Wayne's World* film. The song rather belied the true musical nature of the band, in reality much heavier with funk influences, drawing comparisons with both Mötley Crüe and Faith No More from reviewers. *America's Least Wanted* produced further hits in the shape of 'Neighbor' and 'Cats In The Cradle'. Given a powerful sound by Mark Dodson, the album established the band's credibility without sacrificing their sense of humour, and live shows, including a support slot on Ozzy Osbourne's farewell US tour, further helped the band shake off their novelty tag. Sessions for a second album proper began in 1994 at a rented house in Santa Ynez, California, with new members Dave Fortman (ex-Sugartooth) stepping in for Lahr, and drummer Shannon Larkin (ex-Wrathchild America, Souls At Zero) replacing Davis.

Albums: *As Ugly As They Wanna Be* (Mercury 1992, mini-album), *America's Least Wanted* (Mercury 1992).

Ultraviolence

UK extreme rock band front for one Johnny Violent, who introduced himself via the scorching 'Shout' single, which sold out within in week and drew the attention of DJ John Peel. A session resulted in 1992, which drew further journalistic gasps as the band traversed the sonic boundaries between industrial metal and techno. In its wake Ultraviolence inked a deal with EMI subsidiary Food, but few concessions to the mainstream were advanced on the subsequent *Vengeance* EP. This low-fi but high bpm encounter brought the marriage with Food to an abrupt end, with Violent sustaining himself via live outings with Eskimos In Egypt, Hyperhead and others. Ultraviolence then found a more natural home at Earache Records, debuting with 'I Destructor' and 'Johnny Is A Bastard' (as Johnny Violent). Ever more musically outlandish, the resultant album, *Life Of Destructor*, was a bruising affair, but one with some method in its mayhem. In the light of its favourable response Violent was invited to remix for diverse names including Terrorvision, G.R.O.W.T.H. and Laibach. They then guested with the Orb at a New York show - an appearance guaranteed to startle the assembled onlookers out of their ambient daydreams. 1995 also brought a collaboration with television host

'Krusher' and Wurzel of Motörhead.
Album: *Life Of Destructor* (Earache 1993).

Uncle Sam

Formed in 1987, Uncle Sam were the brainchild of guitarist Larry Millar. With the recruitment of fellow New Yorkers David Gentner (vocals), Bill Purol (bass) and Jeff Mann (drums), they signed with the independent Razor Records. Influenced by both the punk and thrash movements, their songs were short, frantic and sometimes devoid of melody. Gentner's vocals were monotonous, while the back beat lacked depth or colour. At best they came across as an updated, but pale version of the Stooges or MC5, and their were few mourners when the band collapsed in the 90s.
Albums: *Heaven Or Hollywood* (Razor 1988), *Letters From London* (Razor 1990).

Uriah Heep

The critics have scoffed and generally poured derision on Uriah Heep over the years, but the band have sold millions of records and on five occasions placed albums above number 40 in the US charts. A technically brilliant heavy rock band, they deserve most credit for continuing despite almost 30 personnel changes and two deaths along the way. David Byron (b. 29 January 1947, Epping, Essex, England, d. 28 February 1985; vocals) formed the group with Mick Box (b. 8 June 1947, Walthamstow, London, England; lead guitar/vocals). The pair had teamed up in the Stalkers during the mid-60s, and after the group split they assembled another called Spice. This then evolved into Uriah Heep when the duo were joined by Ken Hensley (b. 24 August 1945, London, England; guitar/keyboards/vocals) and Paul Newton (b. 1946, Andover, England; bass). Hensley, a talented musician, had previously played guitar with Kit And The Saracens and the soul group, Jimmy Brown Sound. Before Uriah Heep were bonded under the experienced management of Gerry Bron, Hensley had played alongside Mick Taylor (later to become a member of the Rolling Stones) in the Gods. He had also played on an album by Toe Fat which included Cliff Bennett. The rota of drummers started with former Spice man Alex Napier, followed by Nigel Olsson (later with Elton John). Finding a permanent drummer was to remain one of the band's problems throughout their early years. Their debut, *Very 'eavy, Very 'umble* in 1970 was a simplistic, bass-driven passage from electric folk to a direct, harder sound. They auditioned numerous drummers before offering the job to Keith Baker, who recorded *Salisbury* before deciding that the tour schedule was too rigorous for his liking. *Salisbury* was a drastic development from the debut, with many lengthy, meandering solos and a 16-minute title track embellished by a 26-piece orchestra. The group were near the forefront of a richly embossed, fastidious style of music later to become dubbed 'progressive rock'. During 1971 the line-up was altered again when Lee Kerslake, another former member of the Gods and Toe Fat, replaced Ian Clarke. An ex-member of the Downbeats and Colosseum, Mark Clarke, superseded Paul Newton on bass guitar but lasted just three months before Gary Thain (b. New Zealand; ex-Keef Hartley Band) took over. Gerry Bron had formed Bronze Records by 1971 and *Look At Yourself* became the group's first entry into the UK charts when it reached number 39 in November. The stability of the new line-up enabled the band to enter their most successful period during the early 70s when the fantastical, eccentric nature of their lyrics was supported by a grandiose musical approach. The quintet recorded five albums, beginning with *Demons And Wizards,* their first to enter the US charts. The musical and lyrical themes continued on *Magician's Birthday*, the double set *Uriah Heep Live, Sweet Freedom, Wonderworld* (their last Top 40 entry in the US chart) and *Return To Fantasy* as the band revealed a rare thirst for tough recording and performance schedules. Gary Thain was asked to leave in February 1975 after becoming too unreliable. He died of a drug overdose on 19 March of the following year. John Wetton, formerly of King Crimson, Family and Roxy Music was expected to provide the impetus needed when he took over the bass guitar in March 1975. However, many observers considered that he had taken a retrogressive step in joining a group that was quickly becoming an anachronism. The union, celebrated on *Return To Fantasy*, failed on a creative level although it marked their first and last appearance in the UK Top 10. Wetton left after just over a year to back Bryan Ferry. Early in 1976, Uriah Heep were set to fold when internal arguments broke out and they found the previously winning formula had become archaic and undeniably staid. In Ken Hensley's own words, they were 'a bunch of machines plummeting to a death'. There had been an earlier, brooding row when Thain suffered a near-fatal electric shock in Dallas and said he had not been shown enough regard for his injuries. Hensley walked out during a tour of the USA in the summer of 1976 and in a subsequent power-struggle, Byron was forced to leave. Byron soon afterwards joined Rough Diamond and after their brief lifespan released a series of solo albums before his death in 1985. Hensley had already embarked upon a short, parallel solo career, releasing two albums in 1973 and

1975. John Lawton, previously the singer with Lucifer's Friend, debuted on *Firefly*. The new bassist was David Bowie's former backing musician, Trevor Bolder. The singer's position underwent further changes during the late 70s and early 80s as the group found themselves playing to a cult following that was ever decreasing. Ex-Lone Star singer John Sloman performed on *Conquest* after which Hensley left the group, leaving original member Mick Box to pick up the pieces. A brief hiatus resulted and a new Uriah Heep which included Box, Kerslake, John Sinclair (keyboards), Bob Daisley (bass) and Peter Goalby (vocals, ex-Trapeze) was formed. Daisley would later quit in 1983 and be replaced by the returning Bolder. Bronze Records collapsed in 1984 and the band signed with Portrait Records in the USA. Their earlier extensive touring allowed them to continue appearing at reasonably sized venues, especially across the USA, and in 1987 they had the distinction of becoming the first western heavy metal group to perform in Moscow. Inevitably, there were more personnel changes with the new additions of Bernie Shaw (vocals) and Phil Lanzon (keyboards), both formerly of Grand Prix. The band continues to please itself and its fans, relishing in its longevity, and proving wrong the American critic who once wrote of them: 'If this group makes it, I'll have to commit suicide'.
Albums: *Very 'eavy, Very 'umble* aka *Uriah Heep* (USA) (Bronze 1970), *Salisbury* (Bronze 1971), *Look At Yourself* (Bronze 1971), *Demons And Wizards* (Bronze 1972), *The Magician's Birthday* (Bronze 1972), *Uriah Heep Live* (Bronze 1973), *Sweet Freedom* (Bronze 1973), *Wonderworld* (Bronze 1974), *Return To Fantasy* (Bronze 1975), *High And Mighty* (Bronze 1976), *Firefly* (Bronze 1977), *Innocent Victim* (Bronze 1978), *Fallen Angel* (Bronze 1978), *Conquest* (Bronze 1980), *Abnominog* (Bronze 1982), *Head First* (Bronze 1983), *Equator* (Bronze 1985), *Live In Europe* (Raw Power 1987), *Live At Shepperton '74* (Castle 1988), *Live In Moscow* (Bronze 1988), *Raging Silence* (Legacy 1989), *Still 'eavy, Still Proud* (Legacy 1990), *Different World* (Legacy 1991). Compilations: *The Best Of Uriah Heep* (Bronze 1976), *Anthology* (Raw Power 1986), *The Collection* (Castle 1988, double album), *The Uriah Heep Story* (EMI 1990), *Rarities From The Bronze Age* (Sequel 1991), *CD Box Set* (Castle 1992). Videos: *Easy Livin'* (1988), *Live Legends* (1990), *Gypsy* (1990), *Raging Through The Silence - Live At The Astoria* (1990).

V

Vai, Steve

b. 6 June 1960, Long Island, New York, USA. Vai began his musical career at the age of 13, forming his first rock band, Rayge, while still at school. At this time he was tutored by Joe Satriani, who was to have a profound effect on his style for years to come. He studied jazz and classical music at the Berklee College Of Music in Boston, Massachusetts, before relocating to Los Angeles, California, in 1979. He was recruited by Frank Zappa as the lead guitarist in his backing band, while he was still only 18 years old. By 1984 he had built his own recording studio and had begun experimenting with the fusion of jazz, rock and classical music. These pieces were eventually released as *Flex-able*, and were heavily influenced by Zappa's off-beat and unpredictable style. In 1985 Vai replaced Yngwie Malmsteen in Alcatrazz, then moved on to even greater success with Dave Lee Roth and later Whitesnake. *Passion And Warfare*, released in 1990, was the album that brought Vai international recognition as a solo performer. It welded together jazz, rock, funk, classical and metal nuances within a melodic instrumental framework. It climbed to number 18 on the *Billboard* album chart, earning a gold disc in the process.
Albums: *Flex-able* (Relativity 1984), *Flex-able Leftovers* (Relativity 1984), *Passion And Warfare* (Relativity 1990). As Vai: *Sex & Religion* (Relativity 1993).

Vain

This San Francisco Bay Area band was formed in 1985 by frontman/songwriter (and Death Angel producer) Davy Vain, with James Scott (lead guitar), Danny West (rhythm guitar), Ashley Mitchell (bass), and Tom Rickard (drums). Early shows with Poison and Guns N'Roses, before either was a major act, and a series of impressive demos, brought press interest before a deal with Island Records materialized. *No Respect* was a superb debut crammed with atmospheric driving metal which belied the band's over-the-top glam image, enjoying its own particular ambience due to the live-in-the-studio recording technique. While the lyrics were largely sexually orientated, Davy Vain eschewed the usual glam perspective by drawing inspiration from his own relationships. *No Respect* and attendant single, 'Beat

The Bullet', did well, particularly in the UK, where Vain toured triumphantly with Skid Row. However, the band ran into problems when *All Those Strangers* was rejected after a management/ownership change at Island, and Vain were dropped. Davy Vain, Scott and Mitchell worked briefly with ex-Guns N'Roses drummer Steven Adler in Road Crew, which fell apart during Adler's divorce and litigation with his old band, before re-forming Vain with West and ex-Kill City Dragons' drummer Danny Fury, making an impressive return with *Move On It*.

Albums: *No Respect* (Island 1989), *Move On It* (Heavy Metal 1993).

Van Halen

The origins of this, one of America's most successful heavy metal bands, date back to Pasadena, California, in 1973. Edward (Eddie) Van Halen (b. 26 January 1957, Nijmegen, Netherlands; guitar/keyboards), Alex Van Halen (b. 8 May 1955, Nijmegen, Netherlands; drums) and Michael Anthony (b. 20 June 1955, Chicago, Illinois, USA; bass) who were members of the Broken Combs, persuaded vocalist Dave Lee Roth (b. 10 October 1955, Bloomington, Indianapolis, USA) to leave the Real Ball Jets and become a member. After he consented they changed their name to Mammoth. Specializing in a mixture of 60s and 70s covers plus hard rock originals, they toured the bar and club circuit of Los Angeles, virtually non-stop, during the mid-70s. Their first break came when Gene Simmons (bassist of Kiss) saw one of their club gigs. He was amazed by the energy they generated and the flamboyance of their lead singer. Simmons produced a Mammoth demo, but surprisingly it was refused by many major labels in the USA. It was then discovered that the name Mammoth was already registered, so they would have to find an alternative. After considering Rat Salade, they opted for Roth's suggestion of simply Van Halen. On the strength of Simmons' recommendation, producer Ted Templeman checked out the band, was duly impressed and convinced Warner Brothers Records to sign them. With Templeman at the production desk, Van Halen entered the studio and recorded their self-titled debut in 1978. The album was released to widespread critical acclaim and compared with Montrose's debut in 1973. It featured a unique fusion of energy, sophistication and virtuosity through Eddie Van Halen's extraordinary guitar lines and Roth's self-assured vocal style. Within 12 months it had sold two million units, peaking at number 19 in the *Billboard* chart. Eddie Van Halen was named as Best New Guitarist Of The Year in 1978, by *Guitar Player* magazine. The follow-up, simply titled *Van Halen II*, kept to the same formula and was equally successful. Roth's stage antics became even more sensational - he was the supreme showman, combining theatrical stunts with a stunning voice to entertaining effect. *Women And Children First* saw the band start to explore more musical avenues and experiment with the use of synthesizers. This came to full fruition on *Fair Warning* which was a marked departure from earlier releases. *Diver Down* was the band's weakest album, with the cover versions of 60s standards being the strongest tracks. Nevertheless, the band could do no wrong in the eyes of their fans and the album, as had all their previous releases, went platinum. With *1984*, released on New Year's day of that year, the band returned to form. Nine original tracks re-affirmed their position as the leading exponents of heavy duty melodic metal infused with a pop-sensibility. Spearheaded by 'Jump', a *Billboard* number 1 hit single, the album lodged at number 2 in the US chart for a full five weeks during its one year residency. Eddie Van Halen was also a guest on Michael Jackson's 'Beat It' in the same year. This was easily his most high profile solo outing, though his other select engagements outside Van Halen the band have included work with Private Life and former Toto member Steve Lukather. Roth upset the applecart by quitting in 1985 to concentrate on his solo career, and ex-Montrose vocalist Sammy Hagar (b. 13 October 1947, Monterey, California, USA) eventually filled the vacancy. Retaining the Van Halen name, against record company pressure to change it, the new line-up released *5150* in June 1986. The album name was derived from the police code for the criminally insane, as well as the name of Eddie Van Halen's recording studio. The lead off single, 'Why Can't This Be Love', reached number 3 in the *Billboard* chart, while the album became their first number 1 and their biggest seller to-date. *OU812* was a disappointment in creative terms. The songs were formularized and lacked real direction, but the album became the band's second consecutive number 1 in less than two years. *For Unlawful Carnal Knowledge*, written as the acronym F.U.C.K., stirred up some controversy at the time of release. However, the music on the album transcended the juvenile humour of the title, being an immaculate collection of gritty and uncompromising rockers. The band had defined their identity anew and rode into the 90s on a new creative wave - needless to say, platinum status was attained yet again. A live album prefigured the release of the next studio set, *Balance*, with Van Halen's popularity seemingly impervious to the ravages of time or fashion.

Albums: *Van Halen* (Warners 1978), *Van Halen II* (Warners 1979), *Women And Children First* (Warners 1980), *Fair Warning* (Warners 1981), *Diver Down* (Warners 1982), *1984 (MCMLXXXIV)* (Warners 1984), *5150* (Warners 1986), *OU812* (Warners 1988), *For Unlawful Carnal Knowledge* (Warners 1991), *Live: Right Here, Right Now* (Warners 1993), *Balance* (Warners 1995).
Video: *Live Without A Net* (1987).
Further reading: *Van Halen*, Michelle Craven.

Vandenberg

This Dutch hard rock act were a vehicle for the talents of Adrian Vandenberg (b. 31 January 1954, Holland), formed by the experienced guitarist after the collapse of his previous band, Teaser, and an unsuccessful spell rehearsing with Thin Lizzy. The group, completed by Bert Heerink (vocals), Dick Kemper (bass; ex-Turbo) and Jos Zoomer (drums), quickly signed to Atlantic Records on the strength of an impressive demo, enabling Vandenberg to give up the session work and super-realist art which had financially supported him. The self-produced *Vandenberg* had a heavy sound reminiscent of the Scorpions and Judas Priest, and contained sparkling performances from Vandenberg and Zoomer. The former's songwriting and guitar-playing, compared at the time to Michael Schenker, interested David Coverdale, who twice asked the guitarist to join Whitesnake. However, with the album and 'Burning Heart' single doing well in the USA, Vandenberg declined. *Heading For A Storm* benefited from the band's wider experience, with Heerink particularly improved, but failed to maintain the previous momentum of US success, despite a tour supporting Kiss. *Alibi*, however, saw the band regain much of the lost ground with a better production and more fiery fretwork from Vandenberg, but the departure of Heerink the following year for Picture signalled a downward slide for the band, which dissolved in 1987 when Vandenberg finally accepted a further offer from the persistent Coverdale.
Albums: *Vandenberg* (Atco 1982), *Heading For A Storm* (Atco 1984), *Alibi* (Atco 1985).

Vardis

Taking their central influence from mid-70s Status Quo and adding heavier guitar, *Fireball XL5* fan Steve Zodiac formed Quo Vardis in his home town of Wakefield, England, in 1978, with bassist Alan Selway and drummer Gary Pearson. Zodiac, usually barefoot and bare-chested, with long blonde hair, guitar and screaming vocals, cut the perfect heavy metal stereotype. In 1979, dropping Quo from their name, the group released the *100 M.P.H.* EP, and then set out on tour. By 1980 they had built a major live reputation yet their second single, 'If I Were King', lacked that live aggression. Logo Records remained impressed and signed them up. Realising that performance was their strongest medium, their debut album arose from a live taping. In 1981 they gigged with Hawkwind and released their own version of 'Silver Machine', and an album, *Worlds Insane*, which may be the only heavy metal album ever to feature bagpipes (played by Judd Lander, on a track entitled 'Police Patrol'). This gained them much publicity (appearing naked with bagpipes for photos etc.) while a further tenuous Status Quo link was achieved by having Andy Bown play keyboards on the album. From this point on they remained firm live favourites but falling record sales saw them dropped by Logo. In 1983 Selway quit and Terry Horbury (ex-Dirty Tricks) replaced him and played on their final album. Like most of the New Wave Of British Heavy Metal bands, they eventually faded away rather than burnt out.
Albums: *100 M.P.H.* (Logo 1980), *Worlds Insane* (Logo 1981), *Quo Vardis* (Logo 1982), *The Lion's Share* (Razor 1983), *Vigilante* (Raw Power 1986).

Venom

This influential English black metal band, who were a major influence on thrash pioneers Metallica, Slayer and Possessed, as well as the satanic fraternity, were formed in Newcastle Upon Tyne by Cronos (b. Conrad Lant; bass/vocals), Mantas (b. Geoff Dunn; guitar) and Abaddon (b. Tony Bray; drums). Their debut was the legendary *Welcome To Hell*, a raw collection of brutal songs filled with dark, satanic imagery. *Black Metal* was better in terms of playing and production, and remains Venom's best album, containing the atmospheric 'Buried Alive' amid the more customary speed bursts. *At War With Satan*, a semi-concept album, and numerous singles followed - BBC Radio One DJ Tommy Vance paid £100 to charity when Mike Read span 'Warhead' on his breakfast show for a bet - and Venom played numerous major shows world-wide (club dates were precluded by the nature of Venom's pyrotechnics, which tended to cause structural damage in enclosed spaces), proudly refusing to be anything but headliners. However, the poor *Possessed* and a spate of unofficial live and compilation releases hurt the band, and Mantas left as the *Eine Kleine Nachtmusik* live set emerged. Mike H and Jimi C were recruited for live commitments, and this line-up produced the commendable power metal of *Calm Before The Storm* before Cronos left, taking both guitarists for his Cronos band. Mantas, however, rejoined Abaddon, bringing rhythm guitarist Al Barnes, and the new Venom was completed by ex-Atomkraft bassist/vocalist Tony 'The Demolition Man' Dolan. *Prime Evil* harked back to the early Venom approach, albeit with rather more professionalism, and contained a good cover of Black Sabbath's 'Megalomania', but subsequent releases have yet to emulate these standards. Venom, already the subject of a tribute album, remain among the most important of all heavy metal acts, having originated a style which became a template for much of the music's modern practitioners.

Albums: *Welcome To Hell* (Neat 1981), *Black Metal* (Neat 1982), *At War With Satan* (Neat 1984), *Possessed* (Neat 1985), *Eine Kleine Nachtmusik* (Neat 1985), *Calm Before The Storm* (Filmtrax 1987), *Prime Evil* (Under One Flag 1989), *Tear Your Soul Apart* (Under One Flag 1990), *Temples Of Ice* (Under One Flag 1991), *The Waste Lands* (Under One Flag 1993). Compilations: *The Singles '80 - '86* (Raw Power 1986).

Vicious Rumors

This San Francisco power metal band formed in 1979, making their debut on *US Metal III* after linking with guitar guru Mike Varney. However, by the release of *Soldiers Of The Night*, only one of the original line-up, guitarist Geoff Thorpe, remained, along with bassist Dave Starr, drummer Larry Howe, and vocalist Gary St Pierre. Unable to find a suitable guitar partner, Thorpe drafted in fledgling solo artist Vinnie Moore via Varney, and his blistering guitar solo contributions brought the band considerable attention, although musical differences prevented him from becoming a permanent member, with Terry Montana joining for live work. However, *Digital Dictator* saw the line-up stabilize with the addition of guitarist Mark McGee and vocalist Carl Albert in place of Montana and St Pierre respectively, and the new guitar partnership gelled superbly to produce a more song-based record. The band duly signed a major deal, producing two albums of high quality power metal in *Vicious Rumors* and *Welcome To The Ball*, built on excellent musicianship and Thorpe-McGee guitar interplay, which the band reproduced easily on stage. However, the material lacked the commercial edge to cross over into the mainstream and the band were dropped, although they maintained their popularity in Japan, and returned to independent territory for the Queensrÿche-influenced *Word Of Mouth*.

Albums: *Soldiers Of The Night* (Roadrunner 1986), *Digital Dictator* (Roadrunner 1988), *Vicious Rumors* (Atlantic 1990), *Welcome To The Ball* (Atlantic 1991), *Word Of Mouth* (SPV 1994).

Vincent, Vinnie

b. Vinnie Cusano. Vincent began his musical career as guitar/vocalist in the melodic rock band Treasure in 1977. In 1982 he accepted the offer to join Kiss and contributed to *Creatures Of The Night* and *Lick It Up*, the latter featuring the band without make-up on the cover for the first time. After two years with Kiss, Vincent left to form the autonomous Vinnie Vincent Invasion. Recruiting Robert Fleischman (ex-Journey; vocals), Dana Strum (ex-Ozzy Osbourne group; bass) and Bobby Rock (drums), they secured a deal with Chrysalis Records in 1985. Their self-titled debut album, released the following year, was a critical success. Fleischman was replaced by Mark Slaughter immediately after the album was released, and the cohesion of the band was lost. *All Systems Go* followed a similar pattern to its predecessor, but was not widely purchased by metal fans. Frustrated by the lack of success, Slaughter and Strum left to form Slaughter. Vincent was dropped by Chrysalis, but in 1990 he teamed up with Fleischman again to work on a solo project.

Albums: *Vinnie Vincent Invasion* (Chrysalis 1986), *All Systems Go* (Chrysalis 1988).

Violence

This Bay Area thrash band (also known as Vio-lence due to their logo) formed as Death Penalty in San Francisco in 1985, with a line-up of guitarists Phil Demmel and Troy Fua, Eddie Billy (bass), Perry Strickland (drums) and vocalist Jerry Burr, who was replaced in 1986 by Sean Killian; Robb Flynn and Deen Dell had replaced Fua and Billy respectively before Violence signed a one-album deal with Mechanic. *Eternal Nightmare* was typically riff-heavy Bay Area thrash, with excellent Demmel-Flynn guitar interplay, but Killian's vocals were an acquired taste, and aggressive marketing which included pre-release demo give-aways and the infamous 'vomit' bag for the 'Eternal Nightmare' single (the 'vomit' was in fact a mixture of vegetable soup and vinegar) produced only moderate sales. *Oppressing The Masses* was an impressive effort, but was delayed as Atlantic Records were unwilling to distribute the album due to Killian's lyrics for 'Torture Tactics', inspired by a horrifying documentary on the use of torture as a political weapon by oppressive regimes around the world; the offending track was removed and later released on an independent EP. Violence struggled to broaden their appeal, and after the tired-sounding *Nothing To Gain*, the band faded, only for Flynn to emerge to almost instantaneous success with Machine Head.

Albums: *Eternal Nightmare* (Mechanic 1988), *Oppressing The Masses* (Megaforce 1990), *Nothing To Gain* (Bleeding Hearts 1993).

Vixen (USA)

This glossy, female US rock quartet was put together in 1986 by former Madam X drummer Roxy Petrucci. The line-up initially featured Steve Vai's wife Pia Koko on bass, but she was succeeded by Share Pederson before signing to EMI Records. With Janet Gardner handling vocals and Jan Kuehnemund on guitar, the band had a wealth of musical ability and a strong visual image. Their debut album included much material by outside writers, notably Richard Marx and Jeff Paris. *Rev It Up* was virtually self-penned and it launched the band in the USA. Marketed as the female equivalent of Bon Jovi, they specialised in four-minute pop-rock anthems and the occasional obligatory power-ballad, with memorable choruses including 'Cryin'' and 'How Much Love', plus the Marx-composed epic 'Edge Of A Broken Heart'. Petrucci would later work with Lorraine Lewis (ex-Femme Fatale) in a new all-female outfit. Not to be confused with the Yorkshire, England-based Vixen.

Albums: *Vixen* (EMI 1988), *Rev It Up* (EMI 1990).

Voivod

Formed in Canada in the early 80s, Voivod consisted of Denis Belanger (vocals), Denis D'Amour (guitar), Jean-Yves Theriault (bass) and Michel Langevin (drums). The release of their first album made them one of the first thrash metal bands to make a name for themselves world-wide. The sound of this debut was highly unconventional, with an almost *avant garde* feel at times. A second album continued in this tradition with noisy, neo-industrial elements, and helped them become popular in metal underground circles. Progression was evident on *Killing Technology* which showcased improved musicianship and advanced lyrical content. However, it was the release of *Dimension Hatross* that really saw Voivod assume the role of pioneers in the metal firmament. Leaving behind much of their thrash roots, there was now much more to their sound than that original basic attack, and reviewers, though perplexed, generally agreed that new frontiers were being explored. This trend continued on *Nothingface,* which contained little that could be labelled thrash metal, and *Angel Rat,* which also saw the departure of Jean-Yves Theriault. More than ever influences such as progressive rock were taking hold of song construction and twisting the band's narratives into new and occasionally brilliant shapes. The strength of their ideas and the depth of their musical skills and interpretation has helped them grow steadily and transcend thrash roots while still retaining a strong fan base right across the metal spectrum.

Albums: *War And Pain* (Roadrunner 1984), *RRROOOAAARRR* (Noise 1986), *Killing Technology* (Noise 1987), *Dimension Hatross* (Noise 1988), *Nothingface* (MCA 1989), *Angel Rat* (MCA 1991), *The Outer Limits* (MCA 1993). Compilation: *The Best Of* (MCA 1993).

W

Waite, John

b. 4 July 1955, Lancaster, Lancashire, England. Waite is a singer, bassist and occasional harmonica player who has found greater fame and fortune in the USA than in his native land. A former art student, he began playing in bands in the late 60s and in 1976 formed the Babys with Mike Corby (b. 3 July 1955, England), Tony Brock (b. 31 March 1954, Bournemouth, Dorset, England) and Walter Stocker (b. 17 March 1954, London, England). They were signed to Chrysalis on the strength of a video demo directed by Mike Mansfield - a rather unique sales pitch at the time, but their brand of rock had become unfashionable in the UK and the Babys relocated to the USA where their career flourished. Corby was replaced by Ricky Phillips in 1977 and Jonathan Cain (later of Journey) joined the following year. The Babys split in 1981 after five albums and Waite embarked on a solo career. His debut single, 'Change', was not a chart hit and he had to wait until 'Missing You' was released from his second album for a breakthrough. In the UK the record made a respectable number 9 but in the US it went to the top. Waite formed the No Brakes band, joined by former David Bowie guitarist Earl Slick, to promote the new album, but Waite did not scale the same heights again. Instead he formed the ill-fated Bad English in 1989, before resuming his solo career in the mid-90s.

Albums: *Ignition* (Chrysalis 1982), *No Brakes* (EMI America 1984), *Mask Of Smiles* (Capitol 1985), *Rovers Return* (EMI America 1987), *The Essential* (EMI America 1992), *Temple Bar* (Imago 1995).

Warrant

Warfare

Taking their cue from Venom and Motörhead, this three-piece band were formed in Newcastle in 1984 by former Angelic Upstarts drummer Paul Evo, who also took on vocal duties, guitarist Gunner and bassist Falken. With Algy Ward (Saints/Damned/Tank) at the production helm they recorded an album for Neat Records and put together an excellent set of punk/metal standards. They also recorded one track with their friends, Venom, entitled 'Rose Petals Fall From Her Face', one of the world's most obnoxious songs (the album which housed it ran under the banner *Pure Filth*). Their next recording was a 12-inch single, a wickedly satirical version of Frankie Goes To Hollywood's 'Two Tribes', which brought them to public attention and even secured national airplay. In 1985 they set off on a tour of Europe and enhanced their anarchic image with wild live performances. The only new recording came as another 12-inch single, the *Total Death* EP, which contained wholesome numbers like 'Rape', Destroy' and 'Metal Anarchy'. The latter gave them a title for their second album, produced by Lemmy, which also featured a guest appearance from fellow Motörhead man Wurzel on guitar. They continued in the same vein for 1987's *Mayhem Fuckin' Mayhem*, but soon after release Falken left to be replaced by Zlaughter. The following year's *Conflict Of Hatred* had some surprise guests with Mart Craggs (Lindisfarne) on saxophone and Irene Hume (Prelude) joining the more predictable supporting cast, which included an appearance from Mantas (Venom). They resurfaced in 1990, announcing their intention to record a tribute album to Hammer Horror Films' 49th birthday celebration. An ambitious and ultimately unsuccessful project, this featured many samples of classic Hammer films. After one big promotional concert they were faced with a barrage of press criticisms and announced that they would no longer perform live, stating as an epitaph: 'If our fans want to see us they will have to buy a video'. Since then they have remained largely inactive.
Albums: *Pure Filth* (Neat 1984), *Metal Anarchy* (Neat 1986), *Mayhem Fuckin' Mayhem* (Neat 1987), *Conflict Of Hatred* (Neat 1988), *Hammer Horror* (Hammer Film Music/FM Revolver 1990).
Video: *A Concept Of Hatred* (1988).

Warlock

After two years of constant gigging, the German band Warlock: Doro (b. Dorothee Pesch, 3 June 1964, Dusseldorf, Germany; vocals), Peter Szigeti (guitar), Rudy Graf (guitar), Frank Rittel (bass) and Michael Eurich (drums), finally released an album. Signed to the independent Mausoleum label, they issued *Burning The Witches*, which boasted a sound typical of German bands like the Scorpions and Accept, but with the vocals of Doro sounding strangely like Ronnie James Dio. The album, and the presence of their striking blonde-haired vocalist got them noticed in the rest of the world and they were signed by Vertigo Records, who released *Hellbound* a year later. By 1986 the emphasis on the band was focused mainly on Pesch. Graft left to be replaced by Niko Arvantis and the next single, 'You Hurt My Soul', was withdrawn (the tracks turned up later on a 12-inch EP). *True As Steel* suffered from over-production and Americanization. Pesch then re-located the band to New York where they dissolved. A new line-up, with Eurich the only surviving member, added Tommy Bolan (guitar), Tommy Henriksen (bass) and, eventually, a re-hired Arvantis. The resulting album, *Triumph And Agony*, was definitely the latter, and again the band split. 1989's *Force Majeure*, credited to Doro And Warlock, was essentially a solo effort. Bobby Rondinelli, formerly of Rainbow, played drums on that set. A year later Warlock were confined to history as Pesch fully adopted the American sound and pushed herself forward as a new Lee Aaron or Lita Ford. Her first solo album was produced by Gene Simmons (Kiss), since when her record sales have fallen in line with public indifference.
Albums: *Burning The Witches* (Mausoleum 1984), *Hellbound* (Vertigo 1985), *True As Steel* (Vertigo 1986), *Triumph And Agony* (Vertigo 1987). As Doro and Warlock: *Force Majeure* (Vertigo 1989).
Video: *Metal Racer* (1990).

Warrant

A product of the late 80s Los Angeles club scene, Warrant comprised John 'Jani' Lane (b. 1 February 1964, Akron, Ohio, USA; vocals), guitarists Erik Turner (b. 31 March 1964, Omaha, Nebraska, USA) and Joey Allen (b. 23 June 1964, Fort Wayne, Indiana, USA), Jerry Dixon (b. 15 September 1967, Pasadena, California, USA; bass) and Steven Sweet (b. 29 October 1965, Wadsworth, Ohio, USA; drums). A clever self-promotion campaign and sterling live work turned the band into LA's hottest unsigned outfit, and Columbia Records were quick to step in. *Dirty Rotten Filthy Stinking Rich* was a solid debut, and 'Down Boys', coupled with exhaustive touring made it a hit. However, sales went through the roof as MTV favourite, 'Heaven', rose to number 2 in the US charts. This success, along with that of another ballad, 'Sometimes She Cries', and the band's looks, led to image problems, with Warrant unjustly viewed as a manufactured act in some quarters of the press. The

Warrior Soul

tongue-in-cheek pop metal title-track of *Cherry Pie*, written by Lane in 45 minutes to round off the album, was another enormous hit, but did little to redress the band's credibility problems, although lesser hits 'I Saw Red' and 'Uncle Tom's Cabin' undoubtedly helped. The band's UK debut supporting Dave Lee Roth had little chance to impress the British press, as the dates had to be abandoned when Lane fell and cracked a rib on the first night. *Dog Eat Dog* was a credible attempt at a heavier approach, but during the grunge era it sold dramatically less than either of its multi-million-selling predecessors. Lane went solo, with Columbia reducing both parties to demo deals, and although he later rejoined, Allen and Sweet departed, the latter leaving the music business altogether. Former Kingdom Come/Wild Horses (US) duo Rick Steier and James Kottak, who had worked on Lane's solo project, replaced them respectively.

Albums: *Dirty Rotten Filthy Stinking Rich* (Columbia 1989), *Cherry Pie* (Columbia 1990), *Dog Eat Dog* (Columbia 1992), *Ultraphobic* (CMC International/Music For Nations 1995).

Warrior

Formed in 1982, Los Angeles, California, USA band Warrior occupied a space somewhere between the barbarian machismo of Manowar and the grandiose pomp rock of Queen. The line-up originally comprised Parramore McCarty (vocals), Tommy Asakawa (guitar), Joe Floyd (guitar), Rick Bennett (bass/keyboards) and Liam Jason (drums). The band spent time playing the local clubs and refining their style before recording a three-track demo which led to sold-out local shows and record deals with MCA in the US and 10 Records in Europe. They subsequently endured considerable technical problems during the recording of *Fighting For The Earth* and lost both Bennett and Jason following the sessions, with Bruce Turgon (bass; ex-Black Sheep) and Jimmy Volpe (drums) replacing them. It was a reasonable debut, built on a dense, rhythmic guitar barrage and thunderous drums overlaid by McCarty's near-operatic vocals. Lyrics included some entertaining if daft sub-Nietzchean fantasy scenarios. Similarities to Judas Priest were obvious, although Warrior tended to avoid dual lead guitar work, and the band's stage image, although leather-clad, was in a futuristic armour style befitting their name. However, a bemused public showed little interest and the rock press, convinced they were being sold an industry-hyped act, treated them with disdain. In 1986 the band split leaving the members to join other acts (McCarty joined Steve Steven's Atomic Playboys, while Turgon found himself a job with Shadow King).

Album: *Fighting For The Earth* (MCA 1985).

Warrior Soul

This psychotic art-rock quartet from New York is the brainchild of poetry-reading, one-time video DJ and L7 (the Detroit, rather than all-female Los Angeles version) drummer Kory Clarke. With the help of Pete McClanahan (bass), John Ricco (guitar) and Paul Ferguson (drums), *Last Decade, Dead Century* was released in 1990, with Clarke leading from the front with vocals and lyrics which took few prisoners: 'At that time everybody was hooked on Hollywood and the whole vibe of 80s Republican morality. But all that lame ass shit had no content'. Influences as diverse as the Doors, Metallica, the Stooges and Joy Division were combined to produce a dark, intense, angst-ridden debut album. Lyrically it criticised the establishment's inability to solve contemporary social problems, with references to political and police corruption, the homeless and narcotics. Mark Evans took over as drummer on *Drugs, God And The New Republic*, which built on previous themes, but increased the musical intensity of their delivery, honed on US supports to Queensrÿche, whose philosophical angle, if not musical, they echoed. The message for *Salutations From The Ghetto Nation* was succinct if not polite: 'I don't think you have to be particularly intelligent to understand Fuck The Government!' These works received considerable critical acclaim, but it would be *Chill Pill* and *Space Age Playboys* which converted this into album sales. If anything *Chill Pill* was more resentful and hate-filled than previous offerings, but by *Space Age Playboys* the band looked to have exhausted this avenue. What listeners received instead was an 'up' record, which maintained Clarke's political allegiances, but allied them to a collage of images and events which eschewed earlier didacticism.

Albums: *Last Decade, Dead Century* (Geffen 1990), *Drugs, God And The New Republic* (Geffen 1991), *Salutations From The Ghetto Nation* (Geffen 1992), *Chill Pill* (Geffen 1993), *Space Age Playboys* (Music For Nations 1994).

W.A.S.P.

This theatrical shock-rock troupe emerged from the early 80s Los Angeles club scene with a name which was allegedly an acronym for We Are Sexual Perverts (as opposed to the traditional demographic nomenclature of White Anglo Saxon Protestant). Outrageous live performances included throwing raw meat into the audience and the whipping of a naked woman tied to a 'torture rack' as a backdrop to a primitive metal attack. The band, led by bassist/vocalist Blackie Lawless (b. 4 September 1956) with guitarists Chris Holmes (b. 23 June 1961) and Randy Piper and drummer Tony Richards, were snapped up by Capitol, who then refused to release their debut single, the infamous 'Animal (Fuck Like A Beast)', on legal advice. It was subsequently licensed to independent labels. *W.A.S.P.* was an adequate basic metal debut, although it lacked 'Animal', while *The Last Command* with new drummer Stephen Riley consolidated W.A.S.P.'s status with a more refined approach, producing the excellent 'Wild Child' and 'Blind In Texas'. W.A.S.P. became a major US concert draw, albeit with a stageshow much toned down from the early days. *Inside The Electric Circus* continued in this vein, and saw the debut of bassist Johnny Rod (ex-King Kobra), with Lawless replacing Piper on rhythm guitar, while live shows saw Lawless' trademark buzzsaw-bladed codpiece replaced by a remarkable flame-throwing version. *Live...In The Raw* was a decent live set, but once again lacked 'Animal', which remained the centrepiece of W.A.S.P.'s repertoire. That song, and the band's outrageous approach, made them a constant target for the PMRC, whom Lawless successfully sued for unauthorised use of copyrighted material. As Lawless became a tireless free speech campaigner, he moved the band towards a serious stance on *The Headless Children*, with Quiet Riot drummer Frankie Banali replacing the L.A. Guns-bound Riley. The socio-political and anti-drug commentary of what was W.A.S.P.'s best album was backed by vivid imagery in the live setting, but Holmes departed after the tour, the split catalysed by his drunken appearance in *The Decline And Fall Of Western Civilisation Part II: The Metal Years*. Lawless used session musicians to record *The Crimson Idol*, a Who-influenced concept effort, and toured with Rod, Doug Blair (guitar) and Stet Howland (drums), but went solo after compiling the *First Blood...Last Cuts* retrospective.

Albums: *W.A.S.P.* (Capitol 1984), *The Last Command* (Capitol 1985), *Inside The Electric Circus* (Capitol 1986), *Live...In The Raw* (Capitol 1987), *The Headless Children* (Capitol 1989), *The Crimson Idol* (Parlophone 1992). Compilation: *First Blood...Last*

W.A.S.P.

Cuts (Capitol 1993).
Videos: *Live At The Lyceum* (1985), *W.A.S.P. Videos: In The Raw* (1988).

Watchtower

This experimental four-piece Texan outfit married the power of Metallica with the intricate and sophisticated arrangements of Rush, via the musicianship of Alan Tecchio (vocals), Ron Jarzombek (guitars), Doug Keyser (bass) and Rick Colaluca (drums). Watchtower's playing was of a high order and their songs contained multiple time-changes, including Jarzombek's exemplary performances on lead, acoustic and even reverse-taping guitar. To date, the group's brand of electro-charged techno-thrash has yet to earn them the widespread attention that is due them.
Albums: *Watchtower* (Noise 1988), *Control And Resistance* (Noise 1989).

Waysted

Waysted were formed in 1982 by ex-UFO bassist Pete Way after he failed to get Fastway off the ground with 'Fast' Eddie Clarke. He subsequently set about putting this band together in America, where he was helping Ozzy Osbourne out, and soon found Ronnie Kayfield (ex-Heartbreakers), who was teaching guitar at the time. Returning to the UK, he further enlisted Frank Noon (Def Leppard/Next Band) on drums, UFO guitarist/keyboard player Paul Raymond and vocalist Ian 'Fin' Muir (ex-Flying Squad). Chrysalis Records (home to UFO) showed interest and signed them to a one album deal. The resulting *Vices* featured several excellent compositions including 'Toy With The Passion', 'Love Loaded' and a cover of Jefferson Airplane's 'Somebody To Love'. However, the line-up instabilities which plagued the band began when Raymond was fired on the eve of a UK tour supporting Dio. Guitarist Barry Benedetta (himself about to audition for UFO) was added before a famously riotous US tour with Ozzy and Mötley Crüe, but he, old friend Kayfield and Noon were all sacked afterwards as Waysted and Chrysalis parted company. Ex-Jess Cox guitarist Neil Shepherd barely lasted beyond the recording of *Waysted*, which featured ex-UFO drummer Andy Parker, before he was in turn replaced by another UFO refugee, Paul Chapman, as Waysted toured the UK with Iron Maiden. The album was produced by ex-Ten Years After member Leo Lyons and also featured contributions from former Angelic Upstarts drummer Decca Wade. *The Good, The Bad, The Waysted* proved to be the band's best album as Way and Chapman blended perfectly to provide a weightier blues-rock sound which suited Fin's smoky vocals, but line-up changes continued with the addition of ex-Fastway drummer Jerry Shirley and temporary keyboard/guitar player Jimmy DiLella, formerly with Chapman's DOA band. Any hopes of stability vanished when Fin was replaced by ex-DOA vocalist Danny Vaughn and Johnny DiTeodora joined on drums, but the band gained a new deal with Parlophone for *Save Your Prayers*, which saw Waysted move towards classic UFO in style, with Vaughn's vocals smoothing out the rough edges of his predecessor. The revitalised Waysted embarked on a UK and European tour supporting Status Quo and US tour with Iron Maiden, but Chapman subsequently departed and was replaced by 17-year old American Erik Gamans, who displayed a startling talent on his debut live shows. However, Vaughn quit, forming Tyketto, and the clearly declining band returned to the UK, recording demos with Martin Chaisson (b. Martin Smith) with guest vocals from the Quireboys' Spike Gray before recruiting ex-Tygers Of Pan Tang vocalist Jon Deverill, but the band finally split in late 1987. Way rejoined Phil Mogg in a revamped UFO, DiTeodora joined Britny Fox, and Gamans reappeared in Cold Sweat.

Albums: *Vices* (Chrysalis 1983), *Waysted* (Music For Nations 1984, mini-album), *The Good, The Band And The Waysted* (Music For Nations 1985), *Save Your Prayers* (Parlophone 1986). Compilation: *Completely Waysted* (Raw Power 1985).

Weapon

This sadly neglected metal act were formed in March 1980 by guitarist Jeff Summers (ex-Snatch) and vocalist Danny Hynes, along with Bruce Bisland on drums (ex-Lip Service) and bassist Barry 'Baz' Downes (ex-Inner City Unit, Snatch). After only a handful of gigs they were spotted by 'Fast' Eddie Clarke from Motörhead, who offered them the support slot on their Ace Up Your Sleeve tour. Weapon accepted and rushed into the studio to record two tracks, 'It's A Mad Mad World' and 'Set The Stage Alight', to be released as a single through Virgin. After the tour they recorded enough demos for an album but found no record company interest. Live, however, they excelled, with strong material such as 'Take It Away' and 'Remote Control'. In 1981 Bisland left and was replaced by Jon Phillips who had been playing with Megaton, and the line-up was also boosted by ex-Iron Maiden/Praying Mantis guitarist Bob Angelo. After a series of rehearsals at a studio in Lotts Road they set out on tour but became dogged

by problems which came to a head at the Granary in Bristol where the audience could see the group in its death throes as the set progressed. Summers joined Bisland with ex-More members in Wildfire, Angelo returned to the club circuit with High Roller and later Nitro Blues, while Hynes surfaced in 1986 with ex-Sweet members in Paddy Goes To Hollyhead. In 1986 Summers and Bisland joined Statetrooper before later going to Japan as part of the British All Stars/Praying Mantis supergroup.

West, Leslie

b. 1945, Queens, New York, USA. West, who from an early age suffered from a glandular disorder which affected his weight, began his rock 'n' roll career as a member of the Vagrants, a mid-60s hard rock grouping who released several singles to little commercial recognition. In 1969 he formed Mountain with bass player Felix Pappalardi. Together they would go on to create some of the most timeless power blues compositions of the period, notably 'Mississippi Queen', drawn from their first album, *Mountain Climbing*. Their third gig was in front of nearly half a million people at Woodstock, and they went on to release five albums (two of which went gold). After Pappalardi's defection in 1971, West put together a three-piece with Jack Bruce and Mountain's Corky Laing on drums. Mountain were reformed for two further albums in 1973 following Bruce's departure, before West took the hint and turned solo (having released his first such set in 1969, produced by Pappalardi, which served as a catalyst to the formation of Mountain). *Theme From An Imaginary Western* would see him reunite with Bruce, *The Leslie West Band* paired him with Mick Jones of Foreigner, while *Alligator* saw him work with bassist Stanley Clarke and vocalist Johnette Napoltiano of Concrete Blonde. He also appeared on two IRS compilations of guitar virtuosos, *Guitar Speak* and *Night Of The Guitars* (also a tour). He would go on to work as musical director with DJ Howard Stern, and through him was introduced to comedian Sam Kinison (leading to West arranging the latter's version of 'Wild Thing'). After appearing on four cuts on Billy Joel's *River Of Dreams*, West would also make his screen bow in *The Money Pit*, as the lead singer of a cross-dressing rock band, Lana And The Cheap Girls. However, he returned to the studio and the rock scene with his first album in over four years, *Dodgin' The Dirt*, for Roadrunner Records. With the backing of journeymen Steve Hunter (guitar; ex-Lou Reed, Peter Gabriel), Kevin Neal (drums; ex-Pat Travers) and Randy Coven (bass), it proved an honest attempt to re-establish himself within what he considered to be

Widowmaker (USA)

his natural market.

Albums: *Leslie West Mountain* (Bell 1969), *The Great Fatsby* (RCA 1975), *The Leslie West Band* (RCA 1976), *Theme From An Imaginary Western* (Passport 1988), *Alligator* (IRS 1989), *Dodgin' The Dirt* (Roadrunner 1993).

White Lion

This US group was formed in Brooklyn, New York, during 1983, by Mike Tramp (lead vocals; ex-Mabel) and Vito Bratta (guitar; ex-Dreamer). After a series of false starts, they signed to Elektra Records with Felix Robinson (bass; ex-Angel) and Dave Capozzi (drums) completing the line-up. However, the label were unhappy with the recording of *Fight To Survive* and after refusing to release the album, terminated their contract. RCA-Victor picked up the release option and the album finally surfaced in Japan in 1984. By this stage, James Lomenzo and Gregg D'Angelo had taken over bass and drums, respectively, on a permanent basis. The album did in fact meet with favourable reviews, some critics comparing Mike Tramp to Dave Lee Roth and Vito Bratta to Eddie Van Halen, others likening the songs to those of Europe, Dokken or Journey. Signing to Atlantic

Records, they released *Pride*, which developed their own identity, in particular Mike Tramp's characteristically watery falsetto style. The album catapulted them from obscurity to stardom, climbing to number 11 during its year-long stay on the *Billboard* album chart. It also spawned two US Top 10 hits with 'Wait' and 'When The Children Cry'. *Big Game* was a disappointing follow-up. Nevertheless, it still made the US charts, peaking at number 19. *Mane Attraction* released in 1991, saw the band recapture lost ground over the course of a strong melodic rock collection. Lomenzo and D'Angelo quit due to 'musical differences' shortly after the album's release and were replaced by Tommy 'T-Bone' Caradonna (ex-Alice Cooper; bass) and Jimmy DeGrasso (ex-Y&T; drums).

Albums: *Fight To Survive* (Grand Slamm 1984), *Pride* (Atlantic 1987), *Big Game* (Atlantic 1989), *Mane Attraction* (Atlantic 1991). Compilation: *The Best Of* (Atlantic 1992).

White Spirit

Formed in Hartlepool, England, in 1975 by guitarist Janick Gers and drummer Graeme Crallan, they put together various line-ups before settling in 1979 with

Phil Brady (bass), Malcolm Pearson (keyboards) and Bruce Ruff (vocals). In 1980 they signed to Neat Records, who subsequently released a debut single, 'Backs To The Grind'. This was followed by tours with Iron Maiden and Budgie. MCA were quick to sign them for a second single, 'High Upon High'. A tour with Gillan was planned and Gillan's bassist, John McCoy, produced their album, timed to come out at the same time as the tour. *White Spirit* would, unsurprisingly, offer strong echoes of past bands like Deep Purple. From this point on the group failed to capitalize on their initial success and by 1982 Gers had been invited to replace Bernie Tormé in Gillan. This effectively killed the band off and Ruff also quit. One final attempt to crack the big time offered itself in 1983 with Brian Howe on vocals and Mick Tucker on guitar. This line-up failed to generate any interest and White Spirit joined the large graveyard of the New Wave Of British Heavy Metal. Howe went on to join Bad Company, Tucker joined Tank and Gers later joined Iron Maiden.

Album: *White Spirit* (MCA 1980).

White Zombie

This scuzzy metal band originated in 1985 in New York's Lower East Side, taking their name from a classic horror movie. Led by Rob Straker (later known as Rob Zombie), and female bassist Sean Yseult with drummer Ivan DePlume and guitarist Tom Guay, White Zombie released two albums of primal, noisy and unconventional metal on their own label while they played chaotic shows around local clubs to increasing acclaim from the underground. This eventually helped gain them a deal with Caroline. John Ricci replaced Guay for *Make Them Die Slowly*, adding dynamic lead guitar as the band's more focused approach rid them of the art-noise label thrust upon their earlier albums, with Black Sabbath and Stooges influences becoming more apparent. However, Bill Laswell's production still failed to capture the band's raw onstage power. Musical differences saw Ricci quickly replaced by Jay Yuenger, who made his debut on the *God Of Thunder* EP, a cover of the Kiss classic (rumoured legal action from Gene Simmons over the use of his copyrighted make-up image on the sleeve never materialised). The Andy Wallace production on *La Sexorcisto: Devil Music Vol. 1* finally did White Zombie justice, with Rob Zombie sounding positively demonic as he roared his bizarre stream-of-consciousness lyrics against a monstrous instrumental barrage punctuated by sampled B-movie dialogue. This also proved to be their breakthrough album as White Zombie toured the USA ceaselessly, extending their tours continually as MTV picked up

on 'Thunder Kiss 65' and 'Black Sunshine', with further support coming from cartoon critics *Beavis And Butt-head*. As *La Sexorcisto* took off, Philo replaced DePlume, only to be sacked as the touring finally ended, reinstated, and then replaced by ex-Exodus/Testament drummer John Tempesta as White Zombie returned to the studio.

Albums: *Psycho-Head Blowout* (Silent Explosion 1987, mini-album), *Soul Crusher* (Silent Explosion 1988), *Make Them Die Slowly* (Caroline 1989), *La Sexorcisto: Devil Music Vol. 1* (Geffen 1992).

Whitesnake

This UK-based heavy rock band was led by David Coverdale (b. 21 September 1951, Saltburn, Tyne & Wear, England). The lead vocalist with Deep Purple since 1973, Coverdale left the group in 1976 and recorded two solo albums, *Whitesnake* and *Northwinds*. Shortly afterwards, he formed a touring band from musicians who had played on those records. Entitled David Coverdale's Whitesnake, the group included Micky Moody (guitar), Bernie Marsden (guitar), Brian Johnston (keyboards), Neil Murray (bass) and John Dowle (drums). For much of the late 70s the group toured in the UK, Europe and Japan (the first US tour was in 1980). During this period there were several personnel changes with ex-Deep Purple members Jon Lord and Ian Paice joining on keyboards and drums. Whitesnake's first British hit was 'Fool For Your Loving' (1980), composed by Coverdale, Marsden and Moody, and the double album, *Live in The Heart Of The City* (named after the Bobby Bland song featured on stage by Coverdale) reached the Top 10 the following year. At this point, the illness of Coverdale's daughter caused a hiatus in the group's career and when Whitesnake re-formed in 1982 only Lord and Moody remained from the earlier line-up. The new members were Mel Galley (guitar), ex-Back Door and Alexis Korner bassist Colin Hodgkinson and Cozy Powell (drums). However, this configuration lasted only briefly and by 1984 the long-serving Moody and Lord had left, the latter to join a regenerated Deep Purple. While Coverdale remained the focus of Whitesnake, there were numerous personnel changes in the following years. These had little effect on the band's growing reputation as one of the leading exponents of heavy rock, with unambiguously sexist record sleeves marking out their lyrical and aesthetic territory. Frequent tours finally brought a million-selling album in the USA with 1987's *Whitesnake* and Coverdale's bluesy ballad style brought Top 10 hits with 'Is This Love' and 'Here I Go Again'. They were co-written with ex-Thin Lizzy guitarist John Sykes, a member of Whitesnake from 1983-86. His replacement, Dutch-born Adrian Vandenburg, was co-writer with Coverdale on the band's 1989 album, co-produced by Keith Olsen and Mike Clink. Ex-Dio guitarist Vivian Campbell was also a member of the band in the early 90s. Coverdale joined forces with Jimmy Page for the release of *Coverdale/Page* in early 1993, but when Whitesnake's contract with Geffen Records in the US expired in 1994, it was not renewed.

Albums: *Trouble* (United Artists 1978), *Love Hunter* (United Artists 1979), *Live At Hammersmith* (United Artists 1980), *Ready An' Willing* (United Artists 1980), *Live In The Heart Of The City* (Sunburst 1980), *Come And Get It* (Liberty 1981), *Saints 'N Sinners* (Liberty 1982), *Slide It In* (Liberty 1984), *Whitesnake* (Liberty 1987), *1987* (Liberty 1992), *Slip Of The Tongue* (EMI 1989). Compilations: *Best Of* (EMI 1988), *Greatest Hits* (MCA 1994).

Videos: *Fourplay* (1984), *Whitesnake Live* (1984), *Trilogy* (1988).

Further reading: *Illustrated Biography*, Simon Robinson.

Widowmaker (UK)

A minor 'supergroup' formed in 1975 by ex-Love Affair vocalist Steve Ellis, ex-Spooky Tooth/Mott The Hoople guitarist Luther 'Ariel Bender' Grosvenor, ex-Chicken Shack/Broken Glass bassist Bob Daisley, ex-Skip Bifferty/Lindisfarne drummer Paul Nicholls and ex-Hawkwind/Leo Sayer guitarist Huw Lloyd Langton. They had little trouble getting a record deal, signing to Jet, and soon set up a tour in America where their debut album was a Top 40 hit in 1976. Popular also in the UK, although records failed to chart, they appeared on the *Old Grey Whistle Test*, soon after which Ellis left to be replaced by John Butler, who was at that time fronting his own band. Together they recorded their second and slightly heavier album, *Too Late To Cry*, released in April 1977. It suffered from the media preoccupation with punk, and in July they split up. Daisley went on to work with Ozzy Osbourne, Rainbow and Uriah Heep, while Langton rejoined Hawkwind in November 1979, where he stayed until 1989 when he went solo.

Albums: *Widowmaker* (Jet 1976), *Too Late To Cry* (Jet 1977).

Widowmaker (USA)

Entirely separate from the UK band of similar name, this Widowmaker were formed in 1991 by former Twisted Sister clothes horse/vocalist Dee Snider. Between 1983 and 1987, Twisted Sister sold over 8 million albums, and Snider became one of metal's most distinctive and easily recognised figureheads. Widowmaker sought to blend 90s innovations with 'classic' 80s rock style, Snider bringing along Joe Franco (drums; ex-Good Rats, Leslie West, Doro, Vinny Moore), Al Pitrelli (guitar; ex-Danger Danger, Alice Cooper, Great White, Asia) and Marc Russell (b. London, England; bass; ex-Beki Bondage). As Snider conceded: 'All right, so they're whores, but as the saying goes, it don't matter where they get their appetites, as long as they come home to eat'. Their debut album was released on an independent label before the band signed to CMC International (Music For Nations in the UK). A second set, *Stand By For Pain*, caught the 90s bug for writing about serial killers ('Killing Time'), with other standout tracks like 'Protect And Serve' lambasting corruption in the legal system. Though Snider had hardly been away since the death of Twisted Sister, devising and presenting MTV's *Heavy Metal Mania* (now *Headbanger's Ball*) and hosting *Metal Nation* on radio station WRCN, it was reassuring to have him back as his former fans knew and loved him - fronting a thoroughly rock 'n' roll rock 'n' roll band.

Albums: *Blood And Bullets* (Music For Nations 1991), *Stand By For Pain* (CMC International 1995).

Wild Horses

This melodic hard rock quartet was formed in 1978 by bassist Jimmy Bain (ex-Rainbow) and guitarist Brian Robertson (ex-Thin Lizzy). Deriving their name from a song on the Rolling Stones' *Sticky Fingers*, they enlisted the services of drummer Clive Edwards (ex-Pat Travers) and second guitarist/keyboard player Neil Carter. The line-up never lived up to expectations; Bain's weak vocals did not give the band enough identity, while the material was too derivative of Thin Lizzy and UFO. Live, the band were a different proposition and exuded a raw energy and aggression not evident on their studio work. John Lockton and Dixie Lee (ex-Lone Star) replaced Carter and Edwards for *Stand Your Ground*. This was a marked improvement on their debut, and followed a much more blues-orientated direction. The band finally fell apart in 1981 with Bain going on to work with Ronnie James Dio (in Dio), and Robertson joining Motörhead after a period of session work.

Albums: *Wild Horses* (EMI 1980), *Stand Your Ground* (EMI 1981).

Wildhearts

Following his sacking from the Quireboys and a brief tenure with the Throbs, guitarist/songwriter Ginger

Wildhearts

set about forming the Wildhearts around the nucleus of himself plus ex-Tattooed Love Boys guitarist Chris 'CJ' Jagdhar, with the duo taking on vocal duties after the departure of ex-Torbruk frontman Snake. The line-up stabilized with the recruitment of former Dogs D'Amour drummer Bam and bassist Danny McCormack (ex-Energetic Krusher), and the quartet signed to East West Records in late 1989. Contractual difficulties meant that the Wildhearts' debut EP, *Mondo Akimbo A-Go-Go*, was delayed until early 1992, but the poor production could not obscure the quality of the songs or the band's original style, mixing pop melodies with aggressive, heavy riffing. A Terry Date-remixed version was released as a double-pack with the *Don't Be Happy...Just Worry* EP (later reissued as a single album). This had much greater impact, and the band's following increased as they undertook a succession of support tours. Bam rejoined his old group during this period, with his predecessor Andrew 'Stidi' Stidolph filling the gap. *Earth Vs The Wildhearts* was recorded in a mere seven days, but turned out to be one of the best British rock albums for years, mixing metal, punk and pop into an adrenalized collection of songs, with their commercial appeal tempered only by the liberal use of expletives

in the song-titles. Stidi was ousted shortly afterwards in favour of ex-Radio Moscow drummer Ritch Battersby, and following an acclaimed tour with the Almighty, the band broke into the UK Top 30 with 'Caffeine Bomb'. Subsequent headline dates saw the sound augmented by the keyboards of ex-Grip frontman Willie Dowling, while the summer of 1994 saw guitarist C.J ousted. He would later re-emerge with a new band, Honeycrack, which also featured Dowling. Later that year an exclusive 40 minute mini-album, available only through the Wildhearts' fan club, was released (still featuring CJ on guitar). *Fishing For Luckies* revealed new dimensions to the Wildhearts, stretching even to Pogues influences on 'Geordie In Wonderland', and the commercially available single, 'If Life Is Like A Love Bank I Want An Overdraft' brought a hit, but the band delayed their second album proper until their line-up was restored to a quartet. Auditions for a replacement were held in November, after using Steve Vai guitarist Devin Townsend as a stand-in. With wide acclaim for their live and recorded work, considerable press for their unconventional sense of humour, and a constant flow of impressive new material from Ginger's pen, the Wildhearts still look certain to be one of the biggest rock success stories of the 90s.

Albums: *Earth Vs The Wildhearts* (East West 1993), *Don't Be Happy...Just Worry* (East West 1994, rec. 1992), *Fishing For Luckies* (East West 1994, mini-album).

Wildside

This Los Angeles-based quintet were formed in 1991 by vocalist Drew Hannah and guitarist Brent Wood. With Benny Rhynestone (guitar), Marc Simon (bass) and Jimmy D. (drums) completing the line-up, the band model themselves on the glam-rock tradition embodied by Ratt, Mötley Crüe and Cinderella. Contracted to Capitol Records, *Under The Influence* emerged in July 1992 to a lukewarm reception. Although professionally competent and technically without fault, the material proved to be both derviative and uninspired.

Album: *Under The Influence* (Capitol 1992).

Willard

Named after a character from James Herbert's book, *The Rats*, Willard were formed in Seattle, USA, in 1991, by Johnny Clint (vocals), Mark Spiders (guitar), Steve Wied (drums), Otis P. Otis (guitar) and Darren Peters (bass). They were picked up by Roadracer Records the same year. Subtitled *The Sound Of Fuck!*, their debut album, *Steel Mill*, released in July 1992, was a powerful and uncompromising debut, with influnces ranging from traditional metal sources like Black Sabbath to the more hardcore-derived output of Nirvana and the Henry Rollins Band.

Album: *Steel Mill* (Roadracer 1992).

Winger

This melodic hard rock act was formed by experienced session musicians Kip Winger (bass/vocals) and Paul Taylor (keyboards/guitar) following their work together on Alice Cooper's *Constrictor* tour. Enlisting lead guitarist Reb Beach and drummer Rod Morgenstein (ex-Dixie Dregs), the quartet chose the name Sahara, but were forced to change to Winger at the last moment - the original name still appeared on a corner of the debut sleeve. *Winger* proved to be an immediate success, producing US Top 30 singles in 'Seventeen', 'Madalaine' and 'Headed For A Heartbreak', while the vocalist's rugged good looks turned him into a major sex symbol. This rather worked against the band in press terms, and Winger were never really taken seriously by the UK rock press in particular, despite abilities which kept them in demand for musician-type magazines and a genuinely impressive debut. *In The*

Heart Of The Young consolidated Winger's US success, producing another enormous hit in 'Miles Away', and the band were well-received on their debut European shows, but the heavy touring schedule proved too much for Taylor, who subsequently departed, later working with Steve Perry. The band adopted a heavier approach on the commendable *Pull* to compensate for the lack of keyboards, recruiting a second touring guitarist in John Roth, but were unable to swim against the grunge tide to emulate their earlier successes. After a lengthy US club tour, the band was put on ice.

Albums: *Winger* (Atlantic 1988), *In The Heart Of The Young* (Atlantic 1990), *Pull* (Atlantic 1993).

Witchfinder General

This Midlands-based N.W.O.B.H.M. group are rather better-remembered for two controversial album covers than for any of their actual music. Formed in 1979 by vocalist Zeeb and guitarist Phil Cope, with a name taken from a classic horror film, the initial line-up settled with a rhythm section of Toss McCready (bass) and Steve Kinsell (drums). Their debut single, 'Burning A Sinner' (also jokingly known as 'Burning A Singer'), revealed a primitive, Black Sabbath-influenced doom metal style, and was quickly followed by the *Soviet Invasion* EP, and a track on the *Heavy Metal Heroes* compilation. Saxon producer Peter Hinton was drafted in for *Death Penalty*, recorded in three days with a session drummer - this position remained unstable - and bassist Rod Hawkes replacing the departed Kinsell and McCready. The album showed promise, although it suffered from the rushed recording process. Most attention centred on its sleeve, which featured a mock-sacrifice scene photographed in a graveyard, with a well-known topless model and friend of the band, Joanne Latham, appearing semi-nude. The subsequent publicity reached the UK tabloids, and the band attempted to repeat the formula with *Friends Of Hell*, with the sleeve featuring several semi-naked models daubed with theatrical blood in a similar sacrifice scene, this time photographed in front of a church. This cynical effort succeeded only in losing what little support the band had garnered, and they quickly faded.

Albums: *Death Penalty* (Heavy Metal 1982), *Friends Of Hell* (Heavy Metal 1983).

Witchfynde

This early UK black metal band were formed in the late 70s, and came to prominence with the 'Give 'Em Hell' single, followed by an album of the same name. The quartet of Montalo (guitar), Steve Bridges

Wolfsbane

(vocals), Andro Coulton (bass) and Gra Scoresby (drums) produced a fast and furious brand of Judas Priest and Black Sabbath-influenced metal, mixing heavy riffs with occult lyrics and imagery. *Stagefright*, a live set, followed, but the band were dissatisfied with the level of their record company's support, and took a lengthy break before finding a new label. Witchfynde resurfaced with new members Luther Beltz (vocals) and Pete Surgey (bass) on *Cloak & Dagger*. Although the album was recorded quickly with a low budget, the material again showed genuine quality, and produced the popular 'I'd Rather Go Wild'. However, the long spell of inactivity meant that the band had fallen far behind such early contemporaries as Iron Maiden and Def Leppard, and they were unable to sustain this success without major label backing. A final double set, *Lords Of Sin*, coupled with a live mini-album, *Anthems*, was released before the band disappeared.

Albums: *Give 'Em Hell* (Rondelet 1980), *Stagefright* (Rondelet 1981), *Cloak & Dagger* (Expulsion 1983), *Lords Of Sin/Anthems* (Mausoleum 1985).

Wolfsbane

This UK quartet from Tamworth, Staffordshire, employed a strong biker image to augment their incendiary heavy metal anthems. Featuring Blaze Bayley (vocals), Jase Edwards (guitar), Steve 'Danger' Ellet (drums) and Jeff Hateley (bass), they incorporated elements of Van Halen, Iron Maiden and Zodiac Mindwarp into their own high-energy, and, at times, chaotic style. Picked up by Rick Rubin's Def American label, they released *Live Fast, Die Fast* as an opening philosophical statement. The album failed to match the manic intensity of their live shows and was let down by weak production. Their next two releases saw some development on the songwriting front, with the addition of sci-fi and b-movie imagery, to supplement the well-worn themes of sex, booze and rock 'n' roll. After three albums their style remained loud, aggressive and, to a degree, derivative. 1993 saw them separate both from P Grant Managment and Def American, and by the following year Bayley had quit to replace Bruce Dickinson in Iron Maiden.

Albums: *Live Fast, Die Fast* (Def American 1989), *All Hell's Breaking Loose Down At Little Kathy Wilson's Place* (Def American 1990), *Down Fall The Good Guys* (Def American 1991), *Massive Noise Injection* (Bronze 1993).

World War III

This short-lived American quartet came together when vocalist Mandy Lion and guitarist Tracy G were joined by the former Dio rhythm section of Jimmy Bain (bass) and Vinnie Appice (drums). Their sole, self-titled album, displayed an impressive traditional metal style, with Tracy's G's superb guitar work complemented by a thunderous backing from the Bain/Appice team, although Lion's gruff vocals and a lyrical preoccupation with his own sexual exploits and fantasies tended to detract a little from the overall effect. The album met with limited success, and the band dissolved, with Appice returning briefly to Black Sabbath with Ronnie James Dio before being reunited with Tracy G in a revamped Dio band. Lion later turned up in Jake E Lee's post-Badlands group, Wicked Alliance.

Album: *World War III* (Hollywood 1991).

Wrathchild

Formed in 1980 in Evesham, Worcestershire, England, as a Black Sabbath-influenced band, it was another two years before Wrathchild emerged at the forefront of the new glam rock scene. Original members Rocky Shads (vocals) and Marc Angel (bass) were joined by ex-Medusa personnel Lance Rocket (guitar) and Eddie Starr (drums). They subsequently released an EP on Bullet Records and toured heavily to promote it. By 1983 they had developed a melodramatic live show and perfected their Kiss/Angel influences, whilst retaining an 'English' quality. A year later their hard work paid off with a deal with Heavy Metal Records, but a bad choice of producer (Robin George) led to a slick but flat sound which was not at all representative. Soon after they entered in to a long running legal battle with the company which almost killed the group off. During this time indie label Dojo released a compilation of early material which was far superior to the official album - it also contained the definitive version of live favourite and title-track, 'Trash Queen'. In 1988 they made their comeback with the aptly titled *The Bizz Suxx*. A single, 'Nukklear Rokket', was also released and was followed with a tour that lacked the early aggression and visual drama. The follow-up album in 1989 fared badly against the more established glam rock bands like Mötley Crüe, and the group once again entered a legal battle, this time to stop an American thrash metal band using their moniker. They won, and their namesakes appended America to their tag. None of this, however, did the band any favours, and they disappeared from view shortly thereafter.

Albums: *Stakk Attakk* (Heavy Metal 1984), *Trash Queens* (Dojo 1985), *The Bizz Suxx* (FM Revolver 1988), *Delirium* (FM Revolver 1989).

Video: *War Machine* (1988).

Wrathchild America

This Baltimore quartet seemed set for great things with the release of *Climbing The Walls*, which displayed quality Metallica-influenced thrash infused with melody, although the production didn't quite convey the band's live guitar firepower. However, the good press accrued by Brad Divens (bass/lead vocals), Jay Abbene (guitar), Terry Carter (guitar/vocals) and Shannon Larkin (drums/vocals) went to waste as they became bogged down in litigation over the use of the Wrathchild name with the UK glam outfit of the same title. When the debut finally emerged, with America tagged on to the band's name, the pre-release publicity was long forgotten, and sales were minimal. *3D* proved the band's abilities again with a punchier sound, but stood little chance in a dwindling thrash market. The band lost their recording contract, and subsequently changed their name to Souls At Zero, pursuing a darker direction, although they later lost Larkin to Ugly Kid Joe.
Albums: *Climbing The Walls* (Atlantic 1989), *3D* (Atlantic 1991).

X

XC-NN

This Leeds-based band of electro-industrial rockers were formed as CNN by ex-All About Eve/Sisters Of Mercy guitarist Tim Bricheno with vocalist/guitarist David Tomlinson and drummer Neill Lambert. They made their debut on 1992's *Hot Wired Monstertrux* compilation with 'Looking Forward To The Day (I Stop Breathing)', a quirkily upbeat yet lyrically nihilistic song, with a bizarrely borrowed Buddy Holly lyric in the pre-chorus setting the band's humorous stall out. The *Young, Stupid & White* EP followed with a publicity campaign encouraging fans to nominate celebrities whom they thought fitted that particular bill, with weekly winners featuring on that week's advertising (Jamiroquai's representatives were particularly unimpressed when a caracature of their artist was used). 'Looking Forward To The Day' was re-recorded for the *Copyright* EP with a sampled intro from 2 Unlimited's 'No Limits', bringing legal action from producer Peter Waterman, but the legal muscle of the American news channel CNN proved rather more threatening, enforcing a name change -

although the band retained a sense of identity by becoming XC-NN. They finally recruited a bassist in Nick Witherick, having previously played with sampled bass lines as a three-piece, before recording *XC-NN*. The debut's diversity and quality surprised many people who regarded XC-NN as nothing more than a frivolous gimmick band, with inventive songs ranging from the pop accessibility of '1000 Easy' to indie or industrial guitar-based blasts, while the band's live performances continued to be exhilarating.
Album: *XC-NN* (Transglobal 1994).

Xentrix

Originally known as Sweet Vengeance, this UK rock band was formed in Preston, Lancashire, in 1986 and featured Chris Astley (vocals/guitar), Kristian Havard (guitar), Paul Mackenzie (bass) and Dennis Gasser (drums). The group had done little until signing to Roadrunner Records on the strength of their *Hunger For* demo tape in 1988. (They had already recorded one track, 'Blackmail', for inclusion on the Ebony Records compilation album, *Full Force*, under the Sweet Vengeance moniker). It was their debut, *Shattered Existence*, that bought them to the wider public's attention. Combining Metallica-style power riffs with Bay Area thrash pretensions, the band became popular on the UK club circuit and recorded a cover version of the Ray Parker Jnr. track 'Ghostbusters', a band stage favourite, for their first single release. They had problems with the tracks, however, as they had used the *Ghostbusters* film logo for the cover without Columbia Pictures' permission. The resulting press did the band no harm and the single was released with a new cover in 1990. In the same year the band released their second album, *For Whose Advantage*. Musically similar to previous releases, it nevertheless did much to enhance their profile. With *Dilute To Taste* and *Kin* the band took a more traditional power metal approach which augured well without ever looking like breaking them out into the mainstream.
Albums: *Shattered Existence* (Roadrunner 1989), *For Whose Advantage* (Roadrunner 1990), *Dilute To Taste* (1991), *Kin* (Roadrunner 1992).

XYZ

This French-American Los Angeles-based hard rock act, led by vocalist Terry Ilous with Marc Richard Diglio (guitar), Patt Fontaine (bass) and Paul Monroe (drums), played initially in a blues-based style, but their sound was moulded in the studio by producer Don Dokken into an almost exact replica of Dokken, with Ilous in particular sounding like the producer himself. *XYZ* was not without merit, containing some quality songs with fiery axework from Diglio, although this inevitably led to George Lynch comparisons. However, the debut was reasonably successful as the band toured the USA with Enuff Z'Nuff and Alice Cooper, and Capitol Records signed XYZ for *Hungry*. With George Tutko's production the band established a more characteristic sound with a much heavier approach, also reflecting their bluesier influences with a cover of Free's 'Fire And Water', but the album was a commercial failure, and the band eventually broke up.

Albums: *XYZ* (Enigma 1989), *Hungry* (Capitol 1991).

Y

Y&T

This San Francisco-based band formed in the mid-70s as Yesterday And Today, but David Meniketti (vocals/lead guitar), Joey Alves (rhythm guitar), Phil Kennemore (bass/vocals) and Leonard Haze (drums) failed to make any real impact until they released *Earthshaker* as Y&T. *Earthshaker* was a classic hard rock record built on a blistering guitar barrage, Haze's thunderous rhythms and a superb collection of songs, catapulting the band into the public eye, but also proved to be something of an albatross around the collective Y&T neck. *Black Tiger* was excellent, but subsequent records failed to maintain the standards set on *Earthshaker*. The *Open Fire* live set stopped the rot, and *Down For The Count* signalled a return to form, albeit in a more commercial direction. 'Summertime Girls' was picked up by US radio, but a disenchanted Y&T split with both their record label and drummer, feeling that Haze's image left a lot to be desired. Jimmy DeGrasso made his drumming debut on *Contagious* and Stef Burns replaced Alves for *Ten*, which were both credible hard rock albums, but the band's fortunes were waning and Y&T split in late 1990, with Burns moving on to Alice Cooper's band, DeGrasso joining White Lion and then Suicidal Tendencies, and Meniketti working with Peter Frampton. A brief Y&T reunion came to nothing.

Albums: As Yesterday And Today: *Yesterday And Today* (London 1976), *Struck Down* (London 1978). As Y&T: *Earthshaker* (A&M 1982), *Black Tiger* (A&M 1983), *Mean Streak* (A&M 1983), *In Rock We Trust* (A&M 1984), *Open Fire* (A&M 1985), *Down For The Count* (A&M 1985), *Contagious* (Geffen 1987), *Ten* (Geffen 1990), *Yesterday And Today Live* (Metal Blade 1991).

Z

Zappa, Dweezil

Dweezil is the son of the legendary Frank Zappa. However, it was not his father's guitar playing that prompted Dweezil to form a band, but Eddie Van Halen. Trouble was that this obsession led to an almost direct copy of his hero's style, right down to wielding identical guitars and dressing the same. However, Dweezil still built up a small cult following with early releases, breaking into the mainstream via the album and video, *My Guitar Wants To Kill Your Mama*, one of his father's old tunes given the Van Halen treatment. The video, which achieved mass viewing figures on MTV and music programmes all over the world, featured a 50s cop movie parody in black and white, and guest appearances from, among others, actor Robert Wagner. The album was completed with Bobby Blotzer (Ratt; drums), Steven Smith (Journey; drums), and vocalist Fiona. For *Shampoo Horn* the videos took on a much more surreal nature. Dweezil's brother helped out on vocals but that Van Halen ghost still lurked.

Albums: *Having A Bad Day* (Rykodisc 1987), *My Guitar Wants To Kill Your Mama* (Chrysalis 1988), *Confessions* (Chrysalis 1991), *Shampoo Horn* (Chrysalis 1993).

Zed Yago

Founded in Germany by blues singer Jutta in 1985, Zed Yago were a traditional rock concern very much in keeping with the sound pioneered by fellow nationals, Warlock. Jutta's vocal style owed much to Doro from Warlock, but also saluted American singer Ronnie James Dio. Her band comprised Jimmy and Gunnar on guitar, Tach on bass and a larger-than-life bald powerhouse of a drummer known as Bubi. They first attracted mainstream attention in May 1989 with the release of 'Black Bone Song'. This was followed by their second album and a tour - one concert of which was broadcast live on BBC Radio 1. They vanished in 1990 having failed to make any

Dweezil Zappa

lasting impact.
Albums: *From Over Yonder* (SPV 1988), *Pilgrimage* (BMG 1989).

Znowhite

Standard American power metal team, with the notable exception that it boasted multi-racial membership, who came together late 1983 in Chicago, Illinois, with brothers Ian and Sparks Tafoya on guitar and drums and vocalist Nicole Lee. They spent much of the following year gigging in the Bay Area of San Francisco with Metallica, and supported Raven on their US tour. Their first album was released thanks to help from influential friends Johnny Z and Doc McGhee whose better known credits include Anthrax and Mötley Crüe. A second collection again followed the power metal mantra, but in 1988 they adopted a higher profile when they signed to Roadrunner Records and played gigs outside of the San Francisco scene. Musically they became much heavier and eagerly joined the thrash metal bandwagon - though with results which hardly compared to those of their new peer group. Following disappointing sales the group sundered just after the close of the decade, with members drifting off in to a new conglomeration, Cyclone Temple.

Albums: *All Hail To Thee* (Enigma 1984), *Kick 'Em While They're Down* (Enigma 1985), *Act Of God* (Roadrunner 1988).

Zodiac Mindwarp And The Love Reaction

Formed in 1985, Zodiac Mindwarp And The Love Reaction projected an image encompassing everything from sex maniacs and party animals to leather-clad bikers. Put together by Zodiac (b. Mark Manning), a former graphic designer, their image and attitude was always more interesting than their music. With twin guitarists Cobalt Stargazer and Flash Bastard, plus Trash D. Garbage and Slam Thunderhide on bass and drums respectively, they were the ultimate science-fiction garage band, influenced by Alice Cooper, Motörhead and the Stooges. After releasing the mini-album, *High Priest Of Love*, on the independent Food label, they were picked up by Mercury Records, who funded the recording of *Tattooed Beat Messiah*. Although rigidly formularized, it did spawn the hits 'Prime Mover' and 'Back Seat Education', which were accompanied by expensive and controversial videos. The creative juices soon ran dry, however. Zodiac's backing band disintegrated and Mercury dropped him from its roster in 1989. In 1991 he reformed the band with

Zodiac Mindwarp And The Love Reaction

Stargazer, Thunderhide and new bassist Suzy X, and released the single 'Elvis Died For You'. Despite signing to European label Musidisc, little further progress was made. Manning later lived up to his reputation by collaborating with the KLF's Bill Drummond in 1994 on the semi-pornagraphic work, *A Bible Of Dreams*.

Albums: *High Priest Of Love* (Food 1986), *Tattooed Beat Messiah* (Mercury 1988), *Hoodlum Thunder* (Musidisc 1992), *The Friday Rock Show Sessions At Reading '87* (Windsong 1993).
Video: *Sleazegrinder* (1989).

Z.Z. Top

Formed in Houston, Texas, USA, in 1970, Z.Z. Top evolved out of the city's garage-band circuit and comprise Billy Gibbons (b. 12 December 1949, Houston, Texas, USA; guitar; ex-Moving Sidewalks), Dusty Hill (b. Joe Hill, 1949, Dallas, Texas, USA; bass) and Frank Beard (b. 10 December 1949, Houston, Texas, USA; drums), the last two both ex-American Blues. Z.Z. Top's original line-up; Gibbons, Lanier Greig (bass) and Dan Mitchell (drums), was also the final version of the Moving Sidewalks. This initial trio completed Z.Z. Top's debut single, 'Salt Lick', before Greig was fired. He was replaced by Bill Ethridge. Mitchell was then replaced by Frank Beard while Dusty Hill subsequently joined in place of Ethridge. Initially Z.Z. Top joined a growing swell of southern boogie bands. Their debut album, while betraying a healthy interest in blues, was firmly within this genre, but *Rio Grande Mud* indicated a greater flexibility. It included the rousing 'Francine' which, although indebted to the Rolling Stones, gave the trio their first hit and introduced them to a much wider audience. Their early career coalesced on *Tres Hombres*, a powerful, exciting set which drew from delta music and high energy rock. The group's natural ease was highly affecting and Gibbons' startling guitar work was rarely bettered during these times. However, successive releases failed to attain the same high standard and Z.Z. Top took an extended vacation following their expansive 1976-1977 tour. The reasons, however, were not solely artistic, as the group now wished to secure a more beneficial recording deal. They resumed their career in 1979 with the superb *Deguello*. Revitalized by their break, the trio offered a series of pulsating original songs as well as inspired recreations of Sam And Dave's 'I Thank You' and Elmore James' 'Dust My Broom'. The transitional *El Loco* followed in 1981 and although it lacked the punch of its predecessor, preferring the surreal to the celebratory, the set introduced the growing love of technology which marked the group's subsequent releases. *Eliminator* deservedly became Z.Z. Top's best-selling album. Fuelled by a series of memorable, tongue-in-cheek videos, it provided several international hit singles, including the million-selling 'Gimme All Your Lovin''. 'Sharp Dressed Man' and 'Legs' were also gloriously simple yet enormously infectious songs. The group skilfully wedded computer-age technology to their barrelhouse R&B to create a truly memorable set which established them as one of the world's leading live attractions. The follow-up, *Afterburner*, was a comparative disappointment, although it did feature some excellent individual moments in 'Sleeping Bag' and 'Rough Boy', and the cleverly titled 'Velcro Fly'. Aware of this dichotomy, Z.Z. Top undertook another lengthy break before returning with the impressive *Recycler*. Other notable appearances in 1990 included a cameo, playing themselves, in *Back To The Future 3*. One of rock's maverick attractions, Gibbons, Hill and Beard have retained their eccentric, colourful image, dark glasses and stetson hats, complete with an almost casual musical dexterity which has won over hardened cynics and carping critics. In addition to having produced a fine (but sparse) canon of work, they will stay in the record books as having the longest beards in musical history (although one member, the inappropriately named Frank Beard, is clean-shaven), and are always destined to be the last entry in a popular music encyclopedia.

Albums: *First Album* (London 1971), *Rio Grande Mud* (London 1972), *Tres Hombres* (London 1973), *Fandango!* (London 1975), *Tejas* (London 1976), *Deguello* (Warners 1979), *El Loco* (Warners 1981), *Eliminator* (Warners 1983), *Afterburner* (Warners 1985), *Recycler* (Warners 1990), *Antenna* (RCA 1994). Compilations: *The Best Of Z.Z. Top* (London 1977), *Greatest Hits* (Warners 1992), *One Foot In The Blues* (Warners 1994).
Video: *Greatest Hits* (1992).

INDEX